1 MONTH OF
FREE
READING

at

www.ForgottenBooks.com

By purchasing this book you are eligible for one month membership to ForgottenBooks.com, giving you unlimited access to our entire collection of over 1,000,000 titles via our web site and mobile apps.

To claim your free month visit:
www.forgottenbooks.com/free62429

ISBN 978-0-365-29543-3
PIBN 10062429

This book is a reproduction of an important historical work. Forgotten Books uses
state-of-the-art technology to digitally reconstruct the work, preserving the original format
whilst repairing imperfections present in the aged copy. In rare cases, an imperfection in
the original, such as a blemish or missing page, may be replicated in our edition. We do,
however, repair the vast majority of imperfections successfully; any imperfections that
remain are intentionally left to preserve the state of such historical works.

A

SCRIPTURE MANUAL.

ALPHABETICALLY AND SYSTEMATICALLY ARRANGED,

DESIGNED TO FACILITATE THE FINDING OF

PROOF TEXTS.

BY CHARLES SIMMONS.

SECOND STEREOTYPE REVISION.
First Edition, 2000.

NEW YORK:
M. W. DODD, BRICK CHURCH CHAPEL.
BOSTON: CROCKER & BREWSTER AND JOHN P. JEWETT & CO.
NORTH WRENTHAM, MASS.: CHARLES SIMMONS, PROPRIETOR.
CINCINNATI. J. A. BRAINERD
1850.

Entered according to Act of Congress, in the year 1850, by
CHARLES SIMMONS,
In the Clerk's Office of the District Court of Massachusetts.

ANDOVER: JOHN D. FLAGG,
STEREOTYPER AND PRINTER.

INTRODUCTION;

BY DR. SPRING.

THE object of the present work is clearly announced in its title. It is to collect within a small compass the instructions of unerring wisdom upon a great variety of subjects which relate to the present and eternal interests of men, and comprising the doctrines and duties of a supernatural revelation. A reference to the list of subjects which the work contains, will show that the author's researches have been extensive; while a comparison of the work with others of the same general character evinces patient labor, and cannot fail to give it pre-eminence. While the track pursued is not new, it is more thorough, and more easily followed than that marked out by any previous compiler known to myself. The work contains not merely the *proof texts* on the subjects to which it refers; but, what appears to my own mind one of its excellences, the texts that *illustrate* these great subjects. The work is truly an epitome of the Bible, presenting its great truths in that order in which they will be most easily found by the reader. Though the arrangement of the subjects is alphabetical, in the illustration of the subjects themselves the author has observed that connection between one truth and another which gives to each its proper place. To ministers, Sabbath School teachers, Sabbath Schools, and families the work is of great value. It is fit on every account that the author should be encouraged in this production; but chiefly for its own intrinsic worth. The work is an unpresuming, yet dignified tribute to the word of God, worthy the acceptance of the church, and one which every man may prize.

GARDINER SPRING.

Brick Church Chapel, New York, March, 1845

PREFACE TO THE SECOND STEREOTYPE REVISION.

THE Bible furnishes very ample materials for all needful moral instruction, reproof, and encouragement. But the compilation of a convenient Manual of proof texts from its pages has been unaccountably neglected. The loose manner in which Gaston, and others, have thrown together texts of Scripture for this purpose, has essentially defeated their aims. The SCRIPTURE MANUAL owes its origin to a conviction of the need of a Text-Book, that should assume a more convenient order, bear more effectually against the modern forms of error and vice, and more fully and fearlessly declare "all the counsel of God." The Editor is greatly obliged to the friends of this enterprise, who have aided in the preparation or circulation of the several editions and revisions of the work. The present revision has been stereotyped sooner than was otherwise necessary, in order to embrace the improvements and additions made during the last five years. It has over one hundred additional topics, a much more full and perfect index, a triple or quadruple number of references to kindred subjects, together with no little improvement in the relevancy of its proof texts, and order of the work. Happy would it have been for the purchasers, had all these additions and improvements been secured at an earlier period. But this was impracticable. To atone in some measure for this evil, I will instruct my publishers and agents to exchange copies of the present improved and somewhat enlarged revision, for copies of former editions, on very favorable terms, with those who desire it.

The copy for this work was cut from the pages of Bibles, lately issued from the American Bible Society, and the Manual may be depended upon as accurate Scripture. The italic words are also preserved. The number of the verses is given, that the reader may discover any omissions made, of passages not in point, in any particular extract. Explanatory words are in brackets.

In selecting topics, care has been taken to embrace those which have a prominence in the Bible, and which in all ages have been considered of primary importance in theological and moral inquiry. Such manifestly are those which relate to the perfections, prerogatives, designs, providence, and law of God — the character, rights, and destiny of man — the economy of grace, or way and terms of salvation through Christ — our essential duties towards God and each other, and civil and religious institutions.

Christian nations are far more indebted to the Bible for their elevation above heathenism, than is commonly believed. The revealed facts respecting God and his designs and government — the precepts of his law, clothed with infinite authority — the promises of his grace, and the threatenings of his justice, are the best safeguards against disgraceful and ruinous vices.

It is believed that a convenient and faithful compilation of proofs from the Bible, upon its weighty and practical subjects, may prove one of the most effective auxiliaries to the cause of Christian enterprise. The impressions made upon the public mind in favor of pure and undefiled religion, by a copious and systematic array of proof texts, in a convenient and popular form, must prove a most powerful incentive to virtue, and restraint upon destructive errors, sins and vices.

I now commit the success of this work to the overruling providence of that Being who has mercifully sustained and helped me during its preparation. If it shall tend to confirm the public mind in revealed truth, and become a guard against those errors and vices which lead to death, as is confidently hoped, the labor of preparing it will not have been in vain.

CHARLES SIMMONS.

North Wrentham, Mass., April, 1850.

NOTICE.

Travelling and Sabbath School agents, and especially those who may desire this book by the quantity for gratuitous distribution, will do well to communicate with me by mail.   C. S.

In this first edition of the present revision I have used the old plates for the notices of the work.

INDEX.

N. B. The figures in this Index, and those in brackets at the end of many of the sections in this work, both refer to the number of the sections, or topics, which, to avoid confusion, is placed on the top of the pages, and correspond with those that occur upon the pages. The usual paging is placed at the bottom, and will not be used. A dash between figures, signifies inclusive: for example, 496—8, includes the numbers 496, 497, and 498. *An occasional figure in a parenthesis, refers to some specification under the foregoing numbers, which rarely occurs: for example, 17,(2,) refers to the second specification under the seventeenth topic, or section. The reader will be more sure to find the subject desired, by looking for the principal word first — by looking for the noun before the verb, and both noun and verb before the adjective: for example, for Divine Teaching, look for Teaching, Divine; and for Perfections of God, look for God's Perfections.

SCRIPTURE MANUAL.

ACTIVITY AND DILIGENCE.

1. Activity and diligence required and encouraged — inactivity reproved.

Gen. 3: 19 In the sweat of thy face shalt thou eat bread, till thou return unto the ground.

Ex. 20: 9 Six days shalt thou labor, and do all thy work.

Jud. 5: 23 Curse ye Meroz, said the angel of the Lord, curse ye bitterly the inhabitants thereof; because they came not to the help of the Lord, to the help of the Lord against the mighty.

1 Ch. 22: 16 Arise, *therefore*, and be doing, and the Lord be with thee.

Pr. 10: 4 He becometh poor that-dealeth *with* a slack hand: but the hand of the diligent maketh rich. 5 He that gathereth in summer *is* a wise son: *but* he that sleepeth in harvest *is* a son that causeth shame. — 12: 24 The hand of the diligent shall bear rule: but the slothful shall be under tribute. — 13: 4 The soul of the sluggard desireth, and *hath* nothing: but the soul of the diligent shall be made fat. — 22: 29 Seest thou a man diligent in his business? he shall stand before kings; he shall not stand before mean *men*. — 27: 23 Be thou diligent to know the state of thy flocks, *and* look well to thy herds: 24 For riches *are* not forever. — 28: 19 He that tilleth his land shall have plenty of bread: but he that followeth after vain *persons* shall have poverty enough.

Ec. 5: 12 The sleep of a laboring man *is* sweet, whether he eat little or much. — 9: 10 Whatsoever thy hand findeth to do, do *it* with thy might; for *there is* no work, nor device, nor knowledge, nor wisdom, in the grave, whither thou goest.

Is. 52: 1 Awake, awake, put on thy strength, O Zion; put on thy beautiful garments, O Jerusalem, the holy city.

Am. 6: 1 Wo to them *that are* at ease in Zion.

Rom. 12: 11 Not slothful in business; fervent in spirit; serv-

23

ing the Lord. — 13: 11 Knowing the time, that now *it is* high time to wake out of sleep : for now *is* our salvation nearer than when we believed.

Ep. 4: 28 Let him that stole, steal no more : but rather let him labor, working with *his* hands the thing which is good, that he may have to give to him that needeth.

. 1 Th. 4: 11 Study to be quiet, and to do your own business, and to work with your own hands, as we commanded you ; 12 That ye may walk honestly toward them that are without, and *that* ye may have lack of nothing. [See 63, 358, 738, 749.]

AFFLICTIONS — TRIALS — CHASTISEMENTS.

2. *Afflictions common to man.*

Job 5: 7 Man is born unto trouble, as the sparks fly upward. — 7: 17 What *is* man, that thou shouldest magnify him? and that thou shouldest set thine heart upon him? 18 And *that* thou shouldest visit him every morning, *and* try him every moment? — 14: 1 Man *that is* born of a woman *is* of few days, and full of trouble.

3. *Afflictions from God.*

1 S. 2: 7 The Lord maketh poor, and maketh rich : he bringeth low, and lifteth up.

Job 5: 6 Affliction cometh not forth of the dust, neither doth trouble spring out of the ground. 18 For he maketh sore, and bindeth up : he woundeth, and his hands make whole.

Ps. 39: 9 I was dumb, I opened not my mouth; because thou didst *it.* — 66: 11 Thou broughtest us into the net; thou laidest affliction upon our loins. — 89: 30 If his children forsake my law, and walk not in my judgments; 31 If they break my statutes, and keep not my commandments ; 32 Then will I visit their transgression with the rod, and their iniquity with stripes. — 102: 10 Thou hast lifted me up, and cast me down. 23 He weakened my strength in the way ; he shortened my days.

2 Cor. 12: 7 Lest I should be exalted above measure through the abundance of the revelations, there was given to me a thorn in the flesh, the messenger of Satan to buffet me, lest I should be exalted above measure. [See 147, 260.]

4. *Benefit of afflictions and fatherly chastisements.*

Dt. 8: 2 Thou shalt remember all the way which the LORD thy God led thee these forty years in the wilderness, to humble thee, *and* to prove thee, to know what *was* in thine heart, whether thou wouldest keep his commandments, or no.

Benefit of.

2 Ch. 33: 12 When he was in affliction, he besought the LORD his God, and humbled himself greatly before' the God of his fathers, 13 And prayed unto him : and he was entreated of him, and heard his supplication, and brought him again to Jerusalem into his kingdom.   Then Manasseh knew that the LORD he *was* God.

Job 5: 17 Behold, happy is the man whom God correcteth : therefore despise not thou the chastening of the Almighty. — 23: 10 He knoweth the way that I take : *when* he hath tried me, I shall come forth as gold.

Ps. 78: 34 When he slew them, then they sought him : and they returned and inquired early after God.   35 And they remembered that God *was* their Rock, and the high God their Redeemer. — 94: 12 Blessed *is* the man whom thou chastenest, O LORD, and teachest him out of thy law,   13 That thou mayest give him rest from the days of adversity, until the pit be digged for the wicked. — 119: 67 Before I was afflicted I went astray : but now have I kept thy word. 71 *It is* good for me that I have been afflicted ; that I might learn thy statutes. 75 I know, O LORD, that thy judgments *are* right, and *that* thou in faithfulness hast afflicted me.

Pr. 3: 11 My son, despise not the chastening of the LORD; neither be weary of his correction :   12 For whom the LORD loveth he correcteth ; even as a father the son *in whom* he delighteth.

Is. 26: 9 When thy judgments *are* in the earth, the inhabitants of the world will learn righteousness. — 27: 7 Hath he smitten him, as he smote those that smote him ? *or* is he slain according to the slaughter of them that are slain by him?   9 By this therefore shall the iniquity of Jacob be purged ; and this *is* all the fruit to take away his sin. — 48: 10 Behold, I have refined thee, but not with silver ; I have chosen thee in the furnace of affliction.

Jer. 24: 5 Thus saith the LORD, the God of Israel; Like these good figs, so will I acknowledge them that are carried away captive of Judah, whom I have sent out of this place into the land of the Chaldeans for *their* good.

Lam. 3: 27 *It is* good for a man that he bear the yoke in his youth.

Dan. 11: 35 *Some* of them of understanding shall fall, to try them, and to purge, and to make *them* white, *even* to the time of the end : because *it is* yet for a time appointed. — 12: 10 Many shall be purified, and made white, and tried ; but the wicked shall do wickedly.

Hos. 5: 15 In their affliction they will seek me early.

Benefit of — short.

Zec. 13: 9 I will bring the third part through the fire, and will refine them as silver is refined, and will try them as gold is tried: they shall call on my name, and I will hear them: I will say, It *is* my people; and they shall say, The LORD *is* my God.

Rom. 5: 3 We glory in tribulations also; knowing that tribulation worketh patience; 4 And patience experience; and experience, hope.

1 Cor. 11: 32 When we are judged, we are chastened of the Lord, that we should not be condemned with the world.

2 Cor. 4: 17 Our light affliction, which is but for a moment, worketh for us a far more exceeding *and* eternal weight of glory; 18 While we look not at the things which are seen, but at the things which are not seen: for the things which are seen *are* temporal; but the things which are not seen *are* eternal. — 12: 10 I take pleasure in infirmities, in reproaches, in necessities, in persecutions, in distresses for Christ's sake: for when I am weak, then am I strong.

Heb. 2: 10 It became him, for whom *are* all things, and by whom *are* all things, in bringing many sons unto glory, to make the Captain of their salvation perfect through sufferings. — 12: 10 They verily for a few days chastened *us* after their own pleasure; but he for *our* profit, that *we* might be partakers of his holiness. 11. Now no chastening for the present seemeth to be joyous, but grievous: nevertheless, afterward it yieldeth the peaceable fruit of righteousness unto them which are exercised thereby.

Jam. 1: 2 My brethren, count it all joy when ye fall into divers temptations; 3 Knowing *this*, that the trying of your faith worketh patience. 12 Blessed *is* the man that endureth temptation: for when he is tried, he shall receive the crown of life, which the Lord hath promised to them that love him.

1 Pet. 1: 7 That the trial of your faith, being much more precious than of gold that perisheth, though it be tried with fire, might be found unto praise, and honor, and glory, at the appearing of Jesus Christ. 19 As many as I love, I rebuke and chasten. [See 508, 512, 515.]

5. *The afflictions of the righteous short.*

Job 11: 16 Because thou shalt forget *thy* misery, *and* remember *it* as waters *that* pass away.

Ps. 30: 5 His anger *endureth but* a moment; in his favor *is* life: weeping may endure for a night, but joy *cometh* in the morning.

Lam. 3: 32 Though he cause grief, yet will he have compas-

Support under — demand sympathy.

sion according to the multitude of his mercies. 33 For he doth not afflict willingly, nor grieve the children of men.

2 Cor. 4: 17 Our light affliction, which is but for a moment, worketh for us a far more exceeding *and* eternal weight of glory. [See 225, 585.]

6. *God, the believer's support and helper under afflictions.*

Ps. 23: 4 Yea, though I walk through the valley of the shadow of death, I will fear no evil: for thou *art* with me; thy rod and thy staff they comfort me.—31: 7 I will be glad and rejoice in thy mercy: for thou hast considered my trouble; thou hast known my soul in adversities; 8 And hast not shut me up into the hand of the enemy: thou hast set my foot in a large room.—46: 1 God *is* our refuge and strength, a very present help in trouble.

Is. 25: 4 Thou hast been a strength to the poor, a strength to the needy in his distress, a refuge from the storm, a shadow from the heat, when the blast of the terrible ones *is* as a storm *against* the wall.—49: 13 Sing, O heavens; and be joyful, O earth; and break forth into singing, O mountains: for the LORD hath comforted his people, and will have mercy upon his afflicted.'

Jer. 16: 19 O LORD, my strength and my fortress, and my refuge in the day of affliction.

2 Cor. 1: 3 Blessed *be* God, even the Father of our Lord Jesus Christ, the Father of mercies, and the God of all comfort; 4 Who comforteth us in all our tribulation, that we may be able to comfort them which are in any trouble by the comfort wherewith we ourselves are comforted of God. [See 657, 725.]

7. *Afflictions demand sympathy — examples.*

Job 6: 14 To him that is afflicted pity *should be shewed* from his friend.

Ps. 35: 13 As for me, when they were sick, my clothing *was* sackcloth: I humbled my soul with fasting; and my prayer returned into mine own bosom. 14 I behaved myself as though *he had been* my friend *or* brother: I bowed down heavily, as one that mourneth *for his* mother.

Rom. 12: 15 Rejoice with them that do rejoice, and weep with them that weep.

Ph. 4: 14 Ye have well done that ye did communicate with my affliction.

Heb. 13: 3 Remember them that are in bonds, as bound with them; *and* them which suffer adversity, as being yourselves also in the body. [See 526.]

8. *Afflictions try mankind.*

Dt. 8: 2 Thou shalt remember all the way which the LORD thy God led thee these forty years in the wilderness, to humble thee, *and* to prove thee, to know what *was* in thy heart, whether thou wouldest keep his commandments, or no. 3 And he humbled thee, and suffered thee to hunger, and fed thee with manna. [See 4.]

9. *Afflictions often misimproved and magnified.*

Job 10: 15 I *am* full of confusion; therefore see thou mine affliction; 16 For it increaseth. Thou huntest me as a fierce lion: and again thou shewest thyself marvellous upon me. 17 Thou renewest thy witnesses against me, and increasest thine indignation upon me; changes and war *are* against me. 18 Wherefore then hast thou brought me forth out of the womb? Oh that I had given up the ghost, and no eye had seen me!— 16: 12 I was at ease, but he hath broken me asunder: he hath also taken *me* by my neck, and shaken me to pieces, and set me up for his mark.

Is. 1: 5 Why should ye be stricken any more? ye will revolt more and more: the whole head is sick, and the whole heart faint.—9: 13 The people turneth not unto him that smiteth them, neither do they seek the LORD of hosts.

Jer. 5: 3 O LORD, *are* not thine eyes upon the truth? thou hast stricken them, but they have not grieved; thou hast consumed them, *but* they have refused to receive correction: they have made their faces harder than a rock; they have refused to return.

Lam. 1: 12 *Is it* nothing to you, all ye that pass by? behold, and see if there be any sorrow like unto my sorrow, which is done unto me, wherewith the LORD hath afflicted *me* in the day of his fierce anger. 13 From above hath he sent fire into my bones, and it prevaileth against them: he hath spread a net for my feet, he hath turned me back: he hath made me desolate *and* faint all the day.—3: 10 He *was* unto me *as* a bear lying in wait, *and as* a lion in secret places. 11 He hath turned aside my ways, and pulled me in pieces: he hath made me desolate. 12 He hath bent his bow, and set me as a mark for the arrow.

Am. 4: 6 I also have given you cleanness of teeth in all your cities, and want of bread in all your places: yet have ye not returned unto me, saith the LORD. 7—11.

[See 569, 700.]

28

AGED PERSONS.

10. *Duties to the aged.*

Lev. 19: 32 Thou shalt rise up before the hoary head, and honor the face of the old man, and fear thy God: I *am* the Lord.

1 Tim. 5: 1 Rebuke not an elder, but entreat *him* as a father, *and* the younger men as brethren; 2 The elder women as mothers; the younger as sisters, with all purity.

1 Pet. 5: 5 Likewise, ye younger, submit yourselves unto the elder. [See 730.]

ANGELS.

11. *Angels numerous.*

Heb. 12: 22 Ye are come unto mount Sion, and unto the city of the living God, the heavenly Jerusalem, and to an innumerable company of angels.

Rev. 5: 11 I beheld, and I heard the voice of many angels round about the throne, and the beasts, and the elders: and the number of them was ten thousand times ten thousand, and thousands of thousands.

12. *Employment of good angels.*

2 S. 24: 16 The angel stretched out his hand upon Jerusalem to destroy it.

2 K. 19: 35 It came to pass that night, that the angel of the LORD went out, and smote in the camp of the Assyrians a hundred four score and five thousand.

Job 38: 7 When the morning stars sang together, and all the sons of God shouted for joy?

Ps. 91: 11 For he shall give his angels charge over thee, to keep thee in all thy ways. 12 They shall bear thee up in *their* hands, lest thou dash thy foot against a stone.

Dan. 6: 22 My God hath sent his angel, and hath shut the lions' mouths. — 9: 21 Yea, while I *was* speaking in prayer, even the man Gabriel, whom I had seen in the vision at the beginning, being caused to fly swiftly, touched me about the time of the evening oblation. 22 And he informed *me*, and talked with me, and said, O Daniel, I am now come forth to give thee skill and understanding.

Mat. 13: 39 The harvest is the end of the world; and the reapers are the angels. 41 The Son of man shall send forth his angels, and they shall gather out of his kingdom all things that offend, and them which do iniquity. — 18: 10 Take heed that ye despise not one of these little ones: for I say unto you,

that in heaven their angels do always behold the face of my
Father which is in heaven.

Lk. 16: 22 And it came to pass, that the beggar died, and
was carried by the angels into Abraham's bosom.

Heb. 1: 14 Are they not all ministering spirits, sent forth to
minister to them who shall be heirs of salvation?

ANGELS APOSTATE.

13. *Apostasy of angels.*

2 Pet. 2: 4 God spared not the angels that sinned, but cast
them down to hell, and delivered *them* into chains of darkness,
to be reserved unto judgment.

Jude 6 The angels which kept not their first estate, but left
their own habitation, he hath reserved in everlasting chains,
under darkness, unto the judgment of the great day.

Rev. 12: 7 There was war in heaven: Michael and his
angels fought against the dragon; and the dragon fought and
his angels, 8 And prevailed not; neither was their place
found any more in heaven.

14. *Names of apostate angels.*

Is. 27: 1 Leviathan, the piercing and crooked serpent. —
Mat. 4: 3 And when the tempter came to him, he said, If
thou be the Son of God, command that these stones be made
bread. — 10: 1 Unclean spirits. — 13: 38 The field is the world;
the good seed are the children of the kingdom; but the tares are
the children of the wicked *one;* 39 The enemy that sowed
them is the devil. — Mk. 5: 9 Legion. — Lk. 11: 15 Beelzebub. — Jn. 8: 44 Murderer, liar. — 14: 30 The prince of this
world. — 2 Cor. 4: 4 The god of this world. — Ep. 2: 2 The
prince of the power of the air. — 6: 12 The rulers of the darkness
of this world. — 1 Pet. 5: 8 Your adversary the devil. — Rev.
9: 11 Abaddon, (Heb.) Apollyon, (Gr.) — 12: 9 Great dragon, old serpent, devil, and Satan. — 9: 10 The accuser of the
brethren.

15. *Character, employment and agency of evil spirits.*

Job 1: 7 The LORD said unto Satan, Whence comest thou?
Then Satan answered the LORD, and said, From going to and
fro in the earth, and from walking up and down in it.

Mat. 13: 19 When any one heareth the word of the kingdom, and understandeth *it* not, then cometh the wicked *one,*
and catcheth away that which was sown in his heart. 38 The
field is the world; the good seed are the children of the kingdom; but the tares are the children of the wicked *one;* 39
The enemy that sowed them is the devil.

Their character and employment.

Lk. 4: 5 The devil, taking him up into a high mountain, shewed unto him all the kingdoms of the world in a moment of time.—8: 12 Those by the way-side, are they that hear; then cometh the devil, and taketh away the word out of their hearts, lest they should believe and be saved.—22: 31 The Lord said, Simon, Simon, behold, Satan hath desired *to have* you, that he may sift *you* as wheat.

Jn. 8: 44 Ye are of *your* father the devil, and the lusts of your father ye will do: he was a murderer from the beginning, and abode not in the truth; because there is no truth in him. When he speaketh a lie, he speaketh of his own: for he is a liar, and the father of it.—13: 2 Supper being ended, (the devil having now put into the heart of Judas Iscariot, Simon's *son*, to betray him.)

Ac. 5: 3 Peter said, Ananias, why hath Satan filled thine heart to lie to the Holy Ghost, and to keep back *part* of the price of the land?

2 Cor. 2: 11 Lest Satan should get an advantage of us: for we are not ignorant of his devices.—4: 4 In whom the god of this world hath blinded the minds of them which believe not, lest the light of the glorious gospel of Christ, who is the image of God, should shine unto them.

Ep. 2: 2 Wherein in time past ye walked according to the course of this world, according to the prince of the power of the air, the spirit that now worketh in the children of disobedience.—6: 12 We wrestle not against flesh and blood, but against principalities, against powers, against the rulers of the darkness of this world, against spiritual wickedness in high *places*.

2 Tim. 2: 26 *That* they may recover themselves out of the snare of the devil, who are taken captive by him at his will.

1 Pet. 5: 8 Be sober, be vigilant; because your adversary the devil, as a roaring lion, walketh about, seeking whom he may devour.

Rev. 2: 24 Unto you I say, and unto the rest in Thyatira, As many as have not this doctrine, and which have not known the depths of Satan, as they speak; I will put upon you none other burden.—12: 9 The great dragon was cast out, that old serpent, called the Devil, and Satan, which deceiveth the whole world. 10 I heard a loud voice saying in heaven, Now is come salvation, and strength, and the kingdom of our God, and the power of his Christ: for the accuser of our brethren is cast down which accused them before our God day and night. 12 Therefore rejoice, *ye* heavens, and ye that dwell in them. Wo to the inhabiters of the earth, and of the sea! for the devil is come down unto you, having great wrath, because he knoweth that he.hath but a short time. — 20: 7 When the thousand years are expired, Satan shall be loosed out of his prison, 8 And shall go out to deceive the nations.

16. *By what means and devices do apostate angels lead mankind into sin and death?*

Gen. 3: 13 The serpent beguiled me, and I did eat.

1 Ch. 21: 1 Satan stood up against Israel, and provoked David to number Israel.

2 Cor. 11: 3 I fear, lest by any means, as the serpent beguiled Eve through his subtilty, so your minds should be corrupted from the simplicity that is in Christ. 14 And no marvel; for Satan himself is transformed into an angel of light.

2 Th. 2: 9 *Even him,* whose coming is after the working of Satan, with all power, and signs, and lying wonders. 10 And with all deceivableness of unrighteousness in them that perish.

1 Tim. 4: 1 The Spirit speaketh expressly, that in the latter times some shall depart from the faith, giving heed to seducing spirits, and doctrines of devils.

2 Tim. 2: 26 *That* they may recover themselves out of the snare of the devil, who are taken captive by him at his will.

Rev. 16: 13 I saw three unclean spirits like frogs *come* out of the mouth of the dragon, and out of the mouth of the beast, and out of the mouth of the false prophet. 14 For they are the spirits of devils, working miracles, *which* go forth unto the kings of the earth, and of the whole world, to gather them to the battle of that great day of God Almighty.

[See 474, 702.]

17. *Suggestions of the adversary.*

1. *That sinners will escape threatened punishment.*

Gen. 3: 4 The serpent said unto the woman, Ye shall not surely die: 5 For God doth know, that in the day ye eat thereof, then your eyes shall be opened, and ye shall be as gods, knowing good and evil.

2. *That there is nothing but selfishness in religion.*

Job 1: 9 Satan answered the LORD and said, Doth Job fear God for nought? 10 Hast not thou made a hedge about him, and about his house, and about all that he hath on every side? thou hast blessed the work of his hands and his substance is increased in the land. 11 But put forth thine hand now, and touch all that he hath, and he will curse thee to thy face.

8. *That means are useless, where the end is divinely appointed.*

Mat. 4: 5 The devil taketh him up into the holy city, and setteth him on a pinnacle of the temple, 6 And saith unto him, If thou be the Son of God cast thyself down, for it is written, He shall give his angels charge concerning thee: and in *their* hands they shall bear thee up, lest at any time thou dash thy foot against a stone. [See 257.]

4. *Forbidding matrimony and the use of meats.*

1 Tim. 4: 1 The Spirit speaketh expressly, that in the latter times some shall depart from the faith, giving heed to seducing spirits, and doctrines of devils; 2 Speaking lies in hypocrisy, having their conscience seared with a hot iron; 3 Forbidding to marry, *and commanding* to abstain from meats, which God hath created to be received with thanksgiving of them which believe and know the truth.

18. *Apostate angels to be resisted.*

Ep. 4: 27 Neither give place to the devil. — 6: 12 We wrestle not against flesh and blood, but against principalities, against powers, against the rulers of the darkness of this world, against spiritual wickedness in high *places*. 13 Wherefore take unto you the whole armor of God, that ye may be able to withstand in the evil day, and having done all to stand.

Jam. 4: 7 Resist the devil, and he will flee from you.

1 Pet. 5: 8 Be sober, be vigilant; because your adversary the devil, as a roaring lion, walketh about, seeking whom he may devour. 9 Whom resist steadfast in the faith. [See 477, 738.]

APOSTATES.

19. *Cases of real and supposed apostasy — warnings — fearful end of apostates.*

1 S. 15: 11 It repenteth me that I have set up Saul *to be* king: for he is turned back from following me, and hath not performed my commandments.

1 Ch. 28: 9 And thou, Solomon my son, know thou the God of thy father, and serve him with a perfect heart, and with a willing mind: for the LORD searcheth all hearts, and understandeth all the imaginations of the thoughts: if thou seek him, he will be found of thee; but if thou forsake him, he will cast thee off for ever.

Ezk. 3: 20 When a righteous *man* doth turn from his righteousness, and commit iniquity, and I lay a stumbling-block before him, he shall die: because thou hast not given him warning, he shall die in his sin, and his righteousness which he hath done shall not be remembered; but his blood will I require at thine hand.— 18: 24, 13.— 13: 18 When the righteous turneth from his righteousness, and committeth iniquity, he shall even die thereby.

Hos. 6: 4 O Ephraim, what shall I do unto thee? O Judah, what shall I do unto thee? for your goodness *is* as a morning cloud, and as the early dew it goeth away.

Mat. 25: 8 The foolish said unto the wise, Give us of your oil: for our lamps are gone out.

Lk. 9: 62 Jesus said unto him, No man having put his hand to the plough, and looking back, is fit for the kingdom of God.

Jn. 6: 66 From that *time* many of his disciples went back, and walked no more with him.

Gal. 5: 4 Christ is become of no effect unto you, whosoever of you are justified by the law; ye are fallen from grace.

1 Tim. 1: 19 Holding faith and a good conscience; which some having put away, concerning faith have made shipwreck.

2 Tim. 1: 15 This thou knowest, that all they which are in Asia be turned away from me; of whom are Phygellus, and Hermogenes.

2 Pet. 2: 20 If after they have escaped the pollutions of the world through the knowledge of the Lord and Saviour Jesus Christ, they are again entangled therein, and overcome, the latter end is worse with them than the beginning. 21 For it had been better for them not to have known the way of righteousness, than, after they have known *it*, to turn from the holy commandment delivered unto them. 22 But it is happened unto them according to the true proverb, The dog *is* turned to his own vomit again; and, The sow that was washed, to her wallowing in the mire. [See 23, 27.]

20. *Apostates hard to reclaim.*

Heb. 6: 4 *It is* impossible for those who were once enlightened, and have tasted of the heavenly gift, and were made partakers of the Holy Ghost, 5 And have tasted the good word of God, and the powers of the world to come, 6 If they shall fall away, to renew them again unto repentance; seeing they crucify to themselves the Son of God afresh, and put *him* to an open shame. — 10: 26 If we sin wilfully after that we have received the knowledge of the truth, there remaineth no more sacrifice for sins, 27 But a certain fearful looking for of judgment and fiery indignation, which shall devour the adversaries.

21. *Were Apostates ever truly regenerated?*

Mat. 7: 22 Many will say to me in that day, Lord, Lord, have we not prophesied in thy name? and in thy name have cast out devils? and in thy name done many wonderful works? 23 And then will I profess unto them, I never knew you: depart from me, ye that work iniquity.

Mat. 15: 13 Every plant, which my heavenly Father hath not planted, shall be rooted up.

Mk. 4: 16 These are they likewise which are sown on stony ground; who, when they have heard the word, immediately receive it with gladness; 17 And have no root in themselves, and so endure but for a time: afterward, when affliction or persecution ariseth for the word's sake, immediately they are offended.

Jn. 6: 70 Jesus answered them, Have not I chosen you twelve, and one of you is a devil? — 17: 12 While I was with them in the world, I kept them in thy name: those that thou gavest me I have kept, and none of them is lost, but the son of perdition; that the Scripture might be fulfilled.

1 Jn. 2: 19 They went out from us, but they were not of us; for if they had been of us, they would *no doubt* have continued with us: but *they went out*, that they might be made manifest that they were not all of us. [See 515—517.]

ATHEISM.

22. *Theoretical and practical Atheism.*

Ex. 5: 2 Pharaoh said, Who *is* the LORD, that I should obey his voice to let Israel go? I know not the Lord, neither will I let Israel go.

Job 21: 14 They say unto God, Depart from us; for we desire not the knowledge of thy ways. 15 What *is* the Almighty, that we should serve him? and what profit should we have, if we pray unto him?

Ps. 10: 4 The wicked, through the pride of his countenance, will not seek *after God:* God *is* not in all his thoughts. — 14: 1 The fool hath said in his heart, *There is* no God. — 59: 7 Behold, they belch out with their mouth: swords *are* in their lips: for who, *say they,* doth hear?

Is. 22: 13 Let us eat and drink; for to-morrow we shall die.

Ezk. 8: 12 They say, The LORD seeth us not; the LORD hath forsaken the earth.

Rom. 3: 18 There is no fear of God before their eyes.

Ep. 2: 12 At that time ye were without Christ, being aliens

from the commonwealth of Israel, and strangers from the covenants of promise, having no hope, and without God in the world.

2 Pet. 3: 3 There shall come in the last days scoffers, walking after their own lusts, 4 And saying, Where is the promise of his coming? for since the fathers fell asleep, all things continue as *they were* from the beginning of the creation.

[See 200, 568, 692 (3), 695, 705, 708.]

BACKSLIDING.

23. *Examples of backsliding — cautions.*

Ex. 32: 1 When the people saw that Moses delayed to come down out of the mount, the people gathered themselves together unto Aaron, and said unto him, Up, make us gods which shall go before us: for *as for* this Moses, the man that brought us up out of the land of Egypt, we wot not what is become of him. 2 And Aaron said unto them, Break off the golden ear-rings which *are* in the ears of your wives, of your sons, and of your daughters, and bring *them* unto me. 3 And all the people brake off the golden ear-rings which *were* in their ears, and brought *them* unto Aaron. 4 And he received *them* at their hand, and fashioned it with a graving tool, after he had made it a molten calf: and they said, These *be* thy gods, O Israel, which brought thee up out of the land of Egypt. 5 And when Aaron saw *it*, he built an altar before it; and Aaron made proclamation, and said, To-morrow *is* a feast to the LORD. 6 And they rose up early on the morrow, and offered burnt-offerings, and brought peace-offerings: and the people sat down to eat and to drink, and rose up to play.

2 S. 12: 7 Nathan said to David, Thou *art* the man. 9 Wherefore hast thou despised the commandment of the LORD, to do evil in his sight? thou hast killed Uriah the Hittite with the sword, and hast taken his wife *to be* thy wife, and hast slain him with the sword of the children of Ammon.

1 K. 11: 4 It came to pass, when Solomon was old, *that* his wives turned away his heart after other gods: and his heart was not perfect with the LORD his God, as *was* the heart of David his father.

2 Ch. 16: 7 At that time Hanani the seer came to Asa king of Judah, and said unto him, Because thou hast relied on the king of Syria, and not relied on the LORD thy God, therefore is the host of the king of Syria escaped out of thine hand. 8 Were not the Ethiopians and the Lubims a huge host, with

very many chariots and horsemen? yet, because thou didst rely on the LORD, he delivered them into thine hand. 9 Herein thou hast done foolishly: therefore from henceforth thou shalt have wars. 10 Then Asa was wroth with the seer, and put him in a prison-house; for *he was* in a rage with him because of this *thing.* And Asa oppressed *some* of the people the same time.

Jer. 8: 5 Why *then* is this people of Jerusalem slidden back by a perpetual backsliding? they hold fast deceit, they refuse to return.

Hos. 11: 7 My people are bent to backsliding from me: though they called them to the Most High, none at all would exalt *him.*

Mat. 16: 6 Jesus said unto them, Take heed and beware of the leaven of the Pharisees and of the Sadducees.

[See 19, 695.]

24. Backsliders prone to murmur, despond, and distrust providence.

Gen. 42: 36 Jacob their father said unto them, Me have ye bereaved *of my children:* Joseph *is* not, and Simeon *is* not, and ye will take Benjamin *away:* all these things are against me.

1 K. 19: 4 Elijah went a day's journey into the wilderness, and came and sat down under a juniper-tree: and he requested for himself that he might die: and said, It is enough; now, O LORD, take away my life; for I *am* not better than my fathers.

Job. 3: 1 After this opened Job his mouth, and cursed his day.

Ps. 73: 2 As for me, my feet were almost gone; my steps had well nigh slipped. 3 For I was envious at the foolish, *when* I saw the prosperity of the wicked. 13 Verily I have cleansed my heart *in* vain, and washed my hands in innocency. 14 For all the day long have I been plagued, and chastened every morning.

Is. 49: 14 But Zion said, The LORD hath forsaken me, and my Lord hath forgotten me.

Jer. 20: 14 Cursed be the day wherein I was born.

Lam. 3: 2 He hath led me, and brought *me into* darkness, but not *into* light. 3 Surely against me is he turned; he turneth his hand *against me* all the day. 7 He hath hedged me about, that I cannot get out: he hath made my chain heavy. 8 Also when I cry and shout, he shutteth out my prayer.

Jonah 4: 1 It displeased Jonah exceedingly, and he was very angry. 2 And he prayed unto the LORD, and said, I pray thee, O LORD, *was* not this my saying, when I was yet in my country? Therefore I fled before unto Tarshish; for I knew that thou *art* a gracious God, and merciful, slow to anger, and of great kindness, and repentest thee of the evil. 3 Therefore now, O LORD, take, I beseech thee, my life from me; for *it is* better for me to die than to live. 4 Then said the LORD, Doest thou well to be angry?

[See 9, 171, 272, 700.]

25. *Backsliders insensible of their state.*

Hos. 7: 8 Ephraim is a cake not turned. 9 Strangers have devoured his strength, and he knoweth *it* not: yea, gray hairs are here and there upon him, yet he knoweth not.

Rom. 2: 17 Behold, thou art called a Jew, and restest in the law, and makest thy boast of God, 18 And knowest *his* will, and approvest the things that are more excellent, being instructed out of the law, 19 And art confident that thou thyself art a guide of the blind, a light of them which are in darkness.

Rev. 3: 17 Because thou sayest, I am rich, and increased with goods, and have need of nothing; and knowest not that thou art wretched, and miserable, and poor, and blind, and naked. [See 704.]

26. *Backsliders walk in darkness.*

Job 23: 8 Behold, I go forward, but he *is* not *there;* and backward, but I cannot perceive him: 9 On the left hand, where he doth work, but I cannot behold *him:* he hideth himself on the right hand, that I cannot see *him.*

Is. 59: 2 Your iniquities have separated between you and your God, and your sins have hid *his* face from you, that he will not hear.

Mat. 6: 22 The light of the body is the eye: if therefore thine eye be single, thy whole body shall be full of light. 23 But if thine eye be evil, thy whole body shall be full of darkness. If therefore the light that is in thee be darkness, how great *is* that darkness! [See 707.]

27. *Backsliders threatened and visited with evils.*

Ex. 32: 9 The LORD said unto Moses, I have seen this people, and behold, it *is* a stiff-necked people: 10 Now therefore let me alone, that my wrath may wax hot against them, and that I may consume them: and I will make of thee a great nation.

Ezra 8: 22 The hand of our God *is* upon all them for good that seek him; but his power and his wrath *is* against all them that forsake him.

Pr. 14: 14 The backslider in heart shall be filled with his own ways: and a good man *shall be satisfied* from himself.

Jer. 2: 19 Thine own wickedness shall correct thee, and thy backslidings shall reprove thee: know therefore and see that *it is* an evil *thing* and bitter, that thou hast forsaken the LORD thy God, and that my fear *is* not in thee, saith the Lord GOD of hosts.

Hos. 6: 4 O Ephraim, what shall I do unto thee? O Judah, what shall I do unto thee? for your goodness *is* as a morning cloud, and as the early dew it goeth away. 5 Therefore have I hewed *them* by the prophets; I have slain them by the words of my mouth: and thy judgments *are as* the light *that* goeth forth.

Zep. 1: 4 I will cut off the name of the Chemarims with the priests: 6 And them that are turned back from the LORD.

Heb. 10: 38 The just shall live by faith: but if *any man* draw back, my soul shall have no pleasure in him. [See 19.]

28. *Backsliders called to repentance.*

Jer. 3: 14 Turn, O backsliding children, saith the LORD; for I am married unto you: and I will take you one of a city, and two of a family, and I will bring you to Zion: 22 Return, ye backsliding children, *and* I will heal your backslidings.

Hos. 10: 12 Sow to yourselves in righteousness, reap in mercy; break up your fallow ground: for *it is* time to seek the LORD, till he come and rain righteousness upon you. — 14: 1 O Israel, return unto the LORD thy God; for thou hast fallen by thine iniquity. 2 Take with you words, and turn to the LORD: say unto him, Take away all iniquity, and receive *us* graciously: so will we render the calves of our lips.

Rev. 2: 4 I have *somewhat* against thee, because thou hast left thy first love. 5 Remember therefore from whence thou art fallen, and repent, and do the first works; or else I will come unto thee quickly, and will remove thy candlestick out of his place, except thou repent. — 3: 1 I know thy works, that thou hast a name that thou livest, and art dead. 2 Be watchful, and strengthen the things which remain, that are ready to die: for I have not found thy works perfect before God. 3 Remember therefore how thou hast received and heard, and hold fast, and repent. If therefore thou shalt not watch, I will come on thee as a thief, and thou shalt not know what hour I will come upon thee.

29. *Backsliders hard to reclaim — need re-conversion.*

Lk. 22: 31 The Lord said, Simon, Simon, behold, Satan hath

desired *to have* you, that he may sift *you* as wheat: 32 But I have prayed for thee, that thy faith fail not: and when thou art converted, strengthen thy brethren.

Gal. 4: 19 My little children, of whom I travail in birth again, until Christ be formed in you, 20 I desire to be present with you now, and to change my voice; for I stand in doubt of you. [See 143, 166.]

30. *Backsliders, when reclaimed, heartily repent and confess their sins.*

Job 40: 3 Job answered the LORD, and said, 4 Behold, I am vile; what shall I answer thee? I will lay my hand upon my mouth. 5 Once have I spoken; but I will not answer: yea, twice; but I will proceed no further.

Ps. 102: 3 My days are consumed like smoke, and my bones are burned as an hearth. 4 My heart is smitten, and withered like grass; so that I forget to eat my bread. 5 By reason of the voice of my groaning my bones cleave to my skin. 6 I am like a pelican of the wilderness: I am like an owl of the desert. 7 I watch, and am as a sparrow alone upon the house-top. [See 124, 356, 603.]

BAPTISM.

31. *Mosaic baptisms.*

Ex. 29: 4 Aaron and his sons thou shalt bring unto the door of the tabernacle of the congregation, and shalt wash them with water.

Lev. 8: 5 Moses said unto the congregation, This *is* the thing which the LORD commanded to be done. 6 And Moses brought Aaron and his sons, and washed them with water.

Num. 8: 5 The LORD spake unto Moses, saying, 6 Take the Levites from among the children of Israel, and cleanse them. 7 And thus shalt thou do unto them, to cleanse them: Sprinkle water of purifying upon them, and let them shave all their flesh, and let them wash their clothes, and *so* make themselves clean.

Mk. 7: 2 When they saw some of his disciples eat bread with defiled (that is to say, with unwashen) hands, they found fault. 3 For the Pharisees, and all the Jews, except they wash *their* hands oft, eat not, holding the tradition of the elders. 4 And *when they come* from the market, except they wash [Gr. *Baptisontai,*] they eat not. And many other things there be, which they have received to hold, *as* the washing [Gr. *baptismous*] of cups, and pots, and brazen vessels, and tables.

Lk. 11: 38 When the Pharisee saw *it*, he marvelled that he had not first washed [Gr. *ebaptisthe*] before dinner.

Heb. 9: 10 *Which stood* only in meats and drinks, and divers washings [Gr. *baptismois*,] and carnal ordinances, imposed *on them* until the time of reformation.

32. *Figurative baptism and circumcision.*

Ps. 51: 2 Wash me thoroughly from mine iniquity, and cleanse me from my sin. 7 Purge me with hyssop, and I shall be clean : wash me, and I shall be whiter than snow.

Is. 4: 4 When the LORD shall have washed away the filth of the daughters of Zion.

Mat. 3: 11 He shall baptize you with the Holy Ghost, and *with* fire. — 20: 22 Jesus answered and said, Ye know not what ye ask. Are ye able to drink of the cup that I shall drink of, and to be baptized with the baptism that I am baptized with ?

Lk. 12: 50 I have a baptism to be baptized with ; and how am I straitened till it be accomplished !

Jn. 3: 5 Jesus answered, Verily, verily, I say unto thee, Except a man be born of water, and *of* the Spirit, he cannot enter into the kingdom of God.

Ac. 1: 5 John truly baptized with water ; but ye shall be baptized with the Holy Ghost not many days hence.

Rom. 2: 28 He is not a Jew, which is one outwardly ; neither *is that* circumcision, which is outward in the flesh : 29 But he *is* a Jew which is one inwardly ; and circumcision *is that* of the heart, in the spirit, *and* not in the letter ; whose praise *is* not of men, but of God. — 6: 3 Know ye not that so many of us as were baptized into Jesus Christ, were baptized into his death ? 4 Therefore we are buried with him by baptism into death : that like as Christ was raised up from the dead by the glory of the Father, even so we also should walk in newness of life. 5 For if we have been planted together in the likeness of his death, we shall be also *in the likeness* of *his* resurrection.

1 Cor. 10: 1 Moreover, brethren, I would not that ye should be ignorant how that all our fathers were under the cloud, and all passed through the sea ; 2 And were all baptized unto Moses in the cloud and in the sea. — 12: 13 By one Spirit are we all baptized unto one body, whether *we be* Jews or Gentiles, whether *we be* bond or free, and have been all made to drink into one spirit.

Gal. 3: 27 For as many of you as have been baptized into Christ, have put on Christ.

Col. 2: 11 In whom also ye are circumcised with the circumcision' made without hands, in putting off the body of the sins of the flesh by the circumcision of Christ : 12 Buried with him in baptism, wherein also ye are risen with *him* through the faith of the operation of God, who hath raised him from the dead. 13 And you, being dead in your sins and the uncircumcision of your flesh, hath he quickened together with him, having forgiven you all trespasses.

Tit. 3: 5 Not by works of righteousness which we have done, but according to his mercy he saved us, by the washing of regeneration, and renewing of the Holy Ghost; 6 Which he shed on us abundantly, through Jesus Christ our Saviour.

33. John's baptism, a token of repentance, inward purity, and preparation for Christ's advent.

Mal. 3: 1 Behold, I will send my messenger, and he shall prepare the way before me.

Mk. 1: 4 John did baptize in the wilderness, and preach the baptism of repentance, for the remission of sins.

Lk. 1: 17 He shall go before him in the spirit and power of Elias, to turn the hearts of the fathers to the children, and the disobedient to the wisdom of the just; to make ready a people prepared for the Lord. — 3: 3 He came into all the country about Jordan, preaching the baptism of repentance, for the remission of sins; 4 As it is written in the book of the words of Esaias the prophet, saying, The voice of one crying in the wilderness, Prepare ye the way of the Lord, make his paths straight. [Is. 40: 3.]

Jn. 1: 30 This is he of whom I said, After me cometh a man which is preferred before me; for he was before me. 31 And I knew him not: but that he should be made manifest to Israel, therefore am I come baptizing with water.

34. Was John's baptism in the name of the Holy Ghost?

Ac. 18: 24 A certain Jew, named Apollos, born at Alexandria, an eloquent man, *and* mighty in the Scriptures, came to Ephesus. 25 This man was instructed in the way of the Lord: and being fervent in the spirit, he spake and taught diligently the things of the Lord, knowing only the baptism of John. — 19: 1 And it came to pass, that while Apollos was at Corinth, Paul having passed through the upper coasts, came to Ephesus; and finding certain disciples, 2 He said unto them, Have ye received the Holy Ghost since ye believed? And they said unto him, We have not so much as heard whether there be any Holy Ghost. 3 And he said unto them, Unto what then were ye baptized? And they said, Unto John's baptism. 4 Then said Paul, John verily baptized with the baptism of repentance, saying unto the people, that they should believe on him which should come after him, that is, on

Christ Jesus. 5 When they heard *this*, they were baptized in the name of the Lord Jesus.

35. *Did Christ solicit baptism, to be introduced into the Aaronic priesthood, or to sanction the divine ordinance of John's baptism, and "be made manifest to Israel?"*

Mat. 3: 13 Then cometh Jesus from Galilee to Jordan unto John, to be baptized of him. 14 But John forbade him, saying, I have need to be baptized of thee, and comest thou to me? 15 And Jesus answering said unto him, Suffer *it to be so* now: for.thus it becometh us to fulfil all righteousness. Then he suffered him.

Heb. 7: 11 If therefore perfection were by the Levitical priesthood, (for under it the people received the law,) what further need *was there* that another priest should rise after the order of Melchisedec, and not be called after the order of Aaron? 12 For the priesthood being changed, there is made of necessity a change also of the law. 13 For he of whom these things are spoken pertaineth to another tribe, of which no man gave attendance at the altar. 14 For *it is* evident that our Lord sprang out of Juda; of which tribe Moses spake nothing concerning priesthood.

36. *Christian baptism instituted, and enjoined upon believers.*

Mat. 28: 18 Jesus came, and spake unto them, saying, All power is given unto me in heaven and in earth. 19 Go ye therefore and teach all nations, baptizing them in the name of the Father, and of the Son, and of the Holy Ghost; 20 Teaching them to observe all things whatsoever I have commanded you: and lo, I am with you alway, *even* unto the end of the world.

Mk. 16: 16 He that believeth and is baptized, shall be saved; but he that believeth not, shall be damned.

Ac. 2: 38 Peter said unto them, Repent, and be baptized every one of you in the name of Jesus Christ, for the remission of sins, and ye shall receive the gift of the Holy Ghost. — 10: 48 And he [Peter] commanded them to be baptized in the name of the Lord. — 22: 16 Why tarriest thou? arise, and be baptized, and wash away thy sins, calling on the name of the Lord.

37. *The proper administrators of Christian baptism.*

Mat. 28: 19 Go ye therefore and teach all nations, baptizing them in the name of the Father, and of the Son, and of the Holy Ghost.

Jn. 3: 22 After these things came Jesus and his disciples

into the land of Judea; and there he tarried with them, and baptized.

Ac. 8: 12 When they believed Philip, preaching the things concerning the kingdom of God, and the name of Jesus Christ, they were baptized both men and women.

38. *The proper subjects of baptism.*

Ac. 2: 38 Peter said unto them, Repent, and be baptized every one of you in the name of Jesus Christ, for the remission of sins, and ye shall receive the gift of the Holy Ghost. 39 For the promise is unto you, and to your children, and to all that are afar off, *even* as many as the Lord our God shall call. 40 And with many other words did he testify and exhort, saying, Save yourselves from this untoward generation. 41 Then they that gladly received his word, were baptized: and the same day there were added *unto them* about three thousand souls. — 8: 36 And as they went on *their* way, they came unto a certain water: and the eunuch said, See, *here is* water; what doth hinder me to be baptized? 37 And Philip said, If thou believest with all thine heart, thou mayest. And he answered and said, I believe that Jesus Christ is the Son of God. — 10: 46 Then answered Peter, 47 Can any man forbid water, that these should not be baptized, which have received the Holy Ghost as well as we? 48 And he commanded them to be baptized in the name of the Lord. — 16: 14 A certain woman named Lydia, a seller of purple, of the city of Thyatira, which worshipped God, heard *us:* whose heart the Lord opened, that she attended unto the things which were spoken of Paul. 15 And when she was baptized, and her household, she besought *us,* saying, If ye have judged me to be faithful to the Lord, come into my house, and abide *there:* And she constrained us. 29 Then he called for a light, and sprang in, and came trembling, and fell down before Paul and Silas; 30 And brought them out, and said, Sirs, what must I do to be saved? 31 And they said, Believe on the Lord Jesus Christ, and thou shalt be saved, and thy house. 32 And they spake unto him the word of the Lord, and to all that were in his house. 33 And he took them the same hour of the night, and washed *their* stripes; and was baptized, he and all his, straightway. 34 And when he had brought them into his house, he set meat before them, and rejoiced, believing in God with all his house. — 18: 8 Crispus, the chief ruler of the synagogue, believed on the Lord with all his house: and many of the Corinthians hearing, believed, and were baptized.

44

1 Cor. 1: 16 I baptized also the household of Stephanas; besides, I know not whether I baptized any other. [See 117—121.]

39. Mode of baptism.

1. *Passages referred to by those who immerse.*

Mat. 3: 5 Then went out to him Jerusalem, and all Judea, and all the region round about Jordan, 6 And were baptized of him in Jordan, confessing their sins. 16 And Jesus, when he was baptized, went up straightway out of the water.

Jn. 3: 23 John also was baptizing in Ænon, near to Salim, because there was much water there: and they came, and were baptized.

Ac. 8: 38 He commanded the chariot to stand still: and they went down both into the water, both Philip and the eunuch; and he baptized him. 39 And when they were come up out of the water, the Spirit of the Lord caught away Philip, that the eunuch saw him no more.

Col. 2: 12 Buried with him in baptism, wherein also ye are risen with *him* through the faith of the operation of God, who hath raised him from the dead. Rom. 6: 4. [See 32.]

2. *Passages referred to by those who sprinkle or pour.*

Is. 44: 3 I will pour water upon him that is thirsty, and floods upon the dry ground: I will pour my Spirit upon thy seed, and my blessing upon thine offspring. — 52: 15 So shall he sprinkle many nations.

Ezk. 36: 25 Then will I sprinkle clean water upon you, and ye shall be clean: from all your filthiness, and from all your idols, will I cleanse you. [Num. 8: 7.]

Heb. 10: 22 Let us draw near with a true heart, in full assurance of faith, having our hearts sprinkled from an evil conscience, and our bodies washed with pure water. — 12: 24 To Jesus the Mediator of the new covenant, and to the blood of sprinkling, that speaketh better things than *that of* Abel.

1 Pet. 1: 2 Elect according to the foreknowledge of God the Father, through sanctification of the Spirit, unto obedience and sprinkling of the blood of Jesus Christ. [See 31, 620.]

BIBLE.

40. Bible, the inspired word of God.

2 S. 23: 1 The sweet psalmist of Israel, said, 2 The Spirit of the LORD spake by me, and his word *was* in my tongue.

· **2 K.** 17: 13 The LORD testified against Israel and against Judah, by all the prophets, *and by* all the seers, saying, Turn ye from your evil ways, and keep my commandments, *and* my statutes, according to all the law which I commanded your fathers, and which I sent to you by my servants the prophets.

2 Ch. 34: 21 Our fathers have not kept the word of the LORD, to do after all that is written in this book. — 36: 21 To fulfil the word of the LORD by the mouth of Jeremiah.

Neh. 9: 30 Many years didst thou forbear them, and testifiedst against them by thy Spirit in thy prophets.

Jer. 1: 9 Then the LORD put forth his hand, and touched my mouth. And the LORD said unto me, Behold, I have put my words in thy mouth. — 36: 1 And it came to pass in the fourth year of Jehoiakim the son of Josiah king of Judah, *that* this word came unto Jeremiah from the LORD, saying, 2 Take thee a roll of a book, and write therein all the words that I have spoken unto thee against Israel, and against Judah, and against all the nations, from the day I spake unto thee, from the days of Josiah, even unto this day.

Zec. 7: 12 Yea, they made their hearts *as* an adamant stone, lest they should hear the law, and the words which the LORD of hosts hath sent in his Spirit by the former prophets: therefore came a great wrath from the LORD of hosts. ·

Lk. 1: 70 As he spake by the mouth of his holy prophets, which have been since the world began.

Ac. 1: 16 Men *and* brethren, this scripture must needs have been fulfilled, which the Holy Ghost, by the mouth of David spake before concerning Judas, which was guide to them that took Jesus. — 3: 18 Those things which God before had shewed by the mouth of all his prophets, that Christ should suffer, he hath so fulfilled — 28: 25 And when they agreed not among themselves, they departed, after that Paul had spoken one word, Well spake the Holy Ghost by Esaias the prophet unto our fathers.

Rom. 3: 2 Unto them were committed the oracles of God. [1 Pet. 4: 11.]

1 Cor. 2: 12 Now we have received, not the spirit of the world, but the Spirit which is of God; that we might know the things that are freely given to us of God. 13 Which things also we speak, not in the words which man's wisdom teacheth, but which the Holy Ghost teacheth; comparing spiritual things with spiritual.

Gal. 1: 11 I certify you, brethren, that the gospel which was preached of me is not after man: 12 For I neither received it of man, neither was I taught *it*, but by the revelation of Jesus Christ.

1 Th. 2: 13 For this cause also thank we God without ceasing, because, when ye received the word of God which ye heard of us, ye received *it* not *as* the word of men, but (as it is in truth) the word of God, which effectually worketh also in you that believe.

2 Tim. 3: 16 All scripture *is* given by inspiration of God, and *is* profitable for doctrine, for reproof, for correction, for instruction in righteousness : 17 That the man of God may be perfect, thoroughly furnished unto all good works.

Heb. 1: 1 God, who at sundry times and in divers manners spake in time past unto the fathers by the prophets, 2 Hath in these last days spoken unto us by *his* Son.

2 Pet. 1 18 This voice which came from heaven we heard, when we were with him in the holy mount. 19 We have also a more sure word of prophecy : whereunto ye do well that ye take heed, as unto a light that shineth in a dark place, until the day dawn, and the day-star arise in your hearts ; 20 Knowing this first, that no prophecy of the scripture is of any private interpretation. 21 For the prophecy came not in old time by the will of man; but holy men of God spake *as they were* moved by the Holy Ghost.

41. *Bible, the everlasting truth of God.*

Ps. 19: 9 The fear of the LORD *is* clean, enduring for ever: the judgments of the LORD *are* true *and* righteous altogether. — 93: 5 Thy testimonies are very sure. — 119: 142 Thy law *is* the truth.

Is. 25: 1 *Thy* counsels of old *are* faithfulness *and* truth. — 40: 8 The grass withereth, the flower fadeth : but the word of our God shall stand for ever.

42. *Bible will be fulfilled.*

Mat. 5: 17 Think not that I am come to destroy the law, or the prophets : I am not come to destroy, but to fulfil. 18 For verily, I say unto you, Till heaven and earth pass, one jot or one tittle shall in no wise pass from the law, till all be fulfilled. — 24: 35 Heaven and earth shall pass away, but my words shall not pass away.

Lk. 16: 17 It is easier for heaven and earth to pass, than one tittle of the law to fail. — 24: 44 He said unto to them, These *are* the words which I spake unto you, while I was yet with you, that all things must be fulfilled which were written in the law of Moses, and *in* the prophets, and *in* the psalms, concerning me.

Jn. 10: 35. The scripture cannot be broken.

Ac. 1: 16 Men *and* brethren, this scripture must needs have been fulfilled, which the Holy Ghost by the mouth of David spake before concerning Judas, which was guide to them that took Jesus. — 3: 18. But those things which God before had shewed by the mouth of all his prophets, that Christ should suffer, he hath so fulfilled. [See 284.]

43. *Miracles wrought to confirm the word of God.*

Exod. 4: 4. The LORD said unto Moses, Put forth thine hand, and take it by the tail. And he put forth his hand, and caught it, and it became a rod in his hand: 5 That they may believe that the LORD God of their fathers, the God of Abraham, the God of Isaac, and the God of Jacob, hath appeared unto thee. — 14: 31 Israel saw that great work which the Lord did upon the Egyptians: and the people feared the LORD, and believed the LORD, and his servant Moses. — 19: 9 The Lord said unto Moses, Lo, I come unto thee in a thick cloud, that the people may hear when I speak with thee, and believe thee for ever.

1 K. 18: 38 Then the fire of the LORD fell, and consumed the burnt-sacrifice, and the wood, and the stones, and the dust, and licked up the water that *was* in the trench. 39 And when all the people saw *it*, they fell on their faces: and they said, The LORD, he *is* the God; the LORD he *is* the God.

Mk. 16: 20 They went forth, and preached every where, the Lord working with *them*, and confirming the word with signs following.

Jn. 3: 1 There was a man of the Pharisees named Nicodemus, a ruler of the Jews: 2 The same came to Jesus by night, and said unto him, Rabbi, we know that thou art a teacher come from God; for no man can do these miracles that thou doest, except God be with him.

Ac. 8: 6. The people with one accord gave heed unto those things which Philip spake, hearing and seeing the miracles which he did. — 14: 3 Long time therefore abode they speaking boldly in the Lord, which gave testimony unto the word of his grace, and granted signs and wonders to be done by their hands.

Heb. 2: 4 God also bearing *them* witness, both with signs and wonders, and with divers miracles, and gifts of the Holy Ghost. [See 77.]

44. *Bible confirmed by prophecy.*

Gen. 49: 10 The sceptre shall not depart from Judah, nor a

lawgiver from between his feet, until Shiloh come : and unto him *shall* the gathering of the people *be.*

See also David's prophecy of the resurrection of Christ, (Ps. 16: 10 ;) — and Isaiah's prediction of Christ, (Is. 7: 14, and 35: 3—6 ; and 53d chap. entire ;) — and his prophecy against Babylon, (Is. 13: 17—22, and 14: 22, 23 ; and 47th chap. entire ;) and his prophecy of Cyrus, (Is. 45: 1—3 ;) and Jeremiah's prophecy against Babylon, (Jer. 50: 23—40, and 51: 30—44.;) and Ezekiel's prophecy respecting the overthrow of Tyre, (Ezk. 26: 7—11 ;) and Nebuchadnezzar's invasion of Egypt, (Ezk. 29: 18—20 ;) and Daniel's interpretation of Nebuchadnezzar's dream, (Dan. 2: 31—35 ;) — and his prophecy respecting the rise and power of antichrist, (Dan. 7: 24, 25, and chapters 7, 8, 9, 10, 11, and 12, entire ;) — and Nahum's prophecy respecting the overthrow of Nineveh, in the 2d and 3d chapters of Nahum ; and Zephaniah's prophecy against Nineveh, (Zep. 2: 13—15 ;) — and Zechariah's prediction respecting the 30 pieces of silver paid Judas, (Zec. 11: 12, 13 ;) — and Christ's prophecy respecting the Temple, (Mat. 24: 1, 2, 15, 16, 21 ;) and respecting Jerusalem, (Lk. 19: 43, 44 ;) and Paul's prophecy respecting the man of sin, (2 Th. 2: 3, 4.)

45. Bible confirmed by its internal evidences.

1. By revelations above reason and human capacity.

Gen. 1: 1 In the beginning God created the heaven and the earth.

Ps. 19: 12 Who can understand *his* errors ?—49: 11 Their inward thought *is, that* their houses *shall continue* for ever, *and* their dwelling-places to all generations ; they call *their* lands after their own names.

Pr. 16: 4 The LORD hath made all *things* for himself : yea, even the wicked for the day of evil.

Is. 40: 17 All nations before him *are* as nothing ; and they are counted to him less than nothing, and vanity.

Jer. 17: 9 The heart *is* deceitful above all *things*, and desperately wicked : who can know it ?

1 Cor. 15: 35 Some *man* will say, How are the dead raised up ? and with what body do they come ? 44 It is sown a natural body, it is raised a spiritual body. There is a natural body, and there is a spiritual body.

2 Tim. 1: 10 But it is now made manifest by the appearing of our Saviour Jesus Christ, who hath abolished death, and hath brought life and immortality to light through the gospel.

2 Pet. 3: 10 The day of the Lord will come as a thief in

5

the night; in the which the heavens shall pass away with a great noise, and the elements shall melt with fervent heat, the earth also and the works that are therein shall be burned up.

1 Jn. 4: 8 He that loveth not, knoweth not God; for God is love.—5: 7 There are three that bear record in heaven, the Father, the Word, and the Holy Ghost: and these three are one.

Rev. 20: 11 I saw a great white throne, and him that sat on it, from whose face the earth and the heaven fled away; and there was found no place for them.—22: 16 I am the root and the offspring of David, *and* the bright and morning-star.

. 2. *By the purity of its requirements.*

Ps. 119: 7 The law of the LORD *is* perfect, converting the soul: the testimony of the LORD *is* sure, making wise the simple. 8 The statutes of the LORD *are* right, rejoicing the heart: the commandment of the LORD *is* pure, enlightening the eyes. 9 The fear of the LORD *is* clean, enduring for ever: the judgments of the LORD *are* true *and* righteous altogether.

Pr. 30: 5 Every word of God *is* pure: he *is* a shield unto them that put their trust in him. [See 47, 285.]

46. *Bible, the true standard of faith and practice — danger of false standards.*

Is. 8: 20 To the law and to the testimony: if they speak not according to this word, *it is* because *there is* no light in them.

Mat. 15: 3 He answered and said unto them, Why do ye also transgress the commandment of God by your tradition? 4 For God commanded, saying, Honor thy father and mother: and, He that curseth father or mother, let him die the death. 5 But ye say, Whosoever shall say to *his* father or *his* mother, *It is* a gift, by whatsoever thou mightest be profited by me; 6 And honor not his father or his mother, *he shall be free.* Thus have ye made the commandment of God of none effect by your tradition.

Mk. 7: 7 In vain do they worship me, teaching *for* doctrines the commandments of men. 8 For, laying aside the commandment of God, ye hold the tradition of men, *as* the washing of pots and cups: and many other such like things ye do. 9 He said unto them, Full well ye reject the commandment of God, that ye may keep your own tradition.

Jn. 12: 48 He that rejecteth me, and receiveth not my words, hath one that judgeth him: the word that I have spoken, the same shall judge him in the last day.

Rom. 2: 16 In the day when God shall judge the secrets of men by Jesus Christ, according to my gospel.

2 Cor. 10: 12 We dare not make ourselves of the number, or compare ourselves with some that commend themselves: but they, measuring themselves by themselves, and comparing themselves among themselves, are not wise.

Col. 2: 8 Beware lest any man spoil you through philosophy and vain deceit, after the tradition of men, after the rudiments of the world, and not after Christ.

47. *Bible, the true means of grace.*

Ps. 19: 7 The law of the LORD *is* perfect, converting the soul: the testimony of the LORD *is* sure, making wise the simple.—119: 93 I will never forget thy precepts: for with them thou hast quickened me.

Jn. 15: 3 Ye are clean through the word which I have spoken unto you—17: 17 Sanctify them through thy truth: thy word is truth. 19 And for their sakes I sanctify myself, that they also might be sanctified through the truth.

Rom. 1: 16 I am not ashamed of the gospel of Christ: for it is the power of God unto salvation to every one that believeth; to the Jew first, and also to the Greek.—10: 17 Faith *cometh* by hearing, and hearing by the word of God.

Ep. 6: 17 Take the helmet of salvation, and the sword of the Spirit, which is the word of God.

2 Tim. 3: 15 From a child thou hast known the holy scriptures, which are able to make thee wise unto salvation through faith which is in Christ Jesus.

Jam. 1: 18 Of his own will begat he us with the word of truth, that we should be a kind of first-fruits of his creatures. 21 Wherefore lay apart all filthiness, and superfluity of naughtiness, and receive with meekness the ingrafted word, which is able to save your souls.

1 Pet. 1: 23 Being born again, not of corruptible seed, but of incorruptible, by the word of God, which liveth and abideth for ever. [See 428—432.]

48. *Studying and teaching the Bible required and encouraged.*

Dt. 11: 18 Therefore shall ye lay up these my words in your heart and in your soul, and bind them for a sign upon your hand, that they may be as frontlets between your eyes. 19 And ye shall teach them your children, speaking of them when thou sittest in thine house, and when thou walkest by the way, when thou liest down, and when thou risest up. 20 And thou shalt write them upon the door posts of thine house, and upon thy gates: 21 That your days may be multiplied, and the days of your children, in the land which the LORD sware unto your fathers to give them, as the days of heaven upon the earth.

Jos. 1: 8 This book of the law shall not depart out of thy mouth; but thou shalt meditate therein day and night, that thou mayest observe to do according to all that is written therein: for then thou shalt make thy way prosperous, and then thou shalt have good success.

Ps. 1: 1 Blessed *is* the man that walketh not in the counsel of the ungodly, nor standeth in the way of sinners, nor sitteth in the seat of the scornful. 2 But his delight *is* in the law of the LORD; and in his law doth he meditate day and night.

Pr. 4: 13 Take fast hold of instruction; let *her* not go: keep her: for she *is* thy life. 20 My son, attend to my words; incline thine ear unto my sayings. 21 Let them not depart from thine eyes; keep them in the midst of thine heart. 22 For they *are* life unto those that find them, and health to all their flesh.

Mat. 22: 29 Jesus answered and said unto them, Ye do err, not knowing the scriptures, nor the power of God.

Jn. 5: 39 Search the scriptures; for in them ye think ye have eternal life: And they are they which testify of me.

Ac. 17: 11 These were more noble than those in Thessalonica, in that they received the word with all readiness of mind, and searched the scriptures daily, whether those things were so.

Rom. 15: 4 Whatsoever things were written aforetime, were written for our learning, that we through patience and comfort of the scriptures might have hope.

1 Th. 5: 27 I charge you by the Lord that this epistle be read unto all the holy brethren.

Heb. 2: 1 We ought to give the more earnest heed to the things which we have heard, lest at any time we should let *them* slip.

1 Pet. 2: 2 As new-born babes, desire the sincere milk of the word, that ye may grow thereby.

Rev. 1: 3 Blessed *is* he that readeth, and they that hear the words of this prophecy, and keep those things which are written therein: for the time *is* at hand. [Ps. 19, and 119, entire.]
[See 279, 458, 493.]

49. *Bible a written revelation, and intelligible.*

Dt. 9: 10 The LORD delivered unto me two tables of stone written with the finger of God; and on them *was written* according to all the words which the LORD spake with you in the mount, out of the midst of the fire.

Ps. 102: 18 This shall be written for the generation to come: and the people which shall be created shall praise the LORD.

Ps. 119: 105 Thy word *is* a lamp unto my feet, and a light unto my path. 130 The entrance of thy words giveth light; it giveth understanding unto the simple.

2 Pet. 1: 18 This voice which came from heaven we heard, when we were with him in the holy mount. 19 We have also a more sure word of prophecy; whereunto ye do well that ye take heed, as unto a light that shineth in a dark place, until the day dawn; and the day-star arise in your hearts.

50. *Sin and danger of altering or wresting the Bible.*

Dt. 4: 2 Ye shall not add unto the word which I command you, neither shall ye diminish *aught* from it, that ye may keep the commandments of the LORD your God which I command you.

Pr. 30: 6 Add thou not unto his words, lest he reprove thee, and thou be found a liar.

2 Pet. 3: 15 And account *that* the long-suffering of our Lord *is* salvation; even as our beloved brother Paul also, according to the wisdom given unto him, hath written unto you; 16 As also in all *his* epistles, speaking in them of these things; in which are some things hard to be understood, which they that are unlearned and unstable wrest, as *they do* also the other scriptures, unto their own destruction.

Rev. 22: 18 I testify unto every man that heareth the words of the prophecy of this book, If any man shall add unto these things, God shall add unto him the plagues that are written in this book: 19 And if any man shall take away from the words of the book of this prophecy, God shall take away his part out of the book of life, and out of the holy city, and *from* the things which are written in this book. [See 284.]

51. *The whole Bible profitable and important.*

Dt. 29: 29 The secret *things belong* unto the LORD our God: but those *things which are* revealed *belong* unto us, and to our children for ever, that *we* may do all the words of this law.

2 Tim. 3: 16 All scripture *is* given by inspiration of God, and *is* profitable for doctrine, for reproof, for correction, for instruction in righteousness: 17 That the man of God may be perfect, thoroughly furnished unto all good works.

[See 47, and 279 and 433.]

CHEERFULNESS.

52. Duty and advantages of cheerfulness.

Neh. 8: 10 Neither be ye sorry; for the joy of the LORD is your strength.

Pr. 14: 30 A sound heart *is* the life of the flesh: but envy the rottenness of the bones. [Ps. 119: 80.] — 15: 13 A merry heart maketh a cheerful countenance: but by sorrow of the heart the spirit is broken. 15 He that is of a merry heart *hath* a continual feast. — 17: 22 A merry heart doeth good *like* a medicine: but a broken spirit drieth the bones.

Jn. 16: 33 These things I have spoken unto you, that in me ye might have peace. In the world ye shall have tribulation, but be of good cheer: I have overcome the world.

1 Th. 5: 16 Rejoice evermore. [See 296, 634.]

CHILDREN.

53. Duties of children to parents.

Ex. 20: 12 Honor thy father and thy mother; that thy days may be long upon the land which the Lord thy God giveth thee.

Lev. 19: 3 Ye shall fear every man his mother and his father.

Pr. 1: 8 My son, hear the instruction of thy father, and forsake not the law of thy mother: 9 For they *shall be* an ornament of grace unto thy head, and chains about thy neck. — 6: 20 My son, keep thy father's commandment, and forsake not the law of thy mother: 21 Bind them continually upon thine heart, *and* tie them about thy neck. 22 When thou goest, it shall lead thee; when thou sleepest, it shall keep thee; and *when* thou awakest, it shall talk with thee. — 13: 1 A wise son *heareth* his father's instruction: but a scorner heareth not rebuke. — 23: 22 Hearken unto thy father that begat thee, and despise not thy mother when she is old.

Mat. 15: 4 God commanded, saying, Honor thy father and mother: and, He that curseth father or mother, let him die the death. 5 But ye say, Whosoever shall say to *his* father or *his* mother, *It is* a gift, by whatsoever thou mightest be profited by me; 6 And honor not his father or his mother, *he shall be free.* Thus have ye made the commandment of God of none effect by your tradition.

Lk. 2: 51 He [Christ] went down with them, [his parents] and came to Nazareth, and was subject unto them.

54

Disobedient children punished — Early piety.

Ep. 6: 1 Children, obey your parents in the Lord: for this is right. 2 Honor thy father and mother, (which is the first commandment with promise,) 3 That it may be well with thee, and thou mayest live long on the earth.

Col. 3: 20 Children, obey *your* parents in all things: for this is well-pleasing unto the Lord. [See 10.]

54. *Penalties for disobeying and abusing parents.*

Ex. 21: 15 He that smiteth his father, or his mother, shall be surely put to death. 17 And he that curseth his father or his mother, shall surely be put to death.

Dt. 21: 18 If a man have a stubborn and rebellious son, which will not obey the voice of his father, or the voice of his mother, and *that*, when they have chastened him, will not hearken unto them: 21 And all the men of his city shall stone him with stones, that he die: so shalt thou put evil away from among you, and all Israel shall hear, and fear — 27: 16 Cursed *be* he that setteth light by his father or his mother: and all the people shall say, Amen.

Pr. 20: 20 Whoso curseth his father or his mother, his lamp shall be put out in obscure darkness. — 30: 17 The eye *that* mocketh at *his* father, and despiseth to obey *his* mother, the ravens of the valley shall pick it out, and the young eagles shall eat it. [See 494.]

55. *Early piety exemplified and encouraged.*

1 S. 3: 8 The LORD called Samuel again the third time. And he arose and went to Eli, and said, Here *am* I; for thou didst call me. And Eli perceived that the LORD had called the child.

2 Ch. 34: 1 Josiah *was* eight years old when he began to reign. 3 In the eighth year of his reign, while he was yet young, he began to seek after the God of David his father.

Pr. 8: 17 I love them that love me: and those that seek me early shall find me. — 22: 6 Train up a child in the way he should go: and when he is old, he will not depart from it.

Ec. 12: 1 Remember now thy Creator in the days of thy youth, while the evil days come not, nor the years draw nigh, when thou shalt say, I have no pleasure in them.

Is. 28: 9 Whom shall he teach knowledge? and whom shall he make to understand doctrine? *them that are* weaned from the milk, *and* drawn from the breasts.

2 Tim. 3: 15 And that from a child thou hast known the holy scriptures, which are able to make thee wise unto salvation through faith which is in Christ Jesus.

CHRIST JESUS.

56. *His holiness, righteousness, frankness, and disinterestedness.*

Is. 11: 5 And righteousness shall be the girdle of his loins, and faithfulness the girdle of his reins.

Pr. 8: 50 I seek not mine own glory.

Jn. 18: 19. The high priest then asked Jesus of his disciples, and of his doctrine. 20 Jesus answered him, I spake openly to the world; I ever taught in the synagogue, and in the temple, whither the Jews always resort; and in secret have I said nothing. 21 Why askest thou me? ask them which heard me, what I have said unto them: behold, they know what I said.

Ac. 3: 14 Ye denied the Holy One, and the Just.

2 Cor. 5: 21 He hath made him *to be* sin for us, who knew no sin.

Heb. 4: 15 We have not an high priest which cannot be touched with the feeling of our infirmities; but was in all points tempted like as *we are, yet* without sin.—**7: 26** Such an high priest became us, *who is* holy, harmless, undefiled, separate from sinners, and made higher than the heavens, 27 Who needeth not daily, as those high priests, to offer up sacrifice, first for his own sins, and then for the people's: for this he did once, when he offered up himself.

1 Pet. 2: 21 Christ also suffered for us, leaving us an example, that ye should follow his steps: 22 Who did no sin, neither was guile found in his mouth: 23 Who, when he was reviled, reviled not again; when he suffered, he threatened not; but committed *himself* to him that judgeth righteously.

[See 229, 630.]

57. *Christ obeyed, pleased and honored God.*

Ps. 40: 7 Then said I, Lo, I come: in the volume of the book *it is* written of me, 8 I delight to do thy will, O my God: yea, thy law *is* within my heart.

Mat. 3: 17 Lo, a voice from heaven, saying, This is my beloved Son, in whom I am well pleased.

Jn. 4: 34 Jesus saith unto them, My meat is to do the will of him that sent me, and to finish his work.—**5: 30** I seek not mine own will, but the will of the Father which hath sent me.—**6: 38** I came down from heaven, not to do my own will, but the will of him that sent me.—**8: 29** He that sent me is with me: the Father hath not left me alone; for I do always those things that please him. 49 Jesus answered, I have not a devil, but I honor my Father, and ye do dishonor me.—17: 4 I have glorified thee on the earth: I have finished the work which thou gavest me to do.

58. *Christ's poverty and self-denial.*

Mat. 8: 20 Jesus saith unto him, The foxes have holes, and the birds of the air *have* nests; but the Son of man hath not where to lay *his* head.

Rom. 15: 2 Let every one of us please *his* neighbor for *his* good to edification. 3 For even Christ pleased not himself; but, as it is written, The reproaches of them that reproached thee fell on me.

2 Cor. 8: 9 Ye know the grace of our Lord Jesus Christ, that though he was rich, yet for your sakes he became poor, that ye through his poverty might be rich.

Heb. 12: 2 Looking unto Jesus the author and finisher of *our* faith; who, for the joy [Gr. *Anti—instead of* the joy] that was set before him, endured the cross, despising the shame, and is set down at the right hand of the throne of God.

59. *How did Christ regard the world and its honors?*

Jn. 5: 41 I receive not honor from men.—16: 33 I have overcome the world. — 18: 36 Jesus answered, My kingdom is not of this world. [See 626, 743.]

60. *Christ's love and compassion towards mankind.*

Mat. 9: 35 Jesus went about all the cities and villages, teaching in their synagogues, and preaching the gospel of the kingdom, and healing every sickness, and every disease among the people. 36 But when he saw the multitudes, he was moved with compassion on them, because they fainted, and were scattered abroad, as sheep having no shepherd.—14: 14 Jesus went forth, and saw a great multitude, and was moved with compassion toward them, and he healed their sick.—15: 32 Jesus called his disciples *unto him*, and said, I have compassion on the multitude, because they continue with me now three days, and have nothing to eat: and I will not send them away fasting, lest they faint in the way. — 23: 37 O Jerusalem, Jerusalem, *thou* that killest the prophets, and stonest them which are sent unto thee, how often would I have gathered thy children together, even as a hen gathereth her chickens under *her* wings, and ye would not!

Jn. 13: 34 A new commandment I give unto you, That ye love one another; as I have loved you, that ye also love one another. — 15: 9 As the Father hath loved me, so have I loved you: continue ye in my love.

A Pattern of Condescension.

Ac. 10: 38 God anointed Jesus of Nazareth with the Holy Ghost and with power: who went about doing good, and healing all that were oppressed of the devil; for God was with him.

Rom. 5: 6 When we were yet without strength, in due time Christ died for the ungodly. 7 For scarcely for a righteous man will one die: yet peradventure for a good man some would even dare to die. 8 But God commendeth his love toward us, in that while we were yet sinners, Christ died for us.—8: 37 In all these things we are more than conquerors, through him that loved us.

Ep. 5: 2 Walk in love, as Christ also hath loved us, and hath given himself for us an offering and a sacrifice to God for a sweet-smelling savor.

[See 224–5, 228, and Invitations and Redemption.]

61. *Christ a pattern of condescension.*

Mat. 9: 11 When the Pharisees saw *it*, they said unto his disciples, Why eateth your Master with publicans and sinners? 12 But when Jesus heard *that*, he said unto them, They that be whole need not a physician, but they that are sick.—19: 14 Jesus said, Suffer little children, and forbid them not, to come unto me: for of such is the kingdom of heaven. 15 And he laid *his* hands on them, and departed thence.—20: 27 Whosoever will be chief among you, let him be your servant: 28 Even as the Son of man came not to be ministered unto, but to minister, and to give his life a ransom for many.

Lk. 22: 27 Whether *is* greater, he that sitteth at meat or he that serveth? *is* not he that sitteth at meat? but I am among you as he that serveth.

Jn. 13: 13 Ye call me Master, and Lord: and ye say well; for *so* I am. 14 If I then *your* Lord and Master have washed your feet; ye also ought to wash one another's feet.

Ph. 2: 6 Who, being in the form of God, thought it not robbery to be equal with God: 7 But made himself of no reputation, and took upon him the form of a servant, and was made in the likeness of men: 8 And being found in fashion as a man, he humbled himself, and became obedient unto death, even the death of the cross.

Heb. 2: 11 Both he that sanctifieth, and they who are sanctified, *are* all of one: for which cause he is not ashamed to call them brethren, 12 Saying, I will declare thy name unto my brethren, in the midst of the church will I sing praise unto thee. 16 For verily he took not on *him the nature of* angels; but he took on *him* the seed of Abraham. [See 228.].

62. *Christ's meekness, forbearance, forgiveness, lowliness, modesty, and patience.*

Is. 42: 2 He shall not cry, nor lift up, nor cause his voice to be heard in the street. [Mat. 12: 17—20.] — 50: 6 I gave my back to the smiters, and my cheeks to them that plucked off the hair: I hid not my face from shame and spitting. — 53: 7 He was oppressed, and he was afflicted, yet he opened not his mouth: he is brought as a lamb to the slaughter, and as a sheep before her shearers is dumb, so he opened not his mouth.

Mat. 11: 29 Take my yoke upon you, and learn of me: for I am meek and lowly in heart; and ye shall find rest unto your souls. — 21: 5 Tell ye the daughter of Sion, Behold, thy King cometh unto thee, meek, and sitting upon an ass, and a colt the foal of an ass.

Mk. 15: 4 Pilate asked him again, saying, Answerest thou nothing? behold how many things they witness against thee. 5 But Jesus yet answered nothing: so that Pilate marvelled.

Lk. 23: 34 Then said Jesus, Father, forgive them: for they know not what they do.

2 Cor. 10: 1 I Paul myself beseech you, by the meekness and gentleness of Christ.

1 Pet. 2: 21 Christ also suffered for us, leaving us an example, that ye should follow his steps: 23 Who, when he was reviled, reviled not again; when he suffered, he threatened not; but committed *himself* to him that judgeth righteously.

[See 482, 498, 660.]

63. *Christ diligent in his work.*

Lk. 2: 49 Wist ye not that I must be about my Father's business?

Jn. 5: 17 Jesus answered them, My Father worketh hitherto, and I work. — 9: 4 I must work the works of him that sent me, while it is day: the night cometh, when no man can work.

[See 1.]

64. *Christ's prayerfulness, and prevalence in prayer.*

Ps. 21: 2 Thou hast given him his heart's desire, and hast not withholden the request of his lips.

Mat. 14: 23 When he had sent the multitudes away, he went up into a mountain apart to pray: and when the evening was come, he was there alone. — 26: 36 Sit ye here, while I go and pray yonder. 39 And he went a little further, and fell on his face, and prayed, saying, O my Father, if it be possible, let this cup pass from me: nevertheless, not as I will, but as thou *wilt*. 42 He went away again the second time, and prayed, saying, O my Father, if this cup may not pass away from me, except I drink it, thy will be done. 44 And went away again, and prayed the third time, saying the same words.

Mk. 6: 46 When he had sent them away, he departed into a mountain to pray.

Lk. 5: 16 He withdrew himself into the wilderness, and prayed. — 6: 12 He went out into a mountain to pray, and continued all night in prayer to God. — 9: 18 As he was alone praying, his disciples were with him. 28 He took Peter, and John, and James, and went up into a mountain to pray. — 11: 1 It came to pass, that as he was praying in a certain place, when he ceased, one of his disciples said unto him, Lord, teach us to pray, as John also taught his disciples.

Jn. 11: 41 Jesus lifted up *his* eyes, and said, Father, I thank thee that thou hast heard me : 42 I knew that thou hearest me always. — 14: 15 If ye love me, keep my commandments : 16 And I will pray the Father, and he shall give you another Comforter, that he may abide with you for ever. [See 516.]

65. *Christ a preacher.*

Ps. 40: 9 I have preached righteousness in the great congregation : lo, I have not refrained my lips, O LORD, thou knowest. 10 I have not hid thy righteousness within my heart ; I have declared thy faithfulness and thy salvation : I have not concealed thy loving kindness and thy truth from the great congregation.

Is. 61: 1 The Spirit of the Lord GOD *is* upon me ; because the LORD hath anointed me to preach good tidings unto the meek ; he hath sent me to bind up the broken-hearted, to proclaim liberty to the captives, and the opening of the prison to *them that are* bound ; 2 To proclaim the acceptable year of the LORD, and the day of vengeance of our God. [Lk. 4: 18.]

Mat. 4: 23 Jesus went about all Galilee, teaching in their synagogues, and preaching the gospel of the kingdom. — 7: 28 It came to pass when Jesus had ended these sayings, the people were astonished at his doctrine. 29 For he taught them as *one* having authority, and not as the scribes. — 13: 54 When he was come into his own country, he taught them in their synagogue, insomuch that they were astonished, and said, Whence hath this *man* this wisdom, and *these* mighty works ?

Jn. 7: 14 About the midst of the feast, Jesus went up into the temple and taught. 15 And the Jews marvelled, saying, How knoweth this man letters, having never learned? 46 The officers answered, Never man spake like this man.

66. *Christ a searching reprover.*

Is. 11: 3 And shall make him of quick understanding in the fear of the LORD: and he shall not judge after the sight of his eyes, neither reprove after the hearing of his ears: 4 But with righteousness shall he judge the poor, and reprove with equity for the meek of the earth: and he shall smite the earth with the rod of his mouth, and with the breath of his lips shall he slay the wicked.

Mal. 3: 2 Who may abide the day of his coming? and who shall stand when he appeareth? for he *is* like a refiner's fire, and like fullers' soap. 3 And he shall sit *as* a refiner and purifier of silver: and he shall purify the sons of Levi, and purge them as gold and silver, that they may offer unto the LORD an offering in righteousness.

Lk. 11: 52 Wo unto you, lawyers! for ye have taken away the key of knowledge: ye entered not in yourselves, and them that were entering in ye hindered. — 12: 49 I am come to send fire on the earth, and what will I, if it be already kindled?

Jn. 18: 37 To this end was I born, and for this cause came into the world, that I should bear witness unto the truth. See Mat., chapters 5th and 23d, throughout.] [See 610—11.]

67. *Christ secured some popular favor.*

Mat. 21: 8 A very great multitude spread their garments in the way; others cut down branches from the trees, and strewed *them* in the way. 9 And the multitudes that went before, and that followed, cried, saying, Hosanna to the Son of David: Blessed *is* he that cometh in the name of the Lord: Hosanna in the highest. [Mk. 11: 8—10.]

Mk. 12: 12 They sought to lay hold on him, but feared the people.

Lk. 4: 14 Jesus returned in the power of the Spirit into Galilee: and there went out a fame of him through all the region round about: 15 And he taught in their synagogues, being glorified of all. — 5: 15 So much the more went there a fame abroad of him: and great multitudes came together to hear and to be healed by him of their infirmities.

Jn. 6: 15 When Jesus therefore perceived that they would come and take him by force, to make him a king, he departed

His crucifixion.

again into a mountain himself alone. — 11: 47 Then gathered the chief priests and the Pharisees a council, and said, What do we? for this man doeth many miracles.   48 If we let him thus alone, all *men* will believe on him. — 12: 19 The Pharisees therefore said among themselves, Perceive ye how ye prevail nothing? behold, the world is gone after him.

68. *Christ reviled and persecuted unto death.*

Ps. 2: 1 Why do the heathen rage, and the people imagine a vain thing?   2 The kings of the earth set themselves, and the rulers take counsel together, against the LORD, and against his Anointed, *saying,*   3 Let us break their bands asunder, and cast away their cords from us.

Is. 53: 2 He shall grow up before him as a tender plant, and as a root out of a dry ground: he hath no form nor comeliness; and when we shall see him, *there is* no beauty that we should desire him.   3 He is despised and rejected of men; a man of sorrows, and acquainted with grief: and we hid as it were *our* faces from him; he was despised, and we esteemed him not.   4 Surely he hath borne our griefs, and carried our sorrows: yet we did esteem him stricken, smitten of God, and afflicted.

Mat. 10: 24 The disciple is not above *his* master, nor the servant above his lord.   25 It is enough for the disciple that he be as his master, and the servant as his lord: if they have called the master of the house Beelzebub, how much more *shall they call* them of his household? — 13: 55 Is not this the carpenter's son? is not his mother called Mary? and his brethren, James, and Joses, and Simon, and Judas?   56 And his sisters, are they not all with us?   Whence then hath this *man* all these things?   57 And they were offended in him. But Jesus said unto them, A prophet is not without honor, save in his own country and in his own house. — 26: 66 What think ye?   They answered and said, He is guilty of death. 67 Then did they spit in his face, and buffetted him; and others smote *him* with the palms of their hands,   68 Saying, Prophesy unto us, thou Christ, Who is he that smote thee? — 27: 29 When they had platted a crown of thorns, they put *it* upon his head, and a reed in his right hand: and they bowed the knee before him, and mocked him, saying, Hail, King of the Jews!   30 And they spit upon him, and took the reed, and smote him on the head.   31 And after that they had mocked him, they took the robe off from him, and put his own raiment on him, and led him away to crucify *him*.   34

They gave him vinegar to drink, mingled with gall: and when he had tasted *thereof*, he would not drink.

Mk. 15: 27 With him they crucify two thieves, the one on his right hand, and the other on his left. 28 And the scripture was fulfilled, which saith, And he was numbered with the transgressors. 29 And they that passed by, railed on him, wagging their heads, and saying, Ah, thou that destroyest the temple, and buildest *it* in three days, 30 Save thyself, and come down from the cross. 31 Likewise also the chief priests mocking, said among themselves with the scribes, He saved others; himself he cannot save. 32 Let Christ, the King of Israel, descend now from the cross, that we may see, and believe. And they that were crucified with him, reviled him.

Lk. 4: 2 All they in the synagogue, when they heard these things, were filled with wrath, 29 And rose up, and thrust him out of the city, and led him unto the brow of the hill (whereon their city was built,) that they might cast him down headlong.— 16: 14 The Pharisees also, who were covetous, heard all these things, and they derided him.

Jn. 10: 20 And many of them said, He hath a devil, and is mad; why hear ye him? 31 Then the Jews took up stones again to stone him.—19: 5 Then came Jesus forth, wearing the crown of thorns, and the purple robe. And *Pilate* saith unto them, Behold the man! 6 When the chief priests therefore and officers saw him, they cried out, saying, Crucify *him*, crucify *him*. [See 467, 511, 690.]

CHRIST'S HUMANITY.

69. *Christ's human soul and body.*

Mat. 1: 1 Jesus Christ, the Son of David, the son of Abraham. — 8: 20 The Son of Man hath not where to lay *his* head.*

Lk. 2: 52 Jesus increased in wisdom and stature, and in favor with God and man.

Jn. 1: 14 The Word was made flesh, and dwelt among us, (and we beheld his glory, the glory as of the only begotten of the Father,) full of grace and truth.

1 Tim. 2: 5 *There is* one God, and one mediator between God and men, the man Christ Jesus.

Heb. 2: 14 Forasmuch then as the children are partakers of flesh and blood, he also himself likewise took part of the

* Christ calls himself the Son of Man more than sixty times.

same; that through death he might destroy him that had the
power of death, that is, the devil; 15 And deliver them, who,
through fear of death, were all their life-time subject to bondage. 16 For verily he took not on *him the nature of* angels;
but he took on *him* the seed of Abraham. 17 Wherefore in
all things it behoved him to be made like unto *his* brethren;
that he might be a merciful and faithful High Priest in things
pertaining to God, to make reconciliation for the sins of the
people. 18 For in that he himself hath suffered, being tempted,
he is able to succor them that are tempted. — 4: 15 We have
not a high priest which cannot be touched with the feeling of
our infirmities: but was in all points tempted like as *we are,
yet* without sin.

1 Jn. 4: 3 Every spirit that confesseth not that Jesus Christ
is come in the flesh, is not of God.

70. *Christ's dependence for preservation, knowledge, etc.*

Is. 42: 6 I the LORD have called thee in righteousness, and
will hold thy hand, and will keep thee.

Mk. 13: 32 Of that day and. *that* hour knoweth no man, no,
not the angels which are in heaven, neither the Son, but the
Father. [Mat. 24: 36.]

Jn. 5: 19 Then answered Jesus, and said unto them, Verily,
verily, I say unto you, The Son can do nothing of himself, but
what he seeth the Father do: for what things soever he doeth,
these also doeth the Son likewise. 30 I can of mine own self
do nothing: as I hear, I judge: and my judgment is just;
because I seek not mine own will, but the will of the Father
which hath sent me. — 6: 57 As the living Father hath sent
me, and I live by the Father: so he that eateth me, even he
shall live by me. — 8: 28 Then said Jesus unto them, When
ye have lifted up the Son of man, then shall ye know that I
am *he,* and *that* I do nothing of myself; but as my Father hath
taught me, I speak these things. 29 And he that sent me is
with me: the Father hath not left me alone; for I do always
those things that please him. — 14: 10 Believest thou not that
I am in the Father, and the Father in me? the words that
I speak unto you, I speak not of myself: but the Father, that
dwelleth in me, he doeth the works. — 20: 17 I ascend unto my
Father and your Father, and *to* my God and your God.

2 Cor. 13: 4 For though he was crucified through weakness, yet he liveth by the power of God.

[See his Prayerfulness, 64.]

71. *Christ called the Son of God in reference to his incarnation.*

Ps. 2: 7 I will declare the decree: the LORD hath said unto me, Thou *art* my Son; this day have I begotten thee.

Lk. 1: 35 The angel answered and said unto her, The Holy Ghost shall come upon thee, and the power of the Highest shall overshadow thee: therefore also that holy thing which shall be born of thee, shall be called the Son of God.

Jn. 1: 14 The Word was made flesh, and dwelt among us, (and we beheld his glory, the glory as of the only begotten of the Father,) full of grace and truth. 18 No man hath seen God at any time; the only begotten Son, which is in the bosom of the Father, he hath declared *him.*

Rom. 1: 3 Concerning his Son Jesus Christ our Lord, which was made of the seed of David according to the flesh; 4 And declared *to be* the Son of God with power, according to the Spirit of holiness, by the resurrection from the dead.

Gal. 4: 4 When the fulness of the time was come, God sent forth his Son, made of a woman, made under the law.

Heb. 1: 5 Unto which of the angels said he at any time, Thou art my Son, this day have I begotten thee? And again, I will be to him a Father, and he shall be to me a Son? 6 And again, when he bringeth in the first-begotten into the world, he saith, And let all the angels of God worship him.

72. *Christ's official subjection to his Father.*

Jn. 6: 38 I came down from heaven, not to do mine own will, but the will of him that sent me.—7: 16 Jesus answered them, and said, My doctrine is not mine, but his that sent me.— 8: 29 And he that sent me is with me.—10: 36 Say ye of him whom the Father hath sanctified, and sent into the world, Thou blasphemest; because I said, I am the Son of God?— 12: 49 I have not spoken of myself; but the Father which sent me, he gave me a commandment, what I should say, and what I should speak.—14: 28 I go unto the Father: for my Father is greater than I.—17: 3 This is life eternal, that they might know thee the only true God, and Jesus Christ whom thou hast sent. 8 I have given unto them the words which thou gavest me; and they have received *them,* and have known surely that I came out from thee, and they have believed that thou didst send me.

Rom. 1: 3 Concerning his Son Jesus Christ our Lord, which was made of the seed of David according to the flesh; 4 And declared *to be* the Son of God with power, according to the Spirit of holiness, by the resurrection from the dead.

1 Cor. 3: 23 Ye are Christ's: and Christ *is* God's.—11: 3

The head of Christ *is* God.—15: 27 He hath put all things under his feet. But when he saith all things are put under *him, it is* manifest that he is excepted which did put all things under him. 28 And when all things shall be subdued unto him, then shall the Son also himself be subject unto him that put all things under him, that God may be all in all.

73. *Preëminence of " the man Christ Jesus."*

Ps. 89: 27 I will make him *my* first-born, higher than the kings of the earth.

Jn. 1: 15 John bare witness of him, and cried, saying, This was he of whom I spake, He that cometh after me, is preferred before me ; for he was before me.—3: 31 He that cometh from heaven is above all.

Col. 1: 15 Who is the image of the invisible God, the first-born of every creature. 18 And he is the head of the body, the church : who is the beginning, the first-born from the dead ; that in all *things* he might have the preëminence.

Heb. 1: 4 Being made so much better than the angels, as he hath by inheritance obtained a more excellent name than they. 5 For unto which of the angels said he at any time, Thou art my Son, this day have I begotten thee ? And again, I will be to him a Father, and he shall be to me a Son ? 6 And again, when he bringeth in the first-begotten into the world, he saith, And let all the angels of God worship him.

Rev. 1: 5 The Prince of the kings of the earth.—3: 14 The beginning of the creation of God.

CHRIST'S DIVINITY.

74. *Christ's divine names, titles, and offices.*

*Advocate, 1 Jn. 2: 1—Almighty, Rev. 1: 18—Alpha and Omega, Rev. 22: 13 — Bishop of souls, 1 Pet. 2: 25 — Captain of salvation, Heb. 2: 10 — Counsellor, Is. 9: 6 — Emmanuel, Mat. 1: 23 — Eternal life, 1 Jn. 5: 20 — Father everlasting, Is. 9: 6 — God, and the true God, Ps. 45: 6, and Heb. 1: 8, and 1 Jn. 5: 20 — God over all, Rom. 9: 5 — God, only wise, Jude 25 — Governor, Mat. 2: 6 — Head of all principality and power, Col. 2: 10 — Head over all things to the church, Eph. 1: 22 — Heir of all things, Heb. 1: 2 — High Priest, Heb. 3: 1 — Intercessor, Is. 59: 16, and Heb. 7: 25 — King, Mat. 21: 5 — King of glory, Ps. 24: 7 — King of Israel, Jn. 1: 49 — King of kings, Rev. 17: 14, and 19: 13 — Lamb of God, Jn. 1: 29 — Lion of Juda, Rev. 5: 5 — Lord of lords, Rev. 17: 14, and 19: 13 —
Lord of glory, 1 Cor. 2: 8 — Lord of hosts, Is. 44: 6 — Lord

His divine claims, attributes, and prerogatives.

of all, Ac. 10: 36 — Lord and Master, Jn. 13: 14 — Mediator, 1 Tim. 2: 5 — Messenger of the covenant, Mal. 3: 1 — Mighty God, Is. 9: 6 — Most mighty, Ps. 45: 3 — Passover, 1 Cor. 5: 7 — Prince of life, Ac. 3: 15 — Prince and Saviour, Ac. 5: 31 — Prince of peace, Is. 9: 6 — Prince of kings, Rev. 1: 5 — Prophet, Dt. 18: 15, and Ac. 3: 22 — Redeemer, Is. 44: 6 — Rock, 1 Cor. 10: 4 — Root of David, Rev. 5: 5 — Ruler in Israel, Mic. 5: 2 — Saviour, Lk. 2: 11, and Jude 25 — Shepherd, Jn. 10: 11, and 1 Pet. 2: 25 — Son of God, Jn. 1: 49 — Son of righteousness, Mal. 4: 2 — True God, 1 Jn. 5: 20 — Witness, Rev. 1: 5, and 3: 14 — Wonderful, Is. 9: 6 — Word, Jn. 1: 1 — Word of God, Rev. 19: 13.

75. *Christ's claim to equality and unity with God.*

Jn. 5: 17 My Father worketh hitherto, and I work. 18 Therefore the Jews sought the more to kill him, because he not only had broken the Sabbath, but said also, that God was his Father, making himself equal with God. * — 10: 30 I and my Father are one. 33 The Jews answered him, saying, For a good work we stone thee not; but for blasphemy, and because that thou, being a man, makest thyself God. 36 Say ye of him whom the Father hath sanctified, and sent into the world, Thou blasphemest; because I said, I am the Son of God? 37 If I do not the works of my Father, believe me not. 38 But if I do, though ye believe not me, believe the works: that ye may know and believe that the Father *is* in me, and I in him. — 14: 9 Jesus saith unto him, Have I been so long time with you, and yet hast thou not known me, Philip? he that hath seen me, hath seen the Father; and how sayest thou *then*, Shew us the Father? — 17: 5 O Father, glorify thou me with thine own self, with the glory which I had with thee before the world was. 10 All mine are thine, and thine are mine; and I am glorified in them.

Ph. 2: 5 Let this mind be in you, which was also in Christ Jesus: 6 Who, being in the form of God, thought it not robbery to be equal with God.

76. *Divine attributes and prerogatives claimed and exercised by Christ and ascribed to him.*

1. *Authority supreme,*

Mat. 10: 1 When he had called unto *him* his twelve disciples, he gave them power *against* unclean spirits, to cast them out, and to heal all manner of sickness, and all manner of disease.

* Christ calls God his Father more than fifty times, as recorded by the Evangelists.

His divine Attributes and Prerogatives.

Mk. 2: 5 When Jesus saw their faith, he said unto the sick of the palsy, Son, thy sins be forgiven thee. 6 But there were certain of the scribes sitting there, and reasoning in their hearts, 7 Why doth this *man* thus speak blasphemies? who can forgive sins but God only? 8 And immediately, when Jesus perceived in his spirit that they so reasoned within themselves, he said unto them, Why reason ye these things in your hearts? 9 Whether is it easier to say to the sick of the palsy, *Thy* sins be forgiven thee; or to say, Arise, and take up thy bed, and walk? 10 But that ye may know that the Son of man hath power on earth to forgive sins, (he saith to the sick of the palsy,) 11 I say unto thee, Arise, and take up thy bed and go thy way into thy house.

Col. 1: 18 He is the head of the body, the church: who is the beginning, the first-born from the dead; that in all *things* he might have the preëminence. 19 For it pleased the *Father* that in him should all fulness dwell. — 2: 10 Ye are complete in him, which is the head of all principality and power.

Rev. 1: 18 *I am* he that liveth, and was dead; and behold, I am alive for evermore, Amen; and have the keys of hell and of death.

2. *Authority to seek his own glory supremely.*

Col. 1: 16 All things were created by him and for him. [See 209, 846.]

8. *Eternity.*

Jn. 1: 1 In the beginning was the Word, and the Word was with God, and the Word was God. 2 The same was in the beginning with God. — 8: 58 Jesus said unto them, Verily, verily, I say unto you, Before Abraham was, I am.

Rev. 1: 8 I am Alpha and Omega, the beginning and the ending, saith the Lord, which is, and which was, and which is to come, the Almighty. 17 And when I saw him, I fell at his feet as dead. And he laid his right hand upon me, saying unto me, Fear not; I am the first and the last.

4. *Immutability.*

Heb. 13: 8 Jesus Christ the same yesterday, and to-day, and for ever.

5. *Omnipotence.*

Jn. 1: 3 All things were made by him; and without him was not anything made that was made. 10 He was in the world, and the world was made by him, and the world knew him not. — 2: 19 Jesus answered and said unto them, Destroy this tem-

His divine Attributes and Prerogatives.

ple, and in three days I will raise it up. — 5: 21 As the Father raiseth up the dead, and quickeneth *them;* even so the Son quickeneth whom he will. 25 Verily, verily, I say unto you, The hour is coming, and now is, when the dead shall hear the voice of the Son of God: and they that hear shall live. — 10: 17 Therefore doth my Father love me, because I lay down my life, that I might take it again. 18 No man taketh it from me, but I lay it down of myself. I have power to lay it down, and I have power to take it again. — 11: 25 Jesus said unto her, I am the resurrection, and the life.

1 Cor. 1: 24 Unto them which are called, both Jews and Greeks, Christ the power of God, and the wisdom of God. — 8: 6 To us *there is but* one God, the Father, of whom *are* all things, and we in him; and one Lord Jesus Christ, by whom *are* all things, and we by him.

Ph. 3: 20 Our conversation is in heaven; from whence also we look for the Saviour, the Lord Jesus Christ: 21 Who shall change our vile body, that it may be fashioned like unto his glorious body, according to the working whereby he is able even to subdue all things unto himself.

Col. 1: 16 By him were all things created, that are in heaven, and that are in earth, visible and invisible, whether *they be* thrones, or dominions, or principalities, or powers. 17 And he is before all things, and by him all things consist.

Heb. 1: 3 Who being the brightness of *his* glory, and the express image of his person, and upholding all things by the word of his power, when he had by himself purged our sins, sat down on the right hand of the Majesty on high. [See 218.]

6. *Omnipresence.*

Mat. 18: 20 Where two or three are gathered together in my name, there am I in the midst of them. — 28: 20 I am with you alway, *even* unto the end of the world.

Jn. 3: 13 No man hath ascended up to heaven, but he that came down from heaven, *even* the Son of man which is in heaven. [See 220.]

7. *Omniscience.*

Mat. 9: 4 Jesus, knowing their thoughts, said, Wherefore think ye evil in your hearts? — 11: 27 All things are delivered unto me of my Father; and no man knoweth the Son, but the Father; neither knoweth any man the Father, save the Son, and *he* to whomsoever the Son will reveal *him.* Lk. 10: 22.

Jn. 2: 24 Jesus did not commit himself unto them, because he knew all *men,* 25 And needed not that any should testify of man: for he knew what was in man. — 10: 15 As the

Father knoweth me, even so know I the Father. — 21: 17 He said unto him, Lord, thou knowest all things; thou knowest that I love thee.

Gal. 1: 11 I certify you, brethren, that the gospel which was preached of me is not after man: 12 For I neither received it of man, neither was I taught *it*, but by the revelation of Jesus Christ.

Col. 2: 3 In whom are hid all the treasures of wisdom and knowledge. 9 For in him dwelleth all the fulness of the Godhead bodily. [See 219.]

77. *Christ wrought miracles, in his own name, to confirm his divinity and mission.*

Mat. 8: 3 I will; be thou clean. And immediately his leprosy was cleansed.

Mk. 4: 39 He arose, and rebuked the wind, and said unto the sea, Peace, be still. And the wind ceased, and there was a great calm. 41 And they feared exceedingly, and said one to another, What manner of man is this, that even the wind and the sea obey him?

Lk. 4: 35 Jesus rebuked him, saying, Hold thy peace, and come out of him. And when the devil had thrown him in the midst, he came out of him, and hurt him not. 36 And they were all amazed, and spake among themselves, saying, What a word *is* this! for with authority and power he commandeth the unclean spirits, and they come out.

Jn. 2: 23 Many believed in his name, when they saw the miracles which he did. — 5: 36 I have greater witness than *that* of John: for the works which the Father hath given me to finish, the same works that I do, bear witness of me, that the Father hath sent me. — 7: 31 Many of the people believed on him, and said, When Christ cometh, will he do more miracles than these which this *man* hath done? — 10: 37 If I do not the works of my Father, believe me not. 38 But if I do, though ye believe not me, believe the works: that ye may know and believe that the Father *is* in me, and I in him. — 11: 42 I knew that thou hearest me always: but because of the people which stand by, I said *it*, that they may believe that thou hast sent me. 43 And when he thus had spoken, he cried with a loud voice, Lazarus, come forth. 44 And he that was dead came forth, bound hand and foot with grave-clothes: and his face was bound about with a napkin. Jesus saith unto them, Loose him, and let him go. 45 Then many of the Jews which came to Mary, and had seen the things which Jesus did, believed on him. 47 Then gathered the chief priests and the Pharisees a council, and said, What do we? for this man doeth many miracles. 48 If we let him thus alone, all *men* will believe on him. — 20: 30 Many other signs truly did Jesus in the presence of his disciples, which are not written in this book. 31 But these are written that ye might believe that Jesus is the Christ, the Son of God. [See 43.]

78. *The prophets and apostles acceptably wrought miracles, not in their own names.*

Num. 20: 10 Hear now ye rebels; must we fetch you water out of this rock? 11 And Moses lifted up his hand, and with his rod he smote the rock twice; and the water came out abundantly, and the congregation drank, and their beasts *also*. 12 And the LORD spake unto Moses and Aaron, Because ye believed me not, to sanctify me in the eyes of the children of Israel, therefore ye shall not bring this congregation into the land which I have given them.

Ac. 3: 6 Peter said, Silver and gold have I none; but such as I have give I thee: in the name of Jesus Christ of Nazareth, rise up and walk. 11 As the lame man which was healed held Peter and John, all the people ran together unto them in the porch that is called Solomon's, greatly wondering. 12 And when Peter saw *it*, he answered unto the people, Ye men of Israel, why marvel ye at this? or why look ye so earnestly on us, as though by our own power or holiness we had made this man to walk? — 9: 34 Peter said unto him, Eneas, Jesus Christ maketh thee whole. — 16: 18 Paul being grieved, turned and said to the spirit, I command thee in the name of Jesus Christ to come out of her.

79 *Divine honors paid Christ, and received and claimed by him.*

Ps. 2: 12 Blessed *are* all they that put their trust in him.

Mat. 2: 1 When Jesus was born in Bethlehem of Judea in the days of Herod the king, behold, there came wise men from the east to Jerusalem, 2 Saying, Where is he that is born King of the Jews? for we have seen his star in the east, and are come to worship him. — 8: 2 Behold, there came a leper, and worshipped him, saying, Lord, if thou wilt, thou canst make me clean. — 14: 32 When they were come into the ship, the wind ceased. 33 Then they that were in the ship came and worshipped him, saying, Of a truth thou art the Son of God. — 28: 9 As they went to tell his disciples, behold Jesus met them, saying, All hail. And they came and held him by the feet, and worshipped him. 16 The eleven disciples went away into Galilee, into a mountain where Jesus had appointed them. 17 And when they saw him, they worshipped him : but some doubted. 19 Go ye therefore and teach all nations, baptizing them in the name of the Father, and of the Son, and of the Holy Ghost.

Lk. 24: 51 It came to pass, while he blessed them, he was parted from them, and carried up into heaven. 52 And they worshipped him, and returned to Jerusalem with great joy.

Jn. 5: 22 The Father judgeth no man ; but hath committed all judgment unto the Son : 23 That all *men* should honor the Son, even as they honor the Father. He that honoreth not the Son, honoreth not the Father which hath sent him.

Ac. 7: 59 They stoned Stephen, calling upon *God*, and saying, Lord Jesus, receive my spirit.

2 Cor. 13: 14 The grace of the Lord Jesus Christ, and the love of God, and the communion of the Holy Ghost, *be* with you all.

Ph. 2: 9 God also hath highly exalted him, and given him a name which is above every name : 10 That at the name of Jesus every knee should bow, of *things* in heaven, and *things* in earth, and *things* under the earth ; 11 And *that* every tongue should confess that Jesus Christ *is* Lord, to the glory of God the Father.

Heb. 1: 6 When he bringeth in the first-begotten into the world, he saith, And let all the angels of God worship him.

2 Pet. 1: 17 He received from God the Father honor and glory, when there came such a voice to him from the excellent glory, This is my beloved Son, in whom I am well pleased. — 3: 18 Grow in grace, and *in* the knowledge of our Lord and Saviour Jesus Christ. To him *be* glory both now and for ever.

Rev. 5: 11 I beheld, and I heard the voice of many angels round about the throne, and the beasts, and the elders : and the number of them was ten thousand times ten thousand, and thousands of thousands ; 12 Saying with a loud voice, Worthy is the Lamb that was slain to receive power, and riches, and wisdom, and strength, and honor, and glory, and blessing. 13 And every creature which is in heaven, and on the earth, and under the earth, and such as are in the sea, and all that are in them, heard I saying, Blessing, and honor, and glory, and power, *be* unto him that sitteth upon the throne, and unto the Lamb, for ever and ever. 14 And the four beasts said, Amen. And the four *and* twenty elders fell down and worshipped him that liveth for ever and ever.

80. *Mere creatures not to be divinely honored or worshipped.*

Mat. 4: 10 Then saith Jesus unto him, Get thee hence,

Satan : for it is written, Thou shalt worship the Lord thy God, and him only shalt thou serve.

Ac. 14: 13 The priest of Jupiter, which was before their city, brought oxen and garlands unto the gates, and would have done sacrifice with the people. 14 *Which* when the apostles, Barnabas and Paul, heard *of*, they rent their clothes, and ran in among the people, crying out, 15 And saying, Sirs, why do ye these things ? We also are men of like passions with you, and preach unto you, that ye should turn from these vanities unto the living God, which made heaven and earth, and the sea, and all things that are therein.

Col. 2: 18. Let no man beguile you of your reward in a voluntary humility and worshipping of angels.

Rev. 22: 8 I John saw these things, and heard *them*. And when I had heard and seen, I fell down to worship before the feet of the angel which showed me these things. 9 Then saith he unto me, See *thou do it* not : for I am thy fellow-servant, and of thy brethren the prophets, and of them which keep the sayings of this book : worship God. [Rev. 19: 10.]

81. *Mystery respecting Christ.*

Mat. 1: 23 Behold a virgin shall be with child, and shall bring forth a son, and they shall call his name Emmanuel, which being interpreted is, God with us. — 22: 41 While the Pharisees were gathered together, Jesus asked them, 42 Saying, What think ye of Christ ? whose son is he ? They say unto him, *The son* of David. 43 He saith unto them, How then doth David in spirit call him Lord, saying, 44 The LORD said unto my Lord, Sit thou on my right hand, till I make thine enemies thy footstool ? 45 If David then call him Lord, how is he his son ? 46 And no man was able to answer him a word, neither durst any *man* from that day forth ask him any more *questions*.

Eph. 6: 19 That I may open my mouth boldly, to make known the mystery of the gospel.

1 Tim. 3: 16 Without controversy, great is the mystery of godliness : God was manifest in the flesh.

Rev. 19: 12 His eyes *were* as a flame of fire, and on his head *were* many crowns ; and he had a name written, that no man knew, but he himself. — 22: 16 I Jesus have sent mine angel to testify unto you these things in the churches. I am the root and the offspring of David, *and* the bright and morning-star.

82. *Christ's final triumph and glory.*

Ps. 24: 7 Lift up your heads, O ye gates; and be ye lift up ye everlasting doors; and the King of glory shall come in.

Zec. 6: 13 He shall bear the glory, and shall sit and rule upon his throne: and he shall be a priest upon his throne.

Matt. 24: 30 Then shall appear the sign of the Son of man in heaven: and then shall all the tribes of the earth mourn, and they shall see the Son of man coming in the clouds of heaven, with power and great glory. — 25: 31 When the Son of man shall come in his glory, and all the holy angels with him, then shall he sit upon the throne of his glory: 32 And before him shall be gathered all nations: and he shall separate them one from another, as a shepherd divideth *his* sheep from the goats.

Ep. 1: 19 And what is the exceeding greatness of his power to us-ward who believe, according to the working of his mighty power. 20 Which he wrought in Christ, when he raised him from the dead, and set *him* at his own right hand in the heavenly *places.* 21 Far above all principality, and power, and might, and dominion, and every name that is named, not only in this world, but also in that which is to come.

Ph. 2: 9 God also hath highly exalted him, and given him a name which is above every name: 10 That at the name of Jesus every knee should bow, of *things* in heaven, and *things* in earth, and *things* under the earth; 11 And *that* every tongue should confess that Jesus Christ *is* Lord, to the glory of God the Father.

Heb. 1: 1 God, who at sundry times and in divers manners spake in time past unto the fathers by the prophets, 2 Hath in these last days spoken unto us by *his* Son, whom he hath appointed heir of all things, by whom also he made the worlds; 3 Who being the brightness of *his* glory, and the express image of his person, and upholding all things by the word of his power, when he had by himself purged our sins, sat down on the right hand of the Majesty on high, 4 Being made so much better than the angels, as he hath by inheritance obtained a more excellent name than they.

Rev. 17: 14 These shall make war with the Lamb, and the Lamb shall overcome them: for he is Lord of lords, and King of kings; and they that are with him *are* called, and chosen, and faithful. [See 96.]

CHRIST'S KINGDOM.

83. *Christ a King.*

Ps. 2: 6 Yet have I set my King upon my holy hill of Zion.
—**45:** 6 Thy throne, O God, *is* for ever and ever: the sceptre of thy kingdom *is* a right sceptre. 7 Thou lovest righteousness, and hatest wickedness: therefore God, thy God, hath anointed thee with the oil of gladness above thy fellows.

. **Mic. 5:** 2 Thou, Beth-lehem Ephratah, *though* thou be little among the thousands of Judah, *yet* out of thee shall he come forth unto me *that is* to be Ruler in Israel; whose goings forth *have been* from of old, from everlasting.

Zec. 9: 9 Rejoice greatly, O daughter of Zion; shout, O daughter of Jerusalem: behold, thy King cometh unto thee.

Mat. 27: 11 Jesus stood before the governor: and the governor asked him, saying, Art thou the King of the Jews? And Jesus said unto him, Thou sayest.

Jn. 1: 49 Nathanael answered and saith unto him, Rabbi, thou art the Son of God; thou art the King of Israel.

Rev. 1: 5 Jesus Christ, *who is* the faithful Witness, *and* the First-begotten of the dead, and the Prince of the kings of the earth. [Is: 9: 6. Jer. 23: 5, 6, and 30: 9. Hos. 3: 5. Lk. 1: 32.]

84. *Nature of Christ's kingdom.*

Jn. 18: 36 Jesus answered, My kingdom is not of this world: if my kingdom were of this world, then would my servants fight, that I should not be delivered to the Jews: but now is my kingdom not from hence.

Rom. 14: 17 The kingdom of God is not meat and drink, but righteousness, and peace, and joy in the Holy Ghost.

85. *General opposition to Christ's kingdom, before the flood, and before the first coming of Christ.*

Gen. 6: 5 God saw that the wickedness of man *was* great in the earth, and *that* every imagination of the thoughts of his heart *was* only evil continually.

Is. 53: 3 He is despised and rejected of men; a man of sorrows, and acquainted with grief: and we hid as it were *our* faces from him; he was despised, and we esteemed him not.

86. *Will there be another "falling away," or general opposition to Christ's kingdom before the Millenium?*

Is. 24: 5 The earth also is defiled under the inhabitants thereof; because they have transgressed the laws, changed the ordinance, broken the everlasting covenant.—**59:** 13 In trans-

General opposition to it.

gressing and lying against the LORD, and departing away from our God, speaking oppression and revolt, conceiving and uttering from the heart words of falsehood. 14 And judgment is turned away backward, and justice standeth afar off: for truth is fallen in the street, and equity cannot enter. 15 Yea, truth faileth; and he *that* departeth from evil maketh himself a prey: and the LORD saw *it*, and it displeased him that *there was* no judgment.

Dan. 12: 7 I heard the man clothed in linen, which *was* upon the waters of the river, when he held up his right hand and his left hand unto heaven, and sware by him that liveth for ever, that *it shall be* for a time, times, and an half; and when he shall have accomplished to scatter the power of the holy people, all these *things* shall be finished.

Joel 3: 13 Put ye in the sickle, for the harvest is ripe: come, get you down; for the press is full, the fats overflow; for their wickedness *is* great.

Am. 8: 11 Behold, the days come, saith the Lord GOD, that I will send a famine in the land, not a famine of bread, nor a thirst for water, but of hearing the words of the LORD.

Mat. 24: 24 There shall arise false Christs, and false prophets, and shall shew great signs and wonders; insomuch that, if *it were* possible, they shall deceive the very elect.

Lk. 18: 8 Nevertheless, when the Son of man cometh, shall he find faith on the earth?

2 Th. 2: 3 Let no man deceive you by any means: for *that day shall not come,* except there come a falling away first, and that man of sin be revealed, the son of perdition; 4 Who opposeth and exalteth himself above all that is called God, or that is worshipped; so that he, as God, sitteth in the temple of God, shewing himself that he is God. 7 For the mystery of iniquity doth already work: only he who now letteth *will let,* until he be taken out of the way.

2 Tim. 3: 1 This know also, that in the last days perilous times shall come. 2 For men shall be lovers of their own selves, covetous, boasters, proud, blasphemers, disobedient to parents, unthankful, unholy. 3 Without natural affection, truce-breakers, false accusers, incontinent, fierce, despisers of those that are good, 4 Traitors, heady, high-minded, lovers of pleasures more than lovers of God; 5 Having a form of godliness, but denying the power thereof: from such turn away.

2 Pet. 2: 1 There were false prophets also among the people, even as there shall be false teachers among you, who privily shall bring in damnable heresies, even denying the Lord that

Its Enemies to be destroyed.

bought them, and bring upon themselves swift destruction. 2 And many shall follow their pernicious ways; by reason of whom the way of truth shall be evil spoken of.—3: 3 Knowing this first, that there shall come in the last days scoffers, walking after their own lusts, 4 And saying, Where is the promise of his coming? for since the fathers fell asleep, all things continue as *they were* from the beginning of the creation.

Jude 17 Beloved, remember ye the words which were spoken before of the apostles of our Lord Jesus Christ: 18 How that they told you there should be mockers in the last time, who should walk after their own ungodly lusts. 19 These be they who separate themselves, sensual, having not the Spirit.

Rev. 3: 10 Because thou hast kept the word of my patience, I also will keep thee from the hour of temptation, which shall come upon all the world, to try them that dwell upon the earth. —11: 3 I will give *power* unto my two witnesses, and they shall prophesy a thousand two hundred *and* threescore days, clothed in sackcloth. 7 And when they shall have finished their testimony, the beast that ascendeth out of the bottomless pit shall make war against them, and shall overcome them, and kill them. 10 And they that dwell upon the earth shall rejoice over them; and make merry, and shall send gifts one to another; because these two prophets tormented them that dwelt on the earth.—12: 12 Wo to the inhabiters of the earth, and of the sea! for the devil is come down unto you, having great wrath, because he knoweth that he hath but a short time. —13: 3 I saw one of his heads as it were wounded to death; and his deadly wound was healed: and all the world wondered after the beast. 4 And they worshipped the dragon which gave power unto the beast: and they worshipped the beast, saying, Who *is* like unto the beast? who is able to make war with him?—16: 13 I saw three unclean spirits like frogs *come* out of the mouth of the dragon, and out of the mouth of the beast, and out of the mouth of the false prophet. 14 For they are the spirits of devils, working miracles, *which* go forth unto the kings of the earth, and of the whole world, to gather them to the battle of that great day of God Almighty.

87. *Will the foes of Christ's kingdom be cut off before the millennium?*

Ps. 2: 8 Ask of me, and I shall give *thee* the heathen *for* thine inheritance, and the uttermost parts of the earth *for* thy possession. 9 Thou shalt break them with a rod of iron; thou shalt dash them in pieces like a potter's vessel.—37: 9 Evil

7*

doers shall be cut off: but those that wait upon' the LORD, they shall inherit the earth. [10—13.]—82: 8 Arise, O God, judge the earth: for thou shalt inherit all nations.

Is. 1: 27 Zion shall be redeemed with judgment, and her converts with righteousness. 28 And the destruction of the transgressors and of the sinners *shall be* together, and they that forsake the LORD shall be consumed. — 2: 12 The day of the LORD of hosts *shall be* upon every *one that is* proud and lofty, and upon every *one that is* lifted up; and he shall be brought low. [17—20.]—13: 9 Behold, the day of the LORD cometh, cruel both with wrath and fierce anger, to lay the land desolate: and he shall destroy the sinners thereof out of it. — 24: 1 Behold, the LORD maketh the earth empty, and maketh it waste, and turneth it upside down, and scattereth abroad the inhabitants thereof. 3 The land shall be utterly emptied, and utterly spoiled: for the LORD hath spoken this word. 4 The earth mourneth *and* fadeth away, the world languisheth *and* fadeth away, the haughty people of the earth do languish. 5 The earth also is defiled under the inhabitants thereof; because they have transgressed the laws, changed the ordinance, broken the everlasting covenant. 6 Therefore hath the curse devoured the earth, and they that dwell therein are desolate: therefore the inhabitants of the earth are burned, and few men left. 17 Fear, and the pit, and the snare, *are* upon thee, O inhabitant of the earth. 18 And it shall come to pass, *that* he who fleeth from the noise of the fear shall fall into the pit; and he that cometh up out of the midst of the pit shall be taken in the snare: for the windows from on high are open, and the foundations of the earth do shake. 19 The earth is utterly broken down, the earth is clean dissolved, the earth is moved exceedingly. 20 The earth shall reel to and fro like a drunkard, and shall be removed like a cottage; and the transgression thereof shall be heavy upon it; and it shall fall, and not rise again. 23 Then the moon shall be confounded, and the sun ashamed, when the LORD of hosts shall reign in mount Zion, and in Jerusalem, and before his ancients gloriously. [See the whole Chap.]—26: 20 Come, my people, enter thou into thy chambers, and shut thy doors about thee: hide thyself as it were for a little moment, until the indignation be overpast. 21 For behold, the LORD cometh out of his place to punish the inhabitants of the earth for their iniquity: the earth also shall disclose her blood, and shall no more cover her slain. —28: 21 The LORD shall rise up as *in* mount Perazim, he shall be wroth as *in* the valley of Gibeon, that he may do his work, his strange work; and bring to pass his act, his strange act. 22 Now therefore be ye not mockers, lest your bands be made strong: for I have heard from the Lord GOD of hosts a consumption, even determined upon the whole earth.—34: 1 Come near, ye nations, to hear; and hearken, ye people: let the earth hear, and all that is therein; the world, and all things that come forth of it. 2 For the indignation of the LORD *is* upon all nations, and *his* fury upon all their armies: he hath utterly destroyed them, he hath delivered them to the slaughter. 3 Their slain also shall be cast out, and their stink shall come up out of their carcasses, and the mountains shall be melted with their blood. 4 And all the host of heaven shall be dissolved, and the heavens shall be rolled together as a scroll: and all their host shall fall down, as the leaf falleth off from the vine, and as a falling *fig* from the fig-tree. 8 For *it is* the day of the LORD's vengeance, *and* the year of recompenses for the controversy of Zion. [See verses 5—7, 9, 10 and the following chap.]—63: 1 Who *is* this that cometh from Edom, with dyed garments from Bozrah? this *that is* glorious in his apparel, travelling in the greatness of his strength? I that speak in righteousness, mighty to save. 2 Wherefore *art thou* red in thine apparel, and thy garments like him that treadeth in the wine-fat? 3 I have trodden the wine-press alone; and of the people *there was* none with me: for I will tread them in mine anger, and trample them in my fury, and their blood shall be sprinkled upon my garments, and I will stain all my raiment. 4 For the day of vengeance *is* in mine heart, and the year of my redeemed is come.—66: 15 Behold, the LORD will come with fire, and with his chariots like a whirlwind, to render his anger with fury, and his rebuke with flames of fire. 16 For by fire and by his sword will the LORD plead with all flesh: and the slain of the LORD shall be many.

Jer. 25: 31 A noise shall come *even* to the ends of the earth; for the LORD hath a controversy with the nations, he will plead with all flesh; he will give them *that are* wicked to the sword, saith the LORD. 32 Thus saith the LORD of hosts, Behold, evil shall go forth from nation to nation, and a great whirlwind shall be raised up from the coasts of the earth. 33 And the slain of the LORD shall be at that day from *one* end of the earth even unto the *other* end of the earth: they shall not be lamented, neither gathered, nor buried; they shall be dung upon the ground.

Ezk. 38 [An account of the general gathering of the nations under Gog, upon the mountains of Israel, which concludes thus.] 21 I will call for a sword against him throughout all

Its Enemies to be destroyed.

my mountains, saith the Lord GOD : every man's sword shall be against his brother. 22 And I will plead against him with pestilence and with blood; and I will rain upon him, and upon his bands, and upon the many people that *are* with him, an overflowing rain, and great hailstones, fire, and brimstone.— 39: 1 Thou son of man, prophesy against Gog, and say, Thus saith the Lord GOD ; Behold, I *am* against thee, O Gog, the chief prince of Meshech and Tubal: 2 And I will turn thee back, and leave but the sixth part of thee, and will cause thee to come up from the north parts, and will bring thee upon the mountains of Israel: 3 And I will smite thy bow out of thy left hand, and will cause thine arrows to fall out of thy right hand. 4 Thou shalt fall upon the mountains of Israel, thou and all thy bands, and the people that *is* with thee: I will give thee unto the ravenous birds of every sort, and *to* the beasts of the field, to be devoured. 5 Thou shalt fall upon the open field: for I have spoken *it*, saith the Lord GOD. 6 And I will send a fire on Magog, and among them that dwell carelessly in the isles : and they shall know that I *am* the LORD. 7 So will I make my holy name known in the midst of my people Israel ; and I will not *let them* pollute my holy name any more : and the heathen shall know that I *am* the LORD, the Holy One in Israel. 8 Behold, it is come, and it is done, saith the Lord GOD ; this *is* the day whereof I have spoken. 9 And they that dwell in the cities of Israel shall go forth, and shall set on fire and burn the weapons, both the shields, and the bucklers, the bows and the arrows, and the hand-staves, and the spears, and they shall burn them with fire seven years: 10 So that they shall take no wood out of the field, neither cut down *any* out of the forests ; for they shall burn the weapons with fire : and they shall spoil those that spoiled them, and rob those that robbed them, saith the Lord GOD. 12 And seven months shall the house of Israel be burying of them, that they may cleanse the land. 17 And, thou son of man, thus saith the Lord GOD; Speak unto every feathered fowl, and to every beast of the field, Assemble yourselves, and come ; gather yourselves on every side to my sacrifice that I do sacrifice for you, *even* a great sacrifice upon the mountains of Israel, that ye may eat flesh, and drink blood.

Joel 3: 9 Proclaim ye this among the Gentiles ; Prepare war, wake up the mighty men, let all the men of war draw near ; let them come up : 13 Put ye in the sickle, for the harvest is ripe : come, get you down ; for the press is full, the fats overflow ; for their wickedness *is* great. 14 Multitudes, multitudes in the valley of decision : for the day of the LORD

Its Enemies to be destroyed.

is near in the valley of decision. 15 The sun and the moon shall be darkened, and the stars shall withdraw their shining. 16 The LORD also shall roar out of Zion, and utter his voice from Jerusalem; and the heavens and the earth shall shake: but the LORD *will be* the hope of his people, and the strength of the children of Israel. 17 So shall ye know that I *am* the LORD your God dwelling in Zion my holy mountain: then shall Jerusalem be holy, and there shall no strangers pass through her any more.

Zep. 1: 2 I will utterly consume all *things* from off the land, saith the LORD. 3 I will consume man and beast; I will consume the fowls of the heaven, and the fishes of the sea, and the stumbling-blocks with the wicked; and I will cut off man from off the land, saith the LORD. [17, 18.]—3: 8 Wait ye upon me, saith the LORD, until the day that I rise up to the prey: for my determination *is* to gather the nations, that I may assemble the kingdoms, to pour upon them mine indignation, *even* all my fierce anger: for all the earth shall be devoured with the fire of my jealousy. 9 For then will I turn to the people a pure language, that they may all call upon the name of the LORD, to serve him with one consent. 12 I will also leave in the midst of thee an afflicted and poor people, and they shall trust in the name of the LORD. 13 The remnant of Israel shall not do iniquity, nor speak lies; neither shall a deceitful tongue be found in their mouth: for they shall feed and lie down, and none shall make *them* afraid.

Mal. 4: 1 Behold, the day cometh, that shall burn as an oven; and all the proud, yea, and all that do wickedly, shall be stubble: and the day that cometh shall burn them up, saith the LORD of hosts, that it shall leave them neither root nor branch. 2 But unto you that fear my name, shall the Sun of righteousness arise with healing in his wings; and ye shall go forth, and grow up as calves of the stall. 3 And ye shall tread down the wicked; for they shall be ashes under the soles of your feet in the day that I shall do *this*, saith the LORD of hosts.

Rev. 16: 17 The seventh angel poured out his vial into the air; and there came a great voice out of the temple of heaven, from the throne, saying, It is done. 18 And there were voices, and thunders, and lightnings; and there was a great earthquake, such as was not since men were upon the earth, so mighty an earthquake, *and* so great. 19 And the great city was divided into three parts, and the cities of the nations fell: and great Babylon came in remembrance before God, to give unto her the cup of the wine of the fierceness of his wrath.

20 And every island fled away, and the mountains were not found. 21 And there fell upon men a great hail out of heaven, *every stone* about the weight of a talent: and men blasphemed God because of the plague of the hail; for the plague thereof was exceeding great. — 19: 19 [Contains a description of a general destruction of the kings of the earth, and their armies, by one who sat on a white horse, which concludes thus.] 21 And the remnant were slain with the sword of him that sat upon the horse, which *sword* proceeded out of his mouth: and all the fowls were filled with their flesh. — 20: 1 I saw an angel come down from heaven, having the key of the bottomless pit and a great chain in his hand. 2 And he laid hold on the dragon, that old serpent, which is the Devil, and Satan, and bound him a thousand years. 1 S. 2: 10, Pr. 2: 21, Is. 11: 1—6, and 29: 7, 8, Dan. 12: 1.
[See 381, 486, 513, 566, 630, 733.]

88. *Joy in view of the overthrow of Christ's enemies*

Is. 24: 13 When thus it shall be in the midst of the land among the people, *there shall be* as the shaking of an olive-tree, *and* as the gleaning-grapes when the vintage is done. 14 They shall lift up their voice, they shall sing for the majesty of the LORD, they shall cry aloud from the sea. 15 Wherefore glorify ye the LORD in the fires, *even* the name of the LORD God of Israel in the isles of the sea. 16 From the uttermost part. of the earth have we heard songs, *even* glory to the righteous.

Zep. 3: 14 Sing, O daughter of Zion; shout, O Israel; be glad and rejoice with all the heart, O daughter of Jerusalem. 15 The LORD hath taken away thy judgments, he hath cast out thine enemy: the King of Israel, *even* the LORD, *is* in the midst of thee: thou shalt not see evil any more.
[See 237, 571.]

89. *Christ and his friends warn the wicked before their overthrow.*

Mat. 24: 14 This gospel of the kingdom shall be preached in all the world, for a witness unto all nations; and then shall the end come.

Rev. 11: 3 I will give *power* unto my two witnesses, and they shall prophecy a thousand two hundred *and* three-score days, clothed in sackcloth. — 14: 6 I saw another angel fly in the midst of heaven, having the everlasting gospel to preach unto them that dwell on the earth, and to every nation, and kindred, and tongue, and people, 7 Saying with a loud voice, Fear God, and give glory to him; for the hour of his judgment is come: and worship him that made heaven, and earth, and the sea, and the fountains of waters.

90. *Progress and final triumph of Christ's kingdom upon earth.*

Ps. 72: 8 He shall have dominion also from sea to sea, and from the river unto the ends of the earth. 9 They that dwell in the wilderness shall bow before him; and his enemies shall lick the dust. 10 The kings of Tarshish and of the isles shall bring presents: the kings of Sheba and Seba shall offer gifts. 11 Yea, all kings shall fall down before him: all nations shall serve him.

Is. 9: 7 Of the increase of *his* government and peace *there shall be* no end, upon the throne of David, and upon his kingdom, to order it, and to establish it with judgment, and with justice from henceforth even for ever. The zeal of the LORD of hosts will perform this.

Dan. 2: 35 The stone that smote the image became a great mountain, and filled the whole earth. 44 And in the days of these kings shall the God of heaven set up a kingdom, which shall never be destroyed: and the kingdom shall not be left to other people, *but* it shall break in pieces and consume all these kingdoms, and it shall stand for ever. 45 Forasmuch as thou sawest that the stone was cut out of the mountain without hands, and that it brake in pieces the iron, the brass, the clay, the silver, and the gold; the great God hath made known to the king what shall come to pass hereafter: and the dream *is* certain, and the interpretation thereof sure. —7: 13 I saw in the night visions, and behold, *one* like the Son of man came with the clouds of heaven, and came to the Ancient of days, and they brought him near before him. 14 And there was given him dominion, and glory, and a kingdom, that all people, nations, and languages should serve him.

Zec. 14: 9 The LORD shall be king over all the earth: in that day shall there be one LORD, and his name one.

Mat. 13: 31 Another parable put he forth unto them, saying, The kingdom of heaven is like to a grain of mustard-seed, which a man took, and sowed in his field: 32 Which indeed is the least of all seeds: but when it is grown, it is the greatest among herbs, and becometh a tree, so that the birds of the air come and lodge in the branches thereof. 33 Another parable spake he unto them; The kingdom of heaven is like unto leaven, which a woman took, and hid in three measures of meal, till the whole was leavened.

Rev. 11: 15 The seventh angel sounded; and there were great voices in heaven, saying, The kingdoms of this world are become *the kingdoms* of our Lord, and of his Christ, and he shall reign for ever and ever. — 20: 4 And I saw thrones, and they sat upon them, and judgment was given unto them : and *I saw* the souls of them that were beheaded for the witness of Jesus, and for the word of God, and which had not worshipped the beast, neither his image, neither had received *his* mark upon their foreheads, or in their hands ; and they lived and reigned with Christ a thousand years. [See 440.]

91. *Duration of Christ's kingdom.*

Ps. 45: 6 Thy throne, O God, *is* for ever and ever.

Dan. 7: 14 His dominion *is* an everlasting dominion, which shall not pass away, and his kingdom *that* which shall not be destroyed.

Lk. 1: 33 He shall reign over the house of Jacob for ever ; and of his kingdom there shall be no end.

CHURCH OF GOD.

92. *Design of the church of God.*

Mat. 5: 13 Ye are the salt of the earth : but if the salt have lost his savor, wherewith shall it be salted ? it is thenceforth good for nothing, but to be cast out, and to be trodden under foot of men. 14 Ye are the light of the world. A city that is set on a hill cannot be hid. 15 Neither do men light a candle, and put it under a bushel, but on a candlestick : and it giveth light unto all that are in the house. 16 Let your light so shine before men, that they may see your good works, and glorify your Father which is in heaven.

Ep. 3: 10 To the intent that now unto the principalities and powers in heavenly *places* might be known by the church the manifold wisdom of God, 11 According to the eternal purpose which he purposed in Christ Jesus our Lord.

1 Tim. 3: 15 The church of the living God, the pillar and ground of the truth.

93. *Foundation of the church.*

Mat. 16: 16 Simon Peter answered and said, Thou art the Christ, the Son of the living God. 18 Thou art Peter, and upon this rock [Christ] I will build my church : and the gates of hell shall not prevail against it. — 21: 42 Did ye never read in the scriptures, The stone which the builders rejected, the same is become the head of the corner. [Ps. 118: 22. Is. 28: 16. 1 Pet. 2: 7.]

1 Cor. 3: 9 Ye are God's husbandry, *ye are* God's building.

11 Other foundation can no man lay than that is laid, which is Jesus Christ.

Ep. 2: 20 And are built upon the foundation of the apostles and prophets, Jesus Christ himself being the chief corner-*stone;* 21 In whom all the building fitly framed together, groweth unto an holy temple in the Lord.

94. *The church an object of love and of prayer.*

Ps. 51: 18 Do good in thy good pleasure unto Zion: build thou the walls of Jerusalem.—87: 2 The LORD loveth the gates of Zion more than all the dwellings of Jacob. — 122: 6 Pray for the peace of Jerusalem: they shall prosper that love thee. 7 Peace be within thy walls, *and* prosperity within thy palaces. 8 For my brethren and companions' sakes, I will now say, Peace *be* within thee. 9 Because of the house of the LORD our God I will seek thy good. — 137: 5 If I forget thee, O Jerusalem, let my right hand forget *her cunning.* 6 If I do not remember thee, let my tongue cleave to the roof of my mouth; if I prefer not Jerusalem above my chief joy.

Song 7: 10 I *am* my beloved's, and his desire is toward me.

Is. 62: 6 I have set watchmen upon thy walls, O Jerusalem, *which* shall never hold their peace day nor night: ye that make mention of the LORD, keep not silence. 7 And give him no rest, till he establish, and till he make Jerusalem a praise in the earth.

Ep. 5: 25 Husbands, love your wives, even as Christ also loved the church, and gave himself for it. 29 No man ever yet hated his own flesh; but nourisheth and cherisheth it, even as the Lord the church. [See 111, 504, 585, 672.]

95. *The church safe.*

· Ps. 46: 1 God *is* our refuge and strength, a very present help in trouble. 2 Therefore will we not fear, though the earth be removed, and though the mountains be carried into the midst of the sea; 3 *Though* the waters thereof roar *and* be troubled, *though* the mountains shake with the swelling thereof. 4 *There is* a river, the streams whereof shall make glad the city of God, the holy *place* of the Tabernacles of the Most High. 5 God *is* in the midst of her; she shall not be moved: God shall help her, *and that* right early. 6 The heathen raged, the kingdoms were moved: he uttered his voice, the earth melted. 7 The LORD of hosts *is* with us; the God of Jacob *is* our refuge. — 125: 2 *As* the mountains *are* round about Jerusalem, so the LORD *is* round about his people from henceforth even for ever.

Apostles.

Pr. 18: 10 The name of the LORD *is* a strong tower : the righteous runneth into it, and is safe.

Is. 43: 2 When thou passest through the waters, I *will be* with thee ; and through the rivers, they shall not overflow thee : when thou walkest through the fire, thou shalt not be burned ; neither shall the flame kindle upon thee. 3 For I *am* the LORD thy God, the Holy One of Israel, thy Saviour : I gave Egypt *for* thy ransom, Ethiopia and Seba for thee. 4 Since thou wast precious in my sight, thou hast been honorable, and I have loved thee : therefore will I give men for thee, and people for thy life. 5 Fear not ; for I *am* with thee : I will bring thy seed from the east, and gather thee from the west : 6 I will say to the north, Give up : and to the south, Keep not back : bring my sons from far, and my daughters from the ends of the earth. — 54: 14 In righteousness shalt thou be established : thou shalt be far from oppression ; for thou shalt not fear : and from terror ; for it shall not come near thee. 17 No weapon that is formed against thee shall prosper ; and every tongue *that* shall rise against thee in judgment thou shalt condemn. This *is* the heritage of the servants of the LORD, and their righteousness *is* of me, saith the LORD. [See 515—517, 585.]

96. *Christ the head of the church.*

Mat. 23: 8 Be ye not called Rabbi : for one is your Master, *even* Christ ; and all ye are brethren. 9 And call no *man* your father upon the earth : for one is your Father which is in heaven. 10 Neither be ye called masters : for one is your Master, *even* Christ.

Ep. 1: 22 And hath put all *things* under his feet, and gave him *to be* the head over all *things* to the church, 23 Which is his body, the fulness of him that filleth all in all. [See 76.]

CHURCH OFFICERS.

97. *Apostles, or extraordinary officers, called directly by Christ.*

Mat. 4: 18 Jesus, walking by the sea of Galilee, saw two brethren, Simon called Peter, and Andrew his brother, casting a net into the sea ; for they were fishers. 19 And he saith unto them, Follow me, and I will make you fishers of men. — 10: 5 These twelve Jesus sent forth.

Gal. 1: 1 Paul, an apostle, (not of men, neither by man, but by Jesus Christ, and God the Father, who raised him from the dead.)

98. *The apostles, instructed by direct revelations.*

Mat. 10: 19 When they deliver you up, take no thought how
or what ye shall speak, for it shall be given you in that same
hour what ye shall speak. 20 For it is not ye that speak, but
the Spirit of your Father which speaketh in you.

Gal. 1: 11 I certify you, brethren, that the gospel which
was preached of me is not after man. 12 For I neither received it of man, neither was I taught *it*, but by the revelation
of Jesus Christ.—2: 8 (He that wrought effectually in Peter
to the apostleship of the circumcision, the same was mighty in
me toward the Gentiles.)

99. *Apostles, eye-witnesses of Christ's resurrection.*

Ac. 1: 21 Of these men which have companied with us,
all the time that the Lord Jesus went in and out among us.
22 Beginning from the baptism of John, unto that same day
that he was taken up from us, must one be ordained, to be a
witness with us of his resurrection. — 13: 30 God raised him
from the dead: 31 And he was seen many days of them which
came up with him from Galilee to Jerusalem, who are his witnesses unto the people.

1 Cor. 15: 8 Last of all he was seen of me also, as of one born
out of due time.

100. *Miraculous gifts and authority of the apostles.*

Mat. 10: 1 When he had called unto *him* his twelve disciples, he gave them power *against* unclean spirits, to cast them
out, and to heal all manner of sickness, and all manner of disease. — 16: 19 I will give unto thee the keys of the kingdom of
heaven, and whatsoever thou shalt bind on earth, shall be
bound in heaven; and whatsoever thou shalt loose on earth,
shall be loosed in heaven. — 18: 18 Verily I say unto you,
Whatsoever ye shall bind on earth, shall be bound in heaven:
and whatsoever ye shall loose on earth, shall be loosed in
heaven. 19 If two of you shall agree on earth, as touching
anything that they shall ask, it shall be done for them of my
Father which is in heaven.

Jn. 20: 23 Whose soever sins ye remit, they are remitted
unto them; *and* whose soever *sins* ye retain, they are retained.

Ac. 8: 17 Then laid they *their* hands on them, and they
received the Holy Ghost. 18 And when Simon saw that
through laying on of the apostles' hands the Holy Ghost was
given, he offered them money, 19 Saying, Give me also this
power, that on whomsoever I lay hands, he may receive the
Holy Ghost. — 15: 28 It seemed good to the Holy Ghost and

to us, to lay upon you no greater burden than these necessary things: 29 That ye abstain from meats offered to idols, and from blood, and from things strangled, and from fornication:. from which if ye keep yourselves, ye shall do well.   Fare ye well.

2 Cor. 12: 12 Truly the signs of an apostle were wrought among you in all patience, in signs, and wonders, and mighty deeds. [See 189.]

101. *Elders, Overseers, Ministers, Bishops, Preachers, Teachers, Pastors, Evangelists, (one office,) to instruct, admonish, edify, lead and guide.*

Jer. 3: 15 I will give you pastors according to mine heart, which shall feed you with knowledge and understanding.

Lk. 1: 2 Even as they delivered them unto us, which from the beginning were eye-witnesses, and ministers of the word.

Ac. 15: 6 The apostles and elders came together for to consider of this matter.   23 They wrote *letters* by them after this manner; The apostles, and elders, and brethren, *send* greeting unto the brethren which are of the Gentiles in Antioch, and Syria, and Cilicia. — 20: 28 Take heed therefore unto yourselves, and to all the flock over the which the Holy Ghost hath made you overseers, to feed the church of God, which he hath purchased with his own blood.

Ep. 4: 11 He gave some, apostles; and some, prophets; and some, evangelists; and some, pastors and teachers; 12 For the perfecting of the saints, for the work of the ministry, for the edifying of the body of Christ.

Ph: 1: 1 Paul and Timotheus, the servants of Jesus Christ, to all the saints in Christ Jesus which are at Philippi, with the bishops and deacons.

1 Tim. 2: 7 Whereunto I am ordained a preacher and an apostle, (I speak the truth in Christ, *and* lie not,) a teacher of the Gentiles in faith and verity. — 3: 1 This *is* a true saying, If a man desire the office of a bishop, he desireth a good work.

2 Tim. 1: 11 Whereunto I am appointed a preacher, and an apostle, and a teacher of the Gentiles.

1 Pet. 5: 1 The elders which are among you I exhort, who am also an elder, and a witness of the sufferings of Christ, and also a partaker of the glory that shall be revealed: 2 Feed the flock of God which is among you, taking the oversight *thereof*, not by constraint, but willingly; not for filthy lucre, but of a ready mind; 3 Neither as being lords over *God's* heritage, but being ensamples to the flock. [See 447.]

102. *Deacons, to distribute alms, serve tables, etc.*

Ac. 6: 1 In those days, when the number of the disciples

was multiplied, there arose a murmuring of the Grecians against the Hebrews, because their widows were neglected in the daily ministration. 2 Then the twelve called the multitude of the disciples *unto them*, and said, It is not reason that we should leave the word of God, and serve tables. 3 Wherefore, brethren, look ye out among you seven men of honest report, full of the Holy Ghost and wisdom, whom we may appoint over this business. 4 But we will give ourselves continually to prayer, and to the ministry of the word. 5 And the saying pleased the whole multitude: and they chose Stephen, a man full of faith and of the Holy Ghost, and Philip, and Prochorus, and Nicanor, and Timon, and Parmenas, and Nicolas a proselyte of Antioch. 6 Whom they set before the apostles: and when they had prayed, they laid *their* hands on them.

1 Tim. 3: 8 Likewise *must* the deacons *be* grave, not double-tongued, not given to much wine, not greedy of filthy lucre; 9 Holding the mystery of the faith in a pure conscience. 10 And let these also first be proved; then let them use the office of a deacon, being *found* blameless. 11 Even so *must their* wives *be* grave, not slanderers, sober, faithful in all things. 12 Let the deacons be the husbands of one wife, ruling their children and their own houses well. 13 For they that have used the office of a deacon well, purchase to themselves a good degree, and great boldness in the faith which is in Christ Jesus.

103. *Had any primitive churches a plurality of elders?*

Ac. 14: 23 When they had ordained them elders in every church, and had prayed with fasting, they commended them to the Lord. — 20: 17 From Miletus he sent to Ephesus, and called the elders of the church.

Tit. 1: 5 For this cause left I thee in Crete, that thou shouldest set in order the things that are wanting, and ordain elders in every city, as I had appointed thee.

Jam. 5: 14 Is any sick among you? let him call for the elders of the church.

CHURCH ORDINANCES.

104. *Baptism and Lord's Supper appointed.*

Mat. 26: 26 As they were eating, Jesus took bread, and blessed *it*, and brake *it*, and gave *it* to the disciples, and said, Take, eat; this is my body. 27 And he took the cup, and gave thanks, and gave *it* to them, saying, Drink ye all of it: 28 For this is my blood of the new testament, which is shed for many for the remission of sins. 29 But I say unto you, I will not drink henceforth of this fruit of the vine, until that day when I drink it new with you in my Father's kingdom. 30 And when they had sung a hymn, they went out into the mount of Olives. Mk. 14: 22—25. Lk. 22: 14—20. — Mat. 28: 19 Go ye therefore and teach all nations, baptizing them in the name of the Father, and of the Son, and of the Holy Ghost.

1 Cor. 11: 23 I have received of the Lord, that which also I delivered unto you, That the Lord Jesus, the *same* night in which he was betrayed, took bread : 24 And when he had given thanks, he brake *it*, and said, Take, eat : this is my body, which is broken for you : this do in remembrance of me. 25 After the same manner also *he took* the cup, when he had supped, saying, This cup is the new testament in my blood : this do ye, as oft as ye drink *it*, in remembrance of me. 26 For as often as ye eat this bread, and drink this cup, ye do shew the Lord's death till he come.

105. *Preparation required of partakers at the Lord's Supper.*

1 Cor. 5: 7. Purge out therefore the old leaven, that ye may be a new lump, as ye are unleavened. For even Christ our passover is sacrificed for us : 8 Therefore let us keep the feast, not with old leaven, neither with the leaven of malice and wickedness; but with the unleavened *bread* of sincerity and truth. — 11: 27 Whosoever shall eat this bread, and drink *this* cup of the Lord, unworthily, shall be guilty of the body and blood of the Lord. 28 But let a man examine himself, and so let him eat of *that* bread, and drink of *that* cup. 29 For he that eateth and drinketh unworthily, eateth and drinketh damnation to himself, not discerning the Lord's body. 30 For this cause many *are* weak and sickly among you, and many sleep. [See 397.]

106. *Church ordinances a privilege.*

Ps. 27: 4 One *thing* have I desired of the LORD, that will I seek after; that I may dwell in the house of the LORD all the days of my life, to behold the beauty of the LORD, and to inquire in his temple. — 36: 8 They shall be abundantly satisfied with the fatness of thy house, and thou shalt make them drink of the river of thy pleasures. — 63: 1 O GOD, thou *art* my God; early will I seek thee : my soul thirsteth for thee, my flesh longeth for thee in a dry and thirsty land, where no water is; 2 To see thy power and thy glory, so *as* I have seen thee in the sanctuary. — 65: 4 Blessed *is the man whom* thou choosest, and causest to approach *unto thee, that* he may dwell in thy courts: we shall be satisfied with the goodness of thy house, *even* of thy holy temple. — 84: 1 How amiable *are* thy tabernacles, O LORD of hosts! 2 My soul longeth, yea, even fainteth for the courts of the LORD: my heart and my flesh crieth out for the living God. 3 Yea, the sparrow hath found an house, and the swallow a nest for herself, where she may lay her young, *even* thine altars, O LORD of hosts, my King, and my God. 4 Blessed *are* they that dwell in thy house: they will be still praising thee. 10 For a day in thy courts *is* better than a thousand. I had rather be a door-keeper in the house of my God, than to dwell in the tents of wickedness. — 87: 5 Of Zion it shall be said, This and that man was born in her: and the Highest himself shall establish her. 6 The LORD shall count, when he writeth up the people, *that* this *man* was born there. — 92: 13 Those that be planted in the house of the LORD shall flourish in the courts of our God. 14 They shall still bring forth fruit in old age; they shall be fat and flourishing. [See 658.]

107. *Profession of religion and observance of Christian ordinances exemplified and required.*

Dt. 26: 17 Thou hast avouched the LORD this day to be thy God, and to walk in his ways, and to keep his statutes, and his commandments, and his judgments, and to hearken unto his · voice: 18 And the LORD hath avouched thee this day to be his peculiar people, as he hath promised thee, and that *thou* shouldest keep all his commandments.

Is. 44: 5 One shall say, I *am* the LORD's; and another shall call *himself* by the name of Jacob; and another shall subscribe *with* his hand unto the LORD, and surname *himself* by the name of Israel.

Mat. 5: 15 Neither do men light a candle, and put it under a bushel, but on a candlestick: and it giveth light unto all that are in the house. 16 Let your light so shine before men, that they may see your good works, and glorify your Father which is in heaven. — 10: 32 Whosoever therefore shall confess me before men, him will I confess also before my Father which is in heaven. 33 But whosoever shall deny me before men, him will I also deny before my Father which is in heaven. Lk. 12: 8, 9. — Mat. 26: 27 He took the cup, and gave thanks, and gave *it* to them, saying, Drink ye all of it.

Mk. 8: 38 Whosoever therefore shall be ashamed of me, and of my words, in this adulterous and sinful generation; of him also shall the Son of man be ashamed, when he cometh in the glory of his Father with the holy angels. — 16: 16 He that believeth and is baptized, shall be saved.

Lk. 22: 19 He took bread, and gave thanks, and brake *it*, and gave unto them, saying, This is my body which is given for you: this do in remembrance of me.

Rom. 10: 9 If thou shalt confess with thy mouth the Lord Jesus, and shalt believe in thine heart that God hath raised him from the dead, thou shalt be saved. 10 For with the heart, man believeth unto righteousness; and with the mouth, confession is made unto salvation.

1 Cor. 11: 26 As often as ye eat this bread, and drink this cup, ye do show the Lord's death till he come.

2 Tim. 2: 12 If we suffer, we shall also reign with *him:* if we deny *him*, he also will deny us.

1 Jn. 4: 15 Whosoever shall confess that Jesus is the Son of God, God dwelleth in him, and he in God.

CHURCH ORDER, DISCIPLINE, FELLOWSHIP, ETC.

108. *An early ecclesiastical convention.*

Ac. 15: 5 There rose up certain of the sect of the Pharisees, which believed, saying, That it was needful to circumcise them, and to command *them* to keep the law of Moses. 6 And the apostles and elders came together for to consider of this matter. 22 Then pleased it the apostles and elders, with the whole church, to send chosen men of their own company to Antioch, with Paul and Barnabas; *namely,* Judas surnamed Barsabas, and Silas, chief men among the brethren: 23 And they wrote *letters* by them after this manner; The apostles, and elders, and brethren, *send* greeting unto the brethren which are of the Gentiles in Antioch, and Syria, and Cilicia. 24 Forasmuch as we have heard, that certain which went out from us, have troubled you with words, subverting your souls, saying, *Ye must* be circumcised, and keep the law; to whom we gave no *such* commandment: 25 It seemed good unto us, being assembled with one accord, to send chosen men unto you, with our beloved Barnabas and Paul: 26 Men that have hazarded their lives for the name of our Lord Jesus Christ. 27 We have sent therefore Judas and Silas who shall also tell *you* the same things by mouth. 28 For it seemed good to the Holy Ghost, and to us, to lay upon you no greater burden than these necessary things; 29 That ye abstain from meats offered to idols, and from blood, and from things strangled, and from fornication: from which if ye keep yourselves, ye shall do well. Fare ye well.

109. *Church discipline.*

Ps. 141: 5 Let the righteous smite me; *it shall be* a kindness: and let him reprove me; *it shall be* an excellent oil, *which* shall not break my head.

Mat. 18: 15 If thy brother shall trespass against thee, go and tell him his fault between thee and him alone: if he shall hear thee, thou hast gained thy brother. 16 But if he will not hear *thee, then* take with thee one or two more, that in the mouth of two or three witnesses every word may be established. 17 And if he shall neglect to hear them, tell *it* unto the church: but if he neglect to hear the church, let him be unto thee as a heathen man and a publican. ·

1 Cor. 5: 4 In the name of our Lord Jesus Christ, when ye are gathered together, and my spirit, with the power of our Lord Jesus Christ, 5 To deliver such an one unto Satan for the destruction of the flesh, that the spirit may be saved in the day of the Lord Jesus. 9 I wrote unto you in an epistle, not to company with fornicators: 10 Yet not altogether with the fornicators of this world, or with the covetous, or extortioners, or with idolaters: for then must ye needs go out of the world. 11 But now I have written unto you not to keep company, if any man that is called a brother be a fornicator, or covetous, or an idolater, or a railer, or a drunkard, or an extortioner: with such an one no not to eat. 12 For what have I to do to judge them also that are without? do not ye judge them that are within? 13 But them that are without God judgeth. Therefore put away from among yourselves that wicked person.

Gal. 6: 1 Brethren, if a man be overtaken in a fault, ye which are spiritual, restore such an one in the spirit of meekness; considering thyself, lest thou also be tempted.

2 Th. 3: 6 We command you, brethren, in the name of our Lord Jesus Christ, that ye withdraw yourselves from every brother that walketh disorderly, and not after the tradition which he received of us. 14 And if any man obey not our word by this epistle, note that man, and have no company with him, that he may be ashamed. 15 Yet count *him* not as an enemy, but admonish *him* as a brother.

Tit. 3: 10 A man that is an heretic, after the first and second admonition, reject; 11 Knowing that he that is such, is subverted, and sinneth, being condemned of himself.

Rev. 2: 2 I know thy works, and thy labor, and thy patience, and how thou canst not bear them which are evil; and thou hast tried them which say they are apostles, and are not; and

hast found them liars : 3 And hast borne, and hast patience, and for my name's sake hast labored, and hast not fainted.
[See 610.]

110. *Directions for the edification of churches.*

Rom. 12: 4 As we have many members in one body, and all members have not the same office : 5 So we, *being* many, are one body in Christ, and every one members one of another. 6 Having then gifts, differing according to the grace that is given to us, whether prophecy, *let us prophesy* according to the proportion of faith ; 7 Or ministry, *let us wait* on *our* ministering : or he that teacheth, on teaching : 8 Or he that exhorteth, on exhortation : he that giveth, *let him do it* with simplicity : he that ruleth, with diligence ; he that sheweth mercy, with cheerfulness. 9 *Let* love be without dissimulation. Abhor that which is evil ; cleave to that which is good. 10 *Be* kindly affectioned one to another with brotherly love ; in honor Preferring one another. — 14: 19 Let us therefore follow after the things which make for peace, and things wherewith one may edify another. — 15: 1 We then that are strong ought to bear the infirmities of the weak, and not to please ourselves. 2 Let every one of us please *his* neighbor for *his* good to edification. 3 For even Christ pleased not himself.

Ep. 4: 15 But speaking the truth in love, may grow up into him in all things, which is the head, *even* Christ : 16 From whom the whole body fitly joined together and compacted by that which every joint supplieth, according to the effectual working in the measure of every part, maketh increase of the body unto the edifying of itself in love. 29 Let no corrupt communication proceed out of your mouth, but that which is good to the use of edifying, that it may minister grace unto the hearers.

Col. 3: 16 Let the word of Christ dwell in you richly in all wisdom ; teaching and admonishing one another in psalms, and hymns, and spiritual songs, singing with grace in your hearts to the Lord. [Heb. 10: 24, 25.]

1 Th. 5: 11 Comfort yourselves together, and edify one another, even as also ye do.

Heb. 3: 13 Exhort one another daily, while it is called To-day ; lest any of you be hardened through the deceitfulness of sin. — 10: 24 Let us consider one another, to provoke unto love, and to good works : 25 Not forsaking the assembling of ourselves together, as the manner of some *is ;* but exhorting *one another ;* and so much the more, as ye see the day approaching.

111. *Brotherly love, fellowship, and unity in churches, required and exemplified.*

1 S. 18: 3 Then Jonathan and David made a covenant, because he loved him as his own soul.

2 S. 1: 26 I am distressed for thee, my brother Jonathan: very pleasant hast thou been unto me: thy love to me was wonderful, passing the love of women.

Ps. 133: 1 Behold, how good and how pleasant *it is* for brethren to dwell together in unity! 2 *It is* like the precious ointment upon the head, that ran down upon the beard, *even* Aaron's beard: that went down to the skirts of his garments.

Is. 52: 8 Thy watchmen shall lift up the voice; with the voice together shall they sing: for they shall see eye to eye, when the LORD shall bring again Zion.

Jn. 13: 34 A new commandment I give unto you, That ye love one another; as I have loved you, that ye also love one another. 35 By this shall all *men* know that ye are my disciples, if ye have love one to another.—15: 12 This is my commandment, That ye love one another, as I have loved you.—17: 20 Neither pray I for these alone; but for them also which shall believe on me through their word: 21 That they all may be one; as thou, Father, *art* in me, and I in thee, that they also may be one in us: that the world may believe that thou hast sent me. 22 And the glory which thou gavest me, I have given them; that they may be one, even as we are one.

Ac. 4: 32 The multitude of them that believed were of one heart, and of one soul.—20: 37 They all wept sore, and fell on Paul's neck, and kissed him, 38 Sorrowing most of all for the words which he spake, that they should see his face no more.

Rom. 12: 10 *Be* kindly affectioned one to another with brotherly love; in honor preferring one another.—15: 5 The God of patience and consolation grant you to be like-minded one toward another according to Christ Jesus: 6 That ye may with one mind *and* one mouth glorify God, even the Father of our Lord Jesus Christ.

1 Cor. 1: 10 I beseech you, brethren, by the name of our Lord Jesus Christ, that ye all speak the same thing, and *that* there be no divisions among you; but *that* ye be perfectly joined together in the same mind, and in the same judgment.

2 Cor. 13: 11 Be perfect, be of good comfort, be of one mind, live in peace; and the God of love and peace shall be with you.

Gal. 6: 10 As we have therefore opportunity, let us do good unto all *men*, especially unto them who are of the household of faith.

Ep. 4: 1 I therefore, the prisoner of the Lord, beseech you that ye walk worthy of the vocation wherewith ye are called, 2 With all lowliness and meekness, with long suffering, forbearing one another in love; 3 Endeavoring to keep the unity of the Spirit in the bond of peace.—5: 2 Walk in love, as Christ also hath loved us, and hath given himself for us an offering and a sacrifice to God for a sweet-smelling savor.

Ph. 1: 4 Always in every prayer of mine for you all making request with joy, 5 For your fellowship in the gospel. 27 Only let your conversation be as it becometh the gospel of Christ: that whether I come and see you, or else be absent, I may hear of your affairs, that ye stand fast in one spirit, with one mind striving together for the faith of the gospel.—2: 1 If *there be* therefore any consolation in Christ, if any comfort of love, if any fellowship of the Spirit, if any bowels and mercies, 2 Fulfil ye my joy, that ye be like-minded, having the same love, *being* of one accord, of one mind.

Ph. 3: 16 Whereto we have already attained, let us walk by the same rule, let us mind the same thing.

1 Th. 4: 9 As touching brotherly love ye need not that I write unto you: for ye yourselves are taught of God to love one another. 10 And indeed ye do it toward all the brethren which are in all Macedonia: but we beseech you, brethren, that ye increase more and more.

Heb. 13: 1 Let brotherly love continue.

1 Pet. 1: 22 Seeing ye have purified your souls in obeying the truth through the Spirit unto unfeigned love of the brethren, *see that ye* love one another with a pure heart fervently. —2: 17 Love the brotherhood.

2 Pet. 1: 5 Besides this, giving all diligence, add to your faith, virtue; and to virtue, knowledge; 6 And to knowledge, temperance; and to temperance, patience; and to patience, godliness; 7 And to godliness, brotherly kindness; and to brotherly kindness, charity.

1 Jn. 3: 11 This is the message that ye heard from the beginning, that we should love one another. 12 Not as Cain, *who* was of that wicked one, and slew his brother. 14 We know that we have passed from death unto life, because we love the brethren. 16 Hereby perceive we the love *of God*, because he laid down his life for us: and we ought to lay down *our* lives for the brethren. 17 But whoso hath this world's good, and seeth his brother have need, and shutteth up his

bowels *of compassion* from him, how dwelleth the love of God in him? 18 My little children, let us not love in word, neither in tongue, but in deed and in truth. 19 And hereby we know that we are of the truth, and shall assure our hearts before him. 23 And this is his commandment; That we should believe on the name of his Son Jesus Christ, and love one another, as he gave us commandment.—4: 7 Beloved, let us love one another: for love is of God; and every one that loveth is born of God, and knoweth God. 8 He that loveth not, knoweth not God; for God is love. 10 Herein is love, not that we loved God, but that he loved us, and sent his Son *to be* the propitiation for our sins. 11 Beloved, if God so loved us, we ought also to love one another. 21 This commandment have we from him, That he who loveth God, love his brother also.

2 Jn. 5 Now I beseech thee, lady, not as though I wrote a new commandment unto thee, but that which we had from the beginning, that we love one another. [See 94, 114, 412.]

112. *Limits of Christian fellowship prescribed — Disfellowship.*

2 Ch. 19: 2 Jehu the son of Hanani the seer went out to meet him, and said to king Jehosaphat, Shouldest thou help the ungodly, and love them that hate the LORD? therefore *is* wrath upon thee from before the LORD.

Mat. 10: 11 Into whatsoever city or town ye shall enter, inquire who in it is worthy; and there abide till ye go thence. 12 And when ye come into a house, salute it. 13 And if the house be worthy, let your peace come upon it; but if it be not worthy, let your peace return to you. 14 And whosoever shall not receive you, nor hear your words, when ye depart out of that house, or city, shake off the dust of your feet.

1 Cor. 5: 9 I wrote unto you in an epistle, not to company with fornicators: 10 Yet not altogether with the fornicators of this world, or with the covetous, or extortioners, or with idolaters: for then must ye needs go out of the world. 11 But now I have written unto you not to keep company, if any man that is called a brother be a fornicator, or covetous, or an idolater, or a railer, or a drunkard, or an extortioner: with such a one no not to eat.— 10: 20 I would not that ye should have fellowship with devils.

Ep. 5: 11 Have no fellowship with the unfruitful works of darkness, but rather reprove *them*.

2 Th. 3: 6 We command you, brethren, in the name of our Lord Jesus Christ, that ye withdraw yourselves from every

brother that walketh disorderly, and not after the tradition which he received of us. 14 And if any man obey not our word by this epistle, note that man, and have no company with him, that he may be ashamed. 15 Yet count *him* not as an enemy, but admonish *him* as a brother.

2 Tim. 3: 5 Having a form of godliness, but denying the power thereof: from such turn away.

2 Jn. 10 If there come any unto you, and bring not this doctrine, receive him not into *your* house, neither bid him God speed: 11 For he that biddeth him God speed, is partaker of his evil deeds. [See 115, 122, 177, 477.]

CHURCH-UNITY.

113. *The Church of Christ one body.*

1 Cor. 12: 13 By one Spirit are we all baptized into one body, whether *we be* Jews or Gentiles, whether *we be* bond or free; and have been all made to drink into one Spirit.

Ep. 4: 4 *There is* one body, and one Spirit, even as ye are called in one hope of your calling; 5 One Lord, one faith, one baptism, 6 One God and Father of all, who *is* above all, and through all, and in you all.

114. *Church unity not to be broken by hatred, and selfish divisions.*

Mat. 12: 25 Jesus knew their thoughts, and said unto them, Every kingdom divided against itself, is brought to desolation; and every city or house divided against itself, shall not stand. 26 And if Satan cast out Satan, he is divided against himself; how shall then his kingdom stand?

Rom. 16: 17 I beseech you, brethren, mark them which cause divisions and offences, contrary to the doctrine which ye have learned; and avoid them. 18 For they that are such serve not our Lord Jesus Christ, but their own belly; and by good words and fair speeches deceive the hearts of the simple.

1 Cor. 1: 11 It hath been declared unto me of you, my brethren, by them *which are of the house* of Chloe, that there are contentions among you. 12 Now this I say, that every one of you saith, I am of Paul; and I of Apollos; and I of Cephas; and I of Christ. 13 Is Christ divided?—3: 3 Ye are yet carnal: for whereas *there is* among you envying, and strife, and divisions, are ye not carnal, and walk as men? 4 For while one saith, I am of Paul; and another, I *am* of Apollos; are ye not carnal?—12: 24 Our comely *parts* have no need: but God hath tempered the body together, having

given more abundant honor to that *part* which lacked: 25 That there should be no schism in the body; but *that* the members should have the same care one for another. 26 And whether one member suffer, all the members suffer with it; or one member be honored, all the members rejoice with it. 27 Now ye are the body of Christ, and members in particular.

Gal. 5: 15 If ye bite and devour one another, take heed that ye be not consumed one of another.

1 Jn. 3: 14 He that loveth not *his* brother, abideth in death. 15 Whosoever hateth his brother, is a murderer: and ye know that no murderer hath eternal life abiding in him.—4: 20 If a man say, I love God, and hateth his brother, he is a liar. For he that loveth not his brother, whom he hath seen, how can he love God, whom he hath not seen?

Jude 18 They told you there should be mockers in the last time, who should walk after their own ungodly lusts. 19 These be they who separate themselves, sensual, having not the Spirit. [See 111.]

115. *Church unity and fellowship not to be extended to unbelievers.*

Lk. 12: 51 Suppose ye that I am come to give peace on earth? I tell you, Nay; but rather division.

2 Cor. 6: 14 Be ye not unequally yoked together with unbelievers: for what fellowship hath righteousness with unrighteousness? and what communion hath light with darkness? 15 And what concord hath Christ with Belial? or what part hath he that believeth with an infidel? 16 And what agreement hath the temple of God with idols? for ye are the temple of the living God; as God hath said, I will dwell in them, and walk in *them;* and I will be their God, and they shall be my people. 17 Wherefore come out from among them, and be ye separate, saith the Lord, and touch not the unclean *thing;* and I will receive you; 18 And will be a Father unto you, and ye shall be my sons and daughters, saith the Lord Almighty.

Rev. 18: 4 I heard another voice from heaven, saying, Come out of her, my people, that ye be not partakers of her sins, and that ye receive not of her plagues. [See 112, 122, 177.]

116. *Christian churches, branches of the Abrahamic church.*

Rom. 11: 16 If the first fruit *be* holy, the lump *is* also *holy:* and if the root *be* holy, so *are* the branches. 17 And if some of the branches be broken off, and thou, being a wild olive-tree, wert grafted in among them, and with them partakest of the root and fatness of the olive-tree; 18 Boast not against the branches. But if thou boast, thou hearest not the root, but the root thee. 19 Thou wilt say then, The branches were broken off, that I might be graffed in. 20 Well; because of unbelief they were broken off, and thou standest by faith. Be not high-minded, but fear: 21 For if God spared not the natural branches, *take heed* lest he also spare not thee. 23 And they also, if they abide not still in unbelief, shall be graffed in: for God is able to graff them in again. 24 For if thou wert cut out of the olive-tree which is wild by nature, and wert graffed contrary to nature into a good olive-tree; how much more shall these, which be the natural *branches*, be graffed into their own olive-tree?

Gal. 3: 7 Know ye therefore, that they which are of faith, the same are the children of Abraham. 8 And the scripture, foreseeing that God would justify the heathen through faith, preached before the gospel unto Abraham, *saying*, In thee shall all nations be blessed. 9 So then they which be of faith are blessed with faithful Abraham. [Rom. 4: 11—25. Ac. 7: 38. Ep. 2: 12.]

CHURCH ABRAHAMIC.

117. *God's covenant with the Abrahamic church.*

Mic. 7: 20 Thou wilt perform the truth to Jacob, *and* the mercy to Abraham, which thou hast sworn unto our fathers from the days of old.

Gal. 3: 9 They which be of faith are blessed with faithful Abraham. 14 That the blessing of Abraham might come on the Gentiles through Jesus Christ; that we might receive the promise of the Spirit through faith. 15 Brethren, I speak after the manner of men; Though *it be* but a man's covenant, yet *if it be* confirmed, no man disannulleth or addeth thereto. 16 Now to Abraham and his seed were the promises made. He saith not, And to seeds, as of many; but as of one, And to thy seed, which is Christ. 17 And this I say, *That* the covenant that was confirmed before of God in Christ, the law, which was four hundred and thirty years after, cannot disannul, that it should make the promise of none effect. 18 For if the inheritance *be* of the law, *it is* no more of promise: but God gave *it* to Abraham by promise. 29 And if ye *be* Christ's, then are ye Abraham's seed, and heirs according to the promise.

118. *God's covenant with the Abrahamic church involves true religion.*

Ex. 19: 5 If ye will obey my voice indeed, and keep my covenant, then ye shall be a peculiar treasure unto me above all people.

Lev. 26: 41 If then their uncircumcised hearts be humbled, and they then accept of the punishment of their iniquity: . 42 Then will I remember my covenant with Jacob, and also my covenant with Isaac, and also my covenant with Abraham will I remember; and I will remember the land.

1 K. 8: 23 He said, LORD God of Israel, *there is* no God like thee, in heaven above, or on earth beneath, who keepest covenant and mercy with thy servants that walk before thee with all their heart.

Ps. 78: 10 They kept not the covenant of God, and refused to walk in his law.

Rom. 2: 28 He is not a Jew, which is one outwardly; neither *is that* circumcision, which is outward in the flesh: 29 But he *is* a Jew which is one inwardly; and circumcision *is that* of the heart, in the spirit, *and* not in the letter; whose praise *is* not of men, but of God.

Gal. 3: 9 So then they which be of faith are blessed with faithful Abraham. 29 And if ye *be* Christ's, then are ye Abraham's seed, and heirs according to the promise. [See 502.]

119. *Circumcision, the seal of the Abrahamic Covenant.*

Gen. 17: 10 This *is* my covenant, which ye shall keep, between me and you, and thy seed after thee; every man-child among you shall be circumcised. 11 And ye shall circumcise the flesh of your foreskin; and it shall be a token of the covenant betwixt me and you. 12 And he that is eight days old shall be circumcised among you, every man-child in your generations, he that is born in the house, or bought with money of any stranger which *is* not of thy seed. 13 He that is born in thy house, and he that is bought with thy money, must needs be circumcised: and my covenant shall be in your flesh for an everlasting covenant.

Rom. 4: 11 He received the sign of circumcision, a seal of the righteousness of the faith which *he had yet* being uncircumcised: that he might be the father of all them that believe, though they be not circumcised, that righteousness might be imputed unto them also.

120. *Did the Abrahamic covenant include blessings for the posterity of believers?*

Gen. 17: 7 I will establish my covenant between me and thee, and thy seed after thee, in their generations, for an everlasting covenant; to be a God unto thee, and to thy seed after thee. 19 And God said, Sarah thy wife shall bear thee a son

9*

Good and Bad.

indeed: and thou shalt call his name Isaac : and I will estab-. lish.my covenant with him for an everlasting covenant, *and* with his seed after him. — 26: 24 The LORD appeared unto him the same night, and said, I *am* the God of Abraham thy father: fear not, for I *am* with thee, and will bless thee, and multiply thy seed, for my servant Abraham's sake.

Dt. 30: 19 Choose life, that both thou and thy seed may live.

2 K. 13: 23 The LORD was gracious unto them, and had compassion on them, and had respect unto them, because of his covenant with Abraham, Isaac, and Jacob, and would not destroy them, neither cast he them from his presence as yet.

Ps. 103: 17 The mercy of the LORD *is* from everlasting to everlasting upon them that fear him, and his righteousness unto children's children; 18 To such as keep his covenant, and to those that remember his commandments to do them.

Is. 59: 21 As for me, this *is* my covenant with them, saith the LORD ; My 'Spirit that *is* upon thee, and my words which I have put in thy mouth, shall not depart out of thy mouth, nor out of the month of thy seed, nor out of the mouth of thy seed's seed, saith the Lord, from henceforth and for ever.

Ac. 2: 39 The promise is unto you and to your children. Gen. 26: 24. [See 496.]

121. *The covenant between God and the Abrahamic church permanent.*

Rom. 15: 8 Jesus Christ was a minister of the circumcision for the truth of God, to confirm the promises made unto the fathers.

Gal. 3: 17 This I say, *That* the covenant that was confirmed before of God in Christ, the law, which was four hundred and thirty years after, cannot disannul, that it should make the promise of none effect. 29 If ye *be* Christ's, then are ye Abraham's seed, and heirs according to the promise.

COMPANIONS.

122. *Good companions to be chosen — bad to be avoided.*

Ex. 34: 12 Take heed to thyself, lest thou make a covenant with the inhabitants of the land whither thou goest, lest it be for a snare in the midst of thee.

Ps. 1: 1 Blessed *is* the man that walketh not in the counsel of the ungodly, nor standeth in the way of sinners, nor sitteth in the seat of the scornful. — 26: 4 I have not sat with vain persons, neither will I go in with dissemblers. 5 I have hated the congregation of evil doers; and will not sit with the wicked. — 101: 7 He that worketh deceit shall not dwell within my house: he that telleth lies shall not tarry in my sight. — 119: 115 Depart from me, ye evil-doers; for I will keep the commandments of my God. — 139: 19 Surely thou wilt slay the wicked, O God: depart from me, therefore, ye bloody men.

Pr. 1: 10 My son, if sinners entice thee, consent thou not. 11 If they say, Come with us, let us lay wait for blood, let us lurk privily for the innocent without cause: 12 Let us swallow them up alive as the grave; and whole, as those that go down into the pit: 13 We shall find all precious substance, we shall fill our houses with spoil: 14 Cast in thy lot among us; let us all have one purse: 15 My son walk not thou in the way with them; refrain thy foot from their path: 16 For their feet run to evil, and make haste to shed blood: 18 And they lay wait for their *own* blood; they lurk privily for their *own* lives. — 4: 14 Enter not into the path of the wicked, and go not in the way of evil *men.* 15 Avoid it, pass not by it, turn from it, and pass away. 16 For they sleep not, except they have done mischief; and their sleep is taken away, unless they cause *some* to fall. 17 For they eat the bread of wickedness, and drink the wine of violence. — 7: 24 Hearken unto me now therefore, O ye children, and attend to the words of my mouth. 25 Let not thine heart decline to her ways, go not astray in her paths. 26 For she hath cast down many wounded: yea, many strong *men* have been slain by her. 27 Her house *is* the way to hell, going down to the chambers of death. — 12: 11 He that followeth vain *persons is* void of understanding. — 13: 20 He that walketh with wise *men* shall be wise: but a companion of fools shall be destroyed. — 14: 7 Go from the presence of a foolish man when thou perceivest not *in him* the lips of knowledge. — 22:24 Make no friendship with an angry man; and with a furious man thou shalt not go: 25 Lest thou learn his ways, and get a snare to thy soul. — 24: 1 Be not thou envious against evil men, neither desire to be with them: 2 For their heart studieth destruction, and their lips talk of mischief. 21 My son, fear thou the LORD and the king: *and* meddle not with them that are given to change. — 28: 7 Whoso keepeth the law *is* a wise son: but he that is a companion of riotous *men* shameth his father. 19 He that tilleth his land shall have plenty of bread: but he that followeth after vain *persons* shall have poverty enough. — 29: 3 Whoso loveth wisdom rejoiceth his father: but he that keepeth company with harlots spendeth *his* substance.

1 Cor. 15: 33 Evil communications corrupt good manners. [See 112, 115.]

CONDESCENSION.

123. *Condescension required.*

Lk. 14: 13 When thou makest a feast, call the poor, the maimed, the lame, the blind ; 14 And thou shalt be blessed : for they cannot recompense thee : for thou shalt be recompensed at the resurrection of the just.

Jn. 13: 14 If I then, *your* Lord and Master, have washed your feet, ye also ought to wash one another's feet.

Rom. 12: 16 *Be* of the same mind one toward another. Mind not high things, but condescend to men of low estate. [See 61, 228.]

CONFESSION OF SIN.

124. *Duty and encouragement to confess sin.*

Lev. 26: 40 If they shall confess their iniquity, and the iniquity of their fathers, with their trespass which they trespassed against me, and that also they have walked contrary unto me; 41 And *that* I also have walked contrary unto them, and have brought them into the land of their enemies ; if then their uncircumcised hearts be humbled, and they then accept of the punishment of their iniquity : 42 Then will I remember my covenant with Jacob, and also my covenant with Isaac, and also my covenant with Abraham will I remember ; and I will remember the land.

Pr. 28: 13 He that covereth his sins shall not prosper : but whoso confesseth and forsaketh *them* shall have mercy.

Dan. 9: 20 While I was speaking, and praying, and confessing my sin, and the sin of my people Israel, and presenting my supplication before the LORD my God for the holy mountain of my God ; 21 Yea, while I *was* speaking in prayer, even the man Gabriel, whom I had seen in the vision at the beginning, being caused to fly swiftly, touched me about the time of the evening oblation.

Hos. 5: 14 I *will be* unto Ephraim as a lion, and as a young lion to the house of Judah : I, *even* I, will tear and go away; I will take away, and none shall rescue *him*. 15 I will go *and* return to my place, till they acknowledge their offence, and seek my face : in their affliction they will seek me early.

Jam. 5: 16 Confess *your* faults one to another, and pray one for another, that ye may be healed.

1 Jn. 1: 8 If we say that we have no sin, we deceive ourselves, and the truth is not in us. 9 If we confess our sins, he is faithful and just to forgive us *our* sins, and to cleanse us from all unrighteousness. [See 537, 603.]

CONSCIENCE.

125. *The faculty of conscience belongs to all.*

Pr. 20: 27 The spirit of man *is* the candle of the LORD, searching all the inward parts of the belly.

Is. 5: 3 O inhabitants of Jerusalem, and men of Judah, judge, I pray you, betwixt me and my vineyard.

Jn. 8: 9 They which heard *it*, being convicted by *their own* conscience, went out one by one.

Rom. 2: 14 When the Gentiles, which have not the law, do by nature the things contained in the law, these having not the law, are a law unto themselves. 15 Which show the work of the law written in their hearts, their conscience also bearing witness, and *their* thoughts the mean while accusing, or else excusing one another.

2 Cor. 4: 2 Have renounced the hidden things of dishonesty; not walking in craftiness, nor handling the word of God deceitfully; but, by manifestation of the truth, commending ourselves to every man's conscience in the sight of God. [See 632.]

126. *A seared and defiled conscience.*

Jer. 6: 15 Were they ashamed when they had committed abomination? nay, they were not at all ashamed, neither could they blush.

Zep. 3: 5 The unjust knoweth no shame.

1 Cor. 8: 7 Their conscience, being weak, is defiled. Heb. 9: 14.

1 Tim. 4: 2 Speaking lies in hypocrisy, having their conscience seared with a hot iron.

Tit. 1: 15 Unto the pure all things *are* pure: but unto them that are defiled and unbelieving *is* nothing pure; but even their mind and conscience is defiled.

127. *Conscience, when misinformed, misleads.*

Jn. 16: 2 The time cometh, that whosoever killeth you, will think that he doeth God service.

Ac. 26: 9 I verily thought with myself, that I ought to do many things contrary to the name of Jesus of Nazareth. 10 Which thing I also did in Jerusalem: and many of the saints did I shut up in prison, having received authority from the chief priests; and when they were put to death, I gave my voice against *them*. 11 And I punished them oft in every synagogue, and compelled *them* to blaspheme; and being exceedingly mad against them, I persecuted *them* even unto strange cities. [See 363.]

128. *Conscience will not always sleep.*

Gen. 42: 21 They said one to another, We *are* verily guilty concerning our brother, in that we saw the anguish of his soul, when he besought us, and we would not hear; therefore is this distress come upon us.

Ex. 9: 27 Pharaoh sent and called for Moses and Aaron, and said unto them, I have sinned this time: the LORD *is* righteous, and I and my people *are* wicked.

Mat. 22: 11 When the king came in to see the guests, he saw there a man which had not on a wedding-garment: 12 And he saith unto him, Friend, how earnest thou in hither, not having a wedding-garment? And he was speechless.

Rom. 3: 19 Now we know that what things soever the law saith, it saith to them who are under the law: that every mouth may be stopped, and all the world may become guilty before God. [See 573(2.)]

129. *Conscience should be enlightened and obeyed.*

Ac. 23: 1 Paul, earnestly beholding the council, said, Men *and* brethren, I have lived in all good conscience before God until this day. — 24: 16 Herein do I exercise myself, to have always a conscience void of offence toward God, and *toward* men.

Rom. 13: 5 *Ye* must needs be subject, not only for wrath, but also for conscience' sake.

1 Tim. 1: 19 Holding faith and a good conscience; which some having put away, concerning faith have made shipwreck.

Heb. 13: 18 Pray for us: for we trust we have a good conscience, in all things willing to live honestly.

1 Pet. 2: 19 This *is* thankworthy, if a man for conscience toward God endure grief, suffering wrongfully. — 3: 16 Having a good conscience; that, whereas they speak evil of you, as of evil doers, they may be ashamed that falsely accuse your good conversation in Christ.

130. *Conscientious feelings of others to be respected.*

1 Cor. 8: 10 If any man see thee which hast knowledge, sit at meat in the idol's temple, shall not the conscience of him which is weak be emboldened to eat those things which are offered

to. idols; 11 And through thy knowledge shall the weak brother perish, for whom Christ died? 12 But when ye sin so against the brethren, and wound their weak conscience, ye sin against Christ. 13 Wherefore, if meat make my brother to offend, I will eat no flesh while the world standeth, lest I make my brother to offend. — 10: 27 If any of them that believe not bid you *to a feast*, and ye be disposed to go'; whatsoever is set before you, eat, asking no question for conscience' sake. 28 But if any man say unto you, This is offered in sacrifice unto idols, eat not for his sake that shewed it, and for conscience' sake: for the earth *is* the Lord's, and the fulness thereof: 29 Conscience, I say, not thine own, but of the other: for why is my liberty judged of another *man's* conscience?

131. *Conscience, the cause of great comfort or sorrow.*

Pr. 14: 14 The backslider in heart shall be filled with his own ways: and a good man *shall be satisfied* from himself. — 18: 14 The spirit of a man will sustain his infirmity; but a wounded spirit who can bear?

2 Cor. 1: 12 Our rejoicing is this, the testimony of our conscience, that in simplicity and godly sincerity, not with fleshly wisdom, but by the grace of God, we have had our conversation in the world. [See 573.]

CONSIDERATION.

132. *Consideration required — inconsideration reproved.*

Dt. 4: 39 Know therefore this day, and consider *it* in thine heart, that the LORD he *is* God. — 32: 29 Oh that they were wise, *that* they understood this, *that* they would consider their latter end!

Job 37: 14 Hearken unto this, O Job: stand still, and consider the wondrous works of God.

Ps. 28: 5 Because they regard not the works of the LORD, nor the operation of his hands, he shall destroy them, and not build them up. — 50: 21 These *things* hast thou done, and I kept silence; thou thoughtest that I was altogether *such a one as* thyself: *but* I will reprove thee, and set *them* in order before thine eyes. 22 Now consider this, ye that forget God, lest I tear *you* in pieces, and *there be* none to deliver. — 111: 4 He hath made his wonderful works to be remembered.

Pr. 4: 26 Ponder the path of thy feet, and let all thy ways be established. — 6: 6 Go to the ant, thou sluggard: consider her ways, and be wise.

Ec. 7: 13 Consider the work of God: for who can make *that* straight, which he hath made crooked?   14 In the day of prosperity be joyful, but in the day of adversity consider.

Is. 1: 3 The ox knoweth his owner, and the ass his master's crib: *but* Israel doth not know, my people doth not consider. 5: 12 The harp, and the viol, the tabret, and pipe, and wine, are in their feasts: but they regard not the work of the LORD, neither consider the operation of his hands.   13 Therefore my people are gone into captivity, because *they have* no knowledge.

Hos. 7: 2 They consider not in their hearts, *that* I remember all their wickedness.

Hag. 1: 5 Thus saith the LORD of hosts; Consider your ways. [See 693.]

CONTENTMENT.

133. *Duty and advantages of contentment.*

Ph. 4: 11 Not that I speak in respect of want: for I have learned, in whatsoever state I am, *therewith* to be content.

1 Tim. 6: 6 Godliness with contentment is great gain.   7 For we brought nothing into *this* world, *and it is* certain we can carry nothing out.   8 And having food and raiment, let us be therewith content.

Heb. 13: 5 *Let your* conversation *be* without covetousness; *and be* content with such things as ye have: for he hath said, I will never leave thee, nor forsake thee.   [See 626.]

COURAGE.

134. *Courage and resolution required and exemplified — promises.*

Dt. 31: 6 Be strong and of a good courage, fear not, nor be afraid of them: for the LORD thy God, he *it is* that doth go with thee, he will not fail thee, nor forsake thee.

Josh. 1: 9 Be strong and of a good courage; be not afraid, neither be thou dismayed: for the LORD thy God *is* with thee whithersoever thou goest.

1 Ch. 28: 20 David said to Solomon his son, Be strong, and of good courage, and do *it:* fear not, nor be dismayed, for the LORD God, *even* my God *will be* with thee; he will not fail thee, nor forsake thee, until thou hast finished all the work for the service of the house of the LORD.

2 Ch. 19: 11 Deal courageously, and the LORD shall be with the good.

Ezra 10: 2 Shechaniah the son of Jehiel, *one* of the sons of Elam, answered and said unto Ezra, We have trespassed against our God, and have taken strange wives of the people of the land: yet now there is hope in Israel concerning this thing. 3 Now therefore let us make a covenant with our God to put away all the wives, and such as are born of them, according to the counsel of my lord, and of those that tremble at the commandment of our God ; and let it be done according to the law. 4 Arise ; for *this* matter *belongeth* unto thee : we also *will be* with thee : be of good courage, and do *it*. 5 Then arose Ezra, and made the chief priests, the Levites, and all Israel, to swear that they should do according to this' word.

Neh. 6: 11 I said, should such a man as I flee ? and who *is there*, that, *being* as I *am*, would go into the temple to save his life ? I will not go in.

Ps. 27: 14 Wait on the LORD : be of good courage, and he shall strengthen thine heart : wait, I say, on the LORD.

31: 24 Be of good courage, and he shall strengthen your heart, all ye that hope in the LORD. [See 460, 461.]

COURTESY.

135. *Courtesy exemplified and required.*

Mat. 26: 50 Jesus said unto him, [Judas] Friend, wherefore art thou come ?

Ac. 27: 3 Julius courteously entreated Paul, and gave *him* liberty to go unto his friends to refresh himself.

28: 7 In the same quarters were possessions of the chief man of the island, whose name was Publius ; who received us, and lodged us three days courteously.

1 Pet. 3: 8 Finally, *be ye* all of one mind, having compassion one of another ; love as brethren, *be* pitiful, *be* courteous. [See 459.]

COVETOUSNESS.

136. *Prevalence of covetousness.*

Ph. 2: 21 All seek their own, not the things which are Jesus Christ's. [See 689, and " Spurious" in the Index.]

137. *Covetousness forbidden — cautions.*

Ex. 20: 17 Thou shalt not covet thy neighbor's house, thou shalt not covet thy neighbor's wife, nor his man servant, nor his maid-servant, nor his ox, nor his ass, nor any thing that *is* thy neighbor's.

Pr. 28: 16 The prince that wanteth understanding *is* also a great oppressor : *but* he that hateth covetousness shall prolong *his* days.

Lk. 12: 15 He said unto them, Take heed, and beware of covetousness: for a man's life consisteth not in the abundance of the things which he possesseth. 16 And he spake a parable unto them, saying, The ground of a certain rich man brought forth plentifully: 17 And he thought within himself, saying, What shall I do, because I have no room where to bestow my fruits? 17 And he said, This will I do: I will pull down my barns, and build greater; and there will I bestow all my fruits and my goods. 19 And I will say to my soul, Soul, thou hast much goods laid up for many years; take thine ease, eat, drink *and* be merry: 20 But God said unto him, *Thou* fool, this night thy soul shall be required of thee: then whose shall those things be which thou hast provided? 21 So *is* he that layeth up treasure for himself, and is not rich toward God.

Ep. 5: 3 Fornication, and all uncleanness, or covetousness, let it not be once named among you, as becometh saints.

Ph. 2: 4 Look not every man on his own things, but every man also on the things of others.

Col. 3: 5 Mortify therefore your members which are upon the earth; fornication, uncleanness, inordinate affection, evil concupiscence, and covetousness, which is idolatry.

Heb. 13: 5 *Let your* conversation *be* without covetousness; *and be* content with such things as ye have: for he hath said, I will never leave thee, nor forsake thee. [See 174, 413.]

138. *Threats and punishment for the covetous.*

Ps. 10: 3 The wicked boasteth of his heart's desire, and blesseth the covetous, *whom* the LORD abhorreth.

Is. 57: 17 For the iniquity of his covetousness was I wroth, and smote him: I hid me, and was wroth, and he went on frowardly in the way of his heart.

Mic. 2: 2 They covet fields, and take *them* by violence; and houses, and take *them* away: so they oppress a man and his house, even a man and his heritage. 3 Therefore thus saith the LORD; Behold, against this family do I devise an evil, from which ye shall not remove your necks; neither shall ye go haughtily: for this time *is* evil.

Hab. 2: 9 Wo to him that coveteth an evil covetousness to his house, that he may set his nest on high, that he may be delivered from the power of evil!

1 Cor. 5: 11 Now I have written unto you not to keep company, if any man that is called a brother be a fornicator, or covetous, or an idolater, or a railer, or a drunkard, or an extortioner: with such an one no not to eat.

6: 10 Nor thieves, nor covetous, nor drunkards, nor revilers, nor extortioners, shall inherit the kingdom of God.

Ep. 5: 5 This ye know, that no whoremonger, nor unclean person, nor covetous man, who is an idolater, hath any inheritance in the kingdom of Christ and of God.

Jude 11 Wo unto them! for they have gone in the way of Cain, and ran greedily after the error of Balaam for reward, and perished in the gainsaying of Core. [See 733.]

CREATION.

139. *Creation, the effect of divine power.*

Gen. 1: 1 In the beginning God created the heaven and the earth.

Neh. 9: 6 Thou, *even* thou, *art* LORD alone; thou hast made heaven, the heaven of heavens, with all their host, the earth, and all *things* that *are* therein, the seas, and all that *is* therein, and thou preservest them all.

Ps. 33: 6 By the word of the LORD were the heavens made; and all the host of them by the breath of his mouth. 9 For he spake and it was *done;* he commanded, and it stood fast.

Is. 42: 5 Thus saith God the LORD, he that created the heavens, and stretched them out; he that spread forth the earth, and that which cometh out of it; he that giveth breath unto the people upon it, and spirit to them that walk therein.

Jn. 1: 1 In the beginning was the Word, and the Word was with God, and the Word was God. 3 All things were made by him; and without him was not anything made that was made. 14 And the Word was made flesh, and dwelt among us.

Ep. 3: 9 God, who created all things by Jesus Christ.

Col. 1: 16 By him were all things created, that are in heaven, and that are in earth, visible and invisible, whether *they be* thrones, or dominions, or principalities, or powers: all things were created by him, and for him.

Heb. 3: 4 Every house is builded by some *man;* but he that built all things *is* God.

Rev. 4: 11 Thou art worthy, O Lord, to receive glory, and honor, and power: for thou hast created all things, and for thy pleasure they are and were created.

140. *How long was God in creating the world?*

Gen. 2: 1 Thus the heavens and the earth were finished, and all the host of them. 2 And on the seventh day God ended his work which he had made; and he rested on the seventh day from all his work which he had made. 4 These *are* the generations of the heavens and of the earth when they were created, in the day that the LORD God made the earth and the heavens.

Ex. 20: 11 *In* six days the LORD made heaven and earth, the sea and all that in them *is*.

141. *Use of the heavenly bodies, or, astronomic divinity.*

Gen. 1: 14 God said, Let there be lights in the firmament of the heaven, to divide the day from the night; and let them be for signs, and for seasons, and for days, and years. 15 And let them be for lights in the firmament of the heaven to give light upon the earth: and it was so. 16 And God made two great lights; the greater light to rule the day, and the lesser light to rule the night: *he made* the stars also. 17 And God set them in the firmament of the heaven to give light upon the earth, 18 And to rule over the day, and over the night, and to divide the light from the darkness.

Jer. 31: 35 Thus saith the LORD, which giveth the sun for a light by day, *and* the ordinances of the moon and of the stars for a light by night, which divideth the sea when the waves thereof roar; The LORD of hosts *is* his name.

142. *The works of creation indicate wisdom.*

Ps. 19: 1 The heavens declare the glory of God; and the firmament sheweth his handy-work. 2 Day unto day uttereth speech, and night unto night showeth knowledge. — 104: 24 O LORD, how manifold are thy works! in wisdom hast thou made them all: the earth is full of thy riches.

Pr. 3: 19 The LORD by wisdom hath founded the earth; by understanding hath he established the heavens. 20 By his knowledge the depths are broken up, and the clouds drop down the dew.

Jer. 10: 12 He hath made the earth by his power, he hath established the world by his wisdom, and hath stretched out the heavens by his discretion. [See 222.]

CUSTOM.

143. *Power of sinful customs.*

Jer. 10: 2 Thus saith the LORD, Learn not the way of the heathen, and be not dismayed at the signs of heaven; for the heathen are dismayed at them. 3 For the customs of the people *are* vain. — 13: 23 Can the Ethiopian change his skin, or the leopard his spots? *then* may ye also do good, that are accustomed to do evil.

Rom. 7: 19 The good that I would, I do not; but the evil which I would not, that I do. 20 Now if I do that I would not, it is no more I that do it, but sin that dwelleth in me. 21 I find then a law, that when I would do good, evil is present with me. 23 But I see another law in my members warring against the law of my mind, and bringing me into captivity to the law of sin which is in my members. 24 O wretched man that I am! who shall deliver me from the body of this death? [See 166, 507.]

DEATH.

144. *Death, the consequence of sin.*

Rom. 5: 12 As by one man sin entered into the world, and death by sin; and so death passed upon all men, for that all have sinned. 17 For if by one man's offence death reigned by one; much more they which receive abundance of grace, and of the gift of righteousness, shall reign in life by one, Jesus Christ.

145. *All men must die.*

Gen. 3: 19 Dust thou *art*, and unto dust shalt thou return.

Job 16: 22 When a few years are come, then I shall go the way *whence* I shall not return. — 30: 23 I know *that* thou wilt bring me *to* death, and *to* the house appointed for all living.

Ps. 89: 48 What man *is he that* liveth, and shall not see death? shall he deliver his soul from the hand of the grave?

Ec. 8: 8 *There is* no man that hath power over the spirit to retain the spirit: neither *hath he* power in the day of death: and *there is* no discharge in *that* war; neither shall wickedness deliver those that are given to it.

Zech. 1: 5 Your fathers, where *are* they? and the prophets, do they live for ever?

Heb. 9: 27 It is appointed unto men once to die, but after this the judgment.

146. *The time of our death appointed.*

Job 7: 1 *Is there* not an appointed time to man upon earth? *are not* his days also like the days of a hireling? — 14: 5 Seeing his days *are* determined, the number of his months *is* with thee, thou hast appointed his bounds that he cannot pass; 6 Turn from him, that he may rest, till he shall accomplish, as a hireling, his day. 14 All the days of my appointed time will I wait, till my change come.

147. *God giveth and taketh away human life.*

Dt. 32: 39 See now that I, *even* I, *am* he, and *there is* no god with me: I kill, and I make alive: I wound, and I heal: neither *is there any* that can deliver out of my hand.

1 S. 2: 6 The Lord killeth, and maketh alive: he bringeth down to the grave, and bringeth up.

Ps. 68: 20 Unto God the Lord *belong* the issues from death.

Dan. 5: 23 The God in whose hand thy breath *is*, and whose *are* all thy ways, hast thou not glorified. [See 3.]

148. *Shortness and vanity of life.*

Gen 47: 9 Jacob said unto Pharaoh, The days of the years of my pilgrimage *are* an hundred and thirty years: few and evil have the days of the years of my life been.

1 Ch. 29: 15 We *are* strangers before thee, and sojourners, as *were* all our fathers: our days on the earth *are* as a shadow, and *there is* none abiding.

Job 8: 9 (We *are but of* yesterday, and know nothing, because our days upon earth *are* a shadow.) — 9: 25 My days are swifter than a post: they flee away, they see no good. 26 They are passed away as the swift ships: as the eagle *that* hasteth to the prey. — 14: 1 Man *that is* born of a woman *is* of few days, and full of trouble. 2 He cometh forth like a flower, and is cut down: he fleeth also as a shadow, and continueth not.

Ps. 39: 5 Behold, thou hast made my days *as* an handbreadth; and mine age *is* as nothing before thee: verily every man at his best state *is* altogether vanity. — 90: 10 The days of our years *are* threescore years and ten; and if by reason of strength *they be* fourscore years, yet is their strength labor and sorrow; for it is soon cut off, and we fly away. — 103: 15 *As for* man, his days *are* as grass: as a flower of the field, so he flourisheth. 16 For the wind passeth over it, and it is gone; and the place thereof shall know it no more. — 144: 4 Man is like to vanity: his days *are* as a shadow that passeth away.

Is. 40: 6 The voice said, Cry. And he said, What shall I cry? All flesh *is* grass, and all the goodliness thereof *is* as the flower of the field: 7 The grass withereth, the flower fadeth: because the spirit of the LORD bloweth upon it: surely the people *is* grass. — 64: 6 We all do fade as a leaf; and our iniquities, like the wind, have taken us away.

Jam. 4: 14 Whereas ye know not what *shall be* on the morrow. For what *is* your life? It is even a vapor, that appeareth for a little time, and then vanisheth away.

114

1 Pet. 1: 24 All flesh *is* as grass, and all the glory of man as the flower of grass. The grass withereth, and the flower thereof falleth away. [See 726–7.]

149. *Death often sudden and unexpected.*

1 S. 20: 3 *There is* but a step between me and death.

Ps. 102: 23 He weakened my strength in the way, he shortened my days. 24 I said, O my God, take me not away in the midst of my days.

Ec. 9: 12 Man also knoweth not his time: as the fishes that are taken in an evil net, and as the birds that are caught in the snare; so *are* the sons of men snared in an evil time, when it falleth suddenly upon them. [See 385.]

150. *Death closes intercourse with earth.*

Job 7: 8 The eye of him that hath seen me shall see me no *more.* 9 *As* the cloud is consumed and vanisheth away: so he that goeth down to the grave shall come up no *more.* 10 He shall return no more to his house, neither shall his place know him any more. — 14: 7 There is hope of a tree, if it be cut down, that it will sprout again, and that the tender branch thereof will not cease. 8 Though the root thereof wax old in the earth, and the stock thereof die in the ground; 9 *Yet* through the scent of water it will bud, and bring forth boughs like a plant. 10 But man dieth, and wasteth away.: yea, man giveth up the ghost, and where *is* he? 11 *As* the waters fail from the sea, and the flood decayeth and drieth up: 12 So man lieth down, and riseth not: till the heavens *be* no more, they shall not awake, nor be raised out of their sleep. 19 Thou destroyest the hope of man. 20 Thou prevailest for ever against him, and he passeth: thou changest his countenance, and sendest him away. 21 His sons come to honor, and he knoweth *it* not; and they are brought low, but he perceiveth *it* not of them.

Lk. 16: 27 He said, I pray thee therefore, father, that thou wouldest send him to my father's house: 28 For I have five brethren; that he may testify unto them, lest they also come into this place of torment. 29 Abraham saith unto him, They have Moses and the prophets; let them hear them.

151. *A late death, or old age desirable.*

Gen. 15: 15 Thou shalt go to thy fathers in peace: thou shalt be buried in a good old age.

Ps. 91: 16 With long life will I satisfy him, and shew him my salvation. — 102: 24 I said, O my God, take me not away in (the midst of my days: thy years *are* throughout all generations.

Pr. 3: 16 Length of days *is* in her right hand; *and* in her left hand riches and honor.

Is. 38: 18 The grave cannot praise thee, death cannot celebrate thee: they that go down into the pit cannot hope for thy truth. 19 The living, the living, he shall praise thee, as I *do* this day: the father to the children shall make known thy truth.

152. *Death does not destroy, or hold the soul in slumber.*

Ec. 3: 21 Who knoweth the spirit of man that goeth upward, and the spirit of the beast that goeth downward to the earth?—12: 7 Then shall the dust return to the earth as it was: and the spirit shall return unto God who gave it.

Mat. 22: 32 I am the God of Abraham, and the God of Isaac, and the God of Jacob. God is not the God of the dead, but of the living.

Lk. 16: 22 It came to pass, that the beggar died, and was carried by the angels into Abraham's bosom. The rich man also died, and was buried: 23 And in hell he lifted up his eyes, being in torments, and seeth Abraham afar off, and Lazarus in his bosom. — 23: 43 Jesus said unto him, Verily I say unto thee, To-day shalt thou be with me in paradise.

Ac. 7: 59 They stoned Stephen, calling upon *God*, and saying, Lord Jesus, receive my spirit.

2 Cor. 5: 8 We are confident, *I say*, and willing rather to be absent from the body, and to be present with the Lord.

Ph. 1: 23 I am in a strait betwixt two, having a desire to depart, and to be with Christ; which is far better.

Heb. 12: 23 The spirits of just men made perfect.

Rev. 6: 9 When he had opened the fifth seal, I saw under the altar the souls of them that were slain for the word of God, and for the testimony which they held. [See 422.]

153. *Death desirable to the righteous — fear of, overcome.*

Job 3: 17 There the wicked cease *from* troubling; and there the weary be at rest. 18 *There* the prisoners rest together; they hear not the voice of the oppressor. — 7: 16 I would not live alway.

Ps. 23: 4 Though I walk through the valley of the shadow of death, I will fear no evil: for thou *art* with me; thy rod and thy staff they comfort me. — 31: 5 Into thine hand I commit my spirit: thou hast redeemed me, O LORD God of truth. — 37: 37 Mark the perfect *man*, and behold the upright: for the end of *that* man *is* peace. — 116: 15 Precious in the sight of the Lord *is* the death of his saints.

Pr. 14: 32 The wicked is driven away in his wickedness: but the righteous hath hope in his death.

Is. 57: 1 The righteous perisheth, and no man layeth *it* to heart: and merciful men *are* taken away, none considering that the righteous is taken away from the evil to *come.* 2 He shall enter into peace: they shall rest in their beds, *each one* walking *in* his uprightness.

1 Cor. 3: 22 Or life, or death, or things present, or things to come; all are yours. — 15: 54 So when this corruptible shall have put on incorruption, and this mortal shall have put on immortality, then shall be brought to pass the saying that is written, Death is swallowed up in victory. 55 O death, where *is* thy sting? O grave, where *is* thy victory? 56 The sting of death *is* sin, and the strength of sin *is* the law. 57 But thanks *be* to God, which giveth us the victory, through our Lord Jesus Christ.

2 Cor. 5: 1 We know that if our earthly house of *this* tabernacle were dissolved, we have a building of God, an house not made with hands, eternal in the heavens. 8 We are confident, *I say*, and willing rather to be absent from the body, and to be present with the Lord.

Ph. 1: 21 To me to live *is* Christ, and to die *is* gain.

Rev. 14: 13 I heard a voice from heaven saying unto me, Write, Blessed *are* the dead which die in the Lord from henceforth: Yea, saith the Spirit, that they may rest from their labors; and their works do follow them.

154. *Patient waiting for death.*

Job 14: 14 If a man die, shall he live *again?* all the days of my appointed time will I wait, till my change come.

Lam. 3: 26 *It is* good that *a man* should both hope and quietly wait for the salvation of the LORD.

Ph. 1: 23 I am in a strait betwixt two, having a desire to depart, and to be with Christ; which is far better: 24 Nevertheless, to abide in the flesh *is* more needful for you. 25 And having this confidence, I know that I shall abide and continue with you all for your furtherance and joy of faith. [See 498.]

155. *Death dreadful to the wicked.*

Job 27: 19 The rich man shall lie down, but he shall not be gathered: he openeth his eyes, and he *is* not. 20 Terrors take hold on him as waters, a tempest stealeth him away in the night. 21 The east wind carrieth him away, and he departeth: and as a storm hurleth him out of his place. 22 For *God* shall cast upon him, and not spare: he would fain flee out of his hand.

Préparation for.

Lk. 12: 20 God said unto him, *Thou* fool, this night thy soul shall be required of thee: then whose shall those things be which thou hast provided?

Heb. 10: 31 *It is* a fearful thing to fall into the hands of the living God. [See 564.]

156. *Preparation for death required and exemplified.*

Ps. 90: 12 So teach *us* to number our days, that we may apply *our* hearts unto wisdom.

Ec. 9: 10 Whatsoever thy hand findeth to do, do *it* with thy might; for *there is* no work, nor device, nor knowledge, nor wisdom, in the grave, whither thou goest.

Mat. 24: 44 Be ye also ready: for in such an hour as ye think not, the Son of man cometh.

Lk. 12: 35 Let your loins be girded about, and *your* lights burning; 36 And ye yourselves like unto men that wait for their lord, when he will return from the wedding; that, when he cometh and knocketh, they may open unto him immediately. 37 Blessed *are* those servants, whom the lord when he cometh shall find watching.

1 Cor. 1: 7 So that ye come behind in no gift; waiting for the coming of our Lord Jesus Christ: 8 Who shall also confirm you unto the end, *that ye may be* blameless in the day of our Lord Jesus Christ.

2 Cor. 4: 18 While we look not at the things which are seen, but at the things which are not seen: for the things which are seen *are* temporal; but the things which are not seen *are* eternal.

Ph. 3: 20 Our conversation is in heaven; from whence also we look for the Saviour.

Tit. 2: 11 The grace of God that bringeth salvation hath appeared to all men, 12 Teaching us, that denying ungodliness, and worldly lusts, we should live soberly, righteously, and godly, in this present world; 13 Looking for that blessed hope, and the glorious appearing of the great God and our Saviour Jesus Christ.

1 Pet. 4: 7 The end of all things is at hand: be ye therefore sober, and watch unto prayer.

2 Pet. 3: 11 *Seeing* then *that* all these things shall be dissolved, what manner *of persons* ought ye to be in *all* holy conversation and godliness. [See 727.]

N. B. — For Spiritual Death, see 165; and, for the Second Death, see 563.

DEPRAVITY.

157. *Fall of man, and its immediate effects.*

Gen. 3: 4 The serpent said unto the woman, Ye shall not surely die: 5 For God doth know, that in the day ye eat thereof, then your eyes shall be opened; and ye shall be as gods, knowing good and evil. 6 And when the woman saw that the tree *was* good for food, and that it *was* pleasant to the eyes, and a tree to be desired to make *one* wise; she took of the fruit thereof, and did eat; and gave also unto her husband with her, and he did eat. 14 The LORD God said unto the serpent, Because thou hast done this, thou *art* cursed above all cattle, and above every beast of the field. 16 Unto the woman he said, I will greatly multiply thy sorrow and thy conception; in sorrow thou shalt bring forth children: and thy desire *shall be* to thy husband, and he shall rule over thee. 17 And unto Adam he said, Because thou hast hearkened unto the voice of thy wife, and hast eaten of the tree of which I commanded thee, saying, Thou shalt not eat of it: cursed *is* the ground for thy sake; in sorrow shalt thou eat *of* it all the days of thy life; 18 Thorns also and thistles shall it bring forth to thee; and thou shalt eat the herb of the field: 19 In the sweat of thy face shalt thou eat bread, till thou return unto the ground; for out of it wast thou taken: for dust thou *art*, and unto dust shalt thou return.

Ec. 7: 29 Lo, this only have I found, that God hath made man upright; but they have sought out many inventions.

158. *Consequences of Adam's fall upon his posterity.*

Rom. 5: 12 As by one man sin entered into the world, and death by sin; and so death passed upon all men, for that all have sinned. 18 Therefore as by the offence of one *judgment came* upon all men to condemnation, even so by the righteousness of one *the free gift came* upon all men unto justification of life. 19 For as by one man's disobedience many were made sinners, so by the obedience of one shall many be made righteous.

1 Cor. 15: 22 As in Adam all die, even so in Christ shall all be made alive.

159 *Ill-desert not imputed, without personal transgression.*

Dt. 24: 16 The father shall not be put to death for the children, neither shall the children be but to death for the fathers: every man shall be put to death for his own sin. [2 K. 14: 6.]

119

Ezk. 18: 2 What mean ye, that ye use this proverb concerning the land of Israel, saying, The fathers have eaten sour grapes, and the children's teeth are set on edge? 20 The soul that sinneth, it shall die. The son shall not bear the iniquity of the father, neither shall the father bear the iniquity of the son: the righteousness of the righteous shall be upon him and the wickedness of the wicked shall be upon him. [Jer. 31: 29, 30.]

160. *Nature of moral depravity.*

Hos. 10: 1 Israel *is* an empty vine, he bringeth forth fruit unto himself.

Col. 3: 5 Covetousness, which is idolatry.

1 Jn. 5: 17 All unrighteousness is sin. [See 689.]

161. *No sin, without law and knowledge.*

Jn. 9: 41 If ye were blind, ye should have no sin. — 15: 22 If I had not come and spoken unto them, they had not had sin; but now they have no cloak for their sin.

Rom. 3: 19 We know that what things soever the law saith, it saith to them who are under the law: that every mouth may be stopped, and all the world become guilty before God. — 4: 15 Where no law is, *there is* no transgression. — 5: 13 (For until the law, sin was in the world: but sin is not imputed when there is no law.)

Jam. 4: 17 To him that knoweth to do good, and doeth *it* not, to him it is sin. [See 309.]

162. *Depravity, not founded in mere ignorance.*

Rom. 1: 21 When they knew God they glorified *him* not as God, neither were thankful. [See 690.]

163. *Human depravity universal.*

Gen. 6: 12 God looked upon the earth, and behold, it was corrupt: for all flesh had corrupted his way upon the earth.

Ps. 14: 1 They are corrupt, they have done abominable works, *there is* none that doeth good. 2 The LORD looked down from heaven upon the children of men, to see if there were any that did understand, *and* seek God. 3 They are all gone aside, they are *all* together become filthy: *there is* none that doeth good, no, not one.

Rom. 3: 9 What then, are we better *than they?* No, in no wise: for we have before proved both Jews and Gentiles, that they are all under sin; 10 As it is written, There is none righteous, no, not one: 11 There is none that understandeth, there is none that seeketh after God. 12 They are all gone out of the way, they are together become unprofitable: there is none that doeth good, no, not one. 23 All have sinned, and come short of the glory of God. — 5: 12 As by one man sin entered into the world, and death by sin; and so death passed upon all men, for that all have sinned.

Gal. 3: 21 If there had been a law given which could have given life, verily righteousness should have been by the law. 22 But the scripture hath concluded all under sin, that the promise by faith of Jesus Christ might be given to them that believe. [See 576.]

164. *Native depravity.*

Job. 11: 12 Vain man would be wise, though man be born *like* a wild ass's colt. — 14: 4 Who can bring a clean *thing* out of an unclean? not one. — 15: 14 What *is* man, that he should be clean? and *he which is* born of a woman, that he should be righteous?

Ps. 51: 5 Behold I was shapen in iniquity; and in sin did my mother conceive me. — 58: 3 The wicked are estranged from the womb: they go astray as soon as they be born, speaking lies.

Pr. 22: 15 Foolishness *is* bound in the heart of a child.

Is. 48: 8 I knew that thou wouldest deal very treacherously, and wast called a transgressor from the womb.

Jn. 3: 6 That which is born of the flesh, is flesh; and that which is born of the Spirit, is spirit.

Rom. 3: 10 There is none righteous, no not one. 20 Therefore by the deeds of the law, there shall no flesh be justified in his sight. 23 For all have sinned, and come short of the glory of God. — 5: 12 Death passed upon all men, for that all have sinned. 14 Death reigned from Adam to Moses, even over them that had not sinned after the similitude of Adam's transgression.

2 Cor. 5: 14 If one died for all, then were all dead.

Ep. 2: 3 And were by nature the children of wrath, even as others.

165. *Total sinfulness by nature.*

Gen. 6: 5 GOD saw that the wickedness of man *was* great in the earth, and that every imagination of the thoughts of his heart *was* only evil continually.

Ps. 5: 9 *There is* no faithfulness in their mouth; their inward part *is* very wickedness; their throat *is* an open sepulchre; they flatter with their tongue.

11   121

Pr. 21: 4 The ploughing of the wicked *is* sin.

Ec. 8: 11 Because sentence against an evil work is not exe-cuted speedily, therefore the heart of the sons of men is fully set in them to do evil.—9: 3 This *is* an evil among all *things* that are done under the sun, that *there is* one event unto all: yea, also the heart of the sons of men is full of evil.

2 Cor. 5: 14 If one died for all, then were all dead.

Ep. 2: 1 You *hath he quickened,* who were dead in trespasses and sins; 2 Wherein in time past ye walked according to the course of this world, according to the prince of the power of the air, the spirit that now worketh in the children of disobe-dience: 3 Among whom also we all had our conversation in times past in the lusts of our flesh, fulfilling the desires of the flesh and of the mind; and were by nature the children of wrath, even as others. 12 That at that time ye were without Christ, being aliens from the commonwealth of Israel, and strangers from the covenants of promise, having no hope, and without God in the world.

Col. 2: 13 You, being dead in your sins and the uncircum-cision of your flesh, hath he quickened.

[See 546, 589, 688—690.]

166. *Strength and obstinacy of human depravity — Moral inability.*

Gen. 37: 4 When his brethren saw that their father loved him more than all his brethren, they hated him, and could not speak peaceably unto him.

Ex. 32: 9 The Lord said unto Moses, I have seen this peo-ple, and behold, it *is* a stiff-necked people. [Dt. 9: 6, 13.]

Jos. 24: 19 Joshua said unto the people, Ye cannot serve the LORD: for he *is* an holy God.

Pr. 5: 22 His own iniquities shall take the wicked himself, and he shall be holden with the cords of his sins.—27: 22 Though thou shouldest bray a fool in a mortar among wheat with a pestle, *yet* will not his foolishness depart from him.

Ec. 9: 3 This *is* an evil among all *things* that are done un-der the sun, that *there is* one event unto all: yea, also the heart of the sons of men is full of evil, and madness *is* in their heart while they live, and after that *they go* to the dead.

Is. 48: 4 I knew that thou *art* obstinate, and thy neck *is* an iron sinew, and thy brow brass.

Jer. 2: 22 Though thou wash thee with nitre, and take thee much soap, *yet* thine iniquity is marked before me, saith the Lord God.—3: 5 Behold, thou hast spoken and done evil things as thou couldest.—6: 10 Behold, their ear *is* uncircum-cised, and they cannot hearken: behold, the word of the LORD is unto them a reproach; they have no delight in it. — 13: 23 Can the Ethiopian change his skin, or the leopard his spots? *then* may ye also do good that are accustomed to do evil. — 17: 1 The sin of Judah *is* written with a pen of iron, *and* with the point of a diamond: *it is* graven upon the table of their heart, and upon the horns of your altars. 9 The heart *is* deceitful above all *things*, and desperately wicked: who can know it?

Mat. 7: 18 A good tree cannot bring forth evil fruit, neither *can* a corrupt tree bring forth good fruit. — 12: 34 O generation of vipers, how can ye, being evil, speak good things? for out of the abundance of the heart, the mouth speaketh. — 17: 17 Then Jesus answered and said, O faithless and perverse generation, how long shall I be with you? how long shall I suffer you? — 23: 33 *Ye* serpents, *ye* generation of vipers, how can ye escape the damnation of hell?

Jn. 6: 44 No man can come to me, except the Father which hath sent me draw him. 65 And he said, Therefore said I unto you, that no man can come unto me, except it were given unto him of my Father.

Rom. 8: 7 Because the carnal mind *is* enmity against God: for it is not subject to the law of God, neither indeed can be. 8 So then they that are in the flesh cannot please God. [See 689, 690, 740.]

167. Works of darkness described and denounced.

Job 24: 14 The murderer rising with the light killeth the poor and needy, and in the night is as a thief. 15 The eye also of the adulterer waiteth for the twilight, saying, No eye shall see me: and disguiseth *his* face. 16 In the dark they dig through houses, *which* they had marked for themselves in the day-time: they know not the light. 17 For the morning *is* to them even as the shadow of death: if *one* know *them,* *they are in* the terrors of the shadow of death.

Pr. 7: 6 At the window of my house I looked through my casement, 7 And beheld among the simple ones, I discerned among the youths, a young man void of understanding. 8 Passing through the street near her corner; and he went the way to her house, 9 In the twilight, in the evening, in the black and dark night.

Is. 29: 15 Wo unto them that seek deep to hide their counsel from the LORD, and their works are in the dark, and they say, Who seeth us? and who knoweth us?

Ezk. 8: 12 Then said he unto me, Son of man, hast thou seen what the ancients of the house of Israel do in the dark,

every man in the chambers of his imagery? for they say, The
LORD seeth us not; the LORD hath forsaken the earth.

Ep. 5: 11 Have no fellowship with the unfruitful works of
darkness, but rather reprove *them.* 12 It is a shame even to
speak of those things which are done of them in secret.

168. *Removing restraints develops depravity.*

Ex. 8: 15 When Pharaoh saw that there was respite, he
hardened his heart. — 32: 22 Aaron said, Let not the anger of
my lord wax hot: thou knowest the people, that they *are set*
on mischief. 23 For they said unto me, Make us gods which
shall go before us: for *as for* this Moses, the man that brought
us up out of the land of Egypt, we wot not what is become
of him.

Jud. 2: 7 The people served the LORD all the days of Joshua,
and all the days of the elders that outlived Joshua, who had
seen all the great works of the LORD, that he did for Israel.
8 And Joshua the son of Nun, the servant of the LORD, died.
10 And also all that generation were gathered unto their fathers: and there arose another generation after them, which
knew not the LORD, nor yet the works which he had done for
Israel. 11 And the children of Israel did evil in the sight of
the LORD, and served Baalim.

Ec. 8: 11 Because sentence against an evil work is not ex-
ecnted speedily, therefore the heart of the sons of men is fully
set in them to do evil.

169. *Human nature essentially the same in all ages.*

Pr. 27: 19 As in water face *answereth* to face, so the heart
of man to man.

Mat. 23: 31 Wherefore ye be witnesses unto yourselves,
that ye are the children of them which killed the prophets.
[See 163.]

170. *Human nature untrusty — Cautions.*

Ps. 146: 3 Put not your trust in princes, *nor* in the son of
man, in whom *there is* no help. 4 His breath goeth forth, he
returneth to his earth; in that very day his thoughts perish.

Pr. 25: 19 Confidence in an unfaithful man in time of trouble
is like a broken tooth, and a foot out of joint. — 28: 26 He that
trusteth in his own heart is a fool.

Is. 2: 22 Cease ye from man, whose breath *is* in his nostrils:
for wherein is he to be accounted of?

Jer. 17: 5 Thus saith the LORD; Cursed *be* the man that
trusteth in man, and maketh flesh his arm, and whose heart

departeth from the LORD.   6 For he shall be like the heath in the desert, and shall not see when good cometh; but shall inhabit the parched places in the wilderness, *in* a salt land and not inhabited.

Mic. 7: 5 Trust ye not in a friend, put ye not confidence in a guide: keep the doors of thy mouth from her that lieth in thy bosom.

DESPONDENCY.

171. *Despondency exemplified'and reproved.*

Gen. 37: 34 Jacob rent his clothes, and put sackcloth upon his loins, and mourned for his son many days.   35 And all his sons and all his daughters rose up to comfort him; but he refused to be comforted; and he said, For I will go down into the grave unto my son mourning.

Jos. 7: 6 Joshua rent his clothes, and fell to the earth upon his face before the ark of the LORD until the even-tide, he and the elders of Israel, and put dust upon their heads.   7 And Joshua said, Alas! O Lord GOD, wherefore hast thou at all brought this people over Jordan, to deliver us into the hand of the Amorites, to destroy us?   10 And the LORD said unto Joshua, Get thee up; wherefore liest thou thus upon thy face?

Ps. 42: 5 Why art thou cast down, O my soul? and *why* art thou disquieted in me? hope thou in God: for I shall yet praise him *for* the help of his countenance.

Pr. 12: 25 Heaviness in the heart of man maketh it stoop.

Jer. 18: 11 Thus saith the LORD; Behold, I frame evil against you, and devise a device against you: return ye now every one from his evil way, and make your ways and your doings good.   12 And they said, There is no hope: but we will walk after our own devices, and we will every one do the imagination of his evil heart.

Mat. 27: 5 He cast down the pieces of silver in the temple, and departed, and went and hanged himself.   [See 24, 700.]

DISCRETION — PRUDENCE — ECONOMY.

172. *Duty and advantage of discretion, etc.*

Pr. 2: 11 Discretion shall preserve thee, understanding shall keep thee: 12 To deliver thee from the way of the evil *man*, from the man that speaketh froward things.—3: 21 My son, let not them depart from thine eyes: keep sound wisdom and discretion: 22 So shall they be life unto thy soul, and grace to thy neck.   23 Then shalt thou walk in thy way safely, and

11*

thy foot shalt not stumble.—8: 12 I Wisdom dwell with prudence, and find out knowledge of witty inventions.—11: 22 *As* a jewel of gold in a swine's snout, *so is* a fair woman which is without discretion.—12: 16 A fool's wrath is presently known: but a prudent *man* covereth shame.—19: 11 The discretion of a man deferreth his anger; and *it is* his glory to pass over a transgression.

Jn. 6: 12 When they were filled, he said unto his disciples, Gather up the fragments that remain, that nothing be lost.

DRESS.

173. *Plain dress recommended.*

1 Tim. 2: 9 In like manner also, that women adorn themselves in modest apparel, with shamefacedness and sobriety; not with broidered hair, or gold, or pearls, or costly array, 10 But (which becometh women professing godliness) with good works.

1 Pet. 3: 3 Whose adorning let it not be that outward *adorning* of plaiting the hair, and of wearing of gold, or of putting on of apparel; 4 But *let it be* the hidden man of the heart, in that which is not corruptible, *even the ornament* of a meek and quiet spirit, which is in the sight of God of great price. 5 For after this manner in the old time the holy women also, who trusted in God, adorned themselves, being in subjection unto their own husbands.

ENVY.

174. *Envy a common and foolish sin — prohibitions.*

Gen. 30: 1 When Rachel saw that she bare Jacob no children, Rachel envied her sister; and said unto Jacob, Give me children, or else I die.

Job 5: 2 Wrath killeth the foolish man, and envy slayeth the silly one.

Ps. 37: 1 Fret not thyself because of evil doers, neither be thou envious against the workers of iniquity.—106: 16 They envied Moses also in the camp, *and* Aaron the saint of the LORD.

Pr. 3: 31 Envy thou not the oppressor, and choose none of his ways.—14: 30 A sound heart *is* the life of the flesh, but envy the rottenness of the bones.—23: 17 Let not thy heart envy sinners.—24: 1 Be not thou envious against evil men, neither desire to be with them: 2 For their heart studieth destruction, and their lips talk of mischief. 19 Fret not thyself because of evil *men*, neither be thou envious at the wicked; 20 For there shall be no reward to the evil *man;* the candle of the wicked shall be put out.—27: 4 Wrath *is* cruel, and anger *is* outrageous; but who *is* able to stand before envy?

Ec. 4: 4 Again, I considered all travail, and every right work, that for this a man is envied of his neighbor.

Mat. 27: 17 Whom will ye that I release unto you? Barabbas, or Jesus, which is called Christ? 18 (For he knew that for envy they had delivered him.)

Ac. 7: 9 The patriarchs, moved with envy, sold Joseph into Egypt.—13: 45 When the Jews saw the multitudes, they were filled with envy, and spake against those things which were spoken by Paul, contradicting and blaspheming.—17: 5 The Jews which believed not, moved with envy, took unto them certain lewd fellows of the baser sort, and gathered a company, and set all the city on an uproar, and assaulted the house of Jason, and sought to bring them out to the people.

Rom. 13: 13 Let us walk honestly, as in the day: not in rioting and drunkenness, not in chambering and wantonness, not in strife and envying.

Tit. 3: 3 We ourselves also were sometimes foolish, disobedient, deceived, serving divers lusts and pleasures, living in malice and envy, hateful, *and* hating one another.

Jam. 3: 14 If ye have bitter envying and strife in your hearts, glory not, and lie not against the truth. 15 This wisdom descendeth not from above, but *is* earthly, sensual, devilish. 16 For where envying and strife *is*, there *is* confusion and every evil work.

1 Pet. 2: 1 Laying aside all malice, and all guile, and hypocrisies, and envies, and all evil-speakings, 2 As new-born babes, desire the sincere milk of the word, that ye may grow thereby. [See 137.]

ERROR.

175. *Error prevalent, corrupting and ruinous.*

Ps. 19: 12 Who can understand *his* errors? cleanse thou me from secret *faults.*

Pr. 19: 27 Cease, my son, to hear the instruction *that causeth* to err from the words of knowledge.

Ec. 7: 29 Lo, this only have I found, that God hath made man upright; but they have sought out many inventions.

Mat. 16: 12 Then understood they how that he bade *them* not beware of the leaven of bread, but of the doctrine of the Pharisees and of the Sadducees.

1 Cor. 15: 33 Be not deceived: Evil communications corrupt good manners.

Gal. 1: 6 I marvel that ye are so soon removed from him that called you into the grace of Christ, unto another gospel: 7 Which is not another; but there be some that trouble you, and would pervert the gospel of Christ. — 5: 9 A little leaven leaveneth the whole lump.

2 Th. 2: 11 For this cause God shall send them strong delusion, that they should believe a lie: 12 That they all might be damned who believed not the truth, but had pleasure in unrighteousness.

2 Tim. 2: 16 Shun profane *and* vain babblings: for they will increase unto more ungodliness. 17 And their word will eat as doth a canker; of whom is Hymeneus and Philetus; 18 Who concerning the truth have erred, saying that the resurrection is past already, and overthrow the faith of some.

Jam. 5: 20 Let him know, that he which converteth the sinner from the error of his way shall save a soul from death, and shall hide a multitude of sins.

2 Pet. 2: 1 There were false prophets also among the people, even as there shall be false teachers among you, who privily shall bring in damnable heresies, even denying the Lord that bought them, and bring upon themselves swift destruction. — 3: 17 Ye therefore, beloved, seeing ye know *these things* before, beware lest ye also, being led away with the error of the wicked, fall from your own steadfastness. [See 183, 477.]

176. *Heresies and errors designed and adapted to try mankind.*

1 Cor. 11: 19 There must be also heresies among you, that they which are approved may be made manifest among you. [See 243.]

177. *Fellowship with errorists to be avoided.*

Gal. 1: 8 Though we, or an angel from heaven, preach any other gospel unto you than that which we have preached unto you, let him be accursed. 9 As we said before, so say I now again, If any *man* preach any other gospel unto you than that ye have received, let him be accursed.

1 Tim. 6: 5 Perverse disputings of men of corrupt minds, and destitute of the truth, supposing that gain is godliness: from such withdraw thyself.

Tit. 3: 10 A man that is a heretic, after the first and second admonition, reject; 11 Knowing that he that is such, is subverted, and sinneth, being condemned of himself.
[See 112, 115, 477.]

EXAMPLE.

178. *Good examples required.*

Mat. 5: 16 Let your light so shine before men, that they may see your good works, and glorify your Father which is in heaven.

Col. 4: 5 Walk in wisdom toward them that are without, redeeming the time.

1 Tim. 4: 12 Let no man despise thy youth; but be thou an example of the believers, in word, in conversation, in charity, in spirit, in faith, in purity.

Tit. 2: 7 In all things shewing thyself a·pattern of good works: in doctrine *shewing* uncorruptness, gravity, sincerity, 8 Sound speech that cannot be condemned; that he that is of the contrary part may be ashamed, having no evil thing to say of you.

179. *Good examples to be followed — bad, to be avoided.*

Ex. 23: 2 Thou shalt not follow a multitude to *do* evil.

Mat. 23: 3 All therefore whatsoever they bid you observe, *that* observe and do; but do not ye after their works: for they say, and do not.

1 Cor. 11: 1 Be ye followers of me, even as I also *am* of Christ.

Ph. 3: 17 Brethren, be followers together of me, and mark them which walk so as ye have us for an ensample.

Heb. 6: 12 That ye be not slothful, but followers of them who through faith and patience inherit the promises. — 13: 7 Remember them which have the rule over you, who have spoken unto you the word of God: whose faith follow, considering the end of *their* conversation.

Jam. 5: 10 Take, my brethren, the prophets, who have spoken in the name of the Lord, for an example of suffering affliction and of patience.

1 Pet. 2: 21 For even hereunto were ye called: because Christ also suffered for us, leaving us an example, that ye should follow his steps.

3 Jn. 11 Beloved, follow not that which is evil, but that which is good.

EXTRAVAGANCE — PRODIGALITY.

180. *Extravagance and prodigality sinful — Examples.·*

1 K. 11: 1 King Solomon loved many strange women, together with the daughter of Pharaoh, women of the Moabites,

Ammonites, Edomites, Zidonians, *and* Hittites: 3 He had seven hundred wives, princesses, and three hundred concubines: and his wives turned away his heart.

Ec. 2: 10 Whatsoever mine eyes desired I kept not from them, I withheld not my heart from any joy.

Lk. 15: 13 Not many days after, the younger son gathered all together, and took his journey into a far country, and there wasted his substance with riotous living. 17 And when he came to himself, he said, How many hired servants of my father's have bread enough and to spare, and I perish with hunger! 18 I will arise and go to my father, and will say unto him, Father, I have sinned against heaven, and before thee. — 16: 19 There was a certain rich man, which was clothed in purple and fine linen and fared sumptuously every day: 22 The rich man also died, and was buried: 23 And in hell he lifted up his eyes, being in torments. [See 173, 199, 625.]

FAITH.

181. *Nature of true faith.*

Rom. 10: 9 If thou shalt confess with thy mouth the Lord Jesus, and shalt believe in thine heart that God hath raised him from the dead, thou shalt be saved. 10 For with the heart, man believeth unto righteousness; and with the mouth, confession is made unto salvation.

Heb. 11: 1 Faith is the substance of things hoped for, and the evidence of things not seen.

182. *Faith counted for righteousness.*

Rom. 4: 3 What saith the scripture? Abraham believed God, and it was counted unto him for righteousness. 4 Now to him that worketh, is the reward not reckoned of grace, but of debt. 5 But to him that worketh not, but believeth on him that justifieth the ungodly, his faith is counted for righteousness. 6 Even as David also describeth the blessedness of the man unto whom God imputeth righteousness without works, 7 *Saying*, Blessed *are* they whose iniquities are forgiven, and whose sins are covered. 8 Blessed *is* the man to whom the Lord will not impute sin. 11 He received the sign of circumcision, a seal of the righteousness of the faith which *he had yet* being uncircumcised: that he might be the father of all of them that believe, though they be not circumcised, that righteousness might be imputed unto them also.

183. *Faith in Christ, and belief of the truth, required as necessary to salvation.*

Mk. 16: 15 He said unto them, Go ye into all the world, and preach the gospel to every creature. 16 He that believeth and is baptized, shall be saved; but he that believeth not, shall be damned.

Jn. 1: 12 As many as received him, to them gave he power to become the sons of God, *even* to them that believe on his name. — 3: 16 God so loved the world, that he gave his only begotten Son, that whosoever believeth on him, should not perish, but have everlasting life. 18 He that believeth in him, is not condemned: but he that believeth not, is condemned already, because he hath not believed in the name of the only begotten Son of God. 36 He that believeth on the Son hath everlasting life: and he that believeth not the Son, shall not see life; but the wrath of God abideth on him. — 6: 28 Then said they unto him, What shall we do, that we might work the works of God? 29 Jesus answered and said unto them, This is the work of God, that ye believe on him whom he hath sent. 40 This is the will of him that sent me, that every one which seeth the Son, and believeth on him, may have everlasting life: and I will raise him up at the last day. 53 Then Jesus said unto them, Verily, verily, I say unto you, Except ye eat the flesh of the Son of man, and drink his blood, ye have no life in you. 54 Whoso eateth my flesh, and drinketh my blood, hath eternal life; and I will raise him up at the last day. — 8: 24 If ye believe not that I am *he*, ye shall die in your sins. 47 He that is of God, heareth God's words: ye therefore hear *them* not, because ye are not of God. — 11: 25 Jesus said unto her, I am the resurrection, and the life: he that believeth in me, though he were dead, yet shall he live: 26 And whosoever liveth, and believeth in me, shall never die.

Ac. 10: 43 To him give all the prophets witness, that through his name whosoever believeth in him shall receive remission of sins. — 16: 31 Believe on the Lord Jesus Christ, and thou shalt be saved, and thy house.

Rom. 10: 4 Christ *is* the end of the law for righteousness to every one that believeth.

Gal. 2: 16 Knowing that a man is not justified by the works of the law, but by the faith of Jesus Christ, even we have believed in Jesus Christ, that we might be justified by the faith of Christ, and not by the works of the law: for by the works of the law shall no flesh be justified.

2 Th. 2: 10 With all deceivableness of unrighteousness in them that perish; because they received not the love of the truth, that they might be saved. 11 And for this cause God shall send them strong delusion, that they should believe a lie: 12 That they all might be damned who believed not the truth, but had pleasure in unrighteousness.

Heb. 11: 6 Without faith *it is* impossible to please *him:* for he that cometh to God must believe that he is, and *that* he is a rewarder of them that diligently seek him.

1 Jn. 2: 23 Whosoever denieth the Son, the same hath not the Father: [*but he that acknowledgeth the Son hath the Father also.*] — 5: 10 He that believeth on the Son of God hath the witness in himself: he that believeth not God, hath made him a liar, because he believeth not the record that God gave of his Son. 11 And this is the record, that God hath given to us eternal life: and this life is in his Son. 12 He that hath the Son, hath life; *and* he that hath not the Son of God, hath not life. 13 These things have I written unto you that believe on the name of the Son of God; that ye may know that ye have eternal life, and that ye may believe on the name of the Son of God.

2 Jn. 9 Whosoever transgresseth, and abideth not in the doctrine of Christ, hath not God. He that abideth in the doctrine of Christ, he hath both the Father and the Son. 10 If there come any unto you, and bring not this doctrine, receive him not into *your* house, neither bid him God speed: 11 For he that biddeth him God speed, is partaker of his evil deeds.

3 Jn. 4 I have no greater joy than to hear that my children walk in truth. [See 175, 601.]

184. *Examples of faith.*

Rom. 4: 20 He [Abraham] staggered not at the promise of God through unbelief; but was strong in faith, giving glory to God; 21 And being fully persuaded, that what he had promised, he was able also to perform.

2 Cor. 5: 7 (For we walk by faith, not by sight:) 8 We are confident, *I say,* and willing rather to absent from the body, and to be present with the Lord.

Gal. 2: 20 I am crucified with Christ: nevertheless, I live; yet not I, but Christ liveth in me: and the life which I now live in the flesh, I live by the faith of the Son of God, who loved me, and gave himself for me.

Heb. 11: 7 By faith Noah, being warned of God of things not seen as yet, moved with fear, prepared an ark to the saving of his house; by the which he condemned the world, and became heir of the righteousness which is by faith. 8 By faith

Abraham, when he was called to go out into a place which he should after receive for an inheritance, obeyed ; and he went out not knowing whither he went. 9 By faith he sojourned in the land of promise, as *in* a strange country, dwelling in tabernacles with Isaac and Jacob, the heirs with him of the same promise : 10 For he looked for a city which hath foundations, whose builder and maker *is* God. 13 These all died in faith, not having received the promises, but having seen them afar off, and were persuaded of *them*, and embraced *them*, and confessed that they were strangers and pilgrims on the earth. [See 664.]

185. *Effects of faith.*

Heb. 11: 32 What shall I more say ? for the time would fail me to tell of Gedeon, and *of* Barak, and *of* Samson, and *of* Jephthae, *of* David also, and Samuel, and *of* the prophets : 33 Who through faith subdued kingdoms, wrought righteousness, obtained promises, stopped the mouths of lions, 34 Quenched the violence of fire, escaped the edge of the sword, out of weakness were made strong, waxed valiant in fight, turned to flight the armies of the aliens. [See the whole chapter.]

1 Pet. 1: 8 Whom having not seen, ye love ; in whom, though now ye see *him* not, yet believing, ye rejoice with joy unspeakable, and full of glory : 9 Receiving the end of your faith, *even* the salvation of *your* souls.

1 Jn. 5: 4 Whatsoever is born of God, overcometh the world : and this is the victory that overcometh the world, *even* our faith. 5 Who is he that overcometh the world, but he that believeth that Jesus is the Son of God ?

186. *Evidence of faith.*

Jam. 2: 14 What *doth it* profit, my brethren, though a man say he hath faith, and have not works ? can faith save him ? 15 If a brother or sister be naked, and destitute of daily food, 16 And one of you say unto them, Depart in peace, be *ye* warmed and filled, notwithstanding ye give them not those things which are needful to the body : what *doth it* profit ? 17 Even so faith, if it hath not works, is dead, being alone. 18 Yea, a man may say, Thou hast faith, and I have works : shew me thy faith without thy works, and I will shew thee my faith by my works. [See 302, 602.]

187. *Strength of faith required.*

Ep. 6: 10 Finally, my brethren, be strong in the Lord, and in the power of his might. 11 Put on the whole armor of God,

12   133

that ye may be able to stand against the wiles of the devil.
12 For we wrestle not against flesh and blood, but against
principalities, against powers, against the rulers of the darkness of this world, against spiritual wickedness in high *places*.
13 Wherefore take unto you the whole armor of God, that
ye may be able to withstand in the evil day, and having done
all, to stand. [See 712.]

188. *Contending for the faith exemplified and required.*

Jn. 18: 37 Jesus answered, To this end was I born, and for
this cause came I into the world, that I should bear witness
unto the truth.

Ac. 6: 9 There arose certain of the synagogue, which is
called *the synagogue* of the Libertines, and Cyrenians, and
Alexandrians, and of them of Cilicia, and of Asia, disputing
with Stephen. 10 And they were not able to resist the wisdom and the spirit by which he spake. — 9: 29 He [Paul]
spake boldly in the name of the Lord Jesus, and disputed
against the Grecians : but they went about to slay him. — 17: 16
While Paul waited for them at Athens, his spirit was stirred
in him, when he saw the city wholly given to idolatry. 17
Therefore disputed he in the synagogue with the Jews, and
with the devout persons, and in the market daily with them
that met with him. — 19: 8 He went into the synagogue, and
spake boldly for the space of three months, disputing and persuading the things concerning the kingdom of God. 9 But
when divers were hardened, and believed not, but spake evil
of that way before the multitude, he departed from them, and
separated the disciples, disputing daily in the school of one
Tyrannus. 10 And this continued by the space of two years ;
so that all they which dwelt in Asia heard the word of the Lord
Jesus, both Jews and Greeks.

Ph. 1: 27 Stand fast in one spirit, with one mind striving
together for the faith of the gospel.

Jude 3 Earnestly contend for the faith which was once
delivered unto the saints. [See 458.]

189. *Faith of miracles, and the peculiar promises to it.*

Mat. 14: 29 When Peter was come down out of the ship, he
walked on the water to go to Jesus. 30 But when he saw the
wind boisterous, he was afraid ; and beginning to sink, he cried,
saying, Lord, save me. 31 And immediately Jesus stretched
forth *his* hand, and caught him, and said unto him, O thou of
little faith, wherefore didst thou doubt? — 21: 20 When the
disciples saw *it*, they marvelled, saying, How soon is the fig-tree

withered away! 21 Jesus answered and said unto them, Verily, I say unto you, If ye have faith, and doubt not, ye shall not only do this *which is done* to the fig-tree, but also, if ye shall say unto this mountain, Be thou removed, and be thou cast into the sea; it shall be done. 22 And all things whatsoever ye shall ask in prayer, believing, ye shall receive.

Mk. 11: 23 Verily I say unto you, That whosoever shall say unto this mountain, Be thou removed, and be thou cast into the sea; and shall not doubt in his heart, but shall believe that those things which he saith shall come to pass; he shall have whatsoever he saith. 24 Therefore I say unto you, What things soever ye desire when ye pray, believe that ye receive *them*, and ye shall have *them*. — 16: 17 These signs shall follow them that believe: In my name shall they cast out devils; they shall speak with new tongues: 18 They shall take up serpents; and if they drink any deadly thing, it shall not hurt them; they shall lay hands on the sick, and they shall recover.

Jn. 14: 12 Verily, verily, I say unto you, He that believeth on me, the works that I do shall he do also; and greater *works* than these shall he do; because I go unto my Father. 13 And whatsoever ye shall ask in my name, that will I do, that the Father may be glorified in the Son.

Jam. 5: 14 Is any sick among you? let him call for the elders of the church; and let them pray over him, anointing him with oil in the name of the Lord: 15 And the prayer of faith shall save the sick, and the Lord shall raise him up; and if he have committed sins, they shall be forgiven him. [See 100.]

190. *Was the faith of miracles saving faith?*

Mat. 7: 22 Many will say to me in that day, Lord, Lord, have we not prophesied in thy name? and in thy name have cast out devils? and in thy name done many wonderful works? 23 And then will I profess unto them, I never knew you: depart from me, ye that work iniquity.

1 Cor. 13: 1 Though I speak with the tongues of men and of angels, and have not charity, I am become *as* sounding brass, or a tinkling cymbal. 2 And though I have *the gift of* prophecy, and understand all mysteries, and all knowledge; and though I have all faith, so that I could remove mountains, and have not charity, I am nothing.

191. *Spurious faith, formalism, and selfish religion common and ruinous to the soul.*

Ps. 106: 12 Then believed they his words; they sang his

praise.   13 They soon forgat his works, they waited not for his counsel.

Is. 29: 13 This people draw near *me* with their mouth, and with their lips do honor me, but have removed their heart far from me, and their fear toward me is taught by the precept of men. — 58: 2 They seek me daily, and delight to know my ways, as a nation that did righteousness, and forsook not the ordinance of their God : they ask of me the ordinances of jus- tice : they take delight in approaching to God.   3 Wherefore have we fasted, *say they*, and thou seest not ? *wherefore* have we afflicted our soul, and thou takest no knowledge ?

Jer. 3: 10 Her treacherous sister Judah hath not turned unto me with her whole heart, but feignedly, saith the Lord.

Ezk. 33: 31 They come unto thee as the people cometh, and they sit before thee *as* my people, and they hear thy words, but they will not do them : for with their mouth they shew much love, *but* their heart goeth after their covetousness.

Mat. 13: 20 He that received the seed into stony places, the same is he that heareth the word, and anon with joy receiveth it ; 21 Yet hath he not root in himself, but dureth for a while : for when tribulation or persecution ariseth because of the word, by and by he is offended — 15: 7 Ye hypocrites, well did Esaias prophesy of you, saying, 8 This people draweth nigh unto me with their mouth, and honoreth me with *their* lips ; but their heart is far from me.

Jn. 6: 26 Jesus answered them and said, Verily, verily, I say unto you, Ye seek me, not because ye saw the miracles, but because ye did eat of the loaves, and were filled.

Ac. 8: 13 Simon himself believed also : and when he was baptized, he continued with Philip, and wondered, beholding the miracles and signs which were done.   21 Thou hast neither part nor lot in this matter : for thy heart is not right in the sight of God.

Rom. 10: 2 I bear them record that they have a zeal of God, but not according to knowledge.

1 Cor. 13: 1 Though I speak with the tongues of men and of angels, and have not charity, I am become *as* sounding brass, or a tinkling cymbal.   2 And though I have *the gift of* prophecy, and understand all mysteries, and all knowledge ; and though I have all faith, so that I could remove mountains, and have not charity, I am nothing.   3 And though I bestow all my goods to feed *the poor*, and though I give my body to be burned, and have not charity, it profiteth me nothing.

Gal. 1: 13 Ye have heard of my conversation in time past in the Jews' religion, how that beyond measure I persecuted the church of God, and wasted it; 14 And profited in the Jews' religion above many my equals in mine own nation, being more exceedingly zealous of the traditions of my fathers.—5: 6 In Jesus Christ neither circumcision availeth any thing, nor uncircumcision; but faith which worketh by love.

2 Tim. 3: 5 Having a form of godliness, but denying the power thereof: from such turn away.

Jam. 2: 19 Thou believest that there is one God; thou doest well: the devils also believe, and tremble.

• [See 194, 333, 411, 609, 623, 689, 702, 704.]

FASTING.

192. *Directions for fasting.*

Is. 58: 4 Behold, ye fast for strife and debate, and to smite with the fist of wickedness: ye shall not fast as *ye do this* day, to make your voice to be heard on high. 5 Is it such a fast that I have chosen? a day for a man to afflict his soul? *is it* to bow down his head as a bulrush, and to spread sackcloth and ashes *under him?* wilt thou call this a fast, and an acceptable day to the LORD? 6 *Is* not this the fast that I have chosen? to loose the bands of wickedness, to undo the heavy burdens, and to let the oppressed go free, and that ye break every yoke? 7 *Is it* not to deal thy bread to the hungry, and that thou bring the poor that are cast out to thy house? when thou seest the naked, that thou cover him; and that thou hide not thyself from thine own flesh?

Mat. 6: 16 When ye fast, be not as the hypocrites, of a sad countenance : for they disfigure their faces, that they may appear unto men to fast. Verily, I say unto you, They have their reward. 17 But thou, when thou fastest, anoint thine head, and wash thy face ; 18 That thou appear not unto men, to fast, but unto thy Father, which is in secret: and thy Father, which seeth in secret, shall reward thee openly.

193. *Fasting exemplified.*

Ezra 8: 21 Then I proclaimed a fast there, at the river of Ahava, that we might afflict ourselves before our God, to seek of him a right way for us, and for our little ones, and for all our substance. 22 For I was ashamed to require of the king a band of soldiers and horsemen to help us against the enemy in the way: because we had spoken unto the king, saying. The hand of our God *is* upon all them for good that seek him ; but his power and his wrath *is* against all them that forsake him.

23 So we fasted and besought our God for this : and he was entreated of us.

Dan. 9: 3 I set my face unto the Lord GOD, to seek by prayer and supplications, with fasting, and sackcloth, and ashes.

Jonah 3: 5 So the people of Nineveh believed God, and proclaimed a fast, and put on sackcloth, from the greatest of them even to the least of them. 6 For word came unto the king of Nineveh, and he arose from his throne, and he laid his robe from him, and covered *him* with sackcloth, and sat in ashes. 7 And he caused it to be proclaimed and published through Nineveh by the decree of the king and his nobles, saying, Let neither man nor beast, herd nor flock, taste any thing: let them not feed, nor drink water: 8 But let man and beast be covered with sackcloth, and cry mightily unto God: yea, let them turn every one from his evil way, and from the violence that *is* in their hands. 9 Who can tell if God will turn and repent, and turn away from his fierce anger, that we perish not? 10 And God saw their works, that they turned from their evil way ; and God repented of the evil that he had said that he would do unto them ; and he did *it* not.

Mat. 4: 1 Then was Jesus led up of the Spirit into the wilderness, to be tempted of the devil. 2 And when he had fasted forty days and forty nights, he was afterwards an hungered.

Lk. 2: 36 There was one Anna, a prophetess, the daughter of Phanuel, of the tribe of Aser : she was of a great age, and had lived with an husband seven years from her virginity ; 37 And she *was* a widow of about fourscore and four years, which departed not from the temple, but served *God* with fastings and prayers night and day.

Ac. 10: 30 Cornelius said, Four days ago I was fasting unto this hour ; and at the ninth hour I prayed in my house, and behold, a man stood before me in bright clothing, 31 And said, Cornelius, thy prayer is heard. — 13: 2 As they ministered to the Lord, and fasted, the Holy Ghost said, Separate me Barnabas and Saul, for the work whereunto I have called them. 3 And when they had fasted and prayed, and laid *their* hands on them, they sent *them* away. — 14: 23 When they had ordained them elders in every church, and had prayed with fasting, they commended them to the Lord.

2 Cor. 6: 5 In labors, in watchings, in fastings. — 11: 27 In weariness and painfulness, in watchings often, in hunger and thirst, in fastings often, in cold and nakedness. 28 Besides those things that are without, that which cometh upon me daily, the care of all the churches.

194. *Spurious fasting.*

Is. 58: 3 Wherefore have we fasted, *say they*, and thou seest not? *wherefore* have we afflicted our soul, and thou takest no knowledge? Behold, in the day of your fast ye find pleasure, and exact all your labors. 4 Behold, ye fast for strife and debate, and to smite with the fist of wickedness: ye shall not fast as *ye do this* day, to make your voice to be heard on high. 5 Is it such a fast that I have chosen? a day for a man to afflict his soul? *is it* to bow down his head as a bulrush, and to spread sackcloth and ashes *under him?* wilt thou call this a fast, and an acceptable day to the LORD?

Zec. 7: 5 Speak unto all the people of the land, and to the priests, saying, When ye fasted and mourned in the fifth and seventh *month*, even those seventy years, did ye at all fast unto me, *even* to me? 6 And when ye did eat, and when ye did drink, did not ye eat *for yourselves*, and drink *for yourselves?*

Lk. 18: 11 The Pharisee stood and prayed thus with himself, God, I thank thee, that I am not as other men *are*, extortioners, unjust, adulterers, or even as this publican. 12 I fast twice in the week, I give tithes of all that I possess.

[See 191, 411, 609, 623, 689.]

FEMALES.

195. *Female industry and enterprize.*

Pr. 31: 13 She seeketh wool, and flax, and worketh willingly with her hands. 14 She is like the merchants' ships; she bringeth her food from afar. 15 She riseth also while it is yet night, and giveth meat to her household, and a portion to her maidens. 16 She considereth a field, and buyeth it: with the fruit of her hands she planteth a vineyard. 17 She girdeth her loins with strength, and strengtheneth her arms. 18 She perceiveth that her merchandize *is* good: her candle goeth not out by night. 19 She layeth her hands to the spindle, and her hands hold the distaff. 21 She is not afraid of the snow for her household: for all her household *are* clothed with scarlet. 22 She maketh herself coverings of tapestry; her clothing *is* silk and purple. 23 Her husband is known in the gates, when he sitteth among the elders of the land. 24 She maketh fine linen, and selleth *it*; and delivereth girdles unto the merchant. 25 Strength and honor *are* her clothing; and she shall rejoice in time to come.

Ac. 9: 39 And all the widows stood by him weeping, and shewing the coats and garments which Dorcas made, while she was with them.

196. *Female piety, sympathy, and kindness.*

Pr. 31: 20 She stretcheth out her hand to the poor ; yea, she reacheth forth her hands to the needy.   26 She openeth her mouth with wisdom ; and in her tongue *is* the law of kindness. 27 She looketh well to the ways of her household, and eateth not the bread of idleness.   28 Her children arise up, and call her blessed ; her husband *also*, and he praiseth her.

Mat. 27: 55 Many women were there (beholding afar off) which followed Jesus from Galilee, ministering unto him :   56 Among which was Mary Magdalene, and Mary the mother of James and Joses, and the mother of Zebedee's children.

Mk. 12: 43 He called *unto him* his disciples, and saith unto them, Verily, I say unto you, That this poor widow hath cast more in, than all they which have cast into the treasury.   44 For all *they* did cast in of their abundance : but she of her want did cast in all that she had, *even* all her living.

Lk. 24: 1 Upon the first *day* of the week, very early in the morning, they came unto the sepulchre, bringing the spices which they had prepared, and certain *others* with them.   10 It was Mary Magdalene, and Joanna, and Mary *the mother* of James, and other *women that were* with them.

197. *Female subordination and speaking.*

Gen. 3: 16 Thy desire *shall be* to thy husband, and he shall rule over thee.

Num. 30: 13 Every vow, and every binding oath to afflict the soul, her husband may establish it, or her husband may make it void.

1 Cor. 11: 3 I would have you know, that the head of every man is Christ ; and the head of the woman *is* the man ; and the head of Christ *is* God.   4 Every man praying or prophesying, having *his* head covered, dishonoreth his head.   5 But every woman that prayeth or prophesieth with *her* head uncovered, dishonoreth her head : for that is even all one as if she were shaven.   6 For if the woman be not covered, let her also be shorn : but if it be a shame for a woman to be shorn or shaven, let her be covered.   7 For a man indeed ought not to cover *his* head, forasmuch as he is the image and glory of God : but the woman is the glory of the man.   8 For the man is not of the woman, but the woman of the man.   9 Neither was the man created for the woman, but the woman for the man.   13 Judge in yourselves : Is it comely that a woman pray unto God uncovered ?   14 Doth not even nature itself teach you, that if a man have long hair, it is a shame unto him ?   15 But if a woman have long hair, it is a glory to her : for *her* hair is

140

given' her for a covering. — 14: 34 Let your women keep
silence in the churches; for it is not permitted unto them-to
speak: but *they are commanded* to be under obedience, as also
saith the law.   35 And if they will learn any thing, let them
ask their husbands at home: for it is a shame for women to
speak in the church.

Eph. 5: 22 Wives, submit yourselves unto your own husbands; as unto the Lord.   23 For the husband is the head of
the wife, even as Christ is the head of the church: and he is
the Saviour of the body.   24 Therefore as the church is
subject unto Christ, so *let* the wives *be* to their own husbands
in every thing.

Col. 3: 18 Wives, submit yourselves unto your own husbands,
as it is fit in the Lord.

1 Tim. 2: 11 Let the woman learn in silence with all subjection.   12 But I suffer not a woman to teach, nor to usurp
authority over the man, but to be in silence.   13 For Adam
was first formed, then Eve.

1 Pet. 3: 1 Likewise, ye wives, *be* in subjection to your own
husbands; that, if any obey not the word, they also may
without the word be won by the conversation of the wives;
2 While they behold your chaste conversation *coupled* with
fear.   6 Even as Sarah obeyed Abraham, calling him lord:
whose daughters ye are, as long as ye do well, and are not
afraid with any amazement.   7 Likewise, ye husbands, dwell
with *them* according to knowledge, giving honor unto the wife,
as unto the weaker vessel, and as being heirs together of the
grace of life; that your prayers be not hindered.   [See 425.]

FLATTERY.

198. *Flattery a common and dangerous sin.*

Job 17: 5 He that speaketh flattery to his friends, even the
eyes of his children shall fail.   32: 21 Let me not, I pray you,
accept any man's person, neither let me give flattering titles
unto man.   22 For I know not to give flattering titles; *in so
doing* my Maker would soon take me away.

Ps. 12: 3 The LORD shall cut off all flattering lips, *and* the
tongue that speaketh proud things.

Pr. 20: 19 He that goeth about *as* a tale-bearer revealeth
secrets: therefore meddle not with him that flattereth with his
lips. — 24: 24 He that saith unto the wicked, Thou *art* righteous; him shall the people curse, nations shall abhor him.
26: 28 A lying tongue hateth *those that are* afflicted by it; and
a flattering mouth worketh ruin. — 28: 23 He that rebuketh a
man, afterwards shall find more favor than he that flattereth

with the tongue.—29: 5 A man that flattereth his neighbor spreadeth a net for his feet. [See 474–5, 702, 728.]

FOOD.

199. Instructions respecting food — gluttony reproved.

Gen. 1: 29 God said, Behold, I have given you every herb bearing seed, which *is* upon the face of all the earth, and every tree, in the which *is* the fruit of a tree yielding seed; to you it shall be for meet.—9: 3 Every moving thing that liveth shall be meat for you; even as the green herb have I given you all things. 4 But flesh with the life thereof, *which is* the blood thereof, shall ye not eat.

Dt. 21: 20 This our son *is* stubborn and rebellious, he will not obey our voice; *he is* a glutton, and a drunkard. 21 And all the men of his city shall stone him with stones, that he die.

Pr. 23: 1 When thou sittest to eat with a ruler, consider diligently what *is* before thee: 2 And put a knife to thy throat, if thou *be* a man given to appetite. 3 Be not desirous of his dainties: for they *are* deceitful meat. 20 Be not among winebibbers; among riotous eaters of flesh: 21 For the drunkard and the glutton shall come to poverty: and drowsiness shall clothe *a man* with rags.

Dan. 1: 12 Prove thy servants, I beseech thee, ten days; and let them give us pulse to eat, and water to drink. 15 And at the end of ten days their countenances appeared fairer and fatter in flesh than all the children which did eat the portion of the king's meat.

Mat. 6: 31 Take no thought, saying, What shall we eat? or, what shall we drink? or, wherewithal shall we be clothed? 32 (For after all these things do the Gentiles seek) for your heavenly Father knoweth that ye have need of all these things. 33 But seek ye first the kingdom of God, and his righteousness, and all these things shall be added unto you.

Lk. 16: 19 There was a certain man, which was clothed in purple and fine linen and fared sumptuously every day: 25 But Abraham said, Son, remember that thou in thy life-time receivedst thy good things, and likewise Lazarus evil things: but now he is comforted, and thou art tormented.—21: 34 And take heed to yourselves, lest at any time your hearts be overcharged with surfeiting and drunkenness, and cares of this life, and so that day come upon you unawares.

Rom. 14: 21 *It is* good neither to eat flesh, nor to drink wine, nor *any thing* whereby thy brother stumbleth, or is offended, or is made weak.

A looking-glass.

1 Cor. 8: 13 If meàt make my brother to offend, I will eat no flesh while the world standeth, lest I make my brother to offend.

1 Tim. 4: 3 Forbidding to marry, *and commanding* to abstain from meats, which God hath created to be received with thanksgiving of them which believe and know the truth. [368, 721.]

FOOLS.

200. *Who are fools?* [*A looking-glass.*]

1. *Atheists.*

Ps. 14: 1 ,The fool hath said in his heart, *There is* no God. 94: 6 They slay the widow and the stranger, and murder the fatherless. 7 Yet they say, The LORD shall not see, neither shall the God of Jacob regard *it*. 8 Understand, ye brutish among the people : and *ye* fools, when will ye be wise. [See 22.]

2. *Blabbers.*

Pr. 13: 16 Every prudent *man* dealeth with knowledge; but a fool layeth open *his* folly. — 14: 33 Wisdom resteth in the heart of him that hath understanding : but *that which is* in the midst of fools is máde known. — 18: 7 A fool's mouth *is* his destruction, and his lips *are* the snare of his soul. — 29: 11 A fool uttereth all his mind : but a wise *man* keepeth it in till afterwards. 20 Seest thou a man *that is* hasty in his words? *there is* more hope of a fool than of him. [See 729.]

3. *Blasphemers.*

Ps. 74: 18 The foolish people have blasphemed thy name. 22 Arise, O God, plead thine own cause : remember how the foolish man reproacheth thee daily. [See 718.]

4. *Boasters.*

Rom. 1: 22 Professing themselves to be wise, they became fools. [See 703.]

5. *Children, disobedient.*

Pr. 15: 5 A fool despiseth his father's instruction. 20 A wise son maketh a glad father : but a foolish man despiseth his mother. — 22: 15 Foolishness is bound in the heart of a child ; *but* the rod of correction shall drive it far from him. [See 54.]

6. *Deceivers—self-deceivers—hypocrites.*

Pr. 12: 15 The way of a fool *is* right in his own eyes : but he that hearkeneth unto counsel *is* wise. — 14: 8 The wisdom of the prudent *is* to understand his way : but the folly of fools *is* deceit. — 26: 12 Seest thou a man wise in his own conceit? *there is* more hope of a fool than of him. — 28: 26 He that trusteth in his own heart is a fool.

Lk. 11: 39 The Lord said unto him, Now do ye Pharisees make clean the outside of the cup and the platter; but your inward part is full of ravening and wickedness. 40 *Ye* fools, did not he that made that which is without, make that which is within also?

Tit. 3: 3 We ourselves were sometimes foolish, disobedient, deceived, serving divers lusts and pleasures, living in malice and envy, hateful, *and* hating one another. [See 702.]

7. *Obstinate offenders.*

Dt. 32: 5 They have corrupted themselves, their spot *is* not *the spot* of his children: *they are* a perverse and crooked generation. 6 Do ye thus requite the LORD, O foolish people and unwise? *is* not he thy father *that* hath bought thee? hath he not made thee and established thee?

Pr. 13: 19 *It is* abomination to fools to depart from evil. — 27: 22 Though thou shouldest bray a fool in a mortar among wheat with a pestle, *yet* will not his foolishness depart from him. [See 488.]

8. *Drunkards.*

Pr. 20: 1 Wine *is* a mocker, strong drink *is* raging: and whosoever is deceived thereby is not wise.

9. *Gossips.*

Pr. 10: 8 The wise in heart will receive commandments: but a prating fool shall fall. — 15: 2 The tongue of the wise useth knowledge aright: but the mouth of fools poureth out foolishness. — 18: 7 A fool's mouth *is* his destruction, and his lips *are* the snare of his soul.

Ec. 5: 3 A fool's voice *is known* by multitude of words. — 10: 12 The words of a wise man's mouth *are* gracious; but the lips of a fool will swallow up himself. 13 The beginning of the words of his mouth *is* foolishness: and the end of his talk *is* mischievous madness. 14 A fool also is full of words. [See 729.]

10. *Ignoramuses.*

Ps. 92: 5 O LORD, how great are thy works! *and* thy thoughts are very deep. 6 A brutish man knoweth not: neither doth a fool understand this.

Pr. 1: 7 Fools despise wisdom and instruction. 22 How long, ye simple ones, will ye love simplicity? and the scorners delight in their scorning, and fools hate knowledge? — 15: 14 The heart of him that hath understanding seeketh knowledge: but the mouth of fools feedeth on foolishness. — 18: 2 A fool hath no delight in understanding, but that his heart may discover itself. [See 363.]

A looking-glass.

11. *Knaves.*

Jer. 17: 11 *As* the partridge sitteth *on eggs*, and hatcheth *them* **not** ; *so* he that getteth riches and not by right, shall leave them in the midst of his days, and at his end shall be a fool.

12. *Libertines.*

Pr. 7: 6 At the window of my house I looked through my casement, 7 And behold among the simple ones, I discerned among the youths, a young man void of understanding, 8 Passing through the street near her corner ; and he went the way to her house, 9 In the twilight, in the evening, in the black and dark night : 22 He goeth after her straightway, as an ox goeth to the slaughter, or as a fool to the correction of the stocks ; 23 Till a dart strike through his liver ; as a bird hasteth to the snare, and knoweth not that it *is* for his life. [See 405.]

13. *Meddlers.*

Pr. 20: 3 *It is* an honor for a man to cease from strife; but every fool will be meddling.

14. *Misers.*

Pr. 1: 32 The turning away of the simple shall slay them, and the prosperity of fools shall destroy them.

Lk. 12: 19 I will say to my soul, Soul, thou hast much goods laid up for many years ; take thine ease, eat, drink, *and* be merry. 20 But God said unto him, *Thou* fool, this night thy soul shall be required of thee: then whose shall those things be which thou hast provided ? 21 So *is* he that layeth up treasure for himself, and is not rich toward God. [See 625-6.]

15. *Mockers.*

Pr. 14: 9 Fools make a mock at sin.

16. *Rovers.*

Pr. 17: 24 Wisdom *is* before him that hath understanding ; but the eyes of a fool *are* in the ends of the earth.

17. *Slanderers.*

Pr. 10: 18 He that hideth hatred *with* lying lips, and he that uttereth a slander, *is* a fool.

18. *Sots.*

Pr. 17: 16 Wherefore *is there* a price in the hand of a fool to get wisdom, seeing *he hath* no heart *to it ?*

Jer. 4: 22 My people *is* foolish, they have not known me ; they *are* sottish children, and they have none understanding: they *are* wise to do evil, but to do good they have no knowledge. [See 693.]

19. *Spendthrifts.*

Pr. 21: 20 *There is* treasure to be desired, and oil in the dwelling of the wise ; but a foolish man spendeth it up.

13

20. *Sportsmen.*

Pr. 10: 23 *It is* as sport to a fool to do mischief.

Ec. 7: 4 The heart of fools *is* in the house of mirth. [See 479.]

21. *Warriors.*

Job 5: 2 Wrath killeth the foolish man, and envy slayeth the silly one.

Pr. 12: 16 A fool's wrath is presently known: but a prudent *man* covereth shame. — 14: 16 The fool rageth, and is confident. — 18: 6 A fool's lips enter into contention, and his mouth calleth for strokes. — 20: 3 *It is* an honor for a man to cease from strife: but every fool will be meddling. — 27: 3 A stone *is* heavy, and the sand weighty: but a fool's wrath *is* heavier than them both.

Ec. 7: 9 Anger resteth in the bosom of fools. [See 735.]

FORBEARANCE.

201. *Forbearance required and commended.*

Pr. 19: 11 The discretion of a man deferreth his anger; and *it is* his glory to pass over a transgression.

1 Cor. 13: 4 Charity suffereth long, *and* is kind; charity envieth not; charity vaunteth not itself, is not puffed up, 5 Doth not behave itself unseemly, seeketh not her own, is not easily provoked, thinketh no evil: 7 Beareth all things, believeth all things, hopeth all things, endureth all things.

Ep. 4: 1 I therefore, the prisoner of the Lord, beseech you that ye walk worthy of the vocation wherewith ye are called, 2 With all lowliness and meekness, with long-suffering, forbearing one another in love.

1 Pet. 2: 18 Servants, *be* subject to *your* masters, with all fear; not only to the good and gentle, but also to the froward. 19 For this *is* thankworthy, if a man for conscience toward God endure grief, suffering wrongfully. 20 For what glory *is it*, if, when ye be buffeted for your faults, ye shall take it patiently? but if, when ye do well, and suffer *for it*, ye take it patiently, this *is* acceptable with God. 21 For even hereunto were ye called: because Christ also suffered for us, leaving us an example, that ye should follow his steps. 23 Who, when he was reviled, reviled not again; when he suffered, he threatened not; but committed *himself* to him that judgeth righteously. — 3: 8 Finally, *be ye* all of one mind, having compassion one of another; love as brethren, *be* pitiful, *be* courteous: 9 Not rendering evil for evil, or railing for railing: but con-

trariwise, blessing; knowing that ye are thereunto called, that ye should inherit a blessing.
[See 203, 437—9, 498, 499, 737.]

202. *Sinners abuse forbearance.*

Ec. 8: 11 Because sentence against an evil work is not executed speedily, therefore the heart of the sons of men is fully set in them to do evil.

FORGIVENESS.

203. *Duty to forgive, as we hope to be forgiven — Threats to the implacable.*

Mat. 6: 12 Forgive us our debts, as we forgive our debtors. 14 For, if ye forgive men their trespasses, your heavenly Father will also forgive you: 15 But if ye forgive not men their trespasses, neither will your Father forgive your trespasses.— 18: 21 Then came Peter to him, and said, Lord, how oft shall my brother sin against me, and I forgive him? till seven times? 22 Jesus saith unto him, I say not unto thee, Until seven times: but, Until seventy times seven. 27 Then the lord of that servant was moved with compassion, and loosed him, and forgave him the debt. 28 But the same servant went out, and found one of his fellow-servants, which owed him an hundred pence: and he laid hands on him, and took *him* by the throat, saying, Pay me that thou owest. 29 And his fellow-servant fell down at his feet, and besought him, saying, Have patience with me, and I will pay thee all. 30 And he would not; but went and cast him into prison, till he should pay the debt. 32 Then his lord, after that he had called him, said unto him, O thou wicked servant, I forgave thee all that debt, because thou desiredst me: 33 Shouldest not thou also have had compassion on thy fellow-servant, even as I had pity on thee? 34 And his lord was wroth, and delivered him to the tormentors, till he should pay all that was due unto him. 35 So likewise shall my heavenly Father do also unto you, if ye from your hearts forgive not every one his brother their trespasses.

Mk. 11: 25 When ye stand praying, forgive, if ye have aught against any: that your Father also which is in heaven may forgive you your trespasses. 26 But if ye do not forgive, neither will your Father which is in heaven forgive your trespasses.

Lk. 6: 37 Judge not, and ye shall not be judged: condemn not, and ye shall not be condemned: forgive, and ye shall be forgiven.— 17: 3 Take heed to yourselves: If thy brother

147

trespass against thee, rebuke him; and if he repent, forgive him. 4 And if he trespass against thee seven times in a day, and seven times in a day turn again to thee, saying, I repent; thou shalt forgive him.

Ep. 4: 32 Be ye kind one to another, tender-hearted, forgiving one another, even as God, for Christ's sake, hath forgiven you.

Col. 3: 12 Put on therefore, as the elect of God, holy and beloved, bowels of mercies, kindness, humbleness of mind, meekness, long-suffering; 13 Forbearing one another, and forgiving one another, if any man have a quarrel against any: even as Christ forgave you, so also *do* ye.

[See 62, 539, 737.]

N. B. — For Divine Forgiveness, see 583.

FRIENDSHIP.

204. *True friendship desirable — how to make friends.*

2 S. 1: 26 I am distressed for thee, my brother Jonathan: very pleasant hast thou been unto me: thy love to me was wonderful, passing the love of women.

Pr. 17: 17 A friend loveth at all times, and a brother is born for adversity. — 18: 24 A man *that hath* friends must show himself friendly: and there is a friend *that* sticketh closer than a brother. — 19: 6 Many will entreat the favor of the prince: and every man *is* a friend to him that giveth gifts. — 27: 9 Ointment and perfume rejoice the heart: so *doth* the sweetness of a man's friend by hearty counsel. [See 737.]

205. *Spurious friendship — Ingratitude.*

Job 19: 14 My kinsfolk have failed, and my familiar friends have forgotten me. 19 All my inward friends abhorred me; and they whom I loved are turned against me.

Ps. 38: 11 My lovers and my friends stand aloof from my sore; and my kinsmen stand afar off. — 55: 12 *It was* not an enemy *that* reproached me; then I could have borne *it;* neither *was it* he that hated me *that* did magnify *himself* against me; then I would have hid myself from him: 13 But *it was* thou, a man mine equal, my guide and mine acquaintance. 14 We took sweet counsel together, *and* walked unto the house of God in company.

Mat. 26: 56 Then all the disciples forsook him, and fled.

2 Tim. 4: 16 At my first answer no man stood with me, but all *men* forsook me: I *pray God* that it may not be laid to their charge. [See 701.]

148

GOD.

206. *Have mankind any intuitive knowledge of God?*

Job 32: 8 *There is* a spirit in man; and the inspiration of the Almighty giveth them understanding.

Ac. 17: 28 In him we live, and move, and have our being; as certain also of your own poets have said, For we are also his offspring.   29 Forasmuch then as we are the offspring of God, we ought not to think that the Godhead is like unto gold, or silver, or stone, graven by art and man's device.

Rom. 1: 19 Because that which may be known of God is manifest in them: for God hath shewed *it* unto them. — 2: 14 When the Gentiles, which have not the law, do by nature the things contained in the law, these having not the law, are a law unto themselves.   15 Which shew the work of the law written in their hearts, their conscience also bearing witness, and *their* thoughts the mean while accusing, or else excusing one another. [See 394.]

207. *God made known by his works.*

Ps. 19: 1 The heavens declare the glory of God; and the firmament sheweth his handy work.   2 Day unto day uttereth speech, and night unto night sheweth knowledge. — 75: 1 Unto thee, O God, do we give thanks, *unto thee* do we give thanks: for *that* thy name *is* near, thy wondrous works declare.

Ac. 14: 17 He left not himself without witness, in that he did good, and gave us rain from heaven, and fruitful seasons, filling our hearts with food and gladness.

Rom. 1: 20 For the invisible things of him from the creation of the world are clearly seen, being understood by the things that are made, *even* his eternal power and Godhead; so that they are without excuse. — 11: 36 Of him, and through him, and to him, *are* all things: to whom *be* glory for ever.

Heb. 3: 4 Every house is builded by some *man;* but he that built all things *is* God.   Ps. 9 16.

208. *God, a moral agent, with affections and passions.*

Gen. 6: 6 It repented the Lord that he had made man on the earth, and it grieved him at his heart.

Ps. 7: 11 God is angry *with the wicked* every day. — 103: 13 As a father pitieth *his* children, *so* the Lord pitieth them that

13*

149

fear him. — 147: 11 The Lord taketh pleasure in them that fear him.

Hos. 11: 8 How shall I give thee up, Ephraim? *how* shall I deliver thee, Israel?˙ how shall I make thee as Admah? *how* shall I set thee as Zeboim? mine heart is turned within me, my repentings are kindled together.

Zep. 3: 17 The LORD thy God in the midst of thee *is* mighty; he will save, he will rejoice over thee with joy: he will rest in his love, he will joy over thee with singing.

Mat. 3: 17 This is my beloved Son, in whom I am well pleased.

1 Jn. 4: 8 God is love.   [See 223, 230, 238.]

209. *God's chief end — his regard for himself.*

Ps. 106: 8 He saved them for his name's sake, that he might make his mighty power to be known.

Pr. 16: 4 The Lord hath made all *things* for himself: yea, even the wicked for the day of evil.

Is. 42: 8 I *am* the Lord: that *is* my name: and my glory will I not give to another, neither my praise to graven images. — 43: 7 *Even* every one that is called by my name; for I have created him for my glory, I have formed him; yea, I have made him. 21 This people have I formed for myself; they shall shew forth my praise. — 48: 11 For mine own sake, *even* for mine own sake, will I do *it;* for how should *my name* be polluted? and I will not give my glory unto another.

Ezk. 20: 9 I wrought for my name's sake, that it should not be polluted before the heathen. — 36: 32 Not for your sakes do I *this*, saith the Lord GOD, be it known unto you: be ashamed and confounded for your own ways, O house of Israel.

1 Cor. 15: 28 When all things shall be subdued unto him, then shall the Son also himself be subject unto him that put all things under him, that God may be all in all.

Col. 1: 16 All things were created by him and for him.

Rev. 4: 11 Thou art worthy, O Lord, to receive glory, and honor, and power: for thou hast created all things, and for thy pleasure they are and were they created.   [See 276—7, 570.]

GOD'S MODE OF EXISTENCE.

210. *Divine unity, or only one true God.*

Dt. 4: 35 The Lord he *is* God: *there is* none else beside him. [39.] — 6: 4 The Lord our God *is* one Lord. — 32: 39 See now that I, *even I am* he, and *there is* no god with me.

2 S. 7: 22 *There is* none like thee, neither *is there any* God beside thee.

2 K. 19: 15 Thou art the God, *even* thou alone, of all the kingdoms of the earth.

Neh. 9: 6 Thou, *even* thou, *art* Lord alone.

Is. 44: 6 Thus saith the Lord, the King of Israel, and his Redeemer the Lord of hosts; I *am* the first and I *am* the last; and besides me *there is* no God. 8 Is there a God besides me? Yea, *there is* no God; I know not *any*. — 45: 5 I *am* the Lord, and *there is* none else, *there is* no God besides me.

Jn. 17: 3 This is life eternal, that they might know thee the only true God, and Jesus Christ whom thou hast sent.

1 Cor. 8: 6 To us *there is but* one God, the Father, of whom *are* all things, and we in him.

1 Tim. 1: 17 Now unto the King eternal, immortal, invisible, the only wise God, *be* honor and glory for ever and ever.

Jam. 2: 19 Thou believest that there is one God; thou doest well.

211. *Are there more persons than one in the Godhead?*

Gen. 1: 26 And God said, Let us make man in our image, after our likeness. Gen. 3: 22, and 11: 7, Is. 6: 8.

Dan. 4: 17 This matter *is* by the decree of the watchers, and the demand by the word of the holy ones.

Mat. 28: 19 Teach all nations, baptizing them in the name of the Father, and of the Son, and of the Holy Ghost.

2 Cor. 13: 14 The grace of the Lord Jesus Christ, and the love of God, and the communion of the Holy Ghost, *be* with you all. Amen.

Ep. 2: 18 Through him we both have access by one Spirit unto the Father. 1 Pet. 1: 2.

1 Jn. 5: 7 There are three that bear record in heaven, the Father, the Word, and the Holy Ghost: and these three are one. [See 75—6, 346.]

GOD'S NATURAL ATTRIBUTES.

212. *Eternity of God.*

Dt. 33: 27 The eternal God *is thy* refuge.

Ps. 90: 2 Before the mountains were brought forth, or ever thou hadst formed the earth and the world, even from everlasting to everlasting, thou *art* God. — 93: 2 Thy throne *is* established of old: thou *art* from everlasting.. — 102: 27 Thou *art* the same, and thy years shall have no end.

Is. 44: 6 Thus saith the LORD the King of Israel, and his Redeemer the LORD of hosts; I *am* the first, and I *am* the last, and besides me *there is* no God. — 57: 15 Thus saith the high and lofty One that inhabiteth eternity, whose name *is* Holy.

Hab. 1: 12 *Art* thou not from everlasting, O LORD my God, mine Holy One?

1 Tim. 1: 17 Unto the King eternal, immortal, invisible, the only wise God, *be* honor and glory for ever and ever — 6: 15 Which in his times he shall shew, *who is* the blessed and only Potentate, the King of kings and Lord of lords; 16 Who only hath immortality. [See 76,(3.)]

213. *Foreknowledge of God.*

Is. 46: 9 Remember the former things of old: for I *am* God, and *there is* none else; *I am* God, and *there is* none like me, 10 Declaring the end from the beginning, and from ancient times *the things* that are not *yet* done, saying, My counsel shall stand, and I will do all my pleasure.

Ac. 2: 23 Him, being delivered by the determinate counsel and foreknowledge of God, ye have taken, and by wicked hands have crucified and slain. — 15: 18 Known unto God are all his works from the beginning of the world. [See 219.]

214. *Greatness, majesty, and supremacy of God.*

1 Ch. 29: 11 Thine, O LORD, *is* the greatness, and the power, and the glory, and the victory, and the majesty: for all *that is* in the heaven and in the earth *is thine;* thine *is* the kingdom, O LORD, and thou art exalted as head above all. 12 Both riches and honor *come* of thee, and thou reignest over all; and in thy hand *is* power and might; and in thy hand *it is* to make great, and to give strength unto all.

Neh. 9: 6 Thou, *even* thou, *art* LORD alone; thou hast made heaven, the heaven of heavens, with all their host, the earth, and all *things* that *are* therein, the seas, and all that *is* therein,

152

Greatness and Majesty.

and thou preservest them all; and the host of heaven worshippeth thee.

Job. 11: 7 Canst thou by searching find out God? canst thou find out the Almighty unto perfection? 8 *It is* as high as heaven; what canst thou do? deeper than hell; what canst thou know? 9 The measure thereof *is* longer than the earth, and broader than the sea.—26: 14 Lo, these *are* parts of his ways; but how little a portion is heard of him? but·the thunder of his power who can understand.—36: 26 Behold, God *is* great, and we know *him* not, neither can the number of his years be searched out.—37: 22 With God *is* terrible majesty. 23 *Touching* the Almighty, we cannot find him out: *he is* excellent in power, and in judgment, and in plenty of justice.

Ps. 29: 4 The voice of the LORD *is* powerful; the voice of the LORD *is* full of majesty.—47: 7 For God *is* the King of all the earth.—93: 1 The LORD reigneth, he is clothed with majesty.—104: 1 Bless the LORD, O my soul. O LORD my God, thou art very great; thou art clothed with honor and majesty: 2 Who coverest *thyself* with light as *with* a garment: who stretchest out the heavens like a curtain: 3 Who láyeth the beams of his chambers in the ·waters: who maketh the clouds his chariot: who walketh upon the wings of the wind: 4 Who maketh his angels spirits; his ministers a flaming fire. —145: 3 Great *is* the Lord, and greatly to be praised; and his greatness *is* unsearchable.

Is. 40: 12 Who hath measured the waters in the hollow of his hand, and meted out heaven with the span, and comprehended the dust of the earth in a measure, and weighed the mountains in scales, and the hills in a balance? 13 Who hath directed the Spirit of the LORD, or *being* his counsellor hath taught him? 14 With whom took he counsel, and *who* instructed him, and taught him in the path of judgment, and taught him knowledge, and shewed to him the way of understanding? 15 Behold, the nations *are* as a drop of a bucket, and are counted as the small dust of the balance: behold, he taketh up the isles as a very little thing. 16 And Lebanon *is* not sufficient to burn, nor the beasts thereof sufficient for a burnt-offering. 17 All nations before him *are* as nothing, and they are counted to him less than nothing, and vanity. 18 To whom then will ye liken God? or what likeness will ye compare unto him? [Dan. 4: 35.]

Nah. 1: 3 The LORD *hath* his way in the whirlwind and in the storm, and the clouds *are* the dust of his feet. 4 He rebuketh the sea, and maketh it dry, and drieth up all the rivers: Bashan languisheth, and Carmel, and the flower of Lebanon languisheth.   5 The mountains quake at him, and the hills melt, and the earth is burned at his presence, yea, the world, and all that dwell therein.   6 Who can stand before his indignation? and who can abide in the fierceness of his anger? his fury is poured out like fire, and the rocks are thrown down by him.   [See 45, 234, 275.] .

215. *Essential happiness of God.*

Rom. 1: 25 Who is blessed for ever.—9: 5 Whose *are* the fathers, and of whom, as concerning the flesh, Christ *came,* who is over all, God blessed for ever.

2 Cor. 11: 31 The God and Father of our Lord Jesus Christ, which is blessed .for evermore.

1 Tim. 1: 11 The glorious gospel of the blessed God.—6: 15. The blessed and only Potentate.   [See 223.]

216. *Invisibility of God.*

Jn. 1: 18 No man hath seen God at any time; the only begotten Son, which is in the bosom of the Father, he hath declared *him.*—4: 24 God *is* a spirit.

Col. 1: 15 Who is the image of the invisible God, the first-born of every creature.

1 Tim. 6: 16 Whom no man hath seen, nor can see; to whom *be* honor and power everlasting.

Heb. 11: 27 By faith he forsook Egypt, not fearing the wrath of the king: for he endured, as seeing him who is invisible.

217. *Immutability of God.*

Num. 23: 19 God *is* not a man, that he should lie; neither the son of man, that he should repent: hath he said, and shall he not do *it?* or hath he spoken, and shall he not make it good?

1 S. 15: 29 And also the Strength of Israel will not lie nor repent: for he *is* not a man, that he should repent. .

Job 23: 13 He *is* in one *mind,* and who can turn him?

Ps. 102: 25 Of old hast thou laid the foundation of the earth: and the heavens *are* the work of thy hands.   26 They shall perish, but thou shalt endure: yea, all of them shall wax old like a garment; as a vesture shalt thou change them, and they shall be changed: 27 But thou *art* the same, and thy years shall have no end.

Mal. 3: 6 I *am* the LORD, I change not.

Heb. 13: 8 Jesus Christ the same yesterday, and to-day, and for ever.

Jam. 1: 17 Every good gift and every perfect gift is from

above, and cometh down from the Father of lights, with whom is no variableness, neither shadow of turning. [See 250.]

218. *Omnipotence of God.*

Gen. 17: 1 I *am* the Almighty God.

Job 9: 12 Behold, he taketh away, who can hinder him?

Is. 43: 13 *There is* none that can deliver out of my hand: I will work, and who shall let it?

Jer. 32: 17 Ah Lord GOD! behold, thou hast' made the heaven and the earth by thy great power and stretched out arm, *and* there is nothing too hard for thee.

Mat. 19: 26 With God all things are possible.

Rev. 1: 8 I am Alpha and Omega, the beginning and the ending, saith the Lord, which is, and which was, and which is to come, the Almighty.—11: 17 We give thee thanks, O Lord God Almighty, which art, and wast, and art to come; because thou hast taken to thee thy great power, and hast reigned. —19: 6 The Lord God omnipotent reigneth.

[See 76,(5) 234, 259, 588.]

219. *Omniscience of God.*

1 S. 2: 3 Talk no more so exceeding proudly; let *not* arrogancy come out of your mouth: for the LORD *is* a God of knowledge, and by him actions are weighed.—16: 7 *The Lord seeth* not as man seeth; for man looketh on the outward appearance, but the LORD looketh on the heart.

1 K. 8: 39 Then hear thou in heaven thy dwelling-place, and forgive, and do, and give to every man according to his ways, whose heart thou knowest; (for thou, *even* thou only, knowest the hearts of all the children of men.)

1 Ch. 28: 9 The Lord searcheth all hearts, and understandeth all the imaginations of the thoughts.

Job 11: 11 He knoweth vain men: he seeth wickedness also; will he not then consider *it?*—34: 21 His eyes *are* upon the ways of man, and he seeth all his goings. 22 *There is* no darkness, nor shadow of death, where the workers of iniquity may hide themselves.

Ps. 11: 4 The Lord's throne *is* in heaven: his eyes behold, his eyelids try the children of men.—44: 21 Shall not God search this out? for he knoweth the secrets of the heart.— 94: 9 He that planted the ear, shall he not hear? he that formed the eye, shall he not see?—139: 1 O LORD, thou hast searched me, and known *me.* 2 Thou knowest my down-sitting and mine up-rising, thou understandest my thought afar off. 3 Thou compassest my path and my lying down, and art acquainted *with* all my ways. 4 For *there is* not a word in my tongue, *but* lo, O LORD, thou knowest it altogether. 5 Thou hast beset me behind and before, and laid thine hand upon me. 6 *Such* knowledge *is* too wonderful for me; it is high, I cannot *attain* unto it. 11 If I say, Surely the darkness shall cover me; even the night shall be light about me. 12 Yea, the darkness hideth not from thee; but the night shineth as the day: the darkness and the light *are* both alike *to thee.* —147: 5 Great *is* our Lord, and of great power: his understanding *is* infinite.

Pr. 5: 21 For the ways of man *are* before the eyes of the Lord, and he pondereth all his goings.—15: 3 The eyes of the Lord *are* in every place, beholding the evil and the good. 11 Hell and destruction *are* before the Lord: how much more then the hearts of the children of men? 17: 3 The fining-pot *is* for silver, and the furnace for gold: but the Lord trieth the hearts.—21: 2 Every way of a man *is* right in his own eyes: but the Lord pondereth the hearts.—24: 11 If thou forbear to deliver *them that are* drawn unto death, and *those that are* ready to be slain; 12 If thou sayest, Behold, we knew it not; doth not he that pondereth the heart consider *it?* and he that keepeth thy soul, doth *not* he know *it?*

Is. 40: 28 *There is* no searching of his understanding.

Jer. 23: 23 *Am* I a God at hand, saith the LORD, and not a God afar off? 24 Can any hide himself in secret places that I shall not see him? saith the LORD.—32: 19 Great in counsel, and mighty in work: for thine eyes *are* open upon all the ways of the sons of men; to give every one according to his ways, and according to the fruit of his doings.

Ezk. 11: 5 And the Spirit of the LORD fell upon me, and said unto me, Speak; Thus saith the LORD; Thus have ye said, O house of Israel: for I know the things that come into your mind, *every one of* them.

Ac. 1: 24 Thou, Lord, which knowest the hearts of all *men,* shew whether of these two thou hast chosen.

Heb. 4: 13 Neither is there any creature that is not manifest in his sight: but all things *are* naked and opened unto the eyes of him with whom we have to do.

1 Jn. 3: 20 For if our heart condemn us, God is greater than our heart, and knoweth all things. [See 76,(7) 213.]

220. *Omnipresence of God.*

Ps. 139: 3 Thou compassest my path and my lying down, and art acquainted *with* all my ways. 5 Thou hast beset me behind and before, and laid thine hand upon me. 7 Whither shall I go from thy Spirit? or whither shall I flee from thy presence? 8 If I ascend up into heaven, thou *art* there: if I make my bed in hell, behold, thou *art there.* 9 *If* I take the wings of the morning, *and* dwell in the uttermost parts of the sea; 10 Even there shall thy hand lead me, and thy right hand shall hold me.

Jer. 23: 23 *Am* I a God at hand, saith the LORD, and not a God afar off? 24 Can any hide himself in secret places that I·shall not see him? saith the LORD. Do not I fill heaven and earth? saith the LORD.

Mat. 18: 20 For where two or three are gathered together in my name, there am I in the midst of them.

Ep. 1: 23 The fulness of him that filleth all in all.
[See 76,(6).]

221. *Self-existence of God.*

Ex. 3: 14 God said unto Moses, I AM THAT I AM: And he said, Thus shalt thou say unto the children of Israel, I AM hath sent me unto you.

Dt. 32: 40 I lift my hand to heaven, and say, I live for ever.

Jer. 10: 10 The Lord *is* the true God, he *is* the living God, and an everlasting King.

Jn. 5: 26 As the Father hath life in himself, so hath he given to the Son to have life in himself.—6: 57 The living Father hath sent me.

Ac. 17: 24 God that made the world, and all things therein, seeing that he is Lord of heaven and earth, dwelleth not in temples made with hands; 25 Neither is worshipped with men's hands, as though he needed anything, seeing he giveth to all life, and breath, and all things.

1 Tim. 6: 15 Which in his times he shall shew, *who is* the blessed and only Potentate, the King of kings, and Lord of lords; 16 Who only hath immortality, dwelling in the light which no man can approach unto: whom no man hath seen, nor can see; to whom *be* honor and power everlasting.

222. *Wisdom of God.*

Job. 5: 13 He taketh the wise in their own craftiness: and the counsel of the froward is carried headlong.

Ps. 104: 24 O LORD, how manifold are thy works! in wisdom hast thou made them all: the earth is full of thy riches.

Is. 28: 29 This also cometh forth from the LORD of hosts, *which* is wonderful in counsel, *and* excellent in working.

Rom. 11: 33 O the depth of the riches both of the wisdom **and** knowledge of God! how unsearchable *are* his judgments, and his ways past finding out! 34 For who hath known the mind of the Lord? or who hath been his counsellor?— 16: 27 To God only wise, *be* glory through Jesus Christ for ever. Amen.

1 Cor. 1: 25 The foolishness of God is wiser than men.

Ep. 1: 8 He hath abounded toward us in all wisdom and prudence.—3: 9 To make all *men* see. what *is* the fellowship of the mystery, which from the beginning of the world hath been bid in God, who created all things by Jesus Christ: 10 To the intent that now unto the principalities and powers in heavenly *places* might be known by the church the manifold wisdom of God.

Col. 2: 2 The mystery of God and of the Father, and of Christ; 3 In whom are hid all the treasures of wisdom and knowledge.

Jude 25 To the only wise God our Saviour, *be* glory and majesty, dominion and power, both now and ever. [See 142, 275.]

GOD'S MORAL PERFECTION.

223. *Blessedness or joy of God, arising from his benevolent designs and works.*

Ps. 104: 31 The glory of the LORD shall endure for ever: the LORD shall rejoice in his works.

Is. 62: 5 *As* the bridegroom rejoiceth over the bride, *so* shall thy God rejoice over thee.—65: 19 I will rejoice in Jerusalem, and joy in my people.

Jer. 9: 24 I *am* the Lord which exercise loving-kindness, judgment, and righteousness in the earth: for in these things I delight, saith the Lord.

Ezk. 5: 13 Thus shall mine anger be accomplished, and I will cause my fury to rest upon them, and I will be comforted: and they shall know that I the LORD have spoken *it* in my zeal, when I have accomplished my fury in them.

Zep. 3: 17 The LORD thy God in the midst of thee *is* mighty; he will save, he will rejoice over thee with joy; he will rest in his love, he will joy over thee with singing.

[See 208, 215.]

224. *Benevolence of God — he desires good, and deprecates evil.*

Dt. 5: 29 O that there were such a heart in them, that they would fear me, and keep all my commandments always, that it might be well with them, and with their children for ever!— 32: 29 O that they were wise, *that* they understood this, *that* they would consider their latter end!

Ps. 119: 68 Thou *art* good, and doest good.

Ezk. 18: 32 I have no pleasure in the death of him that dieth, saith the Lord GOD: wherefore turn *yourselves,* and live ye.

Mat. 5: 44 I say unto you, Love your enemies, bless them that curse you, do good to them that hate you and pray for them which despitefully use you, and persecute you; 45 That ye may be the children of your Father which is in heaven: for he maketh his sun to rise on the evil and on the good, and sendeth rain on the just and on the unjust.

Jn. 3: 14 As Moses lifted up the serpent in the wilderness, even so must the Son of man be lifted up. 15 That whosoever believeth in him should not perish, but have eternal life. 16 For God so loved the world, that he gave his only-begotten Son, that whosoever believeth in him, should not perish, but have everlasting life. 17 For God sent not his Son into the world to condemn the world, but that the world through him might be saved.

Rom. 5: 8 God commendeth his love toward us, in that while we were yet sinners, Christ died for us. — 8: 32 He that spared not his own Son, but delivered him up for us all, how shall he not with him also freely give us all things?

1 Th. 4: 3 This is the will of God, *even* your sanctification.

1 Tim. 2: 3 This *is* good and acceptable in the sight of God our Saviour; 4 Who will have all men to be saved, and to come unto the knowledge of the truth.

2 Pet. 3: 9 The Lord is not slack concerning his promise, as some men count slackness; but is long-suffering to us-ward, not willing that any should perish, but that all should come to repentance.

1 Jn. 4: 7 Beloved, let us love one another: for love is of God; and every one that loveth is born of God, and knoweth God. 8 He that loveth not, knoweth not God; for God is love. 9 In this was manifested the love of God toward us, because that God sent his only-begotten Son into the world, that we might live through him. 10 Herein is love, not that we loved God, but that he loved us, and sent his Son *to be* the propitiation for our sins.

[See 60, 228, 233, 254, 370—2, 585, 672.]

225. *Compassion of God.*

Ex. 32: 14 The Lord repented of the evil which he thought to do unto his people.

Jud. 10: 16 His soul was grieved for the misery of Israel.

Ps. 25: 6 Remember, O Lord, thy tender mercies and thy

loving-kindness; for they *have been* ever of old. — 36: 7 How excellent *is* thy loving-kindness, O God! therefore the children of men put their trust under the shadow of thy wings. — 69: 16 Hear me, O Lord; for thy loving-kindness *is* good: turn unto me according to the multitude of thy tender mercies. — 78: 38 He, *being* full of compassion, forgave *their* iniquity, and destroyed *them* not: yea, many a time turned he his anger away, and did not stir up all his wrath. — 86: 15 Thou, O Lord, *art* a God full of compassion, and gracious, long-suffering, and plenteous in mercy and truth. — 103: 13 Like as a father pitieth *his* children, *so* the Lord pitieth them that fear him. — 145: 8 The LORD *is* gracious, and full of compassion; slow to anger, and of great mercy. 9 The LORD *is* good to all: and his tender mercies *are* over all his works.

Lam. 3: 22 *It is* of the Lord's mercies, that we are not consumed, because his compassions fail not. 32 But though he cause grief, yet will he have compassion according to the multitude of his mercies. 33 For he doth not afflict willingly, nor grieve the children of men.

Hos. 11: 8 How shall I give thee up, Ephraim? *how* shall I deliver thee, Israel? how shall I make thee as Admah? *how* shall I set thee as Zeboim? my heart is turned within me, my repentings are kindled together.

Lk. 6: 35 He is kind unto the unthankful and *to* the evil.

Jam. 5: 11 The Lord is very pitiful, and of tender mercy. [See 233, 522, 585.]

226. *Faithfulness of God.*

Dt. 7: 9 Know therefore that the LORD thy God, he *is* God, the faithful God, which keepeth covenant and mercy with them that love him and keep his commandments to a thousand generations.

Jos. 21: 45 There failed not aught of any good thing which the LORD had spoken unto the house of Israel; all came to pass. — 23: 14 Behold, this day I *am* going the way of all the earth; and ye know in all your hearts and in all your souls, that not one thing hath failed of all the good things which the LORD your God spake concerning you; all are come to pass unto you, *and* not one thing hath failed thereof.

Ps. 36: 5 Thy mercy, O LORD, *is* in the heavens; *and* thy faithfulness *reacheth* unto the clouds. — 89: 2 Thy faithfulness shalt thou establish in the very heavens. 33 Nevertheless, my loving-kindness will I not utterly take from him, nor suffer my faithfulness to fail. 34 My covenant will I not break, nor alter the thing *that is* gone out of my lips. — 119: 90 Thy faithfulness *is* unto all generations.

1 Th. 5: 24 Faithful *is* he that calleth you, who also will do it. [See 4, 235, 515—517, 725.]

227. *Forbearance and long-suffering of God.*

Neh. 9: 30 Yet many years didst thou forbear them, and testifiedst against them by thy Spirit in thy prophets; yet would they not give ear.

Ec. 8: 11 Because sentence against an evil work is not executed speedily, therefore the heart of the sons of men is fully set in them to do evil.

Rom. 2: 4 Or despisest thou the riches of his goodness, and forbearance, and long-suffering; not knowing that the goodness of God leadeth thee to repentance? — 9: 22 *What* if God, willing to show *his* wrath, and to make his power known, endured with much long-suffering the vessels of wrath fitted to destruction?

1 Tim. 1: 16 Howbeit, for this cause I obtained mercy, that in me first Jesus Christ might show forth all long-suffering, for a pattern to them which should hereafter believe on him to life everlasting.

1 Pet. 3: 19 By which also he went and preached unto the spirits in prison; 20 Which sometime were disobedient, when once the long-suffering of God waited in the days of Noah, while the ark was a preparing, wherein few, that is, eight souls, were saved by water.

2 Pet. 3: 9 The Lord is not slack concerning his promise, as some men count slackness; but is long-suffering to us-ward, not willing that any should perish, but that all should come to repentance. [See 67·]

228. *Goodness and condescension of God.*

Ex. 34: 6 The LORD passed by before him, and proclaimed, The LORD, The LORD God, merciful and gracious, long-suffering, and abundant in goodness and truth.

1 Ch. 16: 34 O give thanks unto the LORD; for *he is* good; for his mercy *endureth* for ever.

Ps. 8: 3 When I consider thy heavens, the work of thy fingers, the moon and the stars, which thou hast ordained; 4 What is man, that thou art mindful of him? and the son of man, that thou visitest him? — 33: 5 He loveth righteousness and judgment: the earth is full of the goodness of the LORD. — 52: 1 Why boastest thou thyself in mischief, O mighty man? the goodness of God *endureth* continually. — 107: 8 Oh that *men* would praise the LORD *for* his goodness, and *for* his

Holiness and beauty of God.

wonderful works to the children of men! 9 For he satisfieth the longing soul, and filleth the hungry soul with goodness. — 113: 4 The LORD *is* high above all nations, *and* his glory above the heavens. 5 Who *is* like unto the LORD our God, who dwelleth on high, 6 Who humbleth *himself* to behold *the things that are* in heaven, and in the earth? — 119: 68 Thou *art* good, and doest good; teach me thy statutes. — 145: 7 They shall abundantly utter the memory of thy great goodness, and shall sing of thy righteousness. 9 The LORD *is* good to all: and his tender mercies *are* over all his works.

Is. 57: 15 Thus saith the high and lofty One that inhabiteth eternity, whose name *is* Holy; I dwell in the high and holy *place*, with him also *that is* of a contrite and humble spirit.

Zec. 9: 17 How great *is* his goodness, and how great *is* his beauty!

Mat. 19: 17 He said unto him, Why callest thou me good? *there is* none good but one, *that is*, God.

[See 60, 61, 224, 233, 254, 372, 672.]

229. *Holiness and beauty of God.*

Ex. 15: 11 Who *is* like unto thee, O LORD, among the gods? who *is* like thee, glorious in holiness, fearful *in* praises, doing wonders?

Lev. 11: 44 Ye shall be holy; for I *am* holy.

1 S. 2: 2 *there is* none holy as the LORD.

Job 4: 17 Shall mortal man be more just than God? shall a man be more pure than his Maker? 18 Behold, he put no trust in his servants; and his angels he charged with folly. — 34: 10 Therefore hearken unto me, ye men of understanding: far be it from God, *that he should do* wickedness; and *from* the Almighty, *that he should commit* iniquity.

Ps. 5: 4 Thou *art* not a God that hath pleasure in wickedness: neither shall evil dwell with thee. 5 The foolish shall not stand in thy sight: thou hatest all workers of iniquity. — 22: 3 Thou *art* holy, O *thou* that inhabitest the praises of Israel. — 27: 4 One *thing* have I desired of the LORD, that will I seek after; that I may dwell in the house of the LORD all the days of my life to behold the beauty of the LORD, and to inquire in his temple. — 45: 7 Thou lovest righteousness, and hatest wickedness. — 71: 22 I will also praise thee with the psaltery, *even* thy truth, O my God: unto thee will I sing with the harp, O thou Holy One of Israel. — 90: 17 And let the beauty of the LORD our God be upon us. — 99: 9 Exalt the LORD our God, and worship at his holy hill; for the LORD our God *is* holy. — 111: 9 Holy and reverend is his name. — 145: 17 The LORD *is* righteous in all his ways, and holy in all his works.

Is. 6: 3 And one cried unto another, and said, Holy, holy, holy, *is* the LORD of hosts: the whole earth *is* full of his glory. — 28: 5 In that day shall the LORD of hosts be for a crown of glory, and for a diadem of beauty, unto the residue of his people. — 33: 17 Thine eyes shall see the King in his beauty: they shall behold the land that is very far off.

Hab. 1: 13 *Thou art* of purer eyes than to behold evil, and canst not look on iniquity.

Zec. 9: 17 How great *is* his goodness, and how great *is* his beauty!

Rev. 15: 4 Who shall not fear thee, O Lord, and glorify thy name? for *thou* only *art* holy: for all nations shall come and worship before thee; for thy judgments are made manifest. 56.]

230. *God's holy grief, displeasure and controversy with sinners.*

Gen. 6: 5 GOD saw that the wickedness of man *was* great in the earth, and *that* every imagination of the thoughts of his heart *was* only evil continually. 6 And it repented the LORD that he had made man on the earth, and it grieved him at his heart.

Num. 32: 14 Behold, ye are risen up in your fathers' stead, an increase of sinful men, to augment yet the fierce anger of the LORD toward Israel.

Dt. 25: 16 All that do such things, *and* all that do unrighteously, *are* an abomination unto the LORD thy God.

Ps. 7: 11 God judgeth the righteous, and God is angry *with the wicked* every day. 12 If he turn not, he will whet his sword; he hath bent his bow, and made it ready. 13 He hath also prepared for him the instruments of death; he ordaineth his arrow against the persecutors. — 10: 3 The wicked boasteth of his heart's desire, and blesseth the covetous *whom* the LORD abhorreth. — 11: 5 The LORD trieth the righteous: but the wicked and him that loveth violence his soul hateth. — 78: 40 How oft did they provoke him in the wilderness, *and* grieve him in the desert? — 95: 8 Harden not your heart, as in the provocation, *and* as *in* the day of temptation in the wilderness: 9 When your fathers tempted me, proved me, and saw my work. 10 Forty years long was I grieved with *this* generation.

Pr. 11: 20 They that are of a froward heart *are* abomination to the LORD: but *such as are* upright in *their* way *are* his delight. — 15: 9 The way of the wicked *is* an abomination unto the LORD; but he loveth him that followeth after righteousness:

26 The thoughts of the wicked *are* an abomination to the LORD : but *the words* of the pure *are* pleasant words.

Jer. 12: 8 Mine heritage is unto me as a lion in the forest; it crieth out against me; therefore have I hated it.

Hos. 7: 2 They consider not in their hearts, *that* I remember all their wickedness : now their own doings have beset them about; they are before my face — 9: 15 All their wickedness *is* in Gilgal: for there I hated them : for the wickedness of their doings I will drive them out of mine house, I will love them no more: all their princes *are* revolters. — 12: 2 The LORD hath also a controversy with Judah, and will punish Jacob according to his ways: according to his doings will he recompense him. — 13: 7 I will be unto them as a lion : as a leopard by the way will I observe *them*. 8 I will meet them as a bear *that is* bereaved *of her whelps,* and will rend the caul of their heart, and there will I devour them like a lion.

Nah. 1: 6 Who can stand before his indignation? and who can abide in the fierceness of his anger? his fury is poured out like fire, and the rocks are thrown down by him.

Mic. 6: 2 Hear ye, O mountains, the LORD's controversy, and ye strong foundations of the earth : for the LORD hath a controversy with his people, and he will plead with Israel.

Mk. 3: 5 When he had looked round about on them with anger, being grieved for the hardness of their hearts, he saith unto the man; Stretch forth thine hand.

Heb. 3: 17 With whom was he grieved forty years ? *was it* not with them that had sinned, whose carcasses fell in the wilderness? 18 And to whom sware he that they should not enter into his rest, but to them that believed not ?

Rev. 6: 16 And said to the mountains and rocks, Fall on us, and hide us from the face of him that sitteth on the throne, and from the wrath of the Lamb : 17 For the great day of his wrath is come, and who shall be able to stand ?

[See 208, 236, 362, 418, and Punishment, Future.]

231. *Impartiality of God.*

Gen. 18: 25 That be far from thee to do after this manner to slay the righteous with the wicked ; and that the righteous should be as the wicked, that be far from thee : Shall not the Judge of all the earth do right ?

Dt. 10: 17 For the LORD your God *is* God of gods, and Lord of lords, a great God, a mighty and a terrible, which regardeth not persons, nor taketh reward : 18 He doth execute the judgment of the fatherless and widow, and loveth the stranger, in giving him food and raiment.

2 Ch. 19: 7 Wherefore now let the fear of the LORD be upon you : take heed and do *it :* for *there is* no iniquity with the LORD our God, nor respect of persons, nor taking of gifts.

Ezk. 18: 25 Yet ye say, The way of the LORD is not equal. Hear now, O house of Israel ; Is not my way equal? are not your ways unequal?

Ac. 10: 34 Then Peter opened *his* mouth, and said, Of a truth I perceive that God is no respecter of persons.

Rom. 2: 11 There is no respect of persons with God.

Ep. 6: 9 And ye, masters, do the same things unto them, forbearing threatening : knowing that your Master also is in heaven ; neither is there respect of persons with him.

1 Pet. 1: 17 And if ye call on the Father, who without respect of persons judgeth according to every man's work, pass the time of your sojourning *here* in fear. [See 556.]

232. *Justice and righteousness of God.*

2 Ch. 19: 7 Wherefore now let the fear of the LORD be upon you : take heed and do *it :* for *there is* no iniquity with the LORD our God, nor respect of persons, nor taking of gifts.

Job 8: 3 Doth God pervert judgment? or doth the Almighty pervert justice? — 34: 12 Yea, surely, God will not do wickedly, neither will the Almighty pervert judgment. — 37: 23 *Touching* the Almighty, we cannot find him out : *he is* excellent in power, and in judgment, and in plenty of justice ; he will not afflict.

Ps. 33: 4 The word of the LORD *is* right ; and all his works *are done* in truth. 5 He loveth righteousness and judgment. — 48: 10 Thy right hand is full of righteousness. — 92: 15 To show that the LORD *is* upright : *he is* my rock, and *there is* no unrighteousness in him. — 97: 2 Clouds and darkness *are* round about him : righteousness and judgment *are* the habitation of his throne. — 111: 3 His work *is* honorable and glorious, and his righteousness endureth for ever. — 119: 137 Righteous *art* thou, O LORD, and upright *are* thy judgments. 138 Thy testimonies *that* thou hast commanded *are* righteous and very faithful. 142 Thy righteousness *is* an everlasting righteousness, and thy law *is* the truth. — 145: 17 The LORD *is* righteous in all his ways, and holy in all his works.

Jer. 9: 24 Let him that glorieth, glory in this, that he understandeth and knoweth me, that I *am* the LORD which exercise loving-kindness, judgment, and righteousness, in the earth : for in these *things* I delight, saith the LORD.

Rev. 15: 3 They sing the song of Moses, the servant of God, and the song of the Lamb, saying, Great and marvellous *are* thy works, Lord God Almighty; just and true *are* thy ways, thou King of saints. 4 Who shall not fear thee, O Lord, and glorify thy name? for *thou* only *art* holy : for all nations shall come and worship before thee; for thy judgments are made manifest. [See 236.]

233. *Mercy, grace, and kindness of God.*

Ex. 34: 6 The LORD passed by before him, and proclaimed, The LORD, the LORD God, merciful and gracious, long-suffering and abundant in goodness and truth, 7 Keeping mercy for thousands, forgiving iniquity and transgression and sin, and that will by no means clear *the guilty.*

Num. 14: 18 The LORD *is* long-suffering, and of great mercy, forgiving iniquity and transgression, and by no means clearing *the guilty.*

Dt. 4: 31 (The LORD thy God *is* a merciful God;) he will not forsake thee, neither destroy thee, nor forget the covenant of thy fathers, which he sware unto them.

Ps. 25: 6 Remember, O LORD, thy tender mercies and thy loving-kindnesses; for they *have been* ever of old. — 36: 7 How excellent *is* thy loving kindness, O God! therefore the children of men put their trust under the shadow of thy wings. — 86: 5 Thou, LORD, *art* good, and ready to forgive; and plenteous in mercy unto all them that call upon thee. — 100: 5 The LORD *is* good; his mercy *is* everlasting; and his truth *endureth* to all generations. — 103: 8 The LORD *is* merciful and gracious, slow to anger and plenteous in mercy. 9 He will not always chide; neither will he keep *his anger* for ever. 10 He hath not dealt with us after our sins; nor rewarded us according to our iniquities. — 106: 44 He regarded their affliction when he heard their cry: 45 And he remembered for them his covenant, and repented according to the multitude of his mercies. — 116: 5 Gracious *is* the LORD, and righteous; yea, our God *is* merciful. — 119: 64 The earth, O LORD, *is* full of thy mercy. — 138: 8 The LORD will perfect *that which* concerneth me: thy mercy, O LORD, *endureth* for ever: forsake not the works of thine own hands.

Dan. 9: 9 To the Lord our God *belong* mercies and forgivenesses; though we have rebelled against him.

Joel 2: 13 Rend your heart, and not your garments, and turn unto the LORD your God: for he *is* gracious and merciful, slow to anger, and of great kindness, and repenteth him of the evil.

Jonah 4: 2 I fled before unto Tarshish: for I knew that thou *art* a gracious God, and merciful, slow to anger, and of great kindness, and repentest thee of the evil.

Lk. 6: 35 Love ye your enemies, and do good, and lend, hoping for nothing again; and your reward shall be great, and ye shall be the children of the Highest: for he is kind unto the unthankful and *to* the evil. 36 Be ye therefore merciful, as your Father also is merciful.

Ep. 2: 4 God, who is rich in mercy, for his great love wherewith he loved us, 5 Even when we were dead in sins, hath quickened us together with Christ; (by grace ye are saved;) 6 And hath raised *us* up together, and made *us* sit together in heavenly *places*, in Christ Jesus: 7 That in the ages to come he might show the exceeding riches of his grace in *his* kindness toward us, through Christ Jesus.

[See 225, 228, 372, 585, 672.]

234. Sovereignty, freedom, and independence of God.

Job 23: 13 He *is* in one *mind*, and who can turn him? and *what* his soul desireth, even that he doeth. — 33: 13 Why dost thou strive against him? for he giveth not account of any of his matters.

Ps. 115: 3 Our God *is* in the heavens; he hath done whatsoever he pleased. — 135: 6 Whatsoever the LORD pleased, *that* did he in heaven, and in earth, in the seas, and all deep places.

Is. 55: 10 As the rain cometh down, and the snow from heaven, and returneth not thither, but watereth the earth, and maketh it bring forth and bud, that it may give seed to the sower, and bread to the eater: 11 So shall my word be that goeth forth out of my mouth: it shall not return unto me void, but it shall accomplish that which I please, and it shall prosper *in the thing* whereto I sent it.

Dan. 4: 35 All the inhabitants of the earth *are* reputed as nothing: and he doeth according to his will in the army of heaven, and *among* the inhabitants of the earth: and none can stay his hand, or say unto him, What doest thou?

Mat. 11: 25 At that time Jesus answered and said, I thank thee, O Father, Lord of heaven and earth, because thou hast hid these things from the wise and prudent, and hast revealed them unto babes. 26 Even so, Father, for so it seemed good in thy sight. — 20: 12 These last have wrought *but* one hour, and thou hast made them equal unto us, which have borne the burden and heat of the day. 13 But he answered one of them, and said, Friend, I do thee no wrong: didst thou not agree with me for a penny? 14 Take *that* thine *is* and go thy way: I will give unto this last, even as unto thee. 15 Is it not lawful for me to do what I will with mine own? is thine eye evil because I am good? 16 So the last shall be first, and the first last: for many be called, but few chosen.

Rom. 9: 15 He saith to Moses, I will have mercy on whom I will have mercy, and I will have compassion on whom I will have compassion. 16 So then, *it is* not of him that willeth, nor of him that runneth, but of God that sheweth mercy. 17 For the scripture saith unto Pharaoh, Even for this same purpose have I raised thee up, that I might shew my power in thee, and that my name might be declared throughout all the earth. 18 Therefore hath he mercy on whom he will *have mercy*, and whom he will he hardeneth.

Ep. 1: 11 Who worketh all things after the counsel of his own will.

Ph. 2: 13 For it is God which worketh in you both to will and to do of *his* good pleasure. [See 240–8.]

235. *Truth of God.*

Ex. 34: 6 The LORD passed by before him, and proclaimed, The LORD, the LORD God, merciful and gracious, long-suffering, and abundant in goodness and truth.

Num. 23: 19 God *is* not a man, that he should lie; neither the son of man, that he should repent: hath he said, and shall he not do *it?* or hath he spoken, and shall he not make it good?

Dt. 32: 4 *He is* the Rock, his work *is* perfect: for all his ways *are* judgment: a God of truth and without iniquity, just and right *is* he.

1 S. 15: 29 The Strength of Israel will not lie nor repent: for he *is* not a man, that he should repent.

Ps. 19: 9 The fear of the LORD *is* clean, enduring for ever: the judgments of the LORD *are* true *and* righteous altogether. — 89: 14 Justice and judgment *are* the habitation of thy throne: mercy and truth shall go before thy face. — 100: 5 The LORD *is* good; his mercy *is* everlasting; and his truth *endureth* to all generations. — 119: 142 Thy righteousness *is* an everlasting righteousness, and thy law *is* the truth. — 146: 6 Which keepeth truth for ever.

Is. 25: 1 Thy counsels of old *are* faithfulness *and* truth.

Dan. 4: 37 I Nebuchadnezzar praise and extol and honor the King of heaven, all of whose works *are* truth, and his ways judgment.

Rev. 15: 3 They sing the song of Moses, the servant of God,

and the song of the Lamb, saying, Great and marvellous *are* thy works, Lord God Almighty; just and true *are* thy ways, thou King of saints. [See 226.]

236. *Vindicative justice of God.*

Ex. 15: 3 The Lord *is* a man of war: the Lord *is* his name.

Dt. 4: 24 For the LORD thy God *is* a consuming fire, *even* a jealous God. — 32: 35 To me *belongeth* vengeance, and recompense; their foot shall slide in *due* time: for the day of their calamity *is* at hand, and the things that shall come upon them make haste. 39 See now that I, *even* I, *am* he, and *there is* no god with me: I kill, and I make alive: I wound, and I heal: neither *is there any* that can deliver out of my hand. 40 For I lift up my hand to heaven, and say, I live for ever. 41 If I whet my glittering sword, and mine hand take hold on judg-ment; I will render vengeance to mine enemies, and will reward them that hate me. 42 I will make mine arrows drunk with blood, and my sword shall devour flesh; *and that* with the blood of the slain and of the captives from the beginning of revenges upon the enemy.

Ps. 78: 49 He cast upon them the fierceness of his anger, wrath, and indignation, and trouble, by sending evil angels *among them.* 50 He made a way to his anger; he spared not their soul from death, but gave their life over to the pestilence; 51 And smote all the first-born in Egypt; the chief of *their* strength, in the tabernacles of Ham.—97: 3 A fire goeth before him, and burneth up his enemies round about.

Is. 30: 27 Behold, the name of the LORD cometh from far, burning *with* his anger, and the burden *thereof is* heavy: his lips are full of indignation, and his tongue as a devouring fire. — 35: 4 Say to them *that are* of a fearful heart, Be strong, fear not: behold, your God will come *with* vengeance, *even* God *with* a recompense; he will come and save you. — 59: 17 He put on righteousness as a breastplate, and an helmet of salvation upon his head; and he put on the garments of vengeance *for* clothing, and was clad with zeal as a cloak. 18 According to *their* deeds, accordingly he will repay, fury to his adversaries, recompense to his enemies; to the islands he will repay recompense. 19 So shall they fear the name of the LORD from the west, and his glory from the rising of the sun. — 66: 14 The hand of the LORD shall be known toward his servants, and *his* indignation toward his enemies. 15 For behold the LORD will come with fire, and with his chariots like a whirlwind, to render his anger with fury, and his rebuke with flames of fire.

Vindicative Justice amiable.

Lam. 2: 4 He hath bent his bow like an enemy: he stood with his right hand as an adversary, and slew all *that* were pleasant to the eye in the tabernacle of the daughter of Zion: he poured out his fury like fire.

Ezk. 7: 8 Now will I shortly pour out my fury upon thee, and accomplish mine anger upon thee: and I will judge thee according to thy ways, and will recompense thee for all thine abominations.

Nah. 1: 2 God *is* jealous, and the LORD revengeth: the LORD revengeth, and *is* furious: the LORD will take vengeance on his adversaries, and he reserveth *wrath* for his enemies. 6 Who can stand before his indignation? and who can abide in the fierceness of his anger? his fury is poured out like fire, and the rocks are thrown down by him.

Rom. 3: 5 *Is* God unrighteous, who taketh vengeance? (I speak as a man,) 6 God forbid: for then how shall God judge the world? — 11: 22 Behold therefore the goodness and severity of God: on them which fell, severity: but toward thee, goodness, if thou continue in *his* goodness: otherwise thou also shalt be cut off. — 12: 19 Dearly beloved, avenge not yourselves, but *rather* give place unto wrath: for it is written, Vengeance *is* mine; I will repay, saith the Lord.

2 Cor. 5: 11 Knowing therefore the terror of the Lord, we persuade men; but we are made manifest unto God; and I trust also are made manifest in your consciences.

2 Th. 1: 6 Seeing *it is* a righteous thing with God to recompense tribulation to them that trouble you; 7 And to you, who are troubled, rest with us, when the Lord Jesus shall be revealed from heaven with his mighty angels, 8 In flaming fire taking vengeance on them that know not God, and that obey not the gospel of our Lord Jesus Christ.

Heb. 12: 29 Our God *is* a consuming fire. [Ps. 18: 6—14.] [See 230, 232, and Punishment future.]

237. *God's vindicative justice amiable, desirable and comforting.*

Dt. 32: 43 Rejoice, O ye nations, *with* his people: for he will avenge the blood of his servants, and will render vengeance to his adversaries, and will be merciful unto his land, *and to* his people.

Ps. 28: 4 Give them according to their deeds, and according to the wickedness of their endeavors: give them after the work of their hands; render to them their desert. 5 Because they regard not the works of the LORD, nor the operation of his hands. — 48: 11 Let mount Zion rejoice, let the daughters of Judah be glad, because of thy judgments. — 58: 9 He shall take them away as with a whirlwind, both living and in *his* wrath. 10 The righteous shall rejoice when he seeth the vengeance: he shall wash his feet in the blood of the wicked.—97: 8 Zion heard, and was glad; and the daughters of Judah rejoiced because of thy judgments, O LORD.—136: 1 O give thanks unto the LORD; for *he is* good: for his mercy *endureth* for ever. 10 To him that smote Egypt in their first-born: for his mercy *endureth* for ever: 11 And brought out Israel from among them: for his mercy *endureth* for ever. [See the whole Psalm.]

Jer. 11: 19 I *was* like a lamb *or* an ox *that* is brought to the slaughter; and I knew not that they had devised devices against me, *saying*, Let us destroy the tree with the fruit thereof, and let us cut him off from the land of the living, that his name may be no more remembered. 20 But, O LORD of hosts, that judgest righteously, that triest the reins and the heart, let me see thy vengeance on them: for unto thee have I revealed my cause.

Ezk. 5: 13 Thus shall mine anger be accomplished, and I will cause my fury to rest upon them, and I will be comforted: and they shall know that I the LORD have spoken *it* in my zeal, when I have accomplished my fury in them.

[See 88, 571.]

238. *Zeal of God.*

Dt. 7: 10 He will not be slack to him that hateth him, he will repay him to his face.

Is. 9: 7 Of the increase of *his* government and peace *there shall be* no end, upon the throne of David, and upon his kingdom to order it, and to establish it with judgment and with justice from henceforth even for ever. The zeal of the LORD of hosts will perform this.—40: 28 Hast thou not known? hast thou not heard, *that* the everlasting God, the LORD, the Creator of the ends of the earth, fainteth not, neither is weary?—59: 17 He put on righteousness as a breastplate, and a helmet of salvation upon his head; and he put on the garments of vengeance *for* clothing, and was clad with zeal as a cloak.

Ezk. 5: 13 Thus shall mine anger be accomplished, and I will cause my fury to rest upon them, and I will be comforted: and they shall know that I the LORD have spoken *it* in my zeal, when I have accomplished my fury in them.

2 Pet. 3: 9 The Lord is not slack concerning his promise, as some men count slackness. [See 208.]

PREROGATIVES, OR RIGHTS OF GOD.

239. *God's right of property in his creatures.*

1 Ch. 29: 11 All *that is* in the heaven and in the earth *is thine.*

Ps. 24: 1 The earth *is* the LORD's, and the fulness thereof; the world, and they that dwell therein. — 50: 10 Every beast of the forest *is* mine, *and* the cattle upon a thousand hills. 11 I know all the fowls of the mountains: and the wild beasts of the field *are* mine. 12 If I were hungry, I would not tell thee: for the world *is* mine and the fulness thereof.— 95: 5 The sea *is* his, and he made it: and his hands formed the dry *land.* 6 O come, let us worship and bow down: let us kneel before the LORD our maker. 7 For he *is* our God; and we *are* the people of his pasture, and the sheep of his hand. — 100: 3 The Lord he *is* God: *it is* he *that* hath made us, and not we ourselves; *we are* his people, and the sheep of his pasture.

Ezk. 18: 4 Behold, all souls are mine; as the soul of the father, so also the soul of the son is mine.

Rom. 14: 8 Whether we live, therefore, or die, we are the Lord's.

240. *God's right to establish and control natural law.*

Job 38: 33 Knowest thou the ordinances of heaven?

Ps. 119: 90 Thou hast established the earth, and it abideth. 91 They continue this day according to thine ordinances.

Pr. 3: 19 The LORD by wisdom hath founded the earth; by understanding hath he established the heavens.

Jer. 31: 35 Thus saith the LORD, which giveth the sun for a light by day, *and* the ordinances of the moon and of the stars for a light by night, which divideth the sea when the waves thereof roar; The LORD of hosts *is* his name.— 33: 25 Thus saith the LORD; If my covenant *be* not with day and night, *and if* I have not appointed the ordinances of heaven and earth; 26 Then will I cast away the seed of Jacob.

241. *God's right to give supreme moral law.*

Ex. 20: 2 I *am* the LORD thy God, which have brought thee out of the land of Egypt, out of the house of bondage. 3 Thou shalt have no other gods before me.

1 Ch. 29: 11 Thine *is* the kingdom, O LORD, and thou art exalted as head above all.

Mat. 4: 10 Then saith Jesus unto him, Get thee hence, Satan: for it is written, Thou shalt worship the Lord thy God, and him only shalt thou serve.—22: 37 Jesus said unto him, Thou shalt love the Lord thy God with all thy heart, and with all thy soul, and with, all thy mind.   38 This is the first and great commandment.   [See 280.]

242. *God's right to regenerate, or not — to give or withhold success to means — and to form, turn and control the hearts of men.*

Dt. 29: 4 The LORD hath not given you an heart to perceive, and eyes to see, and ears to hear, unto this day.

1 S. 26: 19 Now therefore, I pray thee, let my lord the king hear the words of his servant.   If the LORD have stirred thee up against me, let him accept an offering: but if *they be* the children of men, cursed *be* they before the LORD; for they have driven me out this day from abiding in the inheritance of the LORD, saying, Go serve other gods.

Ps. 33: 14 From the place of his habitation he looketh upon all the inhabitants of the earth.   15 He fashioneth their hearts alike; he considereth all their works.

Is. 45: 9 Wo unto him that striveth with his Maker! *Let* the potsherd *strive* with the potsherds of the earth.   Shall the clay say to him that fashioneth it, What makest thou? or thy work, He hath no hands?

Mat. 13: 10 The disciples came, and said unto him, Why speakest thou unto them in parables?   11 He answered and said unto them, Because it is given unto you to know the mysteries of the kingdom of heaven, but to them it is not given.— 20: 15 Is it not lawful for me to do what I will with mine own? is thine eye evil because I am good?   16 So the last shall be first, and the first last: for many be called, but few chosen.

Rom. 9: 20 Nay but, O man, who art thou that repliest against God?   Shall the thing formed say to him that formed *it*, Why hast thou made me thus?   21 Hath not the potter power over the clay, of the same lump to make one vessel unto honor, and another unto dishonor?   22 *What* if God, willing to shew *his* wrath, and to. make his power known, endured with much long-suffering the vessels of wrath fitted to destruction: 23 And that he might make known the riches of his glory on the vessels of mercy, which he had afore prepared unto glory.

2 Tim. 2: 25 In meekness instructing those that oppose themselves: if God peradventure will give them repentance to the acknowledging of the truth.

[See 234, 264, 435.]

243. *God's right to try us by tempters, temptations, and stumbling-blocks.*

Dt. 13: 1 If there arise among you a prophet, or a dreamer of dreams, and giveth thee a sign or a wonder, 2 And the sign or the wonder come to pass, whereof he spake unto thee, saying, Let us go after other gods, which thou hast not known, and let us serve them; 3 Thou shalt not hearken unto the words of that prophet, or that dreamer of dreams: for the LORD your God proveth you, to know whether ye love the LORD your God with all your heart and with all your soul.

1 K. 22: 20 The LORD said, Who shall persuade Ahab, that he may go up and fall at Ramoth-gilead? And one said on this manner, and another said on that manner. 21 And there came forth a spirit, and stood before the LORD, and said, I will persuade him. 22 And the LORD said unto him, Wherewith? And he said, I will go forth, and I will be a lying spirit in the mouth of all his prophets. And he said, Thou shalt persuade *him*, and prevail also: go forth, and do so. 23 Behold, the LORD hath put a lying spirit in the mouth of all these thy prophets, and the LORD hath spoken evil concerning thee.

Job 2: 6 The LORD said unto Satan, Behold, he *is* in thine hand; but save his life. 7 So went Satan forth from the presence of the LORD, and smote Job with sore boils from the sole of his foot unto his crown.

Jer. 6: 21 Thus saith the LORD, Behold, I will lay stumbling-blocks before this people, and the fathers and the sons together shall fall upon them; the neighbor and his friend shall perish.

Ezk. 3: 20 When a righteous *man* doth turn from his righteousness, and commit iniquity, and I lay a stumbling-block before him, he shall die.

Mat. 4: 1 Then was Jesus led up of the Spirit into the wilderness to be tempted of the devil.

1 Cor. 11: 19 There must be also heresies among you, that they which are approved may be made manifest among you.

244. *God's right to require human life at his pleasure.*

Gen 22: 2 He said, Take now thy son, thine only *son* Isaac, whom thou lovest, and get thee into the land of Moriah; and offer him there as a burnt-offering.

Dt. 20: 16 Of the cities of these people which the LORD thy God doth give thee *for* an inheritance, thou shalt save alive nothing that breatheth: 17 But thou shalt utterly destroy them, *namely*, the Hittites, and the Amorites, the Canaanites, and the Perizzites, the Hivites, and the Jebusites, as the LORD thy God hath commanded thee: 18 That they teach you not to do after all their abominations which they have done unto their gods; so should ye sin against the LORD your God.

1 S. 15: 3 Go and smite Amalek, and utterly destroy all that they have, and spare them not; but slay both man and woman, infant and suckling, ox and sheep, camel and ass.

245. *God's right to appoint rulers and statutes in judgment.*

1 K. 19: 15 The LORD said unto him, Go, return on thy way to the wilderness of Damascus: and when thou comest, anoint Hazael *to be* king over Syria.

2 K. 8: 12 Hazael said, Why weepeth my lord? And he answered, Because I know the evil that thou wilt do unto the children of Israel.

Ezk. 20: 24 Because they had not executed my judgments, but had despised my statutes, and had polluted my Sabbaths, and their eyes were after their fathers' idols. 25 Wherefore I gave them also statutes *that were* not good, and judgments whereby they should not live; 26 And I polluted them in their own gifts, in that they caused to pass through *the fire* all that openeth the womb, that I might make them desolate, to the end that they might know that I *am* the LORD.

Dan. 4: 17 The Most High ruleth in the kingdom of men, and giveth it to whomsoever he will, and setteth up over it the basest of men.

Hos. 13: 11 I gave thee a king in mine anger, and took *him* away in my wrath.

246. *God's right to visit the iniquity of fathers upon children, etc.*

Ex. 20: 5 I the LORD thy God *am* a jealous God, visiting the iniquity of the fathers upon the children unto the third and fourth *generation* of them that hate me: 6 And shewing mercy unto thousands of them that love me, and keep my commandments. [See 497.]

247. *God's right to use men instrumentally.*

1 Ch. 6: 15 Jehozadak went *into captivity,* when the LORD carried away Judah and Jerusalem by the hand of Nebuchadnezzar. [See 265.]

248. *God's right to vindicate himself and servants.*

Dt. 32: 35 To me *belongeth* vengeance, and recompense. [See 558.]

PURPOSES OF GOD.

246. *God has a perfect plan of operations.*

Dt. 32: 4 *He is* the Rock, his work *is* perfect.

Ec. 3: 14 I know that, whatsoever God doeth, it shall be for ever: nothing can be put to it, nor any thing taken from it: and God doeth *it*, that *men* should fear before him. [See 304.]

250. The purposes of God eternal and immutable.

Ps. 33: 11 The counsel of the LORD standeth for ever, the thoughts of his heart to all generations.

Pr. 19: 21 *There are* many devices in a man's heart; nevertheless the counsel of the LORD, that shall stand.

Is. 14: 24 The LORD of hosts hath sworn, saying, Surely as I have thought, so shall it come to pass; and as I have purposed, *so* shall it stand. 27 For the LORD of hosts hath purposed, and who shall disannul *it*? and his hand *is* stretched out, and who shall turn it back? — 46: 9 I *am* God, and *there is* none else; *I am* God, and *there is* none like me, 10 Declaring the end from the beginning, and from ancient times *the things* that are not *yet* done, saying, My counsel shall stand, and I will do all my pleasure.

Ep. 3: 11 According to the eternal purpose which he purposed in Christ Jesus our Lord. [See 217.]

251. The purposes of God universal and particular.

Job 14: 5 Seeing his days *are* determined, the number of his months *are* with thee, thou hast appointed his bounds that he cannot pass.

Is. 14: 26 This *is* the purpose that is purposed upon the whole earth: and this *is* the hand that is stretched out upon all the nations.

Ac. 17: 26 Hath made of one blood all nations of men for to dwell on all the face of the earth, and hath determined the times before appointed, and the bounds of their habitation.

Ep. 1: 11 In whom also we have obtained an inheritance, being predestinated according to the purpose of him who worketh all things after the counsel of his own will. See [307.]

252. Purposes of God include natural and moral evil.

Ac. 2: 23 Him, being delivered by the determinate counsel and foreknowledge of God, ye have taken, and by wicked hands have crucified and slain. — 4: 27 Of a truth against thy holy child Jesus, whom thou hast anointed, both Herod, and

Pontius Pilate, with the Gentiles, and the people of Israel, were gathered together, 28 For to do whatsoever thy hand and thy counsel determined before to be done. — 13: 29 When they had fulfilled all that was written of him, they took *him* down from the tree, and laid *him* in a sepulchre.

1 Pet. 2: 8 A stone of stumbling, and a rock of offence, *even to them* which stumble at the word, being disobedient: whereunto also they were appointed.

Jude 4 There are certain men crept in unawares, who were before of old ordained to this condemnation, ungodly men, turning the grace of our God into lasciviousness, and denying the only Lord God, and our Lord Jesus Christ.

Rev. 17: 17 God hath put in their hearts to fulfil his will, and to agree, and give their kingdom unto the beast, until the words of God shall be fulfilled. [See 3, 264-7.]

253. *National election.*

Dt. 4: 20 The LORD hath taken you, and brought you forth out of the iron furnace, *even* out of Egypt, to be unto him a people of inheritance, as *ye are* this day. — 7: 6 Thou *art* an holy people unto the LORD thy God: the LORD thy God hath chosen thee to be a special people unto himself, above all people that *are* upon the face of the earth. — 32: 9 The LORD's portion *is* his people; Jacob *is* the lot of his inheritance. 10 He found him in a desert land, and in the waste howling wilderness; he led him about, he instructed him, he kept him as the apple of his eye.

Ps. 33: 12 Blessed *is* the nation whose God *is* the LORD; *and* the people *whom* he hath chosen for his own inheritance.

Is. 45: 4 For Jacob my servant's sake, and Israel mine elect, I have even called thee by thy name.

Rom. 3: 1 What advantage then hath the Jew? or what profit *is* there of circumcision? 2 Much every way: chiefly, because unto them were committed the oracles of God. — 9: 4 Who are Israelites; to whom *pertaineth* the adoption, and the glory, and the covenants, and the giving of the law, and the service *of God*, and the promises.

254. *Individual election.*

Mat. 20: 16 So the last shall be first, and the first last: for many be called, but few chosen. — 24: 22 For the elect's sake those days shall be shortened.

Jn. 13: 18 I speak not of you all; I know whom I have chosen. — 15: 16 Ye have not chosen me, but I have chosen you, and ordained you, that ye should go and bring forth fruit, and *that* your fruit should remain. 19 If ye were of the world, the world would love his own; but because ye are not of the world, but I have chosen you out of the world, therefore the world hateth you.

Ac. 13: 48. When the Gentiles heard this, they were glad, and glorified the word of the Lord: and as many as were ordained to eternal life, believed.

Rom. 8: 28 We know that all things work together for good to them that love God, to them who are called according to *his* purpose. 29 For whom he did foreknow, he also did predestinate *to be* conformed to the image of his Son, that he might be the first-born among many brethren. — 9: 10 Not only *this;* but when Rebecca also had conceived by one, *even* by our father Isaac. 11 (For *the children* being not yet born, neither having done any good or evil, that the purpose of God, according to election might stand, not of works, but of him that calleth;) 12 It was said unto her, The elder shall serve the younger. 13 As it is written, Jacob have I loved, but Esau have I hated. 14 What shall we say then? *Is there* unrighteousness with God? God forbid. 15 For he saith to Moses: I will have mercy on whom I will have mercy, and I will have compassion on whom I will have compassion. — 11: 5 Even so then at this present time also there is a remnant according to the election of grace. 7 What then? Israel hath not obtained that which he seeketh for; but the election hath obtained it, and the rest were blinded.

Ep. 1: 4 According as he hath chosen us in him, before the foundation of the world, that we should be holy and without blame before him in love: 5 Having predestinated us unto the adoption of children by Jesus Christ to himself, according to the good pleasure of his will, 6 To the praise of the glory of his grace, wherein he hath made us accepted in the Beloved. 11 In whom also we have obtained an inheritance, being predestinated according to the purpose of him who worketh all things after the counsel of his own will.

. 1 Th. 1: 4 Knowing, brethren beloved, your election of God. — 5: 9 God hath not appointed us to wrath, but to obtain salvation by our Lord Jesus Christ.

2 Th. 2: 13 We are bound to give thinks always to God for you, brethren beloved of the Lord, because God hath from the beginning chosen you to salvation, through sanctification of the Spirit, and belief of the truth.

1 Pet. 1: 2 Elect according to the foreknowledge of God the Father, through sanctification of the Spirit, unto obedience and sprinkling of the blood of Jesus Christ. [See 234, 242, 584.]

255. *Election previous to faith.*

Ep. 1: 2 According as he hath chosen us in him, before the foundation of the world, that we should be holy and without blame before him in love.

Rev. 17: 8 The beast that thou sawest, was, and is not; and shall ascend out of the bottomless pit, and go into perdition: and they that dwell on the earth shall wonder, (whose names were not written in the book of life from the foundation of the world,) when they behold the beast that was, and is not, and yet is.

256. *Purposes respecting the "vessels of wrath"—reprobation.*

Ex. 9: 16 In very deed for this *cause* have I raised thee up, for to shew *in* thee my power; and that my name may be declared throughout all the earth.

Pr. 16: 4 The LORD hath made all *things* for himself: yea even the wicked for the day of evil.

Mk. 4: 11 He said unto them, Unto you it is given to know the mystery of the kingdom of God: but unto them that are without, all *these* things are done in parables: 12 That seeing they may see, and not perceive; and hearing they may hear, and not understand; lest at any time they should be converted, and *their* sins should be forgiven them.

Rom. 9: 17 The Scripture saith unto Pharaoh, Even for this same purpose have I raised the up, that I might shew my power in thee, and that my name might be declared throughout all the earth. 22 *What* if God, willing to shew *his* wrath, and to make his power known, endured with much long-suffering the vessels of wrath fitted to destruction: 23 And that he might make known the riches of his glory on the vessels of mercy, which he had afore prepared unto glory.

2 Cor. 13: 5 Examine yourselves, whether ye be in the faith; prove your own selves. Know ye not your own selves, how that Jesus Christ is in you, except ye be reprobates? 6 But I trust that ye shall know that we are not reprobates.

2 Pet. 2: 12 These, as natural brute beasts, made to be taken and destroyed, speak evil of the things that they understand not; and shall utterly perish in their own corruption.

[See 252, 260, 267, 435, 436, 560.]

257. *God's purposes include means and ends.*

Ac. 27: 22 Now I exhort you to be of good cheer: for there shall be no loss of *any man's* life among you, but of the ship. 23 For there stood by me this night the angel of God, whose I am, and whom I serve, 24 Saying, Fear not, Paul; thou must be brought before Cesar: and lo, God hath given thee all them that sail with thee. 30 And as the shipmen were about to flee out of the ship, when they had let down the boat into the sea, under color as though they would have cast anchors out of the foreship, 31 Paul said to the centurion, and to the soldiers, Except these abide in the ship, ye cannot be saved.

2 Th. 2: 13 We are bound to give thanks always to God for you, brethren beloved of the Lord, because God hath from the beginning chosen you to salvation, through sanctification of the Spirit, and belief of the truth.

1 Pet. 1: 2 Elect according to the foreknowledge of God the Father, through sanctification of the Spirit, unto obedience and sprinkling of the blood of Jesus Christ. [See 17, (3).]

258. *God's purposes encourage the use of means.*

Dan. 9: 2 In the first year of his reign I Daniel understood by books the number of the years, whereof the word of the LORD came to Jeremiah the prophet, that he would accomplish seventy years in the desolations of Jerusalem. And I set my face unto the Lord GOD, to seek by prayer and supplications, with fasting, and sackcloth, and ashes.

Ac. 18: 9 Then spake the Lord to Paul in the night by a vision, Be not afraid, but speak, and hold not thy peace: 10 For I am with thee, and no man shall set on thee, to hurt thee: for I have much people in this city. 11 And he continued *there* a year and six months, teaching the word of God among them. [See 431.]

PROVIDENCE OR AGENCY OF GOD.

259. *Nature and efficacy of God's providence.*

Gen. 1: 3 God said, Let there be light: and there was light.

Ps. 29: 4 The voice of the LORD *is* powerful; the voice of the LORD *is* full of majesty. 5 The voice of the LORD breaketh the cedars; yea, the LORD breaketh the cedars of Lebanon. 6 He maketh them also to skip like a calf; Lebanon and Sirion like a young unicorn. 7 The voice of the LORD divideth the flames of fire. 8 The voice of the LORD shaketh the wilderness; the LORD shaketh the wilderness of Kadesh. 9 The voice of the LORD maketh the hinds to calve. —33: 6 By the word of the LORD were the heavens made; and all the host of them by the breath of his mouth. 8 Let all the earth fear the LORD: let all the inhabitants of the world stand in awe of him. 9 He spake and it was *done;* he commanded, and it stood fast. — 66: 7 He ruleth by his power for ever; his eyes behold the nations: let not the rebellious exalt themselves.

Heb. 11: 3 Through faith we understand that the worlds were framed by the word of God, so that things which are seen were not made of things which do appear. [See 218.]

260. *Particularity and extent of God's providence.*

1 Ch. 29: 12 Both riches and honor *come* of thee, and thou reignest over all; and in thine hand *is* power and might; and in thine hand *it is* to make great, and to give strength unto all.

Ps. 135: 6 Whatsoever the LORD pleased, *that* did he in heaven, and in earth, in the seas, and all deep places. 7 He causeth the vapors to ascend from the ends of the earth: he maketh lightnings for the rain: he bringeth the wind out of his treasuries. — 147: 8 Who covereth the heaven with clouds, who prepareth rain for the earth, who maketh grass to grow upon the mountains. 9 He giveth to the beast his food, *and* to the young ravens which cry. 15 He sendeth forth his commandment *upon* earth: his word runneth very swiftly. 16 He giveth snow like wool: he scattereth the hoar-frost like ashes. 17 He casteth forth his ice like morsels: who can stand before his cold? 18 He sendeth out his word, and melteth them: he causeth his wind to blow, *and* the waters flow.

Pr. 16: 33 The lot is cast into the lap; but the whole disposing thereof *is* of the LORD.

Is. 26: 12 Lord, thou wilt ordain peace for us: for thou also hast wrought all our works in us. — 45: 7 I form the light, and create darkness: I make peace, and create evil: I the LORD do all these *things.*

Jer. 10: 13 When he uttereth his voice, *there is* a multitude of waters in the heavens, and he causeth the vapors to ascend from the ends of the earth: he maketh lightnings with rain, and bringeth forth the wind out of his treasures.

Am. 3: 6 Shall there be evil in a city, and the Lord hath not done *it?*

Mat. 10: 29 Are not two sparrows sold for a farthing? and one of them shall not fall on the ground without your Father. 30 But the very hairs of your head are all numbered.

Rom. 11: 36 For of him, and through him, and to him *are* all things: to whom *be* glory for ever.

1 Cor. 12: 6 There are diversities of operations, but it is the same God, which worketh all in all.

Ep. 1: 11 In whom also we have obtained an inheritance, being predestinated according to the purpose of him who worketh all things after the counsel of his own will.

Ph. 2: 13 It is God which worketh in you both to will and to do of *his* good pleasure.

Heb. 13: 20 The God of peace, that brought again from the dead our Lord Jesus, that great Shepherd of the sheep, through the blood of the everlasting covenant, 21 Make you perfect in every good work, to do his will, working in you that which is well-pleasing in his sight, through Jesus Christ; to whom *be* glory for ever and ever. [See 3, 264—7.]

261. *Providence supplies temporal wants.*

Ps. 104: 14 He causeth the grass to grow for the cattle, and herb for the service of man: that he may bring forth food out of the earth. 21 The young lions roar after their prey, and seek their meat from God. 27 These wait all upon thee; that thou mayest give *them* their meat in due season. 28 *That* thou givest them, they gather: thou openest thy hand, they are filled with good.

Mat. 5: 45 He maketh his sun to rise on the evil and on the good, and sendeth rain on the just and on the unjust. — 6: 26 Behold the fowls of the air: for they sow not, neither do they reap, nor gather into barns; yet your heavenly Father feedeth them. 28 And why take ye thought for raiment? Consider the lilies of the field how they grow; they toil not, neither do they spin; 29 And yet I say unto you, That even Solomon in all his glory was not arrayed like one of these. 30 Wherefore, if God so clothe the grass of the field, which to-day is, and to-morrow is cast into the oven, *shall he* not much more *clothe* you, O ye of little faith?

262. *All creatures dependant upon God's providence.*

Job. 12: 10 In whose hand *is* the soul of every living thing, and the breath of all mankind. [Dan. 5: 23.]

Ps. 22: 29 None can keep alive his own soul. — 87: 7 All my springs *are* in thee.

Jer. 10: 23 O LORD, I know that the way of man *is* not in himself: *it is* not in man that walketh to direct his steps. — 18: 6 Behold, as the clay *is* in the potter's hand, so *are* ye in my hand, O house of Israel.

Jn. 15: 5 Without me ye can do nothing.

Ac. 17: 26 Hath made of one blood all nations of men

for to dwell on all the face of the earth, and hath determined the times before appointed, and the bounds of their habitation; 27 That they should seek the Lord, if haply they might feel after him, and find him, though he be not far from every one of us: 28 For in him we live, and move, and have our being; as certain also of your own poets have said, For we are also his offspring.

2 Cor. 3: 5 Not that we are sufficient of ourselves to think any thing as of ourselves; but our sufficiency *is* of God.

263. *All creatures preserved by God's providence.*

Neh. 9: 6 Thou, *even* thou, *art* LORD alone; thou hast made heaven, the heaven of heavens, with all their host, the earth, and all *things* that *are* therein, the seas, and all that *is* therein, and thou preservest them all.

Job. 7: 20 I have sinned; what shall I do unto thee, O thou Preserver of men? — 10: 12 Thy visitation hath preserved my spirit. — 34: 14 If he set his heart upon man, *if* he gather unto himself his spirit and his breath; 15 All flesh shall perish together, and man shall turn again unto dust.

Ps. 36: 6 O Lord, thou preservest man and beast. — 63: 8 Thy right hand upholdeth me. — 66: 8 O bless our God, ye people, and make the voice of his praise to be heard: 9 Which holdeth our soul in life, and suffereth not our feet to be moved. — 121: 7 The LORD shall preserve thee from all evil: he shall preserve thy soul.

Pr. 24: 12 He that keepeth thy soul, doth *not* he know *it?*

Heb. 1: 3 Upholding all things by the word of his power.

264. *God forms, turns and governs the heart.*

1 Ch. 5: 26 The God of Israel stirred up the spirit of Pul king of Assyria, and the spirit of Tilgath-pilneser king of Assyria, and he carried them away, even the Reubenites, and the Gadites, and the half-tribe of Manasseh.

2 Ch. 18: 31 They compassed about him to fight: but Jehoshaphat cried out, and the LORD helped him; and God moved them *to depart* from him.

Ezra 6: 22 And kept the feast of unleavened bread seven days with joy: for the LORD had made them joyful, and turned the heart of the king of Assyria unto them, to strengthen their hands in the work of the house of God, the God of Israel. — 7: 27 Blessed *be* the LORD God of our fathers, which hath put *such a thing* as this in the king's heart, to beautify the house of the LORD which *is* in Jerusalem.

Pr. 16: 1 The preparations of the heart in man, and the

answer of the tongue, *is* from the Lord. 9 A man's heart deviseth his way : but the Lord directeth his steps.—21: 1 The king's heart *is* in the hand of the LORD, *as* the rivers of water : he turneth it whithersoever he will.

Is. 64: 8 Now, O LORD, thou *art* our Father; we *are* the clay, and thou our potter; and we all *are* the work of thy hand.

Zec. 12: 1 The burden of the word of the LORD for Israel, saith the LORD, which stretcheth forth the heavens, and layeth the foundation of the earth, and formeth the spirit of man within him.

Ac. 16: 14 A certain woman named Lydia, a seller of purple, of the city of Thyatira, which worshipped God, heard *us:* whose heart the Lord opened, that she attended unto the things which were spoken of Paul. [See 242—6.]

265. *God employs men as his instruments.*

2 S. 7: 14 I will be his father, and he shall be my son. If he commit iniquity, I will chasten him with the rod of men, and with the stripes of the children of men.

2 K. 5: 1 Now Naaman, captain of the host of the king of Syria, was a great man with his master, and honorable, because by him the LORD had given deliverance unto Syria.

1 Ch. 6: 15 Jehozadak went *into captivity* when the LORD carried away Judah and Jerusalem by the hand of Nebuchadnezzar.

Job 1: 15 The Sabeans fell *upon them*, and took them away. 17 The Chaldeans made out three bands, and fell upon the camels, and have carried them away, yea, and slain the servants with the edge of the sword. 21 The Lord gave, and the Lord hath taken away; blessed be the name of the Lord.

Ps. 17: 13 Arise, O LORD, disappoint him, cast him down: deliver my soul from the wicked, *which is* thy sword : 14 From men *which are* thy hand, O LORD, from men of the world, *which have* their portion in *this* life.

Is. 10: 5 O Assyrian, the rod of mine anger, and the staff in their hand is mine indignation. 6 I will send him against a hypocritical nation, and against the people of my wrath will I give him a charge; to take the spoil, and to take the prey, and to tread them down like the mire of the streets. 7 Howbeit he meaneth not so; neither doth his heart think so ; but *it is* in his heart to destroy and cut off nations not a few. 12 Wherefore it shall come to pass, *that* when the LORD hath performed his whole work upon mount Zion and on Jerusalem, I will punish the fruit of the stout heart of the king of Assyria, and

the glory of his high looks. 15 Shall the axe boast itself
against him that heweth therewith? or shall the saw magnify
itself against him that shaketh it? as if the rod should shake
itself against them that lift it up, *or* as if the staff should lift
up *itself, as if it were* no wood.—13: 5 They come from a far
country, from the end of heaven, even the LORD, and the
weapons of his indignation, to destroy the whole land.—37: 7
Behold, I will send a blast upon him, and he shall hear a ru-
mor, and return to his own land; and I will cause him to fall
by the sword in his own land.

Jer. 27: 8 It shall come to pass, *that* the nation and kingdom
which will not serve the same Nebuchadnezzar the king of
Babylon, and that will not put their neck under the yoke of
the king of Babylon, that nation will I punish, saith the LORD,
with the sword, and with the famine, and with the pestilence,
until I have consumed them by his hand.—50: 9 For lo, I
will raise and cause to come up against Babylon an assembly
of great nations from the north country: and they shall set
themselves in array against her; from thence she shall be
taken.

Ezk. 25: 14 I will lay my vengeance upon Edom by the
hand of my people Israel.

Hab. 1: 6 For lo, I raise up the Chaldeans, *that* bitter and
hasty nation, which shall march through the breadth of the
land, to possess the dwelling-places *that are* not theirs.   12 O
Lord, thou hast ordained them for judgment: and, O mighty
God, thou hast established them for correction.   [See 278.]

266. *God's control of popular favor and frowns.*

Gen. 39: 21 The LORD was with Joseph, and shewed him
mercy, and gave him favor in the sight of the keeper of the
prison.

Ex. 3: 21 I will give this people favor in the sight of the
Egyptians: and it shall come to pass, then, when ye go, ye
shall not go empty.

Ps. 75: 6 Promotion *cometh* neither from the east, nor from
the west, nor from the south.   7 But God *is* the judge: he
putteth down one, and setteth up another.

Dan. 1: 9 God had brought Daniel into favor and tender
love with the prince of the eunuchs.

Ac. 7: 9 The patriarchs, moved with envy, sold Joseph into
Egypt: but God was with him.   10 And delivered him out of
all his afflictions, and gave him favor and wisdom in the sight
of Pharaoh king of Egypt; and he made him governor over
Egypt, and all his house.

16*

267. *God's providence in moral evils and delusions.*

Ex. 7: 3 I will harden Pharaoh's heart, and multiply my signs and my wonders in the land of Egypt.—9: 12 The Lord hardened the heart of Pharaoh, and he hearkened not unto them; as the Lord had spoken unto Moses.—10: 1 The Lord said unto Moses, Go in unto Pharaoh: for I have hardened his heart, and the heart of his servants; that I might shew these my signs before him.—14: 8 The Lord hardened the heart of Pharaoh king of Egypt, and he pursued after the children of Israel. 17 And I, behold, I will harden the hearts of the Egyptians, and they shall follow them: and I will get me honor upon Pharaoh, and upon all his host.

Dt. 2: 30 Sihon king of Heshbon would not let us pass by him: for the LORD thy God hardened his spirit, and made his heart obstinate, that he might deliver him into thine hand, as *appeareth* this day.

Jos. 11: 19 There was not a city that made peace with the children of Israel, save the Hivites the inhabitants of Gibeon: all *other* they took in battle. 20 For it was of the LORD to harden their hearts, that they should come against Israel in battle, that he might destroy them.

Jud. 7: 22 The Lord set every man's sword against his fellow, even throughout all the host.

2 S. 24: 1 Again the anger of the LORD was kindled against Israel, and he moved David against them to say, Go, number Israel and Judah.

1 K. 22: 23 Behold, the Lord hath put a lying spirit in the mouth of all these thy prophets.

Job 17: 4 Thou hast hid their heart from understanding; therefore shalt thou not exalt *them.*

Ps. 28: 3 Draw me not away with the wicked, and with the workers of iniquity.—105: 25 He turned their heart to hate his people, to deal subtilely with his servants.—119: 36 Incline my heart unto thy testimonies, and not to covetousness. —141: 4 Incline not my heart to *any* evil thing, to practise wicked works with men that work iniquity.

Is. 19: 14 The Lord hath mingled a perverse spirit in the midst thereof.—29: 10 The Lord hath poured out upon you the spirit of deep sleep, and hath closed your eyes: the prophets and your rulers, the seers hath he covered.—44: 18 They have not known nor understood: for he hath shut their eyes, that they cannot see; *and* their hearts, that they cannot understand.—45: 7 I form the light, and create darkness: I make peace, and create evil: I the Lord do all these *things.*—63: 17

Brings Good out of Evil.

O Lord, why hast thou made us to err from thy ways, *and* hardened our heart from thy fear?

Ezk. 14: 9 If the prophet be deceived when he .hath spoken a thing, I the LORD have deceived that prophet, and I will stretch out my hand upon him, and will destroy him from the midst of my people Israel.

Zec. 8: 10 Before these days there was no hire for man, nor any hire for beast; neither *was there any* peace to him that went out or came in because of the affliction : for I set all men every one against his neighbor.

Lk. 10: 21 In that hour Jesus rejoiced in spirit, and said, I thank thee, O Father, Lord of heaven and earth, that thou hast hid these things from the wise and prudent, and hast revealed them unto babes: even so, Father; for so it seemed good in thy sight.

Jn. 12: 39 They could not believe, because that Esaias said again, 40 He hath blinded their eyes, and hardened their heart; that they should not see with *their* eyes, nor understand with *their* heart, and be converted, and I should heal them. 41 These things said Esaias, when he saw his glory, and spake of him.

Rom. 9: 18 Therefore hath he mercy on whom he will *have mercy,* and whom he will he hardeneth.—11: 7 What then? Israel hath not obtained that which he seeketh for; but the election hath obtained it, and the rest were blinded. 8 (According as it is written, God hath given them the spirit of slumber, eyes that they should not see, and ears that they should not hear;) unto this day.

2 Thes. 2: 10 They received not the love of the truth, that they might be saved. 11 And for this cause God shall send them strong delusion, that they should believe a lie: 12 That they all might be damned who believed not the truth, but had pleasure in unrighteousness.

Rev. 17: 17 God hath put in their hearts to fulfil his will, and to agree, and give their kingdom unto the beast, until the words of God shall be fulfilled. [See 252, 256, 435.]

268. *God brings good out of evil — or sin the occasion of good.*

Gen. 45: 5 Be not grieved, nor angry with yourselves, that ye sold me hither: for God did send me before you to preserve life.

Ex. 9: 16 In very deed for this *cause* have I raised thee up, for to shew *in* thee my power; and that my name may be declared throughout all the earth.—10: 1 The LORD said unto Moses, Go in unto Pharaoh: for I have hardened his heart, and the heart of his servants; that I might shew these my signs before him: 2 And that thou mayest tell in the ears of thy son, and of thy son's son, what things I have wrought in Egypt, and my signs which I have done among them; that ye may know how that I *am* the LORD.

Ps. 76: 10 Surely the wrath of man shall praise thee: the remainder of wrath shalt thou restrain.

Mat. 18: 7 Wo unto the world because of offences! for it must needs be that offences come; but wo to that man by whom the offence cometh!

Rom. 3: 5 If our unrighteousness commend the righteousness of God, what shall we say? *Is* God unrighteous who taketh vengeance? (I speak as a man,) 6 God forbid: for then how shall God judge the world? 7 For if the truth of God hath more abounded through my lie unto his glory; why yet am I also judged as a sinner? 8 And not *rather* (as we be slanderously reported, and as some affirm that we say) Let us do evil, that good may come? whose damnation is just.— 5: 20 Where sin abounded, grace did much more abound. —6: 17 God be thanked, that ye were the servants of sin; but ye have obeyed from the heart that form of doctrine which was delivered you.—8: 28 We know that all things work together for good, to them that love God.

1 Cor. 11: 19 There must be also heresies among you, that they which are approved may be made manifest among you.

[See 277.]

269. *God, not the actor, or instigator of sin.*

Jer. 7: 9 Will ye steal, murder, and commit adultery, and swear falsely, and burn incense unto Baal, and walk after other gods whom ye know not; 10 And come and stand before me in this house, which is called by my name, and say, We are delivered to do all these abominations?

1 Cor. 14: 33 God is not *the author* of confusion, but of peace, as in all churches of the saints.

Jam. 1: 13 Let no man say when he is tempted, I am tempted of God: for God cannot be tempted with evil, neither tempteth he any man: 14 But every man is tempted, when he is drawn away of his own lust, and enticed. 15 Then, when lust hath conceived, it bringeth forth sin; and sin, when it is finished, bringeth forth death. 16 Do not err, my beloved brethren. 17 Every good gift and every perfect gift is from above, and cometh down from the Father of lights, with whom is no variableness, neither shadow of turning.—3: 14 If ye have bitter envying and strife in your hearts, glory not, and lie not against the truth. 15 This wisdom descendeth not from above, but *is* earthly, sensual, devilish. 16 For where envying and strife *is*, there *is* confusion and every evil work. 17 But the wisdom that is from above is first pure, then peaceable, gentle, *and* easy to be entreated, full of mercy and good fruits, without partiality, and without hypocrisy.

1 Jn. 2: 16 All that *is* in the world, the lust of the flesh, and the lust of the eyes, and the pride of life, is not of the Father, but is of the world.

270. *God and mankind often have different motives in effecting the same events.*

Gen. 45: 4 Joseph said unto his brethren, Come near to me, I pray you: and they came near: and he said, I *am* Joseph your brother, whom ye sold into Egypt. 5 Now therefore be not grieved, nor angry with yourselves, that ye sold me hither: for God did send me before you to preserve life. 6 For these two years *hath* the famine *been* in the land: and yet *there are* five years, in the which *there shall* neither *be* earing nor harvest.—50: 19 Joseph said unto them, Fear not: for *am* I in the place of God? 20 But as for you, ye thought evil against me; *but* God meant it unto good, to bring to pass, as *it is* this day, to save much people alive.

Is. 10: 5 O Assyrian, the rod of mine anger, and the staff in their hand is mine indignation. 6 I will send him against a hypocritical nation, and against the people of my wrath will I give him a charge, to take the spoil, and to take the prey, and to tread them down like the mire of the streets. 7 Howbeit he meaneth not so, neither doth his heart think so; but *it is* in his heart to destroy and cut off nations not a few. 12 Wherefore it shall come to pass, *that* when the Lord hath performed his whole work upon mount Zion and on Jerusalem, I will punish the fruit of the stout heart of the king of Assyria, and the glory of his high looks.

Mk. 15: 9 Pilate answered them saying, Will ye that I release unto you the King of the Jews? 10 (For he knew that the chief priests had delivered him for envy.)

Jn. 3: 16 God so loved the world, that he gave his only-begotten Son, that whosoever believeth in him, should not perish, but have everlasting life.

Ac. 2: 23 Him, being delivered by the determinate counsel and foreknowledge of God, ye have taken, and by wicked hands have crucified and slain.

271. *Freedom and activity, under the providence of God.*

Ex. 8: 32 Pharaoh hardened his heart at this time also, neither would he let the people go. — 9: 27 And Pharaoh sent and called for Moses and Aaron, and said unto them, I have sinned this time: the LORD *is* righteous, and I and my people *are* wicked. — 10: 16 Pharaoh called for Moses and Aaron in haste; and he said, I have sinned against the LORD your God, and against you. 17 Now therefore forgive, I pray thee, my sin only this once, and entreat the LORD your God that he may take away from me this death only.

Dt. 30: 19 I call heaven and earth to record this day against you, *that* I have set 'before you life and death, blessing and cursing: therefore choose life, that both thou and thy seed may live.

Jos. 24: 15 If it seem evil unto you to serve the Lord, choose you this day whom ye will serve.

2 S. 24: 1 Again the anger of the LORD was kindled against Israel, and he moved David against them to say, Go, number Israel and Judah. 10 And David's heart smote him after that he had numbered the people. And David said unto the LORD, I have sinned greatly in that I have done: and now, I beseech thee, O LORD, take away the iniquity of thy servant; for I have done very foolishly.

Pr. 1: 29 They hated knowledge, and did not choose the fear of the LORD: 30. They would none of my counsel: they despised all my reproof. 31 Therefore shall they eat of the fruit of their own way, and be filled with their own devices. — 16: 9 A man's heart deviseth his way: but the LORD directeth his steps. — 23: 26 My son, give me thy heart.

Song 1: 4 Draw me, we will run after thee.

Is. 66: 3 Yea, they have chosen their own ways, and their soul delighteth in their abominations.

Hos. 13: 9 O Israel, thou hast destroyed thyself.

Mat. 13: 15 For, this people's heart is waxed gross, and *their* ears are dull of hearing, and their eyes they have closed. — 18: 7 Wo unto the world because of offences! for it must needs be that offences come; but wo to that man by whom the offence cometh!

Lk. 22: 22 Truly the Son of man goeth as it was determined: but wo unto that man by whom he is betrayed!

Jn. 5: 40 Ye will not come to me, that ye might have life.

Ac. 4: 27 Of a truth against thy holy child Jesus, whom thou hast anointed, both Herod, and Pontius Pilate, with the Gentiles, and the people of Israel, were gathered together,

28 For to do whatsoever thy hand and thy counsel determined before to be done.

Rom. 2: 15 (Which shew the work of the law written in their hearts, their conscience also bearing witness, and *their* thoughts the meanwhile accusing, or else excusing one another.)

Ph. 2: 12 Work out your own salvation with fear and trembling: 13 For it is God which worketh in you both to will and to do of *his* good pleasure. [See 128, 329, 373, 556, 600-1.]

272. *Objections against God's providential government.*

Ezk. 33: 20 Yet ye say, The way of the LORD is not equal. O ye house of Israel, I will judge you every one after his ways.

Mat. 25: 24 Then he which had received the one talent came, and said, Lord, I knew thee that thou art an hard man, reaping where thou hast not sown, and gathering where thou hast not strewed: 25 And I was afraid, and went and hid thy talent in the earth: lo, *there* thou hast *that is* thine.

Rom. 3: 7 If the truth of God hath more abounded through my lie unto his glory; why yet am I also judged as a sinner? 8 And not *rather* (as we be slanderously reported, and as some affirm that we say) Let us do evil, that good may come? whose damnation is just.—9: 19 Thou wilt say then unto me, Why doth he yet find fault? for who hath resisted his will? 20 Nay, but, O man, who art thou that repliest against God? Shall the thing formed say to him that formed *it*, Why hast thou made me thus? 21 Hath not the potter power over the clay, of the same lump to make one vessel unto honor, and another unto dishonor? [See 373, 695, 706.]

273. *Objectors against Providence reproved.*

Job 40: 2 Shall he that contendeth with the Almighty instruct *him*? he that reproveth God, let him answer it.

Is. 45: 9 Wo unto him that striveth with his Maker! *Let* the potsherd *strive* with the potsherds of the earth. Shall the clay say to him that fashioneth it, What makest thou? or thy work, He hath no hands? 10 Wo unto him that saith to *his* father, What begettest thou? or to the woman, What hast thou brought forth?

Mat. 20: 15 Is it not lawful for me to do what I will with mine own? Is thine eye evil because I am good?

Lk. 19: 27 Those mine enemies, which would not that I should reign over them, bring hither, and slay *them* before me.

Rom. 9: 20 Nay but, O man, who art thou that repliest against God? Shall the thing formed say to him that formed *it*, Why

Wonderful ; and incomprehensible.

hast thou made me thus ? 21 Hath not the potter power over the clay, of the same lump to make one vessel unto honor, and another unto dishonor?

274. *The works and ways of Providence wonderful.*

Ex. 15: 11 Who *is* like unto thee, O LORD, among the gods? who *is* like thee, glorious in holiness, fearful *in* praises, doing wonders?

Dt. 4: 32 Ask now of the days that are past, which were before thee, since the day that God created man upon the earth, and *ask* from the one side of heaven unto the other, whether there hath been *any such thing* as this great thing *is*, or hath been heard like it? 33 Did *ever* people hear the voice of God speaking out of the midst of the fire, as thou hast heard, and live? 34 Or hath God assayed to go *and* take him a nation from the midst of *another* nation, by temptations, by signs, and by wonders, and by war, and by a mighty hand, and by a stretched-out arm, and by great terrors, according to all that the LORD your God did for you in Egypt before your eyes?

Job 5: 8 I would seek unto God, and unto God would I commit my cause : 9 Which doeth great things and unsearchable, marvellous things without number.

Ps. 77: 11 I will remember the works of the LORD : surely I will remember thy wonders of old. 12 I will meditate also of all thy work, and talk of thy doings. 13 Thy way, O God, *is* in the sanctuary : who *is* so great a God as *our* God! 14 Thou *art* the God that doest wonders : thou hast declared thy strength among the people.

Dan. 4: 3 How great *are* his signs! and how mighty *are* his wonders! his kingdom *is* an everlasting kingdom, and his dominion *is* from generation to generation.

275. *The Providence of God incomprehensible.*

Ps. 36: 6 Thy righteousness *is* like the great mountains; thy judgments *are* a great deep : O LORD, thou preservest man and beast. — 77: 19 Thy way *is* in the sea, and thy path in the great waters, and thy footsteps are not known. — 97: 2 Clouds and darkness *are* round about him : righteousness and judgment *are* the habitation of his throne.

Pr. 25: 2 *It is* the glory of God to conceal a thing : but the honor of kings *is* to search out a matter.

Ec. 3: 11 He hath made every *thing* beautiful in his time : also he hath set the world in their heart, so that no man can find out the work that God maketh from the beginning to the end.

Rom. 11: 33 O the depth of the riches both of the wisdom

His Revelations make men know Him.

and knowledge of God! how unsearchable *are* his judgments, and his ways past finding out! 34 For who hath known the mind of the Lord? or who hath been his counsellor? 35 Or who hath first given to him, and it shall be recompensed unto him again? 36 For of him, and through him, *and* to him *are* all things: to whom *be* glory for ever. [See 214, 222.]

276. *Revelations and wonders of Providence make men know the Lord.*

Ex. 8: 22 I will sever in that day the land of Goshen, in which my people dwell, that no swarms *of flies* shall be there; to the end thou mayest know that I *am* the LORD in the midst of the earth. — 9: 16 In very deed for this *cause* have I raised thee up, for to shew *in* thee my power; and that my name may be declared throughout all the earth.

Dt. 4: 34 Or hath God assayed to go *and* take him a nation from the midst of *another* nation, by temptations, by signs, and by wonders, and by war, and by a mighty hand, and by a stretched out-arm, and by great terrors, according to all that the LORD your God did for you in Egypt before your eyes? 35 Unto thee it was shewed, that thou mightest know that the LORD he is God: *there is* none else beside him. 36 Out of heaven he made thee to hear his voice, that he might instruct thee: and upon earth he shewed thee his great fire; and thou heardest his words out of the midst of the fire. 37 And because he loved thy fathers, therefore he chose their seed after them, and brought thee out in his sight with his mighty power out of Egypt; 38 To drive out nations from before thee, greater and mightier than thou *art*, to bring thee in, to give thee their land *for* an inheritance, as *it is* this day. 39 Know therefore this day, and consider *it* in thine heart, that the LORD he *is* God in heaven above, and upon the earth beneath: *there is* none else.

Jos. 4: 23 The LORD your God dried up the waters of Jordan from before you, until ye were passed over, as the LORD your God did to the Red sea, which he dried up from before us, until we were gone over: 24 That all the people of the earth might know the hand of the LORD, that it *is* mighty, that ye might fear the LORD your God for ever.

1 K. 18: 37 Hear me, O LORD, hear me, that this people may know that thou *art* the LORD God, and *that* thou hast turned their heart back again. 38 Then the fire of the LORD fell, and consumed the burnt sacrifice, and the wood, and the stones, and the dust, and licked up the water that *was* in the trench. 39 And when all the people saw *it*, they fell on their faces: and they said, The LORD he *is* the God; the LORD, he *is* the God.

17

Will glorify him — is desirable, etc.

Ezk. 25: 7 Behold, therefore I will stretch out mine hand upon thee, and will deliver thee for a spoil to the heathen; and I will cut thee off from the people, and I will cause thee to perish out of the countries: I will destroy thee; and thou shalt know that I *am* the LORD.

Dan. 4: 25 That they shall drive thee from men, and thy dwelling shall be with the beasts of the field, and they shall make thee to eat grass as oxen, and they shall wet thee with the dew of heaven, and seven times shall pass over thee, till thou know that the Most High ruleth in the kingdom of men, and giveth it to whomsoever he will. [See 4, 207, 570.]

277. God will be glorified by all his works — Satan defeated.

Num. 14: 20 The LORD said, I have pardoned according to thy word: 21 But *as* truly *as* I live, all the earth shall be filled with the glory of the LORD.

Ps. 46: 10 Be still, and know that I *am* God: I will be exalted among the heathen, I will be exalted in the earth. — 86: 9 All nations whom thou hast made shall come and worship before thee, O LORD; and shall glorify thy name. — 104: 31 The glory of the LORD shall endure for ever: the LORD shall rejoice in his works. — 145: 10 All thy works shall praise thee, O LORD; and thy saints shall bless thee. 11 They shall speak of the glory of thy kingdom, and talk of thy power; 12 To make known to the sons of men his mighty acts, and the glorious majesty of his kingdom.

Lk. 10: 18 He said unto them, I beheld Satan as lightning fall from heaven.

1 Jn. 3: 8 For this purpose the Son of God was manifested, that he might destroy the works of the devil. [See 209, 268, 587.]

278. The providential government of God desirable, and a foundation for hope, joy, and submission.

1 S. 3: 18 It *is* the Lord: let him do what seemeth him good.

2 S. 16: 10 The king said, What have I to do with you, ye sons of Zeruiah? so let him curse, because the LORD hath said unto him, Curse David. Who shall then say, Wherefore hast thou done so? 11 And David said to Abishai, and to all his servants, Behold, my son, which came forth from my bowels, seeketh my life: how much more now *may this* Benjamite *do it?* let him alone, and let him curse; for the LORD hath bidden him.

Job 1: 15 The Sabeans fell *upon them*, and took them away; yea, they have slain the servants with the edge of the sword; and I only am escaped alone to tell thee. 21 The LORD gave,

God the rightful Lawgiver.

and the LORD hath taken away; blessed be the name of the LORD. 22 In all this Job sinned not, nor charged God foolishly.

Ps. 39: 9 I was dumb, I opened not my mouth; because thou didst *it.* — 97: 1 The LORD reigneth; let the earth rejoice; let the multitude of isles be glad *thereof.*

Is. 52: 7 How beautiful upon the mountains are the feet of him that bringeth good tidings, that publisheth peace; that bringeth good tidings of good, that publisheth salvation; that saith unto Zion, Thy God reigneth!

Jn. 18: 11 Then said Jesus unto Peter, Put up thy sword into the sheath: the cup which my Father hath given me, shall I not drink it? [See 296-9.]

279. *The wisdom of studying and exhibiting the perfections, purposes, and providential government of God.*

Dt. 32: 2 My doctrine shall drop as the rain, my speech shall distil as the dew, as the small rain upon the tender herb, and as the showers upon the grass: 3 Because I will publish the name of the LORD.

Ps. 36: 9 With thee *is* the fountain of life: in thy light shall we see light.

Jn. 17: 25 O righteous Father, the world hath not known thee: but I have known thee, and these have known that thou hast sent me. 26 And I have declared unto them thy name, and will declare *it;* that the love wherewith thou hast loved me, may be in them, and I in them.

2 Cor. 3: 18 We all, with open face, beholding as in a glass the glory of the Lord, are changed into the same image from glory to glory, *even* as by the Spirit of the Lord. [See 48, 51, 433, 458.]

LAW OF GOD.

280. *God the supreme and rightful Lawgiver and Governor.*

Ps. 22: 28 The kingdom *is* the LORD's: and he *is* the governor among the nations. — 47: 2 The LORD Most High *is* terrible; *he is* a great King over all the earth. 7 For God *is* the King of all the earth: sing ye praises with understanding. 8 God reigneth over the heathen: God sitteth upon the throne of his holiness. — 89: 18 The Lord *is* our defence; and the Holy One of Israel *is* our King. — 99: 1 The LORD reigneth; let the people tremble: he sitteth *between* the cherubims, let the earth be moved. — 103: 19 The LORD hath prepared his throne in the heavens; and his kingdom ruleth over all. — 146: 10 The LORD shall reign for ever, *even* thy God, O Zion, unto all generations. Praise ye the LORD.

Is. 33: 22 The LORD *is* our judge, the LORD *is* our lawgiver, the LORD *is* our King ; he will save us.

Dan. 4: 34 At the end of the days, I Nebuchadnezzar lifted up mine eyes unto-heaven, and mine understanding returned unto me, and I blessed the Most High, and I praised and honored him that liveth for ever, whose dominion *is* an everlasting dominion, and his kingdom *is* from generation to generation.

Rev. 19: 6 The Lord God omnipotent reigneth.   16 And he hath on *his* vesture and on his thigh a name written, KING OF KINGS AND LORD OF LORDS.

[See 241, 260, 744.]

281. *Decalogue, or comprehensive precepts of the law of God.*

Preface.

Ex. 20: 1 God spake all these words, saying,   2 I *am* the LORD thy God which have brought thee out of the land of Egypt, out of the house of bondage.

First Commandment.

3 Thou shalt have no other gods before me.

Second Commandment.

4 Thou shalt not make unto thee any graven image, or any likeness of *any thing* that *is* in heaven above, or that *is* in the earth beneath, or that *is* in the water under the earth.   5 Thou shalt not bow down thyself to them, nor serve them : for I the LORD thy God *am* a jealous God, visiting the iniquity of the fathers upon the children unto the third and fourth *generation* of them that hate me ;   6 And showing mercy unto thousands of them that love me, and keep my commandments.

Third Commandment.

7 Thou shalt not take the name of the LORD thy God in vain: for the LORD will not hold him guiltless that taketh his name in vain.

Fourth Commandment.

8 Remember the sabbath-day to keep it holy.   9 Six days shalt thou labor, and do all thy work: 10 But the seventh day *is* the sabbath of the LORD thy God : *in it* thou shalt not do any work, thou, nor thy son, nor thy daughter, thy man-servant, nor thy maid-servant, nor thy cattle, nor thy stranger that *is* within thy gates :   11 For *in* six days the LORD made heaven and earth, the sea, and all that in them *is*, and rested the seventh day : wherefore the LORD blessed the sabbath-day and hallowed it.

Fifth Commandment.

12 Honor thy father and thy mother; that thy days may be long upon the land which the LORD thy God giveth thee.

Sixth Commandment.

13 Thou shalt not kill.

Seventh Commandment.

14 Thou shalt not commit adultery.

Eighth Commandment.

15 Thou shalt not steal.

Ninth Commandment.

16 Thou shalt not bear false witness against thy neighbor.

Tenth Commandment.

17 Thou shalt not covet thy neighbor's house, thou shalt not covet thy neighbor's wife, nor his man-servant, nor his maid-servant, nor his ox, nor his ass, nor any thing that *is* thy neighbor's.

Eleventh Commandment.

Jn. 13: 34 A new commandment I give unto you, That ye love one another; as I have loved you, that ye also love one another. 35 By this shall all *men* know that ye are my disciples, if ye have love one to another.

282. *Circumstances connected with the promulgation of the Decalogue.*

Ex. 19: 10 The LORD said unto Moses, Go unto the people, and sanctify them to-day and to-morrow, and let them wash their clothes, 11 And be ready against the third day: for the third day the LORD will come down in the sight of all the people upon mount Sinai. 12 And thou shalt set bounds unto the people round about, saying, Take heed to yourselves, *that ye go not* up into the mount, or touch the border of it: whosoever toucheth the mount shall be surely put to death: 13 There shall not a hand touch it, but he shall surely be stoned or shot through: whether *it be* beast or man, it shall not live: when the trumpet soundeth long, they shall come up to the mount. 16 It came to pass on the third day in the morning, that there were thunders and lightnings, and a thick cloud upon the mount, and the voice of the trumpet exceeding loud; so that all the people that *was* in the camp trembled. 17 And Moses brought forth the people out of the camp to meet with God; and they stood at the nether part of the mount. 18 And mount Sinai was altogether on a smoke, because the LORD descended upon it in fire: and the smoke thereof ascended as the smoke of a furnace, and the whole mount quaked greatly. 19 And when the voice of the trumpet sounded long, and waxed louder and louder, Moses spake, and God answered him by a voice. 20 And the LORD came down upon mount Sinai, on the top of the mount; and the LORD called Moses *up* to the top of the mount; and Moses went up. 21 And the LORD said unto Moses, Go down, charge the people, lest they break through unto the LORD to gaze, and many of them perish. 22 And let the priests also which come near to the LORD, sanctify themselves, lest the LORD break forth upon them. 23 And Moses said unto the LORD, The people cannot come up to Mount Sinai: for thou chargedst us, saying, Set bounds about the mount, and sanctify it. 24 And the LORD said unto him, Away, get thee down, and thou shalt come up, thou, and Aaron with thee: but let not the priests and the people break through, to come up unto the LORD, lest he break forth upon them. 25 So Moses went down unto the people, and spake unto them.

Dt. 5: 22 These words the LORD spake unto all your assembly in the mount, out of the midst of the fire, of the cloud, and of the thick darkness, with a great voice; and he added no more: and he wrote them in two tables of stone, and delivered them unto me. 23 And it came to pass, when ye heard the voice out of the midst of the darkness, (for the mountain did burn with fire,) that ye came near unto me, *even* all the heads of your tribes, and your elders. 24 And ye said, Behold, the LORD our God hath shewed us his glory, and his greatness, and we have heard his voice out of the midst of the fire.

283. *Illustrations and summaries of the Decalogue.*

Mat. 5: 43 Ye have heard that it hath been said, Thou shalt love thy neighbor, and hate thine enemy: 44 But I say unto you, Love your enemies, bless them that curse you, do good to them that hate you, and pray for them which despitefully use you, and persecute you. 45 That ye may be the children of your Father which is in heaven: for he maketh his sun to rise on the evil and on the good, and sendeth rain on the just and on the unjust. 46 If ye love them which love you, what reward have ye? do not even the publicans the same? 47 And if ye salute your brethren only, what do ye more *than others?* do not even the publicans so? 48 Be ye therefore perfect, even as your Father which is in heaven is perfect—7: 12 All things whatsoever ye would that men should do to you, do ye even so to them: for this is the law and the prophets.—22: 35 One of them, *which was* a lawyer, asked *him a question,* tempting him, and saying, 36 Master, which *is* the great commandment in the law? 37 Jesus said unto him, Thou shalt love the Lord thy God with all thy heart, and with all thy soul, and with all thy mind. 38 This is the first and great commandment. 39 And the second *is* like unto it, Thou shalt love thy neighbor as thyself. 40 On these two commandments hang all the law and the prophets.

Rom. 13: 8 Owe no man any thing, but to love another: for he that loveth one another hath fulfilled the law. 9 For this, Thou shalt not commit adultery, Thou shalt not kill, Thou shalt not steal, Thou shalt not bear false witness, Thou shalt not covet; and if *there be* any other commandment, it is briefly comprehended in this saying, namely, Thou shalt love thy neighbor as thyself. 10 Love worketh no ill to his neighbor: therefore love *is* the fulfilling of the law.

Gal. 5: 14 All the law is fulfilled in one word, *even* in this, Thou shalt love thy neighbor as thyself.

Jam. 2: 8 If ye fulfil the royal law according to the scripture, Thou shalt love thy neighbor as thyself, ye do well: 9 But if ye have respect to persons, ye commit sin, and are convinced of the law as transgressors. 10 For whosoever shall keep the whole law, and yet offend in one *point,* he is guilty of all. [See 413, 414.]

284. *God's regard for his law.*

Is. 42: 21 The LORD is well pleased for his righteousness' sake; he will magnify the law, and make *it* honorable.—66: 2 To this *man* will I look, *even* to *him that is* poor, and of a contrite spirit, and trembleth at my word.

Mat. 5: 19 Whosoever therefore shall break one of these least commandments, and shall teach men so, he shall be called the least in the kingdom of heaven: but whosoever shall do, and teach *them,* the same shall be called great in the kingdom of heaven. [See 42, 50.]

285 *The law of God requires moral perfection.*

Gen. 17: 1 I *am* the Almighty God; walk before me, and be thou perfect.

Dt. 18: 13 Thou shalt be perfect with the Lord thy God.

1 K. 8: 61 Let your heart therefore be perfect with the Lord our God, to walk in his statutes, and to keep his commandments.

Pr. 23: 17 Let not thine heart envy sinners: but *be thou* in the fear of the LORD all the day long.

Mat. 5: 48 Be ye therefore perfect, even as your Father which is in heaven is perfect. — 22: 37 Jesus said unto him,

Thou shalt love the Lord thy God with all thy heart, and with all thy soul, and with all thy mind. 38 This is the first and great commandment. 39 And the second *is* like unto it, Thou shalt love thy neighbor as thyself.

1 Cor. 10: 31 Whether therefore ye eat or drink, or whatsoever' ye do, do all to the glory of God.

2 Cor. 7: 1 Having therefore these promises, dearly beloved, let us cleanse ourselves from all filthiness of the flesh and spirit, perfecting holiness in the fear of God. — 13: 11 Be perfect, be of good comfort, be of one mind, live in peace.

Jam. 1: 4 Let patience have *her* perfect work, that ye may be perfect and entire, wanting nothing.

1 Pet. 1: 15 As he which hath called you is holy, so be ye holy in all manner of conversation; 16 Because it is written, Be ye holy; for I am holy.

2 Pet. 3: 11 *Seeing* then *that* all these things shall be dissolved, what manner *of persons* ought ye to be in *all* holy conversation and godliness, 12 Looking for and hasting unto the coming of the day of God.

Jude 21 Keep yourselves in the love of God.

[See 501, 629.]

286 *The law of God reasonable — obeying it perfectly our highest happiness and privilege.*

Dt. 6: 24 The LORD commanded us to do all these statutes, to fear the LORD our God, for our good always, that he might preserve us alive, as *it is* at this day. 25 And it shall be our righteousness, if we observe to do all these commandments before the LORD our God, as he hath commanded us. — 10: 12 Now, Israel, what doth the LORD thy God require of thee but to fear the LORD thy God, to walk in all his ways, and to love him, and to serve the LORD thy God with all thine heart and with all thy soul. 13 To keep the commandments of the LORD, and his statutes, which I command thee this day for thy good?

Neh. 9: 13 Thou camest down also upon mount Sinai, and spakest with them from heaven, and gavest them right judgments, and true laws, good statutes and commandments.

Ps. 19: 7 The law of the LORD *is* perfect, converting the soul: the testimony of the LORD *is* sure, making wise the simple. 8 The statutes of ·the LORD *are* right, rejoicing the heart: the commandment of the LORD *is* pure, enlightening the eyes. 9 The fear of the LORD *is* clean, enduring for ever: the judgments of the LORD *are* true *and* righteous altogether. 10 More to be desired *are they* than gold, yea, than

much fine gold: sweeter also than honey and the honey-comb. 11 Moreover, by them is thy servant warned: *and* in keeping of them *there is* great reward. — Ps. 33: 4 The word of the LORD *is* right; and all his works *are done* in truth. — 119: 86 All thy commandments *are* faithful. 128 Therefore I esteem all *thy* precepts *concerning* all *things to be* right; *and·* I hate every false way. 172 My tongue shall speak of thy word: for all thy commandments *are* right-eousness.

Rom. 7: 12 Wherefore the law *is* holy, and the command-ment holy, and just, and good.

1 Jn. 5: 3 His commandments are not grievous.

[See Promises in the Index, and 485, 630.]

287. *Penalty of the law of God.*

Gen. 2: 17 Of the tree of the knowledge of good and evil, thou shalt not eat of it: for in the day that thou eatest thereof thou shalt surely die.

Ezk. 18: 4 The soul that sinneth, it shall die. — 33: 11 Say ·unto them, *As* I live, saith the Lord GOD, I have no pleasure in the death of the wicked; but that the wicked turn from his way and live: turn ye, turn ye from your evil ways; for why will ye die, O house of Israel?

Mat. 25: 41 Then shall he say also unto them on the left hand, Depart from me, ye cursed, into everlasting fire, prepared for the devil and his angels.

Jn. 8: 51 Verily, verily, I say unto you, If a man keep my saying, he shall never see death.

Rom. 6: 23 The wages of sin *is* death: but the gift of God *is* eternal life, through Jesus Christ our Lord.

Gal. 3: 10 As many as are of the works of the law, are under the curse: for it is written, Cursed *is* every one that continueth not in all things which are written in the book of the law to do them. 13 Christ hath redeemed us from the curse of the law, being made a curse for us: for it is written, Cursed *is* every one that hangeth on a tree.

Jam. 1: 15 Sin, when it is finished, bringeth forth death.

Rev. 2: 11 He that overcometh, shall not be hurt of the second death. [See 309, 560-3, 567.]

PRIMARY DUTIES TOWARDS GOD.

288. *Love to God required.*

Dt. 6: 5 Thou shalt love the Lord thy God with all thy heart, and with all thy soul, and with all thy might. — 11: 1 Thou shalt love the Lord thy God, and keep his charge, and his statutes, and his judgments, and his commandments, always. — 30: 15 See, I have set before thee this day life and good, and death and evil; 16 In that I command thee this day to love the LORD thy God, to walk in his ways, and to keep his commandments, and his statutes, and his judgments, that thou mayest live and multiply.

Jos. 22: 5 But take diligent heed to do the commandment and the law, which Moses the servant of the LORD charged you, to love the LORD your God, and to walk in all his ways, and to keep his commandments, and to cleave unto him, and to serve him with all your heart, and with all your soul.

Pr. 23: 26 My son, give me thine heart.

Mat. 22: 37 Jesus said unto him, Thou shalt love the Lord thy God with all thy heart, and with all thy soul, and with all thy mind. 38 This is the first and great commandment. [Mk. 12: 30, and Lk. 10: 27.]

Jude 21 Keep yourselves in the love of God.
[See 283, 601.]

289. *Promises to those who love God.*

Ex. 20: 6 Shewing mercy unto thousands of them that love me, and keep my commandments.

Dt. 7: 9 Know therefore that the LORD thy God, he *is* God, the faithful God, which keepeth covenant and mercy with them that love him and keep his commandments to a thousand generations. — 11: 13 It shall come to pass, if ye shall hearken diligently unto my commandments which I command you this day, to love the LORD your God, and to serve him with all your heart and with all your soul, 14 That I will give *you* the rain of your land in his due season, the first rain and the latter rain, that thou mayest gather in thy corn, and thy wine, and thine oil. 15 And I will send grass in thy fields for thy cattle, that thou mayest eat and be full.

Ps. 91: 14 Because he hath set his love upon me, therefore will I deliver him: I will set him on high, because he hath known my name. — 145: 20 The LORD preserveth all them that love him: but all the wicked will he destroy.

Pr. 8: 17 I love them that love me: and those that seek me early shall find me.

Fear of God required.

Jn. 14: 21 He that hath my commandments, and keepeth them, he it is that loveth me : and he that loveth me, shall be loved of my Father, and I will love him, and will manifest myself to him.   22 Judas saith unto him, (not Iscariot) Lord, how is it that thou wilt manifest thyself unto us, and not unto the world?   23 Jesus answered and said unto him, If a man love me, he will keep my words : and my Father will love him, and we will come unto him, and make our abode with him.

Rom. 8: 28 We know that all things work together for good, to them that love God, to them who are the called according to *his* purpose.

1 Cor. 2: 9 Eye hath not seen, nor ear heard, neither have entered into the heart of man, the things which God hath prepared for them that love him.

Jam. 1: 12 Blessed *is* the man that endureth temptation : for when he is tried, he shall receive the crown of life, which the Lord hath promised to them that love him.   [See 302, 630.]

290. *The fear of God required.*

Dt. 6: 24 The LORD commanded us to do all these statutes, to fear the LORD our God, for our good always, that he might preserve us alive, as *it is* at this day. — 10: 12 Now, Israel, what doth the LORD thy God require of thee but to fear the LORD thy God, to walk in all his ways, and to love him, and to serve the LORD thy God with all thine heart and with all thy soul.   20 Thou shalt fear the LORD thy God; him shalt thou serve, and to him shalt thou cleave, and swear by his name.

Jos. 24: 14 Now therefore, fear the LORD, and serve him in sincerity and in truth.

2 K. 17: 35 Ye shall not fear other gods, nor bow yourselves to them, nor serve them, nor sacrifice to them :   36 But the LORD, who brought you up out of the land of Egypt with great power and a stretched-out arm, him shall ye fear, and him shall ye worship, and to him shall ye do sacrifice.

Ps. 33: 8 Let all the earth fear the LORD : let all the inhabitants of the world stand in awe of him. — 89: 7 God is greatly to be feared in the assembly of the saints, and to be had in reverence of all *them that are* about him.

Pr. 23: 17 Let not thine heart envy sinners : but *be thou* in the fear of the LORD all the day long.

Ec. 12: 13 Let us hear the conclusion of the whole matter : Fear God, and keep his commandments : for this *is* the whole *duty* of man.

Is. 8: 13 Sanctify the Lord of hosts himself; and *let* him *be* your fear, and *let* him *be* your dread.

Lk. 12: 5 I will forewarn you whom ye shall fear: Fear him which after he hath killed, hath power to cast into hell; yea I say unto you, Fear him.

291. *Promises to those who fear God.*

Job 28: 28 Unto man he said, Behold, the fear of the LORD, that *is* wisdom; and to depart from evil *is* understanding.

Ps. 25: 12 What man *is* he that feareth the LORD? him shall he teach in the way *that* he shall choose. 13 His soul shall dwell at ease; and his seed shall inherit the earth. 14 The secret of the LORD *is* with them that fear him; and he will shew them his covenant. — 31: 19 *Oh* how great *is* thy goodness, which thou hast laid up for them that fear thee; *which* thou hast wrought for them that trust in thee before the sons of men! 20 Thou shalt hide them in the secret of thy presence from the pride of man: thou shalt keep them secretly in a pavilion from the strife of tongues. — 33: 18 Behold, the eye of the LORD *is* upon them that fear him, upon them that hope in his mercy; 19 To deliver their soul from death, and to keep them alive in famine. — 34: 7 The angel of the LORD encampeth round about them that fear him, and delivereth them. 8 O taste and see that the LORD *is* good: blessed *is* the man *that* trusteth in him. 9 O fear the LORD, ye his saints; for *there is* no want to them that fear him. — 103: 11 As the heaven is high above the earth, *so* great is his mercy toward them that fear him. 12 As far as the east is from the west, *so* far hath he removed our transgressions from us. 13 Like as a father pitieth *his* children, *so* the LORD pitieth them that fear him. — 111: 5 He hath given meat unto them that fear him: he will ever be mindful of his covenant. 10 The fear of the LORD *is* the beginning of wisdom: a good understanding have all they that do *his commandments:* his praise endureth for ever. [Pr. 9: 10.] 145: 19 He will fulfil the desire of them that fear him: he also will hear their cry, and will save them. — 147: 11 The Lord taketh pleasure in them that fear him, in those that hope for mercy.

Pr. 14: 26 In the fear of the LORD *is* strong confidence: and his children shall have a place of refuge. 27 The fear of the LORD *is* a fountain of life, to depart from the snares of death.

Ec. 8: 12 Though a sinner do evil a hundred times, and his *days* be prolonged, yet surely I know that it shall be well with them that fear God, which fear before him.

Mal. 3: 16 They that feared the LORD spake often one to another: and the LORD hearkened, and heard *it:* and a book of remembrance was written before him for them that feared the LORD, and that thought upon his name. 17 And they shall •be mine, saith the LORD of hosts, in that day when I make up my jewels; and I will spare them, as a man spareth his own son that serveth him.—4: 2 Unto you that fear my name, shall the Sun of righteousness arise with healing in his wings; and ye shall go forth, and grow up as calves of the stall.

Lk. 1: 50 His mercy *is* on them that fear him, from generation to generation.

292. *Trust and hope in God required.*

Ps. 4: 5 Put your trust in the Lord.—42: 5 Why art thou cast down, O my soul? and *why* art thou disquieted in me? hope thou in God: for I shall yet praise him *for* the help of his countenance.—62: 8 Trust in him at all times; ye people, pour out your heart before him: God *is* a refuge for us.—115: 9 O Israel, trust thou in the LORD: he *is* their help and their shield. 10 O house of Aaron, trust in the LORD: he *is* their help and their shield. 11 Ye that fear the LORD, trust in the LORD: he *is* their help and their shield.

Pr. 3: 5 Trust in the Lord with all thy heart; and lean not unto thine own understanding.

Is. 26: 4 Trust ye in the Lord for ever: for in the Lord JEHOVAH *is* everlasting strength.—50: 10 Who *is* among you that feareth the LORD, that obeyeth the voice of his servant, that walketh *in* darkness, and hath no light? let him trust in the name of the LORD, and stay upon his God.

[See 170, 352.]

293. *Trust and hope in God encouraged—promises.*

2 S. 22: 31 He *is* a buckler to all them that trust in him.

Ps. 2: 12 Blessed *are* all they that put their trust in him.—17: 7 Shew thy marvellous loving-kindness, O thou that savest by thy right hand them which put their trust *in thee* from those that rise up *against them.*—28: 7 The LORD *is* my strength, and my shield; my heart trusted in him, and I am helped: therefore my heart greatly rejoiceth: and with my song will I praise him.—31: 19 *Oh* how great *is* thy goodness, which thou hast laid up for them that fear thee; *which* thou hast wrought for them that trust in thee before the sons of men! 20 Thou shalt hide them in the secret of thy presence from the pride of man: thou shalt keep them secretly in a pavilion from the strife of tongues. 24 Be of good courage, and he shall strengthen your heart, all ye that hope in the LORD. — 32: 10 Many sorrows *shall be* to the wicked: but he that trusteth in. the LORD, mercy shall compass him about. — 34: 8 O taste and see that the LORD *is* good : blessed *is* the man *that* trusteth in him.   22 The LORD redeemeth the soul of his servants: and none of them that trust in him shall be desolate. — 37: 3 Trust in the LORD, and do good; *so* shalt thou dwell in the land, and verily thou shalt be fed. — 38: 15 In thee O LORD, do I hope : thou wilt hear, O LORD my God. — 40: 4 Blessed *is* that man that maketh the LORD his trust, and respecteth not the proud, nor such as turn aside to lies. — 112: 6 Surely he shall not be moved for ever : the righteous shall be in everlasting remembrance.   7 He shall not be afraid of evil tidings : his heart is fixed, trusting in the LORD.   8 His heart *is* established, he shall not be afraid, until he see *his desire* upon his enemies. — 118: 8 *It is* better to trust in the LORD than to put confidence in man.   9 *It is* better to trust in the LORD than to put confidence in princes. — 125: 1 They that trust in the LORD *shall be* as mount Zion, *which* cannot be removed, *but* abideth for ever. — 146: 5 Happy *is* he that *hath* the God of Jacob for his help, whose hope *is* in the LORD his God.

Pr. 18: 10 The name of the Lord *is* a strong tower : the righteous runneth into it, and is safe. — 28: 25 He that putteth his trust in the Lord shall be made fat. — 29: 25 The fear of man bringeth a snare : but whoso putteth his trnst in the Lord shall be safe. — 30: 5 Every word of God *is* pure : he *is* a shield unto them that put their trust in him.

Is. 26: 3 Thou wilt keep *him* in perfect peace *whose* mind *is* stayed *on thee :* because he trusteth in thee. — 57: 13 He that putteth his trust in me shall possess the land, and shall inherit my holy mountain.

Jer. 17: 7 Blessed *is* the man that trusteth in the LORD, and whose hope the LORD is.   8 He shall be as a tree planted by the waters, and *that* spreadeth out her roots by the river, and shall not see when heat cometh, but her leaf shall be green; and shall not be careful in the year of drought, neither shall cease from yielding fruit.

294. *Examples of trust and hope in God.*

1 S. 17: 37 David said moreover, The LORD that delivered me out of the paw of the lion, and out of the paw of the bear, he will deliver me out of the hand of this Philistine.

2 K. 18: 5 He [Hezekiah] trusted in the LORD God of Israel : so that after him was none like him among all the kings of Judah, nor *any* that were before him.   6 For he

clave to the LORD, *and* departed not from following him, but kept his commandments, which the LORD commanded Moses. 7 And the LORD was with him : *and* he prospered whithersoever he went forth : and he rebelled against the king of Assyria, and served him not.

Job 13: 15 Though he slay me, yet will I trust in him.

Ps. 7: 1 O LORD my God, in thee do I put my trust : save me from all·them that persecute me, and deliver me. — 56: 4 In God I will praise his word, in God I have put my trust ; I will not fear what flesh can do unto me. — 71: 5 For thou *art* my hope, O Lord GOD : *thou art* my trust from my youth.

Dan. 3: 16 Shadrach, Meshach, and Abed-nego, answered and said to the king, O Nebuchadnezzar, we *are* not careful to answer thee in this matter. 17 If it be *so*, our God whom we serve is able to deliver us from the burning fiery furnace, and he will deliver *us* out of thine hand, O king. 18 But if not, be it known unto thee, O king, that we will not serve thy gods, nor worship the golden image which thou hast set up. [See 659.]

295. *Obedience, homage, and supreme devotion to God required.*

Dt. 13: 4 Ye shall walk after the LORD your God, and fear him, and keep his commandments, and obey his voice, and ye shall serve him, and cleave unto him.

Ps. 95: 6 O come, let us worship and bow down : let us kneel before the LORD our maker. 7 For he *is* our God ; and we *are* the people of his pasture, and the sheep of his hand. To-day if ye will hear his voice, 8 Harden not your heart, as in the provocation, *and* as *in* the day of temptation in the wilderness. — 96: 9 O worship the LORD in the beauty of holiness : fear before him, all the earth.'— 99: 5 Exalt ye the LORD our God, and worship at his footstool ; *for* he *is* holy.

Ec. 12: 13 Let us hear the conclusion of the whole matter : Fear God, and keep his commandments : for this *is* the whole *duty* of man.

Rom. 12: 1 I beseech you therefore, brethren, by the mercies of God, that ye present your bodies a living sacrifice, holy, acceptable unto God, *which is* your reasonable service.

Col. 3: 23 Whatsoever ye do, do *it* heartily, as to the Lord, and not unto men ; 24 Knowing that of the Lord ye shall receive the reward of the inheritance: for ye serve the Lord Christ. [See 285, 288, 290, 661, 744–5.]

296. *Joy in God required.*

1 Ch. 16: 31 Let the heavens be glad, and let the **earth**

rejoice: and let *men* say among the nations, The LORD reigneth. 32 Let the sea roar, and the fulness thereof: let the fields rejoice, and all that *is* therein.

Ps. 5: 11 But let all those that put their trust in thee rejoice: let them ever shout for joy, because thou defendest them: let them also that love thy name be joyful in thee. — 32: 11 Be glad in the LORD, and rejoice ye righteous: and shout for joy, all *ye that are* upright in heart. — 33: 1 Rejoice in the LORD, O ye righteous: *for* praise is comely for the upright. — 37: 4 Delight thyself also in the LORD; and he shall give thee the desires of thine heart. — 40: 16 Let all those that seek thee rejoice and be glad in thee: let such as love thy salvation say continually, the LORD be magnified. — 68: 3 Let the righteous be glad: let them rejoice before God: yea, let them exceedingly rejoice. 4 Sing unto God, sing praises to his name: extol him that rideth upon the heavens by his name JAH, and rejoice before him. — 97: 1 The LORD reigneth: let the earth rejoice; let the multitude of isles be glad *thereof.* 2 Clouds and darkness *are* round about him: righteousness and judgment *are* the habitation of his throne. — 149: 2 Let Israel rejoice in him that made him: let the children of Zion be joyful in their King.

Is. 41: 16 Thou shalt rejoice in the Lord, *and* shalt glory in the Holy One of Israel.

Ph. 3: 1 Finally, my brethren, rejoice in the Lord. — 4: 4 Rejoice in the Lord always: *and* again I say, Rejoice.

[See 52.]

297. *Examples of joy in God.*

1 S. 2: 1 Hannah prayed, and said, My heart rejoiceth in the LORD, mine horn is exalted in the LORD; my mouth is enlarged over mine enemies; because I rejoice in thy salvation.

Neh. 8: 10 He said unto them, Go your way, eat the fat, and drink the sweet, and send portions unto them for whom nothing is prepared: for *this* day *is* holy unto our LORD: neither be ye sorry; for the joy of the LORD is your strength.

Hab. 3: 17 Although the fig-tree shall not blossom, neither *shall* fruit *be* in the vines; the labor of the olive shall fail, and the field shall yield no meat; the flock shall be cut off from the fold, and *there shall be* no herd in the stalls: 18 Yet I will rejoice in the LORD, I will joy in the God of my salvation. 19 The Lord GOD *is* my strength, and he will make my feet like hinds' *feet,* and he will make me to walk upon mine high places.

1 Pet. 1: 8 Whom having not seen, ye love; in whom, though now ye see *him* not, yet believing, ye rejoice with joy unspeakable, and full of glory.

298. *Submission to God required — rebellion forbidden.*

Lev. 26: 41 If then their uncircumcised hearts be humbled, and they then accept of the punishment of their iniquity: 42 Then will I remember my covenant with Jacob, and also my covenant with Isaac, and also my covenant with Abraham will I remember; and I will remember the land. 43 The land also shall be left of them, and shall enjoy her sabbaths, while she lieth desolate without them: and they shall accept of the punishment of their iniquity; because, even because they despised my judgments, and because their soul abhorred my statutes.

Dt. 27: 26 Cursed *be* he that confirmeth not *all* the words of this law to do them: and all the people shall say, Amen.

Is. 45: 9 Wo unto him that striveth with his Maker!

Mat. 6: 9 After this manner therefore pray ye: Our Father which art in heaven, Hallowed be thy name. 10 Thy kingdom come. Thy will be done in earth as *it is* in heaven.

Jam. 4: 7 Submit yourselves therefore to God.

[See 278, 536.]

299. *Submission unconditional to God, exemplified.*

Lev. 10: 1 Nadab and Abihu, the sons of Aaron, took either of them his censer, and put fire therein, and put incense thereon, and offered strange fire before the LORD, which he commanded them not. 2 And there went out fire from the LORD, and devoured them, and they died before the LORD. 3 Moses said unto Aaron, This *it is* that the LORD spake, saying, I will be sanctified in them that come nigh me, and before all the people I will be glorified. And Aaron held his peace.

1 S. 3: 14 Therefore I have sworn unto the house of Eli, that the iniquity of Eli's house shall, not be purged with sacrifice nor offering for ever. 18 And Samuel told him every whit, and hid nothing from him. And he said, It *is* the LORD: let him do what seemeth him good.

2 S. 15: 25 The king [David] said unto Zadok, Carry back the ark of God into the city: If I shall find favor in the eyes of the LORD, he will bring me again, and shew me *both* it, and his habitation: 26 But if he thus say, I have no delight in thee; behold, *here am* I, let him do to me as seemeth good unto him.

Honoring God required.

Job 1: 19 Behold, there came a great wind from the wilderness, and 'smote the four corners of the house, and it fell upon the young men, and they are dead; and I only am escaped alone to tell thee. 20 Then Job arose, and rent his mantle, and shaved his head, and fell down upon the ground, and worshipped, 21 And said, Naked came I out of my mother's womb, and naked shall I return thither: The LORD gave, and the LORD hath taken away; blessed be the name of the LORD.

Ps. 39: 9 I was dumb, I opened not my mouth; because thou didst *it*.

Mat. 26: 39 He went a little further and fell on his face, and prayed, saying, O my Father, if it be possible, let this cup pass from me: nevertheless, not as I will, but as thou *wilt*.

Lk. 15: 18 I will arise and go to my father, and will say unto him, Father, I have sinned against heaven and before thee. 19 And am no more worthy to be called thy son: make me as one of thy hired servants. — 23: 40 The other answering, rebuked him, saying, Dost not thou fear God, seeing thou art in the same condemnation? 41 And we indeed, justly; for we receive the due reward of our deeds: but this man hath done nothing amiss.

Ac. 21: 14 When he would not be persuaded, we ceased, saying, The will of the Lord be done.

Rev. 19: 1 After these things I heard a great voice of much people in heaven, saying, Alleluia: Salvation, and glory, and honor, and power, unto the Lord our God: 2 For true and righteous *are* his judgments: for he hath judged the great whore, which did corrupt the earth with her fornication, and hath avenged the blood of his servants at her hand. 3 And again they said, Alleluia. And her smoke rose up for ever and ever. [See 356, 414, 674.]

300. *Honoring and glorifying God required and exemplified.*

1 Ch. 16: 28 Give unto the LORD, ye kindreds of the people, give unto the LORD glory and strength. 29 Give unto the LORD the glory *due* unto his name: bring an offering, and come before him: worship the LORD in the beauty of holiness.

Job 36: 24 Remember that thou magnify his work which men behold.

Ps. 115: 1 Not unto us, O Lord, not unto us, but unto thy name give glory, for thy mercy, *and* for thy truth's sake.

Pr. 3: 9 Honor the LORD with thy substance, and with the first-fruits of all thine increase.

God displeased, when we do not honor him.

Jer. 13: 16 Give glory to the LORD your God, before he cause darkness, and before your feet stumble upon the dark mountains, and while ye look for light, he turn it into the shadow of death, *and* make *it* gross darkness.

Mal. 1: 6 A son honoreth *his* father, and a servant his master: if then I *be* a father, where *is* mine honor? and if I *be* a master, where *is* my fear? saith the LORD of hosts unto you, O priests, that despise my name.

Jn. 5: 22 The Father judgeth no man; but hath committed all judgment unto the Son: 23 That all *men* should honor the Son, even as they honor the Father. He that honoreth not the Son, honoreth not the Father which hath sent him.— 8: 49 Jesus answered, I have not a devil; but I honor my Father, and ye do dishonor me.

1 Cor. 6: 20 Ye are bought with a price: therefore glorify God in your body, and in your spirit, which are God's.—10: 31 Whether therefore ye eat or drink, or whatsoever ye do, do all to the glory of God.

1 Tim. 1: 17 Now unto the King eternal, immortal, invisible, the only wise God, *be* honor and glory for ever and ever.

Rev. 4: 11 Thou art worthy, O Lord, to receive glory, and honor, and power: for thou hast created all things, and for thy pleasure they are and were created. [See 538.]

301. God displeased with those who will not honor and glorify him.

1 S. 2: 30 Them that honor me I will honor, and they that despise me shall be lightly esteemed.

Dan. 5: 23 The God in whose hand thy breath *is*, and whose *are* all thy ways, hast thou not glorified. 24 Then was the part of the hand sent from him; and this writing was written. 25 And this *is* the writing that was written, MENE, MENE, TEKEL, UPHARSIN.

Mal. 2: 2 If ye will not hear, and if ye will not lay *it* to heart, to give glory unto my name, saith the LORD of hosts, I will even send a curse upon you, and I will curse your blessings; yea, I have cursed them already, because ye do not lay *it* to heart.

Ac. 12: 23 Immediately the angel of the Lord smote him, because he gave not God the glory: and he was eaten of worms, and gave up the ghost.

Rom. 1: 21 When they knew God, they glorified *him* not as God, neither were thankful, but became vain in their imaginations, and their foolish heart was darkened. 24 God also gave them up to uncleanness, through the lusts of their own hearts, to dishonor their own bodies between themselves. [See 230.]

GOD'S MORAL GOVERNMENT.

302. *Promises of temporal good and eternal life to the obedient.*

Ex. 20: 6 Shewing mercy unto thousands of them that love me, and keep my commandments.

Lev. 18: 5 Ye shall therefore keep my statutes and my judgments : which if a man do, he shall live in them : I *am* the LORD.

Dt. 32: 46 He said unto them, Set your hearts unto all the words which I testify among you this day, which ye shall command your children to observe to do, all the words of this law. 47 For it *is* not a vain thing for you: because it *is* your life.

Neh. 9: 29 And testified against them, that thou mightest bring them again unto thy law: yet they dealt proudly, and hearkened not unto thy commandments, but sinned against thy judgments, (which if a man do, he shall live in them.)

Ps. 19: 11 Moreover, by them is thy servant warned, *and* in keeping of them *there is* great reward. — 25: 10 All the paths of the LORD *are* mercy and truth unto such as keep his covenant and his testimonies. — 103: 17 The mercy of the LORD *is* from everlasting to everlasting upon them that fear him, and his righteousness unto children's children ; 18 To such as keep his covenant, and to those that remember his commandments to do them.

Pr. 3: 1 My son, forget not my law ; but let thine heart keep my commandments : 2 For length of days, and long life, and peace shall they add to thee.

Is. 1: 19 If ye be willing and obedient, ye shall eat the good of the land. 20 But if ye refuse and rebel, ye shall be devoured with the sword: for the mouth of the LORD hath spoken *it*.

Ezk. 18: 5 But if a man be just, and do that which is lawful and right, 9 Hath walked in my statutes, and hath kept my judgments, to deal truly ; he *is* just, he shall surely live, saith the LORD GOD. — 20: 13 The house of Israel rebelled against me in the wilderness ; they walked not in my statutes, and they despised my judgments, which *if* a man do, he shall even live in them.

Mat. 7: 21 Not every one that saith unto me, Lord, Lord, shall enter into the kingdom of heaven, but he that doeth the will of my Father which is in heaven. 24 Therefore, whosoever heareth these sayings of mine, and doeth them, I will liken him unto a wise man, which built his house upon a rock : 25

And the rain descended, and the floods came, and the winds blew, and beat upon that house; and it fell not: for it was founded upon a rock.—19: 17 He said unto him, Why callest thou me good? *there is* none good but one, *that is,* God: but if thou wilt enter into life, keep the commandments.

Lk. 10: 27 He answering said, Thou shalt love the Lord thy God with all thy heart, and with all thy soul, and with all thy strength, and with all thy mind; and thy neighbor as thyself. 28 And he said unto him, Thou hast answered right: this do, and thou shalt live.

Jn. 12: 26 If any man serve me, let him follow me, and where I am, there shall also my servant be: if any man serve me, him will *my* Father honor.

Rom. 10: 5 Moses describeth the righteousness which is of the law, That the man which doeth those things shall live by them.

1 Tim. 4: 8 Godliness is profitable unto all things, having promise of the life that now is, and of that which is to come.

Rev. 22: 14 Blessed *are* they that do his commandments, that they may have right to the tree of life, and may enter in through the gates into the city. [See 485, 602, 630.]

303. *Threats of present and future evils to the disobedient.*

Ps. 34: 16 The face of the LORD *is* against them that do evil, to cut off the remembrance of them from the earth.

Is. 1: 20 If ye refuse and rebel, ye shall be devoured with the sword: for the mouth of the LORD hath spoken *it.*

Rom. 2: 7 To them who by patient continuance in well-doing, seek for glory, and honor, and immortality; eternal life: 8 But unto them that are contentious, and do not obey the truth, but obey unrighteousness: indignation and wrath, 9 Tribulation and anguish, upon every soul of man that doeth evil; of the Jew first, and also of the Gentile. 10 But glory, honor, and peace, to every man that worketh good; to the Jew first, and also to the Gentile.

1 Cor. 6: 9 Know ye not that the unrighteous shall not inherit the kingdom of God? [See 486, 561–7, 733.]

GOSPEL, OR PLAN OF REDEMPTION.

304. *Its origin in God's eternal purpose.*

Ep. 1: 3 Blessed *be* the God and Father of our Lord Jesus Christ, who hath blessed us with all spiritual blessings in heavenly *places* in Christ: 4 According as he hath chosen us

in him, before the foundation of the world, that we should be
holy and without blame before him in love.—3: 11 According
to the eternal purpose which he purposed in Christ Jesus our
Lord.

1 Pet. 1: 19 With the precious blood of Christ, as of a lamb
without blemish and without spot: 20 Who verily was fore-
ordained before the foundation of the world, but was manifest
in these last times for you. [See 249—251.]

305. *Gospel a scheme of grace.*

Ac. 20: 24 None of these things move me, neither count I
my life dear unto myself, so that I might finish my course with
joy, and the ministry which I have received of the Lord Jesus,
to testify the gospel of the grace of God.

Rom. 5: 21 That as sin hath reigned unto death, even so
might grace reign through righteousness unto eternal life, by
Jesus Christ our Lord. [See 586.]

306. *Its terms, as distinguished from those of the law.*

Mk. 16: 15 And he said unto them, Go ye into all the world,
and preach the gospel to every creature. 16 He that believeth and is baptized, shall be saved; but he that believeth not,
shall be damned.

Ac. 2: 38 Then Peter said unto them, Repent, and be baptized every one of you in the name of Jesus Christ, for the
remission of sins, and ye shall receive the gift of the Holy
Ghost.

2 Cor. 5: 18 All things *are* of God, who hath reconciled us
to himself by Jesus Christ, and hath given to us the ministry
of reconciliation; 19 To wit, that God was in Christ, reconciling the world unto himself, not imputing their trespasses
unto them; and hath committed unto us the word of reconciliation. 20 Now then we are ambassadors for Christ, as
though God did beseech *you* by us: we pray *you* in Christ's
stead, be ye reconciled to God.

Gal. 3: 10 As many as are of the works of the law, are
under the curse: for it is written, Cursed *is* every one that
continueth not in all things which are written in the book of
the law to do them. 11 But that no man is justified by the
law in the sight of God, *it is* evident: for, The just shall live
by faith. 12 And the law is not of faith: but, The man that
doeth them shall live in them.

Col. 1: 20 Having made peace through the blood of his
cross, by him to reconcile all things unto himself; by him, *I say,*
whether *they be* things in earth, or things in heaven. 21 And

you, that were sometime alienated and enemies in *your* mind by wicked works, yet now hath he reconciled. [See 183, 606.]

307. *Plan of the gospel, all-comprehensive.*

Ep. 1: 9 Having made known unto us the mystery of his will, according to his good pleasure, which he hath purposed in himself: 10 That in the dispensation of the fulness of times he might gather together in one all things in Christ, both which are in heaven, and which are on earth; *even* in him: 11 In whom also we have obtained an inheritance, being predestinated according to the purpose of him who worketh all things after the counsel of his own will: 12 That we should be to the praise of his glory, who first trusted in Christ.— 3: 8 Unto me, who am less than the least of all saints, is this grace given, that I should preach among the Gentiles the unsearchable riches of Christ; 9 And to make all *men* see what *is* the fellowship of the mystery, which from the beginning of the world hath been hid in God, who created all things by Jesus Christ: 10 To the intent that now unto the principalities and powers in heavenly *places* might be known by the church the manifold wisdom of God, 11 According to the eternal purpose which he purposed in Christ Jesus our Lord: 12 In whom we have boldness and access with confidence by the faith of him. [See 251.]

308. *The gospel requires as high moral perfection as the law.*

Mat. 5: 48 Be ye therefore perfect, even as your Father which is in heaven is perfect.

Rom. 6: 15 What then? shall we sin, because we are not under the law, but under grace? God forbid. [See 285, 501.]

309. *Fearful penalty of the gospel for resisting its light.*

Mat. 7: 26 And every one that heareth these sayings of mine, and doeth them not, shall be likened unto a foolish man, which built his house upon the sand: 27 And the rain descended, and the floods came, and the winds blew, and beat upon that house; and it fell: and great was the fall of it.— 11: 20 Then began he to upbraid the cities wherein most of his mighty works were done, because they repented not. 21 Wo unto thee, Chorazin! wo unto thee, Bethsaida! for if the mighty works which were done in you, had been done in Tyre and Sidon, they would have repented long ago in sackcloth and ashes. 22 But I say unto you, It shall be more tolerable for Tyre and Sidon at the day of judgment, than for you. 23 And thou, Capernaum, which art exalted unto heaven, shalt be brought down to-hell: for if the mighty works which have been done in thee, had been done in Sodom, it would have remained until this day. 24 But I say unto you, That it shall be more tolerable for the land of Sodom, in the day of judgment, than for thee.—12: 41 The men of Nineveh shall rise in judgment with this generation, and shall condemn it: because they repented at the preaching of Jonas; and behold, a greater than Jonas is here. [Lk. 11: 31, 32.]

Lk. 12: 47 That servant which knew his lord's will, and prepared not *himself*, neither did according to his will, shall be beaten with many *stripes.* 48 But he that knew not, and did commit things worthy of stripes, shall be beaten with few *stripes.* For unto whomsoever much is given, of him shall be much required; and to whom men have committed much, of him they will ask the more.

Jn. 3: 19 This is the condemnation, that light is come into the world, and men loved darkness rather than light, because their deeds were evil.

Heb. 10: 26 If we sin wilfully after that we have received the knowledge of the truth, there remaineth no more sacrifice for sins, 27 But a certain fearful looking for of judgment and fiery indignation, which shall devour the adversaries. 28 He that despised Moses' law, died without mercy under two or three witnesses: 29 Of how much sorer punishment, suppose ye, shall he be thought worthy, who hath trodden under foot the Son of God, and hath counted the blood of the covenant, wherewith he was sanctified, an unholy thing, and hath done despite unto the Spirit of grace? [See 161, 348.]

CIVIL GOVERNMENT.

310. *Divine authority for civil government.*

Ex. 18: 25 Moses chose able men out of all Israel, and made them heads over the people, rulers of thousands, rulers of hundreds, rulers of fifties, and rulers of tens. 26 And they judged the people at all seasons: the hard causes they brought unto Moses, but every small matter they judged themselves.

Num. 11: 11 And Moses said unto the LORD, Wherefore hast thou afflicted thy servant? and wherefore have I not found favor in thy sight, that thou layest the burden of all this people upon me? 16 And the LORD said unto Moses, Gather unto me seventy men of the elders of Israel, whom thou knowest to be the elders of the people, and officers over them; and bring them unto the tabernacle of the congregation, that they may stand there with thee. 17 And I will come down and talk with thee there; and I will take of the spirit which *is* upon thee, and will put *it* upon them: and they shall bear the burden of the people with thee, that thou bear *it* not thyself alone. [Dt. 1: 9—18.]

Num. 27: 15 Moses spake unto the LORD, saying, 16 Let the LORD, the God of the spirits of all flesh, set a man over the congregation, 17 Which may go out before them, and which may go in before them, and which may lead them out, and which may bring them in; that the congregation of the LORD be not as sheep which have no shepherd. 18 And the LORD said unto Moses, Take thee Joshua the son of Nun, a man in whom *is* the spirit, and lay thine hand upon him; 19 And set him before Eleazar the priest, and · before all the congregation: and give him a charge in their sight. 20 And thou shalt put *some* of thine honor upon him, that all the congregation of the children of Israel may be obedient.

Dt. 16: 18 Judges and officers shalt thou make thee in all thy gates, which the LORD thy God giveth thee, throughout thy tribes: and they shall judge the people with just judgment. 19 Thou shalt not wrest judgment; thou shalt not respect persons, neither take a gift: for a gift doth blind the eyes of the wise, and pervert the words of the righteous.

Pr. 8: 12 I wisdom dwell with prudence. 15 By me kings reign, and princes decree justice. 16 By me princes rule, and nobles, *even* all the judges of the earth.

Ac. 13: 20 After that, he gave *unto them* judges, about the space of four hundred and fifty years, until Samuel the prophet.

Rom. 13: 3 Rulers are not a terror to good works, but to the evil. Wilt thou then not be afraid of the power? do that which is good, and thou shalt have praise of the same: 4 For he is the minister of God to thee for good. But if thou do that which is evil, be afraid; for he heareth not the sword in vain: for he is the minister of God, a revenger to *execute* wrath upon him that doeth evil. 5 Wherefore *ye* must needs be subject, not only for wrath, but also for conscience' sake. 6 For, for this cause pay ye tribute also: for they are God's ministers, attending continually upon this very thing.

311. *Expediency of civil government with penalties.*

Dt. 13: 10 Thou shalt stone him with stones that he die; because he hath sought to thrust thee away from the LORD thy God, which brought thee out of the land of Egypt from the house of bondage. 11 And all Israel shall hear, and fear, and shall do no more any such wickedness as this is among you. —

19: 18 The judges shall make diligent inquisition : and behold, *if* the witness *be* a false witness, *and* hath testified falsely against his brother; 19 Then shall ye do unto him, as he had thought to have done unto his brother: so shalt thou put the evil away from among you. 20 And those which remain shall hear, and fear, and shall henceforth commit no more any such evil among you.

2 Ch. 9: 8 Blessed he the LORD thy God, which delighted in thee to set thee on his throne, *to be* king for the LORD thy God : because thy God loved Israel, to establish them for ever, therefore made he thee [Solomon] king over them, to do judgment and justice.

Pr. 20: 8 A king that sitteth in the throne of judgment, scattereth away all evil with his eyes. 26 A wise king scattereth the wicked and bringeth the wheel over them.

Is. 1: 26 I will restore thy judges as at the first, and thy counsellors as at the beginning : afterward thou shalt be called, The city of righteousness, the faithful city.

1 Tim. 1: 8 We know that the law *is* good, if a man use it lawfully ; 9 Knowing this, that the law is not made for a righteous man, but for the lawless and disobedient, for the ungodly and for sinners, for unholy and profane, for murderers of fathers, and murderers of mothers, for manslayers, 10 For whoremongers, for them that defile themselves with mankind, for menstealers, for liars, for perjured persons, and if there be any other thing that is contrary to sound doctrine.

Pr. 26: 3, and 20: 30. [See 494.]

312. *Qualifications of civil rulers.*

Ex. 18: 21 Thou shalt provide out of all the people, able men, such as fear God, men of truth, hating covetousness ; and place *such* over them *to be* rulers.

Dt. 1: 13 Take you wise men, and understanding, and known among your tribes, and I will make them rulers over you. 15 So I took the chief of your tribes, wise men, and known, and made them heads over you, captains over thousands, and captains over hundreds, and captains over fifties, and captains over tens, and officers among your tribes.

2 S. 23: 3 The God of Israel said, the Rock of Israel spake to me, He that ruleth over men *must be* just, ruling in the fear of God.

313. *Duties of civil rulers.*

Dt. 1: 16 I charged your judges at that time, saying, Hear *the causes* between your brethren, and judge righteously between *every* man and his brother, and the stranger *that is* with him. 17 Ye shall not respect persons in judgment; *but* ye shall hear the small as well as the great; ye shall not be afraid of the face of man; for the judgment *is* God's. [Dt. 16: 19.] 17: 15 Thou shalt in any wise set *him* king over thee whom the LORD thy God shall choose. 18 And it shall be when he sitteth upon the throne of his kingdom, that he shall write him a copy of this law in a book out of *that which is* before the priests and Levites. 19 And it shall be with him, and he shall read therein all the days of his life: that he may learn to fear the LORD his God, to keep all the words of this law and these statutes, to do them: 20 That his heart be not lifted up above his brethren, and that he turn not aside from the commandment *to* the right hand or *to* the left. — 19: 18 The judges shall make diligent inquisition: and behold, *if* the witness *be* a false witness, *and* hath testified falsely against his brother; 19 Then shall ye do unto him, as he had thought to have done unto his brother. — 25: 1 If there be a controversy between men, and they come unto judgment, that *the judges* may judge them: then they shall justify the righteous, and condemn the wicked. 2 And it shall be, if the wicked man *be* worthy to be beaten, that the judge shall cause him to lie down and to be beaten before his face, according to his fault.

Ps. 82: 2 How long will ye judge unjustly, and accept the persons of the wicked? 3 Defend the poor and fatherless: do justice to the afflicted and needy. 4 Deliver the poor and needy: rid *them* out of the hand of the wicked.

Pr. 16: 12 *It is* an abomination to kings to commit wickedness: for the throne is established by righteousness. — 20: 28 Mercy and truth preserve the king: and his throne is upholden by mercy. — 29: 14 The king that faithfully judgeth the poor, his throne shall be established for ever. — 31: 4 *It is* not for kings, O Lemuel, *it is* not for kings to drink wine; nor for princes strong drink: 5 Lest they drink, and forget the law, and pervert the judgment of any of the afflicted.

Jer. 22: 2 Say, Hear the word of the LORD, O king of Judah, that sittest upon the throne of David, thou, and thy servants, and thy people that enter in by these gates: 3 Thus saith the LORD; Execute ye judgment and righteousness, and deliver the spoiled out of the hand of the oppressor: and do no wrong, do no violence to the stranger, the fatherless, nor the widow, neither shed innocent blood in this place. 15 Shalt thou reign, because thou closest *thyself* in cedar? did not thy father eat and drink, and do judgment and justice, *and* then *it was* well with him? 16 He judged the cause of the poor and needy; then *it was* well *with him: was* not this to know me? saith the LORD.

Ezk. 45: 9 Thus saith the Lord GOD; Let it suffice you, O princes of Israel: remove violence and spoil, and execute judgment and justice, take away your exactions from my people, saith the Lord GOD. 10 Ye shall have just balances, and a just ephah, and a just bath. — 46: 18 The prince shall not take of the people's inheritance by oppression, to thrust them out of their possession; *but* he shall give his sons inheritance out of his own possession: that my people be not scattered every man from his possession.

314. *Duties of subjects toward civil rulers.*

Ex. 22: 28 Thou shalt not revile- the gods, nor curse the ruler of thy people. [Ac. 23: 4, 5.]

Dt. 17: 9 Thou shalt come unto the priests the Levites, and unto the judge that shall be in those days, and inquire; and they shall shew thee the sentence of judgment: 10 And thou shalt do according to the sentence, which they of that place which the LORD shall choose shall shew thee; and thou shalt observe to do according to all that they inform thee: 11 According to the sentence of the law which they shall teach thee, and according to the judgment which they shall tell thee, thou shalt do: thou shalt not decline from the sentence which they shall shew thee, *to* the right hand nor *to* the left.

Ec. 8: 2 I *counsel thee* to keep the king's commandment, and *that* in regard of the oath of God.

Mat. 17: 24 When they were come to Capernaum, they that received tribute-*money*, came to Peter, and said, Doth not your Master pay tribute? 25 He saith, Yes. And when he was come into the house, Jesus prevented him, saying, What thinkest thou, Simon? of whom do the kings of the earth take custom or tribute? of their own children, or of strangers? 26 Peter said unto him, Of strangers. Jesus said unto him, Then are the children free. 27 Notwithstanding, lest we should offend them, go thou to the sea, and cast an hook, and take up the fish that first cometh up: and when thou hast opened his mouth, thou shalt find a piece of money: that take, and give unto them for me and thee. — 22: 20 He saith unto them, Whose *is* this image, and superscription? 21 They say unto him, Cesar's. Then saith he unto them, Render therefore unto Cesar, the things which are Cesar's; and unto God, the things that are God's.

Rom. 13: 1 Let every soul be subject unto the higher powers. For there is no power but of God: the powers that be, are ordained of God. 2 Whosoever therefore resisteth the power, resisteth the ordinance of God: and they that resist shall receive to themselves damnation. 5 Wherefore *ye* must needs be subject, not only for wrath, but also for conscience' sake. 6 For this cause pay ye tribute also: for they are God's ministers, attending continually upon this very thing. 7 Render therefore to all their dues: tribute to whom tribute *is due;* custom to whom custom; fear to whom fear; honor to whom honor.

1 Tim. 2: 1 I exhort therefore, that, first of all, supplications prayers, intercessions, *and* giving of thanks be made for all men: 2 For kings, and *for* all that are in authority; that we may lead a quiet and peaceable life in all godliness and honesty. 3 For this *is* good and acceptable in the sight of God our Saviour.

Tit. 3: 1 Put them in mind to be subject to principalities and powers, to obey magistrates, to be ready to every good work.

1 Pet. 2: 13 Submit yourselves to every ordinance of man for the Lord's sake: whether it be to the king as supreme; 14 Or unto governors, as unto them that are sent by him for the punishment of evil-doers, and for the praise of them that do well. 15 For so is the will of God, that with well-doing ye may put to silence the ignorance of foolish men: 16 As free, and not using *your* liberty for a cloak of maliciousness, but as the servants of God. 17 Honor all *men.* Love the brotherhood. Fear God. Honor the king.

315. *Civil penalties divinely appointed.*

Gen. 9: 5 Surely your blood of your lives will I require: at the hand of every beast will I require it, and at the hand of man; at the hand of every man's brother will I require the life of man. 6 Whoso sheddeth man's blood, by man shall his blood be shed: for in the image of God made he man.

Ex. 21: 12 He that smiteth a man, so that he die, shall be surely put to death. 13 And if a man lie not in wait, but God deliver *him* into his hand; then I will appoint thee a place whither he shall flee. 14 But if a man come presumptuously upon his neighbor, to slay him with guile; thou shalt take him from mine altar, that he may die. 15 And he that smiteth his father, or his mother, shall be surely put to death. 16 And he that stealeth a man and selleth him, or if he be found in his hand, he shall surely be put to death. 17 And he that curseth his father or his mother, shall surely be put to death.

19*

Num. 35: 30 Whoso killeth any person, the murderer shall be put to death by the mouth of witnesses: but one witness shall not testify against any person *to cause him* to die. 31 Moreover, ye shall take no satisfaction for the life of a murderer, which *is* guilty of death: but he shall be surely put to death. 32 And ye shall take no satisfaction for him that is fled to the city of his refuge, that he should come again to dwell in the land, until the death of the priest. 33 So ye shall not pollute the land wherein *ye are;* for blood it defileth the land: and the land cannot be cleansed of the blood that is shed therein, but by the blood of him that shed it. 34 Defile not, therefore, the land which ye shall inhabit, wherein I dwell: for I the Lord dwell among the children of Israel.

Dt. 19: 18 Behold, *if* the witness *be* a false witness, *and* hath testified falsely against his brother;. 19 Then shall ye do unto him, as he had thought to have done unto his brother. — 25: 1 If there be a controversy between men, and they come unto judgment, that *the judges* may judge them; then they shall justify the righteous, and condemn the wicked. 2 And it shall be, if the wicked man *be* worthy to be beaten, that the judge shall cause him to lie down, and to be beaten before his face, according to his fault, by a certain number. 3 Forty stripes he may give him, *and* not exceed; lest *if* he should exceed, and beat him above these with many stripes, then thy brother should seem vile unto thee.

Pr. 20: 26 A wise king scattereth the wicked, and bringeth the wheel over them. — 28: 17 A man that doeth violence to the blood of *any* person shall flee to the pit; let no man stay him.

Ac. 25: 10 Then said Paul, I stand at Cesar's judgment-seat, where I ought to be judged: to the Jews I have done no wrong, as thou very well knowest. 11 For if I be an offender, or have committed any thing worthy of death, I refuse not to die: but if there be none of these things whereof these accuse me, no man may deliver me unto them. I appeal unto Cesar.

Rom. 13: 4 He is the minister of God to thee for good. But if thou do that which is evil, be afraid; for he beareth not the sword in vain: for he is the minister of God, a revenger to *execute* wrath upon him that doeth evil.

316 *Capital crimes under the Mosaic code.*

1. *Murder.*—Num. 35: 16 The murderer shall surely be put to death.

2. *Blasphemy.*— Lev. 24: 16 He that blasphemeth the name of the Lord, he shall surely be put to death.

3. *Manstealing.* — Ex. 21: 16 He that stealeth a man, and selleth him, or if he be found in his hand, he shall surely be put to death. 1 Tim. 1: 9.

4. *Idolatry.* — Ex. 22: 20 He that sacrificeth unto *any* god, save unto the LORD only, he shall be utterly destroyed. [Dt. 17: 2.]

5. *Enticement to Idolatry.* — Dt. 13: 6 If thy brother —— entice thee secretly, saying, Let us go and serve other gods: 9 Thou shalt surely kill him.

6. *Adultery.*— Lev. 20: 10 The adulterer and the adulteress shall surely be put to death.

7. *Sodomy and Uncleanness.*— Lev. 20: 13 If a man also lie with mankind as he lieth with a woman, both of them have committed an abomination: they shall surely be put to death. 17—20.

8. *Incest.* — Lev. 20: 14 If a man take a wife and her mother, it *is* wickedness: they shall be burnt with fire. [V. 21.]

9. *Bestiality.* — Lev. 20: 15 If a man lie with a beast, he shall surely be put to death. [16.]

10. *Witchcraft.* — Ex. 22: 18 Thou shalt not suffer a witch to live.

11. *Smiting Parents.* — Ex. 21: 15 He that smiteth his father, or his mother, shall be surely put to death. [See 54.]

12. *Cursing Parents.* — Ex. 21: 17 He that curseth his father, or his mother, shall surely be put to death. [Lev. 20: 9.]

13. *Disobeying Parents.* — Dt. 21: 20 This our son *is* stubborn and rebellious, he will not obey our voice; *he is* a glutton and a drunkard. 21 And all the men of his city shall stone him with stones, that he die.

14. *Sabbath Profanation.*— Ex. 35: 2 Whosoever doeth work therein shall be put to death. [Num. 15: 32.]

15. *Endangering Human Life.* — Ex. 21: 29 If the ox were wont to push with his horn in time past, and it hath been testified to his owner, and he hath not kept him in, but that he hath killed a man or a woman; the ox shall be stoned, and his owner also shall be put to death.

817. *Opposition to rightful government frequent — its penalty.*

Num. 16: 3 They gathered themselves together against Moses and against Aaron, and said unto them, *Ye take* too much upon you, seeing all the congregation *are* holy, every one of them, and the LORD *is* among them: wherefore then

lift ye up yourselves above the congregation of the LORD?
4. And when Moses heard *it*, he fell upon his face: 5 And.
he spake unto Korah and unto all his company, saying, Even
to-morrow the LORD will shew who *are* his, and *who is* holy;
and will cause *him* to come near unto him: even *him* whom
he hath chosen will he cause to come near unto him.' 6 This
do; Take you censers, Korah and all his company; 7 And
put fire therein, and put incense in them before the LORD to-
morrow: and it shall be *that* the man whom the LORD doth
choose, he *shall* be holy; *ye take too* much upon you, ye sons
of Levi. 32 And the earth opened her mouth, and swallowed
them up.

Dt. 17: 12 The man that will do presumptuously, and will
not hearken unto the priest that standeth to minister there
before the LORD thy God, or unto the judge, even that man
shall die: and thou shalt put away the evil from Israel. 13
And all the people shall hear, and fear, and do no more presumptuously.

2 Pet. 2: 9 The Lord knoweth how to deliver the godly out
of temptations, and to reserve the unjust unto the day of judgment to be punished: 10 But chiefly them that walk after the
flesh in the lust of uncleanness, and despise government. Presumptuous *are they*, self-willed; they are not afraid to speak
evil of dignities.

Jude 8 Likewise also these *filthy* dreamers defile the flesh,
despise dominion, and speak evil of dignities.

318. *Wicked rulers injurious.*

1 K. 14: 16 He shall give Israel up because of the sins of
Jeroboam, who did sin, and who made Israel to sin.

2 Ch. 33: 9 So Manasseh made Judah and the inhabitants
of Jerusalem to err, *and* to do worse than the heathen, whom
the LORD had destroyed before the children of Israel. 10 And
the LORD spake to Manasseh, and to his people: but they
would not hearken. 11 Wherefore the LORD brought upon
them the captains of the host of the king of Assyria, which
took Manasseh among the thorns, and bound him with fetters,
and carried him to Babylon.

Ps. 12: 8 The wicked walk on every side, when the vilest
men are exalted. — 94: 20 Shall the throne of iniquity have
fellowship with thee, which frameth mischief by a law? 21
They gather themselves together against the soul of the righteous, and condemn the innocent blood.

Pr. 28: 15 *As* a roaring lion, and a ranging bear: *so is* a
wicked ruler over the poor people. 16 The prince that want-

eth understanding *is* also a great oppressor.—29: 2 When the righteous are in authority, the people rejoice: but when the wicked beareth rule, the people mourn. 4 The king by judgment establisheth the land: but he that receiveth gifts overthroweth it.

319. *Disobeying the wicked commands of civil rulers justifiable.*

Ex. 1: 17 The midwives feared God, and did not as the king of Egypt commanded them, but saved the men-children alive. 20 Therefore God dealt well with the midwives.

1 S. 14: 44 Saul answered, God do so, and more also: for thou shalt surely die, Jonathan. 45 And the people said unto Saul, Shall Jonathan die, who hath wrought this great salvation in Israel? God forbid: *as* the LORD liveth, there shall not one hair of his head fall to the ground; for he hath wrought with God this day.

Dan. 3: 16 Shadrach, Meshach, and Abed-nego, answered and said to the king, O Nebuchadnezzar, we *are* not careful to answer thee in this matter. 17 If it be *so,* our God whom we serve is able to deliver us from the burning fiery furnace, and he will deliver *us* out of thine hand, O king. 18 But if not, be it known unto thee, O king, that we will not serve thy gods, nor worship the golden image which thou hast set up.— 6: 13 Then answered they and said before the king, That Daniel, which *is* of the children of the captivity of Judah, regardeth not thee, O king, nor the decree that thou hast signed, but maketh his petition three times a day.

Ac. 4: 19 Peter and John answered and said unto them, Whether it be right in the sight of God to hearken unto you more than unto God, judge ye.—5: 27 When they had brought them, they set *them* before the council: and the high priest asked them, 28 Saying, Did not we straitly command you, that ye should not teach in this name? and behold, ye have filled Jerusalem with your doctrine, and intend to bring this man's blood upon us. 29 Then Peter and the *other* apostles answered and said, We ought to obey God rather than men.

GRATITUDE.

320. *Gratitude exemplified and rewarded.*

2 S. 9: 6 David said, Mephibosheth. And he answered, Behold thy servant! 7 And David said unto him, Fear not: for I will surely shew thee kindness for Jonathan thy father's sake, and will restore thee all the land of Saul thy father: and

thou shalt eat bread at my table continually.—19: 32 Barzillai was a very aged man, *even* fourscore years old: and he had provided the king of sustenance while he lay at Mahanaim: for he *was* a very great man. 33 And the king said unto Barzillai, Come thou over with me, and I will feed thee with me in Jerusalem.

Mat. 25: 34 Then shall the King say unto them on his right hand, Come, ye blessed of my Father, inherit the kingdom prepared for you from the foundation of the world: 35 For I was an hungered, and ye gave me meat: I was thirsty, and ye gave me drink: I was a stranger and ye took me in: 36 Naked, and ye clothed me: I was sick, and ye visited me: I was in prison, and ye came unto me.

HAPPINESS.

321. *Vanity of sensual happiness.*

Ec. 2: 1 I said in my heart, Go to now, I will prove thee with mirth; therefore enjoy pleasure: and behold, this also *is* vanity. 10 And whatsoever mine eyes desired I kept not from them, I withheld not my heart from any joy; for my heart rejoiced in all my labor: and this was my portion of all my labor. 11 Then I looked on all the works that my hands had wrought, and on the labor that I had labored to do: and behold, all *was* vanity and vexation of spirit. [See 627.]

322. *Intellectual happiness, invaluable.*

Pr. 3: 13 Happy *is* the man *that* findeth wisdom, and the man *that* getteth understanding. 14 For the merchandise of it *is* better than the merchandise of silver, and the gain thereof than fine gold. [See 391–2.]

323. *The happiness of self-denial, and of doing good.*

2 Cor. 6: 10 As sorrowful, yet always rejoicing: as poor, yet making many rich; as having nothing, and *yet* possessing all things. [See 408, 527, 630, 674.]

324. *The happiness of holy obedience.*

Ps. 119: 1 Blessed *are* the undefiled in the way, who walk in the law, of the LORD. 2 Blessed *are* they that keep his testimonies, *and that* seek him with the whole heart.

Pr. 29: 18 Where *there is* no vision, the people perish: but he that keepeth the law, happy *is* he. [See 286, 630.]

325. *The happiness of loving God.*

1 Pet. 1: 8 Whom having not seen, ye love; in whom,

though now ye see *him* not, yet believing, ye rejoice with joy unspeakable, and full of glory. [See 289.]

326. *The happiness of trusting in God.*

Ps. 40: 4 Blessed *is* that man that maketh the LORD his trust. [See 293–4.]

327. *The happiness of an approving conscience.*

2 Cor. 1: 12 Our rejoicing is this, the testimony of our conscience, that in simplicity and godly sincerity, not with fleshly wisdom, but by the grace of God, we have had our conversation in the world. [See 131.]

328. *The happiness of Heaven.*

1 Pet. 4: 13 Rejoice, inasmuch as ye are partakers of Christ's sufferings; that, when his glory shall be revealed, ye may be glad also with exceeding joy. [See 339, 672.]

HEART.

329. *The heart voluntary, or human activity and responsibility in determining its moral state and changes.*

Ex. 8: 15 When Pharaoh saw that there was respite, he hardened his heart.

2 S. 15: 6 Absalom stole the hearts of the men of Israel.

2 Ch. 30: 18 Hezekiah prayed for them, saying, The good Lord pardon every one *that* prepareth his heart to seek God.

Ezra 7: 10 Ezra had prepared his heart to seek the law of the Lord.

Esther 7: 5 Where is he, that durst presume in his heart to do so?

Ps. 73: 13 Verily, I have cleansed my heart *in* vain, and washed my hands in innocency.—119: 112 I have inclined my heart to perform thy statutes alway.

Pr. 4: 23 Keep thy heart with all diligence.—23: 26 My son, give me thine heart.

Mat. 5: 28 Whosoever looketh on a woman to lust after her, hath committed adultery with her already in his heart.

[See 264, 271, 592, 600.]

330. *A 'divided,' 'double heart.'*

Ps. 12: 2 *With* flattering lips *and* with a double heart do they speak.—86: 11 Unite my heart to fear thy name.

Hos. 10: 2 Their heart is divided.

331. *Do moral good and evil lie in the heart?*

1 K. 8: 18 Whereas it was in thy heart to build a house unto my name, thou didst well that it was in thy heart.

2 Ch. 32: 26 Hezekiah humbled himself for the pride of his heart.

Ps. 55: 21 *The words* of his mouth were smoother than butter, but war *was* in his heart.—78: 72 He fed them according to the integrity of his heart.—95: 10 It *is* a people that do err in their heart.

Pr. 6: 14 Frowardness *is* in his heart.—23: 7 As he thinketh in his heart, so *is* he.

Ec. 9: 3 The heart of the sons of men is full of evil, and madness *is* in their heart while they live.

Is. 10: 7 *It is* in his heart to destroy and cut off nations not a few.

Jer. 48: 29 His pride, and the haughtiness of his heart.

Mat. 5: 8 Blessed *are* the pure in heart.—15: 18 But those things which proceed out of the mouth come forth from the heart; and they defile the man.   19 For out of the heart proceed evil thoughts, murders, adulteries, fornications, thefts, false witness, blasphemies.

Rom. 10: 10 For with the heart, man believeth unto righteousness.

Heb. 3: 12 Take heed, brethren, lest there be in any of you an evil heart of unbelief.

332. *Controlling influence of the heart.*

Job. 15: 12 Why doth thine heart carry thee away?

Pr. 4: 23 Keep thy heart with all diligence; for out of it *are* the issues of life. — 16: 9 A man's heart deviseth his way.

Mat. 12: 34 Out of the abundance of the heart, the mouth speaketh.   35 A good man, out of the good treasure of the heart, bringeth forth good things : and an evil man, out of the evil treasure, bringeth forth evil things.   [Lk. 6: 45.]

333. *Religious duties demand sincerity of heart.*

Dt. 26: 16 This day the LORD thy God hath commanded thee to do these statutes and judgments : thou shalt therefore keep and do them with all thy heart, and with all thy soul.

1 S. 16: 7 *The LORD seeth* not as man seeth ; for man looketh on the outward appearance, but the LORD looketh on the heart.

Jer. 29: 13 Ye shall seek me, and find *me*, when ye shall search for me with all your heart.

Mat. 22: 37 Thou shalt love the Lord thy God with all thy

A Place — Its Holiness.

heart.—23: 26 *Thou* blind Pharisee, cleanse first that *which is* within the cup and platter, that the outside of them may be clean also.

Jn. 4: 24 God *is* a Spirit: and they that worship him, must worship *him* in spirit and in truth.

Ac. 8: 21 Thou hast neither part nor lot in this matter: for thy heart is not right in the sight of God. 37 If thou believest with all thy heart, thou mayest.

Rom. 2: 28 He is not a Jew, which is one outwardly; neither *is that* circumcision, which is outward in the flesh: 29 But he *is* a Jew which is one inwardly; and circumcision *is that* of the heart, in the spirit, *and* not in the letter; whose praise *is* not of men, but of God. — 10: 10 With the heart, man believeth unto righteousness.

1 Tim. 1: 5 Now the end of the commandment is charity out of a pure heart, and *of* a good conscience. and *of* faith unfeigned. [See 529, 542.]

HEAVEN.

334. *Heaven a place.*

Jn. 14: 2 In my Father's house are many mansions: if *it were* not *so*, I would have told you. I go to prepare a place for you. 3 And if I go and prepare a place for you, I will come again and receive you unto myself: that where I am, *there* ye may be also.

Ep. 3: 10 To the intent that now unto the principalities and powers in heavenly *places* might be known by the church the manifold wisdom of God.

335. *Perfection of heavenly light.*

Ps. 36: 9 With thee *is* the fountain of life: in thy light shall we see light.

Is. 2: 5 O house of Jacob, come ye, and let us walk in the light of the LORD.

Rev. 21: 23 The city had no need of the sun, neither of the moon, to shine in it: for the glory of God did lighten it, and the Lamb *is* the light thereof. — 22: 5 There shall be no night there; and they need no candle, neither light of the sun; for the Lord God giveth them light: and they shall reign for ever and ever. [See 398.]

336. *Universal and perfect holiness in heaven.*

Ps. 17: 15 As for me, I will behold thy face in righteousness: I shall be satisfied, when I awake, with thy likeness

Ep. 5: 25 Husbands, love your wives, even as Christ also loved the church, and gave himself for it; 26 That he might sanctify and cleanse it with the washing of water by the word, 27 That he might present it to himself a glorious church, not having spot or wrinkle, or any such thing; but that it should be holy and without blemish.

1 Jn. 3: 2 Beloved, now are we the sons of God, and it doth not yet appear what we shall be: but we know that, when he shall appear, we shall be like him; for we shall see him as he is.

Rev. 21: 27 There shall in no wise enter into it any thing that defileth, neither *whatsoever* worketh abomination, or *maketh* a lie.

337. *Heaven a place of rest.*

2 Th. 1: 6 Seeing *it-is* a righteous thing with God to recompense tribulation to them that trouble you; 7 And to you, who are troubled, rest with us, when the Lord Jesus shall be revealed.

Heb. 4: 3 We which have believed do enter into rest, as he said, As I have sworn in my wrath, if they shall enter into my rest: although the works were finished from the foundation of the world. 9 There remaineth therefore a rest to the people of God.

Rev. 14: 13 I heard a voice from heaven, saying unto me, Write, Blessed *are* the dead which die in the Lord from henceforth: Yea, saith the Spirit, that they may rest from their labors. [See 512.]

338. *Nearness to God and to Christ in heaven.*

Jn. 17: 22 The glory which thou gavest me, I have given them; that they may be one, even as we are one; 23 I in them, and thou in me, that they may be made perfect in one; and that the world may know that thou hast sent me, and hast loved them as thou hast loved me. 24 Father, I will that they also whom thou hast given me be with me where I am; that they may behold my glory.

Rev. 22: 4 They shall see his face; and his name *shall be* in their foreheads. [See 657.]

339. *Perfect and perpetual happiness in heaven.*

Ps. 16: 11 Thou wilt shew me the path of life: in thy presence *is* fulness of joy; at thy right hand *there are* pleasures for evermore.—They 36, 8 shall be abundantly satisfied with the fatness of thy house; and thou shalt make them drink of the river of thy pleasures. — 84: 11 The LORD God *is* a sun and shield: the LORD will give grace and glory; no good *thing* will he withhold from them that walk uprightly. — 97: 11 Light is sown for the righteous, and gladness for the upright in heart.

Is. 51: 11 The redeemed of the LORD shall return, and come with singing unto Zion; and everlasting joy *shall be* upon their head: they shall obtain gladness and joy; *and* sorrow and mourning shall flee away.

1 Pet. 4: 13 Rejoice, inasmuch as ye are partakers of Christ's sufferings; that, when his glory shall be revealed, ye may be glad also with exceeding joy.

Jude 24 Now unto him that is able to keep you from falling, and to present *you* faultless before the presence of his glory with exceeding joy.

Rev. 7: 15 Therefore are they before the throne of God, and serve him day and night in his temple; and he that sitteth on the throne shall dwell among them. 16 They shall hunger no more, neither thirst any more; neither shall the sun light on them, nor any heat. 17 For the Lamb which is in the midst of the throne shall feed them, and shall lead them unto living fountains of waters: and God shall wipe away all tears from their eyes. — 21: 3 I heard a great voice out of heaven, saying, Behold, the tabernacle of God *is* with men, and he will dwell with them, and they shall be his people, and God himself shall be with them, *and be* their God. 4 And God shall wipe away all tears from their eyes; and there shall be no more death, neither sorrow, nor crying, neither shall there be any more pain.

340. *Possessions, honors, rewards, and glory in heaven.*

Mat. 13: 43 Then shall the righteous shine forth as the sun in the kingdom of their Father. — 19: 28 Jesus said unto them, Verily, I say unto you, That ye which have followed me in the regeneration, when the Son of man shall sit in the throne of his glory, ye also shall sit upon twelve thrones, judging the twelve tribes of Israel.

Lk. 22: 28 Ye are they which have continued with me in my temptations. 29 And I appoint unto you a kingdom, as my Father hath appointed unto me; 30 That ye may eat and drink at my table in my kingdom, and sit on thrones, judging the twelve tribes of Israel.

Rom. 8: 17 If children, then heirs: heirs of God, and joint-heirs with Christ; if so be that we suffer with *him*, that we may be also glorified together. 18 For I reckon, that the sufferings of this present time *are* not worthy *to be compared* with the glory which shall be revealed to us. 32 He that spared not his own Son, but delivered him up for us all, how shall he not with him also freely give us all things?

1 Cor. 2: 9 Eye hath not seen, nor ear heard, neither have entered into the heart of man, the things which God hath prepared for them that love him. [Is 64: 4.] — 3: 21 Let no man glory in men; for all things are yours; 22 Whether Paul, or Apollos, or Cephas, or the world, or life, or death, or things present, or things to come; all are yours; 23 And ye are Christ's: and Christ *is* God's.

2 Cor. 4: 17 Our light affliction, which is but for a moment, worketh for us, a far more exceeding *and* eternal weight of glory.

Heb. 11: 16 Now they desire a better *country*, that is, a heavenly: wherefore God is not ashamed to be called their God: for he hath prepared for them a city.

Rev. 1: 5 Unto him that loved us, and washed us from our sins in his own blood, 6 And hath made us kings and priests unto God and his Father; to him *be* glory and dominion for ever and ever. — 21: 2 I John saw the holy city, new Jerusalem, coming down from God out of heaven, prepared as a bride adorned for her husband. 7 He that overcometh shall inherit all things: and I will be his God, and he shall be my son. — 22: 5 There shall be no night there; and they need no candle, neither light of the sun; for the Lord God giveth them light: and they shall reign for ever and ever.

[See 672.]

341. *Heaven spiritual, unfading, and eternal.*

Is. 60: 20 Thy sun shall no more go down; neither shall thy moon withdraw itself: for the LORD shall be thine everlasting light, and the days of thy mourning shall be ended.

Mat. 6: 20 Lay up for yourselves treasures in heaven, where neither moth nor rust doth corrupt. — 22: 30 In the resurrection they neither marry, nor are given in marriage, but are as the angels of God in heaven. — 25: 46 These shall go away into everlasting punishment: but the righteous into life eternal.

1 Cor. 15: 50 This I say, brethren, that flesh and blood cannot inherit the kingdom of God; neither doth corruption inherit incorruption.

1 Pet. 1: 4 An inheritance incorruptible, and undefiled, and that fadeth not away, reserved in heaven for you. 5 Who are

kept by the power of God through faith unto salvation, ready to be revealed in the last time.

342. *Do saints merit their heavenly inheritance?*

Ezk. 36: 32 Not for your sakes do I *this*, saith the Lord GOD, be it known unto you; be ashamed and confounded for your own ways, O house of Israel. [See 586, 663, 668.]

HELL.

343. *Hell a place of punishment by fire.*

Ps. 21: 9 Thou shalt make them as a fiery oven in the time of thine anger: the LORD shall swallow them up in his wrath, and the fire shall devour them.

Is. 30: 33 For Tophet *is* ordained of old; yea, for the king it is prepared; he hath· made *it* deep *and* large: the pile thereof *is* fire and much wood: the breath of the LORD, like a stream of brimstone, doth kindle it. — 33: 14 Who among us shall dwell with the devouring fire? who among us shall dwell with everlasting burnings?

Lk. 16: 24 And he cried, and said, Father Abraham, have mercy on me, and send Lazarus, that he may dip the tip of his finger in water, and cool my tongue; for I am tormented in this flame.

2 Th. 1: 8 In flaming fire, taking vengeance on them that know not God, and that obey not the gospel.

Rev. 21: 8 The fearful, and unbelieving, and the abominable, and murderers, and whoremongers, and sorcerers, and idolaters, and all liars, shall have their part in the lake which burneth with fire and brimstone: which is the second death. [See 561.]

HOLINESS.

344. *Holiness intrinsically and supremely valuable.*

Job 28: 12 Where shall wisdom be found?· and where *is* the place of understanding? 13 Man knoweth not the price thereof; neither is it found in the land of the living. 14 The depth saith, It *is* not in me: and the sea saith, *It is* not with me. 15 It cannot be gotten for gold, neither shall silver be weighed *for* the price thereof. 18 No mention shall be made of coral, or of pearls; for the price of wisdom *is* above rubies. 19 The topaz of Ethiopia shall not equal it, neither shall it be

20*

valued with pure gold.   28 And unto man he said, Behold, the fear of the LORD, that *is* wisdom; and to depart from evil *is* understanding.

Pr. 3: 13 Happy *is* the man *that* findeth wisdom, and the man *that* getteth understanding.   14 For the merchandise of it *is* better than the merchandise of silver, and the gain thereof than fine gold.   15 She *is* more precious than rubies: and all the things thou canst desire are not to be compared unto her. 16 Length of days *is* in her right hand: *and* in her left hand riches and honor.   17 Her ways *are* ways of pleasantness, and all her paths *are* peace.   18 She *is* a tree of life to them that lay hold upon her: and happy *is* *every one* that retaineth her. —4: 7 Wisdom *is* the principal thing; *therefore* get wisdom: and with all thy getting get understanding.   8 Exalt her, and she shall promote thee: she shall bring thee to honor, when thou dost embrace her.   9 She shall give to thine head an ornament of grace; a crown of glory shall she deliver to thee. —8: 11 Wisdom *is* better than rubies; and all the things that may be desired are not to be compared to it.   [See 630.]

HOLY SPIRIT.

345. *Personality of the Holy Spirit.*

Mat. 28: 19 Go ye therefore and teach all nations, baptizing them in the name of the Father, and of the Son, and of the Holy Ghost.

Lk. 3: 22 And the Holy Ghost descended in a bodily shape like a dove upon him.

Jn. 14: 16 And I will pray the Father, and he shall give you another Comforter, that he may abide with you for ever.

2 Cor. 13: 14 The grace of the Lord Jesus Christ, and the love of God, and the communion of the Holy Ghost, *be* with you all.   Amen.

Ep. 2: 18 For through him we both have access by one Spirit unto the Father.

1 Pet. 1: 2 Elect according to the foreknowledge of God the Father, through sanctification of the Spirit, unto obedience.

1 Jn. 5: 7. There are three that bear record in heaven, the Father, the Word, and the Holy Ghost; and these three are one.

346. *Divine attributes of the Holy Spirit.*

Mic. 2: 7 O *thou that art* named the house of Jacob, is the Spirit of the LORD straitened?

His Office-work

Jn. 14: 26 The Comforter, *which is* the Holy Ghost, whom the Father will send in my name, he shall teach you all things, and bring all things to your remembrance, whatsoever I have said unto you.

Ac. 5: 3 Peter said, Ananias, why hath Satan-filled thine heart to lie to the Holy Ghost, and to keep back part of the price of the land? 4 While it remained, was it not thine own? and after it was sold, was it not in thine own power? why hast thou conceived this thing in thine heart? thou hast not lied unto men, but unto God.

Rom. 15: 19 Through mighty signs and wonders, by the power of the Spirit of God; so that from Jerusalem, and round about unto Illyricum, I have fully preached the gospel of Christ.

1 Cor. 2: 10 But God hath revealed *them* unto us by his Spirit; for the Spirit searcheth all things, yea, the deep things of God. 11 For what man knoweth the things of a man, save the spirit of man which is in him? even so the things of God knoweth no man, but the Spirit of God.—12: 3 I give you to understand, that no man speaking by the Spirit of God, calleth Jesus accursed: and *that* no man can say that Jesus is the Lord, but by the Holy Ghost.

Heb. 9: 14 How much more shall the blood of Christ, who through the eternal Spirit offered himself without spot to God, purge your conscience from dead works to serve the living God? [See 76, 211.]

347. *Office-work of the Holy Spirit.*

1. *To awaken and convince sinners.*

Gen. 6: 3 The LORD said, My Spirit shall not always strive with man, for that he also *is* flesh.

Job 36: 9 He sheweth them their work, and their transgressions that they have exceeded. 10 He openeth also their ear to discipline, and commandeth that they return from iniquity.

Jn. 16: 7 I tell you the truth: It is expedient for you that I go away: for if I go not away, the Comforter will not come unto you; but if I depart, I will send him unto you. 8 And when he is come, he will reprove [convince] the world of sin, and of righteousness, and of judgment.

2. *To confer miraculous gifts.*

1 S. 10: 10 When they came thither to the hill, behold; a company of prophets met him; and the Spirit of God came upon him, and he prophesied among them.

Lk. 1: 67 Zacharias was filled with the Holy Ghost, and prophesied.

Ac. 2: 4 They were all filled with the Holy Ghost, and began to speak with other tongues, as the Spirit gave them utterance.—10: 45 They of the circumcision which believed, were astonished, as many as came with Peter, because that on the Gentiles also was poured out the gift of the Holy Ghost. 46 For they heard them speak with tongues, and magnify God. —11: 15 As I began to speak, the Holy Ghost fell on them, as on us at the beginning.

3. To reveal divine truth, as a witness against sinners, and for God and his people.

Dt. 31: 19 Write ye this song for you, and teach it the children of Israel: put it in their mouths, that this song may be a witness for me against the children of Israel.

Neh. 9: 20. Thou gavest also thy good Spirit to instruct them.

Mat. 24: 14 This gospel of the kingdom shall be preached in all the world, for a witness unto all nations; and then shall the end come.

Lk. 2: 26 It was revealed unto him by the Holy Ghost, that he should not see death, before he had seen the Lord's Christ.—12: 11 When they bring you unto the synagogues, and *unto* magistrates, and powers, take ye no thought how or what thing ye shall answer, or what ye shall say: 12 For the Holy Ghost shall teach you in the same hour what ye ought to say.

Jn. 14: 26 The Comforter, *which is* the Holy Ghost, whom the Father will send in my name, he shall teach you all things, and bring all things to your remembrance, whatsoever I have said unto you.

Ac. 11: 28 There stood up one of them named Agabus, and signified by the Spirit, that there should be great dearth throughout all the world: which came to pass in the days of Claudius Cesar.

1 Jn. 5: 8 There are three that bear witness in earth, the spirit, and the water, and the blood; and these three agree in one. 9 If we receive the witness of men, the witness of God is greater: for this is the witness of God which he hath testified of his Son. [See 40.]

4. To cause holy affections, which become the "witness of the Spirit" that saints "are the children of God."

Jn. 14: 16 I will pray the Father, and he shall give you another Comforter, that he may abide with you for ever; 17 *Even* the Spirit of truth; whom the world cannot receive, because it seeth him not, neither knoweth him: but ye know him; for he dwelleth with you, and shall be in you.—16: 13 When he, the Spirit of truth, is come, he will guide you into all truth: for he shall not speak of himself; but whatsoever he shall hear, *that* shall he speak: and he will shew you things to come.

Rom. 8: 14 As many as are led by the Spirit of God, they are the sons of God. 15 For ye have not received the spirit of bondage again to fear; but ye have received the Spirit of adoption, whereby we cry, Abba, Father. 16 The Spirit itself beareth witness with our Spirit, that we are the children of God.

Gal. 4: 6 Because ye are sons, God hath sent forth the Spirit of his Son into your hearts, crying, Abba, Father.

Heb. 10: 15 *Whereof* the Holy Ghost also is a witness to us: for after that he had said before, 16 This *is* the covenant that I will make with them after those days, saith the Lord; I will put my laws into their hearts, and in their minds will I write them.

1 Jn. 2: 5 Whosó keepeth his word, in him verily is the love of God perfected: hereby know we that we are in him.— 3: 24 He that keepeth his commandments, dwelleth in him, and he in him. And hereby we know that he abideth in us, by the Spirit which he hath given us.—5: 10 He that believeth on the Son of God hath the witness in himself.

[See 594–6, 598.]

5. *To seal the heirs of glory.*

Ep. 4: 30 Grieve not the Holy Spirit of God, whereby ye are sealed unto the day of redemption. [See 517.]

348. *Guilt and danger of sinning against the Holy Spirit.*

Is. 63: 10 They rebelled, and vexed his Holy Spirit: therefore he was turned to be their enemy, and he fought against them.

Mat. 12: 31 I say unto you, All manner of sin and blasphemy shall be forgiven unto men: but the blasphemy *against* the *Holy* Ghost shall not be forgiven unto men. 32 And whosoever speaketh a word against the Son of man, it shall be forgiven him: but whosoever speaketh against the Holy Ghost, it shall not be forgiven him, neither in this world, neither in the *world* to come.

Ac. 7: 51 Ye stiff-necked, and uncircumcised in heart and ears, ye do always resist the Holy Ghost: as your fathers *did*, so *do* ye.

Ep. 4: 30 Grieve not the Holy Spirit of God, whereby ye are sealed unto the day of redemption.

1 Th. 5: 19 Quench not the Spirit.

Heb. 10: 28 He that despised Moses' law, died without mercy under two or three witnesses: 29 Of how much sorer punishment, suppose ye, shall he be thought worthy, who hath trodden under foot the Son of God, and hath counted the blood of the-covenant, wherewith he was sanctified, an unholy thing, and hath done despite unto the Spirit of grace? [See 309.]

349. *Judicial departure of the Holy Spirit.*

Gen. 6: 3 The LORD said, My Spirit shall not always strive with man.

Ps. 81: 11 My people would not hearken to my voice; and Israel would none of me. 12 So I gave them up unto their own hearts' lust: *and* they walked in their own counsels. 13 Oh that my people had hearkened unto me, *and* Israel had walked in my ways! 14 I should soon have, subdued their enemies, and turned my hand against their adversaries. 15 The haters of the LORD should have submitted themselves unto him: but their time should have endured for ever.

Is. 55: 6 Seek ye the LORD while he may be found, call ye upon him while he is near.

Hos. 5: 6 They shall go·with their flocks and with their herds to seek the LORD; but they shall not find *him;* he hath withdrawn himself from them.—9: 12 Though they bring up their children, yet will I bereave them, *that there shall* not *be* a man *left:* yea, wo also to them when I depart from them!

Rom. 1: 24 God also gave them up to uncleanness, through the lusts of their own hearts, to dishonor their own bodies between themselves: 25 Who changed the truth of God into a lie, and worshipped and served the creature more than the Creator, who is blessed for ever. 26 For this cause God gave them up unto vile affections. 28 And even as they did not like to retain God in *their* knowledge, God gave them over to a reprobate mind, to do those things which are not convenient.

350. *The Holy Spirit promised believers.*

Lk. 11: 13 If ye then, being evil, know how to give good gifts unto your children: how much more shall *your* heavenly Father give the Holy Spirit to them that ask him?

Jn. 14: 16 I will pray the Father, and he shall give you another Comforter, that he may abide with you for ever; 17 *Even* the Spirit of truth; whom the world cannot receive, because it seeth him not, neither knoweth him: but ye know him; for he dwelleth with you, and shall be in you.

2 Cor. 1: 21 Now he which establisheth us with you in

Christ, and hath anointed us, *is* God; 22 Who hath also sealed us, and given the earnest of the Spirit in our hearts.

HOME.

351. *Keeping at home recommended — roving disapproved.*

Pr. 25: 17 Withdraw thy foot from thy neighbor's house; lest he be weary of thee, and so hate thee. — 27: 8 As a bird that wandereth from her nest, so *is* a man that wandereth from his place.

Tit. 2: 4 Teach the young women to be sober, to love their husbands, to love their children, 5 To *be* discreet, chaste, keepers at home.

HOPE.

352. *The proper and-chief object of hope.*

Ps. 42: 5. Hope thou in God.
Rom. 5: 2 Rejoice in hope of the glory of God.
1 Pet. 1: 21 That your faith and hope might be in God.

353. *Full assurance of hope inculcated and exemplified.*

Job 19: 25 I know *that* my Redeemer liveth.

Rom. 8: 35 Who shall separate us from the love of Christ? *shall* tribulation, or distress, or persecution, or famine, or nakedness, or peril, or sword? 37 Nay, in all these things we are more than conquerors, through him that loved us.

2 Tim. 4: 6 I am now ready to be offered, and the time of my departure is at hand. 7 I have fought a good fight, I have finished *my* course, I have kept the faith: 8 Henceforth there is laid up for me a crown of righteousness, which the Lord, the righteous Judge, shall give me at that day: and not to me only, but unto all them also that love his appearing.

Heb. 6: 11 We desire that every one of you do shew the same diligence to the full assurance of hope unto the end. 12 That ye be not slothful, but followers of them who through faith and patience inherit the promises. 17 Wherein God, willing more abundantly to shew unto the heirs of promise the immutability of his counsel, confirmed *it* by an oath: 18 That by two immutable things, in which *it was* impossible for God to lie, we might have a strong consolation, who have fled for refuge to lay hold upon the hope set before us. 19 Which *hope* we have as an anchor of the soul, both sure and steadfast, and which entereth into that within the vail; 20 Whither the forerunner is for us entered, *even* Jesus, made an high priest for ever after the order of Melchisedec.

1 Jn. 3: 18 My little children, let us not love in word, neither in tonge, but in deed and in truth. 19 And hereby we know that we are of the truth, and shall assure our hearts before him.

HOSPITALITY.

354. *Hospitality required and encouraged.*

Rom. 12: 10 *Be* kindly affectioned one to another with broth-erly love; in honor preferring one another; 13 Distributing to the necessity of saints: given to hospitality.

1 Tim. 3: 2 A bishop then must be blameless, the husband of one wife, vigilant, sober, of good behavior, given to hospitality, apt to teach. [Tit. 1: 8.]

Heb. 13: 2 Be not forgetful to entertain strangers: for thereby some have entertained angels unawares.

1 Pet. 4: 9 Use hospitality one to another without grudging. Mat. 10: 40—42. [See 715].

355. *Hospitality exemplified.*

Gen. 18: 2 He lifted up his eyes and looked, and lo, three men stood by him: and when he saw *them*, he ran to meet them from the tent-door, and bowed himself toward the ground, 3 And said, My Lord, if now I have found favor in thy sight, pass not away, I pray thee, from thy servant: 4 Let a little water, I pray you, be fetched, and wash your feet, and rest yourselves under the tree: 5 And I will fetch a morsel of bread, and comfort ye your hearts; after that ye shall pass on: for therefore are ye come to your servant. And they said, So do, as thou hast said. 6 Abraham hastened into the tent unto Sarah, and said, Make ready quickly three measures of fine meal, knead *it*, and make cakes upon the hearth. 7 And Abraham ran unto the herd, and fetched a calf tender and good, and gave *it* unto a young man; and he hasted to dress it. — 19: 1 And there came two angels to Sodom at even; and Lot sat in the gate of Sodom; and Lot seeing *them*, rose up to meet them; and he bowed himself with his face toward the ground; 2 And he said, Behold now, my lords, turn in, I pray you, into your servant's house, and tarry all night, and, wash your feet, and ye shall rise up early, and go on your ways. And they said, Nay; but we will abide in the street all night. 3 And he pressed upon them greatly; and they turned in unto him, and entered into his house; and he made

them a feast, and did bake unleavened bread, and they did
eat.

Job 31: 32 The stranger did not lodge in the street : *but* I
opened my doors to the traveller.

Ac. 28: 7 In the same quarters were possessions of the chief
man of the island, whose name was Publius ; who received us,
and lodged us three days courteously.

3 Jn. 5 Beloved, thou doest faithfully whatsoever thou doest
to the brethren and to strangers; 6 Which have borne witness
of thy charity before the church : whom if thou bring forward
on their journey after a goodly sort, thou shalt do well.
[See 135, 407.]

HUMILITY.

356. *Nature and manifestations of humility.*

Jud. 10: 15 The children of Israel said unto the LORD, We
have sinned : do thou unto us whatsoever seemeth good unto
thee.

2 S. 24: 17 David spake unto the LORD when he saw the
angel that smote the people, and said, Lo, I have sinned, and I
have done wickedly : but these sheep, what have they done ?
Let thy hand, I pray thee, be against me, and against my
father's house.

Job 2: 10 He said unto her, Thou speakest as one of the
foolish women speaketh. What! shall we receive good at the
hand of God, and shall we not receive evil ?

Lk. 15: 18 I will arise and go to my father, and will say
unto him, Father, I have sinned against heaven and before
thee, 19 And am no more worthy to be called thy son: make
me as one of thy hired servants. — 23: 40 But the other
answering, rebuked him, saying, Dost not thou fear God, seeing thou art in the same condemnation? 41 And we indeed
justly ; for we receive the due reward of our deeds.
[See 299, 414, 537, 603, 674.]

357. *Humility required and encouraged.*

Lev. 26: 41 If then their uncircumcised hearts be humbled,
and they then accept of the punishment of their iniquity, 42
Then will I remember my covenant with Jacob, and also my
covenant with Isaac, and also my covenant with Abraham will
I remember ; and I will remember the land.

Job 22: 29 When *men* are cast down, then thou shalt say,
There is lifting up ; and he shall save the humble person.

Ps. 9: 12 When he maketh inquisition for blood, he remem_

bereth them: he forgetteth not the cry of the humble.—10: 17 LORD, thou hast heard the desire of the humble: thou wilt prepare their heart, thou wilt cause thine ear to hear.—138: 6 Though the LORD *be* high, yet hath he respect unto the lowly: but the proud he knoweth afar off.

Pr. 3: 34 Surely he scorneth the scorners: but he giveth grace unto the lowly. — 15: 33 The fear of the LORD *is* the instruction of wisdom: and before honor is humility. — 22: 4 By humility *and* the fear of the LORD *are* riches, and honor, and life. — 29: 23 A man's pride shall bring him low: but honor shall uphold the humble in spirit.

Is. 57: 15 Thus saith the high and lofty One that inhabiteth eternity, whose name *is* Holy; I dwell in the high and holy *place*, with him also *that is* of a contrite and humble spirit, to revive the spirit of the humble, and to revive the heart of the contrite ones.

Mic. 6: 8 He hath shewed thee, O man, what *is* good; and what doth the LORD require of .thee, but to do justly, and to love mercy, and to walk humbly with thy God?

Mat. 5: 3 Blessed *are* the poor in spirit: for theirs is the kingdom of heaven.

Lk. 18: 14. I tell you, this man went down to his house justified *rather* than the other: for every one that exalteth himself shall be abased: and he that humbleth himself shall be exalted.

Jam. 4: 6 God resisteth the proud, but giveth grace unto the humble. 10 Humble yourselves in the sight of the Lord, and he shall lift you up.

1 Pet. 5: 5 God resisteth the proud, and giveth grace to the humble. 6 Humble yourselves, therefore, under the mighty hand of God, that he may exalt you in due time.

[See 606–7.]

IDLENESS.

358. *Idleness described, reproved, and punished.*

Pr. 6: 6 Go to the ant, thou sluggard; consider her ways, and be wise: 7 Which having no guide, overseer, or ruler, 8 Provideth her meat in the summer, *and* gathereth her food in the harvest. 9 How long wilt thou sleep, O sluggard? when wilt thou arise out of thy sleep?—15: 19 The way of the slothful *man* is as a hedge of thorns: but the way of the righteous *is* made plain.—18: 9 He also that is slothful in his work is brother to him that is a great waster. — 19: 15 Slothfulness casteth into a deep sleep; and an idle soul shall suffer hunger. — 20: 4 The sluggard will not plough by reason of the cold; *therefore* shall he beg in harvest, and *have* nothing. 13 Love not sleep, lest thou come to poverty; open thine eyes, *and* thou shalt be satisfied with bread. — 21: 25 The desire of the slothful killeth him; for his hands refuse to labor. 26 He coveteth greedily all the day long: but the righteous giveth and spareth not. — 23: 21 The drunkard and the glutton shall come to poverty: and drowsiness shall clothe *a man* with rags. — 24: 30 I went by the field of the slothful, and by the vineyard of the man void of understanding; 31 And lo, it was all grown over with thorns, *and* nettles had covered the face thereof, and the stone wall thereof was broken down. 32 Then I saw, *and* considered *it* well: I looked upon *it, and* received instruction. 33 *Yet* a little sleep, a little slumber, a little folding of the hands to sleep: 34 So shall thy poverty come *as* one that travelleth; and thy want as an armed man.

Ec. 10: 18 By much slothfulness the building decayeth; and through idleness of the hands the house droppeth through.

2 Thes. 3: 10 Even when we were with you, this we commanded you, that if any would not work, neither should he eat. 11 We hear that there are some which walk among you disorderly, working not at all, but are busy-bodies. 12 Now them that are such, we command and exhort by our Lord Jesus Christ, that with quietness they work, and eat their own bread.

1 Tim. 5: 13 They learn *to be* idle, wandering about from house to house : and not only idle, but tattlers also, and busy-bodies, speaking things which they ought not. [See 1, 709.]

IDOLATRY AND HEATHENISM.

359. Character of heathen idolaters.

2 K. 16: 3 But he [Ahaz] walked in the way of the kings of Israel, yea, and made his son to pass through the fire, according to the abominations of the heathen, whom the LORD cast out from before the children of Israel.

Rom. 1: 21 When they knew God, they glorified *him* not as God, neither were thankful, but became vain in their imaginations, and their foolish heart was darkened. 22 Professing themselves to be wise, they became fools ; 23 And changed the glory of the incorruptible God into an image made like to corruptible man, and to birds, and four-footed beasts, and creeping things. 24 Wherefore God also gave them up to uncleanness, through the lusts of their own hearts, to dishonor their own bodies between themselves : 29 Being filled with all unrighteousness, fornication, wickedness, covetousness, maliciousness ; full of envy, murder, debate, deceit, malignity ; whisperers, 30 Backbiters, haters of God, despiteful, proud, boasters, inventors of evil things, disobedient to parents, 31 Without understanding, covenant-breakers, without natural affection, implacable, unmerciful.

Ep. 4: 17 This I say therefore, and testify in the Lord, that ye henceforth walk not as other Gentiles walk, in the vanity of their mind, 18 Having the understanding darkened, being alienated from the life of God through the ignorance that is in them, because of the blindness of their heart: 19 Who, being past feeling, have given themselves over unto lasciviousness, to work all uncleanness with greediness. [See 480.]

360. *Heathen gods destitute of divinity.*

Ps. 115: 4 Their idols *are* silver and gold, the work of men's hands. 5 They have mouths, but they speak not: eyes have they, but they see not : 6 They have ears, but they hear not : noses have they, but they smell not : 7 They have hands, but they handle not : feet have they, but they walk not : neither speak they through their throat. 8 They that make them are like unto them; *so is* every one that trusteth in them.

Is. 46: 6 They lavish gold out of the bag, and weigh silver in the balance, *and* hire a goldsmith; and he maketh it a god: they fall down, yea they worship. 7 They bear him upon the shoulder, they carry him, and set him in his place, and he standeth ; from his place shall he not remove : yea, *one* shall cry unto him yet can he not answer, nor save him out of his trouble.

361. *Idolatry and image-worship forbidden.*

Ex. 20: 3 Thou shalt have no other gods before me. 4 Thou shalt not make unto thee any graven image, or any likeness *of any thing* that *is* in heaven above, or that *is* in the earth beneath, or that *is* in the water under the earth : 5 Thou shalt not bow down thyself to them, nor serve them for I the LORD thy God *am* a jealous God, visiting the iniquity of the fathers upon the children unto the third and fourth *generation* of them that hate me. — 23: 24 Thou shalt not bow down to their gods, nor serve them, nor do after their works : but thou shalt utterly overthrow them, and quite break down their images. — 34: 17 Thou shalt make thee no molten gods.

Common — Displeasing to God.

Lev. 19: 4 Turn ye not unto idols, nor make to yourselves molten gods: I *am* the LORD your God. — 26: 1 Ye shall make you no idols nor graven image, neither rear you up a standing image, neither shall ye set up *any* image of stone in your land, to bow down unto it: for I *am* the LORD your God.

Dt. 6: 14 Ye shall not go after other gods, of the gods of the people which *are* round about you; 15 (For the LORD thy God *is* a jealous God among you;) lest the anger of the LORD thy God be kindled against thee, and destroy thee from off the face of the earth — 28: 14 Thou shalt not go aside from any of the words which I command thee this day, *to* the right hand or *to* the left, to go after other gods to serve them.

362. *Idolatry common — Threats.*

Ex. 22: 20 He that sacrificeth unto *ang* god, save unto the LORD only, he shall be utterly destroyed.

Dt. 8: 19 It shall be, if thou do at all forget the LORD thy God, and walk after other gods, and serve them, and worship them, I testify against you this day that ye shall surely perish. — 27: 15 Cursed *be* the man that maketh *any* graven or molten image, an abomination unto the LORD, the work of the hands of the craftsman, and putteth *it* in *a* secret *place:* and all the people shall answer and say, Amen. — 30: 17 If thy heart turn away, so that thou wilt not hear, but shalt be drawn away, and worship other gods, and serve them; 18 I denounce unto you this day, that ye shall surely perish.

Jud. 2: 11 The children of Israel did evil in the sight of the LORD, and served Baalim: 12 And they forsook the LORD God of their fathers, which brought them out of the land of Egypt, and followed other gods, of the gods of the people that *were* round about them, and bowed themselves unto them, and provoked the LORD to anger. 13 And they forsook the LORD, and served Baal and Ashtaroth. 14 And the anger of the LORD was hot against Israel, and he delivered them into the hands of spoilers. — 10: 6 The children of Israel did evil again in the sight of the LORD, and served Baalim, and Ashtaroth, and the gods of Syria, and the gods of Zidon, and the gods of Moab, and the gods of the children of Ammon, and the gods of the Philistines, and forsook the LORD, and served not him. 7 And the anger of the LORD was hot against Israel, and he sold them into the hands of the Philistines, and into the hands of the children of Ammon.

1 K. 9: 6 If ye shall at all turn from following me, ye or your children, and will not keep my commandments *and* my

Displeasing to God.

statutes which I have set before you, but go and serve other
gods and worship them: 7 Then will I cut off Israel out of the
land which I have given them; and this house which I have
hallowed for my name, will I cast out of my sight; and Israel
shall be a proverb and a bye-word among all people.

2 K. 17: 9 The children of Israel did secretly *those* things
that *were* not right against the LORD their God, and they built
them high places in all their cities, from the tower of the
watchmen to the fenced city. 10 And they set them up images
and groves in every high hill, and under every green tree:
11 And there they burnt incense in all the high places, as *did*
the heathen whom the LORD carried away before them; and
wrought wicked things to provoke the LORD to anger: 12 For
they served idols, whereof the LORD had said unto them, Ye
shall not do this thing. 16 And they left all the commandments of the LORD their God, and made them molten images,
even two calves, and made a grove, and worshipped all the host
of heaven, and served Baal. 18 Therefore the LORD was
very angry with Israel, and removed them out of his sight:
there was none left but the tribe of Judah only. 19 Judah
kept not the commandments of the LORD their God, but walked
in the statutes of Israel which they made. 20 And the LORD
rejected all the seed of Israel, and afflicted them, and delivered
them into the hand of spoilers, until he had cast them out of
his sight. — 22: 17 Because they have forsaken me, and have
burned incense unto other gods, that they might provoke me
to anger with all the works of their hands; therefore my
wrath shall be kindled against this place, and shall not be
quenched.

Ps. 78: 58 They provoked him to anger with their high
places, and moved him to jealousy with their graven images.
59 When God heard *this*, he was wroth, and greatly abhorred
Israel.

Jer. 44: 2 Thus saith the LORD of hosts, the God of Israel;
Ye have seen all the evil that I have brought upon Jerusalem,
and upon all the cities of Judah; and behold, this day they
are a desolation, and no man dwelleth therein; 3 Because of
their wickedness which they have committed to provoke me to
anger, in that they went to burn incense, *and* to serve other
gods, whom they knew not, *neither* they, ye, nor your fathers.
4 I sent unto you all my servants the prophets, rising early
and sending *them*, saying, Oh, do not this abominable thing
that I hate.

Ezk. 36: 18 Wherefore, I poured my fury upon them for the
blood that they had shed upon the land, and for their idols

wherewith they had polluted it : 19 And I scattered them among the heathen, and they were dispersed through the countries : according to their way and according to their doings I judged them. [See 486, 699.]

IGNORANCE.

363. *The sin and danger of ignorance — knowledge required.*

Ps. 32: 9 Be ye not as the horse, *or* as the mule, *which* have no understanding : whose mouth must be held in with bit and bridle, lest they come near unto thee.

Pr. 13: 18 Poverty and shame *shall be to* him that refuseth instruction : but he that regardeth reproof shall be honored. — 15: 32 He that refuseth instruction despiseth his own soul : but he that heareth reproof getteth understanding. — 19: 2 Also, *that* the soul *be* without knowledge, *it is* not good ; and he that hasteth with *his* feet sinneth.

Is. 5: 13 My people are gone into captivity, because *they have* no knowledge : and their honorable men *are* famished, and their multitude dried up with thirst.

Hos. 4: 1 Hear the word of the LORD, ye children of Israel : for the LORD hath a controversy with the inhabitants of the land, because *there is* no truth, nor mercy, nor knowledge of God in the land. 6 My people are destroyed for lack of knowledge : because thou hast rejected knowledge, I will also reject thee, that thou shalt be no priest to me : seeing thou hast forgotten the law of thy God, I will also forget thy children.

Jn. 16: 2 They shall put you out of the synagogues : yea, the time cometh, that whosoever killeth you, will think that he doeth God service. 3 And these things will they do unto you, because they have not known the Father, nor me.

1 Cor. 2: 7 We speak the wisdom of God in a mystery, *even* the hidden *wisdom* which God ordained before the world unto our glory ; 8 Which none of the princes of this world knew : for had they known *it*, they would not have crucified the Lord of glory. — 14: 20 Brethren, be not children in understanding : howbeit, in malice be ye children, but in understanding be men.

2 Th. 1: 7 To you, who are troubled, rest with us, when the Lord Jesus shall be revealed from heaven with his mighty angels, 8 In flaming fire taking vengeance on them that know not God, and that obey not the gospel of our Lord Jesus Christ. [See 127, 200,(10) 391.]

INSTABILITY.

364. Instability reproved—Unstable persons to be avoided.

Gen. 49: 4 Unstable as water, thou shalt not excel.

Pr. 24: 21 Meddle not with them that are given to change.

Ep. 4: 14 That we *henceforth* be no more children, tossed to and fro, and carried about with every wind of doctrine, by the sleight of men, *and* cunning craftiness, whereby they lie in wait to deceive.

Heb. 13: 9 Be not carried about with divers and strange doctrines: for *it is* a good thing that the heart be established with grace. [See 712.]

INTEMPERANCE.

365. Intemperance a prevalent, deceitful, loathsome and destructive vice.

Gen. 9: 20 Noah began *to be* an husbandman, and he planted a vineyard: 21 And he drank of the wine, and was drunken; and he was uncovered within his tent.

Pr. 20: 1 Wine *is* a mocker, strong drink *is* raging: and whosoever is deceived thereby is not wise.—23: 21 The drunkard and the glutton shall come to poverty. 29 Who hath wo? who hath sorrow? who hath contentions? who hath babbling? who hath wounds without cause? who hath redness of eyes? 30 They that tarry long at the wine; they that go to seek mixed wine. 34 Yea, thou shalt be as he that lieth down in the midst of the sea, or as he that lieth upon the top of a mast. 35 They have stricken me, *shalt thou say, and* I was not sick; they have beaten me, *and* I felt *it* not: when shall I awake? I will seek it yet again.

Is. 28: 7 They also have erred through wine, and through strong drink are out of the way; the priest and the prophet have erred through strong drink, they are swallowed up of wine, they are out of the way through strong drink; they err in vision, they stumble *in* judgment. 8 For all tables are full of vomit *and* filthiness, *so that there is* no place *clean.*—56: 12 Come ye, *say they,* I will fetch wine, and we will fill ourselves with strong drink.

Jer. 25: 27 Thou shalt say unto them, Thus saith the LORD of hosts, the God of Israel; Drink ye, and be drunken, and spue, and fall, and rise no more, because of the sword which I will send among you.

Dan. 5: 1 Belshazzar the king made a great feast to a thousand of his lords, and drank wine before the thousand. 4 They drank wine, and praised the gods of gold, and of silver.

Hos. 4: 11 Whoredom and wine and new wine take away the heart.

1 Cor. 11: 21 In eating every one taketh before *other* his own supper: and one is hungry, and another is drunken.

366. *Intemperance forbidden — penalty of — cautions.*

Dt. 21: 20 They shall say unto the elders of his city, This our son *is* stubborn and rebellious, he will not obey our voice; *he is* a glutton, and a drunkard. 21 And all the men of his city shall stone him with stones, that he die : so shalt thou put evil away from among you, and all Israel shall hear, and fear.

Pr. 23: 20 Be not among wine-bibbers ; among riotous eaters of flesh. 31 Look not thou upon the wine when it is red, when it giveth his color in the cup, *when* it moveth itself aright. 32 At the last it biteth like a serpent, and stingeth like an adder.

Is. 5: 11 Wo unto them that rise up early in the morning, *that* they may follow strong drink ; that continue until night, *till* wine inflame them! 12 And the harp, and the viol, the tabret, and pipe, and ·wine, are in their feasts : 22 Wo unto *them that are* mighty to drink wine, and men of strength to mingle strong drink. — 28: 1 Wo to the crown of pride, to the drunkards of Ephraim, whose glorious beauty *is* a fading flower, which *are* on the head of the fat valleys of them that are overcome with wine!

Mat. 24: 48 If that evil servant shall say in his heart, My lord delayeth his coming ; 49 And shall begin to smite *his* fellow-servants, and to eat and drink with the drunken ; 50 The lord of that servant shall come in a day when he looketh not for *him*, and in an hour that he is not aware of, 51 And shall cut him asunder, and appoint *him* his portion with the hypocrites : there shall be weeping and gnashing of teeth.

Rom. 13: 13 Let us walk honestly, as in the day : not in rioting and drunkenness, not in chambering and wantonness, not in strife and envying.

1 Cor. 6: 10 Nor thieves, nor covetous, nor drunkards, nor revilers, nor extortioners, shall inherit the kingdom of God.

Gal. 5: 19 The works of the flesh are manifest, which are *these*, Adultery, fornication, uncleanness, lasciviousness, 20 Idolatry, witchcraft, hatred, variance, emulations, wrath, strife, seditions, heresies, 21 Envyings, murders, drunkenness, revellings, and such like : of the which I tell you before, as I have also told *you* in time past, that they which do such things shall not inherit the kingdom of God.

Ep. 5: 18 And be not drunk with wine, wherein is excess; but be ye filled with the Spirit. [See 199, 721.]

367. *The liquor seller virtually and explicitly condemned.*

Gen. 4: 9 The LORD said unto Cain, Where *is* Abel thy brother? And he said, I know not: *Am* I my brother's keeper? 10 And he said, What hast thou done? the voice of thy brother's blood crieth unto me from the ground. 11 And now *art* thou cursed from the earth, which hath opened her mouth to receive thy brother's blood from thy hand.

Ex. 21. 28 If an ox gore a man or a woman, that they die: then the ox shall be surely stoned, and his flesh shall not be eaten; but the owner of the ox *shall be* quit. 29 But if the ox were wont to push with his horn in time past, and it hath been testified to his owner, and he hath not kept him in, but that he hath killed a man or a woman; the ox shall be stoned, and his owner also shall be put to death. 30 If there be laid on him a sum of money, then he shall give for the ransom of his life whatsoever is laid upon him.

Dt. 32: 33 Their wine *is* the poison of dragons, and the cruel venom of asps. 34 *Is* not this laid up in store with me, *and* sealed up among my treasures? 35 To me *belongeth* vengeance, and recompense; their foot shall slide in *due* time: for the day of their calamity *is* at hand, and the things that shall come upon them make haste.

2 K. 21: 9 Manasseh seduced them to do more evil than did the nations whom the LORD destroyed before the children of Israel. 10 The LORD spake by his servants, the prophets, saying, 11 Because Manasseh king of Judah hath done these abominations, *and* hath done wickedly above all that the Amorites did, which *were* before him, and hath made Judah also to sin. 12 Therefore thus saith the LORD God of Israel, Behold, I *am* bringing *such* evil upon Jerusalem and Judah, that whosoever heareth of it, both his ears shall tingle.

Hab. 2: 15 Wo unto him that giveth his neighbor drink, that puttest thy bottle to *him*, and makest *him* drunken also, that thou mayest look on their nakedness!

Jn. 3: 19 And this is the condemnation, that light has come into the world. [See 685.]

368. *The wisdom of total abstinence and watchfulness.*

Dan. 1: 8 Daniel purposed in his heart that he would not defile himself with the portion of the king's meat, nor with the

Founded on the promises of the Gospel.

wine which he drank. 12 Prove thy servants, I beseech thee, ten days ; and let them give us pulse to eat, and water to drink. 15 And at the end of ten days their countenances appeared fairer and fatter in flesh than all the children which did.eat the portion of the king's meat.

Lk. 1: 15 He [John] shall be great in the sight of the Lord, and shall drink neither wine nor strong drink.

Rom. 14: 21 It is good neither to eat flesh, nor to drink wine, nor any thing whereby thy brother stumbleth, or is offended, or is made weak.

1 Cor. 5: 11 Now I have written unto you not to keep company, if any man that is called a brother be a fornicator or covetous, or an idolater, or a railer, or a drunkard, or an extortioner: with such a one no not to eat. [See 199.]

369. *Priests, Nazarites, and civil rulers specially forbidden the use of strong drink.*

Lev. 10: 8 The Lord spake unto Aaron, saying, 9 Do not drink wine nor strong drink, thou, nor thy sons with thee, when ye go into the tabernacle of the congregation, lest ye die: *it shall be* a statute for ever throughout your generations : 10 And that ye may put difference between holy and unholy, and between unclean and clean ; 11 And that ye may teach the children of Israel all the statutes which the Lord hath spoken unto them by the hand of Moses.

Num. 6: 1 The Lord spake unto Moses, saying, 2 Speak unto the children of Israel, and say unto them, When either man or woman shall separate *themselves* to vow a vow of a Nazarite, to separate *themselves* unto the Lord : 3 He shall separate *himself* from wine and strong drink, and shall drink no vinegar of wine, or vinegar of strong drink, neither shall he drink any liquor of grapes, nor eat moist grapes, or dried. 4 All the days of his separation shall he eat nothing that is made of the vine-tree, from the kernels even to the husk.

Pr. 31: 4 It is not for kings, O Lemuel, it is not for kings to drink wine ; nor for princes strong drink : 5 Lest they drink, and forget the law, and pervert the judgment of any of the afflicted. [See 457.]

INVITATIONS.

370. *Invitations, founded upon the provisions of the Gospel.*

Is. 45: 22 Look unto me, and be ye saved, all the ends of the earth : for I am God, and there is none else. — 55: 1 Ho, every one that thirsteth, come ye to the waters, and he that

hath no money; come ye, buy, and eat; yea, come, buy wine
and milk without money and without price. 2 Wherefore do
ye spend money for *that which is* not bread? and your labor
for *that which* satisfieth not? hearken diligently unto me, and
eat ye *that which is* good, and let your soul delight itself in
fatness. 3 Incline your ear, and come unto me: hear, and
your soul shall live: and I will make an everlasting covenant
with you, *even* the sure mercies of David.

Mat. 11: 28 Come unto me, all *ye* that labor, and are heavy
laden, and I will give you rest. 29 Take my yoke upon you,
and learn of me: for I am meek and lowly in heart; and ye
shall find rest unto your souls. 30 For my yoke *is* easy, and
my burden is light. — 22: 2 The kingdom of heaven is like
unto a certain king, which made a marriage for his son, 3 And
sent forth his servants to call them that were bidden to the
wedding, and they would not come. 4 Again, he sent forth
other servants, saying, Tell them which are bidden, Behold, I
have prepared my dinner: my oxen and *my* fatlings *are* killed,
and all things *are* ready: come unto the marriage.

Lk. 14: 17 And sent his servant at supper-time, to say to
them that were bidden, Come, for all things are now ready.

Jn. 7: 37 In the last day, that great *day* of the feast, Jesus
stood and cried, saying, If any man thirst, let him come unto
me, and drink.

Rev. 3: 20 Behold, I stand at the door, and knock: If any
man hear my voice, and open the door, I will come in to him,
and will sup with him, and he with me. — 22: 17 The spirit and
the bride say, Come. And let him that heareth say, Come.
And let him that is athirst come. And whosoever will, let him
take the water of life freely. [See 233, 580.]

371. *Expostulatory Invitations.*

Pr. 1: 20 Wisdom crieth without; she uttereth her voice in
the streets; 21 She crieth in the chief place of concourse, in
the openings of the gates: in the city she uttereth her words,
saying, 22 How long, ye simple ones, will ye love simplicity?
and the scorners delight in their scorning, and fools hate knowledge? 23 Turn you at my reproof: behold, I will pour out
my spirit unto you, I will make known my words unto you.

Is. 1: 18 Come now, and let us reason together, saith the
LORD: though your sins be as scarlet, they shall be as white
as snow; though they be red like crimson, they shall be as
wool.

Jer. 22: 29 O earth, earth, earth, hear the word of the LORD.

Ezk. 33: 11 Say unto them, *As* I live, saith the Lord God,

I have no pleasure in the death of the wicked; but that the wicked turn from his way and live : turn ye, turn ye from your evil ways; for why will ye die, O house of Israel?

Mic. 6: 1 Hear ye now what the LORD saith; Arise, contend thou before the mountains and let the hills hear thy voice. 2 Hear ye, O mountains, the LORD's controversy, and ye strong foundations of the earth: for the LORD hath a controversy with his people, and he will plead with Israel. 3 O my people, what have I done unto thee? and wherein have I wearied thee? testify against me. [See 60, 224–5.]

372. *Sincerity of God's invitations apparent, or good desired and evil deprecated.*

Ps. 81: 13 Oh that my people had hearkened unto me, *and* Israel had walked in my ways! 14 I should soon have subdued their enemies, and turned my hand against their adversaries. 15 The haters of the LORD should have submitted themselves unto him.

Is. 48: 18 O that thou hadst hearkened to my commandments! then had thy peace been as a river, and thy righteousness as the waves of the sea.

Lk. 19: 41 When he was come near, he beheld the city, and wept over it, 42 Saying, If thou hadst known, even thou, at least in this thy day, the things *which belong* to thy peace! but now they are hid from thine eyes. [See 224, 228, 233.]

373. *Invitations rejected — excuses of sinners.*

Ps. 58: 4 *They are* like the deaf adder *that* stoppeth her ear: 5 Which will not hearken to the voice of charmers, charming never so wisely.

Pr. 1: 24 I have called and ye refused, I have stretched out my hand, and no man regarded; 25 But ye have set at nought all my counsel, and would none of my reproof.

Zec. 7: 11 They refused to hearken, and pulled away the shoulder, and stopped their ears, that they should not hear. 12 Yea, they made their hearts as an adamant stone, lest they should hear the law, and the words which the LORD of hosts hath sent in his Spirit by the former prophets: therefore came a great wrath from the LORD of hosts. 13 Therefore it is come to pass, *that* as he cried, and they would not hear; so they cried, and I would not hear, saith the LORD of hosts.

Mat. 22: 2 The kingdom of heaven is like unto a certain king, which made a marriage for his son, 3 And sent forth his servants to call them that were bidden to the wedding: and they would not come. 4 Again, he sent forth other servants, saying, Tell them which are bidden, Behold, I have prepared my dinner: my oxen and *my* fatlings *are* killed, and all things *are* ready: come unto the marriage. 5 But they made light of *it*, and went their ways, one to his farm, another to his merchandise. 6 And the remnant took his servants, and entreated *them* spitefully, and slew *them*.

Lk. 14: 17 And sent his servant at supper-time to say to them that were bidden, Come, for all things are now ready. 18 And they all with one *consent* began to make excuse. The first said unto him, I have bought a piece of ground, and I must needs go and see it: I pray thee have me excused. 19 And another said, I have bought five yoke of oxen, and I go to prove them: I pray thee have me excused. 20 And another said, I have married a wife: and therefore I cannot come. [See 272, 696–7, 706.]

IRONY.

374. *Ironical language sometimes used in the Bible.*

Jud. 10: 14 Go and cry unto the gods which ye have chosen; let them deliver you in the time of your tribulation.

1 K. 18: 27 It came to pass at noon, that Elijah mocked them, and said, Cry aloud: for he *is* a god: either he is talking, or he is pursuing, or he is in a journey, or peradventure he sleepeth, and must be awaked.

Job 12: 1 Job answered and said, 2 No doubt but ye *are* the people, and wisdom shall die with you.

Ee. 11: 9 Rejoice, O young man, in thy youth; and let thy heart cheer thee in the days of thy youth, and walk in the ways of thy heart, and in the sight of thine eyes: but know thou, that for all these *things* God will bring thee into judgment.

JEWS, OR SEED OF ABRAHAM.

375. *Predicted population of the Jews.*

Gen. 13: 16 I will make thy seed as the dust of the earth: so that if a man can number the dust of the earth, *then* shall thy seed also be numbered. — 26: 4 I will make thy seed to multiply as the stars of heaven, and will give unto thy seed all these countries: and in thy seed shall all the nations of the earth be blessed.

Is. 27: 6 He shall cause them that come of Jacob to take root: Israel shall blossom and bud, and fill the face of the world with fruit. — 60: 22 A little one shall become a thousand, and a small one a strong nation: I the LORD will hasten it in his time. — 37: 26 I will make a covenant of peace with them; it shall be an everlasting covenant with them: and I will place them, and multiply them, and will set my sanctuary in the midst of them for evermore.

Hos. 1: 10 The number of the children of Israel shall be as the sand of the sea, which cannot be measured nor numbered; and it shall come to pass, *that* in the place where it was said unto them, Ye *are* not my people, *there* it shall be said unto them, *Ye are* the sons of the living God.
[Gen. 15: 5, and 16: 10, and 22: 17, and 28: 14. Num. 23: 10. Is. 65: 23.]

376. *Extent of their territory, and nature of the grant to them.*

Gen. 15: 18 In that same day the LORD made a covenant with Abram, saying, Unto thy seed have I given this land, from the river of Egypt unto the great river, the river Euphrates. — 17: 8 I will give unto thee, and to thy seed after thee, the land wherein thou art a stranger, all the land of Canaan, for an everlasting possession; and I will be their God.

Dt. 32: 8 When the Most High divided to the nations their inheritance, when he separated the sons of Adam, he set the bounds of the people according to the number of the children of Israel. 9 For the LORD's portion *is* his people; Jacob *is* the lot of his inheritance.

· Jos. 1: 4 From the wilderness and this Lebanon even unto the great river, the river Euphrates, all the land of the Hittites, and unto the great sea toward the going down of the sun, shall be your coast.
[Num. 34: 2—12. Gen. 12: 7, and 13: 14—17. Ex. 6: 4, and 32: 13.]

377. *Wickedness and predicted dispersion of the Jews.*

Dt. 28: 65 The LORD shall scatter thee among all people from the one end of the earth even unto the other; and there thou shalt serve other gods, which neither thou nor thy fathers have known, *even* wood and stone. 65 And among these nations shalt thou find no ease, neither shall the sole of thy foot have rest: but the LORD shall give thee there a trembling heart, and failing of eyes, and sorrow of mind. 66 And thy life shall hang in doubt before thee: and thou shalt fear day and night, and shalt have none assurance of **thy** life.

2 K. 17: 6 In the ninth year of Hoshea the king of Assyria took Samaria, and carried Israel away into Assyria, and placed them in Halah and in Habor *by* the river of Gozan, and in the cities of the Medes. 18 Therefore the LORD was very angry with Israel, and removed them out of his sight: there was none left but the tribe of Judah only. 19 Also Judah kept not the commandments of the LORD their God, but walked in the statutes of Israel which they made. 20 And the LORD rejected all the seed of Israel, and afflicted them, and delivered them into the hand of spoilers, until he had cast them out of his sight. 23 So was Israel carried away out of their own land to Assyria unto this day.

Ezk. 2: 3 He said unto me, Son of man, I send thee to the children of Israel, to a rebellious nation that hath rebelled against me: they and their fathers have transgressed against me, *even* unto this very day. 7 Thou shalt speak my words unto them, whether they will hear, or whether they will forbear: for they *are* most rebellious. — 5: 5 Thus saith the Lord GOD; This *is* Jerusalem; I have set it in the midst of the nations and countries *that are* round about her. 6 And she hath changed my judgments into wickedness more than the nations, and my statutes more than the countries that *are* round about her: for they have refused my judgments and my statutes, they have not walked in them. 9 I will do in thee that which I have not done, and whereunto I will not do any more the like, because of all thine abominations. — 9: 9 Then said he unto me, The iniquity of the house of Israel and Judah *is* exceeding great, and the land is full of blood, and the city full of perverseness: for they say, The LORD hath forsaken the earth, and the LORD seeth not.

Hos. 9: 16 Ephraim is smitten, their root is dried up, they shall bear no fruit: yea, though they bring forth, yet will I slay *even* the beloved *fruit* of their womb. 17 My God will cast them away, because they did not hearken unto him: and they shall be wanderers among the nations.

378. *Predicted resuscitation, reunion, and return of the Jews to the promised land, with peculiar subsequent prosperity.*

Is. 11: 11 It shall come to pass in that day, *that* the LORD shall set his hand again the second time to recover the remnant of his people, which shall be left, from Assyria, and from Egypt, and from Pathros, and from Cush, and from Elam, and from Shinar, and from Hamath, and from the islands of the sea. 12 And he shall set up an ensign for the nations, and shall assemble the outcasts of Israel, and gather together the dispersed of Judah from the four corners of the earth. 13 The envy also of Ephraim shall depart, and the adversaries of Judah shall be cut off: Ephraim shall not envy Judah, and Judah shall not vex Ephraim. 16 And there shall be an highway for the remnant of his people, which shall be left, from Assyria: like as it was to Israel in the day that he came up out of the land of Egypt. — 27: 6 He shall cause them that come of Jacob to take root; Israel shall blossom and bud, and fill the face of the world with fruit. 13 And it shall come to pass in that day, *that* the great trumpet shall be blown, and they shall come which were ready to perish in the land of Assyria, and the outcasts in the land of Egypt, and shall worship the LORD in the holy mount at Jerusalem. — 49: 22 Thus saith the Lord GOD, Behold, I will lift up my hand to the Gentiles, and set up my standard to the people: and they shall bring thy sons in *their* arms, and thy daughters shall be carried upon *their* shoulders. 23 And kings shall be thy nursing fathers, and their queens thy nursing mothers.

Jer. 3: 17 At that time they shall call Jerusalem the throne of the LORD; and all the nations shall be gathered unto it, to the name of the LORD, to Jerusalem: neither shall they walk any more after the imagination of their evil heart. 18 In those days the house of Judah shall walk with the house of Israel, and they shall come together out of the land of the north to the land that I have given for an inheritance unto your fathers. — 16: 14 Behold, the days come, saith the LORD, that it shall no more be said, The LORD liveth, that brought up the children of Israel out of the land of Egypt. 15 But, The LORD liveth, that brought up the children of Israel from the land of the north, and from all the lands whither he had driven them: and I will bring them again into their land that I gave unto their fathers. 16 Behold, I will send for many fishers, saith the LORD, and they shall fish them; and after will I send for many hunters, and they shall hunt them from every mountain, and from every hill, and out of the holes of the rocks.

Ezk. 20: 40 For in my holy mountain, in the mountain of the height of Israel, saith the Lord GOD, there shall all the house of Israel, all of them in the land, serve me: there will I accept them, and there will I require your offerings, and the first fruits of your oblations, with all your holy things. 41 I will accept you with your sweet savor, when I bring you out from the people, and gather you out of the countries wherein ye have been scattered; and I will be sanctified in you before the heathen. 42 And ye shall know that I *am* the LORD when I shall bring you into the land of Israel, into the country *for* the which I lifted up my hand to give it to your fathers. — 34: 13 I will bring them out from the people, and gather them from the countries, and will bring them to their own land, and feed them upon the mountains of Israel by the rivers, and in all the inhabited places of the country. 23 And I will set up one Shepherd over them, and he shall feed them, *even* my servant David; he shall feed them, and he shall be their shepherd. 24 And I the LORD will be their God, and my servant David a prince among them; I the LORD have spoken *it*. 25 And I will make with them a covenant of peace, and will cause the evil beasts to cease out of the land: and they shall dwell safely in the wilderness, and sleep in the woods. 26 And I will make them and the places round about my hill a blessing; and I will cause the shower to come down in his season; there shall be showers of blessing. 27 And the tree of the field shall yield her fruit, and the earth shall yield her increase, and they shall be safe in their land, and shall know that I *am* the LORD, when I have broken the bands of their yoke, and delivered them out of the hand of those that served themselves of them. 28 And they shall no more be a prey to the heathen, neither shall the beasts of the land devour them; but they shall dwell safely, and none shall make *them* afraid. 29 And I will raise up for them a plant of renown, and they shall be no more consumed with hunger in the land, neither bear the shame of the heathen any more. — 36: 1 Also, thou son of man, prophesy unto the mountains of Israel, and say, Ye mountains of Israel, hear the word of the LORD: 2 Thus saith the Lord GOD; Because the enemy hath said against you, Aha, even the ancient high places are ours in possession: 3 Therefore prophesy and say, Thus saith the Lord GOD; Because they have made *you* desolate, and swallowed you up on every side, that ye might be a possession unto the residue of the heathen, and ye are taken up in the lips of talkers, and *are* an infamy of the people: 4 Therefore, ye mountains of Israel, hear the word of the Lord GOD; Thus saith the Lord GOD to the mountains, and to the hills, to the rivers, and to the valleys, to the desolate wastes, and to the cities that are forsaken, which became a prey and derision to the residue of the heathen that *are* round about; 5 Therefore thus saith the Lord GOD; Surely in the fire of my jealousy have I spoken against the residue of the heathen, and against all Idumea, which have appointed my land into their possession with the joy of all *their* heart, with despiteful minds, to cast it out for a prey. 6 Prophesy therefore concerning the land of Israel, and say unto the mountains, and to the hills, to the rivers, and to the valleys, Thus saith the Lord GOD ; Behold, I have spoken in my jealousy and in my fury, because ye have borne the shame of the heathen : 7 Therefore thus saith the Lord GOD ; I have lifted up mine hand : Surely the heathen that *are* about you, they shall bear their shame. 8 But ye, O mountains of Israel, ye shall shoot forth your branches, and yield your fruit to my people of Israel ; for they are at hand to come. 9 For behold, I *am* for you, and I will turn unto you, and ye shall be tilled and sown : 10 And I will multiply men upon you, all the house of Israel, *even* all of it : and the cities shall be inhabited, and the wastes shall be builded : 11 And I will multiply upon you man and beast ; and they shall increase and bring fruit : and I will settle you after your old estates, and will do better *unto you* than at your beginnings : and ye shall know that I *am* the LORD. 12 Yea, I will cause men to walk upon you *even* my people Israel ; and they shall possess thee, and thou shalt be their inheritance, and thou shalt no more henceforth bereave them *of men.* 13 Thus saith the Lord GOD ; Because they say unto you, Thou *land* devourest up men, and hast bereaved thy nations ; 14 Therefore, thou shalt devour men no more, neither bereave thy nations any more, saith the Lord GOD. 15 Neither will I cause *men* to hear in thee the shame of the heathen any more, neither shalt thou bear the reproach of the people any more, neither shalt thou cause thy nations to fall any more, saith the Lord God. 33 Thus saith the Lord GOD ; In the day that I shall have cleansed you from all your iniquities I will also cause *you* to dwell in the cities, and the wastes shall be builded. 34 And the desolate land shall be tilled, whereas it lay desolate in the sight of all that passed by. 35 And they shall say, This land that was desolate is become like the garden of Eden ; and the waste and desolate and ruined cities *are become* fenced, *and* are inhabited. 36 Then the heathen that are left round about you shall know that I the LORD build the ruined *places,* *and* plant that that was desolate : I the LORD have spoken *it,* and I will do *it.* — 37: 1 The hand of the LORD was upon me, and carried me out in the Spirit of the LORD, and set me down in the midst of the valley which *was* full of bones, 2 And caused me to pass by them round about : and behold, *there were* very many in the open valley ; and lo, *they were* very dry. 3 And he said unto me, Son of man, can these bones live ? and I answered, O Lord GOD, thou knowest. 11 Then he said unto me, Son of man, these bones are the whole house of Israel : behold, they say, Our bones are dried, and our hope is lost : we are cut off for our parts. 12 Therefore prophesy and say unto them, Thus saith the Lord GOD ; Behold, O my people, I will open your graves, and cause you to come up out of your graves, and bring you into the land of Israel. 13 And ye shall know that I *am* the LORD, when I have opened your graves, O my people, and brought you up out of your graves, 14 And shall put my Spirit in you, and ye shall live, and I shall place you in your own land : then shall ye know that I the LORD have spoken *it*, and performed *it*, saith the LORD. 16 Moreover, thou son of man, take thee one stick, and write upon it, For Judah, and for the children of Israel his companions : then take another stick, and write upon it, For Joseph, the stick of Ephraim, and *for* all the house of Israel his companions : 17 And join them one to another into one stick ; and they shall become one in thy hand. 18 And when the children of thy people shall speak unto thee, saying, Wilt thou not shew us what thou *meanest* by these ? 19 Say unto them, Thus saith the Lord GOD ; Behold, I will take the stick of Joseph, which *is* in the hand of Ephraim, and the tribes of Israel his fellows, and will put them with him, *even* with the stick of Judah, and make them one stick, and they shall be one in my hand. 20 And the sticks whereon thou writest shall be in thy hand before their eyes. 21 And say unto them, Thus saith the Lord GOD ; Behold, I will take the children of Israel from among the heathen, whither they be gone, and will gather them on every side, and bring them into their own land : 22 And I will make them one nation in the land upon the mountains of Israel ; and one king shall be king to them all : and they shall be no more two nations, neither shall they be divided into two kingdoms any more at all : 23 Neither shall they defile themselves any more with their idols, nor with their detestable things, nor with any of their transgressions : but I will save them out of all their dwelling-places, wherein they have sinned; and will cleanse them : so shall they be my people, and I will be their God. 25 And they shall dwell in the land that I have given unto Jacob my servant, wherein your fathers have dwelt, and they shall dwell therein, *even* they, and their children, and their children's children for ever : and my servant David *shall be* their prince for ever. 26 Moreover I will make a covenant of peace with them ; it shall be an everlasting covenant with them : and I will place them, and multiply them, and will set my sanctuary in the midst of them for evermore. 27 My tabernacle also shall be with them : yea, I will be their God, and they shall be my people. 28 And the heathen shall know that I the LORD do sanctify

Israel, when my sanctuary shall be in the midst of them for evermore. — 39: 24 According to their uncleanness and according to their transgressions have I done unto them, and hid my face from them. 25 Therefore thus saith the Lord GOD; Now will I bring again the captivity of Jacob, and have mercy upon the whole house of Israel, and will be jealous for my holy name; 28 Then shall they know that I *am* the LORD their God, which caused them to be led into captivity among the heathen: but I have gathered them unto their own land, and have left none of them any more there. 29 Neither will I hide my face any more from them: for I have poured out my Spirit upon the house of Israel, saith the Lord GOD.

Hos. 1: 10 Yet the number of the children of Israel shall be as the sand of the sea, which cannot be measured nor numbered; and it shall come to pass, *that* in the place where it was said unto them, *Ye are* not my people, *there* it shall be said unto them, *Ye are* the sons of the living God. 11 Then shall the children of Judah and the children of Israel be gathered together, and appoint themselves one head, and they shall come up out of the land: for great *shall be* the day of Jezreel. — 3: 4 For the children of Israel shall abide many days without a king, and without a prince, and without a sacrifice, and without an image, and without an ephod, and *without* teraphim: 5 Afterward shall the children of Israel return, and seek the LORD their God, and David their king; and shall fear the LORD and his goodness in the latter days. — 14: 5 I will be as the dew unto Israel: he shall grow as the lily, and cast forth his roots as Lebanon. 6 His branches shall spread, and his beauty shall be as the olive tree, and his smell as Lebanon. 7 They that dwell under his shadow shall return; they shall revive *as* the corn, and grow as the vine: the scent thereof *shall be* as the wine of Lebanon.

Am. 9: 14 I will bring again the captivity of my people Israel, and they shall build the waste cities, and inhabit *them:* and they shall plant vineyards, and drink the wine thereof; they shall also make gardens, and eat the fruit of them. 15 And I will plant them upon their land, and they shall no more be pulled up out of their land which I have given them, saith the LORD thy God.

Mic. 2: 12 I will surely assemble, O Jacob, all of thee; I will surely gather the remnant of Israel; I will put them together as the sheep of Bozrah, as the flock in the midst of their fold: they shall make great noise by reason of *the multitude of* men. 13 The breaker is come up before them: they **have** broken up, and have passed through the gate, and are gone out by it; and their king shall pass before them, and the LORD on the head of them. — 4: 6 In that day, saith the LORD, will I assemble her that halteth, and I will gather her that is driven out, and her that I have afflicted; 7 And I will make her that halted a remnant, and her that was cast far off a strong nation : and the LORD shall reign over them in Mount Zion from henceforth, even for ever.

~ Zec. 10: 6 I will strengthen the house of Judah, and I will save the house of Joseph, and I will bring them again to place them; for I have mercy upon them: and they shall be as though I had not cast them off : for I *am* the LORD their God, and will hear them.   7 And *they of* Ephraim shall be like a mighty *man*, and their heart shall rejoice as through wine : yea, their children shall see *it*, and be glad ; their heart shall rejoice in the LORD.   8 I will hiss for them, and gather them ; for I have redeemed them ; and they shall increase as they have increased.   10 I will bring them again also out of the land of Egypt, and gather them out of Assyria ; and I will bring them into the land of Gilead and Lebanon ; and *place* shall not be found for them.

Lk. 21: 24 They shall fall by the edge of the sword, and shall be led away captive into all nations : and Jerusalem shall be trodden down of the Gentiles, until the times of the Gentiles be fulfilled.   [Dt. 30: 1—6, Jer. 23: 6—8, and 46 ; 27, 28, Mic. 5th chap.]

379. *Removal of obstructions to the return of the Jews.*

Is. 11: 15 The LORD shall utterly destroy the tongue of the Egyptian sea; and with his mighty wind shall he shake his hand over the river, and shall smite it in the seven streams, and make *men* go over dry-shod. — 27: 12 It shall come to pass in that day, *that* the LORD shall beat off from the channel of the river unto the stream of Egypt, and ye shall be gathered one by one, O ye children of Israel.

Rev. 16: 12 The sixth angel poured out his vial upon the great river Euphrates ; and the water thereof was dried up, that the way of the kings of the east might be prepared.

380. *Enlarged possessions predicted.*

Is. 11: 14 They shall fly upon the shoulders of the Philistines toward the west; they shall spoil them of the east together : they shall lay their hand upon Edom and Moab; and the children of Ammon shall obey them.

Am. 9: 11 In that day will I raise up the tabernacle of David that is fallen, and close up the breaches thereof ; and I will raise up his ruins, and I will build it as in the days of old: 12 That they may possess the remnant of Edom, and of all the heathen which are called by my name, saith the LORD that doeth this.

Ob. 18 The house of Jacob shall be a fire, and the house of Joseph a flame, and the house of Esau for stubble, and they shall kindle in them, and devour them; and there shall not be *any* remaining of the house of Esau; for the LORD hath spoken *it.* 19 And *they of* the south shall possess the mount of Esau; and *they of* the plain the Philistines: and they shall possess the fields of Ephraim, and the fields of Samaria: and Benjamin *shall possess* Gilead. 20 And the captivity of this host of the children of Israel *shall possess* that of the Canaanites, *even* unto Zarephath; and the captivity of Jerusalem, which *is* in Sephared, shall possess the cities of the south. [See Is. 54: 3.]

381. *Trials and revolutions connected with the return of the Jews to Palestine.*

Is. 11: 14 They shall fly upon the shoulders of the Philistines toward the west; they shall spoil them of the east together: they shall lay their hands upon Edom and Moab; and the children of Ammon shall obey them.

Jer. 30: 7 Alas! for that day *is* great, so that none *is* like it: it *is* even the time of Jacob's trouble, but he shall be saved out of it. 11 For I *am* with thee, saith the LORD, to save thee: though I make a full end of all nations whither I have scattered thee, yet will I not make a full end of thee: but I will correct thee in measure, and will not leave thee altogether unpunished.

Ezk. 20: 33 *As* I live, saith the Lord GOD, surely with a mighty hand, and with a stretched out arm, and with fury poured out, will I rule over you: 34 And I will bring you out from the people, and will gather you out of the countries wherein ye are scattered, with a mighty hand, and with a stretched out arm, and with fury poured out. 35 And I will bring you into the wilderness of the people, and there will I plead with you face to face. 36 Like as I pleaded with your fathers in the wilderness of the land of Egypt, so will I plead with you, saith the Lord GOD. 37 And I will cause you to pass under the rod, and I will bring you into the bond of the covenant: 38 And I will purge out from among you the rebels, and them that transgress against me: I will bring them forth out of the country where they sojourn, and they shall not enter into the land of Israel: and ye shall know that I *am* the LORD. — 38: 8 After many days thou shalt be visited: in the latter years thou shalt come into the land *that is* brought back from the sword, *and is* gathered out of many people, against the mountains of Israel, which have been always waste: but it is brought forth out of the nations, and they shall dwell safely all of them. 9 Thou shalt ascend and come like a storm, thou shalt be like a cloud to cover the land, thou, and all thy bands, and many people with thee. 11 And thou shalt say, I will go up to the land of unwalled villages; I will go to them that are at rest, that dwell safely, all of them dwelling without walls, and having neither bars nor gates, 12 To take a spoil and to take a prey; to turn thy hand upon the desolate places *that are now* inhabited, and upon the people *that are* gathered out of the nations, which have gotten cattle and goods, that dwell in the midst of the land. 16 And thou shalt come up against my people of Israel, as a cloud to cover the land; it shall be in the latter days, and I will bring thee against my land, that the heathen may know me, when I shall be sanctified in thee, O Gog, before their eyes. 21 And I will call for a sword against him throughout all my mountains, saith the Lord GOD: every man's sword shall be against his brother. 22 And I will plead against him with pestilence and with blood; and I will rain upon him, and upon his bands, and upon the many people that *are* with him, an overflowing rain, and great hailstones, fire, and brimstone.

Joel 3: 1 Behold, in those days, and in that time, when I shall bring again the captivity of Judah and Jerusalem, 2 I will also gather all nations, and will bring them down into the valley of Jehoshaphat, and will plead with them there for my people and *for* my heritage Israel, whom they have scattered among the nations, and parted my land. 12 Let the heathen be wakened, and come up to the valley of Jehoshaphat: for there will I sit to judge all the heathen round about. 17 So shall ye know that I *am* the LORD your God dwelling in Zion my holy mountain: then shall Jerusalem be holy, and there shall no strangers pass through her any more.

Mic. 4: 11 Many nations are gathered against thee, that say, Let her be defiled, and let our eye look upon Zion. 12 But they know not the thoughts of the LORD, neither understand they his counsel: for he shall gather them as the sheaves into the floor. 13 Arise and thresh, O daughter of Zion: for I will make thine horn iron, and I will make thy hoofs brass: and thou shalt beat in pieces many people: and I will consecrate their gain unto the LORD, and their substance unto the Lord of the whole earth.

Zec. 10: 11 He shall pass through the sea with affliction, and shall smite the waves in the sea, and all the deeps of the river shall dry up: and the pride of Assyria shall be brought down, and the sceptre of Egypt-shall depart away. — 12: 2 Behold, I will make Jerusalem a cup of trembling unto all the people round about, when they shall be in the siege both against Judah *and* against Jerusalem. 3 And in that day will I make Jerusalem a burdensome stone for all people: all that burden themselves with it shall be cut in pieces, though all the people of the earth be gathered together against it. 6 In that day will I make the governors of Judah like a hearth of fire among the wood, and like a torch of fire in a sheaf; and they shall devour all the people round about, on the right hand and on the left: and Jerusalem shall be inhabited again in her own place, *even* in Jerusalem. 9 And it shall come to pass in that day, *that* I will seek to destroy all the nations that come against Jerusalem. — 13: 8 It shall come to pass, *that* in all the land, saith the LORD, two parts therein shall be cut off *and* die; but the third shall be left therein. 9 And I will bring the third part through the fire, and will refine them as silver is refined, and will try them as gold is tried: they shall call on my name, and I will hear them: I will say, It *is* my people; and they shall say, The LORD *is* my God. — 14: 1 Behold, the day of the LORD cometh, and thy spoil shall be divided in the midst of thee. 2 For I will gather all nations against Jerusalem to battle; and the city shall be taken, and the houses rifled, and the women ravished; and half of the city shall go forth into captivity, and the residue of the people shall not be cut off from the city. 3 Then shall the LORD go forth, and fight against those nations, as when he fought in the day of battle. 12 And this shall be the plague wherewith the LORD will smite all the people that have fought against Jerusalem; Their flesh shall consume away while they stand upon their feet, and their eyes shall consume away in their holes, and their tongue shall consume away in their mouth. 13 And it shall come to pass in that day, *that* a great tumult from the LORD shall be among them; and they shall lay hold every one on the hand of his neighbor, and his hand shall rise up against the hand of his neighbor. 14 And Judah also shall fight at Jerusalem: and the wealth of all the heathen round about shall be gathered together, gold, and silver, and apparel, in great abundance. 16 And it shall come to pass *that* every one that is left of all the nations which came against Jerusalem, shall even go up from year to year to worship the King, the LORD of hosts, and to keep the feast of tabernacles. 20 In that day shall there be upon the bells of the horses, HOLINESS UNTO THE LORD; and the pots in the LORD's house be like the bowls before the altar. [Zec. 10: 10—12. Jer. 30: 7—11.]—[See 86, 87, 486, 566, 630.]

382. *Conversion of the Jews.*

Is. 27: 7 Hath he smitten him, as he smote those that smote him? *or* is he slain according to the slaughter of them that are slain by him? 9 By this therefore shall the iniquity of Jacob be purged; and this *is* all the fruit to take away his sin; when he maketh all the stones of the altar as chalk-stones that are beaten in sunder, the groves and images shall not stand up.

Jer. 31: 1 At the same time, saith the LORD, will I be the God of all the families of Israel, and they shall be my people. 18 I have surely heard Ephraim bemoaning himself *thus;* Thou hast chastised me, and I was chastised, as a bullock unaccustomed *to the yoke:* turn thou me, and I shall be turned; for thou *art* the LORD my God. 19 Surely after that I was turned, I repented; and after that I was instructed, I smote upon *my* thigh: I was ashamed, yea, even confounded, because I did bear the reproach of my youth. 20 *Is* Ephraim my dear son? *is he* a pleasant child? for since I spake against him, I do earnestly remember him still: therefore my bowels are troubled for him; I will surely have mercy upon him, saith the LORD. 31 Behold, the days come, saith the LORD, that I will make a new covenant with the house of Israel, and with the house of Judah: 32 Not according to the covenant that I made with their fathers, in the day *that* I took them by the hand to bring them out of the land of Egypt; which my covenant they brake, although I was a husband unto them, saith the LORD: 33 But this *shall be* the covenant that I will make with the house of Israel; After those days, saith the LORD, I will put my law in their inward parts, and write it in their hearts; and will be their God, and they shall be my people. 34 And they shall teach no more every man his neighbor, and every man his brother, saying, Know the LORD: for they shall all know me, from the least of them unto the greatest of them, saith the LORD: for I will forgive their iniquity, and I will remember their sin no more.—33: 8 I will cleanse them from all their iniquity, whereby they have sinned against me; and I will pardon all their iniquities, whereby they have sinned, and whereby they have transgressed against me.

Ezk. 36: 21 I had pity for mine holy name, which the house of Israel had profaned among the heathen, whither they went. 22 Therefore, say unto the house of Israel, Thus saith the Lord GOD; I do not *this* for your sakes, O house of Israel, but for mine holy name's sake, which ye have profaned among the heathen, whither ye went.   23 And I will sanctify my great name, which was profaned among the heathen, which ye have profaned in the midst of them; and the heathen shall know that I *am* the LORD, saith the Lord GOD, when I shall be sanctified in you before their eyes.   24 For I will take you from among the heathen, and gather you out of all countries, and will bring you into your own land.   25 Then will I sprinkle clean water upon you, and ye shall be clean: from all your filthiness, and from all your idols, will I cleanse you. 26 A new heart also will I give you, and a new spirit will I put within you: and I will take away the stony heart out of your flesh, and I will give you an heart of flesh.   27 And I will put my Spirit within you, and cause you to walk in my statutes, and ye shall keep my judgments, and do *them*.   28 And ye shall dwell in the land that I gave to your fathers; and ye shall be my people, and I will be your God.   31 Then shall ye remember your own evil ways, and your doings that *were* not good, and shall loathe yourselves in your own sight for your iniquities, and for your abominations.   32 Not for your sakes do I *this*, saith the Lord GOD, be it known unto you: be ashamed and confounded for your own ways, O house of Israel.

Hos. 14: 4 I will heal their backsliding, I will love them freely: for mine anger is turned away from him.   8 Ephraim *shall say*, What have I to do any more with idols?

Mic. 4: 2 Many nations shall come, and say, Come, and let us go up to the mountain of the LORD, and to the house of the God of Jacob; and he will teach us of his ways, and we will walk in his paths: for the law shall go forth of Zion, and the word of the LORD from Jerusalem.

Zec. 12: 10 I will pour upon the house of David, and upon the inhabitants of Jerusalem, the spirit of grace and of supplications: and they shall look upon me whom they have pierced, and they shall mourn for him as one mourneth for *his* only *son*, and shall be in bitterness for him, as one that is in bitterness for *his* first-born.   11 In that day shall there be a great mourning in Jerusalem, as the mourning of Hadadrimmon in the valley of Megiddon.

Rom. 11: 15 If the casting away of them *be* the reconciling of the world, what *shall* the receiving *of them be*, but life from the dead?   16 For if the first fruit *be* holy, the lump *is* also *holy:* and if the root *be* holy, so *are* the branches.   24 For if thou wert cut out of the olive-tree which is wild by nature, and wert grafted contrary to nature into a good olive-tree, how much more shall these, which be the natural *branches*, be graffed into their own olive-tree? 25 For I would not, breth-ren, that ye should be ignorant of this mystery, (lest ye should be wise in your own conceits) that blindness in part is happened to Israel, until the fulness of the Gentiles be come in. 26 And so all Israel shall be saved: as it is written, There shall come out of Sion the Deliverer, and shall turn away ungodliness from Jacob: 27 For this *is* my covenant unto them, when I shall take away their sins.

2 Cor. 3: 15 Even unto this day, when Moses is read, the vail is upon their heart. 16 Nevertheless, when it shall turn to the Lord, the vail shall be taken away.

GENERAL JUDGMENT.

383. *General judgment appointed.*

Ps. 50: 3 Our God shall come, and shall not keep silence: a fire shall devour before him, and it shall be very tempestuous round about him. 4 He shall call to the heavens from above, and to the earth, that he may judge his people. 5 Gather my saints together unto me; those that have made a covenant with me by sacrifice. 6 And the heavens shall declare his right-eousness: for God *is* judge himself.

Mat. 11: 24 I say unto you, That it shall be more tolera-ble for the land of Sodom, in the day of judgment, than for thee.

Ac. 17: 31 He hath appointed a day, in the which he will judge the world in righteousness, by *that* man whom he hath ordained: *whereof* he hath given assurance unto all *men*, in that he hath raised him from the dead.—24: 25 As he reasoned of righteousness, temperance, and judgment to come, Felix trembled.

Rom. 14: 10 Why dost thou judge thy brother? or why dost thou set at nought thy brother? for we shall all stand before the judgment-seat of Christ. 12 So then every one of us shall give account of himself to God.

2 Cor. 5: 10 We must all appear before the judgment-seat of Christ; that every one may receive the things *done* in *his* body, according to that he hath done, whether *it be* good or bad.

2 Tim. 4: 1 I charge *thee* therefore before God, and the Lord Jesus Christ, who shall judge the quick and the dead at his appearing and his kingdom.

Heb. 9: 27 It is appointed unto men once to die, but after this the judgment.

2 Pet. 3: 7 The heavens and the earth, which are now, by

the same word are kept in store, reserved unto fire against the day of judgment and perdition of ungodly men.

Jude 6 The angels which kept not their first estate, but left their own habitation, he hath reserved in everlasting chains under darkness unto the judgment of the great day.

Rev. 20: 12 I saw the dead, small and great, stand before God: and the books were opened: and another book was opened, which is *the book* of life: and the dead were judged out of those things which were written in the books, according to their works. 13 And the sea gave up the dead which were in it; and death and hell delivered up the dead which were in them: and they were judged every man according to their works.

384. *Design of the general judgment.*

Rom. 2: 5 After thy hardness and impenitent heart, treasurest up unto thyself wrath against the day of wrath, and revelation of the righteous judgment of God.

Jude 14 Enoch also, the seventh from Adam, prophesied of these, saying, Behold, the Lord cometh with ten thousand of his saints, 15 To execute judgment upon all, and to convince all that are ungodly among them of all their ungodly deeds which they have ungodly committed, and of all their hard *speeches* which ungodly sinners have spoken against him.

385. *The Judgment day will come suddenly and unexpectedly.*

Mat. 24: 37 As the days of Noe *were*, so shall also the coming of the Son of man be. 38 For as in the days that were before the flood, they were eating and drinking, marrying and giving in marriage, until the day that Noe entered into the ark, 39 And knew not until the flood came, and took them all away: so shall also the coming of the Son of man be.— 25: 13 Watch therefore, for ye know neither the day nor the hour wherein the Son of man cometh:

Mk. 13: 32 Of that day and *that* hour knoweth no man, no, not the angels which are in heaven, neither the Son, but the Father. 33 Take ye heed, watch and pray: for ye know not when the time is. 35 Watch ye therefore: for ye know not when the master of the house cometh, at even, or at midnight, or at the cock-crowing, or in the morning: 36 Lest coming suddenly, he find you sleeping.

Lk. 17: 24 As the lightning that lighteneth out of the one *part* under heaven, shineth unto the other *part* under heaven; so shall also the Son of man be in his day. 28 Likewise also as it was in the days of Lot: they did eat, they drank, they

23*

bought, they sold, they planted, they builded; 29 But the same day that Lot went out of Sodom, it rained fire and brimstone from heaven, and destroyed *them* all: 30 Even thus shall it be in the day when the Son of man is revealed. — 21: 35 As a snare shall it come on all them that dwell on the face of the whole earth. 36 Watch ye therefore, and pray always, that ye may be accounted worthy to escape all these things that shall come to pass, and to stand before the Son of man.

Ac. 1: 7 He said unto them, It is not for you to know the times or the seasons which the Father hath put in his own power. [See 149.]

386. *Destruction of the material heavens and earth.*

Ps. 102: 25 Of old hast thou laid the foundation of the earth: and the heavens *are* the work of thy hands. 26 They shall perish, but thou shalt endure : yea, all of them shall wax old like a garment; as a vesture shalt thou change them, and they shall be changed.

Is. 51: 6 Lift up your eyes to the heavens, and look upon the earth beneath : for the heavens shall vanish away like smoke, and the earth shall wax old like a garment, and they that dwell therein shall die in like manner.

2 Pet. 3: 7 The heavens and the earth, which are now, by the same word are kept in store, reserved unto fire against the day of judgment and perdition of ungodly men. 10 But the day of the Lord will come as a thief in the night; in the which the heavens shall pass away with a great noise, and the elements shall melt with fervent heat, the earth also and the works that are therein shall be burned up. 11 *Seeing* then *that* all these things shall be dissolved, what manner *of persons* ought ye to be in *all* holy conversation and godliness, 12 Looking for and hasting unto the coming of the day of God, wherein the heavens being on fire shall be dissolved, and the elements shall melt with fervent heat ?

Rev. 20: 11 I saw a great white throne, and him that sat on it, from whose face the earth and the heaven fled away ; and there was found no place for them.

387. *The righteous and wicked separated at judgment.*

Mat. 13: 30 Let both grow together until the harvest: and in the time of harvest I will say to the reapers, Gather ye together first the tares, and bind them in bundles to burn them : but gather the wheat into my barn. — 22: 11 When the king came in to see the guests, he saw there a man which had not on a wedding-garment: 12 And he saith unto him, Friend, how camest thou in hither, not having a wedding-garment? And he was speechless. 13 Then said the king to the servants, Bind him hand and foot, and take him away, and cast *him* into outer darkness: there shall be weeping and gnashing of teeth.— 25: 31 When the Son of man shall come in his glory, and all the holy angels with him, then shall he sit upon the throne of his glory: 32 And before him shall be gathered all nations: and he shall separate them one from another, as a shepherd divideth *his* sheep from the goats: 33 And he shall set the sheep on his right hand, but the goats on the left.

Lk. 16: 26 Between us and you there is a great gulf fixed: so that they which would pass from hence to you cannot; neither can they pass to us, that *would come* from thence. [See 560.]

388. *Judgment committed to Christ.*

Jn. 5: 22 The Father judgeth no man; but hath committed all judgment unto the Son: 23 That all *men* should honor the Son, even as they honor the Father. 27 And hath given him authority to execute judgment also, because he is the Son of man.

Ac. 10: 40 Him God raised up the third day, and shewed him openly: 42 And he commanded us to preach unto the people, and to testify that it is he which was ordained of God *to be* the Judge of quick and dead.

2 Tim. 4: 1 I charge *thee* therefore before God, and the Lord Jesus Christ, who shall judge the quick and the dead at his appearing and his kingdom.

389. *Particular disclosures at the day of judgment.*

Ec. 11: 9 Rejoice, O young man, in thy youth: and let thy heart cheer thee in the days of thy youth, and walk in the ways of thine heart, and in the sight of thine eyes: but know thou, that for all these *things* God will bring thee into judgment. — 12: 14 God shall bring every work into judgment, with every secret thing, whether *it be* good, or whether *it be* evil.

Mat. 12: 36 I say unto you, That every idle word that men shall speak, they shall give account thereof in the day of judgment.

Lk. 12: 2 There is nothing covered, that shall not be revealed; neither hid, that shall not be known. 3 Therefore, whatsoever ye have spoken in darkness, shall be heard in the light: and that which ye have spoken in the ear in closets, shall be proclaimed upon the house-tops.

Rom. 2: 16 In the day when God shall judge the secrets of men by Jesus Christ, according to my gospel.

1 Cor. 3: 13 Every man's work shall be made manifest: for the day shall declare it, because it shall be revealed by fire; and the fire shall try every man's work, of what sort it is. — 4: 5 Judge nothing before the time, until the Lord come, who both will bring to light the hidden things of darkness, and will make manifest the counsels of the hearts: and then shall every man have praise of God.

390. *Irrevocable decisions of the judgment.*

Lk. 13: 26 Then shall ye begin to say, We have eaten and drunk in thy presence, and thou hast taught in our streets. 27 But he shall say, I tell you, I know you not whence ye are; depart from me, all *ye* workers of iniquity. — 16: 26 Between us and you there is a great gulf fixed: so that they which would pass from hence to you, cannot; neither can they pass to us, that *would come* from thence.

Rev. 22: 11 He that is unjust, let him be unjust still: and he which is filthy, let him be filthy still: and he that is righteous, let him be righteous still: and he that is holy, let him be holy still. 12 And behold, I come quickly; and my reward *is* with me, to give every man according as his work shall be.
[See 553, 567, 572.]

KNOWLEDGE.

391. *True knowledge required and encouraged.*

Pr. 4: 7 Wisdom *is* the principal thing; *therefore* get wisdom: and with all thy getting get understanding. 8 Exalt her, and she shall promote thee: she shall bring thee to honor, when thou dost embrace her. 9 She shall give to thine head an ornament of grace: a crown of glory shall she deliver to thee. 13 Take fast hold of instruction; let *her* not go: keep her; for she *is* thy life. — 8: 10 Receive my instruction, and not silver: and knowledge rather than choice gold. — 22: 17 Bow down thine ear, and hear the words of the wise, and apply thine heart unto my knowledge. — 23: 12 Apply thine heart unto instruction, and thine ears to the words of knowledge. 23 Buy the truth, and sell *it* not, *also* wisdom, and instruction, and understanding. [See 363, 633.]

392. *The benefit of true knowledge.*

Pr. 2: 10 When wisdom entereth into thine heart, and knowledge is pleasant unto thy soul; 11 Discretion shall pre-

serve thee, understanding shall keep thee: 12 To deliver thee
from the way of the evil *man*, from the man that speaketh
froward things. — 3: 13 Happy *is* the man *that* findeth wisdom,
and the man *that* getteth understanding. 14 For the merchandise of it *is* better than the merchandise of silver, and the gain
thereof than fine gold. 15 She *is* more precious than rubies:
and all the things thou canst desire are not to be compared
unto her. 16 Length of days *is* in her right hand; *and* in her
left riches and honor. 17 Her ways *are* ways of pleasantness,
and all her paths *are* peace. ` 18 She *is* a tree of life to them
that lay hold upon her: and happy *is every one* that retaineth
her. 35 The wise shall inherit glory: but shame shall be the
promotion of fools. — 4: 5 Get wisdom, get understanding:
forget *it* not; neither decline from the words of my mouth.
6 Forsake her not, and she shall preserve thee: love her, and
she shall keep thee.` 8 Exalt her, and she shall promote thee:
she shall bring thee to honor, when thou dost embrace her.
9 She shall give to thine head an ornament of grace: a crown
of glory shall she deliver to thee. — 16: 22 Understanding *is*
a well-spring of life unto him that hath it: but the instruction
of fools *is* folly.

Ec. 7: 12 Wisdom *is* a defence, *and* money *is* a defence: but
the excellency of knowledge *is, that* wisdom giveth life to them
that have it.

393. *True knowledge, essential to true love.*

Ph. 1: 9 This I pray, that your love may abound yet more
and more in knowledge and *in* all judgment; 10 That ye may
approve things that are excellent; that ye may be sincere and
without offence till the day of Christ.

2 Pet. 1: 2 Grace and peace be multiplied unto you through
the knowledge of God, and of Jesus our Lord. 3 According
as his divine power hath given unto us all things that *pertain*
unto life and godliness, through the knowledge of him that hath
called us to glory and virtue. [See 47.]

394. *The certain knowledge of divine truth.*

Job 19: 25 I know *that* my Redeemer liveth, and *that* he
shall stand at the latter *day* upon the earth.

Pr. 22: 20 Have not I written to thee excellent things in
counsels and knowledge, 21 That I might make thee know the
certainty of the words of truth; that thou mightest answer the
words of truth to them that send unto thee?

Jn. 6: 69 We believe, and are sure that thou art that Christ,
the Son of the living God.

2 Tim. 1: 12 For the which cause I also suffer these things:

nevertheless I am not ashamed: for I know whom I have believed, and am persuaded that he is able to keep that which I have committed unto him against that day.

1 Jn. 2: 20 Ye have an unction from the Holy One, and ye know all things. 21 I have not written unto you because ye know not the truth, but because ye know it, and that no lie is of the truth. [See 206, 240.]

395. *How can knowledge and wisdom be attained?*

Pr. 2: 3 Yea, if thou criest after knowledge, *and* liftest up thy voice for understanding; 4 If thou seekest her as silver, and searchest for her as *for* hid treasures; 5 Then shalt thou understand the fear of the LORD, and find the knowledge of God. 6 For the LORD giveth wisdom: out of his mouth *cometh* knowledge and understanding. 7 He layeth up sound wisdom for the righteous: *he is* a buckler to them that walk uprightly. — 18: 1 Through desire, a man, having separated himself, seeketh *and* intermeddleth with all wisdom.

Jam. 1: 5 If any of you lack wisdom, let him ask of God, that giveth to all *men* liberally, and upbraideth not; and it shall be given him. 6 But let him ask in faith, nothing wavering. For he that wavereth is like a wave of the sea driven with the wind and tossed.

396. *Knowledge should be imparted.*

Pr. 27: 9 Ointment and perfume rejoice the heart: so *doth* the sweetness of a man's friend by hearty counsel.

Mat. 5: 19 Whosoever therefore shall break one of these least commandments, and shall teach men so, he shall be called the least in the kingdom of heaven: but whosoever shall do, and 'teach *them*, the same shall be called great in the kingdom of heaven. [See 110.]

397. *Self-knowledge required.*

Ps. 4: 4 Stand in awe, and sin not: commune with your own heart upon your bed, and be still.

Lam. 3: 40 Let us search and try our ways, and turn again to the LORD.

1 Cor. 11: 28 Let a man examine himself, and so let him eat of *that* bread, and drink of *that* cup.

2 Cor. 13: 5 Examine yourselves, whether ye be in the faith; prove your own selves. Know ye not your own selves, how that Jesus Christ is in you, except ye be reprobates?

Gal. 6: 4 But let every man prove his own work, and then shall he have rejoicing in himself alone, and not in another.

[See 105, 704.]

KNOWLEDGE—LAYING ON OF HANDS. 398—400

Future Knowledge more Perfect—Laying on of Hands—In working Miracles.

398. *Knowledge more perfect hereafter.*

Jn. 13: 7 Jesus answered and said unto him, What I do thou knowest not now; but thou shalt know hereafter.—16: 25 These things have I spoken unto you in proverbs: but the time cometh when I shall no more speak unto you in proverbs, but I shall show you plainly of the Father.

1 Cor. 13: 9 We know in part, and we prophesy in part. 10 But when that which is perfect is come, then that which is in part shall be done away. 12 For now we see through a glass, darkly; but then face to face: now I know in part; but then shall I know even as also I am known.

LAYING ON OF HANDS.

399. *Laying on of hands in communicating ordinary blessings.*

Gen. 48: 14 Israel stretched out his right hand, and laid *it* upon Ephraim's head, who *was* the younger, and his left hand upon Manasseh's head, guiding his hands wittingly; for Manasseh *was* the first-born. 15 And he blessed Joseph, and said, God, before whom my fathers Abraham and Isaac did walk, the God which fed me all my life long unto this day, 16 The Angel which redeemed me from all evil, bless the lads; and let my name be named on them, and the name of my fathers Abraham and Isaac: and let them grow into a multitude in the midst of the earth.

Mat. 19: 13 Then were there brought unto him little children, that he should put *his* hands on them, and pray: and the disciples rebuked them. 14 But Jesus said, Suffer little children, and forbid them not, to come unto me: for of such is the kingdom of heaven. 15 And he laid *his* hands on them, and departed thence.

Rev. 1: 17 When I saw him, I fell at his feet as dead. And he laid his right hand upon me, saying unto me, Fear not; I am the first and the last.

400. *Laying on of hands in working miracles.*

Mk. 6: 5 He laid his hand upon a few sick folk, and healed *them*.—16: 18 They shall lay hands on the sick, and they shall recover.

Lk. 4: 40 When the sun was setting, all they that had any sick with divers diseases, brought them unto him: and he laid his hands on every one of them, and healed them.

Ac. 8: 17 Then laid they *their* hands on them, and they received the Holy Ghost. 18 And when Simon saw **that** through laying on of the apostles' hands the Holy Ghost was given, he offered them money, 19 Saying, Give me also this power, that on whomsoever I lay hands, he may receive the Holy Ghost. — 28: 8 Paul entered in, and prayed, and laid his hands on him, and healed him.

401. *Laying on of hands in giving charges and designating to office.*

Num. 27: 22 Moses did as the LORD commanded him : and he took Joshua, and set him before Eleazar the priest, and before all the congregation : 23 And he laid his hands upon him, and gave him a charge, as the LORD commanded by the hand of Moses.

Ac. 13: 2 As they ministered to the Lord, and fasted, the Holy Ghost said, Separate me Barnabas and Saul, for the work whereunto I have called them. 3 And when they had fasted and prayed, and laid *their* hands on them, they sent *them* away.

1 Tim. 4: 14 Neglect not the gift that is in thee, which was given thee by prophecy, with the laying on of the hands of the presbytery. — 5: 22 Lay hands suddenly on no man, neither be partaker of other men's sins : keep thyself pure.

2 Tim. 1: 6 Wherefore I put thee in remembrance, that thou stir up the gift of God, which is in thee by the putting on of my hands.

LEWDNESS.

402. *Lewdness a common vice.*

Jer. 9: 2 Oh that I had in the wilderness a lodging-place of way-faring men; that I might leave my people, and go from them! for they *be* all adulterers, an assembly of treacherous men. — 23: 10 The land is full of adulterers.

Ezk. 22: 9 In thee are men that carry tales to shed blood : and in thee they eat upon the mountains : in the midst of thee they commit lewdness. 11 And one hath committed abomination with his neighbor's wife ; and another hath lewdly defiled his daughter-in-law; and another in thee hath humbled his sister, his father's daughter.

Mat. 12: 39 He answered and said to them, An evil and adulterous generation.

Jn. 8: 7 When they continued asking him, he lifted up himself and said unto them, He that is without sin among you, let him first cast a stone at her. 9 And they which heard *it* being convicted by *their own* conscience, went out one by one, beginning at the eldest, *even* unto the last.

Gal. 5: 19 The works of the flesh are manifest, which are *these*, Adultery, fornication, uncleanness, lasciviousness.

'1 **Pet. 4:** 3 The time past of *our* life may suffice us to have wrought the will of the Gentiles, when we walked in lasciviousness, lusts, excess of wine, revellings, banquetings, and abominable adolatries: 4 Wherein they think it strange that ye run not with *them* to the same excess of riot, speaking evil of *you*. [Gen. 19: 5. Lev. 18: 22—25. 1 S. 2: 22. Hos. 7: 4.]

403. *Lewdness deceitful and alluring.*

Pr. 5: 3 The lips of a strange woman drop *as* a honey-comb, and her mouth *is* smoother than oil. — 6: 23 The commandment *is* a lamp; and the law *is* light; and reproofs of instruction *are* the way of life: 24 To keep thee from the evil woman, from the flattery of the tongue of a strange woman. 25 Lust not after her beauty in thy heart; neither let her take thee with her eyelids. [Pr. 7: 10—18.]

404. *Lewdness forbidden.*

Ex. 20: 14 Thou shalt not commit adultery.

Mat. 5: 27 Ye have heard that it was said by them of old time, Thou shalt not commit adultery: 28 But I say unto you, That whosoever looketh on a woman to lust after her, hath committed adultery with her already in his heart.

Ac. 15: 20 We write unto them that they abstain from pollutions of idols, and *from* fornication, and *from* things strangled, and *from* blood.

Rom. 13: 13 Let us walk honestly, as in the day: not in rioting and drunkenness, not in chambering and wantonness, not in strife and envying.

Ep. 5: 3 Fornication, and all uncleanness, or covetousness, let it not be once named among you, as becometh saints; 4 Neither filthiness, nor foolish talking, nor jesting, which are not convenient: but rather giving of thanks.

Col. 3: 5 Mortify therefore your members which are upon the earth; fornication, uncleanness, inordinate affection, evil concupiscence, and covetousness, which is idolatry: 6 For which things' sake the wrath of God cometh on the children of disobedience.

1 **Tim. 1:** 10 For whoremongers, for them that defile themselves with mankind, for men-stealers, for liars, for perjured persons, and if there be any other thing that is contrary to sound doctrine.

1 **Pet. 2:** 11 Dearly beloved, I beseech *you*, as strangers and pilgrims, abstain from fleshly lusts, which war against the soul.

24   277

[Gen. 39: 7—9. Lev. 18: 20—23, and 19: 29. Pr. 31: 3. Hab. 2: 15, 1 Th. 4: 3—5.]

405. *Guilt and condemnation of lewdness — cautions.*

Gen. 39: 9 How then can I do this great wickedness, and sin against God?

Lev. 20: 10 The man that committeth adultery with *another* man's wife, *even he* that committeth adultery with his neighbor's wife, the adulterer and the adulteress shall surely be put to death.

Pr. 2: 18 Her house inclineth unto death, and her paths unto the dead. 19 None that go unto her return again, neither take they hold of the paths of life. — 5: 3 The lips of a strange woman drop *as* a honey-comb, and her mouth *is* smoother than oil: 4 But her end is bitter as wormwood, sharp as a two-edged sword. 8 Remove thy way far from her, and come not nigh the door of her house: 9 Lest thou give thine honor unto others, and thy years unto the cruel: 10 Lest strangers be filled with thy wealth; and thy labors *be* in the house of a stranger; 11 And thou mourn at the last, when thy flesh and thy body are consumed. 12 And say, How have I hated instruction, and my heart despised reproof. — 7: 22 He goeth after her straightway as an ox goeth to the slaughter, or as a fool to the correction of the stocks; 23 Till a dart strike through his liver; as a bird hasteth to the snare, and knoweth not that it *is* for his life. 24 Hearken unto me now therefore, O ye children, and attend to the words of my mouth. 25 Let not thy heart decline to her ways, go not astray in her paths. 26 For she hath cast down many wounded: yea, many strong *men* have been slain by her. 27 Her house *is* the way to hell, going down to the chambers of death.

Ec. 7: 26 I find more bitter than death the woman whose heart *is* snares and nets, *and* her hands *as* bands: whoso pleaseth God shall escape from her: but the sinner shall be taken by her.

Jer. 23: 14 I have seen also in the prophets of Jerusalem an horrible thing: they commit adultery, and walk in lies: they strengthen also the hands of evil-doers, that none doth return from his wickedness: they are all of them unto me as Sodom, and the inhabitants thereof as Gomorrah. 15 Therefore thus saith the LORD of hosts concerning the prophets; Behold, I will feed them with wormwood, and make them drink the water of gall.

Mal. 3: 5 I will come near to you to judgment: and I will be a swift witness against the sorcerers, and against the adul-

Condemned and punished.

terers, and against false swearers, and against those that oppress the hireling in *his* wages, the widow, and the fatherless, and that turn aside the stranger *from his right,* and fear not me, saith the LORD of hosts.

1 Cor. 5: 11 Now I have written unto you not to keep company, if any man that is called a brother be a fornicator, or covetous, or an idolater, or a railer, or a drunkard, or an extortioner: with such an one no not to eat. — 6: 9 Know ye not that the unrighteous shall not inherit the kingdom of God? Be not deceived; neither fornicators, nor idolaters, nor adulterers, nor effeminate, nor abusers of themselves with mankind, 10 Nor thieves, nor covetous, nor drunkards, nor revilers, nor extortioners, shall inherit the kingdom of God. — 10: 8 Neither let us commit fornication, as some of them committed, and fell in one day three and twenty thousand.

[See Numbers 25: 1—9.]

Gal. 5: 19 The works of the flesh are manifest, which are *these,* Adultery, fornication, uncleanness, lasciviousness, 20 Idolatry, witchcraft, hatred, variance, emulations, wrath, strife, seditions, heresies, 21 Envyings, murders, drunkenness, revellings, and such like: of the which I tell you before, as I have also told *you* in time past, that they which do such things shall not inherit the kingdom of God.

Ep. 5: 5 This ye know, that no whoremonger, nor unclean person, nor covetous man, who is an idolater, hath any inheritance in the kingdom of Christ and of God. 6 Let no man deceive you with vain words: for because of these things cometh the wrath of God upon the children of disobedience.

Heb. 13: 4 Marriage *is* honorable in all, and the bed undefiled :- but whoremongers and adulterers God will judge.

Jude 7 As Sodom and Gomorrah, and the cities about them in like manner, giving themselves over to fornication, and going after strange flesh, are set forth for an example, suffering the vengeance of eternal fire.

Rev. 21: 8 The fearful, and unbelieving, and the abominable, and murderers, and whoremongers, and sorcerers, and idolaters, and all liars, shall have their part in the lake which burneth with fire and brimstone: which is the second death. — 22: 15 Without *are* dogs, and sorcerers, and whoremongers, and murderers, and idolaters, and whosoever loveth and maketh a lie.

[Pr. 6: 26—34, and 9: 16—18, and 29: 3. Ec. 7: 25, 26. Jer. 5: 7—9. Hos. 4: 11. Rom. 1: 27.]

LIBERALITY.

406. *Liberality enjoined.*

Ec. 11: 1 Cast thy bread upon the waters : for thou shalt find it after many days. 2 Give a portion to seven, and also to eight ; for thou knowest not what evil shall be upon the earth.

- Mat. 10: 8 Freely ye have received, freely give.

Lk. 3: 11 He answereth and saith unto them, He that hath two coats, let him impart to him that hath none : and he that hath meat, let him do likewise. — 12: 33 Sell that ye have, and give alms : provide yourselves bags which wax not old, a treasure in the heavens that faileth not, where no thief approacheth, neither moth corrupteth. 34 For where your treasure is, there will your heart be also. — 16: 9 I say unto you, Make to yourselves friends of the mammon of unrighteousness, that when ye fail, they may receive you into everlasting habitations. 11 If therefore ye have not been faithful in the unrighteous mammon, who will commit to your trust the true *riches?* 13 Ye cannot serve God and mammon. 14 And the Pharisees also, who were covetous, heard all these things, and they derided him.

Ac. 20: 35 I have shewed you all things, how that so laboring ye ought to support the weak, and to remember the words of the Lord Jesus, how he said, It is more blessed to give than to receive.

2 Cor. 8: 7 As ye abound in every *thing, in* faith, and utterance, and knowledge, and *in* all diligence, and *in* your love to us, *see* that ye abound in this grace also.

Gal. 6: 9 Let us not be weary in well-doing: for in due season we shall reap if we faint not. 10 As we have therefore opportunity, let us do good unto all *men,* especially unto them who are of the household of faith.

1 Tim. 6: 17 Charge them that are rich in this world, that they be not high-minded, nor trust in uncertain riches, but in the living God, who giveth us richly all things to enjoy ; 18 That they do good, that they be rich in good works, ready to distribute, willing to communicate ; 19 Laying up in store for themselves a good foundation against the time to come, that they may lay hold on eternal life.

Heb. 13: 16 To do good, and to communicate, forget not : for with such sacrifices God is well pleased.

[See 412, 526.]

407. *Liberality exemplified.*

Ac. 10: 4 He said unto him, [Cornelius] Thy prayers and thine alms are come up for a memorial before God.
[See 355, 414, 661.]

408. *Rewards of liberality, and evils of covetousness.*

2 Ch. 31: 10 Azariah the chief priest of the house of Zadok answered him, and said, Since *the people* began to bring the offerings into the house of the LORD, we have had enough to eat, and have left plenty: for the LORD hath blessed his people: and that which is left *is* this great store.

Ps. 37: 3 Trust in the LORD, and do good; *so* shalt thou dwell in the ·land, and verily thou shalt be fed. 25 I have been young, and *now* am old; yet I have not seen the righteous forsaken, nor his seed begging bread. 26 *He is* ever merciful, and lendeth; and his seed *is* blessed.—112: 5 A good man sheweth favor, and lendeth: he will guide his affairs with discretion. 6 Surely he shall not be moved for ever: the righteous shall be in everlasting remembrance.

Pr. 3: 9 Honor the LORD with thy substance, and with the first-fruits of all thine increase: 10 So shall thy barns be filled with plenty, and thy presses shall burst out with new wine.— 11: 24 There is that scattereth, and yet increaseth; and *there is* that withholdeth more than is meet, but *it tendeth* to poverty. 25 The liberal soul shall be made fat: and he that watereth shall be watered also himself. 26 He that withholdeth corn, the people shall curse him: but blessing *shall be* upon the head of him that selleth *it.*— 13: 7 There is that maketh himself rich, yet *hath* nothing: *there is* that maketh himself poor, yet *hath* great riches.

Is. 32: 8 The liberal deviseth liberal things; and by liberal things shall he stand.

Mal. 3: 9 Ye *are* cursed with a curse: for ye have robbed me, *even* this whole nation. 10 Bring ye all the tithes into the storehouse, that there may be meat in mine house, and prove me now herewith saith the LORD of hosts, if I will not open you the windows of heaven, and pour you out a blessing, that *there shall* not *be room* enough *to receive it.* 11 And I will rebuke the devourer for your sakes, and he shall not destroy the fruits of your ground; neither shall your vine cast her fruit before the time in the field, saith the LORD of hosts. 12 And all nations shall call you blessed.

Lk. 6: 38 Give, and it shall be given unto you; good measure, pressed down, and shaken together, and running over, shall men give into your bosom. For with the same measure that ye mete withal, it shall be measured to you again.

Ac. 20: 35 I have shewed you all things, how that so laboring ye ought to support the weak, and to remember the words of the Lord Jesus, how he said, It is more blessed to give than to receive.

2 Cor. 9: 6 This *I say,* He which soweth sparingly, shall reap also sparingly; and he which soweth bountifully, shall reap also bountifully. 7 Every man according as he purposeth in his heart, *so let him give;* not grudgingly, or of necessity: for God loveth a cheerful giver. 8 And God *is* able to make all grace abound toward you; that ye, always having all sufficiency in all *things,* may abound to every good work.
[See 415, 527, 630, 674.]

LOVE TO GOD.

409. *Love to God our primary duty.*

Mat. 22: 37 Jesus said unto him, Thou shalt love the LORD thy God with all thy heart, and with all thy soul, and with all thy mind. 38 This is the first and great commandment.
[See 288.]

410. *Why should we love God?*

Ps. 99: 9 Exalt the Lord our God, and worship at his holy hill; for the Lord our God *is* holy.—107: 8 Oh that men would praise the LORD *for* his goodness, and *for* his wonderful works to the children of men! 145: 3 Great *is* the LORD, and greatly to be praised; and his greatness *is* unsearchable. 148: 13 Let them praise the name of the Lord: for his name alone is excellent; his glory *is* above the earth and heaven.

411. *Spurious love to God.*

Ps. 106: 12 They sang his praise. 13 They soon forgat his works.
Ezk. 33: 31 With their mouth they shew much love, *but* their heart goeth after their covetousness.
[See 191, 194, 609, 623, 689, 702.]

LOVE TO MAN.

412. *Love to man an essential duty.*

Rom. 13: 8 Owe no man any thing, but to love one another: for he that loveth another hath fulfilled the law. 9 For this,

Thou shalt not commit adultery, Thou shalt not kill, Thou shalt not steal, Thou shalt not bear false witness, Thou shalt not covet; and if *there be* any other commandment, it is briefly comprehended in this saying, namely, Thou shalt love thy neighbor as thyself. 10 Love worketh no ill to his neighbor: therefore love *is* the fulfilling of the law.

1 Cor. 13: 13 Now abideth faith, hope, charity, these three; but the greatest of these *is* charity.—16: 14 Let all your things be done with charity.

Gal. 5: 13 Brethren, ye have been called unto liberty; only *use* not liberty for an occasion to the flesh, but by love serve one another. 22 The fruit of the Spirit is love, joy, peace, long-suffering, gentleness, goodness, faith, 23 Meekness, temperance.

Col. 3: 14 Above all these things *put on* charity, which is the bond of perfectness.

1 Th. 3: 12 The Lord make you to increase and abound in love one toward another, and toward all *men*, even as we *do* toward you.

1 Pet. 4: 8 Above all things have fervent charity among yourselves: for charity shall cover the multitude of sins.

[See 406, 629, 685, 715.]

LOVE DISINTERESTED.

413. *Disinterested love required as indispensable.*

Mat. 5: 43 Ye have heard that it hath been said, Thou shalt love thy neighbor, and hate thine enemy: 44 But I say unto you, Love your enemies, bless them that curse you, do good to them that hate you, and pray for them which despitefully use you, and persecute you; 45 That ye may be the children of your Father which is in heaven: for he maketh his sun to rise on the evil and on the good, and sendeth rain on the just and on the unjust.—6: 33 Seek ye first the kingdom of God, and his righteousness, and all these things shall be added unto you. —7: 12 All things whatsoever ye would that men should do to you, do ye even so to them: for this is the law and the prophets.—22: 39 The second *is* like unto it, Thou shalt love thy neighbor as thyself.

Lk. 6: 35 Love ye your enemies, and do good, and lend, hoping for nothing again.

Rom. 8: 9 Ye are not in the flesh, but in the Spirit, if so be that the Spirit of God dwell in you. Now, if any man have not the Spirit of Christ, he is none of his. —15: 1 We then that are strong ought to bear the infirmities of the weak, and not to please ourselves. 2 Let every one of us please *his* neighbor for *his* good to edification. 3 For even Christ pleased not himself; but, as it is written, The reproaches of them that reproached thee fell on me.

1 Cor. 10: 24 Let no man seek his own, but every man another's *wealth.* 33 Even as I please all *men* in all *things,* not seeking mine own profit, but the *profit* of many, that they may be saved.—13: 4 Charity suffereth long, *and* is kind; charity envieth not; charity vaunteth not itself, is not puffed up, 5 Doth not behave itself unseemly, seeketh not her own, is not easily provoked, thinketh no evil; 6 Rejoiceth not in iniquity, but rejoiceth in the truth; 7 Beareth all things, believeth all things, hopeth all things, endureth all things.

2 Cor. 5: 15 He died for all, that they which live should not henceforth live unto themselves, but unto him which died for them, and rose again.

Gal. 5: 14 All the law is fulfilled in one word, *even* in this, Thou shalt love thy neighbor as thyself.

Ph. 2: 3 *Let* nothing *be done* through strife or vain-glory; but in lowliness of mind let each esteem other better than themselves. 4 Look not every man on his own things, but every man also on the things of others.

Jam. 2: 8 If ye fulfil the royal law according to the scripture, Thou shalt love thy neighbor as thyself, ye do well: 9 But if ye have respect to persons, ye commit sin, and are convinced of the law as transgressors.

1 Jn. 3: 16 Hereby perceive we the love *of God,* because he laid down his life for us: and we ought to lay down *our* lives for the brethren.

[See 111, 137–8, 283, 299, 356, 674, 689.]

414. *Examples of disinterested love.*

Ex. 32: 31 Moses returned unto the LORD, and said, Oh, this people have sinned a great sin, and have made them gods of gold. 32 Yet now, if thou wilt forgive their sin: and if not, blot me, I pray thee, out of thy book which thou hast written. 33 And the LORD said unto Moses, Whosoever hath sinned against me, him will I blot out of my book.

1 S. 24: 16 Saul lifted up his voice and wept. 17 And he said to David, Thou *art* more righteous than I: for thou hast rewarded me good, whereas I have rewarded thee evil. 18 And thou hast shewed this day how that thou hast dealt well with me; forasmuch as when the LORD had delivered me into thine hand, thou killedst me not.

Job 1: 9 Then Satan answered the LORD and said, Doth Job fear God for nought? 21 The LORD gave, and the LORD hath taken away; blessed be the name of the LORD.—13: 15 Though he slay me, yet will I trust in him: but I will maintain mine own ways before him.—29: 12 I delivered the poor that cried, and the fatherless, and *him that had* none to help him. 13 The blessing of him that was ready to perish came upon me; and I caused the widow's heart to sing for joy.

Dan. 3: 16 Shadrach, Meshach, and Abed-nego, answered and said to the king, O Nebuchadnezzar, we *are* not careful to answer thee in this matter. 17 If it be *so*, our God whom we serve is able to deliver us from the burning fiery furnace, and he will deliver *us* out of thine hand, O king. 18 But if not, be it known unto thee, O king, that we will not serve thy gods, nor worship the golden image which thou hast set up.—6: 10 Now when Daniel knew that the writing was signed, he went into his house; and his windows being open in his chamber toward Jerusalem, he kneeled upon his knees three times a day, and prayed, and gave thanks before his God, as he did aforetime.

Lk. 10: 33 A certain Samaritan, as he journeyed, came where he was: and when he saw him, he had compassion *on him*, 34 And went to *him*, and bound up his wounds, pouring in oil and wine, and set him on his own beast, and brought him to an inn, and took care of him.

Ac. 2: 44 All that believed were together, and had all things common; 45 And sold their possessions and goods, and parted them to all *men*, as every man had need.—4: 32 The multitude of them that believed were of one heart, and of one soul: neither said any *of them* that aught of the things which he possessed was his own; but they had all things common. 34 Neither was there any among them that lacked: for as many as were possessors of lands or houses sold them, and brought the prices of the things that were sold, 35 And laid *them* down at the apostles' feet: and distribution was made unto every man according as he had need.

Rom. 9: 1 I say the truth in Christ, I lie not, my conscience also bearing me witness in the Holy Ghost, 2 That I have great heaviness and continual sorrow in my heart. 3 For I could wish that myself were accursed from Christ, for my brethren, my kinsmen according to the flesh.

2 Cor. 8: 9 Ye know the grace of our Lord Jesus Christ, that though he was rich, yet for your sakes he became poor, that ye through his poverty might be rich.—12: 14 Behold,

the third time I am ready to come to you ; and I will not be burdensome to you : for I seek not yours, but you.

Heb. 11: 24 By faith Moses, when he was come to years, refused to be called the son of Pharaoh's daughter ; 25 Choosing rather to suffer affliction with the people of God, than to enjoy the pleasures of sin for a season ; 26 Esteeming the reproach of Christ greater riches than the treasures in Egypt.
[See 56, 299, 356, 407, 674.]

415. Disinterested love rewarded.

Mk. 10: 28 Then Peter began to say unto him, Lo, we have left all, and have followed thee.   29 And Jesus answered and said, Verily, I say unto you, There is no man that hath left house, or brethren, or sisters, or father, or mother, or wife, or children, or lands, for my sake, and the gospel's,   30 But he shall receive an hundred-fold now in this time, houses, and brethren, and sisters, and mothers, and children, and lands, with persecutions ; and in the world to come, eternal life.
[See 408, 527, 630.]

LYING.

416. Lying a prevalent sin.

Is. 59: 3 Your hands are defiled with blood, and your fingers with iniquity ; your lips have spoken lies, your tongue hath muttered perverseness.   4 None calleth for justice, nor *any* pleadeth for truth : they trust in vanity, and speak lies ; they conceive mischief. and bring forth iniquity.   13 In transgressing and lying against the LORD, and departing away from our God, speaking oppression and revolt, conceiving and uttering from the heart words of falsehood.   14 And judgment is turned away backward, and justice standeth afar off : for truth is fallen in the street, and equity cannot enter.

Jer. 9: 2 Oh that I had in the wilderness a lodging-place of way-faring men ; that I might leave my people, and go from them ! for they *be* all adulterers, an assembly of treacherous men.   3 And they bend their tongues *like* their bow *for* lies : but they are not valiant for the truth upon the earth ; for they proceed from evil to evil, and they know not me, saith the LORD. 4 Take ye heed every one of his neighbor, and trust ye not in any brother : for every brother will utterly supplant, and every neighbor will walk with slanders.   5 And they will deceive every one his neighbor, and will not speak the truth : they have taught their tongue to speak lies, *and* weary themselves to commit iniquity.   6 Thine habitation *is* in the midst of deceit; through deceit they refuse to know me, saith the LORD. 8 Their tongue *is as* an arrow shot out; it speaketh deceit: *one* speaketh peaceably to his neighbor with his mouth, but in heart he layeth his wait.

Hos. 4: 1 Hear the word of the LORD, ye children of Israel: for the LORD hath a controversy with the inhabitants of the land, because *there is* no truth, nor mercy, nor knowledge of God in the land. 2 By swearing, and lying, and killing, and stealing, and committing adultery, they break out, and blood toucheth blood.

Mic. 6: 12 The rich men thereof are full of violence, and the inhabitants thereof have spoken lies, and their tongue *is* deceitful in their mouth.

Jn. 8: 44 Ye are of *your* father the devil, and the lusts of your father ye will do: he was a murderer from the beginning, and abode not in the truth; because there is no truth in him. When he speaketh a lie, he speaketh of his own: for he is a liar, and the father of it. [See 702.]

417. *Lying forbidden.*

Ex. 20: 16 Thou shalt not bear false witness against thy neighbor.

Lev. 19: 11 Ye shall not steal, neither deal falsely, neither lie one to another. 12 And ye shall not swear by my name falsely, neither shalt thou profane the name of thy God: I *am* the LORD.

Ps. 34: 13 Keep thy tongue from evil, and thy lips from speaking guile.

Pr. 4: 24 Put away from thee a froward mouth, and perverse lips put far from thee.

Ep. 4: 25 Putting away lying, speak every man truth with his neighbor: for we are members one of another.

Col. 3: 9 Lie not one to another, seeing that ye have put off the old man with his deeds.

1 Pet. 3: 10 He that will love life, and see good days, let him refrain his tongue from evil, and his lips that they speak no guile. [See 729, 730.]

418. *Lying displeasing to God.*

Ps. 5: 6 Thou shalt destroy them that speak leasing: the LORD will abhor the bloody and deceitful man — 59: 12 *For* the sin of their mouth *and* the words of their lips let them even be taken in their pride: and for cursing and lying *which* they speak. 13 Consume *them* in wrath, consume *them*, that they *may* not *be:* and let them know that God ruleth in Jacob

His Origin, Powers, and Dignity.

unto the ends of the earth. — 63: 11 The king shall rejoice in God; every one that sweareth by him shall glory: but the mouth of them that speak lies shall be stopped.

Pr. 6: 16 These six *things* doth the LORD hate; yea, seven *are* an abomination unto him: 17 A proud look, a lying tongue, and hands that shed innocent blood, 18 A heart that deviseth wicked imaginations, feet that be swift in running to mischief, 19 A false witness *that* speaketh lies, and him that soweth discord among brethren. — 10: 18 He that hideth hatred *with* lying lips, and he that uttereth a slander, *is* a fool. — 12: 19 The lip of truth shall be established for ever: but a lying tongue *is* but for a moment. 22 Lying lips *are* abomination to the LORD: but they that deal truly *are* his delight. — 19: 9 A false witness shall not be unpunished, and *he that* speaketh lies shall perish.

Is. 28: 17 Judgment also will I lay to the line, and righteousness to the plummet: and the hail shall sweep away the refuge of lies, and the waters shall overflow the hiding-place.

Ac. 5: 3 Peter said, Ananias, why hath Satan filled thine heart to lie to the Holy Ghost, and to keep back *part* of the price of the land? 4 While it remained, was it not thine own? and after it was sold, was it not in thine own power? why hast thou conceived this thing in thine heart? thou hast not lied unto men, but unto God. 5 And Ananias hearing these words, fell down, and gave up the ghost. And great fear came on all them that heard these things.

Rev. 21: 8 The fearful, and unbelieving, and the abominable, and murderers, and whoremongers, and sorcerers, and idolaters, and all liars, shall have their part in the lake which burneth with fire and brimstone: which is the second death. — 22: 15 Without *are* dogs, and sorcerers, and whoremongers, and murderers, and idolaters, and whosoever loveth and maketh a lie. [Ps. 62: 3, 4. Pr. 21: 6. Zec. 8: 16, 17.]
[See 230.]

MAN.

419. *Man's common origin and dignity.*

Gen. 1: 27 God created man in his *own* image, in the image of God created he him; male and female created he them. 28. And God blessed them, and God said unto them, Be fruitful, and multiply, and replenish the earth, and subdue it: and have dominion over the fish of the sea, and over the fowl of the air, and over every living thing that moveth upon the earth.

Ps. 8: 3 When I consider thy heavens, the work of thy fingers ; the moon and the stars, which thou hast ordained ; 4 What is man, that thou art mindful of him ? and the son of man, that thou visitest him ? 5 For thou hast made him a little lower than the angels, and hast crowned him with glory and honor. 6 Thou madest him to have dominion over the works of thy hands : thou hast put all *things* under his feet.

Mal. 2: 10 Have we not all one father ? hath not one God created us ? why do we deal treacherously every man against his brother, by profaning the covenant of our fathers ?

Ac. 17: 26 And hath made of one blood all nations of men for to dwell on all the face of the earth, and hath determined the times before appointed, and the bounds of their habitation. 28 For in him we live, and move, and have our being ; as certain also of your own poets have said, For we are also his offspring.

420. Man's power of intuition, or perception of self-evident truths.

Job 32: 8 *There is* a spirit in man : and the inspiration of the Almighty giveth them understanding.

Lk. 12: 57 Why even of yourselves judge ye not what is right ? [See 206.]

421. Man's power of reason, and capacity for knowledge, holiness, and progress.

Pr. 18: 1 Through desire, a man, having separated himself, seeketh *and* intermeddleth with all wisdom.

Ezk. 12: 2 Son of man, thou dwellest in the midst of a rebellious house, which have eyes to see, and see not ; they have ears to hear, and hear not : for they *are* a rebellious house. [Jer. 5: 21.]

2 Cor. 8: 12 For if there be first a willing mind, *it is* accepted according to that a man hath *and* not according to that he hath not.

Heb. 5: 14 Strong meat belongeth to them that are of full age, *even* those who by reason of use have their senses exercised to discern both good and evil. — 6: 1 Leaving the principles of the doctrine of Christ, let us go on unto perfection. [See 667.]

422. Man's immortality.

Jn. 10: 27 My sheep hear my voice, and I know them, and they follow me : 28 And I give unto them eternal life ; and they shall never perish, neither shall any pluck them o t of my hand.

Rom. 2: 6 Who will render to every man according to his deeds: 7 To them who by patient continuance in well-doing, seek for glory, and honor, and immortality ; eternal life.

2 Tim. 1: 10 But is now made manifest by the appearing of our Saviour Jesus Christ, who hath abolished death, and hath brought life and immortality to light through the gospel. [See 152, 617.]

MARRIAGE.

423. Marriage instituted and recommended.

Gen. 2: 18 The LORD God said, *It is* not good that the man should be alone : I will make him an help meet for him. 21 And the LORD God caused a deep sleep to fall upon Adam, and he slept ; and he took one of his ribs, and closed up the flesh instead thereof: 22 And the rib, which the LORD God had taken from man, made he a woman, and brought her unto the man.

Pr. 18: 22 *Whoso* findeth a wife, findeth a good *thing*, and obtaineth favor of the LORD.

Ep. 5: 31 For this cause shall a man leave his father and mother, and shall be joined unto his wife, and they two shall be one flesh.

1 Tim. 3: 2 A bishop then must be blameless, the husband of one wife, vigilant, sober, of good behavior, given to hospitality, apt to teach. — 4: 1 The Spirit speaketh expressly, that in the latter times some shall depart from the faith, giving heed to seducing spirits, and doctrines of devils; 2 Speaking lies in hypocrisy, having their conscience seared with a hot iron; 3 Forbidding to marry, *and commanding* to abstain from meats, which God hath created to be received with thanksgiving of them which believe and know the truth. — 5: 14 I will therefore that the younger women marry, bear children, guide the house, give none occasion to the adversary to speak reproachfully. 15 For some are already turned aside after Satan.

Heb. 13: 4 Marriage *is* honorable in all, and the bed unde-filed: but whoremongers and adulterers God will judge. [Ps. 68: 6 : and 107: 41, 42. 1 Cor. 7: 2.]

424. Matrimonial instructions and warnings.

Gen. 6: 2 The sons of God saw the daughters of men that

they *were* fair; and they took them wives of all which they chose.

Dt. 7: 3 Neither shalt thou make marriages with them : thy daughter thou shalt not give unto his son, nor his daughter shalt thou take unto thy son. 4 For they will turn away thy son from following me, that they may serve other gods : so will the anger of the LORD be kindled against you, and destroy thee suddenly.

Am. 3: 3 Can two walk together, except they be agreed?

1 Cor. 7: 39 The wife is bound by the law as long as her husband liveth; but if her husband be dead, she is at liberty to be married to whom she will; only in the Lord.

2 Cor. 6: 14 Be ye not unequally yoked together with unbelievers : for what fellowship hath righteousness with unrighteousness? and what communion hath light with darkness?

425. *Mutual duties of husbands and wives.*

Ep. 5: 21 Submitting yourselves one to another in the fear of God. 22 Wives, submit yourselves unto your own husbands, as unto the Lord. 23 For the husband is the head of the wife, even as Christ is the head of the church : and he is the Saviour of the body. 24 Therefore as the church is subject unto Christ, so *let* the wives *be* to their own husbands in every thing. 25 Husbands, love your wives, even as Christ also loved the church, and gave himself for it; 28 So ought men to love their wives, as their own bodies. He that loveth his wife loveth himself. 33 Neverthelesss, let every one of you in particular so love his wife even as himself: and the wife *see* that she reverence *her* husband.

Tit. 2: 4 That they may teach the young women to be sober, to love their husbands, to love their children, 5 *To be* discreet, chaste, keepers at home, good, obedient to their own husbands, that the word of God be not blasphemed.

[See 197.]

426. *Polygamy forbidden — its tendency.*

Dt. 17: 15 Thou shalt in any wise set. *him* king over thee whom the LORD thy God shall choose. 17 Neither shall he multiply wives to himself, that his heart turn not away : neither shall he greatly multiply to himself silver and gold.

1 K. 11: 1 King Solomon loved many strange women. 3 And he had seven hundred wives, princesses, and three hundred concubines : and his wives turned away his heart.

Mal. 2: 15 Did not he make one? Yet had he the residue

of the Spirit. And wherefore one? That he might seek a godly seed. Therefore take heed to your spirit, and let none deal treacherously against the wife of his youth.

Mat. 19: 9 I say unto you, Whosoever shall put away his wife, except *it be* for fornication, and shall marry another, committeth adultery: and whoso marrieth her which is put away, doth commit adultery.

Mk. 10: 11 He saith unto them, Whosoever shall put away his wife, and marry another, committeth adultery against her. 12 And if a woman shall put away her husband, and be married to another, she committeth adultery.

1 Tim. 3: 2 A bishop then must be blameless, the husband of one wife. 12 Let the deacons be the husbands of one wife, ruling their children and their own houses well.

427. *Divorce discountenanced.*

Gen. 2: 23 Adam said, This *is* now bone of my bones, and flesh of my flesh: she shall be called Woman, because she was taken out of man. 24 Therefore shall a man leave his father and his mother, and shall cleave unto his wife: and they shall be one flesh.

Mal. 2: 15 Did not he make one? Yet had he the residue of the Spirit. And wherefore one? That he might seek a godly seed. Therefore take heed to your spirit, and let none deal treacherously against the wife of his youth. 16 For the LORD, the God of Israel, saith, that he hateth putting away: for *one* covereth violence with his garment, saith the LORD of hosts: therefore take heed to your spirit, that ye deal not treacherously.

Mat. 19: 4 He answered and said unto them, Have ye not read, that he which made *them* at the beginning, made them male and female, 5 And said, For this cause shall a man leave father and mother, and shall cleave to his wife: and they twain shall be one flesh? 6 Wherefore they are no more twain, but one flesh. What therefore God hath joined together, let not man put asunder. 8 He saith unto them, Moses, because of the hardness of your hearts, suffered you to put away your wives: but from the beginning it was not so. 9 And I say unto, Whosoever shall put away his wife, except *it be* for fornication, and shall marry another, committeth adultery: and whoso marrieth her which is put away, doth commit adultery. [Mk. 10: 2—12.]

Lk. 16: 18 Whosoever putteth away his wife, and marrieth another, committeth adultery; and whosoever marrieth her that is put away from *her* husband, committeth adultery.

Rom. 7: 2 The woman which hath an husband, is bound by the law to *her* husband so long as he liveth; but if the husband be dead, she is loosed from the law of *her* husband. 3 So then, if while *her* husband liveth, she be married to another man, she shall be called an adulteress: but if her husband be dead, she is free from that law; so that she is no adulteress, though she be married to another man.

1 Cor. 7: 10 Unto the married I command, *yet* not I, but the Lord, Let not the wife depart from *her* husband: 11 But and if she depart, let her remain unmarried, or be reconciled to *her* husband: and let not the husband put away *his* wife.

MEANS OF GRACE.

428. *Means and instruments of grace appointed.*

Pr. 6: 23 The commandment *is* a lamp, and the law *is* light; and reproofs of instruction *are* the way of life.

Ec. 11: 6 In the morning sow thy seed, and in the evening withhold not thine hand: for thou knowest not whether shall prosper, either this or that, or whether they both *shall be* alike good.

Mat. 20: 1 The kingdom of heaven is like unto a man *that is* an householder, which went out early in the morning to hire laborers into his vineyard.

Mk. 4: 14 The sower soweth the word.

Lk. 10: 2 Therefore said he unto them, The harvest truly *is* great, but the laborers *are* few; pray ye therefore the Lord of the harvest, that he would send forth laborers into his harvest.

Jn. 4: 35 Say not ye, There are yet four months, and *then* cometh harvest? behold, I say unto you, Lift up your eyes, and look on the fields; for they are white already to harvest. 36 And he that reapeth receiveth wages, and gathereth fruit unto life eternal: that both he that soweth, and he that reapeth, may rejoice together.

1 Cor. 3: 8 He that planteth and he that watereth are one: and every man shall receive his own reward, according to his own labor. 9 For we are laborers together with God.

[See 47.]

429. *Use of means required as indispensable.*

Ezk. 33: 8 When I say unto the wicked, () wicked *man*, thou shalt surely die; if thou dost not speak to warn the **wicked** from his way, that wicked *man* shall die in his iniquity; but his blood will I require at thy hand. — 36: 37 Thus saith the Lord GOD; I will yet *for* this be inquired of by the house of Israel, to do *it* for them; I will increase them with men like a flock.

Ac. 27: 31 Paul said to the centurion, and to the soldiers, Except these abide in the ship, ye cannot be saved.

Rom. 10: 14 How then shall they call on him in whom they have not believed? and how shall they believe in him of whom they have not heard? and how shall they hear without a preacher? 15 And how shall they preach, except they be sent? 17 So then faith *cometh* by hearing, and hearing by the word of God. [See 257.]

430. Preaching, the principal means of grace.

1 Cor. 1: 17 Christ sent me not to baptize, but to preach the gospel: not with wisdom of words, lest the cross of Christ should be made of none effect. 18 The preaching of the cross is to them that perish, foolishness; but unto us which are saved, it is the power of God. 21 After that in the wisdom of God the world by wisdom knew not God, it pleased God by the foolishness of preaching to save them that believe.

Ep. 4: 11 He gave some, apostles; and some, prophets; and some, evangelists; and some, pastors and teachers: 12 For the perfecting of the saints, for the work of the ministry, for the edifying of the body of Christ: 13 Till we all come in the unity of the faith, and of the knowledge of the Son of God unto a perfect man, unto the measure of the stature of the fulness of Christ.

2 Tim. 4: 1 I charge *thee* therefore before God, and the Lord Jesus Christ, who shall judge the quick and the dead at his appearing and his kingdom; 2 Preach the word; be instant in season, out of season; reprove, rebuke, exhort with all long-suffering and doctrine. 3 For the time will come, when they will not endure sound doctrine; but after their own lusts shall they heap to themselves teachers, having itching ears; 4 And they shall turn away *their* ears from the truth, and shall be turned unto fables. 5 But watch thou in all things, endure afflictions, do the work of an evangelist, make full proof of thy ministry. [See 458.]

431. Use of means encouraged by promises and predictions.

Ps. 126: 5 They that sow in tears shall reap in joy. 6 He that goeth forth and weepeth, bearing precious seed, shall doubtless come again with rejoicing, bringing his sheaves *with him.*

Pr. 11: 18 The wicked worketh a deceitful work : but to him that soweth righteousness *shall be* a sure reward.   30 The fruit of the righteous *is* a tree of life; and he that winneth souls *is* wise.

Is. 66: 8 Who hath heard such a thing? who hath seen such things? shall the earth be made to bring forth in one day? *or* shall a nation be born at once? for as soon as Zion travailed, she brought forth her children.

Dan. 12: 3 They that be wise, shall shine as the brightness of the firmament ; and they that turn many to righteousness, as the stars for ever and ever.

Mk. 1: 17· Jesus said unto them, Come ye after me, and I will make you to become fishers of men.

Lk. 1: 16 Many of the children of Israel shall he [John] turn to the Lord their God.

Jn. 17: 20 Neither pray I for these alone ; but for them also which shall believe on me through their word.

Jam. 5: 20 Let him know, that he which converteth the sinner from the error of his way shall save a soul from death, and shall hide a multitude of sins.   [See 1, 258, 545.]

432. *Means, successfully used.*

Ac. 14: 1 It came to pass in Iconium, that they [Paul and Barnabas] went both together into the synagogue of the Jews, and so spake that a great multitude, both of the Jews, and also of the Greeks believed.

Gal. 4: 19 My little children, of whom I travail in birth again, until Christ be formed in you.

1 Cor. 4: 15 Though ye have ten thousand instructors in Christ, yet *have ye* not many fathers : for in Christ Jesus I have begotten you through the gospel.

Philemon 10 I beseech thee for my son Onesimus, whom I have begotten in my bonds.   [See 468, 545.]   ▪

433. *Superiority of the true means of grace.*

Jer. 23 28 The prophet that hath a dream, let him tell a dream ; and he that hath my word, let him speak my word faithfully.   What *is* the chaff to the wheat? saith the LORD. 29 *Is* not my word like as a fire? saith the LORD ; and like a hammer *that* breaketh the rock in pieces?

Lk. 16: 31 He said unto him, If they hear not Moses and the prophets, neither will they be persuaded, though one rose from the dead.

2 Cor. 10: 4 (The weapons of our warfare *are* not carnal, but mighty through God to the pulling down of strong holds.) 5 Casting down imaginations, and every high thing that exalteth itself against the knowledge of God, and bringing into captivity every thought to the obedience of Christ.

Heb. 4: 12 The word of God *is* quick, and powerful, and sharper than any two-edged sword, piercing even to the dividing asunder of soul and spirit, and of the joints and marrow, and *is* a discerner of the thoughts and intents of the heart. [See 47.]

434. *Use of means made effectual by divine power.*

Ps. 51: 12 Restore unto me the joy of thy salvation; and uphold me *with thy* free Spirit. 13 *Then* will I teach transgressors thy ways; and sinners shall be converted unto thee.

Zec. 4: 6 He answered and spake unto me, saying, This *is* the word of the LORD unto Zerubbabel, saying, Not by might, nor by power, but by my Spirit, saith the LORD of hosts.

2 Tim. 2: 25 In meekness instructing those that oppose themselves; if God peradventure will give them repentance to the acknowledging of the truth. [See 594—6.]

435. *The means of grace have different and sometimes destructive effects.*

Is. 6: 9 He said, Go, and tell this people, Hear ye indeed, but understand not; and see ye indeed, but perceive not. 10 Make the heart of this people fat, and make their ears heavy, and shut their eyes; lest they see with their eyes, and hear with their ears, and understand with their heart, and convert, and be healed. 11 Then said I, LORD, how long? And he answered, Until the cities be wasted without inhabitant, and the houses without man, and the land be utterly desolate; 12 And the LORD have removed men far away, and *there be* a great forsaking in the midst of the land. — 28: 13 The word of the LORD was unto them, precept upon precept, precept upon precept: line upon line, line upon line; here a little, *and* there a little; that they might go, and fall backward, and be broken, and snared, and taken.

Jer. 5: 14 Wherefore thus saith the LORD God of hosts, Because ye speak this word, behold, I will make my words in thy mouth fire, and this people wood, and it shall devour them.

Mk. 4: 3 Hearken; Behold, there went out a sower to sow. 4 And it came to pass as he sowed, some fell by the way-side, and the fowls of the air came and devoured it up. 5 And some fell on stony ground, where it had not much earth; and immediately it sprang up, because it had no depth of earth:

6 But when the sun was up, it was scorched; and because it had no root, it withered away. 7 And some fell among thorns, and the thorns grew up, and choked it, and it yielded no fruit. 8 And other fell on good ground, and did yield fruit that sprang up, and increased, and brought forth, some thirty, and some sixty, and some an hundred.

2 Cor. 2: 15 We are unto God a sweet savor of Christ, in them that are saved, and in them that perish: 16 To the one *we are* the savor of death unto death; and to the other the savor of life unto life. And who *is* sufficient for these things?

Heb. 4: 2 Unto us was the gospel preached, as well as unto them: but the word preached did not profit them, not being mixed with faith in them that heard *it.* [Mic. 2: 7.] [See 242.]

436. *Cases of discouragement in using means.*

Pr. 9: 7 He that reproveth a scorner getteth to himself shame: and he that rebuketh a wicked *man, getteth* himself a blot. 8 Reprove not a scorner, lest he hate thee: rebuke a wise man, and he will love thee—13: 1 A wise son *heareth* his father's instruction: but a scorner heareth not rebuke. — 14: 7 Go from the presence of a foolish man, when thou perceivest not *in him* the lips of knowledge.—23: 9 Speak not in the ears of a fool: for he will despise the wisdom of thy words.

Mat. 7: 6 Give not that which is holy unto the dogs, neither cast ye your pearls before swine, lest they trample them under their feet, and turn again and rend you.

1 Jn. 5: 16 If any man see his brother sin a sin *which is* not unto death, he shall ask, and he shall give him life for them that sin not unto death. There is a sin unto death: I do not say that he shall pray for it. [See 256, 562.]

MEEKNESS.

437. *Meekness required.*

Zep. 2: 3 Seek ye the LORD, all ye meek of the earth, which have wrought his judgment; seek righteousness, seek meekness: it may be ye shall be hid in the day of the LORD's anger.

Mat. 10: 16 Behold, I send you forth as sheep in the midst of wolves: be ye therefore wise as serpents, and harmless as doves.

Gal. 6: 1 Brethren, if a man be overtaken in a fault, ye which are spiritual, restore such a one in the spirit of meekness; considering thyself, lest thou also be tempted.

Ep. 4: 1 I therefore, the prisoner of the Lord, beseech. you that ye walk worthy of the vocation wherewith ye are called, 2 With all lowliness and meekness, with long-suffering, forbearing one another in love; 3 Endeavoring to keep the unity of the Spirit in the bond of peace.

Col. 3: 12 Put on therefore, as the elect of God, holy and beloved, bowels of mercies, kindness, humbleness of mind, meekness, long-suffering; 13 Forbearing one another, and forgiving one another, if any man have a quarrel against any: even as Christ forgave you, so also *do* ye.

1 Tim. 6: 11 Thou, O man of God, flee these things; and follow after righteousness, godliness, faith, love, patience, meekness.

2. Tim. 2: 25 In meekness instructing those that oppose themselves.

1 Pet. 3: 3 Whose adorning let it not be that outward *adorning* of plaiting the hair, and of wearing of gold, or of putting on of apparel; 4 But *let it be* the hidden man of the heart, in that which is not corruptible, *even the ornament* of a meek and quiet spirit, which is in the sight of God of great price. [See 201, 482, 498–9, 737.]

438. *Meekness encouraged.*

Ps. 25: 9 The meek will he guide in judgment: and the meek will he teach his way. — 37: 11 The meek shall inherit the earth, and shall delight themselves in the abundance of peace. — 76: 8 Thou didst cause judgment to be heard from heaven; the earth feared and was still, 9 When God arose to judgment, to save all the meek of the earth. — 147: 6 The LORD lifted up the meek: he casteth the wicked down to the ground. — 149: 4 The LORD taketh pleasure in his people: he will beautify the meek with salvation.

Ec. 7: 8 Better *is* the end of a thing than the beginning thereof: *and* the patient in spirit *is* better than the proud in spirit.

Mat. 5: 5 Blessed *are* the meek: for they shall inherit the earth.

439. *Meekness exemplified.*

Ac. 7: 59 They stoned Stephen, calling upon *God,* and saying, Lord Jesus, receive my spirit. [See 62, 660.]

MILLENNIUM.

440. *A millennium of holiness and happiness upon this earth predicted.*

Ps. 22: 27 All the ends of the world shall remember and turn unto the LORD: and all the kindreds of the nations shall worship before thee. — 37: 11 The meek shall inherit the earth, and shall delight themselves in the abundance of peace. — 72: 6 He shall come down like rain upon the mown grass: as showers *that* water the earth. 7 In his days shall the righteous flourish: 11 Yea, all kings shall fall down before him: all nations shall serve him. — 86: 9 All nations whom thou hast made shall come and worship before thee, O LORD; and shall glorify thy name.

Is. 2: 2 It shall come to pass in the last days, *that* the mountain of the LORD's house shall be established in the top of the mountains, and shall be exalted above the hills; and all nations shall flow unto it. 4 And he shall judge among the nations, and shall rebuke many people: and they shall beat their swords into plough-shares, and their spears into pruning-hooks: nation shall not lift up sword against nation, neither shall they learn war any more. 17 And the loftiness of man shall be bowed down, and the haughtiness of men shall be made low: and the LORD alone shall be exalted in that day. 20 In that day a man shall cast his idols of silver, and his idols of gold, which they made *each one* for himself to worship, to the moles and to the bats. — 25: 6 In this mountain shall the LORD of hosts make unto all people a feast of fat things, a feast of wines on the lees; of fat things full of marrow, of wines on the lees well refined. 7 And he will destroy in this mountain the face of the covering cast over all people, and the vail that is spread over all nations. 8 He will swallow up death in victory; and the Lord GOD will wipe away tears from off all faces; and the rebuke of his people shall he take away from off all the earth: for the LORD hath spoken *it*. — 32: 15 Until the Spirit be poured upon us from on high, and the wilderness be a fruitful field, and the fruitful field be counted for a forest. 16 Then judgment shall dwell in the wilderness, and righteousness remain in the fruitful field. — 45: 22 Look unto me, and be ye saved, all the ends of the earth: for I *am* God, and *there is* none else. 23 I have sworn by myself, the word is gone out of my mouth *in* righteousness, and shall not return, That unto me every knee shall bow, every tongue shall swear. — 49: 6 I will also give thee for a light to the Gentiles, that thou mayest be my salvation unto the end

299

of the earth. — 60: 18 Violence shall no more be heard in thy land, wasting nor destruction within thy borders ; but thou shalt call thy walls Salvation, and thy gates Praise. [See the whole chapter.] — 65: 17 Behold, I create new heavens and a new earth : and the former shall not be remembered, nor come into mind. 18 But be ye glad and rejoice for ever *in that* which I create : for behold, I create Jerusalem a rejoicing, and her people a joy. 19 And I will rejoice in Jerusalem, and joy in my people : and the voice of weeping shall be no more heard in her, nor the voice of crying. 20 There shall be no more thence an infant of days, nor an old man that hath not filled his days : for the child shall die an hundred years old : but the sinner *being* an hundred years old shall be accursed. 21 And they shall build houses and inhabit *them ;* and they shall plant vineyards, and eat the fruit of them. 22 They shall not build, and another inhabit ; they shall not plant, and another eat : for as the days of a tree *are* the days of my people, and mine elect shall long enjoy the work of their hands. — 66: 23 It shall come to pass, *that* from one new moon to another, and from one Sabbath to another, shall all flesh come to worship before me, saith the LORD.

Dan. 7: 27 The kingdom and dominion, and the greatness of the kingdom under the whole heaven, shall be given to the people of the saints of the Most High, whose kingdom *is* an everlasting kingdom, and all dominions shall serve and obey him.

Mic. 4: 1 In the last days it shall come to pass, *that* the mountain of the house of the LORD shall be established in the top of the mountains, and it shall be exalted above the hills ; and people shall flow unto it. 2 And many nations shall come, and say, Come, and let us go up to the mountain of the LORD, and to the house of the God of Jacob ; and he will teach us of his ways, and we will walk in his paths : for the law shall go forth of Zion, and the word of the LORD from Jerusalem.

Hab. 2: 14 The earth shall be filled with the knowledge of the glory of the LORD, as the waters cover the sea.

Mal. 1: 11 From the rising of the sun even unto the going down of the same, my name *shall be* great among the Gentiles ; and in every place incense *shall be* offered unto my name, and a pure offering : for my name *shall be* great among the heathen, saith the LORD of hosts.

Rom. 11: 25 I would not, brethren, that ye should be ignorant of this mystery, (lest ye should be wise in your own conceits) that blindness in part is happened to Israel, until the fulness of the Gentiles be come in. 26 And so all Israel shall be saved ;

as it is written, There shall come out of Zion the Deliverer, and shall turn away ungodliness from Jacob: 27 For this *is* my covenant unto them, when I shall take away their sins.

2 Pet. 3: 13 We, according to his promise, look for new heavens and a new earth, wherein dwelleth righteousness.

Rev. 20: 1 I saw an angel come down from heaven, having the key of the bottomless pit and a great chain in his hand. 2 And he laid hold on the dragon, that old serpent, which is the Devil, and Satan, and bound him a thousand years, 3 And cast him into the bottomless pit, and shut him up, and set a seal upon him, that he should deceive the nations no more, till the thousand years should be fulfilled; and after that he must be loosed a little season.' [Num. 14: 21. Ps. 67: 4—7, and 82: 8. Is. 49: 8, 9, and 65: 17—23. Ac. 3: 20—25. Rev. 15: 4.] [See 90.]

441 Millennium a time of general holiness.

Is. 60: 21 Thy people also *shall be* all righteous: they shall inherit the land for ever, the branch of my planting, the work of my hands, that I may be glorified. — 65: 25 They shall not hurt nor destroy in all my holy mountain, saith the LORD.

Jer. 31: 33 This *shall be* the covenant that I will make with the house of Israel; After those days, saith the LORD, I will put my law in their inward parts, and write it in their hearts: and will be their God, and they shall be my people. 34 And they shall teach no more every man his neighbor, and every man his brother, saying, Know the LORD; for they shall all know me, from the least of them unto the greatest of them, saith the LORD: for I will forgive their iniquity, and I will remember their sin no more.

Ezk. 36: 25 Then will I sprinkle clean water upon you, and ye shall be clean: from all your filthiness, and from all your idols, will I cleanse you. 26 A new heart also will I give you, and a new spirit will I put within you: and I will take away the stony heart out of your flesh, and I will give you an heart of flesh. 27 And I will put my Spirit within you, and cause you to walk in my statutes, and ye shall keep my judgments, and do *them*. 28 And ye shall dwell in the land that I gave to your fathers; and ye shall be my people, and I will be your God. 29 I will also save you from all your uncleannesses; and I will call for the corn, and will increase it, and lay no famine upon you.—37: 23 Neither shall they defile themselves any more with their idols, nor with their detestable things, nor with any of their transgressions: but I will save them out of all their dwelling-places, wherein they have sinned, and will cleanse them: so shall they be my people, and I will be their God. 24 And David my servant *shall be* king over them; and they all shall have one shepherd: they shall also walk in my judgments, and observe my statutes.

Zep. 3: 13 The remnant of Israel shall not do iniquity, nor speak lies, neither shall a deceitful tongue be found in their mouth; for they shall feed and lie down, and none shall make *them* afraid.

Zec. 14: 20 In that day shall there be upon the bells of the horses, HOLINESS UNTO THE LORD; and the pots in the LORD's house shall be like the bowls before the altar.

Rom. 11: 25 I would not, brethren, that ye should be ignorant of this mystery, (lest ye should be wise in your own conceits) that blindness in part has happened to Israel, until the fulness of the Gentiles be come in. 26 And so all Israel shall be saved: as it is written, [Dt. 18: 15,] There shall come out of Zion the Deliverer, and shall turn away ungodliness from Jacob: 27 For this is my covenant unto them, when I shall take away their sins. [See 506.]

442. *Millennium a time of peace and unity.*

Ps. 37: 11 The meek shall inherit the earth, and shall delight themselves in the abundance of peace. — 72: 3 The mountains shall bring peace to the people, and the little hills, by righteousness. 7 In his days shall the righteous flourish: and abundance of peace so long as the moon endureth.

Is. 52: 8 Thy watchmen shall lift up the voice: with the voice together shall they sing: for they shall see eye to eye, when the LORD shall bring again Zion. — 60: 17 I will also make thy officers peace, and thine exactors righteousness. 18 Violence shall no more be heard in thy land, wasting nor destruction within thy borders; but thou shalt call thy walls Salvation, and thy gates Praise. — 66: 12 Thus saith the LORD, Behold I will extend peace to her like a river, and the glory of the Gentiles like a flowing stream: then shall ye suck, ye shall be borne upon *her* sides, and be dandled upon *her* knees.

Mic. 4: 3 He shall judge among many people, and rebuke strong nations afar off; and they shall beat their swords into plough-shares, and their spears into pruning-hooks; nation shall not lift up a sword against nation, neither shall they learn war any more. 4 But they shall sit every man under his vine and under his fig-tree; and none shall make *them* afraid: for the mouth of the LORD of hosts hath spoken *it*.
[Is. 2: 4. Ps. 72: 4—6. Is. 2: 4, and 11: 6—9.]

443. *Millennium a time of true knowledge.*

Is. 11: 9 They shall not hurt nor destroy in all my holy mountain: for the earth shall be full of the knowledge of the LORD, as the waters cover the sea. [Hab. 2: 14.] — 29: 18 In that day shall the deaf hear the words of the book, and the eyes of the blind shall see out of obscurity and out of darkness. 24 They also that erred in spirit shall come to understanding, and they that murmured shall learn doctrine. — 33: 6 Wisdom and knowledge shall be the stability of thy times, *and* strength of salvation: the fear of the LORD *is* his treasure.

Jer. 3: 15 I will give you pastors according to mine heart, which shall feed you with knowledge and understanding.

Heb. 8: 11 They shall not teach every man his neighbor, and every man his brother, saying, Know the Lord: for all shall know me, from the least to the greatest.

444. *Millennium a time of prosperity.*

Ps. 72: 16 There shall be an handful of corn in the earth upon the top of the mountains; the fruit thereof shall shake like Lebanon: and *they* of the city shall flourish like grass of the earth.

Is. 60: 5 Then thou shalt see, and flow together, and thine heart shall fear and be enlarged; because the abundance of the sea shall be converted unto thee, the forces of the Gentiles shall come unto thee. 6 The multitude of camels shall cover thee, the dromedaries of Midian and Ephah; all they from Sheba shall come: they shall bring gold and incense; and they shall shew forth the praises of the LORD. 7 All the flocks of Kedar shall be gathered together unto thee, the rams of Nebaioth shall minister unto thee: they shall come up with acceptance on mine altar, and I will glorify the house of my glory. 13 The glory of Lebanon shall come unto thee, the fir-tree, the pine-tree, and the box together, to beautify the place of my sanctuary; and I will make the place of my feet glorious.

Joel 2: 21 Fear not, O land; be glad and rejoice: for the LORD will do great things. 22 Be not afraid, ye beasts of the field; for the pastures of the wilderness do spring, for the tree beareth her fruit, the fig-tree and the vine do yield their strength. 23 Be glad, then, ye children of Zion, and rejoice in the LORD your God: for he hath given you the former rain moderately, and he will cause to come down for you the rain, the former rain, and the latter rain in the first *month*. 24 And the floors shall be full of wheat, and the fats shall overflow with wine and oil.   25 And I will restore to you the years that the locust hath eaten, the canker-worm, and the caterpiller, and the palmer-worm, my great army, which I sent among you.   26 And ye shall eat in plenty, and be satisfied, and praise the name of the LORD your God, that hath dealt wondrously with you : and my people shall never be ashamed. — 3: 18 And it shall come to pass in that day, *that* the mountains shall- drop down new wine, and the hills shall flow with milk, and all the rivers of Judah shall flow with waters, and a fountain shall come forth of the house of the LORD, and shall water the valley of Shittim.   [Is. 25: 6 ; and 35th entire, and 41: 18.]   [See 446.]

445. *Millennium a time of enjoyment.*

Is. 25: 8 He will swallow up death in victory; and the Lord GOD will wipe away tears from off all faces ; and the rebuke of his people shall he take away from off all the earth : for the LORD hath spoken *it.* — 35: 10 The ransomed of the LORD shall return, and come to Zion with songs and everlasting joy upon their heads ; they shall obtain joy and gladness, and sorrow and sighing shall flee away. — 52: 9 Break forth into joy, sing together, ye waste places of Jerusalem ; for the LORD hath comforted his people, he hath redeemed Jerusalem. — 65: 18 Be ye glad and rejoice for ever *in that* which I create : for behold, I create Jerusalem a rejoicing, and her people a joy.   19 And I will rejoice in Jerusalem, and joy in my people : and the voice of weeping shall be no more heard in her, nor the voice of crying.

Zep. 3: 14 Sing, O daughter of Zion; shout, O Israel ; be glad, and rejoice with all the heart, O daughter of Jerusalem. 15 The LORD hath taken away thy judgments, he hath cast out thine enemy : the King of Israel, *even* the LORD, *is* in the midst of thee : thou shalt not see evil any more.   16 In that day it shall be said to Jerusalem, Fear thou not : *and to* Zion, Let not thy hands be slack.   17 The LORD thy God in the midst of thee *is* mighty: he will save, he will rejoice over thee with joy ; he will rest in his love, he will joy over thee with singing.

446. *Millennium a contrast to previous times.*

Is. 11: 6 The wolf also shall dwell with the lamb, and the leopard shall lie down with the kid ; and the calf and the young lion and the fatling together ; and a little child shall lead them.   7 And the cow and the bear shall feed ; their young ones shall lie down together : and the lion shall eat straw like the ox. 8 And the suckling child shall play on the hole of the asp, and the weaned child shall put his hand on the cockatrice's den. — 40: 4 Every valley shall be exalted, and every mountain and hill shall be made low : and the crooked shall be made straight, and the rough places plain. 5 And the glory of the LORD shall be revealed, and all flesh shall see it together : for the mouth of the LORD hath spoken it. — 41: 18 I will open rivers in high places, and fountains in the midst of the valleys : I will make the wilderness a pool of water, and the dry land springs of water. 19 I will plant in the wilderness the cedar, the shittah-tree, and the myrtle, and the oil-tree : I will set in the desert the fir-tree, and the pine, and the box-tree together : 20 That they may see, and know, and consider, and understand together, that the hand of the LORD hath done this, and the Holy One of Israel hath created it. — 55: 13 Instead of the thorn shall come up the fir-tree, and instead of the brier shall come up the myrtle-tree : and it shall be to the LORD for a name, for an everlasting sign that shall not be cut off. — 65: 25 The wolf and the lamb shall feed together, and the lion shall eat straw like the bullock : and dust shall be the serpent's meat. [Is. 35: 6, 7. Ezk. 47: 8, 9. Ac. 3: 21.]

MINISTRY OF THE WORD.

447. *Design and use of the Christian ministry.*

Jer. 3: 15 I will give you pastors according to mine heart, which shall feed you with knowledge and understanding. — 15: 19 If thou take forth the precious from the vile, thou shalt be as my mouth.

Ezk. 3: 17 Son of man, I have made thee a watchman unto the house of Israel : therefore hear the word at my mouth, and give them warning from me.

Mat. 5: 13 Ye are the salt of the earth : but if the salt have lost his savor, wherewith shall it be salted ? it is thenceforth good for nothing, but to be cast out, and to be trodden under foot of men. 14 Ye are the light of the world. A city that is set on a hill cannot be hid.

Ac. 26: 17 Delivering thee from the people, and *from* the Gentiles, unto whom now I send thee, 18 To open their eyes, *and* to turn *them* from darkness to light, and *from* the power of Satan unto God, that they may receive forgiveness of sins, and inheritance among them which are sanctified by faith that is in me.

Rom. 10: 14 How then shall they call on him in whom they have not believed? and how shall they believe in him of whom they have not heard? and how shall they hear without a preacher? 15 And how shall they preach, except they be sent? as it is written, How beautiful are the feet of them that preach the gospel of peace, and bring glad tidings of good things! [Is. 52: 7.]

1 Cor. 1: 21 After that in the wisdom of God the world by wisdom knew not God, it pleased God by the foolishness of preaching to save them that believe.

2 Cor. 1: 24 Not for that we have dominion over your faith, but are helpers of your joy: for by faith ye stand. — 5: 20 We are ambassadors for Christ, as though God did beseech *you* by us: we pray *you* in Christ's stead, be ye reconciled to God.

Ep. 4: 11 He gave some, apostles; and some, prophets; and some, evangelists; and some, pastors and teachers; 12 For the perfecting of the saints, for the work of the ministry, for the edifying of the body of Christ: 13 Till we all come in the unity of the faith, and of the knowledge of the Son of God, unto a perfect man, unto the measure of the stature of the fulness of Christ. [1 Tim. 3: 1. Heb. 13: 17.] [See 101.]

448. Ministers divinely appointed and qualified.

Is. 62: 6 I have set watchmen upon thy walls, O Jerusalem, *which* shall never hold their peace day nor night: ye that make mention of the LORD keep not silence.

Mal. 2: 7 For the priest's lips should keep knowledge, and they should seek the law at his mouth: for he *is* the messenger of the LORD of hosts.

Lk. 10: 1 After these things, the Lord appointed other seventy also, and sent them two and two before his face into every city, and place, whither he himself would come. 2 Therefore said he unto them, The harvest truly *is* great, but the laborers *are* few: pray ye therefore the lord of the harvest, that he would send forth laborers into his harvest.

Ac. 20: 24 But none of these things move me, neither count I my life dear unto myself, so that I might finish my course with joy, and the ministry which I have received of the Lord Jesus, to testify the gospel of the grace of God. 28 Take heed therefore unto yourselves, and to all the flock over the which the Holy Ghost hath made you overseers, to feed the church of God, which he hath purchased with his own blood. — 26: 16 Rise and stand upon thy feet: for I have appeared unto thee for this purpose to make thee a minister and a wit-

Call to preach — Ordination.

ness both of these things which thou hast seen, and of those things in the which I will appear unto thee. 17 Delivering thee from the people, and *from* the Gentiles, unto whom now I send thee, 18 To open their eyes, *and* to turn *them* from darkness to light, and *from* the power of Satan unto God, that they may receive forgiveness of sins, and inheritance among them which are sanctified by faith that is in me.

Rom. 12: 6 Having then gifts, differing according to the grace that is given to us, whether prophecy, *let us prophesy*, according to the proportion of faith; 7 Or ministry, *let us wait* on *our* ministering: or he that teacheth, on teaching: 8 Or he that exhorteth, on exhortation.

1 Cor. 1: 1 Paul, called *to be* an apostle of Jesus Christ through the will of God, and Sosthenes *our* brother. 17 For Christ sent me not to baptize, but to preach the gospel.

2 Cor. 5: 18 All things *are* of God, who hath reconciled us to himself by Jesus Christ, and hath given to us the ministry of reconciliation.

Col. 4: 17 Say to Archippus, Take heed to the ministry which thou hast received in the Lord, that thou fulfil it.

1 Tim. 1: 12 I thank Christ Jesus our Lord, who hath enabled me, for that he counted me faithful, putting me into the ministry.

Tit. 1: 3 But hath in due times manifested his word through preaching, which is committed unto me, according to the commandment of God our Saviour. [1 Cor. 12: 7—11.] [See 480.]

449. *Call to preach the gospel.*

1 Cor. 9: 16 Though I preach the Gospel, I have nothing to glory of: for necessity is laid upon me ; yea, wo is unto me, if I preach not the gospel !

Gal. 1: 15 When it pleased God, who separated me from my mother's womb, and called *me* by his grace, 16 To reveal his Son in me, that I might preach him among the heathen ; immediately I conferred not with flesh and blood.

Heb. 5: 4 No man taketh this honor unto himself, but he that is called of God, as *was* Aaron.

450. *Ordination of ministers.*

Mk. 3: 14 He ordained twelve, that they should be with him, and that he might send them forth to preach.

Ac. 13: 2 As they ministered to the Lord, and fasted, the Holy Ghost said, Separate me Barnabas and Saul, for the work whereunto I have called them. 3 And when they had fasted and prayed, and laid *their* hands on them, they sent *them* away. — 14: 23 When they had ordained them elders in every church, and had prayed with fasting, they commended them to the Lord, on whom they believed.   •

2 Tim. 2: 2 The things that thou hast heard of me among many witnesses, the same commit thou to faithful men, who shall be able to teach others also.

Tit. 1:5 For this cause left I thee in Crete, that thou shouldest set in order the things that are wanting, and ordain elders in every city, as I had appointed thee.   [See 401.]

451. *Oriental priesthood.*

Gen. 47: 22 Only the land of the priests bought he not ; for the priests had a portion *assigned them* of Pharaoh, and did eat their portion which Pharaoh gave them; wherefore they sold not their lands.

Ex. 3: 1 Now Moses kept the flock of Jethro his father-in-law, the priest of Midian: and he led the flock to the back side of the desert, and came to the mountain of God, *even* to Horeb.

452. *Primitive mode of preaching.*

Ac. 17: 2 Paul, as his manner was, went in unto them, and three Sabbath-days reasoned with them out of the scriptures.

1 Cor. 2: 4 My speech and my preaching *was* not with enticing words of man's wisdom, but in demonstration of the Spirit, and of power: 5 That your faith should not stand in the wisdom of men, but in the power of God.

2 Cor. 3: 12 Seeing then that we have such hope, we use great plainness of speech. — 4: 1 Seeing we have this ministry, as we have received mercy, we faint not; 2 But have renounced the hidden things of dishonesty; not walking in craftiness, nor handling the word of God deceitfully; but, by manifestation of the truth, commending ourselves to every man's conscience in the sight of God.   [See 447, 458, 461.]

453. *Ministerial qualifications.*

1 Tim. 3: 2 A bishop then must be blameless, the husband of one wife, vigilant, sober, of good behavior, given to hospitality, apt to teach; 3 Not given to wine, no striker, not greedy of filthy lucre; but patient; not a brawler; not covetous; 4 One that ruleth well his own house, having his children in subjection with all gravity; 5 (For if a man know not how to rule his own house, how shall he take care of the church of God?) 6 Not a novice, lest being lifted up with pride he fall into the condemnation of the devil. 7 Moreover, he must

have a good report of them which are without; lest he fall into reproach and the snare of the devil.

2 Tim. 2: 2 The things that thou hast heard of me among many witnesses, the same commit thou to faithful men, who shall be able to teach others also. 24 And the servant of the Lord must not strive; but be gentle unto all *men*, apt to teach, patient; 25 In meekness instructing those that oppose.

Tit. 1: 6 If any be blameless, the husband of one wife, having faithful children, not accused of riot, or unruly. 7 For a bishop must be blameless, as the steward of God: not self-willed, not soon angry, not given to wine, no striker, not given to filthy lucre; 8 But a lover of hospitality, a lover of good men, sober, just, holy, temperate; 9 Holding fast the faithful word as he hath been taught, that he may be able by sound doctrine both to exhort and to convince the gainsayers. [Mat. 13: 52. 1 Cor. 4: 2.]

454. *Significant names of ministers.*

2 Cor. 5: 20 Ambassadors for Christ. — Tit. 1: 7 Bishops. — 1 Tim. 5: 17 Elders. — Ep. 4: 11 Evangelists. — 2 Cor. 1: 24 Helpers. — 1 Cor. 3: 9, and 2 Cor. 6: 1 Laborers with God. — Lk. 1: 2 Ministers of the Word. — 2 Cor. 11: 15 Ministers of righteousness. — Mat. 2: 7 Messengers of the Lord. — Ac. 20: 28 Overseers. — Ep. 4: 11 Pastors and teachers. — 1 Tim. 5: 17 Rulers. — Mat. 5: 13 Salt of the earth. — Jam. 1: 1 Servants of God. — 2 Cor. 4: 5 Servants for Jesus' sake. — Jer. 23: 4 Shepherds. — Tit. 1: 7 Stewards of God. — Is. 26: 6 Watchmen. — Ac. 26: 16 and Rev. 11: 3 Witnesses.

455. *Ministerial authority and rights.*

Ac. 20: 17 And called the elders of the church. 28 Take heed therefore unto yourselves, and to all the flock over the which the Holy Ghost hath made you overseers, [bishops] to feed the church of God, which he hath purchased with his own blood.

2 Cor. 10: 8 Though I should boast somewhat more of our authority, which the Lord hath given us for edification, and not for your destruction, I should not be ashamed. — 13: 10 I write these things being absent, lest being present I should use sharpness, according to the power which the Lord hath given me to edification, and not to destruction.

1 Tim. 5: 17 Let the elders that rule well, be counted worthy of double honor, especially they who labor in the word and doctrine.

2 Tim. 4: 1 I charge *thee* therefore before God, and the

Lord Jesus Christ, who shall judge the quick and the dead at his appearing and his kingdom; 2 Preach the word; be instant in season, out of season; reprove, rebuke, exhort with all long-suffering and doctrine.

Tit. 2: 15 These things speak, and exhort, and rebuke with all authority. Let no man despise thee.

Heb. 13: 7 Remember them which have the rule over you, who have spoken unto you the word of God: whose faith follow, considering the end of *their* conversation. 17 Obey them that have the rule over you, and submit yourselves: for they watch for your souls, as they that must give account, that they may do it with joy, and not with grief: for that *is* unprofitable for you.

456. *Limits of ministerial authority.*

Mat. 20: 25 Jesus called them *unto him*, and said, Ye know that the princes of the Gentiles exercise dominion over them, and they that are great exercise authority upon them. 26 But it shall not be so among you: but whosoever will be great among you, let him be your minister: 27 And whosoever will be chief among you, let him be your servant: 28 Even as the Son of man came not to be ministered unto, but to minister, and to give his life a ransom for many. Mk. 10: 42. — 23: 8 Be not ye called Rabbi: for one is your Master, *even* Christ; and all ye are brethren. 9 And call no *man* your father upon the earth: for one is your father which is in heaven. 10 Neither be ye called masters: for one is your Master, *even* Christ.

1 Pet. 5: 3 Neither as being lords over *God's* heritage, but being ensamples to the flock.

MINISTERIAL DUTIES.

457. *The cultivation of knowledge, piety and wisdom required and exemplified.*

Ezk. 2: 8 Son of man, hear what I say unto thee. Be not thou rebellious like that rebellious house: open thy mouth, and eat that I give thee.

Mat. 10: 16 Behold, I send you forth as sheep in the midst of wolves: be ye therefore wise as serpents, and harmless as doves.

Ac. 6: 4 We will give ourselves continually to prayer, and to the ministry of the word. — 20: 28 Take heed therefore unto yourselves, and to all the flock over the which the Holy Ghost hath made you overseers, to feed the church of God

Duty to take heed to their own ways

which he hath purchased with his own blood. 29 For I know this, that after my departing shall grevious wolves- enter in among you, not sparing the flock. 30 Also of your own selves shall men arise, speaking perverse things, to draw away disciples after them. 31 Therefore watch, and remember, that by the space of three years I ceased not to warn every one night and day with tears.

Rom. 2: 21 Thou therefore which teachest another, teachest thou not thyself? thou that preachest, a man should not steal, dost thou steal?

1 Cor. 9: 25 Every man that striveth for the mastery is temperate in all things. Now they *do it* to obtain a corruptible crown; but we an incorruptible. 26 I therefore so run, not as uncertainly; so fight I, not as one that beateth the air: 27 But I keep under my body, and bring *it* into subjection: lest that by any means when I have preached to others, I myself should be a cast-away.

1 Th. 2: 10 Ye *are* witnesses, and God *also*, how holily, and justly, and unblamably we behaved ourselves among you that believe.

1 Tim. 4: 12 Let no man despise thy youth; but be thou an example of the believers, in word, in conversation, in charity, in spirit, in faith, in purity. 13 Till I come, give attendance to reading, to exhortation, to doctrine. 14 Neglect not the gift that is in thee, which was given thee by prophecy, with the laying on of the hands of the presbytery. 15 Meditate upon these things, give thyself wholly to them; that thy profiting may appear to all. 16 Take heed unto thyself, and unto the doctrine; continue in them: for in doing this thou shalt both save thyself, and them that hear thee. — 6: 20 O Timothy, keep that which is committed to thy trust, avoiding profane *and* vain babblings, and oppositions of science falsely so called: 21 Which some professing, have erred concerning the faith.

2 Tim. 1: 13 Hold fast the form of sound words, which thou hast heard of me, in faith and love which is in Christ Jesus. — 2: 3 Thou therefore endure hardness, as a good soldier of Jesus Christ. 4 No man that warreth entangleth himself with the affairs of *this* life; that he may please him who hath chosen him to be a soldier. 22 Flee also youthful lusts: but follow righteousness, faith, charity, peace, with them that call on the Lord out of a pure heart. 23 But foolish and unlearned questions avoid, knowing that they do gender strifes.

2 Tim. 4: 5 Watch thou in all things, endure afflictions, do the work of an evangelist, make full proof of thy ministry.

7 I have fought a good fight, I have finished my course, I have kept the faith.

Tit. 2: 7 In all things shewing thyself a pattern of good works : in doctrine *shewing* uncorruptness, gravity, sincerity. 8 Sound speech that cannot be condemned ; that he that is of the contrary part may be ashamed, having no evil thing to say of you. [See 369, 463.]

458. *Preaching faithfully as "ambassadors for Christ" required and exemplified.*

Dt. 33: 10 They shall teach Jacob thy judgments, and Israel thy law.

Neh. 8: 8 They read in the book, in the law of God distinctly, and gave the sense, and caused *them* to understand the reading.

Ec. 12: 9 Because the Preacher was wise, he still taught the people knowledge : yea, he gave good heed, and sought out, *and* set in order many proverbs.

Jer. 1: 17 Thou therefore gird up thy loins, and arise, and speak unto them all that I command thee : be not dismayed at their faces, lest I confound thee before them. — 23: 28 The prophet that hath a dream, let him tell a dream ; and he that hath my word, let him speak my word faithfully. What *is* the chaff to the wheat ? saith the LORD. — 26: 2 Thus saith the LORD ; Stand in the court of the LORD's house, and speak unto all the cities of Judah, which come to worship in the LORD's house, all the words that I command thee to speak unto them ; diminish not a word.

Ezk. 2: 7 Thou shalt speak my words unto them, whether they will hear, or whether they will forbear ; for they *are* most rebellious. — 3: 10 He said unto me, Son of man, all my words that I shall speak unto thee receive in thine heart, and hear with thine ears. 11 And go, get thee to them of the captivity, unto the children of thy people, and speak unto them, and tell them, Thus saith the Lord GOD ; whether they will hear, or whether they will forbear.

Mat. 28: 19 Go ye therefore and teach all nations, baptizing them in the name of the Father, and of the Son, and of the Holy Ghost ; 20 Teaching them to observe all things whatsoever I have commanded you.

Ac. 5: 42 Daily in the temple, and in every house, they ceased not to teach and preach Jesus Christ. — 20: 18 When they were come to him, he said unto them, Ye know, from the first day that I came into Asia, after what manner I have been with you at all seasons. 20 *And* how I kept back nothing that

was profitable *unto you*, but have shewed you, and have taught you publicly, and from house to house. 26 Wherefore I take you to record this day, that I *am* pure from the blood of all *men*, 27 For I have not shunned to declare unto you all the counsel of God. 28 Take heed therefore unto yourselves, and to all the flock over the which the Holy Ghost hath made you overseers, to feed the church of God, which he hath purchased with his own blood.

1 Cor. 4: 1 Let a man so account of us, as of the ministers of Christ, and stewards of the mysteries of God. 2 Moreover, it is required in stewards that a man be found faithful. — 9: 16 Though I preach the Gospel, I have nothing to glory of; for necessity is laid upon me; yea, wo is unto me, if I preach not the Gospel!

2 Cor. 2: 17 We are not as many, which corrupt the word of God: but as of sincerity, but as of God, in the sight of God speak we in Christ. — 4: 1 Seeing we have this ministry, as we have received mercy, we faint not; 2 But have renounced the hidden things of dishonesty; not walking in craftiness, nor handling the word of God deceitfully; but, by manifestation of the truth, commending ourselves to every man's conscience in the sight of God.

Gal. 1: 10 Do I now persuade men, or God? or do I seek to please men? for if I yet pleased men, I should not be the servant of Christ.

1 Th. 2: 3 Our exhortation *was* not of deceit, nor of uncleanness, nor in guile; 4 But as we were allowed of God to be put in trust with the gospel, even so we speak; not as pleasing men; but God, which trieth our hearts. 5. For neither at any time used we flattering words, as ye know, nor a cloak of covetousness; God *is* witness.

2 Tim. 2: 15 Study to shew thyself approved unto God, a workman that needeth not to be ashamed, rightly dividing the word of truth. — 4: 1 I charge *thee* therefore before God, and the Lord Jesus Christ, who shall judge the quick and the dead at his appearing and his kingdom; 2 Preach the word; be instant in season, out of season; reprove, rebuke, exhort with all long-suffering and doctrine. 3 For the time will come, when they will not endure sound doctrine; but after their own lusts shall they heap to themselves teachers, having itching ears; 4 And they shall turn away *their* ears from the truth, and shall be turned into fables. 5 But watch thou in all things, endure afflictions, do the work of an evangelist, make full proof of thy ministry.

Tit. 2: 1 Speak thou the things which become sound doctrine.

1 Pet. 4: 11 If any man speak, *let him speak* as the oracles of God; if any man minister, *let him do it* as of the ability which God giveth; that God in all things may be glorified through Jesus Christ; to whom be praise and dominion for ever and ever. [See 48, 65, 188, 279, 430, 462.]

459. *Duty to be properly inoffensive.*

Mat. 17: 27 Notwithstanding, lest we should offend them, go thou to the sea, and cast an hook, and take up the fish that first cometh up: and when thou hast opened his mouth, thou shalt find a piece of money: that take, and give unto them for me and thee.

Rom. 14: 21 *It is* good neither to eat flesh, nor to drink wine, nor *any thing* whereby thy brother stumbleth, or is offended, or is made weak.

1 Cor. 9: 19 Though I be free from all *men,* yet I have made myself servant unto all, that I might gain the more. 20 And unto the Jews I became as a Jew, that I might gain the Jews; to them that are under the law, as under the law, that I might gain them that are under the law; 22 To the weak became I as weak, that I might gain the weak: I am made all things to all *men,* that I might by all means save some. — 10: 32 Give none offence, neither to the Jews, nor to the Gentiles, nor to the church of God. 33 Even as I please all *men* in all *things,* not seeking mine own profit, but the *profit* of many, that they may be saved.

2 Cor. 6: 3 Giving no offence in any thing, that the ministry be not blamed: 4 But in all *things* approving ourselves as the ministers of God, in much patience, in afflictions, in necessities, in distresses.

2 Tim. 2: 24 The servant of the Lord must not strive; but be gentle unto all *men.* [See 67, 135.]

460. *Duty to fear not man — boldness exemplified.*

Jer. 1: 7 The LORD said unto me, Say not, I *am* a child: for thou shalt go to all that I shall send thee, and whatsoever I command thee thou shalt speak. 8 Be not afraid of their faces: for I *am* with thee to deliver thee, saith LORD. 17 Thou therefore gird up thy loins, and arise, and speak unto them all that I command thee: be not dismayed at their faces, lest I confound thee before them. 18 For behold, I have made thee this day a defenced city, and an iron pillar, and brazen walls against the whole land, against the kings of Judah, against the princes thereof, against the priests thereof, and against the people of the land. 19 And they shall fight against thee; but they shall not prevail against thee; for I *am* with thee, saith the LORD, to deliver thee.

Ezk. 2: 6 Thou, son of man, be not afraid of them, neither be afraid of their words, though briers and thorns *be* with thee, and thou dost dwell among scorpions : be not afraid of their words, nor be dismayed at their looks, though they *be* a rebellious house.

Ac. 4: 13 When they saw the boldness of Peter and John, and perceived that they were unlearned and ignorant men, they marvelled ; and they took knowledge of them, that they had been with Jesus. 18 And they called them, and commanded them not to speak at all, nor teach in the name of Jesus. 19 But Peter and John answered and said unto them, Whether it be right in the sight of God to hearken unto you more than unto God, judge ye. 20 For we cannot but speak the things which we have seen and heard. 29 And now, Lord, behold their threatenings ; and grant unto thy servants, that with all boldness they may speak thy word. — 6: 10 They were not able to resist the wisdom and the spirit by which they spake. — 9: 29 He spake boldly in the name of the Lord Jesus, and disputed against the Grecians : but he went about to slay him. — 18: 9 Then spake the Lord to Paul in the night by a vision, Be not afraid, but speak, and hold not thy peace : 10 For I am with thee, and no man shall set on thee, to hurt thee : for I have much people in this city. — 19: 8 He went into the synagogue, and spake boldly for the space of three months, disputing and persuading the things concerning the kingdom of God.

Ph. 1: 20 According to my earnest expectation, and *my* hope, that in nothing I shall be ashamed, but *that* with all boldness, as always, *so* now also, Christ shall be magnified in my body, whether *it be* by life, or by death. [See 134, 659.]

461. Exposing sins, and reproving transgressors required and exemplified.

1 S. 13: 13 Samuel said to Saul, Thou hast done foolishly : thou hast not kept the commandment of the LORD thy God, which he commanded thee : for now would the LORD have established thy kingdom upon Israel for ever. 14 But now thy kingdom shall not continue.

2 S. 12: 7 Nathan said to David, Thou *art* the man.

1 K. 18: 17 It came to pass when Ahab saw Elijah, that Ahab said unto him, *Art* thou he that troubleth Israel? 18 And he answered, I have not troubled Israel ; but thou, and thy father's house, in that ye have forsaken the commandments

of the LORD, and thou hast followed Baalim. — 21: 20 Ahab said to Elijah, Hast thou found me, O mine enemy?. And he answered, I have found *thee:* because thou hast sold thyself to work evil in the sight of the LORD.

Is. 58: 1 Cry aloud, spare not, lift up thy voice like a trumpet, and shew my people their transgression, and the house of Jacob their sins.

Ezk. 16: 2 Son of man, cause Jerusalem to know her abominations.

Mic. 3: 8 Truly I am full of power by the Spirit of the LORD, and of judgment, and of might, to declare unto Jacob his transgression, and to Israel his sin.

Ac. 2: 23 Him, being delivered by the determinate counsel and foreknowledge of God, ye have taken, and by wicked hands have crucified and slain. — 7: 51 Ye stiff-necked, and uncircumcised in heart and ears, ye do always resist the Holy Ghost: as your fathers *did,* so *do* ye. 52 Which of the prophets have not your fathers persecuted? and they have slain them which shewed before of the coming of the Just One; of whom ye have been now the betrayers and murderers; 53 Who have received the law by the disposition of angels, and have not kept *it.*

1 Tim. 5: 20 Them that sin rebuke before all, that others also may fear.

2 Tim. 4: 2 Preach the word; be instant in season, out of season: reprove, rebuke, exhort with all long-suffering and doctrine.

Tit. 1: 10 There are many unruly and vain talkers and deceivers, especially they of the circumcision: 11 Whose mouths must be stopped, who subvert whole houses, teaching things which they ought not, for filthy lucre's sake. 13 This witness is true: wherefore rebuke them sharply, that they may be sound in the faith. [See 610, 611.]

462. *Duty to distinguish saints from sinners.*

Jer. 15: 19 If thou take forth the precious from the vile, thou shalt be as my mouth: let them return unto thee; but return not thou unto them. 20 And I will make thee unto this people a fenced brazen wall: and they shall fight against thee, but they shall not prevail against thee: for I *am* with thee to save thee and to deliver thee, saith the LORD.

Ezk. 44: 23 And they shall teach my people *the difference* between the holy and profane, and cause them to discern between the unclean and the clean. 24 And in controversy they shall stand in judgment; *and* they shall judge it according to my judgments.

Mal. 3: 18 Then shall ye reutrn and discern between the righteous and the wicked, between him that serveth God and him that serveth him not. [See 458, 645.]

463. *The duties of praying, watching and visiting required and exemplified — negligence reproved.*

1 S. 12: 23 As for me, God forbid that I should sin against the LORD in ceasing to pray for you : but I will teach you the good in the right way.

Jer. 23: 2 Thus saith the LORD God of Israel against the pastors that feed my people; Ye have scattered my flock, and driven them away, and have not visited them: behold, I will visit upon you the evil of your doings saith the LORD.

Joel 2: 17 Let the priests, the ministers of the LORD, weep between the porch and the altar, and let them say, Spare thy people, O LORD, and give not thine heritage to reproach, that the heathen should rule over them: wherefore should they say among the people, Where *is* their God?

Mat. 25: 42 I was an hungered, and ye gave me no meat; I was thirsty, and ye gave me no drink: 43 I was a stranger, and ye took me not in : naked, and ye clothed me not: sick and in prison, and ye visited me not.

Ac. 20: 31 Watch, and remember, that by the space of three years I ceased not to warn every one night and day with tears.

Rom. 1: 9 God is my witness, whom I serve with my spirit in the gospel of his Son, that without ceasing I make mention of you always in my prayers.

2 Cor. 11: 2 I am jealous over you with godly jealousy : for I have espoused you to one husband, that I may present *you as* a chaste virgin to Christ. — 12: 14 Behold the third time I am ready to come to you ; and I will not be burdensome to you: for I seek not yours, but you. For the children ought not to lay up for the parents, but the parents for the children. 15 And I will very gladly spend and be spent for you ; though the more abundantly I love you, the less I be loved.

Gal. 4: 19 My little children, of whom I travail in birth again until Christ be formed in you, 20 I desire to be present with you now, and to change my voice : for I stand in doubt of you.

Ph. 1: 3 I thank my God upon every remembrance of you, 4 Always in every prayer of mine for you all making request with joy, 5 For your fellowship in the gospel from the first day until now; 8 For God is my record, how greatly I long after you all in the bowels of Jesus Christ.

Col. 1: 9 For this cause we also, since the day we heard *it*, do not cease to pray for you, and to desire that ye might be filled with the knowledge of his will in all wisdom and spiritual understanding; 10 That ye might walk worthy of the Lord unto all pleasing, being fruitful in every good work, and increasing in the knowledge of God: 11 Strengthened with all might, according to his glorious power, unto all patience and long-suffering with joyfulness: 28 Whom we preach, warning every man, and teaching every man in all wisdom; that we may present every man perfect in Christ Jesus. — 4: 12 Epaphras, who is *one* of you, a servant of Christ, saluteth you, always laboring fervently for you in prayers, that ye may stand perfect and complete in all the will of God. 13 For I bear him record, that he hath a great zeal for you, and them *that are* in Laodicea, and them in Hierapolis.

1 Th. 2: 6 Nor of men sought we glory, neither of you, nor *yet* of others, when we might have been burdensome, as the apostles of Christ. 7 But we were gentle among you, even as a nurse cherisheth her children: 8 So being affectionately desirous of you we were willing to have imparted unto you, not the gospel of God only, but also our own souls, because ye were dear unto us. 9 For ye remember, brethren, our labor and travail: for laboring night and day, because we would not be chargeable unto any of you, we preached unto you the gospel of God. 10 Ye *are* witnesses, and God *also*, how holily, and justly, and unblamably we behaved ourselves among you that believe: 11 As ye know how we exhorted, and comforted, and charged every one of you, as a father *doth* his children, 12 That ye would walk worthy of God, who hath called you unto his kingdom and glory. [1 Th. 3: 7—10.]

464. *Entire devotion to the calling required and exemplified.*

Lk. 9: 59 He said unto another, Follow me. But he said, Lord, suffer me first to go and bury my father. 60 Jesus said unto him, Let the dead bury their dead: but go thou and preach the kingdom of God.

Ac. 6: 2 Then the twelve called the multitude of the disciples *unto them*, and said, It is not reason that we should leave the word of God, and serve tables. 3 Wherefore, brethren, look ye out among you seven men of honest report, full of the Holy Ghost and wisdom, whom we may appoint over this business. 4 But we will give ourselves continually to prayer and to the ministry of the word.

1 Cor. 2: 2 I determined not to know any thing among you, save Jesus Christ, and him crucified.

1 Tim. 4: 15 Meditate upon these things; give thyself wholly to them; that thy profiting may appear to all.

MINISTERIAL TRUSTS, TRIALS, AND REWARDS.

465. Ministerial responsibility.

Ezk. 33: 7 O son of man, I have set thee a watchman unto the house of Israel; therefore thou shalt hear the word at my mouth, and warn them from me. 8 When I say unto the wicked, O wicked *man*, thou shalt surely die; if thou dost not speak to warn the wicked from his way, that wicked *man* shall die in his iniquity; but his blood will I require at thine hand. 9 Nevertheless, of thou warn the wicked of his way to turn from it; if he do not turn from his way, he shall die in his iniquity; but thou hast delivered thy soul. [Ezk. 3: 17, 19.] — 34: 8 *As* I live, saith the Lord GOD, surely because my flock became a prey, and my flock became meat to every beast of the field, because *there was* no shepherd, neither did my shepherds search for my flock, but the shepherds fed themselves, and fed not my flock; 9 Therefore, O ye shepherds, hear the word of the LORD; 10 Thus saith the Lord GOD; Behold, I *am* against the shepherds; and I will require my flock at their hand, and cause them to cease from feeding the flock, neither shall the shepherds feed themselves any more; for I will deliver my flock from their mouth, and they may not be meat for them.

1 Tim. 1: 11 According to the glorious gospel of the blessed God which was committed to my trust. — 6: 20 O Timothy, keep that which is committed to thy trust, avoding profane *and* vain babblings, and oppositions of science falsely so called; 21 Which some professing, have erred concerning the faith.

466. Ministerial temptations.

1. To please their hearers.

Num. 24: 10 Balak said unto Balaam, I called thee to curse mine enemies, and behold, thou hast altogether blessed *them* these three times. 11 Therefore now flee thou to thy place: I thought to promote thee unto great honor; but lo, the LORD hath kept thee back from honor.

2. *To avoid the frowns of the influential.*

Am. 7: 12 Amaziah said unto Amos, O thou seer, go flee thee away into the land of Judah, and there eat bread, and prophesy there : 13 But prophesy not again any more at Bethel : for it *is* the king's chapel, and it *is* the king's court.

Ac. 4: 18 And they called them, and commanded them not to speak at all, nor teach in the name of Jesus.

3. *To conceal the true God.*

· Is. 30: 9 This *is* a rebellious people, lying children, children *that* will not hear the law of the LORD : 10 Which say to the seers, See not ; and to the prophets, Prophesy not unto us right things, speak unto us smooth things, prophesy deceits : 11 Get ye out of the way, turn aside out of the path, cause the Holy One of Israel to cease from before us.

4. *To countenance popular errors, delusions and vices.*

Ex. 32: 21 Moses said unto Aaron, What did this people unto thee, that thou hast brought so great a sin upon them? 22 And Aaron said, Let not the anger of my lord wax hot : thou knowest the people, that they *are set* on mischief. 23 For they said unto me, Make us gods which shall go before us.

Am. 2: 11 ·I raised up of your sons for prophets, and of your young men for Nazarites. *Is it* not even thus, O ye children of Israel? saith the LORD. 12 But ye gave the Nazarites wine to drink: and commanded the prophets, saying, Prophesy not.

467. *Trials and persecutions of faithful ministers.*

Jer. 2: 30 In vain have I smitten your children ; they received no correction : your own sword hath devoured your prophets, like a destroying lion. — 15: 10 Wo is me, my mother, that thou hast borne me a man of strife and a man of contention to the whole earth ! I have neither lent on usury, nor men have lent to me on usury ; *yet* every one of them doth curse me.

Ezk. 33: 30 Also, thou son of man, the children of thy people still are talking against thee by the walls and in the doors of the houses.

Mat. 10: 16 Behold, I send you forth as sheep in the midst of wolves : be ye therefore wise as serpents, and harmless as doves. 17 But beware of men : for they will deliver you up to the councils, and they will scourge you in their synagogues. 18 And ye shall be brought before governors and kings for my sake, for a testimony against them and the Gentiles. · 22 And ye shall be hated of all *men* for my name's sake : but he·

Trials and Persecutions of Ministers.

that endureth to the end shall be saved. 23 But when they persecute you in this city, flee ye into another: for verily I say unto you, Ye shall not have gone over the cities of Israel till the Son of man be come. 24 The disciple is not above *his* master, nor the servant above his lord. 25 It is enough for the disciple that he be as his master, and the servant as his lord: if they have called the master of the house Beelzebub, how much more *shall they call* them of his household?—23: 34 Behold, I send unto you prophets, and wise men, and scribes; and *some* of them ye shall kill and crucify, and *some* of them shall ye scourge in your synagogues, and persecute *them* from city to city.

Jn. 16: 33 These things I have spoken unto you, that in me ye might have peace. In the world ye shall have tribulation, but be of good cheer: I have overcome the world.—17: 14 I have given them thy word; and the world hath hated them, because they are not of the world, even as I am not of the world.

Ac. 5: 40 To him they agreed: and when they had called the apostles, and beaten *them*, they commanded that they should not speak in the name of Jesus, and let them go. 41 And they departed from the presence of the council, rejoicing that they were counted worthy to suffer shame for his name.

Ac. 7: 52 Which of the prophets have not your fathers persecuted? and they have slain them which shewed before of the coming of the Just One; of whom ye have been now the betrayers and murderers.—9: 15 The Lord said unto him, Go thy way: for he is a chosen vessel unto me, to bear my name before the Gentiles, and kings, and the children of Israel. 16 For I will show him how great things he must suffer for my name's sake.—20: 23 Save that the Holy Ghost witnesseth in every city, saying, that bonds and afflictions abide me.

1 Cor. 4: 9 I think that God hath set forth us the apostles last, as it were appointed to death: for we are made a spectacle unto the world, and to angels, and to men. 11 Even unto this present hour we both hunger, and thirst, and are naked, and are buffeted, and have no certain dwelling-place; 12 And labor, working with our own hands. Being reviled, we bless; being persecuted, we suffer it; 13 Being defamed, we entreat: we are made as the filth of the world, *and are* the off-scouring of all things unto this day.

2 Cor. 1: 5 As the sufferings of Christ abound in us, so our consolation also aboundeth by Christ. 6 And whether we be afflicted, *it is* for your consolation and salvation, which is effectual in the enduring of the same sufferings which we also

821

suffer: or whether we be comforted, *it is* for your consolation
and salvation. 7 And our hope of you *is* steadfast, knowing
that as ye are partakers of the sufferings, so *shall ye be* also of
the consolation.—4: 8 *We are* troubled on every side, yet not
distressed; *we are* perplexed, but not in despair; 9 Persecuted, but not forsaken; cast down, but not destroyed; 10 Always bearing about in the body the dying of the Lord Jesus,
that the life also of Jesus might be made manifest in our body.
11 For we which live are always delivered unto death for
Jesus' sake, that the life also of Jesus might be made manifest
in our mortal flesh.—6: 4 In all *things* approving ourselves as
the ministers of God, in much patience, in afflictions, in necessities, in distresses, 5 In stripes, in imprisonments, in tumults,
in labors, in watchings, in fastings; 8 By honor and dishonor,
by evil report and good report; as deceivers, and *yet* true;
9 As unknown, and *yet* well known; as dying, and behold, we
live; as chastened, and not killed; 10 As sorrowful, yet always rejoicing; as poor, yet making many rich; as having
nothing, and *yet* possessing all things.—11: 23 Are they ministers of Christ? (I speak as a fool) I *am* more; in labors
more abundant, in stripes above measure, in prisons more frequent, in deaths oft. 24 Of the Jews five times received I
forty *stripes* save one. 25 Thrice was I beaten with rods,
once was I stoned, thrice I suffered shipwreck, a night and a
day I have been in the deep; 26 *In* journeyings often, *in*
perils of waters, *in* perils of robbers, *in* perils by *mine own*
countrymen, *in* perils by the heathen, *in* perils in the city, *in*
perils in the wilderness, *in* perils in the sea, *in* perils among
false brethren; 27 In weariness and painfulness, in watchings
often, in hunger and thirst, in fastings often, in cold and nakedness. 32 In Damascus the governor under Aretas the king
kept the city of the Damascenes with a garrison, desirous to
apprehend me: 33 And through a window in a basket was I
let down by the wall, and escaped his hands.

Gal. 1: 10 Do I now persuade men, or God? or do I seek
to please men? for if I yet pleased men, I should not be the
servant of Christ.—5: 11 I, brethren, if I yet preach circumcision, why do I yet suffer persecution? then is the offence of
the cross ceased.

1 Th. 3: 3 That no man should be moved by these afflictions: for yourselves know that we are appointed thereunto.
4 For verily, when we were with you, we told you before that
we should suffer tribulation; even as it came to pass, and ye
know.

2 Tim. 2: 3 Thou therefore endure hardness, as a good

soldier of Jesus Christ. 9 Wherein I suffer trouble, as an evil-doer, *even* unto bonds; but the word of God is not bound. —3: 11 Persecutions, afflictions, which came unto me at Antioch, **at** Iconium, at Lystra, what persecutions I endured: but out of *them* all the Lord delivered me. 12 Yea, and all that will live godly in Christ Jesus shall suffer persecution.

Rev. 1: 9 I John, who also am your brother, and companion in tribulation, and in the kingdom and patience of Jesus Christ, was in the isle that is called Patmos, for the word of God, and for the testimony of Jesus Christ. [See 68, 511.]

468. *Success in preaching promised, encouraged, and exemplified.*

Jer. 23: 22 If they had stood in my counsel, and had caused my people to hear my words, then they should have turned them from their evil way, and from the evil of their doings.

Dan. 12: 3 They that be wise, shall shine as the brightness of the firmament; and they that turn many to righteousness, as the stars for ever and ever.

Mk. 1: 17 Jesus said unto them, Come ye after me, and I will make you to become fishers of men.

Jn. 4: 36 He that reapeth receiveth wages, and gathereth fruit unto life eternal: that both he that soweth, and he that reapeth, may rejoice together.

Ac. 11: 24 He was a good man, and full of the Holy Ghost, and of faith: and much people was added unto the Lord.— 14: 1 It came to pass in Iconium, that they went both together into the synagogue of the Jews, and so spake, that a great multitude, both of the Jews, and also of the Greeks, beheved.

1 Tim. 4: 16 Take heed unto thyself, and unto the doctrine; continue in them: for in doing this thou shalt both save thyself, and them that hear thee. [See 432.]

469. *Is present success always in proportion to faithfulness?*

Is. 49: 4 I said, I have labored in vain, I have spent my strength for nought, and in vain; *yet* surely my judgment *is* with the LORD, and my work with my God. 5 And now, saith the LORD that formed me from the womb *to be* his servant, to bring Jacob again to him, Though Israel be not gathered, yet shall I be glorious in the eyes of the LORD, and my God shall be my strength.—53: 1 Who hath believed our report? and to whom is the arm of the LORD revealed?

Ezk. 3: 7 The house of Israel will not hearken unto thee;

for they will not hearken unto me : for all the house of Israel *are* impudent and hard-hearted.

Jn. 12: 37 Though he had done so many miracles before them, yet they believed not on him : 38 That the saying of Esaias the prophet might be fulfilled, which he spake, Lord, who hath believed our report? and to whom hath the arm of the Lord been revealed? 39 Therefore they could not believe, because that Esaias said again, 40 He hath blinded their eyes, and hardened their heart; that they should not see with *their* eyes, nor understand with *their* heart, and be converted, and I should heal them.

Ac. 13: 46 Then Paul and Barnabas waxed bold, and said, It was necessary that the word of God should first have been spoken to you : but seeing ye put it from you, and judge yourselves unworthy of everlasting life, lo, we turn to the Gentiles. [See 435.]

470. Faithful ministers encouraged and rewarded by God.

Jer. 1: 18 For behold, I have made thee this day a defenced city, and an iron pillar, and brazen walls against the whole land, against the kings of Judah, against the princes thereof, against the priests thereof, and against the people of the land. 19 And they shall fight against thee; but they shall not prevail against thee; for I *am* with thee, saith the LORD, to deliver thee.—15: 19 Thus saith the LORD, If thou return, then will I bring thee again, *and* thou shalt stand before me : and if thou take forth the precious from the vile, thou shalt be as my mouth : let them return unto thee; but return not thou unto them. 20 And I will make thee unto this people a fenced brazen wall : and they shall fight against thee, but they shall not prevail against thee : for I *am* with thee to save thee and to deliver thee, saith the LORD. 21 And I will deliver thee out of the hand of the wicked, and I will redeem thee out of the hand of the terrible.

Ezk. 3: 8 Behold, I have made thy face strong against their faces, and thy forehead strong against their foreheads. 9 As an adamant, harder than flint have I made thy forehead : fear them not, neither be dismayed at their looks, though they *be* a rebellious house.

Mat. 28: 20 Teaching them to observe all things whatsoever I have commanded you : and lo, I am with you alway, *even* unto the end of the world.

Lk. 6: 22 Blessed are ye when men shall hate you, and when they shall separate you *from their company*, and shall reproach *you*, and cast out your name as evil, for the Son of man's sake. 23 Rejoice ye in that day, and leap for joy: for behold, your reward *is* great in heaven.—21: 15 I will give you a mouth and wisdom, which all your adversaries shall not be able to gainsay nor·resist.

2 Tim. 4: 7 I have fought a good fight, I have finished *my* course, I have kept the faith: 8 Henceforth there is laid up for me a crown of·righteousness, which the Lord, the righteous Judge, shall give me at that day: and not to me only, but unto all them also that love his appearing. [See 630.]

471. *Faithful ministers to be prayed for.*

Ep. 6: 18 Praying always with all prayer.and supplication in the Spirit, and watching thereunto with all perseverance and supplication for all saints; 19 And for me, that utterance may be given unto me, that I may open my mouth boldly, to make known the mystery of the gospel.

1 Th. 5: 25 Brethren, pray for us.

2 Th. 3: 1 Finally, brethren, pray for us, that the word of the Lord may have *free* course, and be glorified, even as *it is* with you; 2 And that we may be delivered from unreasonable and wicked men: for all *men* have not faith.

472. *Faithful ministers should be supported.*

Num. 18: 21 Behold, I have given the children of Levi all the tenth in Israel for an inheritance, for their service which they serve, *even* the service of the tabernacle of the congregation.

Mal. 3: 10 Bring ye all the tithes into the storehouse, that there may be meat in my house.

Mat. 10: 9 Provide neither gold, nor silver, nor brass in your purses; 10 Nor scrip for *your* journey, neither two coats, neither shoes, nor yet staves: (for the workman is worthy of his meat.)

Jn. 13: 20 Verily, verily, I say unto you, He that receiveth whomsoever I send, receiveth me; and he that receiveth me, receiveth him that sent me.

1 Cor. 9: 11 If we have sown unto you spiritual things, *is it* a great thing if we shall reap your carnal things? 13 Do ye not know that they which minister about holy things live *of the things* of the temple, and they which wait at the altar are partakers with the altar? 14 Even so hath the Lord ordained that they which preach the gospel should live *of* the gospel.

Gal. 6: 6 Let him that is taught in the word, communicate unto him that teacheth in all good things.

1 Th. 5: 12 We beseech you, brethren, to know them which

labor among you, and are over you in the Lord, and admonish you; 13 And to esteem them very highly in love for their work's sake. *And* be at peace among yourselves.

1 Tim. 5: 17 Let the elders that rule well, be counted worthy of double honor, especially they who labor in the word and doctrine. 18 For the scripture saith, Thou shalt not muzzle the ox that treadeth out the corn. And, The laborer *is* worthy of his reward.

MINISTERS OF SATAN.

473. False and unfaithful ministers numerous.

1 K. 18: 22 Then said Elijah unto the people, I, *even* I only, remain a prophet of the LORD; but Baal's prophets *are* four hundred and fifty men.

Jer. 10: 21 The pastors are become brutish, and have not sought the LORD : therefore they shall not prosper, and all their flocks shall be scattered.

Mat. 7: 22 Many will say to me in that day, Lord, Lord, have we not prophesied in thy name? and in thy name have cast out devils? and in thy name done many wonderful works? 23 And then I will profess unto them I never knew you: depart from me, ye that work iniquity.—24: 5 Many shall come in my name, saying, I am Christ; and shall deceive many. 11 And many false prophets shall rise, and shall deceive many.

1 Jn. 4: 1 Beloved, believe not every spirit, but try the spirits whether they are of God: because many false prophets are gone out into the world.

2 Jn. 7 Many deceivers are entered into the world, who confess not that Jesus Christ is come in the flesh. This is a deceiver, and an antichrist.

474. False and unfaithful ministers deceitful.

Jer. 6: 14 They have healed also the hurt *of the daughter* of my people slightly, saying, Peace, peace; when *there is* no peace.

Ezk. 13: 10 They have seduced my people, saying, Peace; and *there was* no peace; and one built up a wall, and lo, others daubed it with untempered *mortar.* 18 Wo to the *women* that sew pillows to all arm-holes, and make kerchiefs upon the head of every statue to hunt souls! 22 Because with lies ye have made the heart of the righteous sad, whom I have not made sad; and strengthened the hands of the wicked, that he should not return from his wicked way by promising him life.

Mat. 7: 15 Beware of false prophets, which come to you in sheep's clothing, but inwardly they are ravening wolves.— 24: 11 Many false prophets shall rise, and shall deceive many. 24 There shall arise false Christs, and false prophets, and shall shew great signs and wonders; insomuch that, if *it were* possible, they shall deceive 'the very elect.

Rom. 16: 17 I beseech you, brethren, mark them which cause divisions and offences, contrary to the doctrine which ye have learned; and avoid them. 18 For they that are such serve not our Lord Jesus Christ, but their own belly;. and by good words and fair speeches deceive the hearts of the simple.

2 Cor. 11: 13 Such *are* false apostles, deceitful workers, transforming themselves into the apostles of Christ. 14 And no marvel; for Satan himself is transformed into an angel of light. 15 Therefore *it is* no great thing if his ministers also be transformed as the ministers of righteousness; whose end shall be according to their works.

Ep. 4: 14 That we *henceforth* be no more children, tossed to and fro, and carried about with every wind of doctrine, by the sleight of men, *and* cunning craftiness, whereby they lie in wait to deceive.

2 Tim. 3: 13 Evil men and seducers shall wax worse and worse, deceiving, and being deceived.

Tit. 1: 10 There are many unruly and vain talkers and deceivers, especially they of the circumcision: 11 Whose mouths must be stopped, who subvert whole houses, teaching things which they ought not, for filthy lucre's sake.

2 Pet. 2: 3 Through covetousness shall they with feigned words make merchandise of you: whose judgment now of a long time lingereth not, and their damnation slumbereth not.

[See 15, 198, 702:]

475. *False and unfaithful teachers cruel, dangerous and despicable—Threats.*

Is. 3: 12 O my people, they which lead thee cause *thee* to err, and destroy the way of thy paths.—9: 15 The ancient and honorable, he *is* the head; and the prophet that teacheth lies, he *is* the tail. 16 For the leaders of this people cause *them* to err; and *they that are* led of them *are* destroyed.

Jer. 23: 1 Wo be unto the pastors that destroy and scatter the sheep of my pasture! saith the LORD. 2 Therefore thus saith the LORD God of Israel against the pastors that feed my people; Ye have scattered my flock, and driven them away, and have not visited them: behold, I will visit upon you the

Cruel, dangerous and despicable

evil of your doings, saith the LORD. 14 I have seen also in the prophets of Jerusalem a horrible thing : they commit adultery, and walk in lies : they strengthen also the hands of evildoers, that none doth return from his wickedness : they are all of them unto me as Sodom, and the inhabitants thereof as Gomorrah. 15 Therefore thus saith the LORD of hosts concerning the prophets ; Behold, I will feed them with wormwood, and make them drink the water of gall : for from the prophets of Jerusalem is profaneness gone forth into all the land. 32 Behold, I *am* against them that prophesy false dreams, saith the LORD, and do tell them, and cause my people to err by their lies, and by their lightness ; yet I sent them not, nor commanded them : therefore they shall not profit this people at all, saith the LORD.

Ezk. 13: 22 With lies ye have made the heart of the righteous sad, whom I have not made sad ; and strengthened the hands of the wicked, that he should not return from his wicked way, by promising him life.—22: 25 *There is* a conspiracy of her prophets in the midst thereof, like a roaring lion ravening the prey ; they have devoured souls ; they have taken the treasure and precious things ; they have made her many widows in the midst thereof. 26 Her priests have violated my law, and have profaned my holy things : they have put no difference between the holy and profane, neither have they shewed *difference* between the unclean and the clean, and have hid their eyes from my Sabbaths, and I am profaned among them. 27 Her princes in the midst thereof *are* like wolves ravening the prey, to shed blood, *and* to destroy souls, to get dishonest gain. 28 And her prophets have daubed them with untempered *mortar*, seeing vanity, and divining lies unto them, saying, Thus saith the Lord GOD, when the LORD hath not spoken. 31 Therefore, have I poured out mine indignation upon them ; I have consumed them with the fire of my wrath : their own way have I recompensed upon their heads, saith the Lord GOD. —34: 2 Son of man, prophesy against the shepherds of Israel, prophesy, and say unto them, Thus saith the Lord GOD unto the shepherds ; Wo *be* to the shepherds of Israel that do feed themselves ! should not the shepherds feed the flocks ? 3 Ye eat the fat, and ye clothe you with the wool, ye kill them that are fed : *but* ye feed not the flock. 4 The diseased have ye not strengthened, neither have ye healed that which was sick, neither have ye bound up *that which was* broken, neither have ye brought again that which was driven away, neither have ye sought that which was lost ; but with force and with cruelty have ye ruled them. 10 Thus saith the Lord GOD ; Behold,

I *am* against the shepherds; and I will require my flock at their hand, and cause them to cease from feeding the flock; neither shall the shepherds feed themselves any more; for I will deliver my flock from their mouth, that they may not be meat for them.

Mal. 2: 8 Ye are departed out of the way; ye have caused many to stumble at the law; ye have corrupted the covenant of Levi, saith the LORD of hosts. 9 Therefore have I also made you contemptible and base before all the people, according as ye have not kept my ways, but have been partial in the law.

Mat. 23: 14 Wo unto you, scribes and Pharisees, hypocrites! for ye devour widows' houses, and for a pretence make long prayer: therefore ye shall receive the greater damnation. 15 Wo unto you, scribes and Pharisees, hypocrites! for ye compass sea and land to make one proselyte; and when he is made, ye make him two-fold more the child of hell than yourselves. 16 Wo unto you, *ye* blind guides! which say, Whosoever shall swear by the temple, it is nothing; but whosoever shall swear by the gold of the temple, he is a debtor. 17 *Ye* fools, and blind! for whether is greater, the gold, or the temple that sanctifieth the gold? 23 Wo unto you, scribes and Pharisees, hypocrites! for ye pay tithe of mint, and anise, and cummin, and have omitted the weightier *matters* of the law, judgment, mercy, and faith: these ought ye to have done, and not to leave the other undone. 24 *Ye* blind guides, which strain at a gnat, and swallow a camel. 27 Wo unto you, scribes and Pharisees, hypocrites! for ye are like unto whited sepulchres, which indeed appear beautiful outward, but are within full of dead *men's* bones, and of all uncleanness. 28 Even so ye also outwardly appear righteous unto men, but within ye are full of hypocrisy and iniquity. 33 *Ye* serpents, *ye* generation of vipers, how can ye escape the damnation of hell?

Lk. 6: 26 Wo unto you, when all men shall speak well of you! for so did their fathers to the false prophets. — 11: 52 Wo unto you, lawyers! for ye have taken away the key of knowledge: ye entered not in yourselves, and them that were entering in ye hindered.

Ac. 20: 29 I know this, that after my departing shall grievous wolves enter in among you, not sparing the flock. 30 Also of your own selves shall men arise, speaking perverse things, to draw away disciples after them.

2 Pet. 2: 1 There were false prophets also among the people, even as there shall be false teachers among you, who

28*

privily shall bring in damnable heresies, even denying the
Lord that bought them, and bring upon themselves swift
destruction.   2 And many shall follow their pernicious ways;
by reason of whom the way of truth shall be evil spoken of.
3 And through covetousness shall they with feigned words
make merchandise of you: whose judgment now of a long
time lingereth not, and their damnation slumbereth not.
[See 175–7.]

476. *False and unfaithful teachers, sought after.*

Jer. 5: 30 A wonderful and horrible thing is committed in
the land;   31 The prophets prophesy falsely, and the priests
bear rule by their means; and my people love *to have it* so:
and what will ye do in the end thereof?

Jn. 5: 43 I am come in my Father's name, and ye receive
me not: if another shall come in his own name, him ye will
receive.

2 Tim. 4: 2 Preach the word: be instant in season, out of
season; reprove, rebuke, exhort with all long-suffering and
doctrine.   3 The time will come, when they will not endure
sound doctrine; but after their own lusts shall they heap to
themselves teachers, having itching ears;   4 And they shall
turn away *their* ears from the truth, and shall be turned unto
fables.   [See 175, 704.]

477. *False teachers to be avoided — cautions.*

Pr. 19: 27 Cease, my son, to hear the instruction *that causeth*
to err from the words of knowledge.

Mat. 7: 15 Beware of false prophets, which come to you in
sheep's clothing, but inwardly they are ravening wolves. — 15:14
Let them alone: they be blind leaders of the blind. — 24: 4
Jesus answered and said unto them, Take heed that no man
deceive you.

Mk. 4: 24 He said unto them, Take heed what ye hear.

Lk. 21: 8 He said, Take heed that ye be not deceived: for
many shall come in my name, saying, I am *Christ;* and the
time draweth near: go ye not therefore after them.

Rom. 16: 17 I beseech you, brethren, mark them which cause
divisions and offences, contrary to the doctrine which ye have
learned; and avoid them.

1 Cor. 15: 33 Be not deceived: Evil communications corrupt
good manners.

Gal. 1: 7 There be some that trouble you, and would pervert
the gospel of Christ.   8 But though we, or an angel from

heaven, preach any other gospel unto you than that which we have preached unto you, let him be accursed.

Ph. 3: 2 Beware of dogs, beware of evil-workers, beware of the concision; 3 For we are the circumcision, which worship God in the Spirit, and rejoice in Christ Jesus, and have no confidence in the flesh.

1 Tim. 6: 3 If any man teach otherwise, and consent not to wholesome words, *even* the words of our Lord Jesus Christ, and to the doctrine which is according to godliness, 4 He is proud, knowing nothing, but doting about questions and strifes of words, whereof cometh envy, strife, railings, evil surmisings, 5 Perverse disputings of men of corrupt minds, and destitute of the truth, supposing that gain is godliness: from such withdraw thyself.

2 Jn. 10 If there come any unto you, and bring not this doctrine, receive him not into *your* house, neither bid him God speed: 11 For he that biddeth him God speed, is partaker of his evil deeds. [See 18, 112, 175-7.]

478. *False teachers destroy themselves and others.*

Mat 15: 14 Let them alone: they be blind leaders of the blind. And if the blind lead the blind, both shall fall into the ditch. — 23: 13 Wo unto you, scribes and Pharisees, hypocrites! for ye shut up the kingdom of heaven against men: for ye neither go in *yourselves*, neither suffer ye them that are entering, to go in. 15 Wo unto you scribes and Pharisees, hypocrites! for ye compass sea and land to make one proselyte; and when he is made, ye make him two-fold more the child of hell than yourselves.

MIRTH AND LAUGHTER.

479. *Mankind prone to mirth — nature and tendency of.*

Job 21: 11 They send forth their little ones like a flock, and their children dance. 12 They take the timbrel and harp, and rejoice at the sound of the organ. 13 They spend their days in wealth, and in a moment go down to the grave. 14 Therefore they say unto God, Depart from us; for we desire not the knowledge of thy ways.

Pr. 14: 13 Even in laughter the heart is sorrowful; and the end of that mirth *is* heaviness. — 21: 17 He that loveth pleasure *shall be* a poor man: he that loveth wine and oil shall not be rich.

Ec. 2: 1 I said in my heart, Go to now, I will prove thee with mirth; therefore enjoy pleasure: and behold, this also *is* vanity. 2 I said of laughter, *It is* mad: and of mirth, What doeth it? 10 Whatsoever mine eyes desired I kept not from them, I withheld not my heart from any joy; for my heart rejoiced in all my labor: and this was my portion of all my labor. 11 Then I looked on all the works that my hands had wrought, and on the labor that I had labored to do: and behold, all *was* vanity and vexation of spirit, and *there was* no profit under the sun. — 7: 2 *It is* better to go to the house of mourning, than to go to the house of feasting: for that *is* the end of all men; and the living will lay *it* to his heart. 3 Sorrow *is* better than laughter: for by the sadness of the countenance the heart is made better. 4 The heart of the wise *is* in the house of mourning; but the heart of fools *is* in the house of mirth. — 11: 9 Rejoice, O young man, in thy youth; and let thy heart cheer thee in the days of thy youth, and walk in the ways of thine heart, and in the sight of thine eyes: but know thou, that for all these *things* God will bring thee into judgment. 10 Therefore remove sorrow from thy heart, and put away evil from thy flesh: for childhood and youth *are* vanity.

Lk. 6: 25 Wo unto you that are full! for ye shall hunger Wo unto you that laugh now! for ye shall mourn and weep.

1 Cor. 10: 7 Neither be ye idolaters, as *were* some of them: as it is written, The people sat down to eat and drink, and rose up to play.

2 Pet. 2: 13 And shall receive the reward of unrighteousness, *as* they that count it pleasure to riot in the day-time. Spots *they are* and blemishes, sporting themselves with their own deceivings while they feast with you. [See 698, 711.]

MISSIONS.

480. *Missions needed and divinely appointed.*

Ps. 9: 17 The wicked shall be turned into hell, *and* all the nations that forget God — 74: 20 Have respect unto the covenant: for the dark places of the earth are full of the habitations of cruelty.

Mat. 28: 19 Go ye therefore and teach all nations, baptizing them in the name of the Father, and of the Son, and of the Holy Ghost; 20 Teaching them to observe all things whatsoever I have commanded you: and lo, I am with you always, *even* unto the end of the world.

Mk. 16: 15 He said unto them, Go ye into all the world, and preach the gospel to every creature.

· **Rom.** 2: 12 As many as have sinned without law, shall also perish without law : and as many as have sinned in the law, shall be judged by the law. — 10: 14 How then shall they call on him in whom they have not believed? and how shall they believe in him of whom they have not heard? and how shall they hear without a preacher? 15 And how shall they preach, except they be sent? as it is written, How beautiful are the feet of them that preach the gospel of peace, and bring glad tidings of good things! [See 359, 448.]

481. *Encouragement of missions.*

Ps. 68: 31 Princes shall come out of Egypt; Ethiopia shall soon stretch out her hands unto God. — 110: 3 Thy people *shall be* willing in the day of thy power, in the beauties of holiness from the womb of the morning: thou hast the dew of thy youth.

Joel 2: 28 It shall come to pass afterward, *that* I will pour out my Spirit upon all flesh ; and your sons and your daughters shall prophesy, your old men shall dream dreams, your young men shall see visions : 29 And also upon the servants and upon the handmaids in those days will I pour out my Spirit.

Ac. 28: 28 Be it known therefore unto you, that the salvation of God is sent unto the Gentiles, and *that* they will hear it. [See 90, 440.]

MODESTY.

482. *Modesty and lowliness required.*

Pr. 25: 6 Put not forth thyself in the presence of the king ; and stand not in the place of great *men.* 7 For better *it is* that it be said unto thee, Come up hither; than that thou shouldest be put lower in the presence of the prince whom thine eyes have seen.

Mat. 11: 29 Take my yoke upon you, and learn of me : for I am meek and lowly in heart: and ye shall find rest unto your souls. — 20: 26 It shall not be so among you : but whosoever will be great among you, let him be your minister : 27 And whosoever will be chief among you, let him be your servant.

Rom. 12: 3 I say, through the grace given unto me, to every man that is among you, not to think *of himself* more highly than he ought to think: but to think soberly, according as God hath dealt to every man the measure of faith. 10 *Be* kindly affectioned one to another with brotherly love; in honor preferring one another.

1 Cor. 13: 4 Charity suffereth long, *and is* kind; charity envieth not; charity vaunteth not itself, is not puffed up.

Gal. 5: 26 Let us not be desirous of vain-glory, provoking one another, envying one another.

Ep. 4: 1 I therefore, the prisoner of the Lord, beseech you that ye walk worthy of the vocation wherewith ye are called, 2 With all lowliness and meekness, with long-suffering, forbearing one another in love.

Ph. 2: 3 *Let* nothing *be done* through strife or vain-glory; but in lowliness of mind let each esteem other better than themselves. [See 62, 437.]

483. *Modesty in good works.*

Mat. 6: 1 Take heed that ye do not your alms before men, to be seen of them : otherwise ye have no reward of your Father which is in heaven. 2 Therefore, when thou doest *thine* alms, do not sound a trumpet before thee, as the hypocrites do, in the synagogues, and in the streets, that they may have glory of men. Verily I say unto you, They have their reward. 3 But when thou doest alms, let not thy left hand know what thy right hand doeth; 4 That thine alms may be in secret : and thy Father, which seeth in secret, himself shall reward thee openly. [See 703.]

NATIONAL.

484. *National organizations appointed.*

Gen. 21: 13 Of the son of the bond-woman will I make a nation, because he *is* thy seed.

Dt. 32: 8 When the Most High divided to the nations their inheritance, when he separated the sons of Adam, he set the bounds of the people according to the number of the children of Israel.

485. *National promises and favors to the obedient.*

Ex. 19: 5 If ye will obey my voice indeed, and keep my covenant, then ye shall be a peculiar treasure unto me above all people : for all the earth *is* mine : 6 And ye shall be unto me a kingdom of priests, and an holy nation.

Lev. 26: 3 If ye walk in my statutes and keep my commandments, and do them; 4 Then I will give you rain in due season, and the land shall yield her increase, and the trees of the field shall yield their fruit: 6 And I will give peace in the land, and ye shall lie down, and none shall make *you*

Promises to the Obedient.

afraid: and I will rid evil beasts out of the land, neither shall the sword go through your land. 7 And ye shall chase your enemies, and they shall fall before you by the sword. 8 And five of you shall chase an hundred, and an hundred of you shall put ten thousand to flight: and your enemies shall fall before you by the sword. 9 For I will have respect unto you, and make you fruitful, and multiply you, and establish my covenant with you. 10 And ye shall eat old store, and bring forth the old because of the new. 11 And I will set my tabernacle among you: and my soul shall not abhor you. 12 And I will walk among you, and will be your God, and ye shall be my people.

Dt. 4: 5 Behold, I have taught you statutes, and judgments, even as the LORD my God commanded me, that ye should do so in the land whither ye go to possess it. 6 Keep therefore and do *them:* for this *is* your wisdom and your understanding, in the sight of the nations, which shall hear all these statutes, and say, Surely this great nation *is* a wise and understanding people. 40 Thou shalt keep therefore his statutes and his commandments which I command thee this day, that it may go well with thee, and with thy children after thee, and that thou mayest prolong *thy* days upon the earth, which the LORD thy God giveth thee, for ever. — 28: 1 It shall come to pass, if thou shalt hearken diligently unto the voice of the LORD thy God, to observe *and* to do all his commandments which I command thee this day: that the LORD thy God will set thee on high above all nations of the earth: 2 And all these blessings shall come on thee, and overtake thee, if thou shalt hearken unto the voice of the LORD thy God. 3 Blessed *shalt* thou *be* in the city, and blessed *shalt* thou *be* in the field. 4 Blessed *shall be* the fruit of thy body, and the fruit of thy ground, and the fruit of thy cattle, the increase of thy kine, and the flocks of thy sheep. 5 Blessed *shall be* thy basket and thy store. 6 Blessed *shalt* thou *be* when thou comest in, and blessed *shalt* thou *be* when thou goest out. 7 The LORD shall cause thine enemies that rise up against thee to be smitten before thy face; they shall come out against thee one way, and flee before thee seven ways. 8 The LORD shall command the blessing upon thee in thy store-houses, and in all that thou settest thine hand unto; and he shall bless thee in the land which the LORD thy God giveth thee. 9 The LORD shall establish thee a holy people unto himself, as he hath sworn unto thee, if thou shalt keep the commandments of the LORD thy God, and walk in his ways. 10 And all people of the earth shall see that thou art called by the name of the LORD; and they shall be afraid of thee. 11 And the LORD shall make thee plenteous in goods, in the fruit of thy body, and in the fruit of thy cattle, and in the fruit of thy ground, in the land which the LORD sware unto thy fathers to give thee. 12 The LORD shall open unto thee his good treasure, the heaven to give the rain unto thy land in his season, and to bless all the work of thine hand; and thou shalt lend unto many nations, and thou shalt not borrow. 13 And the LORD shall make thee the head, and not the tail; and thou shalt be above only, and thou shalt not be beneath; if that thou hearken unto the commandments of the LORD thy God, which I command thee this day, to observe and to do *them*.

Ps. 81: 13 Oh that my people had hearkened unto me, *and* Israel had walked in my ways! 14 I should soon have subdued their enemies, and turned my hand against their adversaries. 15 The haters of the LORD should have submitted themselves unto him: but their time should have endured for ever. 16 He should have fed them also with the finest of the wheat: and with honey out of the rock should I have satisfied thee. [Lev. 26: 3—12. Dt. 4: 5, 6, 40, and 28: 1—13.]

[See 302, 630, and Promises in the Index.]

486. National threats and calamities for disobedience.

Lev. 26: 14 If ye will not hearken unto me, and will not do all these commandments; 15 And if ye shall despise my statutes, or if your soul abhor my judgments, so that ye will not do all my commandments, *but* that ye break my covenant: 16 I also will do this unto you, I will even appoint over you terror, consumption, and the burning ague, that shall consume the eyes, and cause sorrow of heart: and ye shall sow your seed in vain; for your enemies shall eat it. 17 And I will set my face against you, and ye shall be slain before your enemies: they that hate you shall reign over you, and ye shall flee when none pursueth you. 18 And if ye will not yet for all this hearken unto me, then I will punish you seven times more for your sins. 19 And I will break the pride of your power; and I will make your heaven as iron, and your earth as brass: 20 And your strength shall be spent in vain: for your land shall not yield her increase, neither shall the trees of the land yield their fruits. 21 And if ye walk contrary unto me, and will not hearken unto me, I will bring seven times more plagues upon you, according to your sins. 22 I will also send wild beasts among you, which shall rob you of your children, and destroy your cattle, and make you few in number, and your *high*-ways shall be desolate. 23 And if ye will not be reformed by me by these things, but will walk contrary unto me ;   24 Then will I also walk contrary unto you, and will punish you yet seven times for your sins.   25 And I will bring a sword upon you, that shall avenge the quarrel of *my* covenant; and when ye are gathered together within your cities, I will send the pestilence among you ; and ye shall be delivered into the hand of the enemy.   26 *And* when I have broken the staff of your bread, ten women shall bake your bread in one oven, and they shall deliver *you* your bread again by weight : and ye shall eat, and not be satisfied.   27 And if ye will not for all this hearken unto me, but walk contrary to me :   28 Then I will walk contrary into you also in fury ; and I, even I, will chastise you seven times for your sins.   29 And ye shall eat the flesh of your sons, and the flesh of your daughters shall ye eat.   30 And I will destroy your high places, and cut down your images, and cast your carcasses upon the carcasses of your idols, and my soul shall abhor you. 31 And I will make your cities waste, and bring your sanctuaries unto desolation, and I will not smell the savor of your sweet odors.   32 And I will bring the land unto desolation : and your enemies which dwell therein shall be astonished at it.   33 And I will scatter you among the heathen, and will draw out a sword after you : and your land shall be desolate, and your cities waste.   34 Then shall the land enjoy her sabbaths, as long as it lieth desolate, and ye *be* in your enemies' land : *even* then shall the land rest, and enjoy her sabbaths. 35 As long as it lieth desolate it shall rest ; because it did not rest in your sabbaths, when ye dwelt upon it.   36 And upon them that are left *alive* of you, I will send a faintness into their hearts in the lands of their enemies ; and the sound of a shaken leaf shall chase them ; and they shall flee, as fleeing from a sword ; and they shall fall when none pursueth.   37 And they shall fall one upon another, as it were before a sword, when none pursueth ; and ye shall have no power to stand before your enemies.   38 And ye shall perish among the heathen, and the land of your enemies shall eat you up. 39 And they that are left of you shall pine away in their iniquity in your enemies' lands : and also in the iniquities of their fathers shall they pine away with them.

Dt. 4: 25 When thou shalt beget children, and children's children, and ye shall have remained long in the land, and shall corrupt *yourselves*, and make a graven image, *or* the likeness of any *thing*, and shall do evil in the sight of the LORD thy God, to provoke him to anger, 26 I call heaven and earth to witness against you this day, that ye shall soon utterly per-

ish from off the land whereunto ye go over Jordan to possess
it: ye shall not prolong *your* days upon it, but shall utterly be-
destroyed. 27 And the LORD shall scatter you among the
nations, and ye shall be left few in number among the heathen,
whither the LORD shall lead you. — 28: 15 It shall come to
pass, if thou wilt not hearken unto the voice of the LORD thy
God, to observe to do all his commandments and his statutes
which I command thee this day; that all these curses shall
come upon thee: 16 Cursed *shalt* thou *be* in the city, and
cursed *shalt* thou *be* in the field. 17 Cursed *shall be* thy basket and thy store. 18 Cursed *shall be* the fruit of thy body,
and the fruit of thy land, the increase of thy kine, and the
flocks of thy sheep. 19 Cursed *shalt* thou *be* when thou comest
in, and cursed *shalt* thou *be* when thou goest out. 20 The
LORD shall send upon thee cursing, vexation, and rebuke, in
all that thou settest thine hand unto for to do, until thou be destroyed, and until thou perish quickly: because of the wickedness of thy doings whereby thou hast forsaken me. 21 The
LORD shall make the pestilence cleave unto thee, until he have
consumed thee from off the land, whither thou goest to possess
it. 22 The LORD shall smite thee with a consumption,
and with a fever, and with an inflammation, and with
an extreme burning, and with the sword, and with blast-
ing, and with mildew: and they shall pursue thee until
thou perish. 23 And thy heaven that *is* over thy head shall
be brass, and the earth that *is* under thee *shall be* iron. 24
The LORD shall make the rain of thy land powder and dust:
from heaven shall it come down upon thee, until thou be destroyed. 25 The LORD shall cause thee to be smitten before
thine enemies: thou shalt go out one way against them, and
flee seven ways before them; and shalt be removed into
all the kingdoms of the earth. 33 The fruit of thy land, and
all thy labors, shall a nation which thou knowest not eat up:
and thou shalt be only oppressed and crushed alway. 37 And thou
shalt become an astonishment, a proverb, and a by-word, among
all nations whither the LORD shall lead thee. 38 Thou shalt carry much seed out into the field, and shalt gather *but* little in:
for the locust shall consume it. 39 Thou shalt plant vineyards
and dress *them*, but shalt neither drink *of* the wine, nor gather
the grapes : for the worms shall eat them. 40 Thou shalt have
olive-trees throughout all thy coasts, but thou shalt not anoint
thyself with the oil; for thine olive shall cast *his fruit.* 41
Thou shalt beget sons and daughters, but thou shalt not enjoy
them: for they shall go into captivity. 42 All thy trees and
fruit of thy land shall the locusts consume. 43 The stranger

that *is* within thee shall get up above thee very high; and thou shalt come down very low. 44 He shall lend to thee, and thou shalt not lend to him : he shall be the head, and thou shalt be the tail. 45 Moreover, all these curses shall come upon thee, and shall pursue thee, and overtake thee, till thou be destroyed: because thou hearkenedst not unto the voice of the LORD thy God, to keep his commandments and his statutes which he commanded thee. 46 And they shall be upon thee for a sign and for a wonder, and upon thy seed for ever. 47 Because thou servedst not the LORD thy God with joyfulness and with gladness of heart, for the abundance of all *things ;* 48 Therefore shalt thou serve thine enemies which the LORD shall send against thee, in hunger, and in thirst, and in nakedness, and in want of all *things :* and he shall put a yoke of iron upon thy neck, until he have destroyed thee. 58 If thou wilt not observe to do all the words of this law that are written in this book, that thou mayest fear this glorious and fearful name, THE LORD THY GOD; 59 Then the LORD will make thy plagues wonderful, and the plagues of thy seed, *even* great plagues, and of long continuance, and sore sicknesses, and of long continuance. 62 And ye shall be left few in number, whereas ye were as the stars of heaven for multitude ; because thou wouldest not obey the voice of the LORD thy God. 63 And it shall come to pass, *that* as the LORD rejoiced over you to do you good, and to multiply you ; so the LORD will rejoice over you to destroy you and to bring you to nought : and ye shall be plucked from off the land whither thou goest to possess it. 66 And thy life shall hang in doubt before thee : and thou shalt fear day and night, and shalt have none assurance of thy life : 67 In the morning thou shalt say, Would God it were even ! and at even thou shalt say, Would God it were morning ! for the fear of thine heart wherewith thou shalt fear, and for the sight of thine eyes which thou shalt see.

2 Ch. 24: 20 And the Spirit of God came upon Zechariah the son of Jehoiada the priest, which stood above the people, and said unto them, Thus saith God, Why transgress ye the commandments of the LORD, that ye cannot prosper ? because ye have forsaken the LORD, he hath also forsaken you. 21 And they conspired against him, and stoned him with stones at the commandment of the king, in the court of the house of the LORD. 22 Thus Joash the king remembered not the kindness which Jehoiada his father had done to him, but slew his son. And when he died, he said, The LORD look upon *it*, and require *it*. 23 And it came to pass at the end of the year, *that* the host of Syria came up against him: and they came to

Judah and Jerusalem, and destroyed all the princes of the people from among the people, and sent all the spoil of them unto the king of Damascus. 24 For the army of the Syrians came with a small company of men, and the LORD delivered a very great host into their hand, because they had forsaken the LORD God of their fathers. So they executed judgment against Joash.

Neh. 9: 25 They took strong cities, and a fat land, and possessed houses full of all goods, wells digged, vineyards and olive-yards, and fruit-trees in abundance: so they did eat, and were filled, and became fat, and delighted themselves in thy great goodness. 26 Nevertheless, they were disobedient, and rebelled against thee, and cast thy law behind their backs, and slew thy prophets which testified against them to turn them to thee, and they wrought great provocations. 27 Therefore thou deliveredst them into the hand of their enemies, who vexed them: and in the time of their trouble, when they cried unto thee, thou heardest *them* from heaven; and according to thy manifold mercies thou gavest them saviours, who saved them out of the hand of their enemies. 28 But after they had rest, they did evil again before thee: therefore leftest thou them in the hand of their enemies, so that they had the dominion over them: yet when they returned and cried unto thee, thou heardest *them* from heaven; and many times didst thou deliver them according to thy mercies: 29 And testifiedst against them, that thou mightest bring them again unto thy law: yet they dealt proudly, and hearkened not unto thy commandments, but sinned against thy judgments, (which if a man do, he shall live in them;) and withdrew the shoulder, and hardened their neck, and would not hear. 30 Yet many years didst thou forbear them, and testifiedst against them by thy Spirit in thy prophets: yet would they not give ear: therefore gavest thou them into the hand of the people of the lands.

Jer. 44: 6 My fury and mine anger was poured forth, and was kindled in the cities of Judah and in the streets of Jerusalem; and they are wasted *and* desolate, as at this day. 7 Therefore now thus saith the LORD, the God of hosts, the God of Israel; Wherefore commit ye *this* great evil against your souls, to cut off from you man and woman, child and suckling, out of Judah, to leave you none to remain: 8 In that ye provoke me unto wrath with the works of your hands, burning incense unto other gods in the land of Egypt, whither ye be gone to dwell, that ye might cut yourselves off, and that ye might be a curse and a reproach among all the nations of the earth? 9 Have ye forgotten the wickednesss of your fathers, and the wickedness of the kings of Judah, and the wickedness of their wives, and your own wickedness, and the wickedness of your wives, which they have committed in the land of Judah, and in the streets of Jerusalem ? 10 They are not humbled *even* unto this day, neither have they feared, nor walked in my law, nor in my statutes, that I set before you and before your fathers. 11 Therefore thus saith the LORD of hosts, the God of Israel ; Behold, I will set my face against you for evil, and to cut off all Judah.

Ezk. 39: 23 The heathen shall know that the house of Israel went into captivity for their iniquity : because they trespassed against me, therefore hid I my face from them, and gave them into the hand of their enemies : so fell they all by the sword. [Lev. 26: 14—39. Dt. 28: 15—67. Neh. 9: 27—30. Jer. 25: 8—14, and 44: 6—11.]

[See 87, 303, 362, 381, 566, 630, 733, and Threats, in the Index.]

NEUTRALITY.

487. *Neutrality towards Christ and his cause apparent, not real.*

1 K. 18: 21 Elijah came unto all the people, and said, How long halt ye between two opinions ? if the LORD *be* God, follow him : but if Baal, *then* follow him. And the people answered him not a word.

Mat. 12: 30 He that is not with me, is against me ; and he that gathereth not with me, scattereth abroad.

Mk. 9: 40 He that is not against us, is on our part.

Rev. 3: 15 I know thy works, that thou art neither cold nor hot : I would thou wert cold or hot. 16 Because thou art lukewarm, and neither cold nor hot, I will spue thee out of my mouth.

OPPRESSION.

488. *Specimens of ancient oppression.*

Ex. 5: 15 Then the officers of the children of Israel came and cried unto Pharaoh, saying, Wherefore dealest thou thus with thy servants ? 16 There is no straw given unto thy servants, and they say to us, Make brick : and behold, thy servants *are* beaten ; but the fault *is* in thine own people. 17 But he said, Ye *are* idle, *ye are* idle : therefore ye say, Let us go, *and* do sacrifice to the LORD. 18 Go therefore now, *and* work:

for there shall no straw be given you, yet shall ye deliver the
tale of bricks.   19 And the officers of the children of Israel
did see *that* they *were* in evil *case*, after it was said, Ye shall
not minish *aught* from your bricks of your daily task.

Ezk. 22: 27 Her princes in the midst thereof *are* like wolves
ravening the prey, to shed blood, *and* to destroy souls, to get
dishonest gain.   28 And her prophets have daubed them with
untempered *mortar*, seeing vanity, and divining lies unto them,
saying, Thus saith the Lord GOD, when the LORD hath not
spoken.   29 The people of the land have used oppression, and
exercised robbery, and have vexed the poor and needy : yea,
they have oppressed the stranger wrongfully.

Mic. 3: 2 Who hate the good, and love the evil ; who pluck
off their skin from off them, and their flesh from off their
bones ; 3 Who also eat the flesh of my people, and flay their
skin from off them ; and they break their bones, and chop them
in pieces, as for the pot, and as flesh within the caldron.

Nah. 3: 1 Wo to the bloody city! it *is* all full of lies *and*
robbery ; the prey departeth not.   [See 200(7), 681, 682.]

489. *Effects of oppression upon oppressors.*

Pr. 21: 7 The robbery of the wicked shall destroy them ;
because they refuse to do judgment.

Is. 30: 12 Thus saith the Holy One of Israel, Because ye
despise this word, and trust in oppression and perverseness, and
stay thereon : 13 Therefore this iniquity shall be to you as a
breach ready to fall, swelling out in a high wall, whose breaking cometh suddenly at an instant.   [See 733.]

490. *God notices and hates oppressors — Threats.*

Ex. 3: 7 The LORD said, I have surely seen the affliction
of my people which *are* in Egypt, and have heard their cry by
reason of their taskmasters ; for I know their sorrows : 9 Now
therefore, behold, the cry of the children of Israel is come unto
me : and I have also seen the oppression wherewith the Egyptians oppress them.

Job 27: 13 This *is* the portion of a wicked man with God,
and the heritage of oppressors, *which* thay shall receive of
the Almighty.   14 If his children be multiplied, *it is* for the
sword : and his offspring shall not be satisfied with bread.

Ps. 12: 5 For the oppression of the poor, for the sighing of
the needy, now will I arise, saith the LORD ; I will set *him* in
safety *from him that* puffeth at him. — 72: 4 He shall judge the
poor of the people, he shall save the children of the needy, and
shall break in pieces the oppressor.

Pr. 14: 31 He that oppresseth the poor reproacheth his Maker: but he that honoreth him hath mercy on the poor.

Ec. 5: 8 If thou seest the oppression of the poor, and violent perverting of judgment and justice in a province, marvel not at the matter: for *he that is* higher than the highest regardeth; and *there be* higher than they.

Is. 61: 8 For I the Lord love judgment, I hate robbery for burnt-offering.

Jer. 5: 27 As a cage is full of birds, so *are* their houses full of deceit: therefore they are become great, and waxen rich. 28 They are waxen fat, they shine: yea, they overpass the deeds of the wicked: they judge not the cause, the cause of the fatherless, yet they prosper; and the right of the needy do they not judge. 29 Shall I not visit for these *things?* saith the Lord: shall not my soul be avenged on such a nation as this?

Ezk. 18: 10 If he beget a son *that is* a robber, a shedder of blood, and *that* doeth the like to *any* one of these things, 12 Hath oppressed the poor and needy, hath spoiled by violence, hath not restored the pledge, and hath lifted up his eyes to the idols, hath committed abomination, 13 Hath given forth upon usury, and hath taken increase: shall he then live? he shall not live: he hath done all these abominations; he shall surely die; his blood shall be upon him. — 22: 12 In thee have they taken gifts to shed blood; thou hast taken usury and increase, and thou hast greedily gained of thy neighbors by extortion, and hast forgotten me, saith the Lord God. 13 Behold, therefore I have smitten mine hand at thy dishonest gain which thou hast made, and at thy blood which hath been in the midst of thee. 14 Can thy heart endure or can thy hands be strong, in the days that I shall deal with thee? I the Lord have spoken *it*, and will do *it*. 29 The people of the land have used oppression, and exercised robbery, and have vexed the poor and needy: yea, they have oppressed the stranger wrongfully. 31 Therefore have I poured out mine indignation upon them; I have consumed them with the fire of my wrath: their own way have I recompensed upon their heads, saith the Lord God.

Jam. 2: 13 He shall have judgment without mercy that hath shewed no mercy; and mercy rejoiceth against judgment. — 5: 4 Behold, the hire of the laborers who have reaped down your fields, which is of you kept back by fraud, crieth; and the cries of them which have reaped are entered into the ears of the Lord of Sabaoth. [See 523, 636, 679.]

To set an example, instruct and govern.

---

491. *Infatuation of oppressors.*

Ec. 7: 7 Surely oppression maketh a wise man mad.

Am. 3: 10 They know not to do right, saith the LORD, who store up violence and robbery in their palaces. [See 707.]

PARENTS.

} 492. *Parents should set a good example.*

Jos. 24: 15 As for me and my house, we will serve the LORD.

Ps. 101: 2 I will behave myself wisely in a perfect way. O when wilt thou come unto me? I will walk within my house with a perfect heart.

Tit. 2: 7 In all things shewing thyself a pattern of good works. [See 178.]

493. *Parents should instruct and govern their children.*

Ex. 10: 2 That thou mayest tell in the ears of thy son, and of thy son's son, what things I have wrought in Egypt, and my signs which I have done among them; that ye may know how that I *am* the LORD.

Dt. 6: 6 These words which I command thee this day, shall be in thine heart: 7 And thou shalt teach them diligently unto thy children, and shalt talk of them when thou sittest in thine house, and when thou walkest by the way, and when thou liest down, and when thou risest up. 8 And thou shalt bind them for a sign upon thine hand, and they shall be as frontlets between thine eyes. 9 And thou shalt write them upon the posts of thine house, and on thy gates. [Dt. 11: 18—21.] — 32: 46 He said unto them, Set your hearts unto all the words which I testify among you this day, which ye shall command your children to observe to do, all the words of this law.

Pr. 22: 6 Train up a child in the way he should go: and when he is old, he will not depart from it.

Is. 28: 9 Whom shall he teach knowledge? and whom shall he make to understand doctrine? *them that are* weaned from the milk, *and* drawn from the breasts.

Ep. 6: 4 Ye fathers, provoke not your children to wrath: but bring them up in the nurture and admonition of the Lord. [See 48.]

494. *Parents should correct children for disobedience.*

Pr. 10: 13 A rod is for the back of him that is void of understanding. — 13: 24 He that spareth his rod hateth his son: but he that loveth him chasteneth him betimes. — 19: 18 Chasten thy son while there is hope, and let not thy soul spare for his crying. — 22: 15 Foolishness *is* bound in the heart of a child; *but* the rod of correction shall drive it far from him. — 23: 13 Withhold not correction from the child: for *if* thou beatest him with the rod, he shall not die. 14 Thou shalt beat him with the rod, and shalt deliver his soul from hell. — 26: 3 A whip for the horse, a bridle for the ass, and a rod for the fool's back. — 29: 15 The rod and reproof give wisdom : but a child left *to himself* bringeth his mother to shame. 17 Correct thy son, and he shall give thee rest; yea, he shall give delight unto thy soul.

Heb. 12: 9 We have had fathers of our flesh which corrected *us*, and we gave *them* reverence: shall we not much rather be in subjection unto the Father of spirits, and live? [See 54.]

495. *Parents should provide for their children.*

2 Cor. 12: 14 Behold, the third time I am ready to come to you; and I will not be burdensome to you : for I seek not yours, but you. For the children ought not to lay up for the parents, but the parents for the children.

1 Tim. 5: 8 If any provide not for his own, and especially for those of his own house, he hath denied the faith, and is worse than an infidel.

496. *Happy result of parental faithfulness.*

Gen. 18: 19 I know him, that he will command his children and his household after him, and they shall keep the way of the LORD, to do justice and judgment; that the LORD may bring upon Abraham that which he hath spoken of him.

Ps. 37: 26 *He is* ever merciful, and lendeth, and his seed *is* blessed. — 102: 28 The children of thy servants shall continue, and their seed shall be established before thee.

Pr. 20: 7 The just *man* walketh in his integrity : his children *are* blessed after him. — 22: 6 Train up a child in the way he should go : and when he is old, he will not depart from it.

2 Tim. 1: 5 When I call to remembrance the unfeigned faith that is in thee, which dwelt first in thy grandmother Lois, and thy mother Eunice ; and I am persuaded that in thee also. [See 120.]

497. *Sad result of parental unfaithfulness — judicial visitation.*

Ex. 20: 5 I the LORD thy God *am* a jealous God, visiting the iniquity of the fathers upon their children unto the third and fourth *generation* of them that hate me. Jer. 32: 18.

Num. 14: 33 Your children shall wander in the wilderness

forty years, and bear your whoredoms, until your carcasses be wasted in the wilderness.

1 S. 3: 13 I have told him, that I will judge his house for ever, for the iniquity which he knoweth: because his sons made themselves vile, and he restrained them not. 1 K. 21: 21.

1 K. 16: 3 Behold, I will take away the posterity of Baasha, and the posterity of his house ; and will make thy house like the house of Jeroboam the son of Nebat.

Job 17: 5 He that speaketh flattery to *his* friends, even the eyes of his children shall fail. — 21: 17 How oft is the candle of the wicked put out ? and *how oft* cometh their destruction upon them ? *God* distributeth sorrows in his anger. 18 They are as stubble before the wind, and as chaff that the storm carrieth away. 19 God layeth up his iniquity for his children : he rewardeth him, and he shall know *it*.

Is. 14: 21 Prepare slaughter for his children for the iniquity of their fathers ; that they do not rise, nor possess the land, nor fill the face of the world with cities.

Hos. 4: 6 Seeing thou hast forgotten the law of thy God, I will also forget thy children. [See 733.]

PATIENCE.

498. *Patience required.*

Ps. 37: 1 Fret not thyself because of evil doers, neither be thou envious against the workers of iniquity. 7 Rest in the LORD, and wait patiently for him : fret not thyself because of him who prospereth in his way, because of the man who bringeth wicked devices to pass.

Lk. 21: 19 In your patience possess ye your souls.

Rom. 2: 7 To them who by patient continuance in well-doing, seek for glory, and honor, and immortality ; eternal life. — 12: 12 Rejoicing in hope ; patient in tribulation : continuing instant in prayer.

2 Cor. 6: 4 In all *things* approving ourselves as the ministers of God, in much patience.

1 Th. 5: 14 We exhort you, brethren, warn them that are unruly, comfort the feeble-minded, support the weak, be patient toward all *men*.

Heb. 6: 12 That ye be not slothful, but followers of them who through faith and patience inherit the promises. — 10: 36 Ye have need of patience, that, after ye have done the will of God, ye might receive the promise. — 12: 1 Let us run with patience the race that is set before us,   2 Looking unto Jesus, the author and finisher of *our* faith.

Jam. 1: 4 Let patience have *her* perfect work, that ye may be perfect and entire, wanting nothing.—5: 7 Be patient therefore, brethren, unto the coming of the Lord. Behold, the husbandman waiteth for the precious fruit of the earth, and hath long patience for it, until he receive the early and latter rain. 8 Be ye also patient; establish your hearts: for the coming of the Lord draweth nigh. 10 Take, my brethren, the prophets, who have spoken in the name of the Lord, for an example of suffering-affliction, and of patience. 11 Behold, we count them happy which endure. Ye have heard of the patience of Job, and have seen the end of the Lord; that the Lord is very pitiful, and of tender mercy.

1 Pet. 2: 20 What glory *is it*, if when ye be buffeted for your faults, ye shall take it patiently? but if, when ye do well, and suffer *for it*, ye take it patiently, this *is* acceptable with God.

2 Pet. 1: 5 Giving all diligence, add to your faith, virtue; and to virtue, knowledge;   6 And to knowledge, temperance; and to temperance, patience. [See 201, 437, 737.]

N. B. For examples of patience, see 62, 154, 660.

PEACE.

499. *A peaceable and gentle spirit required, encouraged, and exemplified.*

Ps. 34: 14 Depart from evil, and do good; seek peace, and pursue it.

Pr. 15: 1 A soft answer turneth away wrath: but grievous words stir up anger.

Jer. 29: 7 Seek the peace of the city whither I have caused you to be carried away captives, and pray unto the LORD for it: for in the peace thereof shall ye have peace.

Mat. 5: 9 Blessed *are* the peace-makers: for they shall be called the children of God.

Rom. 12: 10 *Be* kindly affectioned one to another with brotherly love; in honor preferring one another;   18 If it be possible, as much as lieth in you, live peaceably with all men. —14: 19 Let us therefore follow after the things which make for peace, and things wherewith one may edify another.

1 Cor. 7: 15 God hath called us to peace.

2 Cor. 13: 11 Finally, brethren, farewell. Be perfect, be of good comfort, be of one mind, live in peace: and the God of love and peace shall be with you.

Gal. 5: 22 The fruit of the Spirit is love, joy, peace, long-suffering, gentleness, goodness, faith,   23 Meekness, temperance: against such there is no law.

Ep. 4: 1 I therefore, the prisoner of the Lord, beseech you that ye walk worthy of the vocation wherewith ye are called, 2 With all lowliness and meekness, with long-suffering, forbearing one another in love ;   3 Endeavoring to keep the unity of the Spirit in the bond of peace.   32 And be ye kind one to another, tender-hearted, forgiving one another, even as God for Christ's sake hath forgiven you.

Ph. 2: 14 Do all things without murmurings and disputings : 15 That ye may be blameless and harmless, the sons of God, without rebuke, in the midst of a crooked and perverse nation, among whom ye shine as lights in the world.

Col. 3: 8 Now ye also put off all these ; anger, wrath, malice, blasphemy, filthy communication out of your mouth.   15 And let the peace of God rule in your hearts, to the which also ye are called in one body ; and be ye thankful.

1 Th. 2: 7 We were gentle among you, even as a nurse cherisheth her children.—5: 13 Be at peace among yourselves.

2 Tim. 2: 24 And the servant of the Lord must not strive ; but be gentle unto all *men*, apt to teach, patient ;   25 In meekness instructing those that oppose themselves.

Heb. 12: 14 Follow peace with all *men*, and holiness, without which no man shall see the Lord.

Jam. 3: 17 The wisdom that is from above is first pure, then peaceable, gentle, *and* easy to be entreated, full of mercy and good fruits, without partiality, and without hypocrisy.

1 Pet. 3: 10 He that will love life, and see good days, let him refrain his tongue from evil, and his lips that they speak no guile :   11 Let him eschew evil, and do good : let him seek peace, and ensue it.   [See 62, 201, 437, 660, 737.]

500. *False peace-makers.*

Jer. 6: 14 They have healed also the hurt *of the daughter* of my people slightly, saying, Peace, peace ; when *there is* no peace.

Ezk. 13: 10 They have seduced my people, saying, Peace ; and *there was* no peace ; and one built up a wall, and lo, others daubed it with untempered *mortar :*   11 Say unto them which daub *it* with untempered *mortar*, that it shall fall : there shall be an overflowing shower ; and ye, O great hailstones, shall fall ; and a stormy wind shall rend *it*.   [See 191.]

PERFECTION.

501. *Commands and exhortations to be perfect in all good works.*

Mat. 5: 37 Let your communication be, Yea, yea; Nay, nay: for whatsoever *is* more than these cometh of evil. 38 Ye have heard that it hath been said, An eye for an eye, and a tooth for a tooth. 39 But I say unto you, That ye resist not evil: but whosoever shall smite thee on thy right cheek, turn to him the other also. 40 And if any man will sue thee at the law, and take away thy coat, let him have *thy* cloak also. 41 And whosoever shall compel thee to go a mile, go with him twain. 42 Give to him that asketh thee, and from him that would borrow of thee, turn not thou away. 43 Ye have heard that it hath been said, Thou shalt love thy neighbor, and hate thine enemy: 44 But I say unto you, Love your enemies, bless them that curse you, do good to them that hate you, and pray for them which despitefully use you, and persecute you; 45 That ye may be the children of your Father which is in heaven: for he maketh his sun to rise on the evil and on the good, and sendeth rain on the just and on the unjust. 46 For if ye love them which love you, what reward have ye? do not even the publicans the same? 47 And if ye salute your brethren only, what do ye more *than others?* do not even the publicans so? 48 Be ye therefore perfect, even as your Father which is in heaven is perfect.

Rom. 12: 1 I beseech you therefore, brethren, by the mercies of God, that ye present your bodies a living sacrifice, holy, acceptable unto God, *which is* your reasonable service. 2 And be not conformed to this world. 9 *Let* love be without dissimulation. Abhor that which is evil; cleave to that which is good. 10 *Be* kindly affectioned one to another with brotherly love; in honor preferring one another; 11 Not slothful in business; fervent in spirit; serving the Lord; 12 Rejoicing in hope; patient in tribulation; continuing instant in prayer; 13 Distributing to the necessity of saints; given to hospitality. 14 Bless them which persecute you; bless, and curse not. 15 Rejoice with them that do rejoice, and weep with them that weep. 16 *Be* of the same mind one toward another. Mind not high things, but condescend to men of low estate. Be not wise in your own conceits. 17 Recompense to no man evil for evil. Provide things honest in the sight of all men. 18 If it be possible, as much as lieth in you, live peaceably with all men. 19 Dearly beloved, avenge not yourselves, but *rather* give place unto wrath: for it is written, Vengeance *is*

mine; I will repay, saith the Lord. 20 Therefore, if thine
enemy hunger, feed him; if he thirst, give him drink: for in
so doing thou shalt heap coals of fire on his head. 21 Be not
overcome of evil, but overcome evil with good.

2 Cor. 7: 1 Having therefore these promises, dearly beloved,
let us cleanse ourselves from all filthiness of the flesh and
spirit, perfecting holiness in the fear of God.

Ep. 4: 25 Putting away lying, speak every man truth with
his neighbor: for we are members one of another. 26 Be ye
angry, and sin not: let not the sun go down upon your wrath:
27 Neither give place to the devil. 28 Let him that stole,
steal no more: but rather let him labor, working with *his* hands
the thing which is good, that he may have to give to him that
needeth. 29 Let no corrupt communication proceed out of
your mouth, but that which is good to the use of edifying, that
it may minister grace unto the hearers. 31 Let all bitterness,
and wrath, and anger, and clamor, and evil-speaking, be put
away from you, with all malice: 32 And be ye kind one to
another, tender-hearted, forgiving one another, even as God for
Christ's sake hath forgiven you.—5: 1 Be ye therefore followers of God as dear children; 2 And walk in love, as
Christ also hath loved us, and hath given himself for us an
offering and a sacrifice to God for a sweet-smelling savor. 3
But fornication, and all uncleanness, or covetousness, let it not
be once named among you, as becometh saints; 4 Neither
filthiness, nor foolish talking, nor jesting, which are not couve-
nient: but rather giving of thanks. 11 And have no fellowship with the unfruitful works of darkness, but rather reprove
them. 15 See then that ye walk circumspectly, not as fools,
but as wise. 16 Redeeming the time, because the days are
evil.—6: 10 Finally, my brethren, be strong in the Lord, and
in the power of his might. 11 Put on the whole armor of
God, that ye may be able to stand against the wiles of the
devil. 12 For we wrestle not against flesh and blood, but
against principalities, against powers, against the rulers of the
darkness of this world, against spiritual wickedness in high
places. 13 Wherefore take unto you the whole armor of God,
that ye may be able to withstand in the evil day, and having
done all, to stand. 14 Stand therefore, having your loins girt
about with truth, and having on the breast-plate of righteousness; 15 And your feet shod with the preparation of the
gospel of peace; 16 Above all, taking the shield of faith,
wherewith ye shall be able to quench all the fiery darts of the
wicked. 17 And take the helmet of salvation, and the sword
of the Spirit, which is the word of God: 18 Praying always

with all prayer and supplication in the Spirit, and watching thereunto with all perseverance and supplication for all saints.

·1 Pet. 2: 21 For even hereunto were ye called: because Christ also suffered for us, leaving us an example, that ye should follow his steps: 22 Who did no sin, neither was guile found in his mouth. [See 285–6, 629.]

502. *Should perpetual moral perfection be pledged in a covenant with God?*

Ex. 24: 7 He took the book of the covenant, and read in the audience of the people: and they said, All that the LORD hath said will we do, and be obedient. 8 And Moses took the blood, and sprinkled *it* on the people, and said, Behold the blood of the covenant, which the LORD hath made with you concerning all these words.

Dt. 29: 10 Ye stand this day all of you before the LORD your God; your captains of your tribes, your elders, and your officers, *with* all the men of Israel, 11 Your little ones, your wives, and thy stranger that *is* in thy camp, from the hewer of thy wood, unto the drawer of thy water: 12 That thou shouldest enter into covenant with the LORD thy God, and into his oath, which the LORD thy God maketh with thee this day: 13 That he may establish thee to-day for a people unto himself, and *that* he may be unto thee a God, as he hath said unto thee, and as he hath sworn unto thy fathers, to Abraham, to Isaac, and to Jacob.

2 Ch. 15: 12 They entered into a covenant to seek the LORD God of their fathers with all their heart and with all their soul; 14 And they sware unto the LORD with a loud voice, and with shouting, and with trumpets, and with cornets. 15 And all Judah rejoiced at the oath: for they had sworn with all their heart, and sought him with their whole desire; and he was found of them: and the LORD gave them rest round about. —34: 31 And the king stood in his place, and made a covenant before the LORD, to walk after the LORD, and to keep his commandments, and his testimonies, and his statutes, with all his heart, and with all his soul, to perform the words of the covenant which are written in this book. 32 And he caused all that were present in Jerusalem and Benjamin to stand *to it.* And the inhabitants of Jerusalem did according to the covenant of God, the God of their fathers.

Neh. 10: 29 They clave to their brethren, their nobles, and entered into a curse, and into an oath, to walk in God's law, which was given by Moses the servant of God, and to observe and do all the commandments of the LORD our Lord, and his judgments and his statutes.

Ps. 76: 11 Vow, and pay unto the LORD your God.—119: 106 I have sworn, and I will perform *it*, that I will keep thy righteous judgments.

Jer. 50: 5 They shall ask the way to Zion with their faces thitherward, *saying*, Come and let us join ourselves to the LORD in a perpetual covenant *that* shall not be forgotten.

Ezk. 20: 37 I will cause you to pass under the rod, and I will bring you into the bond of the covenant. [2 K. 11: 17, Is. 56: 4.] [See 118.]

503. *The appellation, "perfect," applied to saints.*

Gen. 6: 9 These *are* the generations of Noah: Noah was a just man, *and* perfect in his generations, *and* Noah walked with God.

Job 1: 1 There was a man in the land of Uz, whose name *was* Job; and that man was perfect and upright, and one that feared God, and eschewed evil. 8 And the LORD said unto Satan, Hast thou considered my servant Job, that *there is* none like him in the earth, a perfect and an upright man, one that feareth God, and escheweth evil? [Job 2: 3.]

Ps. 37: 37 Mark the perfect *man*, and behold the upright: for the end of *that* man *is* peace.

Pr. 2: 21 The upright shall dwell in the land, and the perfect shall remain in it.—11: 5 The righteousness of the perfect shall direct his way: but the wicked shall fall by his own wickedness.

1 Cor. 2: 6 We speak wisdom among them that are perfect: yet not the wisdom of this world, nor of the princes of this world, that come to nought.

Ph. 3: 15 Let us therefore, as many as be perfect, be thus minded: and if in any thing ye be otherwise minded, God shall reveal even this unto you.

504. *Do saints attain any moral perfection in which God delights?*

Gen. 5: 24 Enoch walked with God, and he *was* not: for God took him.

Jos. 14: 14 Hebron therefore became the inheritance of Caleb the son of Jephunneh the Kenezite unto this day; because that he wholly followed the LORD God of Israel.

2 K. 20: 3 I beseech thee, O LORD, remember now how I have walked before thee in truth and with a perfect heart, and have done *that which is* good in thy sight. And Hezekiah wept sore.

Ps. 11: 7 The righteous LORD loveth righteousness; his countenance doth behold the upright. — 45: 13 The King's daughter *is* all glorious within: her clothing *is* of wrought gold. — 119: 1 Blessed *are* the undefiled in the way, who walk in the law of the LORD. — 147: 11 The LORD taketh pleasure in them that fear him, in those that hope in his mercy.

Pr. 8: 17 I love them that love me: and those that seek me early shall find me. — 11: 20 They that are of a froward heart *are* abomination to the LORD: but *such as are* upright in *their* way *are* his delight.

Jn. 13: 34 A new commandment I give unto you, That ye love one another; as I have loved you, that ye also love one another. — 16: 27 The Father himself loveth you, because ye have loved me, and have believed that I came out from God.

Rom. 13: 8 Owe no man any thing, but to love one another: for he that loveth another hath fulfilled the law. 10 Love worketh no ill to his neighbor: therefore love *is* the fulfilling of the law.

1 Th. 2: 10 Ye *are* witnesses, and God *also*, how holily, and justly, and unblamably we behaved ourselves among you that believe.

1 Jn. 3: 3 Every man that hath this hope in him purifieth himself, even as he is pure. — 4: 12 No man hath seen God at any time. If we love one another, God dwelleth in us, and his love is perfected in us. 17 Herein is our love made perfect, that we may have boldness in the day of judgment; because as he is, so are we in this world.

Rev. 19: 8 To her was granted that she should be arrayed in fine linen, clean and white: for the fine linen is the righteousness of saints. [See 94, 505, 584–5, 659, 672.]

505. *Can the "perfect love" of saints be blended with sin?*

Ps. 119: 2 Blessed *are* they that keep his testimonies, *and that* seek him with the whole heart. 3 They also do no iniquity: they walk in his ways.

Ezk. 36: 26 I will take away the stony heart out of your flesh, and I will give you a heart of flesh.

Mat. 6: 24 No man can serve two masters: for either he will hate the one, and love the other; or else he will hold to the one, and despise the other. Ye cannot serve God and mammon.

Rom. 13: 10 Love worketh no ill to his neighbor: therefore love *is* the fulfilling of the law.

Gal. 5: 16 *This* I say then, Walk in the Spirit, and ye shall not fulfil the lust of the flesh. 17 For the flesh lusteth against the Spirit, and the Spirit against the flesh: and these are contrary the one to the other.

1 Jn. 2: 15 If any man love the world, the love of the Father is not in him. — 3: 6 Whosoever abideth in him sinneth not. 9 Whosoever is born of God doth not commit sin; for his seed remaineth in him ; and he cannot sin, because he is born of God. — 4: 18 There is no fear in love; but perfect love casteth out fear: because fear hath torment. He that feareth, is not made perfect in love. [See 503.]

506. *Millennial perfection.*

Dt. 30: 6 The LORD thy God will circumcise thine heart, and the heart of thy seed, to love the LORD thy God with all thine heart, and with all thy soul, that thou mayest live.

Jer. 31: 33 This *shall be* the covenant that I will make with the house of Israel; After those days, saith the LORD, I will put my law in their inward parts, and write it in their hearts ; and will be their God, and they shall be my people. — 32: 39 And I will give them one heart and one way, that they may fear me for ever, for the good of them, and of their children after them :- 40 And I will made an everlasting covenant with them, that I will not turn away from them, to do them good ; but I will put my fear in their hearts, that they shall not depart from me. — 50: 20 In those days, and in that time, saith the LORD, the iniquity of Israel shall be sought for, and *there shall be* none ; and the sins of Judah, and they shall not be found : for I will pardon them whom I reserve. [See 441.]

507. *Inconstant perfection of saints in this life.*

2 Ch. 6: 36 If they sin against thee, (for *there is* no man which sinneth not,) and thou be angry with them, and deliver them over before *their* enemies, and they carry them away captives unto a land far off or near.

Job 9: 20 If I justify myself, mine own mouth shall condemn me : *If I say*, I *am* perfect, it shall also prove me perverse. — 40: 4 Behold, I am vile ; what shall I answer thee ? I will lay my hand upon my mouth. — 42: 5 I have heard of thee by the hearing of the ear: but now mine eye seeth thee : 6 Wherefore I abhor *myself*, and repent in dust and ashes.

Ps. 19: 12 Who can understand *his* errors ? cleanse thou me from secret *faults.* 13 Keep back thy servant also from presumptuous *sins ;* let them not have dominion over me. — 38: 4 Mine iniquities are gone over mine head : as a heavy burden they are too heavy for me. 5 My wounds stink, *and* are corrupt because of my foolishness. [6—8.] — 119: 96 I have seen an end of all perfection : *but* thy commandment *is* exceeding broad.

Pr. 20: 9 Who can say, I have made my heart clean, I am pure from my sin ?

Ec. 7: 20 *There is* not a just man upon earth, that doeth good and sinneth not.

Is. 6: 5 Then said I, Wo *is* me! for I am undone; because I *am* a man of unclean lips, and I dwell in the midst of a people of unclean lips : for mine eyes have seen the King, the LORD of hosts.

Mat. 6: 12 Forgive us our debts, as we forgive our debtors.
— 26: 72 Again he denied with an oath, I do not know the man. 73 And after a while came unto *him* they that stood by, and said to Peter, Surely thou also art *one* of them ; for thy speech bewrayeth thee. 74 Then began he to curse and to swear, *saying*, I know not the man.

Rom. 7: 14 We know that the law is spiritual: but I am carnal, sold under sin. 15 For that which I do, I allow not : for 'what I would, that do I not; but what I hate, that do I. [Verses 16—25.]

Gal. 5: 17 The flesh lusteth against the Spirit, and the Spirit against the flesh: and these are contrary the one to the other; so that ye cannot do the things that ye would.

Ph. 3: 12 Not as though I had already attained, either were already perfect: but I follow after, if that I may apprehend that for which also I am apprehended of Christ Jesus.

Jam. 3: 2 In many things we offend all. If any man offend not in word, the same *is* a perfect man, *and* able also to bridle the whole body.

1 Jn. 1: 8 If we say that we have no sin, we deceive ourselves, and the truth is not in us. [See 166, 663.]

508. *Real saints subjected to occasional afflictions and chastisements.*

Heb. 12: 5 Ye have forgotten the exhortation which speaketh unto you as unto children, My son, despise not thou the chastening of the Lord, nor faint when thou art rebuked of him : 6 For whom the Lord loveth he chasteneth, and scourgeth every son whom he receiveth. 7 If ye endure chastening, God dealeth with you as with sons : for what son is he whom the father chasteneth not? 8 But if ye be without chastisement, whereof all are partakers, then are ye bastards, and not sons.

Rev. 3: 19 As many as I love, I rebuke and chasten : be zealous therefore, and repent. [See 2, 3, 4.]

509. *Would God afflict his people, had they attained permanent moral perfection?*

Job 36: 8 If *they* be bound in fetters, *and* be holden in cords of affliction; 9 Then he sheweth them their work, and their transgressions that they have exceeded.

Is. 27: 7 Hath he smitten him, as he smote those that smote him? *or* is he slain according to the slaughter of them that are slain by him? 9 By this therefore shall the iniquity of Jacob be purged; and this *is* all the fruit to take away his sin.

Lam. 3: 32 Though he cause grief, yet will he have compassion according to the multitude of his mercies. 33 For he doth not afflict willingly, nor grieve the children of men.

Heb. 12: 10 They verily for a few days chastened *us* after their own pleasure: but he for *our* profit, that *we* might be partakers of his holiness.

510. *Self-deceived perfectionists.*

Pr. 30: 12 *There is* a generation *that are* pure in their own eyes, and *yet* is not washed from their filthiness.

Mat. 19: 20 The young man saith unto him, All these things have I kept from my youth up: what lack I yet? 21 Jesus said unto him, If thou wilt be perfect, go *and* sell that thou hast, and give to the poor, and thou shalt have treasure in heaven: and come *and* follow me. 22 But when the young man heard that saying, he went away sorrowful: for he had great possessions. [See 696; 703—4.]

PERSECUTION.

511. *The righteous reproached and persecuted.*

Neh. 4: 4 Hear, O our God; for we are despised.

Job 16: 10 They have gaped upon me with their mouth; they have smitten me upon the cheek reproachfully; they have gathered themselves together against me.

Ps. 14: 4 Have all the workers of iniquity no knowledge? who eat up my people *as* they eat bread, and call not upon the LORD. — 22: 6 I *am* a worm, and no man; a reproach of men, and despised of the people. 7 All they that see me laugh me to scorn: they shoot out the lip, they shake the head, *saying*, 8 He trusted on the LORD *that* he would deliver him: let him deliver him, seeing he delighted in him. — 31: 11 I was a reproach among all mine enemies, but especially among my neighbors, and a fear to mine acquaintance: they that did see me without fled from me. 13 For I have heard the slander of many: fear *was* on every side: while

For Righteousness' sake.

they took counsel together against me, they devised to take away my life. — 42: 10 *As* with a sword in my bones, mine enemies reproach me; while they say daily unto me, Where *is* thy God? — 44: 22 Yea, for thy sake are we killed all the day long; we are counted as sheep for the slaughter. — 64: 2 Hide me from the secret counsel of the wicked; from the insurrection of the workers of iniquity: 3 Who whet their tongue like a sword, *and* bend *their bows to shoot* their arrows, *even* bitter words: 4 That they may shoot in secret at the perfect: suddenly do they shoot at him, and fear not. — 69: 4 They that hate me without a cause are more than the hairs of mine head: they that would destroy me, *being* mine enemies wrongfully, are mighty: then I restored *that* which I took not away. 7 Because for thy sake I have borne reproach: shame hath covered my face. 8 I am become a stranger unto my brethren, and an alien unto my mother's children. 9 For the zeal of thine house hath eaten me up; and the reproaches of them that reproached thee are fallen upon me. 10 When I wept, *and chastened* my soul with fasting, that was to my reproach. 19 Thou hast known my reproach, and my shame, and my dishonor: mine adversaries *are* all before thee. 20 Reproach hath broken my heart; and I am full of heaviness: and I looked *for some* to take pity, but *there was* none; and for comforters, but I found none. — 79: 4 We are become a reproach to our neighbors, a scorn and derision to them that are round about us. — 89: 50 Remember, Lord, the reproach of thy servants; *how* I do bear in my bosom *the reproach of* all the mighty people; 51 Wherewith thine enemies have reproached, O LORD; wherewith they have reproached the footsteps of thine anointed. — 102: 8 Mine enemies reproach me all the day; *and* they that are mad against me are sworn against me.

Dan. 7: 25 He shall speak *great* words against the Most High, and shall wear out the saints of the Most High, and think to change times and laws: and they shall be given into his hand until a time and times and the dividing of time.

Jn. 10: 20 And many of them said, He [Christ] hath a devil, and is mad; why hear ye him?

Heb. 11: 36 Others had trial of *cruel* mockings and scourgings, yea, moreover of bonds and imprisonment: 37 They were stoned, they were sawn asunder, were tempted, were slain with the sword: they wandered about in sheep-skins, and goat-skins; being destitute, afflicted, tormented; 38 (Of whom the world was not worthy:) they wandered in deserts, and *in* mountains, and *in* dens and caves of the earth.

Rev. 7: 14 I said unto him, Sir, Thou knowest. And he said to me, These are they which came out of great tribulation, and have washed their robes, and made them white in the blood of the Lamb. [See 68, 86, 467, 740.]

512. *Ultimate triumph of those persecuted for righteousness' sake.*

– Ps. 64: 10 The righteous shall be glad in the LORD, and shall trust in him ; and all the upright in heart shall glory. — 68: 13 Though ye have lien among the pots, *yet shall ye be as* the wings of a dove covered with silver, and her feathers with yellow gold.

Mat. 5: 10 Blessed *are* they which are persecuted for righteousness' sake : for theirs is the kingdom of heaven. 11 Blessed are ye when *men* shall revile you, and persecute *you*, and shall say all manner of evil against you falsely, for my sake. 12 Rejoice, and be exceeding glad : for great *is* your reward in heaven : for so persecuted they the prophets which were before you.

Rom. 8: 17 If children, then heirs : heirs of God, and joint-heirs with Christ ; if so be that we suffer with *him*, that we may be also glorified together. 18 For I reckon, that the sufferings of this present time *are* not worthy *to be compared* with the glory which shall be revealed in us.

2 Tim. 2: 12 If we suffer, we shall also reign with *him :* if we deny *him*, he also will deny us.

1 Pet. 4: 12 Beloved, think it not strange concerning the fiery trial which is to try you, as though some strange thing happened unto you : 13 But rejoice, inasmuch as ye are partakers of Christ's sufferings ; that, when his glory shall be revealed, ye may be glad also with exceeding joy. 14 If ye be reproached for the name of Christ, happy *are ye ;* for the Spirit of glory and of God resteth upon you. On their part he is evil spoken of, but on your part he is glorified.

Rev. 15: 3 They sing the song of Moses the servant of God, and the song of the Lamb. [See 4, 337.]

513. *God will abase persecutors.*

Ps. 37: 12 The wicked plotteth against the just, and gnasheth upon him with his teeth. 13 The LORD shall laugh at him ; for he seeth that his day is coming. 14 The wicked have drawn out the sword, and have bent their bow, to cast down the poor and needy, *and* to slay such as be of upright conversation. 15 Their sword shall enter into their own heart, and their bows shall be broken. — 47: 3 He shall subdue the people under us, and the nations under our feet.

Is. 41: 11 Behold, all they that were incensed against thee shall be ashamed and confounded: they shall be as nothing; and they that strive with thee shall perish. [12.] — 51: 7 Hearken unto me, ye that know righteousness, the people in whose heart *is* my law; fear ye not the reproach of men, neither be ye afraid of their revilings. 8 For the moth shall eat them up like a garment, and the worm shall eat them like wool. — 54: 17 No weapon that is formed against thee shall prosper, and every tongue *that* shall rise against thee in judgment thou shalt condemn. This *is* the heritage of the servants of the LORD, and their righteousness *is* of me, saith the LORD. 60: 14 The sons also of them that afflicted thee shall come bending unto thee: and all they that despised thee shall bow themselves down at the soles of thy feet. — 66: 5 Hear the word of the LORD, ye that tremble at his word; Your brethren that hated you, that cast you out for my name's sake, said, Let the LORD be glorified: but he shall appear to your joy, and they shall be ashamed.

Jer. 20: 11 The LORD *is* with me as a mighty terrible one: therefore my persecutors shall stumble, and they shall not prevail; they shall be greatly ashamed; for they shall not prosper: *their* everlasting confusion shall never be forgotten.

Mic. 7: 9 I will bear the indignation of the LORD, because I have sinned against him, until he plead my cause, and execute judgment for me: he will bring me forth to the light, *and* I shall behold his righteousness. 10 Then *she that is* mine enemy shall see *it*, and shame shall cover her, which said unto me, Where is the LORD thy God? mine eyes shall behold her: now shall she be trodden down as the mire of the streets.

Mal. 4: 2 Unto you that fear my name, shall the Sun of righteousness arise with healing in his wings; and ye shall go forth and grow up as calves of the stall. 3 And ye shall tread down the wicked; for they shall be ashes under the soles of your feet in the day that I shall do *this*, saith the LORD of hosts.

Rom. 16: 20 The God of peace shall bruise Satan under your feet shortly.

2 Th. 1: 4 We ourselves glory in you in the churches of God, for your patience and faith in all your persecutions and tribulations that ye endure: 5 *Which is* a manifest token of the righteous judgment of God, that ye may be counted worthy of the kingdom of God, for which ye also suffer: 6 Seeing *it is* a righteous thing with God to recompense tribulation to them that trouble you: 7 And to you, who are troubled, rest with

us, when the Lord Jesus shall be revealed from heaven with his mighty angels, 8 In flaming fire taking vengeance on them that know not God, and that obey not the gospel of our Lord Jesus Christ.

Rev. 3: 9 Behold, I will, make them of the synagogue of Satan, which say they are Jews, and are not, but do lie; behold I will make them to come and worship before thy feet, and to know that I have loved thee. — 18: 20 Rejoice over her, *thou* heaven, and *ye* holy apostles and prophets; for God hath avenged you on her.— 19: 3 And again they said, Alleluia. And her smoke rose up for ever and ever.

[See 87, 525, 550, 573,(7.)]

PERSEVERANCE.

514. *Perseverance in holiness indispensable.*

Mat. 10: 22 Ye shall be hated of all *men* for my name's sake: but he that endureth to the end shall be saved. [Mat. 24: 13.]

Jn. 15: 6 If a man abide not in me, he is cast forth as a branch, and is withered; and men gather them, and cast *them* into the fire, and they are burned.

Rom. 2: 6 Who will render to every man according to his deeds: 7 To them who by patient continuance in well-doing, seek for glory, and honor, and immortality; eternal life.

1 Cor. 9: 27 I keep under my body, and bring *it* into subjection: lest that by any means when I have preached to others, I myself should be a cast-away.— 10: 12 Let him that thinketh he standeth, take heed lest he fall.

Col. 1: 23 If ye continue in the faith grounded and settled, and *be* not moved away from the hope of the gospel, which ye have heard, *and* which was preached to every creature which is under heaven; whereof I Paul am made a minister.

Heb. 3: 6 Christ as a Son over his own house: whose house are we, if we hold fast the confidence, and the rejoicing of the hope firm unto the end. 12 Take heed, brethren, lest there be in any of you an evil heart of unbelief, in departing from the living God. 13 But exhort one another daily while it is called Today; lest any of you be hardened through the deceitfulness of sin. 14 For we are made partakers of Christ, if we hold the beginning of our confidence steadfast unto the end. — 4: 1 Let us therefore fear, lest a promise being left *us* of entering into his rest, any of you should seem to come short of it. 11 Let us labor therefore to enter into that rest, lest any man fall after the same example of unbelief.

2 Pet. 1: 10 Wherefore the rather, brethren, give diligence to make your calling and election sure: for if ye do these things ye shall never fall.

Rev. 2: 10 Be thou faithful unto death, and I will give thee a crown of life. 11 He that hath an ear, let him hear what the Spirit saith unto the churches; He that overcometh, shall not be hurt of the second death. 17 He that hath an ear, let him hear what the Spirit saith unto the churches: To him that overcometh will I give to eat of the hidden manna, and will give him a white stone, and in the stone a new name written, which no man knoweth, saving he that receiveth *it*. 26 And he that overcometh, and keepeth my works unto the end, to him will I give power over the nations. — 21: 7 He that overcometh shall inherit all things; and I will be his God, and he shall be my son. [Rev. 3: 5, 12: 21, and 2: 7.]

[See 19, 20, 540.]

515. *Predictions and promises of saints' perseverance.*

Job 17: 9 The righteous also shall hold on his way, and he that hath clean hands shall be stronger and stronger.

Ps. 37: 23 The steps of a *good* man are ordered by the Lord: and he delighteth in his way. 24 Though he fall, he shall not be utterly cast down: for the Lord upholdeth *him with* his hand. — 89: 30 If his children forsake my law, and walk not in my judgments; 31 If they break my statutes, and keep not my commandments ; 32 Then will I visit their transgression with the rod, and their iniquity with stripes. 33 Nevertheless, my loving kindness will I not utterly take from him, nor suffer my faithfulness to fail. 34 My covenant will I not break, nor alter the thing *that is* gone out of my lips. 35 Once have I sworn by my holiness that I will not lie unto David. 36 His seed shall endure for ever, and his throne as the sun before me. 37 It shall be established for ever as the moon, and *as* a faithful witness in heaven.

Pr. 4: 18 The path of the just *is* as the shining light, that shineth more and more unto the perfect day.

Is. 54: 10 The mountains shall depart, and the hills be removed: but my kindness shall not depart from thee, neither shall the covenant of my peace be removed, saith the LORD, that hath mercy on thee. — 55: 3 Incline your ear, and come unto me; hear, and your soul shall live: and I will make an everlasting covenant with you, *even* the sure mercies of David.

Jer. 32: 40 I will make an everlasting covenant with them, that I will not turn away from them to do them good; but

I will put my fear in their hearts, that they shall not depart from me.

Mat. 24: 24 There shall arise false Christs, and false prophets, and shall shew great signs and wonders; insomuch that, if *it were* possible, they shall deceive the very elect.·

Jn. 3: 16 God so loved the world, that he gave his only begotten Son, that whosoever believeth on him, should not perish, but have everlasting life. 36 He that believeth on the Son hath everlasting life: and he that believeth not the Son, shall not see life; but the wrath of God abideth on him. — 5: 24 Verily, verily, I say unto you, He that heareth my word, and believeth on him that sent me, hath everlasting life, and shall not come into condemnation; but is passed from death unto life. — 6: 39 This is the Father's will which hath sent me, that of all which he hath given me, I should lose nothing, but should raise it up again at the last day. 40 And this is the will of him that sent me, that every one which seeth the Son, and believeth on him, may have everlasting life: and I will raise him up at the last day. 47 Verily, verily, I say unto you, He that believeth on me hath everlasting life. 51 I am the living bread which came down from heaven: if any man eat of this bread, he shall live for ever: and the bread that I will give is my flesh, which I will give for the life of the world. 54 Whoso eateth my flesh, and drinketh my blood, hath eternal life; and I will raise him up at the last day. — 10: 27 My sheep hear my voice, and I know them, and they follow me: 28 And I give unto them eternal life; and they shall never perish, neither shall any pluck them out of my hand. 29 My Father, which gave *them* me, is greater than all; and none is able to pluck *them* out of my Father's hand.

Rom. 8: 30 Whom he did predestinate, them he also called; and whom he called, them he also justified: and whom he justified, them he also glorified. 38 For I am persuaded, that neither death, nor life, nor angels, nor principalities, nor powers, nor things present, nor things to come, 39 Nor height, nor depth, nor any other creature, shall be able to separate us from the love of God which is in Christ Jesus, our Lord.

Ph. 1: 6 Being confident of this very thing, that he which hath begun a good work in you, will perform *it* until the day of Jesus Christ.

2 Th. 2: 14 Whereunto he called you by our gospel, to the obtaining of the glory of our Lord Jesus Christ.

Heb. 6: 19 Which *hope* we have as an anchor of the soul, both sure and steadfast, and which entereth into that within the vail.

2 Tim. 4: 18 The Lord shall deliver me from every evil work, and will preserve *me* unto his heavenly kingdom; to whom *be* glory for ever and ever.

1 Pet. 1: 3 Blessed *be* the God and Father of our Lord Jesus Christ, which, according to his abundant mercy, hath begotten us again unto a lively hope by the resurrection of Jesus Christ from the dead, 4 To an inheritance incorruptible, and undefiled, and that fadeth not away, reserved in heaven for you, 5 Who are kept by the power of God through faith unto salvation, ready to be revealed in the last time. 9 Receiving the end of your faith, *even* the salvation of *your* souls.

1 Jn. 5: 18 We know that whosoever is born of God, sinneth not; but he that is begotten of God, keepeth himself, and that wicked one toucheth him not. [See 95, 667.]

516. *Christ's intercession for the saints.*

Lk. 22: 31 The Lord said, Simon, Simon, behold, Satan hath desired *to have* you, that he may sift *you* as wheat: 32 But I have prayed for thee, that thy faith fail not: and when thou art converted, strengthen thy brethren.

Jn. 17: 9 I pray for them: I pray not for the world, but for them which thou hast given me; for they are thine. 10 And all mine are thine, and thine are mine; and I am glorified in them. 11 And now I am no more in the world, but these are in the world, and I come to thee. Holy Father, keep through thine own name those whom thou hast given me, that they may be one, as we *are.* 12 While I was with them in the world, I kept them in thy name: those that thou gavest me I have kept, and none of them is lost, but the son of perdition; that the scripture might be fulfilled. 13 And now come I to thee, and these things I speak in the world, that they might have my joy fulfilled in themselves. 14 I have given them thy word; and the world hath hated them, because they are not of the world, even as I am not of the world. 15 I pray not that thou shouldest take them out of the world, but that thou shouldest keep them from the evil. 16 They are not of the world even as I am not of the world. 17 Sanctify them through thy truth: thy word is truth. 18 As thou hast sent me into the world, even so have I also sent them into the world. 19 And for their sakes I sanctify myself, that they also might be sanctified through the truth. 20 Neither pray I for these alone; but for them also which shall believe on me through their word: 21 That they all may be one; as thou, Father, *art* in me, and I in thee, that they also may be one in us: that the world may believe that thou hast sent me.

Rom. 8: 34 Who *is* he that condemneth ? *It is* [is it] Christ that died, yea rather, that is risen again, who is even at the right hand of God, who also maketh intercession for us.

Heb. 7: 25 He is able also to save them to the uttermost that come unto God by him, seeing he ever liveth to make intercession for them. — 9: 24 Christ is not entered into the holy places made with hands, *which are* the figures of the true ; but into heaven itself, now to appear in the presence of God for us.

517. *"Sealing" and "earnest of the Spirit."*

Rom. 8: 23 Not only *they*, but ourselves also, which have the first-fruits of the Spirit, even we ourselves groan within ourselves, waiting for the adoption, *to wit*, the redemption of our body.

2 Cor. 1: 21 He which establisheth us with you in Christ, and hath anointed us, *is* God ; 22 Who hath also sealed us, and given the earnest of the Spirit in our hearts.—5: 5 He that hath wrought us for the selfsame thing *is* God, who also hath given unto us the earnest of the Spirit.

Ep. 1: 13 In whom ye also *trusted*, after that ye heard the word of truth, the gospel of your salvation : in whom also, after that ye believed, ye were sealed with the Holy Spirit of promise, 14 Which is the earnest of our inheritance until the redemption of the purchased possession, unto the praise of his glory. — 4: 30 Grieve not that Holy Spirit of God, whereby ye are sealed unto the day of redemption.

2 Tim. 2: 19 The foundation of God standeth sure, having this seal, The Lord knoweth them that are his. [See 21.]

POPERY.

518. *Popery or the Romish hierarchy predicted.*

Dan. 7: 8 I considered the horns, and behold, there came up among them another little horn, before whom there were three of the first horns plucked up by the roots : and behold, in this horn *were* eyes like the eyes of man, and a mouth speaking great things. 24 And the ten horns out of this kingdom *are* ten kings *that* shall arise : and another shall rise after them ; and he shall be diverse from the first. and he shall subdue three kings. 25 And he shall speak *great* words against the Most High, and shall wear out the saints of the Most High, and think to change times and laws : and they shall be given into his hand until a time and times and the dividing of time. 26 But the judgment shall sit, and they shall take away his dominion to consume and destroy *it* unto the end.

2 Th. 2: 3 Let no man deceive you by any means: for *that day shall not come*, except there come a falling away first, and that man of sin be revealed, the son of perdition ; 4 Who opposeth and exalteth himself above all that is called God, or that is worshipped; so that he, as God, sitteth in the temple of God, shewing himself that he is God. 5 Remember ye not, that when I was yet with you, I told you these things ? 6 And now ye know what withholdeth that he might be revealed in his time. 7 For the mystery of iniquity doth already work : only he who now letteth *will let*, until he be taken out of the way. 8 And then shall that Wicked be revealed, whom the Lord shall consume with the spirit of his mouth, and shall destroy with the brightness of his coming : 9 *Even him*, whose coming is after the working of Satan, with all power, and signs, and lying wonders, 10 And with all deceivableness of unrighteousness in them that perish ; because they received not the love of the truth, that they might be saved.

1 Tim. 4: 1 The Spirit speaketh expressly, that in the latter times some shall depart from the faith, giving heed to seducing spirits, and doctrines of devils ; 2 Speaking lies in hypocrisy, having their conscience seared with a hot iron ; 3 Forbidding to marry, *and commanding* to abstain from meats, which God hath created to be received with thanksgiving of them which believe and know the truth.

Rev. 13: 11 I beheld another beast coming up out of the earth, and he had two horns like a lamb, and he spake as a dragon. 12 And he exerciseth all the power of the first beast before him, and causeth the earth and them which dwell therein to worship the first beast, whose deadly wound was healed. 13 And he doeth great wonders, so that he maketh fire come down from heaven on the earth in the sight of men, 14 And deceiveth them that dwell on the earth by *the means of* those miracles which he had power to do in the sight of the beast ; saying to them that dwell on the earth, that they should make an image to the beast, which had the wound by a sword, and did live. 15 And he had power to give life unto the image of the beast, that the image of the beast should both speak, and cause that as many as would not worship the image of the beast should be killed. 16 And he causeth all, both small and great, rich and poor, free and bond, to receive a mark in their right hand, or in their foreheads ; 17 And that no man might buy or sell, save he that had the mark, or the name of the beast, or the number of his name. 18 Here is wisdom. Let him that hath understanding count the number of the beast : for it is the number of a man ; and his number *is* Six hundred threescore *and* six. — 17: 1 There came one of the seven angels which had the seven vials, and talked with me, saying unto me, Come hither; I will shew unto thee the judgment of the great whore that sitteth upon many waters; 2 With whom the kings of the earth have committed fornication, and the inhabitants of the earth have been made drunk with the wine of her fornication. 3 So he carried me away in the spirit into the wilderness: and I saw a woman sit upon a scarlet-colored beast, full of names of blasphemy, having seven heads and ten horns. 4 And the woman was arrayed in purple and scarlet-color, and decked with gold and precious stones and pearls, having a golden cup in her hand full of abominations and filthiness of her fornication: 5 And upon her forehead-*was* a name written, MYSTERY, BABYLON THE GREAT, THE MOTHER OF HARLOTS AND ABOMINATIONS OF THE EARTH. 6 And I saw the woman drunken with the blood of the saints, and with the blood of the martyrs of Jesus: and when I saw her, I wondered with great admiration. 7 And the angel said unto me, Wherefore didst thou marvel? I will tell thee the mystery of the woman, and of the beast that carrieth her, which hath the seven heads, and ten horns. 18 And the woman which thou sawest is that great city, which reigneth over the kings of the earth.

519. *Was Peter made head of the apostles, or universal bishop?*

Mat. 16: 23 He turned, and said unto Peter, Get thee behind me, Satan; thou art an offence unto me: for thou savorest not the things that be of God, but those that be of men. — 20: 25 Jesus called them *unto him*, and said, Ye know that the princes of the Gentiles exercise dominion over them, and they that are great exercise authority upon them. 26 But it shall not be so among you: but whosoever will be great among you, let him be your minister; 27 And whosoever will be chief among you, let him be your servant: 28 Even as the Son of man came not to be ministered unto, but to minister, and to give his life a ransom for many.

Ac. 8: 14 When the apostles which were at Jerusalem heard that Samaria had received the word of God, they sent unto them Peter and John: 15 Who, when they were come down, prayed for them that they might receive the Holy Ghost. — 15: 6 The apostles and elders came together for to consider of this matter. 7 And when there had been much disputing, Peter rose up and said unto them, Men *and* brethren, ye know how that a good while ago, God made choice among us, that the Gentiles, by my mouth, should hear the word of the gospel, and believe. 12 Then all the multitude kept silence, and gave audience to Barnabas and Paul, declaring what miracles and wonders God had wrought among the Gentiles by them. 13 And after they had held their peace, James answered, saying, Men *and* brethren, hearken unto me. 14 Simeon hath declared how God at the first did visit the Gentiles, to take out of them a people for his name. 15 And to this agree the words of the prophets; as it is written, 16 After this I will return, and will build again the tabernacle of David which is fallen down; and I will build again the ruins thereof, and I will set it up: 17 That the residue of men might seek after the Lord, and all the Gentiles, upon whom my name is called, saith the Lord, who doeth all these things. 18 Known unto God are all his works from the beginning of the world. 19 Wherefore my sentence is, that we trouble not them, which from among the Gentiles are turned to God: 20 But that we write unto them that they abstain from pollutions of idols, and *from* fornication, and *from* things strangled, and *from* blood.

1 Pet. 5: 1 The elders which are among you I exhort, who am also an elder, and a witness of the sufferings of Christ, and also a partaker of the glory that shall be revealed.

520. *Dreadful end of Popery.*

Dan. 7: 11 I beheld then because of the voice of the great words which the horn spake: I beheld *even* till the beast was slain, and his body destroyed, and given to the burning flame. 26 But the judgment shall sit, and they shall take away his dominion to consume and to destroy *it* unto the end.

2 Th. 2: 8 Then shall that Wicked be revealed, whom the Lord shall consume with the spirit of his mouth, and shall destroy with the brightness of his coming.

Rev. 17: 16 The ten horns which thou sawest upon the beast, these shall hate the whore, and shall make her desolate and naked, and shall eat her flesh, and burn her with fire. — 18: 4 I heard another voice from heaven, saying, Come out of her, my people, that ye be not partakers of her sins, and that ye receive not of her plagues. 8 Therefore shall her plagues come in one day, death, and mourning, and famine; and she shall be utterly burned with fire: for strong *is* the Lord God who judgeth her.—19: 1 After these things I heard a great voice of much people in heaven, saying, Alleluia: Salvation, and glory, and honor, and power, unto the Lord our God: 2 For true and righteous *are* his judgments: for he hath judged the great whore, which did corrupt the earth with her fornication, and hath avenged the blood of his servants at her hand. 3 And again they said, Alleluia. And her smoke rose up for ever and ever. 20 And the beast was taken, and with him the false prophet that wrought miracles before him, with which he deceived them that had received the mark of the beast, and them that worshipped his image. These both were cast alive into a lake of fire burning with brimstone.

POVERTY.

521. *Evils of poverty.*

Pr. 10: 15 The rich man's wealth *is* his strong city : the destruction of the poor *is* their poverty. — 14: 20 The poor is hated even of his own neighbor, but the rich *hath* many friends. — 19: 7 All the brethren of the poor do hate him : how much more do his friends go far from him? he pursueth *them, with* words, *yet* they *are* wanting *to him.* — 22: 7 The rich ruleth over the poor, and the borrower *is* servant to the lender.

Ec. 9: 16 Then said I, Wisdom *is* better than strength : nevertheless the poor man's wisdom *is* despised, and his words are not heard.

522 *God pities and helps the poor.*

Dt. 10: 18 He doth execute the judgment of the fatherless and widow, and loveth the stranger, in giving him food and raiment.

Job 5: 15 He saveth the poor from the sword, from their mouth, and from the hand of the mighty. 16 So the poor hath hope, and iniquity stoppeth her mouth.

Ps. 10: 14 Thou hast seen *it ;* for thou beholdest mischief and spite, to requite *it* with thy hand : the poor committeth himself unto thee; thou art the helper of the fatherless. 17 LORD, thou hast heard the desire of the humble : thou wilt prepare their heart, thou wilt cause thine ear to hear : 18 To judge the fatherless and the oppressed, that the man of the earth may no more oppress. — 72: 12 He shall deliver the needy when he crieth : the poor also, and *him* that hath no helper. 13 He shall spare the poor and needy, and shall save the souls of the needy. 14 He shall redeem their soul from deceit and violence : and precious shall their blood be in his sight. — 102: 17 He will regard the prayer of the destitute, and not despise their prayer. — 140: 12 I know that the LORD will maintain the cause of the afflicted, *and* the right of the poor. — 146: 9 The LORD

God hates Oppressors.

preserveth the strangers; he relieveth the fatherless and widow: but the way of the wicked he turneth upside down. [See 224–5.]

523. *Oppression of the poor forbidden — Threats.*

Ex. 22: 21 Thou shalt neither vex a stranger, nor oppress him: for ye were strangers in the land of Egypt. 22 Ye shall not afflict any widow, or fatherless child.

Ps. 12: 5 For the oppression of the poor, for the sighing of the needy, now will I arise, saith the LORD; I will set *him* in safety *from him that* puffeth at him. — 72: 4 He shall judge the poor of the people, he shall save the children of the needy, and shall break in pieces the oppressor.

Pr. 21: 13 Whoso stoppeth his ears at the cry of the poor, he also shall cry himself, but shall not be heard. — 22: 16 He that oppresseth the poor to increase his *riches, and* he that giveth to the rich, *shall* surely *come* to want. 22 Rob not the poor, because he *is* poor: neither oppress the afflicted in the gate. — 23: 10 Remove not the old landmark; and enter not into the fields of the fatherless.

Is. 3: 15 What mean ye *that* ye beat my people to pieces, and grind the faces of the poor? saith the Lord GOD of hosts. — 10: 1 Wo unto them that decree unrighteous decrees, and that write grievousness *which* they have prescribed; 2 To turn aside the needy from judgment, and to take away the right from the poor of my people, that widows may be their prey, and *that* they may rob the fatherless! 3 And what will ye do in the day of visitation, and in the desolation *which* shall come from far? to whom will ye flee for help? and where will ye leave your glory?

Am. 8: 4 Hear this, O ye that swallow up the needy, even to make the poor of the land to fail, 5 Saying, When will the new-moon be gone, that we may sell corn? and the sabbath, that we may set forth wheat, making the ephah small, and the shekel great, and falsifying the balances by deceit? 6 That we may buy the poor for silver, and the needy for a pair of shoes; *yea,* and sell the refuse of the wheat. 7 The LORD hath sworn by the excellency of Jacob, Surely I will never forget any of their works.

Mal. 3: 5 I will come near to you to judgment: and I will be a swift witness against the sorcerers, and against the adulterers, and against false swearers, and against those that oppress the hireling in *his* wages, the widow, and the fatherless, and that turn aside the stranger *from his right* and fear not me, saith the LORD of hosts. [See 490, 679.]

524. *The poor often distinguished by God's special grace.*

Lk. 1: 52 He hath put down the mighty from *their* seats, and exalted them of low degree. 53 He hath filled the hungry with good things, and the rich he hath sent empty away. — 4: 18 The Spirit of the Lord *is* upon me, because he hath anointed me to preach the gospel to the poor ; he hath sent me to heal the broken-hearted, to preach deliverance to the captives, and recovering of sight to the blind, to set at liberty them that are bruised. — 10: 21 In that hour Jesus rejoiced in spirit, and said, I thank thee, O Father, Lord of heaven and earth, that thou hast hid these things from the wise and prudent, and hast revealed them unto babes : even so, Father ; for so it seemed good in thy sight. — 14: 21 So that servant came, and shewed his lord these things. Then the master of the house being angry, said to his servant, Go out quickly into the streets and lanes of the city, and bring in hither the poor, and the maimed, and the halt, and the blind.

1 Cor. 1: 26 Ye see your calling, brethren, how that not many wise men after the flesh, not many mighty, not many noble, *are called :* 27 But God hath chosen the. foolish things of the world to confound the wise; and God hath chosen the weak things of the world to confound the things which are mighty ; 28 And base things of the world, and things which are despised, hath God chosen, *yea,* and things which are not, to bring to nought things that are. 29 That no flesh should glory in his presence.

Jam. 2: 5 Hearken, my beloved brethren, Hath not God chosen the poor of this world rich in faith, and heirs of the kingdom which he hath promised to them that love him ?

525. *Future contrast between the humble poor, and their oppressors.*

1 S. 2: 8 He raiseth up the poor out of the dust, *and* lifteth up the beggar from the dunghill, to set *them* among princes, and to make them inherit the throne of glory.

Lk. 16: 25 Abraham said, Son, remember that thou in thy lifetime receivedst thy good things, and likewise Lazarus evil things : but now he is comforted, and thou art tormented.

[See 513, 550.]

526. *Duty to help the poor and the afflicted, and to avoid prejudice and partiality.*

Lev. 19: 9 When ye reap the harvest of your land, thou shalt not wholly reap the corners of thy field, neither shalt thou gather the gleanings of thy harvest. 10 And thou shalt not glean thy vineyard, neither shalt thou gather *every* grape of thy vineyard; thou shalt leave them for the poor and stranger: I *am* the Lord your God.—25: 35 If thy brother be waxen poor, and fallen in decay with thee; then thou shalt relieve him: *yea, though he be* a stranger, or a sojourner: that he may live with thee.

Dt. 15: 10 Thou shalt surely give him, and thine heart shall not be grieved when thou givest unto him: because that for this thing the LORD thy God shall bless thee in all thy works, and in all that thou puttest thine hand unto. 11 For the poor shall never cease out of the land: therefore I command thee, saying, Thou shalt open thine hand wide unto thy brother, to thy poor, and to thy needy, in thy land.

Dan. 4: 27 Wherefore, O king, let my counsel be acceptable unto thee, and break off thy sins by righteousness, and thine iniquities by shewing mercy to the poor; if it may be a lengthening of thy tranquillity.

Jam. 1: 27 Pure religion and undefiled before God and the Father is this, To visit the fatherless and widows in their affliction, *and* to keep himself unspotted from the world. — 2: 1 My brethren, have not the faith of our Lord Jesus Christ, *the Lord* of glory, with respect of persons. 2 For if there come unto your assembly, a man with a gold ring, in goodly apparel, and there come in also a poor man in vile raiment; 3 And ye have respect to him that weareth the gay clothing, and say unto him, Sit thou here in a good place; and say to the poor, Stand thou there, or sit here under my footstool: 4 Are ye not then partial in yourselves, and are become judges of evil thoughts? 5 Hearken, my beloved brethren, Hath not God chosen the poor of this world rich in faith, and heirs of the kingdom which he hath promised to them that love him? 6 But ye have despised the poor. Do not rich men oppress you, and draw you before the judgment-seats? 7 Do not they blaspheme that worthy name by the which ye are called? 8 If ye fulfil the royal law according to the scripture, Thou shalt love thy neighbor as thyself, ye do well: 9 But if ye have respect to persons, ye commit sin, and are convinced of the law as transgressors.

1 Jn. 3: 17 Whoso hath this world's good, and seeth his brother have need, and shutteth up his bowels *of compassion* from him, how dwelleth the love of God in him.

[See 7, 687.]

527. *Encouragements to help the poor.*

Ps. 41: 1 Blessed *is* he that considereth the poor: the LORD will deliver him in time of trouble. 2 The LORD will preserve him, and keep him alive; *and* he shall be blessed upon the earth: and thou wilt not deliver him unto the will of his enemies.

Ps. 112: 9 He hath dispersed, he hath given to the poor; his righteousness endureth for ever; his horn shall be exalted with honor.

Pr. 19: 17 He that hath pity upon the poor, lendeth unto the LORD; and that which he hath given will he pay him again. — 22: 9 He that hath a bountiful eye shall be blessed; for he giveth of his bread to the poor.

Mat. 5: 7 Blessed *are* the merciful: for they shall obtain mercy. — 25: 34 Then shall the King say unto them on his right hand, Come, ye blessed of my Father, inherit the kingdom prepared for you from the foundation of the world: 35 For I was an hungerd, and ye gave me meat: I was thirsty, and ye gave me drink: I was a stranger, and ye took me in: 36 Naked, and ye clothed me; I was sick, and ye visited me; I was in prison, and ye came unto me.

[See 354, 408, 630, 686.]

PRAISE TO GOD.

528. *Praising God in private and social worship required and exemplified.*

Ps. 9: 11 Sing praises to the LORD, which dwelleth in Zion, declare among the people his doings. — 22: 22 I will declare thy name unto my brethren: in the midst of the congregation will I praise thee. — 35: 18 I will give thee thanks in the great congregation: I will praise thee among much people. — 47: 6 Sing praises to God, sing praises: sing praises unto our King, sing praises. 7 For God *is* the King of all the earth: sing ye praises with understanding. — 95: 1 O come, let us sing unto the LORD: let us make a joyful noise to the Rock of our salvation. 2 Let us come before his presence with thanksgiving, and make a joyful noise unto him with psalms. 3 For the LORD *is* a great God, and a great King above all gods. — 100: 1 Make a joyful noise unto the LORD, all ye lands. 2 Serve the LORD with gladness: come before his presence with singing. 4 Enter into his gates with thanksgiving, *and* into his courts with praise: be thankful unto him *and* bless his name. 5 For the LORD *is* good; his mercy *is* everlasting; and his truth *endureth* to all generations. — 107: 31 O that *men* would praise the LORD *for* his goodness, and *for* his wonderful works to the children of men! 32 Let them exalt him also in the congregation of the people, and praise him in the assembly of the elders. — 150: 1 Praise ye the LORD. Praise God in

his sanctuary: praise him in the firmament of his power.   2
Praise him for his mighty acts: praise him according to his
excellent greatness.   3 Praise him with the sound of the
trumpet: praise him with the psaltery and harp.   4 Praise
him with the timbrel and dance: praise him with stringed instruments and organs.   5 Praise him upon the loud cimbals:
praise him upon the high-sounding cymbals.   6 Let every thing
that hath breath praise the LORD.   Praise ye the LORD.

Mat. 26: 30 When they had sung an hymn, they went out
into the mount of Olives.

Ac. 16: 25 At midnight Paul and Silas prayed, and sang
praises unto God: and the prisoners heard them.

Heb. 13: 15 By him therefore let us offer the sacrifice of
praise to God continually, that is, the fruit of *our* lips, giving
thanks to his name. [Ps. 57: 7—11, and 92: 1—4, and 96: 1—4.]
[See 747.]

529. *Praise should be offered with a devout heart.*

Ps. 111: 1 I will praise the LORD with *my* whole heart, in
the assembly of the upright, and *in* the congregation.

1 Cor. 14: 15 What is it then?   I will pray with the spirit,
and I will pray with the understanding also: I will sing with
the spirit, and I will sing with the understanding also.

Ep. 5: 19 Speaking to yourselves in psalms, and hymns, and
spiritual songs, singing and making melody in your heart to
the Lord.   20 Giving thanks always for all things unto God
and the Father, in the name of our Lord Jesus Christ.

Col. 3: 16 Let the word of Christ dwell in you richly in all
wisdom; teaching and admonishing one another in psalms,
and hymns, and spiritual songs, singing with grace in your
hearts to the Lord.   [See 333.]

PRAYER.

530. *Prayer an important and necessary duty.*

Job. 42: 8 Take unto you now seven bullocks and seven
rams, and go to my servant Job, and offer up for yourselves a
burnt-offering; and my servant Job shall pray for you: for
him will I accept: lest I deal with you *after your* folly, in that
ye have not spoken of me *the thing which is* right, like my
servant Job.

Is. 55: 6 Seek ye the LORD while he may be found, call ye
upon him while he is near. — 62: 6 I have set watchmen upon
thy walls, O Jerusalem, *which* shall never hold their peace day

nor night : ye that make mention of the LORD, keep not silence, 7 And give him no rest, till he establish, and till he make Je-- rusalem a praise in the earth.

Ezk. 36: 37 Thus saith the Lord GOD; I will yet *for* this be inquired of by the house of Israel, to do *it* for them ; I will increase them with men like a flock.

Mat. 5: 44 Pray for them which despitefully use you, and persecute you.—6: 9 After this manner therefore pray ye: Our Father which art in heaven, Hallowed be thy name. 10 Thy kingdom come. Thy will be done in earth as *it is* in heaven. 11 Give us this day our daily bread. 12 And for- give us our debts, as we forgive our debtors. 13 And lead us not into temptation, but deliver us from evil. For thine is the kingdom, and the power, and the glory, for ever.—26: 41 Watch and pray, that ye enter not into temptation: the spirit indeed *is* willing, but the flesh *is* weak.

Lk. 18: 1 He spake a parable unto them *to this end*, that men ought always *to* pray, and not to faint.

Ep. 6: 18 Praying always with all prayer and supplication in the Spirit, and watching thereunto with all perseverance and supplication for all saints.

Ph. 4: 6 Be careful for nothing ; but in every thing by prayer and supplication with thanksgiving let your requests be made known unto God.

Col. 4: 2 Continue in prayer, and watch in the same with thanksgiving.

1 Th. 3: 10 Night and day praying exceedingly that we might see your face, and might perfect that which is lacking in your faith?—5: 17 Pray without ceasing. 18 In every thing give thanks.

1 Tim. 2: 1 I exhort therefore, that, first of all, supplications, prayers, intercessions, *and* giving of thanks be made for all men : 2 For kings, and *for* all that are in authority ; that we may lead a quiet and peaceable life in all godliness and honesty. 3 For this *is* good and acceptable in the sight of God our Saviour. 8 I will therefore that men pray every where, lifting up holy hands, without wrath and doubting.

Heb. 4: 15 We have not a high priest which cannot be touched with the feeling of our infirmities: but was in all points tempted like as *we are*, *yet* without sin. 16 Let us therefore come-boldly unto the throne of grace, that we may obtain mercy, and find grace to help in time of need.

Jam. 5: 13 Is any among you afflicted? let him pray. 16 Confess *your* faults one to another, and pray one for another, that ye may be healed.

374

1 Pet. 4: 7 The end of all things is at hand: be ye therefore sober, and watch unto prayer. [See 64.]

531. *Secret prayer required and exemplified.*

Ps. 119: 62 At midnight I will rise to give thanks unto thee, because of thy righteous judgments.

Mat. 6: 6 When thou prayest, enter into thy closet, and when thou hast shut thy door, pray to thy Father which is in secret; and thy Father, which seeth in secret, shall reward thee openly.—14: 23 When he had sent the multitudes away, he went up into a mountain apart to pray: and when the evening was come, he was there alone.

Mk. 1: 35 In the morning, rising up a great while before day, he went out and departed into a solitary place, and there prayed.

Lk. 5: 16 He withdrew himself into the wilderness, and prayed. [See 665.]

532. *Mental prayer exemplified.*

1 S. 1: 12 It came to pass, as she continued praying before the LORD, that Eli marked her mouth. 13 Now Hannah she spake in her heart; only her lips moved, but her voice was not heard: therefore Eli thought she had been drunken. 14 And Eli said unto her, How long wilt thou be drunken? put away thy wine from thee. 15 And Hannah answered and said, No, my lord, I *am* a woman of a sorrowful spirit: I have drunk neither wine nor strong drink, but have poured out my soul before the LORD. 16 Count not thine handmaid for a daughter of Belial: for out of the abundance of my complaint and grief have I spoken hitherto.

Neh. 2: 4 The king said unto me, For what dost thou make request? So I prayed to the God of heaven. 5 And I said unto the king, If it please the king, and if thy servant have found favor in thy sight, that thou wouldest send me unto Judah, unto the city of my fathers' sepulchres, that I may build it.

533. *Prayer, verbal and audible, required and exemplified.*

1 K. 8: 22 Solomon stood before the altar of the LORD in the presence of all the congregation of Israel, and spread forth his hands toward heaven: 23 And he said, LORD God of Israel, *there is* no God like thee, in heaven above, or on earth beneath, who keepest covenant and mercy with thy servants that walk before thee with all their heart: 28 Yet have thou respect unto the prayer of thy servant, and to his

supplication, O Lord my God, to hearken unto the cry and to the prayer, which thy servant prayeth before thee to-day: 29 That thine eyes may be open toward this house night and day, *even* toward the place of which thou hast said, My name shall be there: that thou mayest hearken unto the prayer which thy servant shall make toward this place. 30 And hearken thou to the supplication of thy servant, and of thy people Israel, when they shall pray toward this place: and hear thou in heaven thy dwelling-place: and when thou hearest, forgive.

Ps. 55: 16 As for me, I will call upon God: and the Lord shall save me. 17 Evening, and morning, and at noon, will I pray, and cry aloud: and he shall hear my voice.—86: 3 Be merciful unto me, O Lord: for I cry unto thee daily.

Dan. 9: 19 O Lord, hear; O Lord, forgive; O Lord, hearken and do; defer not, for thine own sake, O my God: for thy city and thy people are called by thy name. 20 And while I was speaking, and praying, and confessing my sin, and the sin of my people Israel, and presenting my supplication before the Lord my God for the holy mountain of my God; 21 Yea, while I *was* speaking in prayer, even the man Gabriel, whom I had seen in the vision at the beginning, being caused to fly swiftly, touched me about the time of the evening oblation.

Hos. 14: 2 Take with you words, and turn to the Lord: say unto him, Take away all iniquity, and receive *us* graciously: so will we render the calves of our lips.

Joel 1: 14 Sanctify ye a fast, call a solemn assembly, gather the elders *and* all the inhabitants of the land *into* the house of the Lord your God, and cry unto the Lord.

Mat. 26: 39 He went a little further, and fell on his face, and prayed, saying, O my Father, if it be possible, let this cup pass from me: nevertheless, not as I will, but as thou *wilt.* 42 He went away again the second time, and prayed, saying, O my Father, if this cup may not pass away from me, except I drink it, thy will be done.

Mk. 8: 6 He commanded the people to sit down on the ground: and he took the seven loaves, and gave thanks, and brake, and gave to his disciples to set before *them;* and they did set *them* before the people.

Ac. 1: 24 They prayed, and said, Thou, Lord, which knowest the hearts of all *men,* shew whether of these two thou hast chosen.—7: 59 They stoned Stephen, calling upon *God,* and saying, Lord Jesus, receive my spirit. 60 And he kneeled down and cried with a loud voice, Lord, lay not this sin to their

376

charge. And when he had said this, he fell asleep.—20: 36 When he had thus spoken, he kneeled down, and prayed with them all. 37 And they all wept sore, and fell on Paul's neck, and kissed him.—27: 35 When he had thus spoken, he took bread, and gave thanks to God in presence of them all; and when he had broken *it*, he began to eat.

534. *Devout prayer includes love and obedience to God.*

Ps. 37: 4 Delight thyself also in the LORD; and he shall give thee the desires of thy heart.

Pr. 28: 9 He that turneth away his ear from hearing the law, even his prayer *shall be* abomination.

Jn. 9: 31 We know that God heareth not sinners: but if any man be a worshipper of God, and doeth his will, him he heareth.

1 Jn. 3: 22 Whatsoever we ask, we receive of him, because we keep his commandments, and do those things that are pleasing in his sight. [See 289.]

535. *Acceptable prayer includes faith in God.*

Heb. 10: 22 Let us draw near with a true heart, in full assurance of faith, having our hearts sprinkled from an evil conscience, and our bodies washed with pure water.—11: 6 Without faith *it is* impossible to please *him:* for he that cometh to God must believe that he is, and *that* he is a rewarder of them that diligently seek him.

Jam. 1: 5 If any of you lack wisdom, let him ask of God, that giveth to all *men* liberally, and upbraideth not; and it shall be given him. 6 But let him ask in faith, nothing wavering. For he that wavereth is like a wave of the sea driven with the wind and tossed. 7 For let not that man think that he shall receive any thing of the Lord. [See 293.]

536. *True prayer includes submission to God.*

Ps. 37: 7 Rest in the LORD, and wait patiently for him. —40: 1 I waited patiently for the LORD; and he inclined unto me, and heard my cry.

Mat. 6: 9 After this manner therefore pray ye: Our Father which art in heaven, Hallowed be thy name. 10 Thy kingdom come. Thy will be done in earth as *it is* in heaven.— 26: 39 He went a little further, and fell on his face, and prayed, saying, O my Father, if it be possible, let this cup pass from me: nevertheless, not as I will, but as thou *wilt.*

Lk. 22: 41 He was withdrawn from them about a stone's cast, and kneeled down, and prayed, 42 Saying, Father, if thou be willing, remove this cup from me : nevertheless, not my will, but thine, be done.

Ac. 21: 14 When he would not be persuaded, we ceased, saying, The will of the Lord be done. [See 278, 298.]

537. Prayer includes humility, confession, and repentance.

2 Ch. 7: 14 If my people, which are called by my name, shall humble themselves, and p_ra_y, and seek my face, and turn from their wicked ways ; then will I hear from heaven, and will forgive their sin, and will heal their land.—33: 12 When he was in affliction, he besought the LORD his God, and humbled himself greatly before the God of his fathers, 13 And prayed unto him : and he was entreated of him, and heard his supplication, and brought him again to Jerusalem into his kingdom. Then Manasseh knew that the LORD he *was* God.

Ps. 9: 12 When he maketh inquisition for blood, he remembereth them : he forgetteth not the cry of the humble.

Lk. 18: 13 The publican, standing afar off, would not lift up so much as *his* eyes unto heaven, but smote upon his breast, saying, God be merciful to me a sinner. · 14 I tell you, this man went down to his house justified *rather* than the other : for every one that exalteth himself shall be abased ; and he that humbleth himself shall be exalted.

[See 124, 356–7, 663.]

538. Prayer includes a supreme regard for God's glory.

1 K. 18: 36 It came to pass at *the time of* the offering of the *evening* sacrifice, that Elijah the prophet came near and said, LORD God of Abraham, Isaac, and of Israel, let it be known this day that thou *art* God in Israel, and *that* I *am* thy servant, and *that* I have done all these things at thy word. 37 Hear me, O LORD, hear me, that this people may know that thou *art* the LORD God, and *that* thou hast turned their heart back again.

Ps. 25: 11 For thy name's sake, O LORD, pardon mine iniquity ; for it *is* great.—79: 9 Help us, O God of our salvation, for the glory of thy name : and deliver us, and purge away our sins, for thy name's sake.—143: 11 Quicken me, O LORD, for thy name's sake : for thy righteousness' sake bring my soul out of trouble.

Is. 37: 20 O LORD our God, save us from his hand, that all the kingdoms of the earth may know that thou *art* the LORD, *even* thou only.

Dan. 9: 17 O our God, hear the prayer of thy servant, and

his supplications, and cause thy face to shine upon thy sanctuary that is desolate, for the Lord's sake. 18 O my God, incline thine ear, and hear: open thine eyes, and behold our desolations, and the city which is called by thy name: for we do not present our supplications before thee for our righteousness, but for thy great mercies. 19 O Lord, hear; O Lord, forgive; O Lord, hearken and do; defer not, for thine own sake, O my God: for thy city and thy people are called by thy name. [See 300, 662.]

539. *Acceptable prayer includes a forgiving temper.*

Mat. 6: 9 After this manner therefore pray ye: Our Father which art in heaven, Hallowed be thy name. 12 And forgive us our debts, as we forgive our debtors.

Mk. 11: 25 When ye stand praying, forgive, if ye have aught against any: that your Father also which is in heaven may forgive you your trespasses. 26 But, if ye do not forgive, neither will your Father which is in heaven forgive your trespasses.

Lk. 23: 34 Then said Jesus, Father, forgive them: for they know not what they do. [See 203.]

540. *Prayer includes importunity and perseverance.*

Gen. 32: 24 Jacob was left alone; and there wrestled a man with him, until the breaking of the day. 25 And when he saw that he prevailed not against him, he touched the hollow of his thigh: and the hollow of Jacob's thigh was out of joint, as he wrestled with him. 26 And he said, Let me go, for the day breaketh: And he said, I will not let thee go except thou bless me.

Is. 62: 1 For Zion's sake will I not hold my peace, and for Jerusalem's sake I will not rest, until the righteousness thereof go forth as brightness, and the salvation thereof as a lamp *that* burneth. 6 I have set watchmen upon thy walls, O Jerusalem, *which* shall never hold their peace day nor night: ye that make mention of the LORD, keep not silence, 7 And give him no rest, till he establish, and till he make Jerusalem a praise in the earth.

Lk. 6: 12 It came to pass in those days, that he went out into a mountain to pray, and continued all night in prayer to God. — 11: 5 He said unto them, Which of you shall have a friend, and shall go unto him at midnight, and say unto him, Friend, lend me three loaves: 6 For a friend of mine in his journey is come to me, and I have nothing to set before him? 7 And he from within shall answer and say, Trouble me not:

the door is now shut, and my children are with me in bed; I cannot rise and give thee. 8 I say unto you, though he will not rise and give him, because he is his friend, yet because of his importunity he will rise and give him as many as he needeth.—18: 1 He spake a parable unto them *to this end*, that men ought always *to* pray, and not to faint; 5 Yet, because this widow troubleth me, I will avenge her, lest by her continual coming she weary me. 7 And shall not God avenge his own elect, which cry day and night unto him, though he bear long with them? 8 I tell you that he will avenge them speedily.

Rom. 12: 12 Rejoicing in hope; patient in tribulation; continning instant in prayer.

Ep. 6:-18 Praying always with all prayer and supplication in the Spirit, and watching thereunto with all perseverance and supplication for all saints.

Col. 4: 2 Continue in prayer, and watch in the same with thanksgiving.

1 Th. 3: 10 Night and day praying exceedingly that we might see your face, and might perfect that which is lacking in your faith?—5: 17 Pray without ceasing. [See 514.]

541. *Prayer should be offered in Christ's name.*

Jn. 16: 24 Hitherto have ye asked nothing in my name: ask, and ye shall receive, that your joy may be full.

Col. 3: 17 Whatsoever ye do in word or deed, *do* all in the name of the Lord Jesus, giving thanks to God and the Father by him.

542. *Prayer implies godly sincerity.*

Ps. 145: 18 The LORD *is* nigh unto all them that call upon him, to all that call upon him in truth.

Is. 29: 13 The Lord said, Forasmuch as this people draw near *me* with their mouth, and with their lips do honor me, but have removed their heart far from me, and their fear toward me is taught by the precept of men: 14 Therefore behold, I will proceed to do a marvellous work among this people.

Jer. 29: 13 Ye shall seek me, and find *me*, when ye shall search for me with all your heart. [Dt. 4: 29.]

Mat. 15: 7 *Ye* hypocrites, well did Esaias prophesy of you, saying, 8 This people draweth nigh unto me with their mouth, and honoreth me with *their* lips; but their heart is far from me. [See 333.]

543. *Prayer implies holy sympathy and compassion.*

Pr. 21: 13 Whoso stoppeth his ears at the cry of the poor, he also shall cry himself, but shall not be heard.

Is. 58: 7 *Is it* not to deal thy bread to the hungry, and that thou bring the poor that are cast out to thy house? when thou seest the naked, that thou cover him; and that thou hide not thyself from thine own flesh? 9 Then shalt thou call, and the LORD shall answer.

544. *Various postures in prayer — (no sitting.)*

Ex. 9: 29 Moses said unto him, As soon as I am gone out of the city, I will spread abroad my hands unto the LORD; *and* the thunder shall cease, neither shall there be any more hail; that thou mayest know how that the earth *is* the LORD's.

1 K. 8: 22 Solomon stood before the altar of the LORD in the presence of all the congregation of Israel, and spread forth his hands toward heaven.

2 Ch. 6: 13 (Solomon had made a brazen scaffold, of five cubits long, and five cubits broad, and three cubits high, and had set it in the midst of the court: and upon it he stood, and kneeled down upon his knees before all the congregation of Israel, and spread forth his hands toward heaven.)

Mat. 26: 39 He went a little further, and fell on his face, and prayed, saying, O my Father, if it be possible, let this cup pass from me: nevertheless, not as I will, but as thou *wilt*.

Mk. 11: 25 When ye stand praying, forgive, if ye have aught against any.

Lk. 22: 41 He was withdrawn from them about a stone's cast, and kneeled down, and prayed, 42 Saying, Father, if thou be willing, remove this cup from me: nevertheless, not my will, but thine, be done.

Ac. 20: 36 When he had thus spoken, he kneeled down, and prayed with them all.

545. *Prayer heard and answered — its efficacy.*

Gen. 18: 32 He said, Oh, let not the LORD be angry, and I will speak yet but this once: Peradventure ten shall be found there. And he said, I will not destroy *it* for ten's sake. — 32: 28 He said, Thy name shall be called no more Jacob, but Israel: for as a prince hast thou power with God, and with men, and hast prevailed.

Hos. 12: 4 Yea, he had power over the angel, and prevailed: he wept, and made supplication unto him.

Ex. 32: 11 Moses besought the LORD his God, and said, LORD, why doth thy wrath wax hot against thy people, which thou hast brought forth out of the land of Egypt, with great power, and with a mighty hand? 14 And the LORD repented of the evil which he thought to do unto his people. [Dt. 9: 14, 18—20.]

Num. 11: 2 The people cried unto Moses; and when Moses prayed unto the LORD, the fire was quenched. — 14: 19 Pardon, I beseech thee, the iniquity of this people according unto the greatness of thy mercy, and as thou hast forgiven this people, from Egypt even until now. 20 And the LORD said, I have pardoned according to thy word.

Dt. 26: 7 When we cried unto the LORD God of our fathers, the LORD heard our voice, and looked on our affliction, and our labor, and our oppression: 8 And the LORD brought us forth out of Egypt with a mighty hand, and with an out-stretched arm, and with great terribleness, and with signs, and with wonders.

1 S. 1: 27 For this child I prayed; and the LORD hath given me my petition which I asked of him. — 12: 18 So Samuel called unto the LORD; and the LORD sent thunder and rain that day: and all the people greatly feared the LORD and Samuel.

1 K. 17: 22 The LORD heard the voice of Elijah; and the soul of the child came into him again, and he revived. — 18: 37 Hear me, O LORD, hear me, that this people may know that thou *art* the LORD God, and *that* thou hast turned their heart back again. 38 Then the fire of the LORD fell, and consumed the burnt-sacrifice, and the wood, and the stones, and the dust, and licked up the water that *was* in the trench.

2 K. 6: 18 When they came down to him, Elisha prayed unto the LORD, and said, Smite this people, I pray thee, with blindness. And he smote them with blindness, according to the word of Elisha. — 19: 20 Isaiah the son of Amoz sent to Hezekiah, saying, Thus saith the LORD God of Israel, *That* which thou hast prayed to me against Sennacherib king of Assyria I have heard. — 20: 5 Turn again, and tell Hezekiah the captain of my people, Thus saith the LORD, the God of David thy father, I have heard thy prayer, I have seen thy tears: behold, I will heal thee: on the third day thou shalt go up unto the house of the LORD. 6 And I will add unto thy days fifteen years; and I will deliver thee and this city out of the hand of the king of Assyria; and I will defend this city for mine own sake, and for my servant David's sake. 11 And Isaiah the prophet cried unto the LORD: and he brought the shadow ten degrees backward, by which it had gone down in the dial of Ahaz.

1 Ch. 4: 10 Jabez called on the God of Israel, saying, Oh that thou wouldest bless me indeed, and enlarge my coast, and that thine hand might be with me, and that thou wouldest keep *me* from evil, that it may not grieve me! And God granted him that which he requested.

Ps. 18: 6 In my distress I called upon the LORD, and cried unto my God: he heard my voice out of his temple, and my cry came before him, *even* into his ears. — 34: 4 I sought the LORD, and he heard me, and delivered me from all my fears. 5 They looked unto him, and were lightened: and their faces were not ashamed. 6 This poor man cried, and the LORD heard *him*, and saved him out of all his troubles. 10 The young lions do lack, and suffer hunger: but they that seek the LORD shall not want any good *thing.* 34:15 The eyes of the LORD *are* upon the righteous, and his ears *are open* unto their cry. 17 *The righteous* cry, and the LORD heareth, and delivereth them out of all their troubles. — 50: 15 Call upon me in the day of trouble: I will deliver thee, and thou shalt glorify me. — 65: 2 O thou that hearest prayer, unto thee shall all flesh come. — 66: 19 Verily God hath heard *me;* he hath attended to the voice of my prayer. 20 Blessed *be* God, which hath not turned away my prayer, nor his mercy from me. — 84: 11 The LORD God *is* a sun and shield: the LORD will give grace and glory; no good *thing* will he withhold from them that walk uprightly. — 86: 5 Thou, LORD, *art* good, and ready to forgive; and plenteous in mercy unto all them that call upon thee. — 91: 15 He shall call upon me, and I will answer him: I *will be* with him in trouble; I will deliver him, and honor him. — 106: 23 He said that he would destroy them, had not Moses his chosen stood before him in the breach, to turn away his wrath, lest he should destroy *them.* — 118: 5 I called upon the LORD in distress: the LORD answered me, *and set me* in a large place. — 145: 18 The LORD *is* nigh unto all them that call upon him, to all that call upon him in truth. 19 He will fulfil the desire of them that fear him: he also will hear their cry, and will save them.

Is. 45: 19 I said not unto the seed of Jacob, Seek ye me in vain: I the LORD speak righteousness, I declare things that are right. — 65: 24 It shall come to pass, that before they call, I will answer; and while they are yet speaking, I will hear.

Jer. 15: 1 Then said the LORD unto me, Though Moses and Samuel stood before me, *yet* my mind *could* not *be* toward this people: cast *them* out of my sight, and let them go forth. — 33: 3 Call unto me, and I will answer thee, and shew thee great and mighty things, which thou knowest not.

Ezk. 14: 14 Though these three men, Noah, Daniel, and Job, were in it, they should deliver *but* their own souls by their righteousness, saith the Lord GOD. [V. 20.]

Dan. 9: 21 Yea, while I *was* speaking in prayer, even the man Gabriel, whom I had seen in the vision at the beginning, being caused to fly swiftly, touched me about the time of the evening oblation. 22 And he informed *me*, and talked with me, and said, O Daniel, I am now come forth to give thee skill and understanding. 23 At the beginning of thy supplications the commandment came forth, and I am come to shew *thee;* for thou *art* greatly beloved. — 10: 12 Then said he unto me, Fear not, Daniel: for from the first day that thou didst set thine heart to understand, and to chasten thyself before thy God, thy words were heard, and I am come for thy words.

Joel 2: 32 It shall come to pass, *that* whosoever shall call on the name of the LORD shall be delivered.

Mat. 7: 7 Ask, and it shall be given you; seek, and ye shall find; knock, and it shall be opened unto you: 8 For every one that asketh, receiveth; and he that seeketh, findeth; and to him that knocketh, it shall be opened. 9 Or what man is there of you, whom if his son ask bread, will he give him a stone? 10 Or if he ask a fish, will he give him a serpent? 11 If ye then being evil know how to give good gifts unto your children, how much more shall your Father which is in heaven give good things to them that ask him?

Lk. 18: 7 Shall not God avenge his own elect, which cry day and night unto him, though he bear long with them? 8 I tell you that he will avenge them speedily.

Ac. 12: 5 Peter therefore was kept in prison: but prayer was made without ceasing of the Church unto God for him. 7 And behold, the angel of the Lord came upon *him*, and a light shined in the prison; and he smote Peter on the side, and raised him up, saying, Arise up quickly.

Jam. 4: 3 Ye ask, and receive not, because ye ask amiss, that ye may consume *it* upon your lusts. 8 Draw nigh to God, and he will draw nigh to you. Cleanse *your* hands, *ye* sinners, and purify *your* hearts, *ye* double-minded. — 5: 16 Confess *your* faults one to another, and pray one for another, that ye may be healed. The effectual fervent prayer of a righteous man availeth much. 17 Elias was a man subject to like passions as we are, and he prayed earnestly that it might not rain: and it rained not on the earth by the space of three years and six months. 18 And he prayed again, and the heaven gave rain, and the earth brought forth her fruit.

1 Pet. 3: 12 The eyes of the Lord *are* over the righteous,

and his ears *are open* unto their prayers : but the face of the Lord *is* against them that do evil.

Rev. 8: 3 Another angel came and stood at the altar, having a golden censer ; and there was given unto him much incense, that he should offer *it* with the prayers of all saints, upon the golden altar which was before the throne. 4 And the smoke of the incense, *which came* with the prayers of the saints, ascended up before God out of the angel's hand.

[See 431, 670.]

546. *Prayer and worship of the ungodly not acceptable.*

Ps. 50: 16 Unto the wicked God saith, What hàst thou to do to declare my statutes, or *that* thou shouldest take my covenant in thy mouth ? 17 Seeing thou hatest instruction, and castest my words behind thee. — 66: 18 If I regard iniquity in my heart, the LORD will not hear *me.*

Pr. 1: 28 Then' shall they call upon me, but I will not answer ; they shall seek me early, but they shall not find me ; 29 For that they hated knowledge, and did not choose the fear of the LORD. — 15: 8 The sacrifice of the wicked *is* an abomination to the LORD : but the prayer of the upright *is* his delight. 29 The LORD *is* far from the wicked : but he heareth the prayer of the righteous. — 28: 9 He that turneth away his ear from hearing the law, even his prayer *shall be* abomination.

Is. 1: 11 To what purpose *is* the multitude of your sacrifices unto me ? saith the LORD : I am full of the burnt-offerings of rams, and the fat of fed beasts ; and I delight not in the blood of bullocks, or of lambs, or of he-goats. 12 When ye come to appear before me, who hath required this at your hand, to tread my courts ? 13 Bring no more vain oblations : incense is an abomination unto me : the new moons and sabbaths, the calling of assemblies, I cannot away with : *it is* iniquity, even the solemn meeting. 14 Your new moons and your appointed feasts my soul hateth : they are a trouble unto me ; I am weary to bear *them.* 15 And when ye spread forth your hands, I will hide mine eyes from you ; yea, when ye make many prayers, I will not hear ; your hands are full of blood. — 59: 1 Behold, the LORD's hand is not shortened, that it cannot save ; neither his ear heavy, that it cannot hear : 2 But your iniquities have separated between you and your God, and your sins have hid *his* face from you, that he will not hear.

Mat. 7: 18 A good tree cannot bring forth evil fruit, neither can a corrupt tree bring forth good fruit.

Jn. 9: 31 We know that God heareth not sinners : but if any man be a worshipper of God, and doeth his will, him he heareth.

Heb. 11: 6 Without faith *it is* impossible to please *him :* for he that cometh to God must believe that he is, and *that* he is a rewarder of them that diligently seek him.   [See 165, 589.]

547. *Prayer not agreeable to the wicked.*

Job 27: 8 What *is* the hope of the hypocrite, though he hath gained, when God taketh away his soul ?   10 Will he delight himself in the Almighty ? will he always call upon God ? [See 22.]

548. *God displeased with prayerless persons.*

Jer. 10: 25 Pour out thy fury upon the heathen that know thee not, and upon the families that call not on thy name : for they have eaten up Jacob, and devoured him, and consumed him, and have made his habitation desolate.   [See 230.]

PRIDE AND SELF-CONCEIT.

549. *Pride, and self-conceit, prevalent evils.*

Gen. 11: 4 They said, Go to, let us build us a city and a tower, whose top *may reach* unto heaven ; and let us make us a name, lest we be scattered abroad upon the face of the whole earth.

Ps. 10: 2 The wicked in *his* pride doth persecute the poor. — 73: 6 Pride compasseth them about as a chain : violence covereth them *as* a garment.   7 Their eyes stand out with fatness : they have more than heart could wish.   8 They are corrupt, and speak wickedly *concerning* oppression : they speak loftily.   9 They set their mouth against the heavens, and their tongue walketh through the earth.

Ezk. 16: 49 Behold, this was the iniquity of thy sister Sodom, pride, fulness of bread, and abundance of idleness was in her and in her daughters, neither did she strengthen the hand of the poor and needy.   50 And they were haughty, and committed abomination before me: therefore I took them away as I saw *good.*   [See 696, 703.]

550. *Pride and self-conceit, offensive to God — threats.*

2 S. 22: 28 The afflicted people thou wilt save : but thine eyes *are* upon the haughty, *that* thou mayest bring *them* down.

Ps. 12: 3 The LORD shall cut off all flattering lips, *and* the tongue that speaketh proud things : 4 Who have said, With our tongue will we prevail; our lips *are* our own : who *is* lord over us? — 18: 27 Thou wilt save the afflicted people; but wilt bring down high looks. — 119: 21' Thou hast rebuked the proud *that are* cursed, which do err from thy commandments. — 138: 6 Though the LORD *be* high, yet hath he respect unto the lowly; but the proud he knoweth afar off.

Pr. 8: 13 The fear of the LORD *is* to hate evil: pride, and arrogancy, and the evil way, and the froward mouth, do I hate. — 15: 26 The LORD will destroy the house of the proud; but he will establish the border of the widow. — 16: 5 Every one *that is* proud in heart *is* an abomination to the LORD ; *though* hand *join* in hand, he shall not be unpunished.

Is. 2: 12 The day of the LORD of hosts *shall be* upon every *one that is* proud and lofty, and upon every *one that is* lifted up; and he shall be brought low. — 3: 16 The LORD saith, Because the daughters of Zion are haughty, and walk with stretched forth necks and wanton eyes, walking and mincing *as* they go, and making a tinkling with their feet: 17 Therefore the LORD will smite with a scab the crown of the head of the daughters of Zion. 18 In that day the LORD will take away the bravery of *their* tinkling ornaments *about their feet*, and *their* cauls, and *their* round tires like the moon. 19 The chains, and the bracelets, and the mufflers, 20 The bonnets, and the ornaments of the legs, and the head-bands, and the tablets, and the ear-rings, 21 The rings, and nose jewels, 22 The changeable suits of apparel, and the mantles, and the wimples, and the crisping-pins, 23 The glasses, and the fine linen, and the hoods, and the vails. — 13: 11 I will cause the arrogancy of the proud to cease, and will lay down the haughtiness of the terrible. — 26: 5 He bringeth down them that dwell on high; the lofty city, he layeth it low; he layeth it low, *even* to the ground; he bringeth it *even* to the dust. — 65: 5 Stand by thyself; come not near to me; for I am holier than thou. These *are* a smoke in my nose, a fire that burneth all the day.

Dan. '4: 30 The king spake, and said, Is not this great Babylon, that I have built for the house of the kingdom by the might of my power, and for the honor of my majesty? 31 While the word *was* in the king's mouth, there fell a voice from heaven, *saying*, O king Nebuchadnezzar, to thee it is spoken; The kingdom is departed from thee : 32 And they shall drive thee from men, and thy dwelling *shall be* with the beasts of the field: they shall make thee to eat grass as oxen, and seven times shall pass over thee, until thou know that the Most High ' ruleth in the kingdom of men, and giveth it to whomsoever he will.

Mat. 23: 12 Whosoever shall exalt himself, shall be abased: and he that shall humble himself, shall be exalted. 29 Wo unto you, scribes and Pharisees, hypocrites! because ye build the tombs of the prophets, and garnish the sepulchres of the righteous, 30 And say, If we had been in the days of our fathers, we would not have been partakers with them in the blood of the prophets. 31 Wherefore, ye be witnesses unto yourselves, that ye are the children of them which killed the prophets.

2 Th. 2: 4 Who opposeth and exalteth himself above all · that is called God, or that is worshipped ; so that he, as God, sitteth in the temple of God, showing himself that he is God. 8 And then shall that Wicked be revealed, whom the Lord shall consume with the spirit of his mouth, and shall destroy with the brightness of his coming.

Jam. 4: 6. God resisteth the proud, but giveth grace unto the humble. 16 But now ye rejoice in your boastings: all such rejoicing is evil. [See 513.]

551. *Pride tends to a fall.*

Esther 3: 5 When Haman saw that Mordecai bowed not, nor did him reverence, then was Haman full of wrath. 6 · And 'he thought scorn to lay hands on Mordecai alone ; for they had shewed him the people of Mordecai : wherefore Haman sought to destroy all the Jews that *were* throughout the whole kingdom of Ahasuerus, *even* the people of Mordecai. — 7: 9 And Harbonah, one of the chamberlains, said before the king, Behold also the gallows, fifty cubits high, which Haman had made for Mordecai, who had spoken good for the king, standeth in the house of Haman. Then the king said, Hang him thereon.

Pr. 16: 18 Pride *goeth* before destruction, and an haughty spirit before a fall. — 18: 12 Before destruction the heart of man is haughty, and before honor *is* humility. — 26: 12 Seest thou a man wise in his own conceit? *there is* more hope of a fool than of him. — 28: 26 He that trusteth in his own heart is a fool: but whoso walketh wisely, he shall be delivered.—29: 23 A man's pride shall bring him low: but honor shall uphold the humble in spirit. [See 733.]

PROBATION.

552. *Retribution imperfect during this life.*

Ps. 103: 10 He hath not dealt with us after our sins; nor rewarded us according to our iniquities.

Ec. 8: 11 Because sentence against an evil work is not executed speedily, therefore the heart of the sons of men is fully set in them to do evil. — 9: 1 For all this I considered in my heart even to declare all this, that the righteous, and the wise, and their works, *are* in the hand of God: no man knoweth either love or hatred *by* all *that is* before them. 2 All *things* come alike to all: there *is* one event to the righteous and to the wicked; to the good, and to the clean, and to the unclean; to him that sacrificeth, and to him that sacrificeth not: as *is* the good, so *is* the sinner; *and* he that sweareth, as *he* that feareth an oath. [See 565.]

553. *Probation limited to this life — its immeasurable importance.*

Pr. 1: 24 Because I have called and ye refused: I have stretched out my hand, and no man regarded: 25 But ye have set at nought all my counsel, and would none of my reproof: 26 I also will laugh at your calamity: I will mock when your fear cometh: 27 When your fear cometh as desolation, and your destruction cometh as a whirlwind: when distress and anguish cometh upon you. 28 Then shall they call upon me, but I will not answer: they shall seek me early, but they shall not find me.

Ec. 9: 10 Whatsoever thy hand findeth to do, do *it* with thy might; for *there is* no work, nor device, nor knowledge, nor wisdom, in the grave, whither thou goest.

Is. 55: 6 Seek ye the LORD while he may be found, call ye upon him while he is near.

Jer. 8: 20 The harvest is past, the summer is ended, and we are not saved.

Zec. 9: 12 Turn you to the strong hold, ye prisoners of hope.

Mat. 25: 10 While they went to buy, the bridegroom came: and they that were ready went in with him to the marriage: and the door was shut. 11 Afterward came also the other virgins, saying, Lord, Lord, open to us. 12 But he answered and said, Verily, I say unto you, I know you not.

2 Cor. 6: 2 (He saith, I have heard thee in a time accepted, and in the day of salvation have I succored thee: behold, now *is* the accepted time: behold, now *is* the day of salvation.)

[See 390, 572, 727.]

554. *Probation includes danger of losing the soul.*

Mat. 5: 22 Whosoever shall say, Thou fool, shall be in danger of hell-fire. — 16: 25 Whosoever will save his life, shall lose it: and whosoever will lose his life for my sake, shall find it. 26 For what is a man profited, if he shall gain the whole world, and lose his own soul? or what shall a man give in exchange for his soul? [Lk. 9: 24.]

Mk. 9: 43 If thy hand offend thee, cut it off; it is better for thee to enter into life maimed, than having two hands to go into hell, into the fire that never shall be quenched: 44 Where their worm dieth not, and the fire is not quenched. 45 And if thy foot offend thee, cut it off; it is better for thee to enter halt into life, than having two feet to be cast into hell, into the fire that never shall be quenched: 46 Where their worm dieth not, and the fire is not quenched. 47 And if thine eye offend thee, pluck it out: it is better for thee to enter into the kingdom of God with one eye, than having two eyes to be cast into hell-fire: 48 Where their worm dieth not, and the fire is not quenched. [Mat. 18: 8.]

Lk. 12: 4 I say unto you, my friends, Be not afraid of them that kill the body, and after that, have no more that they can do. 5 But I will forewarn you whom ye shall fear: Fear him, which after he hath killed, hath power to cast into hell; yea, I say unto you, Fear him. [Mat. 10: 28.] — 13: 23 Then said one unto him, Lord, are there few that be saved? And he said unto them, 24 Strive to enter in at the strait gate: for many, I say unto you, will seek to enter in, and shall not be able.

Heb. 4: 1 Let us therefore fear, lest a promise being left *us* of entering into his rest, any of you should seem to come short of it.

1 Pet. 4: 17 The time *is come* that judgment must begin at the house of God: and if *it* first *begin* at us, what shall the end *be* of them that obey not the gospel of God? 18 And if the righteous scarcely be saved, where shall the ungodly and the sinner appear? [See 563.]

555. *Probationary conduct determines our final state; or salvation conditional.*

1 Ch. 28: 9 And thou Solomon my son, know thou the God of thy father, and serve him with a perfect heart, and with a willing mind: for the LORD searcheth all hearts, and understandeth all the imaginations of the thoughts: if thou seek him, he will be found of thee; but if thou forsake him, he will cast thee off for ever.

Pr. 1: 29 They hated knowledge, and did not choose the fear of the LORD: 30 They would none of my counsel: they despised all my reproof. 31 Therefore shall they eat of the fruit of their own way, and be filled with their own devices. 32 For the turning away of the simple shall slay them, and the prosperity of fools shall destroy them. — 8: 36 He that sinneth against me wrongeth his own soul: all they that hate me love death. — 9: 12 If thou be wise, thou shalt be wise for thyself: but *if* thou scornest, thou alone shalt bear *it*.—11: 19 As righteousness *tendeth* to life: so he that pursueth evil *pursueth it* to his own death.

Mat. 5: 25 Agree with thine adversary quickly, while thou art in the way with him: lest at any time the adversary deliver thee to the judge, and the judge deliver thee to the officer, and thou be cast into prison. 26 Verily I say unto thee, Thou shalt by no means come out thence, till thou hast paid the uttermost farthing. — 7: 13 Enter ye in at the strait gate ; for wide *is* the gate, and broad *is* the way, that leadeth to destruction, and many there be which go in thereat: 14 Because, strait *is* the gate, and narrow *is* the way, which leadeth unto life, and few there be that find it.

Mk. 16: 16 He that believeth and is baptized, shall be saved: but he that believeth not, shall be damned.

Rom. 2: 5 After thy hardness and impenitent heart, treasurest up unto thyself wrath against the day of wrath, and revelation of the righteous judgment of God ; 6 Who will render to every man according to his deeds: 7 To them who by patient continuance in well-doing, seek for glory, and honor, and immortality, eternal life: 8 But unto them that are contentious, and do not obey the truth, but obey unrighteousness: indignation and wrath, 9 Tribulation and anguish, upon every soul of man that doeth evil: of the Jew first, and also of the Gentile: 10 But glory, honor, and peace, to every man that worketh good.

Gal. 6: 7 Be not deceived: God is not mocked: for whatsoever a man soweth, that shall he also reap. 8 For he that soweth to his flesh, shall of the flesh reap corruption: but he that soweth to the Spirit, shall of the Spirit reap life everlasting.

Rev. 22: 19 If any man shall take away from the words of the book of this prophecy, God shall take away his part out of the book of life, and out of the holy city, and *from* the things which are written in this book.

[See Terms of Salvation, in the Index, and 567, and Mat. 25, (Parable of the ten virgins and of the talents,) and Lk. 19: 12—27, (Parable of the pounds.)]

391

556. *Rewards and punishments according to probationary conduct.*

Job 34: 11 The work of a man shall he render unto him, and cause every man to find according to *his* ways.

Ps. 62: 12 Unto thee, O Lord, *belongeth* mercy: for thou renderest to every man according to his work.

Pr. 24: 12 If thou sayest, Behold, we knew it not; doth not he that pondereth the heart, consider *it*? and he that keepeth thy soul, doth *not* he know *it*? and shall *not* he render to *every* man according to his works?

Is. 3: 10 Say ye to the righteous, that *it shall be* well *with him;* for they shall eat the fruit of their doings. 11 Wo unto the wicked! *it shall be* ill *with him;* for the reward of his hands shall be given him.

Jer. 17: 10 I the LORD search the heart, *I* try the reins, even to give every man according to his ways, *and* according to the fruit of his doings. — 32: 19 Thine eyes *are* open upon all the ways of the sons of men; to give every one according to his ways, and according to the fruit of his doings.

Mat. 5: 19 Whosoever, therefore, shall break one of these least commandments, and shall teach men so, he shall be called the least in the kingdom of heaven; but whosoever shall do, and teach *them*, the same shall be called great in the kingdom of heaven. — 16: 27 The Son of man shall come in the glory of his Father, with his angels, and then he shall reward every man according to his works.

Lk: 19: 16 Then came the first, saying, Lord, thy pound hath gained ten pounds. 17 And he said unto him, Well, thou good servant; because thou hast been faithful in a very little, have thou authority over ten cities. 18 And the second came, saying, Lord, thy pound hath gained five pounds. 19 And he said likewise to him, Be thou also over five cities.

Gal. 6: 7 Be not deceived: God is not mocked: for whatsoever a man soweth, that shall he also reap. 8 For he that soweth to his-flesh, shall of the flesh reap corruption; but he that soweth to the Spirit, shall of the Spirit reap life everlasting.

Rev. 22: 12 Behold, I come quickly; and my reward *is* with me, to give every man according as his work shall be.

[See 231–2.]

Sin exceeding sinful — God's right and disposition to punish.

PUNISHMENT IN A FUTURE STATE.

557. *Sins against God, " exceeding sinful."*

Gen. 39: 9 *There is* none greater in this house than I; neither hath he kept back any thing from me, but thee, because thou *art* his wife : how then·can I do this great wickedness, and sin against God?

1 S. 2: 25 If óne man sin against another, the judge shall judge him : but if a man sin against the LORD, who shall entreat for him?

Ps. 51: 4 Against thee, thee only, have I sinned, and done *this* evil in thy sight : that thou mightest be justified when thou speakest, *and* be clear when thou judgest.

Rom. 7: 13 Sin, that it might appear sin, working death in me by that which is good ; that sin by the commandment might become exceeding sinful. [See 230, 236.]

558. *God's prerogative to punish according to desert.*

Dt. 32: 35 To me *belongeth* vengeance, and recompense ; their foot shall slide in *due* time : for the day of their calàmity *is* at hand, and the things that shall come upon them make haste. 39 See now that I, *even* I *am* he, and *there is* no god with me : I kill, and I make alive ; I wound, and I heal : neither *is there any* that can deliver out of my hand. 40 For I lift up my hand to heaven, and say, I live for ever. 41 If I whet my glittering sword, and my hand take hold on judgment ; I will render vengeance to mine enemies, and will reward them that hate me.

Ps. 94: 1 O LORD God, to whom vengeance belongeth ; O God, to whom vengeance belongeth, shew thyself.

Rom. 12: 19 Dearly beloved, avenge not yourselves, but *rather* give place unto wrath : for it is written, Vengeance *is* mine ; I will repay, saith the Lord.

Heb. 10: 30 We know him that hath said, Vengeance *belongeth* unto me, I will recompense, saith the Lord. And again, The Lord shall judge his people.

559. *Will God's love and compassion save unbelievers?*

Ex. 34: 6 The LORD passed by before him, and proclaimed, The Lord, The LORD God, merciful and gracious, long-suffering, and abundant in goodness and truth. 7 Keeping mercy for thousands, forgiving iniquity and transgression and sin, and that will by no means clear *the guilty.*

Is. 27: 11 It *is* a people of no understanding : therefore he that made them will not have mercy on them, and he that formed them will shew them no favor.

Ezk. 7: 9 Mine eye shall not spare, neither will I have pity: I will recompense thee according to thy ways, and thine abominations *that* are in the midst of thee; and ye shall know that I *am* the LORD that smiteth. ﹏

Nah..1: 3 The LORD *is* slow to anger, and great in power, and will not at all acquit *the wicked.* [See 230, 572, 573,(7).]

560. *The finally impenitent to be separated from the saints, and shut out of heaven.*

Ps. 119: 155 Salvation *is* far from the wicked: for they seek not thy statutes.

Mat. 5: 20 I say unto you, That except your righteousness shall exceed *the righteousness* of the scribes and Pharisees, ye shall in no case enter into the kingdom of heaven. — 7: 21 Not every one that saith unto me, Lord, Lord, shall enter into the kingdom of heaven; but he that doeth the will of my Father which is in heaven. 22 Many will say to me in that day, Lord, Lord, have we not prophesied in thy name? and in thy name have cast out devils? and in thy name done many wonderful works? 23 And then will I profess unto them, I never knew you: depart from me, ye that work iniquity. — 10: 33 Whosoever shall deny me before men, him will I also deny before my Father which is in heaven. —13: 30 Let both grow together until the harvest: and in the time of harvest I will say to the reapers, Gather ye together first the tares, and bind them in bundles to burn them: but gather the wheat into my barn. 49 So shall it be at the end of the world: the angels shall come forth, and sever the wicked from among the just. — 25: 10 While they went to buy, the bridegroom came; and they that were ready, went in with him to the marriage; and the door was shut. 11 Afterward came also the other virgins, saying, Lord, Lord, open to us. 12 But he answered, and said, Verily, I say unto you, I know you not. 31 When the Son of man shall come in his glory, and all the holy angels with him, then shall he sit upon the throne of his glory: 32 And before him shall be gathered all nations: and he shall separate them one from another, as a shepherd divideth *his* sheep from the goats: 33 And he shall set the sheep on his right hand, but the goats on the left.

1 Cor. 6: 9 Know ye not that the unrighteous shall not inherit the kingdom of God? Be not deceived; neither fornicators, nor idolaters, nor adulterers, nor effeminate, nor abusers of themselves with mankind, 10 Nor thieves, nor covetous, nor

drunkards, nor revilers, nor extortioners, shall inherit the kingdom of God.

Gal. 5: 19 The works of the flesh are manifest, which are *these*, Adultery, fornication, uncleanness, lasciviousness, 20 Idolatry, witchcraft, hatred, variance, emulations, wrath, strife, seditions, heresies, 21 Envyings, murders, drunkenness, revellings, and such like: of the which I tell you before, as I have also told *you* in time past, that they which do such things shall not inherit the kingdom of God.

Ep. 5: 5 This ye know, that no whoremonger, nor unclean person, nor covetous man, who is an idolater, hath any inheritance in the kingdom of Christ and of God. 6 Let no man deceive you with vain words: for because of these things cometh the wrath of God upon the children of disobedience.

Rev. 21: 27 There shall in no wise enter into it any thing that defileth, neither *whatsoever* worketh abomination, or *maketh* a lie; but they which are written in the Lamb's book of life.
[See 256, 287, 387, 390, 554.]

561. *The wicked to be cast into hell.*

Job 21: 20 His eyes shall see his destruction, and he shall drink of the wrath of the Almighty. — 31: 3 *Is* not destruction to the wicked? and a strange *punishment* to the workers of iniquity? — 36: 13 The hypocrites in heart heap up wrath.

Ps. 1: 5 Therefore the ungodly shall not stand in the judgment, nor sinners in the congregation of the righteous. 6 For the Lord knoweth the way of the righteous: but the way of the ungodly shall perish. — 9: 17 The wicked shall be turned into hell, *and* all the nations that forget God. — 11: 6 Upon the wicked he shall rain snares, fire and brimstone, and a horrible tempest: *this shall be* the portion of their cup.

Mat. 3: 7 O generation of vipers, who hath warned you to flee from the wrath to come? 10 Now also the axe is laid unto the root of the trees: therefore every tree which bringeth not forth good fruit is hewn down, and cast into the fire. 11 I indeed baptize you with water unto repentance: but he that cometh after me is mightier than I, whose shoes I am not worthy to bear; he shall baptize you with the Holy Ghost, and *with* fire: 12 Whose fan *is* in his hand, and he will thoroughly purge his floor, and gather his wheat into the garner; but he will burn up the chaff with unquenchable fire. — 7: 19 Every tree that bringeth not forth good fruit is hewn down, and cast into the fire. 27 The rain descended, and the floods came, and the winds blew, and beat upon that house; and it fell: and great was the fall of it. — 8: 11 I say unto you, That many shall

Loss of the Soul.

come from the east and west, and shall sit down with Abraham, and Isaac, and Jacob, in the kingdom of heaven: 12 But the children of the kingdom shall be cast out into outer darkness: there shall be weeping and gnashing of teeth. — 13: 40 As therefore the tares are gathered and burned in the fire; so shall it be in the end of this world. 41 The Son of man shall send forth his angels, and they shall gather out of his kingdom all things that offend, and them which do iniquity; 42 And shall cast them into a furnace of fire; there shall be wailing and gnashing of teeth. 47 Again, The kingdom of heaven is like unto a net, that was cast into the sea, and gathered of every kind: 48 Which, when it was full, they drew to shore, and sat down, and gathered the good into vessels, but cast the bad away. 49 So shall it be at the end of the world: the angels shall come forth, and sever the wicked from among the just, 50 And shall cast them into the furnace of fire: there shall be wailing and gnashing of teeth.—11:23 And thou, Capernaum, which art exalted unto heaven, shalt be brought down to hell: for if the mighty works which have been done in thee, had been done in Sodom, it would have remained until this day. 24 But I say unto you, that it shall be more tolerable for the land of Sodom in the day of Judgment, than for thee.— 22: 13 Then said the king to the servants, Bind him hand and foot, and take him away, and cast *him* into outer darkness: there shall be weeping and gnashing of teeth.

Lk. 16: 22 It came to pass, that the beggar died, and was carried by the angels into Abraham's bosom. The rich man also died, and was buried: 23 And in hell he lifted up his eyes, being in torments, and seeth Abraham afar off, and Lazarus in his bosom. 24 And he cried, and said, Father Abraham, have mercy on me, and send Lazarus, that he may dip the tip of his finger in water, and cool my tongue: for I am tormented in this flame.

Jn. 5: 28 Marvel not at this: for the hour is coming, in the which all that are in the graves shall hear his voice, 29 And shall come forth; they that have done good, unto the resurrection of life; and they that have done evil, unto the resurrection of damnation. — 15: 6 If a man abide not in me, he is cast forth as a branch, and is withered; and men gather them, and cast *them* into the fire, and they are burned. — 17: 12 None of them is lost, but the son of perdition. [2 Th. 2: 3.]

1 Cor. 16: 22 If any man love not the Lord Jesus Christ, let him be Anathema, Maranatha.

Ph. 3: 18 *They are* the enemies of the cross of Christ: 19 Whose end *is* destruction.

396

Evinced by the unpardonable sin.

2 Th. 2: 3 Let no man deceive you by any means: for *that day shall not come*, except there come a falling away first, and that man of sin be revealed, the son of perdition ; 9 *Even him*, whose coming is after the working of Satan, with all power, and signs, and lying wonders, 10 And with all deceivableness of unrighteousness of them that perish ; because they received not the love of the truth, that they might be saved.   11 And for this cause God shall send them strong delusion, that they should believe a lie: 12 That they all might be damned who believed not the truth, but had pleasure in unrighteousness.

Heb. 10: 26 For if we sin wilfully after that we have re- cieved the knowledge of the truth, there remaineth no more sacrifice for sins, 27 But a certain fearful looking for of judg- ment and fiery indignation, which shall devour the adversaries. [V. 28—31.]

2 Pet. 2: 4 If God spared not the angels that sinned, but cast *them* down to hell, and delivered *them* into chains of dark- ness, to be reserved unto judgment ; 9 The Lord knoweth how to deliver the godly out of temptations, and to reserve the unjust unto the day of judgment to be punished : 10 But chiefly them that walk after the flesh in the lust of unclean- ness, and despise government.   Presumptuous *are they*, self- willed ; they are not afraid to speak evil of dignities.   17 These are wells without water, clouds that are carried with a tempest: to whom the mist of darkness is reserved for ever. — 3: 7 But the heavens and the earth, which are now, by the same word are kept in store, reserved unto fire against the day of judgment and perdition of ungodly men.

Rev. 19: 20 The beast was taken, and with him the fasle prophet that wrought miracles before him, with which he deceived them that had received the mark of the beast, and them that worshipped his image.   These both were cast alive into a lake of fire burning with brimstone. — 20: 15 Whoso- ever was not found written in the book of life was cast into the lake of fire.   [See 236-7, 287, 343, 387.]

562. *Future punishment evinced by the unpardonable sin.*

Mat. 12: 31 I say unto you, All manner of sin and blas- phemy shall be forgiven unto men : but the blasphemy *against* the *Holy* Ghost shall not be forgiven unto men.   32 And whosoever speaketh a word against the Son of man, it shall be forgiven him : but whosoever speaketh against the Holy Ghost, it shall not be forgiven him, neither in this world, neither in the *world* to come.

Mk. 3: 28 Verily, I say unto you, All sins shall be forgiven unto the sons of men, and blasphemies wherewith soever they shall blaspheme: 29 But he that shall blaspheme against the Holy Ghost hath never forgiveness, but is in danger of eternal damnation.

Lk. 12: 10 Unto him that blasphemeth against the Holy Ghost, it shall not be forgiven.

Heb. 10: 26 If we sin wilfully after that we have received the knowledge of the truth, there remaineth no more sacrifice for sins.

1 Jn. 5: 16 If any man see his brother sin a sin *which is* not unto death, he shall ask, and he shall give him life for them that sin not unto death. There is a sin unto death: I do not say that he shall pray for it.

563. *Future punishment evinced by the second death.*

Ezk. 18: 31 Why will ye die, O house of Israel? 32 For I have no pleasure in the death of him that dieth, saith the Lord GOD: wherefore, turn *yourselves,* and live ye.

Rev. 2: 11 He that overcometh shall not be hurt of the second death. — 20: 6 Blessed and holy *is* he that hath part in the first-resurrection: on such the second death hath no power, but they shall be priests of God and of Christ, and shall reign with him a thousand years. 14 And death and hell were cast into the lake of fire. This is the second death. 15 And whosoever was not found written in the book of life was cast into the lake of fire. — 21: 8 The fearful, and unbelieving, and the abominable, and murderers, and whoremongers, and sorcerers, and idolaters, and all liars, shall have their part in the lake which burneth with fire and brimstone: which is the second death. [See 287.]

564. *Future punishment evinced by death in impenitence.*

Gen. 19: 24 Then the LORD rained upon Sodom and upon Gomorrah brimstone and fire from the LORD out of heaven. 25 And he overthrew those cities, and all the plain, and all the inhabitants of the cities, and that which grew upon the ground.

Lev. 10: 1 Nadab and Abihu, the sons of Aaron, took either of them his censer, and put fire therein, and put incense thereon, and offered strange fire before the LORD, which he commanded them not. 2 And there went out fire from the LORD, and devoured them, and they died before the LORD.

Num. 16: 22 The earth opened her mouth, and swallowed them up, and their houses, and all the men that *appertained* unto Korah, and all *their* goods. 33 They, and all that *appertained* to them, went down alive into the pit, and the earth

Evinced by present prosperity of the wicked

closed upon them: and they perished from among the congregation.

Ps: 58: 9 He shall take them away as with a whirlwind both living, and in *his* wrath.

Pr. 14: 32 The wicked is driven away in his wickedness: but the righteous hath hope in his death.

Mat. 27: 5 He cast down the pieces of silver in the temple, and departed, and went and hanged himself.

Jn. 8: 21 Then said Jesus again unto them, I go my way, and ye shall seek me, and shall die in your sins: whither I go, ye cannot come.

Ac. 5: 5 Ananias hearing these words, fell down, and gave up the ghost. And great fear came on all them that heard these things.

2 Pet. 2: 12 These, as natural brute beasts, made to be taken and destroyed, speak evil of the things that they understand not; and shall utterly perish in their own corruption. 13 And shall receive the reward of unrighteousness, *as* they that count it pleasure to riot in the day-time.

565. *Future punishment evinced by the present prosperity of the wicked, and sufferings of the righteous.*

Job 12: 6 The tabernacles of robbers prosper, and they that provoke God are secure : into whose hand God bringeth *abundantly.* — 21: 7 Wherefore do the wicked live, become old, yea, are mighty in power? 8 Their seed is established in their sight with them, and their offspring before their eyes. 9 Their houses *are* safe from fear, neither *is* the rod of God upon them. 11 They send forth their little ones like a flock, and their children dance. 12 They take the timbrel and harp, and rejoice at the sound of the organ. 13 They spend their days in wealth, and in a moment go down to the grave. 14 Therefore they say unto God, Depart from us ;. for we desire not the knowledge of thy ways. 15 What *is* the Almighty, that we should serve him? and what profit should we have, if we pray unto him? 16 Lo, their good *is* not in their hand.

Ps. 73: 3 I was envious at the foolish, *when* I saw the prosperity of the wicked. 4 For *there are* no hands in their death: but their strength *is* firm. 5 They *are* not in trouble *as other* men; neither are they plagued like *other* men. 6 Therefore pride compasseth them about as a chain; violence covereth them *as* a-garment. 7 Their eyes stand out with fatness : they have more than heart could wish. — 12 Behold, these *are* the ungodly, who prosper in the world : they increase *in* riches. — 92: 7 When the wicked spring as the grass, and when all the workers of iniquity do flourish ; *it is* that they shall be destroyed for ever.

Jer. 12: 1 Righteous *art* thou, O LORD, when I plead with thee; yet let me talk with thee of *thy* judgments. Wherefore doth the way of the wicked prosper? *wherefore* are all they happy that deal very treacherously? 2 Thou hast planted them, yea, they have taken root : they grow, yea, they bring forth fruit : thou *art* near in their mouth, and far from their reins.

Mat. 6: 5 Verily, I say unto you, They have their reward. Lk. 6: 24 Wo unto you that are rich! for ye have received your consolation. 25 Wo unto you that are full! for ye shall hunger. Wo unto you that laugh now! for ye shall mourn and weep. 26 Wo unto you, when all men shall speak well of you! for so did their fathers to the false prophets. — 16: 25 Abraham said, Son, remember that thou in thy lifetime receivedst thy good things, and likewise Lazarus evil things : but now he is comforted, and thou art tormented.

2 Th. 1: 4 We ourselves glory in you in the churches of God, for your patience and faith in all your persecutions and tribulations that ye endure: 5 *Which is* a manifest token of the righteous judgment of God, that ye may be counted worthy of the kingdom of God, for which ye also suffer: 6 Seeing *it is* a righteous thing with God to recompense tribulation to them that trouble you; 7 And to you, who are troubled, rest with us, when the Lord Jesus shall be revealed from heaven with his mighty angels, 8 In flaming fire taking vengeance on them that know not God, and that obey not the gospel of our Lord Jesus Christ. [See 511, 552.]

566. *Future punishment presaged by temporal judgments.*

Gen. 6: 12 God looked upon the earth, and behold, it was corrupt : for all flesh had corrupted his way upon the earth. 13 And God said unto Noah, The end of all flesh is come before me : for the earth is filled with violence through them : and behold, I will destroy them with the earth. — 18: 20 The LORD said, because the cry of Sodom and Gomorrah is great, and because their sin is very grievous, 21 I will go down now, and see whether they have done altogether according to the cry of it, which is come unto me. — 19: 24 Then the LORD rained upon Sodom and upon Gomorrah brimstone and fire from the LORD out of heaven; 25 And he overthrew those cities, and all the plain, and all the inhabitants of the cities, and that which grew upon the ground.

2 Pet. 2: 4 If God spared not the angels that sinned, but

cast *them* down to hell, and delivered *them* into chains of darkness, to be reserved unto judgment; 5 And spared not the old world, but saved Noah the eighth *person*, a preacher of righteousness bringing in the flood upon the world of the ungodly; 6 And turning the cities of Sodom and Gomorrah into ashes, condemned *them* with an overthrow, making *them* an ensample unto those that after should live ungodly; 7 And delivered just Lot, vexed with the filthy conversation of the wicked: 9 The Lord knoweth how to deliver the godly out of temptations, and to reserve the unjust unto the day of judgment to be punished. [See 87, 486, 630, 733.]

567. *Punishment everlasting.*

Mat. 25: 41 Then shall he say also unto them on the left hand, Depart from me, ye cursed, into everlasting fire, prepared for the devil and his angels: 42 For I was an hungered, and ye gave me no meat: L was thirsty, and ye gave me no drink. 46 And these shall go away into everlasting punishment: but the righteous into life eternal.

Mk. 9: 43 If thy hand offend thee, cut it off: it is better for thee to enter into life maimed, than having two hands to go into hell, into the fire that never shall be quenched: 44 Where their worm dieth not, and the fire is not quenched. — 14: 21 The Son of man indeed goeth, as it is written of him: but wo to that man by whom the Son of man is betrayed! good were it for that man if he had never been born. [Mat. 26: 24.]

Lk. 3: 17 Whose fan *is* in his hand, and he will thoroughly purge his floor, and will gather the wheat into his garner; but the chaff he will burn with fire unquenchable.

Jn. 3: 36 He that believeth on the Son, hath everlasting life: and he that believeth not the Son, shall not see life; but the wrath of God abideth on him.

Ph. 3: 18 (For many walk, of whom I have told you often, and now tell you even weeping, *that they are* the enemies of the cross of Christ: 19 Whose end *is* destruction, whose God *is* their belly, and *whose* glory *is* in their shame, who mind earthly things.)

2 Th. 1: 7 The Lord Jesus shall be revealed from heaven with his mighty angels, 8 In flaming fire taking vengeance on them that know not God, and that obey not the gospel of our Lord Jesus Christ: 9 Who shall be punished with everlasting destruction from the presence of the Lord, and from the glory of his power.

Jude 6 The angels which kept not their first estate, but left their own habitation, he hath reserved in everlasting chains un-

der ,darkness unto the judgment of the great day. 7 Even
as Sodom and Gomorrah, and the cities about them in like
manner, giving themselves over to fornication, and going after
strange flesh, are set forth for an example, suffering the vengeance of eternal fire.   13 Raging waves of the sea, foaming
out their own shame ; wandering stars to whom is reserved the
blackness of darkness for ever.

Rev. 14: 9 And the third angel followed them, saying with
a loud voice, If any man worship the beast and his image, and
receive *his* mark in his forehead, or in his hand, 10 The same
shall drink of the wine of the wrath of , God, which is poured
out without mixture into the cup of his indignation ; and he
shall be tormented with fire and brimstone in the presence
of the holy angels, and in the presence of the Lamb : 11
The smoke of their torment ascendeth up for ever and ever :
and they have no rest day nor night, who worship the beast
and his image, and whosoever receiveth the mark of his name.
— 20: 10 The devil that deceived them was cast into the lake
of fire and brimstone, where the beast and the false prophet *are,*
and shall be tormented day and night for ever and ever.
        [See 287, 390, 553—5, 572, 573,(1).]

568. *Future punishment denied or disbelieved by some.*

Gen. 3: 4 The serpent said unto the woman, Ye shall not
surely die.

Dt. 29: 19 And it come to pass, when he heareth the words
of this curse, that he bless himself in his heart, saying, I shall
have peace, though I walk in the imagination of mine heart,
to add drunkenness to thirst.

Ezk. 13: 22 With lies ye have made the heart of the righteous sad, whom I have not made sad ; and strengthened the
hands of the wicked, that he should not return from his wicked
way, by promising him life.

2 Pet. 3: 5 This they willingly are ignorant of, that by the
word of God the heavens were of old, and the earth standing
out of the water and in the water: 6 Whereby the world that
then was, being overflowed with water, perished: 7 But the
heavens and the earth, which are now, by the same word are
kept in store, reserved unto fire against the day of judgment
and perdition of ungodly men.   [See 22, 708.]

569. *The wicked not always purified by punishment.*

Pr. 27: 22 Though thou shouldest bray a fool in a mortar
among wheat with a pestle, *yet* will not his foolishness depart
from him.

Rev. 16: 9 Men were scorched with great heat, and blasphemed the name of God, which hath power over these plagues : and they repented not to give him glory. 10 And the fifth angel poured out his vial *upon the seat of the beast; and his kingdom was full of darkness ; and they gnawed their tongues for pain, 11 And blasphemed the God of heaven, because of their pains and their sores, and repented not of their deeds. 21 And there fell upon men a great hail out of heaven, *every stone* about the weight of a talent : and men blasphemed God because of the plague of the hail; for the plague thereof was exceeding great. [See 9.]

570. *The wicked punished according to their desert, to make known and glorify God.*

Ex. 9: 15 Now I will stretch out my hand that I may smite thee and thy people with pestilence; and thou shalt be cut off from the earth. 16 And in very deed for this *cause* have I raised thee up, for to shew *in* thee my power; and that my name may be declared throughout all the earth.

— 14: 4 I will be honored upon Pharaoh, and upon all his host; that the Egyptians may know that I *am* the LORD.

Ps. 83: 17 Let them be confounded and troubled for ever: yea, let them be put to shame, and perish: 18 That *men* may know that thou, whose name alone *is* JEHOVAH, *art* the Most High over all the earth.

Ezk. 25: 17· I will execute great vengeance upon them with furious rebukes ; and they shall know that I *am* the LORD, when I shall lay my vengeance upon them.

Rom. 9: 17 The scripture saith unto Pharaoh, Even for this same purpose have I raised thee up, that I might shew my ·power in thee, and that my name might be declared throughout all the earth. 22 *What* if God, willing to shew *his* wrath, and to make his power known, endured with much long-suffering the vessels of wrath fitted to destruction : 23 And that he might make known the riches of his glory on the vessels of mercy, which he had afore prepared unto glory, 24 Even us, whom he hath called, not of the Jews only, but also of the Gentiles? [See 209, 276.]

571. *Punishment approved by the righteous.*

Ex. 15: 1 Then sang Moses and the children of Israel this song unto the LORD, and spake, saying. I will sing unto the LORD, for he hath triumphed gloriously; the horse and his rider hath he thrown into the sea. 6 Thy right hand, O LORD, is become glorious in power: thy right hand, O LORD, hath dashed in pieces the enemy. 7 And in the greatness of. thine excellency thou hast overthrown them that rose up against thee.

Ps. 28: 4 Give them according to their deeds, and according to the wickeness of their endeavors: give them after the work of their hands ; render to them their desert. 5 Because they regard not the works of the LORD, nor the operation of his hands, he shall destroy them, and not build them up. — 94: 1. O LORD God, to whom vengeance belongeth ; O God, to whom vengeance belongeth, shew thyself. 2 Lift up thyself, thou Judge of the earth : render a reward to the proud.

Lk. 23: 40 The other answering, rebuked him, saying, Dost not thou fear God, seeing thou art in the same condemnation ? 41 And we indeed justly ; for we receive the due reward of our deeds : but this man hath done nothing amiss.

Rev. 6: 9 When he had opened the fifth seal, I saw under the altar the souls of them that were slain for the word of God, and for the testimony which they held : 10 And they cried with a loud voice, saying, How long, O Lord, holy and true, dost thou not judge and avenge our blood on them that dwell on the earth ? — 15: 3 They sing the song of Moses the servant of God, and the song of the Lamb, saying, Great and marvellous *are* thy works, Lord God Almighty ; just and true *are* thy ways, thou King of saints. 4 Who shall not fear thee, O Lord, and glorify thy name ? for *thou* only *art* holy : for all nations shall come and worship before thee ; for thy judgments are made manifest. — 18: 20 Rejoice over her, *thou* heaven, and *ye* holy apostles and prophets ; for God hath avenged you on her. — 19: 1 After these things I heard a great voice of much people in heaven, saying, Alleluia : Salvation, and glory, and honor, and power, unto the Lord our God : 2 For true and righteous *are* his judgments : for he hath judged the great whore, which did corrupt the earth with her fornication, and hath avenged the blood of his servants at her hand. 3 And again they said, Alleluia. And her smoke rose up for ever and ever. 4 And the four and twenty elders and the four beasts fell down and worshipped God that sat on the throne, saying, Amen ; Alleluia. 5 And a voice came out of the throne, saying, Praise our God, all ye his servants, and ye that fear him, both small and great. 6 And I heard as it were the voice of a great multitude, and as the voice of many waters, and as the voice of mighty thunderings, saying, Alleluia : for the Lord God omnipotent reigneth. 7 Let us be glad and rejoice, and give honor to him : for the marriage of the Lamb is come, and his wife hath made herself ready. [See 88, 237.]

572. *The cries of lost souls unavailing.*

'Job 27: 8 What *is* the hope of the hypocrite, though he hath gained, when God taketh away his soul? 9 Will God hear his cry when trouble cometh upon him?

Pr. 1: 24 Because I have called and ye refused; I have stretched out my hand, and no man regarded; 25 But ye have set at nought all my counsel, and would none of my reproof: 26 I also will laugh at your calamity: I will mock when your fear cometh; 27 When your fear cometh as desolation, and your destruction cometh as a whirlwind; when distress and anguish cometh upon you. 28 Then shall they call upon me, but I will not answer; they shall seek me early, but they shall not find me; 29 For that they hated knowledge, and did not choose the fear of the LORD: 30 They would none of my counsel: they despised all my reproof. 31 Therefore shall they eat of the fruit of their own way, and be filled with their own devices. 32 For the turning away of the simple shall slay them, and the prosperity of fools shall destroy them.

Lk. 13: 25 When once the Master of the house is risen up, and hath shut to the door, and ye begin to stand without, and to knock at the door, saying, Lord, Lord, open unto us; and he shall answer and say unto you, I know you not whence ye are.—16: 24 And he cried, and said, Father Abraham, have mercy on me, and send Lazarus, that he may dip the tip of his finger in water, and cool my tongue: for I am tormented in this flame. 25 But Abraham said, Son, remember that thou in thy lifetime receivedst thy good things, and likewise Lazarus evil things: but now he is comforted, and thou art torment-ed. 26 And besides all this, between us and you there is a great gulf fixed: so that they which would pass from hence to you, cannot; neither can they pass to us, that *would come* from thence. [See 390, 553–55, 559, 567.]

573. *Sources of future misery.*

1. *The loss of all hope, or complete despair.*

· Job 8: 13 The hypocrite's hope shall perish.—11: 20 The eyes of the wicked shall fail, and they shall not escape, and their hope *shall be as* the giving up of the ghost.

Pr. 10: 28 The hope of the righteous *shall be* gladness: but the expectation of the wicked shall perish.—11: 7 When a wicked man dieth, *his* expectation shall perish: and the hope of unjust *men* perisheth.

Lam. 3: 64 Render unto them a recompense, O LORD, ac-cording to the work of their hands. 65 Give them sorrow of heart, thy curse unto them.

Ezk. 22: 14 Can thy heart endure, or can thy hands be strong, in the days that I shall deal with thee? I the LORD have spoken *it*, and will do *it*. [See 390, 567.]

2. *Bitter reflections.*

Pr. 5: 11 And thou mourn at the last, when thy flesh and thy body are consumed, 12 And say, How have I hated instruction, and my heart despised reproof; 13 And have not obeyed the voice of my teachers, nor inclined mine ear to them that instructed me! 14 I was almost in all evil in the midst of the cóngregation and assembly.

Jer. 8: 20 The harvest is past, the summer is ended, and we are not saved.

Lk. 16: 25 Abraham said, Son, remember that thou in thy life-time receivedst thy good things, and likewise Lazarus evil things: but now he is comforted, and thou art tormented. [See 128, 131.]

3. *Deprivation of rest.*

Ps. 95: 11 Unto whom I sware in my wrath, that they should not enter into my rest. [Heb. 3: 18.]

Is. 57: 20 The wicked *are* like the troubled sea, when it cannot rest, whose waters cast up mire and dirt. 21 *There is* no peace, saith my God, to the wicked.

Rev. 14: 11 The smoke of their torment ascendeth up for ever and ever: and they have no rest day nor night.

4. *Banishment from all lovely beings, and suffering, while saints are rejoicing.*

Lk. 13: 28 There shall be weeping and gnashing of teeth, when ye shall see Abraham, and Isaac, and Jacob, and all the prophets, in the kingdom of God, and you *yourselves* thrust out.—16: 23 In hell he lifted up his eyes, being in torments, and seeth Abraham afar off, and Lazarus in his bosom.

Jn. 7: 34 Ye shall seek me, and shall not find *me:* and where I am, *thither* ye cannot come.

Rev. 14: 10 The same shall drink of the wine of the wrath of God, which is poured out without mixture into the cup of his indignation; and he shall be tormented with fire and brimstone in the presence of the holy angels, and in the presence of the Lamb. [See 387.]

5. *Darkness and gloom.*

Jer. 13: 16 Give glory to the LORD your God, before he cause darkness, and before your feet stumble upon the dark mountains, and while ye look for light, he turn it into the shadow of death, *and* make *it* gross darkness.

Its Sources.

Zep. 1: 15 That day *is* a day of wrath, a day of trouble and distress, a day of wasteness and desolation, a day of darkness and gloominess, a day of clouds and thick darkness.

Mat. 8: 12 The children of the kingdom shall be cast out into outer darkness : there shall be weeping and gnashing of teeth.

2 Pet. 2: 17 These are wells without water, clouds that are carried with a tempest; to whom the mist of darkness is reserved for ever.

Jude 12 These are spots in your feasts of charity, when they feast with you, feeding themselves without fear : clouds *they are* without water, carried about of winds ; trees whose fruit withereth, without fruit twice dead, plucked up by the roots ; 13 Raging waves of the sea, foaming out their own shame ; wandering stars, to whom is reserved the blackness of darkness for ever.

6. *Painful fears and terrors.*

Job 6: 4 The arrows of the Almighty *are* within me, the poison whereof drinketh up my spirit : the terrors of God do set themselves in array against me.

Ps. 73: 19 How are they *brought* into desolation, as in a moment : they are utterly consumed with terrors.

Pr. 10: 24 The fear of the wicked, it shall come upon him : but the desire of the righteous shall be granted.

2 Cor. 5: 11 Knowing therefore the terror of the Lord, we persuade men.

Rev. 6: 16 And said to the mountains and rocks, Fall on us, and hide us from the face of him that sitteth on the throne, and from the wrath of the Lamb.

7. *Enduring the just scorn of the universe forever.*

Job 22: 15 Hast thou marked the old way which wicked men have trodden ? 16 Which were cut down out of time, whose foundation was overflown with a flood : 19 The righteous see *it*, and are glad : and the innocent laugh them to scorn.

Ps. 2: 4 He that sitteth in the heavens shall laugh : the LORD shall have them in derision. 5 Then shall he speak unto them in his wrath, and vex them in his sore displeasure. —52: 1 Why boastest thou thyself in mischief, O mighty man ? the goodness of God *endureth* continually. 5 God shall likewise destroy thee for ever, he shall take thee away, and pluck thee out of *thy* dwelling-place, and root thee out of the land of the living. 6 The righteous also shall see, and fear, and shall

407

laugh at him.—59: 7 Behold, they belch out with their mouth: swords *are* in their lips: for who, *say they*, doth hear? 8 But thou, O LORD, shalt laugh at them; thou shalt have all the heathen in derision.

Pr. 1: 26 I also will laugh at your calamity: I will mock when your fear cometh; 27 When your fear cometh as desolation, and your destruction cometh as a whirlwind; when distress and anguish cometh upon you.—3: 34 Surely he scorneth the scorners: but he giveth grace unto the lowly.

Dan. 12: 2 Many of them that sleep in the dust of the earth shall awake, some to everlasting life, and some to shame *and* everlasting contempt. [See 513.]

8. *Pains of body by fire.*

Is. 33: 14 The sinners in Zion are afraid; fearfulness hath surprised the hypocrites. Who among us shall dwell with the devouring fire? who among us shall dwell with everlasting burnings?

Lk. 16: 24 He cried, and said, Father Abraham, have mercy on me, and send Lazarus, that he may dip the tip of his finger in water, and cool my tongue: for I am tormented in this flame. [See 343.]

574. *Degradation of the wicked, here and hereafter.*

Tit. 3: 3 We ourselves also were sometimes foolish, disobedient, deceived, serving divers lusts and pleasures, living in malice and envy, hateful, *and* hating one another.

Rev. 22: 15 Without *are* dogs, and sorcerers, and whoremongers, and murderers, and idolaters, and whosoever loveth and maketh a lie. [See 513.]

N. B. The foregoing pages on Probation and Punishment Future may be had separate, of John P. Jewett & Co, 17 and 19 Cornhill. Boston, and of M. W. Dodd, Brick Chapel, New York, at 25 cents a dozen.

REDEMPTION OF SAINTS.

575. *Redemption — Covenant of.*

Ps. 89: 3 I have made a covenant with my chosen, I have sworn unto David my servant, 4 Thy seed will I establish for ever, and build up thy throne to all generations.

Is. 53: 12 Therefore will I divide him *a portion* with the great, and he shall divide the spoil with the strong; because he hath poured out his soul unto death.

Zec. 6: 12 Thus speaketh the LORD of hosts, saying, Behold the man whose name *is* The BRANCH; and he shall grow up out of his place, and he shall build the temple of the LORD: 13 Even he shall build the temple of the LORD; and he shall bear the glory, and shall sit and rule upon his throne: and he shall be a priest upon his throne: and the counsel of peace shall be between them both.

Jn. 6: 39 This is the Father's will which hath sent me, that of all which he hath given me, I should lose nothing, but should raise it up again at the last day. — 17: 6 I have manifested thy name unto the men which thou gavest me out of the world: thine they were, and thou gavest them me; and they have kept thy word. 11 Holy Father, keep through thine own name those whom thou hast given me, that they may be one, as we *are.*

Heb. 13: 20 The God of peace, that brought again from the dead our Lord Jesus, that great Shepherd of the sheep, through the blood of the everlasting covenant, 21 Make you perfect in every good work.

576. *Necessity of atonement, or the salvation of sinners through obedience to the law of God, hopeless.*

Ps. 143: 2 Enter not into judgment with thy servant: for in thy sight shall no man living be justified.

Mat. 18: 11 The Son of man is come to save that which was lost.

Ac. 4: 12 Neither is there salvation in any other: for there is none other name under heaven given among men, whereby we must be saved. — 13: 38 Be it known unto you therefore, men *and* brethren, that through this man is preached unto you the forgiveness of sins; 39 And by him all that believe are justified from all things, from which ye could not be justified by the law of Moses.

Rom. 3: 19 We know that what things soever the law saith, it saith to them who are under the law: that every mouth may

35

be stopped, and all the world may become guilty before God. 20 Therefore by the deeds of the law, there shall no flesh be justified in his sight: for by the law *is* the knowledge of sin. —5: 6 When we were yet without strength, in due time Christ died for the ungodly.—9: 31 Israel, which followed after the law of righteousness, hath not attained to the law of righteousness. 32 Wherefore? Because *they sought it* not by faith, but as it were by the works of the law. For they stumbled at that stumbling-stone.

Gal. 2: 16 Knowing that a man is not justified by the works of the law, but by the faith of Jesus Christ, even we have believed in Jesus Christ, that we might be justified by the faith of Christ, and not by the works of the law: for by the works of the law shall no flesh be justified. 20 I am crucified with Christ: nevertheless, I live; yet not I, but Christ liveth in me: and the life which I now live in the flesh, I live by the faith of the Son of God, who loved me, and gave himself for me. 21 I do not frustrate the grace of God: for if righteousness *come* by the law, then Christ is dead in vain.—3: 10 As many as are of the works of the law, are under the curse: for it is written, Cursed *is* every one that continueth not in all things which are written in the book of the law to do them. 11 But that no man is justified by the law in the sight of God, *it is* evident: for, The just shall live by faith. 12 And the law is not of faith. 18 For if the inheritance *be* of the law, *it is* no more of promise: But God gave *it* to Abraham by promise. 19 Wherefore then *serveth* the law? It was added because of transgressions, till the seed should come to whom the promise was made; *and it was* ordained by angels in the hand of a mediator. 20 Now, a mediator is not *a mediator* of one; but God is one. 21 *Is* the law then against the promises of God? God forbid: for if there had been a law given which could have given life, verily righteousness should have been by the law. 22 But the scripture hath concluded all under sin, that the promise by faith of Jesus Christ might be given to them that believe. 23 But before faith came, we were kept under the law, shut up unto the faith which should afterwards be revealed. 24 Wherefore the law was our schoolmaster *to bring us* unto Christ, that we might be justified by faith.

Ph. 3: 4 If any other man thinketh that he hath whereof he might trust in the flesh, I more: 5 Circumcised the eighth day, of the stock of Israel, *of* the tribe of Benjamin, an Hebrew of the Hebrews; as touching the law, a Pharisee; 6 Concerning zeal, persecuting the church; touching the righteousness which is in the law, blameless. 7 But what things were gain to me, those I counted loss for Christ.

Heb. 9: 23 *It was* therefore necessary that the patterns of things in the heavens should be purified with these; but the heavenly things themselves with better sacrifices than these.

Jam. 2: 10 Whosoever shall keep the whole law, and yet offend in one *point*, he is guilty of all. [See 183.]

577. Redemption through the death or blood of Christ.

Lev. 17: 11 The life of the flesh *is* in the blood; and I have given it to you upon the altar, to make an atonement for your souls: for it *is* the blood *that* maketh an atonement for the soul.

Is. 53: 5 He *was* wounded for our transgressions, *he was* bruised for our iniquities; the chastisement of our peace *was* upon him; and with his stripes we are healed.

Mat. 20: 28 Even as the Son of man came not to be ministered unto, but to minister, and to give his life a ransom for many. — 26: 28 This is my blood of the new testament, which is shed for many for the remission of sins.

Jn. 3: 14 As Moses lifted up the serpent in the wilderness, even so must the Son of man be lifted up: 15 That whosoever believeth in him should not perish, but have eternal life. — 6: 51 The bread that I will give is my flesh, which I will give for the life of the world.

Ac. 20: 28 Take heed therefore unto yourselves, and to all the flock over the which the Holy Ghost hath made you overseers, to feed the church of God, which he hath purchased with his own blood.

Rom. 3: 25 Whom God hath set forth *to be* a propitiation, through faith in his blood. — 5: 8 God commendeth his love toward us, in that while we were yet sinners, Christ died for us. 9 Much more then, being now justified by his blood, we shall be saved from wrath through him. 11 We also joy in God, through our Lord Jesus Christ, by whom we have now received the atonement.

1 Cor. 5: 7 Christ our passover is sacrificed for us. — 15: 3 Christ died for our sins according to the scriptures.

Gal. 3: 13 Christ hath redeemed us from the curse of the law, being made a curse for us: for it is written, Cursed *is* every one that hangeth on a tree.

Ep. 2: 13 In Christ Jesus, ye, who sometimes were far off, are made nigh by the blood of Christ.

Heb. 9: 12 Neither by the blood of goats and calves, but by his own blood, he entered in once into the holy place, having obtained eternal redemption *for us.* 13 For if the blood of bulls and of goats, and the ashes of an heifer sprinkling the unclean, sanctifieth to the purifying of the flesh: 14 How much more shall the blood of Christ, who through the eternal Spirit offered himself without spot to God, purge your conscience from dead works to serve the living God? 22 And almost all things are by the law purged with blood; and without shedding of blood is no remission. 26 But now once in the end of the world hath he appeared to put away sin by the sacrifice of himself. 27 And as it is appointed unto men once to die, but after this the judgment: 28 So Christ was once offered to bear the sins of many.—10: 10 By the which will we are sanctified through the offering of the body of Jesus Christ once *for all.* 11 And every priest standeth daily ministering and offering oftentimes the same sacrifices, which can never take away sins: 12 But this man, after he had offered one sacrifice for sins, for ever sat down on the right hand of God; 13 From henceforth expecting till his enemies be made his footstool. 14 For by one offering he hath perfected for ever them that are sanctified. 19 Having therefore, brethren, boldness to enter into the holiest by the blood of Jesus, 20 By a new and living way, which he hath consecrated for us, through the vail, that is to say, his flesh.

1 Pet. 1: 18 Forasmuch as ye know that ye were not redeemed with corruptible things, *as* silver and gold, from your vain conversation *received* by tradition from your fathers; 19 But with the precious blood of Christ. — 2: 24 Who his own self bare our sins in his own body on the tree, that we, being dead to sins, should live unto righteousness: by whose stripes ye were healed.—3: 18 Christ also hath once suffered for sins, the just for the unjust, that he might bring us to God, being put to death in the flesh, but quickened by the Spirit.

1 Jn. 1: 7 If we walk in the light, as he is in the light, we have fellowship one with another, and the blood of Jesus Christ his Son cleanseth us from all sin.

[Jn. 1: 29, and 10: 15. Gal. 1: 4, and 2: 20. 1 Tim. 1: 1.]

578. *Efficacy of the atonement, or "the Lord our righteousness."*

Is. 53: 6 The LORD hath laid on him the iniquity of us all.

Jer. 23: 6 In his days Judah shall be saved, and Israel shall dwell safely : and this *is* his name whereby he shall be called, THE LORD OUR RIGHTEOUSNESS.

Dan. 9: 24 Seventy weeks are determined upon thy people and upon thy holy city, to finish the transgression, and to make an end of sins, and to make reconciliation for iniquity, and to bring in everlasting righteousness, and to seal up the vision and prophecy, and to anoint the Most Holy.

Jn. 3: 17 God sent not his Son into the world to condemn the world, but that the world through him might be saved. — 6: 51 I am the living bread which came down from heaven : if any man eat of this bread, he shall live for ever : and the bread that I will give is my flesh, which I will give for the life of the world. 55 My flesh is meat indeed, and my blood is drink indeed. — 10: 9 I am the door : by me if any man enter in, he shall be saved.

Rom. 1: 16 I am not ashamed of the gospel of Christ : for it is the power of God unto salvation to every one that believeth ; to the Jew first, and also to the Greek. 17 For therein is the righteousness of God revealed from faith to faith : as it is written, The just shall live by faith. — 3: 21 But now the righteousness of God without the law is manifested, being witnessed by the law and the prophets ; 22 Even the righteousness of God, *which is* by faith of Jesus Christ unto all, and upon all them that believe ; for there is no difference. — 5: 10 If when we were enemies, we were reconciled to God by the death of his Son ; much more, being reconciled, we shall be saved by his life. 11 And not only *so*, but we also joy in God, through our Lord Jesus Christ, by whom we have now received the atonement. 15 Not as the offence, so also *is* the free gift. For if through the offence of one many be dead, much more the grace of God, and the gift by grace, *which is* by one man, Jesus Christ, hath abounded unto many. 16 And not as *it was* by one that sinned, *so is* the gift. For the judgment *was* by one to condemnation, but the free gift *is* of many offences unto justification. 17 For if by one man's offence death reigned by one ; much more they which receive abundance of grace, and of the gift of righteousness, shall reign in life by one, Jesus Christ. 18 Therefore, as by the offence of one *judgment came* upon all men to condemnation, even so by the righteousness of one *the free gift came* upon all men unto justification of life. 19 For as by one man's disobedience many were made sinners, so by the obedience of one shall many be made righteous. 20 Moreover the law entered, that the offence might abound. But where sin abounded, grace did much more abound: 21 That as sin hath reigned unto death, even so might grace reign through righteousness unto eternal life, by Jesus Christ our Lord. — 10: 3 They, being ignorant of God's righteousness, and going about to establish their own righteousness, have not submitted themselves unto the righteousness of God. 4 For Christ *is* the end of the law for righteousness to every one that believeth.

Ep. 5: 2 Walk in love, as Christ also hath loved us, and hath given himself for us an offering and a sacrifice to God for a sweet-smelling savor.

Ph. 3: 9 And be found in him, not having mine own righteousness, which is of the law, but that which is through the faith of Christ, the righteousness which is of God by faith.

1 Jn. 4: 9 In this was manifested the love of God toward us, because that God sent his only-begotten Son into the world, that we might live through him. 10 Herein is love, not that we loved God, but that he loved us, and sent his Son *to be* the propitiation for our sins. [1 Jn. 3: 5.]

579. *Redemption requires a perfect Redeemer.*

Lev. 22: 19 *Ye shall offer* at your own will a male without blemish of the beeves, of the sheep, or of the goats. 20 *But* whatsoever hath a blemish, *that* shall ye not offer: for it shall not be acceptable for you.

Mal. 1: 8 If ye offer the blind for sacrifice, *is it* not evil? and if ye offer the lame and sick, *is it* not evil? offer it now unto thy governor; will he be pleased with thee, or accept thy person? saith the LORD of hosts.

Heb. 7: 26 Such a high priest became us, who *is* holy, harmless, undefiled, separate from sinners, and made higher than the heavens; 27 Who needeth not daily, as those high priests, to offer up sacrifice, first for his own sins, and then for the people's: for this he did once, when he offered up himself.

1 Pet. 1: 19 With the precious blood of Christ, as of a lamb without blemish and without spot.

580. *The Redeemer "a ransom for all."*

· Jn. 1: 29 Behold the lamb of God, which taketh away the sin of the world! — 3: 17 God sent not his Son into the world to condemn the world, but that the world through him might be saved. — 4: 42 This is indeed the Christ, the Saviour of the world.

Rom. 5: 18 As by the offence of one *judgment came* upon all men to condemnation, even so by the righteousness of one *the free gift came* upon all men unto justification of life.

2 Cor. 5: 14 The love of Christ constraineth us ; because we thus judge, that if one died for all, then were all dead : 15 And *that* he died for all, that they which live should not henceforth live unto themselves, but unto him which died for them, and rose again.

1 Tim. 2: 6 Who gave himself a ransom for all, to be testified in due time.

Heb. 2: 9 We see Jesus, who was made a little lower than the angels for the suffering of death, crowned with glory and honor; that he by the grace of God should taste death for every man.

1 Jn. 2: 2 He is the propitiation for our sins: and not for ours only, but also for *the sins of* the whole world. [See 370.]

581. *Agency of the Father in making atonement.*

Is. 53: 6 All we like sheep have gone astray; we have turned every one to his own way ; and the LORD hath laid on him the iniquity of us all. 10 It pleased the LORD to bruise him; he hath put *him* to grief.

Jn. 3: 16 God so loved the world, that he gave his only-begotten Son, that whosoever believeth in him, should not perish, but have everlasting lfe.

Rom. 3: 25 Whom God hath set forth *to be* a propitiation.

Gal. 4: 4 When the fulness of the time was come, God sent forth his Son, made of a woman, made under the law, 5 To redeem them that were under the law, that we might receive the adoption of sons.

1 Jn. 4: 9 In this was manifested the love of God toward us, because that God sent his only-begotten Son into the world, that we might live through him. 10 Herein is love, not that we loved God, but that he loved us, and sent his Son *to be* the propitiation for our sins.

582. *Redemption includes peace with God.*

Rom. 5: 1 Being justified by faith, we have peace with God, through our Lord Jesus Christ: 2 By whom also we have access by faith into this grace wherein we stand, and rejoice in hope of the glory of God. 10 For if when we were enemies, we were reconciled to God by the death of his Son, much more, being reconciled, we shall be saved by his life.

2 Cor. 5: 18 All things *are* of God, who hath reconciled us to himself by Jesus Christ, and hath given to us the ministry of

reconciliation; 19 To wit, That God was in Christ, reconciling the world unto himself, not imputing their trespasses unto them; and hath committed unto us the word of reconciliation.

Ep. 2: 13 In Christ Jesus, ye, who sometime were far off, are made nigh by the blood of Christ. 14 For he is our peace, who hath made both one, and hath broken down the middle wall of partition *between us;* 15 Having abolished in his flesh the enmity, *even* the law of commandments *contained* in ordinances: for to make in himself of twain one new man, *so* making peace; 16 And that he might reconcile both unto God in one body by the cross, having slain the enmity thereby: 17 And came and preached peace to you which were afar off, and to them that were nigh. 18 For through him we both have access by one Spirit unto the Father. 19 Now therefore ye are no more strangers and foreigners, but fellow-citizens with the saints, and of the household of God.

Col. 1: 20 Having made peace through the blood of his cross, by him to reconcile all things unto himself; by him, *I say,* whether *they be* things in earth, or things in heaven. 21 And you, that were sometime alienated and enemies in *your* mind by wicked works, yet now hath he reconciled, 22 In the body of his flesh through death, to present you holy, and unblamable, and unreprovable, in his sight.

Heb. 2: 17 In all things it behoved him to be made like unto *his* brethren; that he might be a merciful and faithful High Priest in things *pertaining* to God, to make reconciliation for the sins of the people. [See 666.]

583. *Redemption includes forgiveness or justification, and access.*

Ps. 32: 1 Blessed *is he whose* transgression *is* forgiven, *whose* sin *is* covered. 2 Blessed *is* the man unto whom the LORD imputeth not iniquity, and in whose spirit *there is* no guile. — [Rom. 4: 7] — Ps. 85: 2 Thou hast forgiven the iniquity of thy people, thou hast covered all their sin. 3 Thou hast taken away all thy wrath: thou hast turned *thyself* from the fierceness of thine anger. — 130: 4 *There is* forgiveness with thee, that thou mayest be feared.

Is. 43: 25 I, *even* I, *am* he that blotteth out thy transgressions for mine own sake, and will not remember thy sins. — 44: 22 I have blotted out, as a thick cloud, thy transgressions, and as a cloud, thy sins: return unto me; for I have redeemed thee. — 55: 7 Let the wicked forsake his way, and the unrighteous man his thoughts: and let him return unto the LORD, and he will have mercy upon him; and to our God, for he will abundantly pardon.

Includes Forgiveness, and Access.

Mic. 7: 18 Who *is* a God like unto thee, that pardoneth iniquity, and passeth by the transgression of the remnant of his heritage? he retaineth not his anger for ever, because he delighteth *in* mercy. 19 He will turn again, he will have compassion upon us ; he will subdue our iniquities : and thou wilt cast all their sins into the depths of the sea.

Rom. 3: 24 Being justified freely by his grace, through the redemption that is in Christ Jesus. — 6: 14 For sin shall not have dominion over you : for ye are not under the law, but under grace. — 8: 1 *There is* therefore now no condemnation to them which are in Christ Jesus, who walk not after the flesh, but after the Spirit. 2 For the law of the Spirit of life in Christ Jesus, hath made me free from the law of sin and death. 28 We know that all things work together for good, to them that love God, to them who are the called according to *his* purpose. 29 For whom he did foreknow, he also did predestinate *to be* conformed to the image of his Son, that he might be the first-born among many brethren. 30 Moreover, whom he did predestinate, them he also called, and whom he called, them he also justified : and whom he justified, them he also glorified. 33 Who shall lay any thing to the charge of God's elect? *It is* [Is it] God that justifieth : 34 Who *is* he that condemneth? *It is* [Is it] Christ that died, yea rather, that is risen again, who is even at the right hand of God, who also maketh intercession for us. 37 Nay, in all these things we are more than conquerors, through him that loved us.

1 Cor. 6: 11 Ye are justified in the name of the Lord Jesus, and by the Spirit of our God. — 15: 57 Thanks *be* to God, which giveth us the victory, through our Lord Jesus Christ.

Gal. 5: 18 If ye be led by the Spirit, ye are not under the law.

Ep. 1: 6 He hath made us accepted in the Beloved. 7 In whom we have redemption through his blood, the forgiveness of sins, according to the riches of his grace. — 2: 18 Through him we both have access by one Spirit unto the Father. 19 Now therefore ye are no more strangers and foreigners, but fellow-citizens with the saints, and of the household of God. — 3: 12 In whom we have boldness and access with confidence by the faith of him. — 4: 32 Be ye kind one to another, tender-hearted, forgiving one another, even as God for Christ's sake hath forgiven you.

Col. 1: 21 You, that were sometime alienated and enemies in *your* mind by wicked works, yet now hath he reconciled. — 2: 13 You, being dead in your sins and the uncircumcision of your flesh, hath he quickened together with him, having for-

417

Includes Adoption, Mercy, Faithfulness, and Loving-kindness.

given you all trespasses : 14 Blotting out the hand-writing of ordinances that was against us, which was contrary to us, and took it out of the way, nailing it to his cross.

1 Jn. 2: 12 I write unto you, little children, because your sins are forgiven you for his name's sake.

584. *Redemption includes adoption as " sons of God."*

Jn. 1: 12 As many as received him, to them gave he power to become the sons of God, *even* to them that believe on his name.

Rom. 8: 14 As many as are led by the Spirit of God, they are the sons of God. 15 For ye have not received the spirit of bondage again to fear ; but ye have received the Spirit of adoption, whereby we cry, Abba, Father. 16 The Spirit itself beareth witness with our spirit, that we are the children of God : 17 And if children, then heirs : heirs of God, and joint-heirs with Christ ; if so be that we suffer with *him*, that we may be also glorified together.

2 Cor. 6: 17 I will receive you ; 18 And will be a Father unto you, and ye shall be my sons and daughters, saith the Lord Almighty.

Gal. 3: 26 Ye are all the children of God by faith in Christ Jesus. 29 And if ye *be* Christ's, then are ye Abraham's seed, and heirs according to the promise. — 4: 4 When the fulness of the time was come, God sent forth his Son, made of a woman, made under the law, 5 To redeem them that were under the law, that we might receive the adoption of sons. 6 And because ye are sons, God hath sent forth the Spirit of his Son into your hearts, crying, Abba, Father. 7 Wherefore thou art no more a servant, but a son ; and if a son, then an heir of God through Christ.

Ep. 1: 5 Having predestinated us unto the adoption of children by Jesus Christ to himself, according to the good pleasure of his will.

1 Jn. 3: 1 Behold what manner of love the Father hath bestowed upon us, that we should be called the sons of God ! therefore the world knoweth us not, because it knew him not. 2 Beloved, now are we the sons of God, and it doth not yet appear what we shall be : but we know that, when he shall appear, we shall be like him ; for we shall see him as he is.

[See 254–5, 504, 672.]

585. *Redemption includes peculiar mercy, faithfulness, and loving kindness to Zion.*

Dt. 7: 9 Know therefore that the LORD thy God he *is* God,

the faithful God, which keepeth covenant and mercy with them that love him and keep his commandments to a thousand generations. — 32: 9 The LORD's portion *is* his people: Jacob *is* the lot of his inheritance. 10 He found him in a desert land, and in the waste howling wilderness; he led him about, he instructed him, he kept him as the apple of his eye. 11 As an eagle stirreth up her nest, fluttereth over her young, spreadeth abroad her wings, taketh them, beareth them on her wings; 12 So the LORD alone did lead him, and *there was* no strange god with him.

Neh. 9: 17 Thou *art* a God ready to pardon, gracious, and merciful, slow to anger, and of great kindness, and forsookest them not. 18 Yea, when they had made them a molten calf, and said, This *is* thy God that brought thee up out of Egypt, and had wrought great provocations; 19 Yet thou in thy manifold mercies forsookest them not in the wilderness: the pillar of the cloud departed not from them by day to lead them in the way; neither the pillar of fire by night, to shew them light, and the way wherein they should go. 20 Thou gavest also thy good Spirit to instruct them, and withheldest not thy manna from their mouth, and gavest them water for their thirst. 21 Yea, forty years didst thou sustain them in the wilderness, *so that* they lacked nothing; their clothes waxed not old, and their feet swelled not.

· Job 36: 7 He withdraweth not his eyes from the righteous: but with kings *are they* on the throne; yea, he doth establish them for ever, and they are exalted.

Ps. 105: 12 When they were *but* a few men in number; yea, very few, and strangers in it. 13 When they went from one nation to another, from *one* kingdom to another people; 14 He suffered no man to do them wrong: yea, he reproved kings for their sakes; 15 *Saying,* Touch not mine anointed, and do my prophets no harm.

Is. 40: 1 Comfort ye, comfort ye my people, saith your God. — 49: 13 Sing, O heavens, and be joyful, O earth; and break forth into singing, O mountains: for the LORD hath comforted his people, and will have mercy upon his afflicted. 14 But Zion said, The LORD hath forsaken me, and my Lord hath forgotten me. 15 Can a woman forget her sucking child, that she should not have compassion on the son of her womb? yea, they may forget, yet will I not forget thee. 16 Behold I have graven thee upon the palms of *my* hands: thy walls *are* continually before me. — 54: 8 In a little wrath I hid my face from thee for a moment; but with everlasting kindness will I have mercy on thee, saith the LORD, thy Redeemer. 10 For the

mountains shall depart, and the hills be removed: but my
kindness shall not depart from thee, neither shall the covenant
of my peace be removed, saith the LORD that hath mercy on
thee. 17 No weapon that is formed against thee shall prosper, and every tongue *that* shall rise against thee in judgment
thou shalt condemn. This *is* the heritage of the servants of the
LORD, and their righteousness *is* of me, saith the LORD. —
63: 9 In all their affliction he was afflicted, and the angel of
his presence saved them: in his love and in his pity he redeemed them; and he bare them and carried them all the days
of old.

Hos. 2: 19 I will betroth thee unto me for ever; yea, I will
betroth thee unto me in righteousness, and in judgment, and in
loving kindness, and in mercies.

Zec. 2: 8 Thus saith the LORD of hosts: After the glory
hath he sent me unto the nations which spoiled you: for he
that toucheth you, toucheth the apple of his eye.

Mat. 28: 20 Teaching them to observe all things whatsoever
I have commanded you: and lo, I am with you always, *even*
unto the end of the world.

Jn. 14: 16 I will pray the Father, and he shall give you
another Comforter, that he may abide with you for ever; 17
Even the Spirit of truth; whom the world cannot receive, because it seeth him not, neither knoweth him: but ye know him;
for he dwelleth with you, and shall be in you. 18 I will not
leave you comfortless: I will come to you.

Rev. 1: 5 Unto him that loved us, and washed us from our
sins in his own blood, 6 And hath made us kings and priests
unto God and his Father; to him *be* glory and dominion for
ever and ever. [See 60, 94–5, 233, 672.]

586. *Redemption or salvation by grace.*

Ac. 20: 24 The gospel of the grace of God.

Rom. 3: 24 Being justified freely by his grace, through the
redemption that is in Christ Jesus. — 5: 8 God commendeth
his love toward us, in that while we were yet sinners, Christ
died for us. 15 (But not as the offence, so also *is* the free
gift. For if through the offence of one many be dead, much
more the grace of God, and the gift by grace, *which is* by one
man, Jesus Christ, hath abounded unto many. 16 And not as
it was by one that sinned, *so is* the gift. For the judgment
was by one to condemnation, but the free gift *is* of many
offences unto justification. 17 For if by one man's offence
death reigned by one; much more they which receive abundance of grace, and of the gift of righteousness, shall reign in

A Work of Grace — Honorable to God's Law.

life by one, Jesus Christ.) — 9: 16 *It is* not of him that willeth, nor of him that runneth, but of God that showeth mercy. 11: 5 At this present time also there is a remnant according to the election of grace. 6 And if by grace, then *is it* no more of works: otherwise grace is no more grace.

1 Cor. 4: 7 Who maketh thee to differ *from another?* and what hast thou that thou didst not receive? now if thou didst receive *it*, why dost thou glory, as if thou hadst not received *it?* — 15: 10 By the grace of God I am what I am.

Ep. 1: 5 Having predestinated us unto the adoption of children by Jesus Christ to himself, according to the good pleasure of his will, 6 To the praise of the glory of his grace, wherein he hath made us accepted in the Beloved. — 2: 4 God, who is rich in mercy, for his great love wherewith he loved us. 5 Even when we were dead in sins, hath quickened us together with Christ; (by grace ye are saved;) 6 And hath raised *us* up together, and made *us* sit together in heavenly *places*, in Christ Jesus: 7 That in the ages to come he might shew the exceeding riches of his grace in *his* kindness toward us through Christ Jesus. 8 For by grace are ye saved, through faith; and that not of yourselves: *it is* the gift of God: 9 Not of works, lest any man should boast. 10 For we are his workmanship, created in Christ Jesus unto good works, which God hath before ordained that we should walk in them.

2 Tim. 1: 9 Who hath saved us, and called *us* with an holy calling, not according to our works, but according to his own purpose and grace, which was given us in Christ Jesus, before the world began.

Tit. 3: 5 Not by works of righteousness which we have done, but according to his mercy he saved us, by the washing of regeneration, and renewing of the Holy Ghost; 6 Which he shed on us abundantly, through Jesus Christ our Saviour; 7 That being justified by his grace, we should be made heirs according to the hope of eternal life.

1 Pet. 1: 10 Of which salvation the prophets have inquired and searched diligently, who prophesied of the grace *that should come* unto you. [See 305, 668.]

587. *Redemption honorable to God and his law.*

Ps. 85: 10 Mercy and truth are met together: righteousness and peace have kissed *each other*.

Is. 42: 21 The LORD is well pleased for his righteousness' sake; he will magnify the law, and make *it* honorable.

Rom. 3: 26 To declare, *I say*, at this time his righteousness: that he might be just, and the justifier of him which believeth in Jesus. 31 Do we then make void the law through faith? God forbid : yea, we establish the law.

2 Cor. 4: 6 God, who commanded the light to shine out of darkness, hath shined in our hearts, to *give* the light of the knowledge of the glory of God in the face of Jesus Christ.

Ep. 3: 8 Unto me, who am less than the least of all saints in this grace given, that I should preach among the Gentiles the unsearchable riches of Christ; 9 And to make all *men* see what *is* the fellowship of the mystery, which from the beginning of the world hath been hid in God, who created all things by Jesus Christ: 10 To the intent that now unto the principalities and powers in heavenly *places* might be known by the church the manifold wisdom of God, 11 According to the eternal purpose which he purposed in Christ Jesus our Lord.

1 Tim. 1: 11 According to the glorious gospel of the blessed God which was committed to my trust.

1 Pet. 1: 12 Which things the angels desire to look into.

[See 277.]

REGENERATION AND SANCTIFICATION

588. *God able to sanctify us, and to keep us from sin.*

Ps. 110: 3 Thy people *shall be* willing in the day of thy power.

Ezk. 36: 26 I will take away the stony heart out of your flesh, and I will give you an heart of flesh.

Mic. 2: 7 O *thou that art* named The house of Jacob, is the Spirit of the LORD straitened?

2 Cor. 9: 8 God *is* able to make all grace abound toward you; that ye, always having all sufficiency in all *things*, may abound to every good work.

Ep. 1: 18 The eyes of your understanding being enlightened; that ye may know what is the hope of his calling, and what the riches of the glory of his inheritance in the saints,. 19 And what *is* the exceeding greatness of his power to usward who believe, according to the working of his mighty power, 20 Which he wrought in Christ when he raised him from the dead. — 3: 20 Unto him that is able to do exceeding abundantly above all that we ask or think, according to the power that worketh in us. 21 Unto him *be* glory in the church by Christ Jesus throughout all ages, world without end.

Jude 24 Unto him that is able to keep you from falling, and

to present *you* faultless before the presence of his glory with exceeding joy, 25 To the only wise God our Saviour, *be* glory and majesty, dominion and power, both now and ever. [See 218, 234.]

589. *Regeneration necessary, or the total sinfulness of unregenerate doings.*

Ps. 50: 16 Unto the wicked God saith, what hast thou to do to declare my statutes, or *that* thou shouldest take my covenant in thy mouth?

Is. 1: 11 To what purpose is the multitude of your sacrifices unto me ? saith the LORD : I am full of the burnt-offerings of rams, and the fat of fed beasts ; and I delight not in the blood of bullocks, or of lambs, or of he-goats. ·12 When ye come to appear before me, who hath required this at your hand, to tread my courts ? 13. Bring no more vain oblations : incense is an abomination unto me ; the new moons and sabbaths, the calling of assemblies, I cannot away with ; *it is* iniquity, even the solemn meeting. 14 Your new moons and your appointed feasts my soul hateth : they are a trouble unto me ; I am weary to bear *them.* 15 And when ye spread forth your hands, I will hide mine eyes from you ; yea, when ye make many prayers, I will not hear : your hands are full of blood.

Am. 5: 21 I hate, I despise your feast days, and I will not smell in your solemn assemblies. 22 Though ye offer me burnt-offerings and your meat-offerings, I will not accept *them:* neither will I regard the peace-offerings of your fat beasts. 23 Take thou away from me the noise of thy songs ; for I will not hear the melody of thy viols.

Mat. 15: 7 *Ye* hypocrites, well did Esaias prophesy of you, saying, 8 This people draweth nigh unto me with their mouth, and honoreth me with *their* lips ; but their heart is far from me. — 18: 3 Verily, I say unto you, Except ye be converted, and become as little children, ye shall not enter into the kingdom of heaven. — 23: 25 Wo unto you, scribes and Pharisees, hypocrites ! for ye make clean the outside of the cup and of the platter, but within they are full of extortion and excess. 26 *Thou* blind Pharisee, cleanse first that *which is* within the cup and platter, that the outside of them may be clean also.

Jn. 3: 3 Jesus answered, and said unto him, Verily, verily, I say unto thee, Except a man be born again, he cannot see the kingdom of God. 5 Except a man be born of water, and *of* the Spirit, he cannot enter into the kingdom of

God. 7 Marvel not that I said unto thee, Ye must be born again.

Heb. 11: 6 Without faith *it is* impossible to please *him:* for he that cometh to God must believe that he is, and *that* he is a rewarder of them that diligently seek him.

[See 165, 546, 688–9.]

590. *Regeneration preceded by conviction, and the death of false hopes.*

Ac. 2: 37 When they heard *this*, they were pricked in their heart, and said unto Peter and to the rest of the apostles, Men *and* brethren, what shall we do?

Rom. 7: 9 I was alive without the law once: but when the commandment came, sin revived, and I died. 10 And the commandment which *was ordained* to life, I found *to be* unto death. 11 For sin, taking occasion by the commandment, deceived me, and by it slew *me*. [See 356.]

591. *Regeneration, a radical change.*

Ezk. 36: 26 A new heart also will I give you, and a new spirit will I put within you.

Rom. 2: 28 He is not a Jew which is one outwardly; neither *is that* circumcision which is outward in the flesh: 29 But he *is* a Jew which is one inwardly; and circumcision *is that* of the heart, in the spirit, *and* not in the letter; whose praise *is* not of men, but of God.

1 Cor. 5:17 If any man *be* in Christ, *he is* a new creature: old things are passed away; behold, all things are become new.

Gal. 5: 24 They that are Christ's have crucified the flesh, with the affections and lusts. — 6: 15 In Christ Jesus, neither circumcision availeth anything, nor uncircumcision, but a new creature. [See 645.]

592. *Regeneration a moral or spiritual change.*

Jn. 3: 6 That which is born of the flesh is flesh; and that which is born of the Spirit is spirit.

Gal. 5: 22 But the fruit of the Spirit is love, joy, peace, long-suffering, gentleness, goodness, faith.

Ep. 4: 22 That ye put off concerning the former conversation the old man, which is corrupt according to the deceitful lusts: 23 And be renewed in the spirit of your mind.

1 Jn. 4: 7 Beloved, let us love one another, for love is of God; and every one that loveth is born of God, and knoweth God. [See 329, 600.]

593. *Regeneration alarming to sinners.*

Ps. 40: 3 He hath put a new song in my mouth, *even* praise unto our God: many shall see *it,* and fear, and shall trust in the LORD.

Ac. 2: 41 Then they that gladly received his word, were baptized: and the same day there were added *unto them* about three thousand souls. 42 And they continued steadfastly in the apostles' doctrine and fellowship, and in breaking of bread, and in prayers. 43 And fear came upon every soul.

594. *Creative or omnipotent power exerted in regeneration and sanctification.*

Dt. 30: 6 The LORD thy God will circumcise thy heart, and the heart of thy seed, to love the LORD thy God with all thy heart, and with all thy soul, that thou mayest live.

Ps. 51: 10 Create in me a clean heart, O God: and renew a right spirit within me.

Jer. 24: 7 I will give them a heart to know me, that I *am* the LORD : and they shall be my people, and I will be their God ; for they shall return unto me with their whole heart. — 31: 33 This *shall be* the cevenant that I will make with the house of Israel; After those days, saith the LORD, I will put my law in their inward parts, and write it in their hearts; and will be their God, and they shall be my people.

Ezk. 11: 19 I will give them one heart, and I will put a new spirit within you; and I will take the stony heart out of their flesh, and will give them an heart of flesh: 20 That they may walk in my statutes, and keep mine ordinances, and do them : and they shall be my people, and I will be their God. — 36: 25 Then will I sprinkle clean water upon you, and ye shall be clean : from all your filthiness, and from all your idols, will I cleanse you. 26 A new heart also will I give you. and a new spirit will I put within you: and I will take away the stony heart out of your flesh, and I will give you an heart of flesh. 27 And I will put my Spirit within you, and cause you to walk in my statutes, and ye shall keep my judgments, and do *them.*

Jn. 1: 12 As many as received him, to them gave he power to become the sons of God, *even* to them that believe on his name: 13 Which were born, not of blood, nor of the will of the flesh, nor of the will of man, but of God.

Rom. 9: 15 He saith to Moses, I will have mercy on whom I will have mercy, and I will have compassion on whom I will have compassion. 16 So then, *it is* not of him that willeth,

36*

nor of him that runneth, but of God that sheweth mercy. —
15: 16 Being sanctified by the Holy Ghost.

1 Cor. 3: 5 Who then is Paul, and who *is* Apollos, but ministers by whom ye believed, even as the Lord gave to every
man? 6 I have planted, Apollos watered: but God gave the
increase. 7 So then, neither is he that planteth any thing,
neither he that watereth: but God that giveth the, increase.
— 4: 7 Who maketh thee to differ *from another?* and what
hast thou that thou didst not receive? now if thou didst
receive *it,* why dost thou glory, as if thou hadst not received
it?

Ep. 2: 4 God, who is rich in mercy, for his great love wherewith he loved us, 5 Even when we were dead in sins,
hath quickened us together with Christ. 8 For by grace ye
are saved, through faith; and that not of yourselves : *it is* the
gift of God. 10 For we are his workmanship, created in
Christ Jesus unto good works, which God hath before ordained
that we should walk in them. — 4: 24 That ye put on the new
man, which after God is created in righteousness and true holiness.

Col. 1: 12 Giving thanks unto the Father, which hath made
us meet to be partakers of the inheritance of the saints 'in
light: 13 Who hath delivered us from the power of darkness,
and hath translated *us* into the kingdom of his dear Son.

2 Th. 2: 13 God hath from the beginning chosen you to salvation, through sanctification of the Spirit, and belief of the
truth.

Tit. 3: 5 Not by works of righteousness which we have done,
but according to his mercy he saved us, by the washing of
regeneration, and renewing of the Holy Ghost ; 6 Which he
shed on us abundantly, through Jesus Christ, our Saviour.

Heb. 13: 20 The God of peace, 21 Make you perfect in
every good work, to do his will, working in you that which is
well-pleasing in his sight, through Jesus Christ; to whom *be*
glory for ever and ever.

Jam. 1: 18 Of his own will begat he us with the word of
truth, that we should be a kind of first-fruits of his creatures.

[See 347,(4) 434.]

595. *Particular holy exercises the gift of God.*

Ac. 5: 31 Him hath God exalted with his right hand *to be* a
Prince and a Saviour, for to give repentance to Israel, and forgiveness of sins.

Rom. 5: 5 Hope maketh not ashamed: because the love of
God is shed abroad in our hearts by the Holy Ghost which is

given unto us. — 12: 3 I say, through the grace given unto me, to every man that is among you, not to think *of himself* more highly than he ought to think; but to think soberly, according as God hath dealt to every man the measure of faith.·

Ep. 2: 8 By grace are ye saved, through faith: and that not of yourselves: *it is* the gift of God.

2 Tim. 2: 25 In meekness instructing those that oppose themselves; if God peradventure will give them repentance to the acknowledging of the truth.

596. *Saints as dependant as sinners, for holy affections.*

Ps. 17: 5 Hold up my goings in thy paths, *that* my footsteps slip not. — 51: 11 Cast me not away from thy presence; and take not thy Holy Spirit from me. 12 Restore unto me the joy of thy salvation; and uphold me *with thy* free Spirit. — 68: 35 O God, *thou art* terrible out of thy Holy places: the God of Israel *is* he that giveth strength and power unto *his* people. — 119: 32 I will run the way of thy commandments, when thou shalt enlarge my heart. 117 Hold thou me up, and I shall be safe: and I will have respect unto thy statutes continually.

Song 1: 4 Draw me, we will run after thee:

Jn. 15: 5 I am the vine, ye *are* the branches: He that abideth in me, and I in him, the same bringeth forth much fruit: for without me ye can do nothing.

1 Cor. 15: 10 By the grace of God I am what I am: and his grace which *was bestowed* upon me, was not in vain; but I labored more abundantly than they all: yet not I, but the grace of God which was with me.

1 Pet. 1: 5 Who are kept by the power of God through faith unto salvation. [See 262.]

597. *Effectual calling.*

Ac. 2: 39 The promise is unto you, and to your children, and to all that are afar off, *even* as many as the Lord our God shall call.

Rom. 1: 6 Among whom are ye also the called of Jesus Christ: 7 To all that be in Rome, beloved of God, called *to be* saints: Grace to you, and peace from God our Father, and the Lord Jesus Christ. — 8: 30 Whom he did predestinate, them he also called: and whom he called, them he also justified; and whom he justified, them he also glorified. — 9: 23 That he might make known the riches of his glory on the vessels of mercy, which he had afore prepared unto glory, 24 Even us, whom he hath called, not of the Jews only, but also of the Gentiles?

1 Cor. 1: 9 God *is* faithful, by whom ye were called unto the

fellowship of his Son Jesus Christ our Lord. 23 But we preach Christ crucified, unto the Jews a stumbling-block, and unto the Greeks foolishness; 24 But unto them which are .called, both Jews and Greeks, Christ the power of God, and the wisdom of God.

1 Th. 2: 12 Walk worthy of God, who hath called you unto his kingdom and glory. [1 Pet. 2: 9.]

598. *Regeneration and sanctification illuminate.*

Ps. 25: 14 The secret of the LORD *is* with them that fear him; and he will shew them his covenant.

Pr. 1: 7 The fear of the LORD *is* the beginning of knowledge: *but* fools despise wisdom and instruction. — 16: 23 The heart of the wise teacheth his mouth and addeth learning to his lips. — 28: 5 Evil men understand not judgment; but they that seek the Lord understand all *things.*

Ec. 8: 5 Whoso keepeth the commandment shall feel no evil thing: and a wise man's heart discerneth both time and judgment.

Dan. 12: 10 Many shall be purified, and made white, and tried; but the wicked shall do wickedly: and none of the wicked shall understand; but the wise shall understand.

Jn. 7: 17 If any man will do his will, he shall know of the doctrine, whether it be of God, or *whether* I speak of myself.

1 Cor. 2: 14 The natural man receiveth not the things of the Spirit of God: for they are foolishness unto him: neither can he know *them*, because they are spiritually discerned. 15 But he that is spiritual judgeth all things, yet he himself is judged of no man.

2 Cor. 4: 6 God, who commanded the light to shine out of darkness, hath shined in our hearts, to *give* the light of the knowledge of the glory of God in the face of Jesus Christ.

Ep. 5: 8 Ye were sometime darkness, but now *are ye* light in the Lord: walk as children of light.

Col. 1: 12 Giving thanks unto the Father, which hath made us meet to be partakers of the inheritance of the saints in light: 13 Who hath delivered us from the power of darkness, and hath translated *us* into the kingdom of his dear Son.

1 Th. 5: 4 Ye, brethren, are not in darkness, that that day should overtake you as a thief. 5 Ye are all the children of light, and the children of the day: we are not of the night, nor of darkness.

1 Pet. 2: 9 Ye *are* a chosen generation, a royal priesthood, a holy nation, a peculiar people; that ye should shew forth

the praises of him who hath called you out of darkness into his marvellous light.

1 Jn. 2: 8 A new commandment I write unto you, which thing is true in him and in you: because the darkness is past, and the true light now shineth. 9 He that saith he is in the light, and hateth his brother, is in darkness even until now. 10 He that loveth his brother abideth in the light, and there is none occasion of stumbling in him. 11 But he that hateth his brother is in darkness, and walketh in darkness, and knoweth not whither he goeth, because that darkness hath blinded his eyes. 20 But ye have an unction from the Holy One, and ye know all things. 21 I have not written unto you because ye know not the truth, but because ye know it, and that no lie is of the truth. [See 707.]

599. *Regeneration connected with divine teaching.*

Job 36: 22 Behold, God exalteth by his power: who teacheth like him?

Ps. 25: 8 Good and upright *is* the LORD : therefore will he teach sinners in the way. 9 The meek will he guide in judgment: and the meek will he teach his way. 12 What man *is* he that feareth the LORD? him shall he teach in the way *that* he shall choosê.

Is. 54: 13 All thy children *shall be* taught of the LORD ; and great *shall be* the peace of thy children.

Jn. 6: 45 It is written in the prophets, And they shall be all taught of God. Every man therefore that hath heard, and hath learned of the Father, cometh unto me.

600. *Are men active, under the influence of means and instruments, and the agency of the Holy Spirit?*

Ps. 119: 59 I thought on my ways, and turned my feet unto thy testimonies. 112 I have inclined mine heart to perform thy statutes always, *even unto* the end.

Ezk. 18: 27 When the wicked *man* turneth away from his wickedness that he hath committed, and doeth that which is lawful and right, he shall save his soul alive. 28 Because he considereth and turneth away from all his transgressions that he hath committed, he shall surely live, he shall not die.

Ac. 17: 28 In him we live, and move, and have our being.

1 Cor. 4: 15 Though ye have ten thousand instructors in Christ, yet *have ye* not many fathers : for in Christ Jesus I have begotten you through the gospel.

Col. 3: 9 Lie not one to another, seeing that ye have put off the old man with his deeds ; 10 And have put on the new

Required.

man, which is renewed in knowledge after the image of him that created him.

1 Pet. 1: 22 Seeing ye have purified your souls in obeying the truth through the Spirit unto unfeigned love of the brethren, *see that ye* love one another with a pure heart fervently. [See 271, 329, 332, 432, 592.]

601. *Sinners required to "be converted," and holy.*

Dt. 10: 16 Circumcise therefore the foreskin of your heart, and be no more stiff-necked.

Job. 22: 21 Acquaint now thyself with him, and be at peace: thereby good shall come unto thee.

Pr. 23: 26 My son, give me thine heart, and let thine eyes observe my ways.

Is. 1: 16 Wash you, make you clean : put away the evil of your doings from before mine eyes ; cease to do evil ; 17 Learn to do well.—42: 18 Hear, ye deaf ; and look, ye blind, that ye may see.—45: 22 Look unto me, and be ye saved, all the ends of the earth: for I *am* God, and *there is* none else.—55: 7 Let the wicked forsake his way, and the unrighteous man his thoughts : and let him return unto the LORD, and he will have mercy upon him ; and to our God, for he will abundantly pardon.

Jer. 4: 3 Thus saith the LORD to the men of Judah and Jerusalem, Break up your fallow ground, and sow not among thorns. 4 Circumcise yourselves to the LORD, and take away the foreskins of your heart. 14 O Jerusalem, wash thine heart from wickedness, that thou mayest be saved. How long shall thy vain thoughts lodge within thee ?

Ezk. 18: 30 Repent, and turn *yourselves* from all your transgressions ; so iniquity shall not be your ruin. 31 Cast away from you all your transgressions, whereby ye have transgressed: and make you a new heart and a new spirit: for why will ye die, O house of Israel ? 32 For I have no pleasure in the death of him that dieth, saith the Lord GOD : wherefore turn *yourselves*, and live ye.—33: 11 Say unto them, *As* I live, saith the Lord GOD, I have no pleasure in the death of the wicked ; but that the wicked turn from his way and live : turn ye, turn ye from your evil ways ; for why will ye die, O house of Israel?

Mat. 25: 24 He which had received the one talent came, and said, Lord, I knew thee that thou art a hard man, reaping where thou hast not sown, and gathering where thou hast not strewed: 25 And I was afraid, and went and hid thy talent in the earth: lo, *there* thou hast *that is* thine. 26 His lord answered and said unto him, *Thou* wicked and slothful servant, thou knewest that I reap where I sowed not, and gather where I have not strewed : 27 Thou oughtest therefore to have put my money to the exchangers, and *then* at my coming I should have received mine own with usury. [Lk. 19: 20.]

Ac. 3: 19 Repent ye therefore, and be converted, that your sins may be blotted out, when the times of refreshing shall come from the presence of the Lord.—16: 31 They said, Believe on the Lord Jesus Christ, and thou shalt be saved, and thy house.—26: 20 But shewed first unto them of Damascus, and at Jerusalem, and throughout all the coasts of Judea, and *then* to the Gentiles, that they should repent and turn to God, and do works meet for repentance.

Rom. 12: 2 Be not conformed to this world : but be ye transformed by the renewing of your mind, that ye may prove what *is* that good, and acceptable, and perfect will of God.—13: 14 Put ye on the Lord Jesus Christ, and make not provision for the flesh, to *fulfil* the lusts *thereof.*

2 Cor. 5: 20 We are ambassadors for Christ, as though God did beseech *you* by us : we pray *you* in Christ's stead, be ye reconciled to God.

Ep. 4: 22 That ye put off concerning the former conversation the old man, which is corrupt according to the deceitful lusts ; 23 And be renewed in the spirit of your mind : 24 And that ye put on the new man, which after God is created in righteousness and true holiness.

Ep. 5: 14 Wherefore he saith, Awake, thou that sleepest, and arise from the dead, and Christ shall give thee light.

Jam. 4: 7 Submit yourselves therefore to God. Resist the devil, and he will flee from you. 8 Draw nigh to God and he will draw nigh to you. Cleanse *your* hands, *ye* sinners, and purify *your* hearts, *ye* double-minded. [See 183, 288, 606.]

602. *Obedience to God, the evidence of regeneration.*

Ps. 119: 6 Then shall I not be ashamed, when I have respect unto all thy commandments.

Mat. 7: 16 Ye shall know them by their fruits : Do men gather grapes of thorns, or figs of thistles? 17 Even so every good tree bringeth forth good fruit ; but a corrupt tree bringeth forth evil fruit. 18 A good tree cannot bring forth evil fruit, neither *can* a corrupt tree bring forth good fruit. 19 Every tree that bringeth not forth good fruit is hewn down, and cast into the fire. 20 Wherefore, by their fruits ye shall know them. 21 Not every one that saith unto me, Lord, Lord, shall enter into the kingdom of heaven; but he that doeth the will of my Father which is in heaven.

Jn. 8: 47 He that is of God, heareth God's words: ye therefore hear *them* not, because ye are not of God.—13: 35 By this shall all *men* know that ye are my disciples, if ye have love one to another.—14: 21 He that hath my commandments, and keepeth them, he it is that loveth me.   23 Jesus answered and said unto him, If a man love me, he will keep my words: and my Father will love him, and we will come unto him, and make our abode with him.   24 He that loveth me not, keepeth not my sayings: and the word which ye hear is not mine, but the Father's which sent me.

Rom. 8: 9 If any man have not the Spirit of Christ, he is none of-his.   14 As many as are led by the Spirit of God, they are the sons of God.

Jam. 2: 17 Faith, if it hath not works, is dead, being alone.

1 Jn. 2: 3 Hereby we do know that we know him, if we keep his commandments.   4 He that saith, I know him, and keepeth not his commandments, is a liar, and the truth is not in him.   5 But whoso keepeth his word, in him verily is the love of God perfected: hereby know we that we are in him. 6 He that saith he abideth in him, ought himself also so to walk, even as he walked.—3: 14 We know that we have passed from death unto life, because we love the brethren.   He that loveth not *his* brother, abideth in death.   18 My little children, let us not love in word, neither in tongue, but in deed and in truth.   19 And hereby we know that we are of the truth, and shall assure our hearts before him.   24 And he that keepeth his commandments, dwelleth in him, and he in him.   And hereby we know that he abideth in us, by the Spirit which he hath given us.—5: 1 Whosoever believeth that Jesus is the Christ, is born of God: and every one that loveth him that begat, loveth him also that is begotten of him.   2 By this we know that we love the children of God, when we love God, and keep his commandments.   3 For this is the love of God, that we keep his commandments; and his commandments are not grievous.   4 For whatsoever is born of God, overcometh the world: and this is the victory that overcometh the world, *even* our faith.   [See 186.]

432

REPENTANCE.

603. *Nature and manifestations of repentance.*

Job 42: 5 I have heard of thee by the hearing of the ear: but now mine eye seeth thee: 6 Wherefore I abhor *myself*, and repent in dust and ashes.

Ps. 38: 3 *There is* no soundness in my flesh because of thine anger; neither *is there any* rest in my bones because of my sin. 4 For mine iniquities are gone over mine head: as an heavy burden they are too heavy for me. 5 My wounds stink, *and* are corrupt because of my foolishness. 6 I am troubled; I am bowed down greatly; I go mourning all the day long. 7 For my loins are filled with a loathsome *disease:* and *there is* no soundness in my flesh. 8 I am feeble and sore broken: I have roared by reason of the disquietness of my heart. 9 Lord, all my desire *is* before thee; and my groaning is not hid from thee. 10 My heart panteth, my strength faileth me: as for the light of mine eyes, it also is gone. 18 I will declare mine iniquity; I will be sorry for my sin.—51: 3 I acknowledge my transgressions: and. my sin *is* ever before me. 4 Against thee, thee only, have I sinned, and done *this* evil in thy sight: that thou mightest be justified when thou speakest, *and* be clear when thou judgest. 17 The sacrifices of God *are* a broken spirit: a broken and a contrite heart, O God, thou wilt not despise.—119: 59 I thought on my ways, and turned my feet unto thy testimonies. 60 I made haste, and delayed not to keep thy commandments.

Ezk. 36: 31 Then shall ye remember your own evil ways, and your doings that *were* not good, and shall loathe yourselves in your own sight for your iniquities, and for your abominations. [Ezk. 20: 43.]

Mat. 26: 75 Peter remembered the word of Jesus, which said unto him, Before the cock crow, thou shalt deny me thrice. And he went out, and wept bitterly.

Lk. 15: 18 I will arise and go to my father, and will say unto him, Father, I have sinned against heaven, and before thee, 19 And am no more worthy to be called thy son: make me as one of thy hired servants.—18: 13 The publican, standing afar off, would not lift up so much as *his* eyes unto heaven, but smote upon his breast, saying, God be merciful to me a sinner.

2 Cor. 7: 9 I rejoice, not that ye were made sorry, but that ye sorrowed to repentance: for ye were made sorry after a godly manner, that ye might receive damage by us in nothing.

10 For godly sorrow worketh repentance to salvation not to be repented of: but the sorrow of the world worketh death. [See 30, 124, 356–7.]

604. *Moral dignity of true penitence for sin.*

Is. 57: 15 Thus saith the high and lofty One that inhabiteth eternity, whose name *is* Holy; I dwell in the high and holy *place*, with him also *that is* of a contrite and humble spirit, to revive the spirit of the humble, and to revive the heart of the contrite ones.

Lk. 15: 7 I say unto you, that likewise joy shall be in heaven over one sinner that repenteth, more than over ninety and nine just persons which need no repentance. 21 The son said unto him, Father, I have sinned against Heaven, and in thy sight, and am no more worthy to be called thy son. 22 But the father said to his servants, Bring forth the best robe, and put *it* on him. [See 672.]

605. *Effects of repentance and godly sorrow.*

2 Cor. 7: 11 Behold this self-same thing, that ye sorrowed after a godly sort, what carefulness it wrought in you, yea, *what* clearing of yourselves, yea, *what* indignation, yea, *what* fear, yea, *what* vehement desire, yea, *what* zeal, yea, *what* revenge! In all *things* ye have approved yourselves to be clear in this matter. [See 602, 621.]

606. *Repentance required — its necessity.*

Ezk. 14: 6 Say unto the house of Israel, Thus saith the Lord GOD. Repent, and turn *yourselves* from your idols; and turn away your faces from all your abominations. — 18: 30 I will judge you, O house of Israel, every one according to his ways, saith the Lord GOD. Repent, and turn *yourselves* from all your transgressions; so iniquity shall not be your ruin.

Mat. 3: 1 In those days came John the Baptist, preaching in the wilderness of Judea, And saying, Repent ye; for the kingdom of heaven is at hand. — 4: 17 From that time Jesus began to preach, and to say, Repent; for the kingdom of heaven is at hand.

Lk. 13: 3 I tell you, Nay; but except ye repent, ye shall all likewise perish.

Ac. 2: 38 Then Peter said unto them, Repent, and be baptized every one of you in the name of Jesus Christ, for the remission of sins, and ye shall receive the gift of the Holy Ghost. — 3: 19 Repent ye therefore, and be converted, that your sins may be blotted out, when the times of refreshing shall come from the presence of the Lord. — 8: 22 Repent therefore of this thy wickedness, and pray God, if perhaps the thought of thy heart may be forgiven thee. — 17: 30 The times of this ignorance God winked at; but now commandeth all men every where to repent. — 20: 21 Testifying both to the Jews, and also to the Greeks, repentance toward God, and faith toward our Lord Jesus Christ. — 26: 20 But shewed first unto them of Damascus, and at Jerusalem, and throughout all the coasts of Judea, and *then* to the Gentiles, that they should repent and turn to God, and do works meet for repentance.

Rev. 2: 5 Remember therefore from whence thou art fallen, and repent, and do the first works ; or else I will come unto thee quickly, and will remove thy candlestick out of his place, except thou repent. [Mk. 6: 12.] [See 357, 601.]

607. *Repentance encouraged — promises.*

2 Ch: 7: 14 If my people, which are called by my name, shall humble themselves, and pray, and seek my face, and turn from their wicked ways ; then will I hear from heaven, and will forgive their sin, and will heal their land.

Ps. 34: 18 The LORD *is* nigh unto them that are of a broken heart ; and saveth such as be of a contrite spirit. — 51: 17 The sacrifices of God *are* a broken spirit: a broken and a contrite heart, O God, thou wilt not despise. — 147: 3 He healeth the broken in heart, and bindeth up their wounds.

Is. 55: 7 Let the wicked forsake his way, and the unrighteous man his thoughts : and let him return unto the LORD, and he will have mercy upon him ; and to our God, for he will abundantly pardon. — 66: 2 All those *things* hath my hand made, and all those *things* have been, saith the LORD : but to this *man* will I look, *even* to *him that is* poor and of a contrite spirit, and trembleth at my word.

Hos. 6: 1 Come, and let us return unto the LORD : for he hath torn, and he will heal us ; he hath smitten, and he will bind us up. 2 After two days will he revive us : in the third day he will raise us up, and we shall live in his sight. 3 Then shall we know, *if* we follow on to know the LORD : his going forth is prepared as the morning ; and he shall come unto us as the rain, as the latter *and* former rain unto the earth.

Joel 2: 12 Now, saith the LORD, Turn ye *even* to me with all your heart, and with fasting, and with weeping, and with mourning. 13 And rend your heart, and not your garments, and turn unto the LORD your God : for he *is* gracious and merciful, slow to anger, and of great kindness, and repenteth him of the evil.

Zec. 1: 3 Say thou unto them, Thus saith the LORD of hosts: Turn ye unto me, saith the LORD of hosts, and I will turn unto you, saith the LORD of hosts.

Mat. 5: 3 Blessed *are* the poor in spirit: for theirs is the kingdom of heaven. 4 Blessed *are* they that mourn: for they shall be comforted.

Lk. 15: 21 The son said unto him, Father, I have sinned against Heaven, and in thy sight, and am no more worthy to be called thy son. 22 But the father said to his servants, Bring forth the best robe, and put *it* on him; and put a ring on his hand, and shoes on *his* feet: 23 And bring hither the fatted calf, and kill *it;* and let us eat and be merry. [See 357.]

608. *Repentance, as ascribed to God.*

Gen. 6: 6 And it repented the LORD that he had made man on the earth, and it grieved him at his heart.

Jer. 18: 7 *At what* instant I shall speak concerning a nation, and concerning a kingdom, to pluck up, and to pull down, and to destroy *it:* 8 If that nation against whom I have pronounced, turn from their evil, I will repent of the evil that I thought to do unto them. 9 And *at what* instant I shall speak concerning a nation, and concerning a kingdom, to build and to plant *it;* 10 If it do evil in my sight, that it obey not my voice, then I will repent of the good, wherewith I said I would benefit them. — 26: 2 Thus saith the LORD; Stand in the court of the LORD's house, and speak unto all the cities of Judah, which come to worship in the LORD's-house, all the words that I command thee to speak unto them; diminish not a word: 3 If so be they will hearken, and turn every man from his evil way, that I may repent me of the evil, which I purpose to do unto them because of the evil of their doings. 13 Therefore now amend your ways and your doings, and obey the voice of the LORD your God; And the LORD will repent him of the evil that he hath pronounced against you.

Ezk. 33: 14 When I say unto the wicked, Thou shalt surely die; if he turn from his sin, and do that which is lawful and right; 15 *If* the wicked restore the pledge, give again that he had robbed, walk in the statutes of life, without committing iniquity; he shall surely live, he shall not die.

Jonah 3: 10 God saw their works, that they turned from their evil way; and God repented of the evil that he had said that he would do unto them: and he did *it* not.

609. *Spurious repentance.*

Mat. 27: 3 Then Judas, which had betrayed him, when he

saw that he was condemned, repented himself, and brought again the thirty pieces of silver to the chief priests and elders, 4 Saying, I have sinned in that I have betrayed the innocent blood. And they said, What *is that* to us? see thou *to that.* 5 And he cast down the pieces of silver in the temple, and departed, and went and hanged himself.

2 Cor. 7: 10 The sorrow of the world worketh death.

[See 191, 194, 411, 623, 689.]

REPROOF.

610. *Faithful reproof required and encouraged.*

Lev. 19: 17 Thou shalt not hate thy brother in thy heart: thou shalt in any wise rebuke thy neighbor, and not suffer sin upon him.

Pr. 6: 23 The commandment *is* a lamp; and the law *is* light; and reproofs of instruction *are* the way of life. — 19: 25 Reprove one that hath understanding, *and* he will understand knowledge. — 24: 24 He that saith unto the wicked, Thou *art* righteous; him shall the people curse, nations shall abhor him: 25 But to them that rebuke *him* shall be delight, and a good blessing shall come upon them. — 28: 4 They that forsake the law praise the wicked, but such as keep the law contend with them. 23 He that rebuketh a man, afterwards shall find more favor than he that flattereth with the tongue.

Ezk. 16: 1 The word of the LORD came unto me, saying, 2 Son of man, cause Jerusalem to know her abominations.

Mat. 18: 15 If thy brother shall trespass against thee, go and tell him his fault between thee and him alone: if he shall hear thee, thou hast gained thy brother.

Lk. 17: 3 Take heed to yourselves: If thy brother trespass against thee, rebuke him; and if he repent, forgive him.

Ep. 5: 11 Have no fellowship with the unfruitful works of darkness, but rather reprove *them.*

Col. 3: 16 Let the word of Christ dwell in you richly in all wisdom; teaching and admonishing one another in psalms, and hymns, and spiritual songs, singing with grace in your hearts to the Lord.

1 Th. 5: 14 We exhort you, brethren, warn them that are unruly, comfort the feeble-minded, support the weak, be patient toward all *men.* [See 109.]

611. *Reproving others exemplified.*

Neh. 13: 11 Then contended I with the rulers, and said, Why is the house of God forsaken? And I gathered them together, and set them in their place. 17 Then I contended with the nobles of Judah, and said unto them, What evil thing *is* this that ye do, and profane the sabbath day? 18 Did, not your fathers thus, and did not our God bring all this evil upon us, and upon this city? yet ye bring more wrath upon Israel by profaning the sabbath.

Dan. 5: 22 Thou his son, O Belshazzar, hast not humbled thine heart, though thou knewest all this; 23 But hast lifted up thyself against the Lord of heaven; and they have brought the vessels of his house before thee, and thou, and thy lords, thy wives and thy concubines, have drunk wine in them; and thou hast praised the gods of silver, and gold, of brass, iron, wood, and stone, which see not, nor hear, nor know: and the God in whose hand thy breath *is*, and whose *are* all thy ways, hast thou not glorified. 24 Then was the part of the hand sent from him; and this writing was written.

Hos. 5: 2 The revolters are profound to make slaughter, though I *have been* a rebuker of them all.

Mat. 16: 23 He turned, and said unto Peter, Get thee behind me, Satan; thou art an offence unto me: for thou savorest not the things that be of God, but those that be of men.

Lk. 23: 40 The other answering, rebuked him, saying, Dost not thou fear God, seeing thou art in the same condemnation?

Gal. 2: 11 When Peter was come to Antioch, I withstood him to the face, because he was to be blamed. [See 66, 461.]

612. Reproof gratefully received by the humble.

Ps. 141: 5 Let the righteous smite me; *it shall be* a kindness: and let him reprove me: *it shall be* an excellent oil, *which* shall not break my head: for yet my prayer also *shall be* in their calamities.

Pr. 25: 12 *As* an ear-ring of gold, and an ornament of fine gold, *so is* a wise reprover upon an obedient ear. — 28: 23 He that rebuketh a man, afterwards shall find more favor than he that flattereth with the tongue.

613. Reproof rejected by the proud.

Pr. 1: 7 The fear of the LORD *is* the beginning of knowledge: *but* fools despise wisdom and instruction. 25 But ye have set at nought all my counsel, and would none of my reproof. — 13: 1 A wise son *heareth* his father's instruction: but a scorner heareth not rebuke. — 15: 12 A scorner loveth not one that reproveth him: neither will he go unto the wise.

Am. 5: 10 They hate him that rebuketh in the gate, and they abhor him that speaketh uprightly.

Lk. 3: 19 Herod the tetrarch, being reproved by him for Herodias his brother Philip's wife, and for all the evils which Herod had done, 20 Added yet this above all, that he shut up John in prison.

Jn. 3: 20 Every one that doeth evil hateth the light, neither cometh to the light, lest his deeds should be reproved. — 7: 7 The world cannot hate you ; but me it hateth, because I testify of it, that the works thereof are evil.

614. *Wisdom of receiving reproof—folly of rejecting it.*

Pr. 6: 23 The commandment *is* a lamp ; and the law *is* light ; and reproofs of instruction *are* the way of life. — 10: 17 He *is in* the way of life that keepeth instruction : but he that refuseth reproof erreth. — 12: 1 Whoso loveth instruction loveth knowledge: but he that hateth reproof *is* brutish. — 13: 18 Poverty and shame *shall be to* him that refuseth instruction : but he that regardeth reproof shall be honored. — 15: 5 A fool despiseth his father's instruction : but he that regardeth reproof is prudent. 10 Correction *is* grievous unto him that forsaketh the way : *and* he that hateth reproof shall die. 31 The ear that heareth the reproof of life abideth among the wise. 32 He that refuseth instruction despiseth his own soul : but he that heareth reproof getteth understanding. — 29: 1 He that, being often reproved, hardeneth *his* neck, shall suddenly be destroyed, and that without remedy.

Ec. 4: 13 Better *is* a poor and a wise child, than an old and foolish king, who will no more be admonished.

615. *Reprovers should correct their own faults.*

Mat. 7: 3 Why beholdest thou the mote that is in thy brother's eye, but considerest not the beam that is in thine own eye ? 4 Or how wilt thou say to thy brother, Let me pull out the mote out of thine eye ; and behold, a beam *is* in thine own eye ? 5 Thou hypocrite, first cast out the beam out of thine own eye ; and then shalt thou see clearly to cast out the mote out of thy brother's eye.

Rom. 2: 21 Thou therefore which teachest another, teachest thou not thyself ? thou that preachest, a man should not steal, dost thou steal ? 22 Thou that sayest, a man should not commit adultery, dost thou commit adultery ? thou that abhorrest idols, dost thou commit sacrilege ? 23 Thou that makest thy boast of the law, through breaking the law dishonorest thou God ?

REPUTATION.

616. *Value of reputation — sin of abusing it.*

Pr. 22: 1 A *good* name *is* rather to be chosen than great riches, *and* loving favor rather than silver and gold. — 25: 18 A man that heareth false witness against his neighbor *is* a maul, and a sword, and a sharp arrow.

Ec. 7: 1 A good name *is* better than precious ointment; and the day of death than the day of one's birth.

[See 729, 730.]

RESURRECTION OF THE DEAD.

617. *General resurrection of the dead.*

Job 19: 26 *Though* after my skin worms destroy this *body,* yet in my flesh shall I see God.

Hos. 13: 14 I will ransom them from the power of the grave; I will redeem them from death: O death, I will be thy plagues, O grave, I will be thy destruction.

Lk. 20: 37 That the dead are raised, even Moses shewed at the bush, when he calleth the Lord the God of Abraham, and the God of Isaac, and the God of Jacob. 38 For he is not a God of the dead, but of the living.

Jn. 5: 28 Marvel not at this: for the hour is coming, in the which all that are in the graves shall hear his voice, 29 And shall come forth. — 6: 40 This is the will of him that sent me, that every one which seeth the Son, and believeth on him, may have everlasting life : and I will raise him up at the last day. — 11: 23 Jesus saith unto her, Thy brother shall rise again. 24 Martha saith unto him, I know that he shall rise again in the resurrection at the last day.

Ac. 4: 1 As they spake unto the people, the priests and the captain of the temple, and the Sadducees came upon them, 2 Being grieved that they taught the people, and preached through Jesus the resurrection from the dead. — 24: 15 And have hope toward God, which they themselves also allow, that there shall be a resurrection of the dead both of the just and unjust. — 26: 8 Why should it be thought a thing incredible with you, that God should raise the dead?

Rom. 6: 8 If we be dead with Christ, we believe that we shall also live with him: 9 Knowing that Christ, being raised from the dead, dieth no more ; death hath no more dominion over him. — 8: 23 And not only *they,* but ourselves also, which have the first-fruits of the Spirit, even we ourselves groan within ourselves, waiting for the adoption, *to wit,* the redemption of our body.

1 Cor. 6: 14 God hath both raised up the Lord, and will also raise up us by his own power. — 15: 21 Since by man *came* death, by man *came* also the resurrection of the dead. 22 For as in Adam all die, even so- in Christ shall all be made alive. [See the whole chapter.]

2 Cor. 4: 14 Knowing, that he which raised up the Lord Jesus, shall raise up us also by Jesus, and shall present *us* with you.

1 Th. 4: 16 The Lord himself shall descend from heaven with a shout, with the voice of the archangel, and with the trump of God : and the dead in Christ shall rise first : 17 Then we which are alive *and* remain shall be caught up together with them in the clouds, to meet the Lord in the air : and so shall we ever be with the Lord.

618. *The dead raised with incorruptible bodies.*

1 Cor. 15: 35 Some *man* will say, How are the dead raised up ? and with what body do they come ? 36 *Thou* fool, that which thou sowest is not quickened except it die : 37 And that which thou sowest, thou sowest not that body that shall be. 42 So also *is* the resurrection of the dead. It is sown in corruption, it is raised in incorruption : 43 It is sown in dishonor, it is raised in glory : it is sown in weakness, it is raised in power : 44 It is sown a natural body, it is raised a spiritual body. There is a natural body, and there is a spiritual body. 50 Now this I say, brethren, that flesh and blood cannot inherit the kingdom of God ; neither doth corruption inherit incorruption. 52 In a moment, in the twinkling of an eye, at the last trump : for the trumpet shall sound, and the dead shall be raised incorruptible, and we shall be changed. 53 For this corruptible must put on incorruption, and this mortal *must* put on immortality. 54 So when this corruptible shall have put on incorruption, and this mortal shall have put on immortality, then shall be brought to pass the saying that is written, Death is swallowed up in victory.

2 Cor. 5: 2 In this we groan, earnestly desiring to be clothed upon with our house which is from heaven : 3 If so be that -being clothed we shall not be found naked. 4 For we that are in *this* tabernacle do groan, being burdened : not for that we would be unclothed, but clothed upon, that mortality might be swallowed up of life.

Ph. 3: 20 Our conversation is in heaven ; from whence also we look for the Savior, the Lord Jesus Christ : 21 Who shall

441

change our vile body, that it may be fashioned like unto his glorious body, according to the working whereby he is able even to subdue all things unto himself.

REVIVALS.

619. *Ancient revivals of religion.*

Gen. 4: 26 To Seth, to him also there was born a son ; and he called his name Enos : then began men to call upon the name of the LORD.

1 K. 18: 38 Then the fire of the LORD fell, and consumed the burnt-sacrifice, and the wood, and the stones, and the dust, and licked up the water that *was* in the trench. 39 And when all the people saw *it*, they fell on their faces : and they said, The LORD, he *is* the God ; the LORD, he *is* the God.

2 K. 23: 3 The king [Josiah] stood by a pillar, and made a covenant before the LORD, to walk after the LORD, and to keep his commandments, and his testimonies, and his statutes, with all *their* heart, and all *their* soul, to perform the words of this covenant that were written in this book. And all the people stood to the covenant. 21 The king commanded all the people, saying, Keep the passover unto the LORD your God, as *it is* written in the book of this covenant. 22 Surely there was not holden such a passover from the days of the judges that judged Israel, nor in all the days of the kings of Israel, nor of the kings of Judah.

2 Ch. 30: 11 Divers of Asher and Manasseh and of Zebulun humbled themselves, and came to Jerusalem. 12 Also in Judah the hand of God was to give them one heart to do the commandment of the king [Hezekiah] and of the princes, by the word of the LORD. 13 And there assembled at Jerusalem much people to keep the feast of unleavened bread in the second month, a very great congregation. 21 The children of Israel *that were* present at Jerusalem kept the feast of unleavened bread seven days with great gladness : 22 And Hezekiah spake comfortably unto all the Levites that taught the good knowledge of the LORD : and they did eat throughout the feast seven days, offering peace-offerings, and making confession to the LORD God of their fathers. 23 And the whole assembly took counsel to keep other seven days : and they kept *other* seven days with gladness. 26 So there was great joy in Jerusalem : for since the time of Solomon the son of David king of Israel *there was* not the like in Jerusalem. 27 Then the priests the Levites arose and blessed the people : and their

voice was heard, and their prayer came *up* to his holy dwelling-place, *even* unto heaven.

Neh. 8: 2 Ezra the priest brought the law before-the congregation both of men and women, and all that could hear with understanding, upon the first day of the seventh month. 3 And he read therein before the street that *was* before the water-gate from the morning until mid-day, before the men and the women, and those that could understand; and the ears of all the people *were attentive* unto the book of the law. 6 And Ezra blessed the LORD, the great God. And all the people answered, Amen, Amen, with lifting up their hands: and they bowed their heads, and worshipped the LORD with *their* faces to the ground. 9 And Nehemiah, which *is* the Tirshatha, and Ezra the priest the scribe, and the Levites that taught the people, said unto all the people, This day *is* holy unto the LORD your God; mourn not, nor weep. For all the people wept, when they heard the words of the law.

Jer. 2: 2 Go, and cry in the ears of Jerusalem, saying, Thus saith the LORD; I remember thee, the kindness of thy youth, the love of thine espousals, when thou wentest after me in the wilderness, in a land *that was* not sown. 3 Israel *was* holiness unto the LORD, *and* the first-fruits of his increase.

Ac. 2: 41 Then they that gladly received his word, were baptized: and the same day there were added *unto them* about three thousand souls. 42 And they continued steadfastly in the apostles' doctrine and fellowship, and in breaking of bread, and in prayers. 43 And fear came upon every soul: and many wonders and signs were done by the apostles. — 4: 4 Many of them which heard the word, believed, and the number of the men was about five thousand. — 5: 14 Believers were the more added to the Lord, multitudes both of men and women. — 8: 5 Then Philip went down to the city of Samaria, and preached Christ unto them. 6 And the people with one accord gave heed unto those things which Philip spake, hearing and seeing the miracles which he did. 7 For unclean spirits, crying with loud voice, came out of many that were possessed *with them:* and many taken with palsies, and that were lame, were healed. — 11: 19 They which were scattered abroad upon the persecution that arose about Stephen, travelled as far as Phenice, and Cyprus, and Antioch, preaching the word to none but unto the Jews only. 20 And some of them were men of Cyprus and Cyrene, which when they were come to Antioch, spake unto the Grecians, preaching the Lord Jesus. 21 And the hand of the Lord was with them: and a great number believed, and turned unto the Lord. 22 Then tidings of these things came unto the ears of the church which was in Jerusalem: and they sent forth Barnabas, that he should go as far as Antioch. 23 Who, when he came, and had seen the grace of God, was glad, and exhorted them all, that with purpose of heart they would cleave unto the Lord. 24 For he was a good man, and full of the Holy Ghost, and of faith: and much people was added unto the Lord.—14: 1 It came to pass in Iconium, that they went both together into the synagogue of the Jews, and so spake, that a great multitude, both of the Jews, and also of the Greeks, believed.

620. *The influences of the Spirit compared to rain, or the pouring of water.*

Ps. 72: 6 He shall come down like rain upon the mown grass: as showers *that* water the earth.

Pr. 1: 23 Turn you at my reproof: behold, I will pour out my spirit unto you, I will make known my words unto you.

Is. 32: 15 Until the Spirit be poured upon us from on high, and the wilderness be a fruitful field, and the fruitful field be counted for a forest.—44: 3 I will pour water upon him that is thirsty, and floods upon the dry ground: I will pour my Spirit upon thy seed, and my blessing upon thine offspring.

Ezk. 39: 29 Neither will I hide my face any more from them: for I have poured out my Spirit upon the house of Israel, saith the Lord GOD.

Joel 2: 28 It shall come to pass afterward, *that* I will pour out my Spirit upon all flesh; and your sons and your daughters shall prophesy, your old men shall dream dreams, your young men shall see visions: 29 And also upon the servants and upon the handmaids in those days will I pour out my Spirit.

Zec. 12: 10 I will pour upon the house of David, and upon the inhabitants of Jerusalem, the spirit of grace and of supplications: and they shall look upon me whom they have pierced, and they shall mourn for him, as one mourneth for *his* only *son*, and shall be in bitterness for him, as one that is in bitterness for *his* first-born.

1 Pet. 1: 12 Unto whom it was revealed, that not unto themselves, but unto us they did minister the things which are now reported unto you by them that have preached the gospel unto you, with the Holy Ghost sent down from heaven.

621. *Happy effects of genuine revivals.*

2 K. 23: 24 The *workers with* familiar spirits, and the wizards, and the images, and the idols, and all the abominations that were spied in the land of Judah and in Jerusalem, did Josiah put away, that he might perform the words of the law
444

which were written in the book that Hilkiah the priest found in the house of the LORD. 25 And like unto him was there no king before him, that turned to the LORD with all his heart, and with all his soul, and with all his might, according to all the law of Moses; neither after him arose there *any* like him.

2 Ch. 31: 5 As soon as the commandment came abroad, the children of Israel brought in abundance the first-fruits of corn, wine, and oil, and honey, and of all the increase of the field; and the tithe of all *things* brought they in abundantly. 8 And when Hezekiah and the princes came and saw the heaps, they blessed the LORD, and his people Israel.

Ps. 14: 7 When the LORD bringeth back the captivity of his people, Jacob shall rejoice, *and* Israel shall be glad.

Ac. 2: 44 All that believed were together, and had all things common; 45 And sold their possessions and goods, and parted them to all *men*, as every man had need. 46 And they, continuing daily with one accord in the temple, and breaking bread from house to house, did eat their meat with gladness and singleness of heart, 47 Praising God, and having favor with all the people. ' And the Lord added to the church daily such as should be saved. — 8: 8 And there was great joy in that city. — 19: 18 Many that believed came, and confessed, and shewed their deeds. 19 Many of them also which used curious arts, brought their books together, and burned them before all *men ;* and they counted the price of them, and found *it* fifty thousand *pieces* of silver. 20 So mightily grew the word of God prevailed.

Col. 2: 5 Though I be absent in the flesh, yet am I with you in the spirit, joying and beholding your order, and the steadfastness of your faith in Christ. [See 605.]

622. *Praying for revivals required and exemplified.*

Ps. 80: 14 Return, we beseech thee, O God of hosts: look down from heaven, and behold, and visit this vine; 15 And the vineyard which thy right hand hath planted, and the branch *that* thou madest strong for thyself. 16 *It is* burnt with fire, *it is* cut down: they perish at the rebuke of thy countenance. — 85: 6 Wilt thou not revive us again: that thy people may rejoice in thee? 7 Shew us thy mercy, O LORD, and grant us thy salvation. — 122: 6 Pray for the peace of Jerusalem: they shall prosper that love thee.

Song 4: 16 Awake, O north wind; and come, thou south; blow upon my garden, *that* the spices thereof may flow out. Let my beloved come into his garden, and eat his pleasant fruits.

Is. 62: 6 Ye that make mention of the LORD, keep not silence, 7 And give him no rest, till he establish, and till he make Jerusalem a praise in the earth. — 64: 1 Oh that thou wouldest rend the heavens, that thou wouldest come down, that the mountains might flow down at thy presence, 2 As *when* the melting fire burneth, the fire causeth the waters to boil, to make thy name known to thine adversaries, *that* the nations may tremble at thy presence!

Jer. 14 20 We acknowledge, O LORD, our wickedness, *and* the iniquity of our fathers: for we have sinned against thee. 21 Do not abhor *us;* for thy name's sake, do not disgrace the throne of thy glory: remember, break not thy covenant with us.

Dan. 9: 17 O our God, hear the prayer of thy servant, and his supplications, and cause thy face to shine upon thy sanctuary that is desolate, for the Lord's sake.

Hab. 3: 2 O LORD, I have heard thy speech *and* was afraid: O LORD, revive thy work in the midst of the years, in the midst of the years make known; in wrath remember mercy.

Mat. 6: 10 Thy kingdom come. Thy will be done in earth as *it is* in heaven.

623. *Spurious revivals.*

Mat. 23: 15 Wo unto you, scribes and Pharisees, hypocrites! for ye compass sea and land to make one proselyte; and when he is made, ye make him two-fold more the child of hell than yourselves.

Gal. 4: 17 They zealously affect you, *but* not well; yea, they would exclude you, that ye might affect them.

[See 191, 194, 411, 609, 689.]

RICHES.

624. *Riches, the idol of many.*

Mat. 19: 21 Jesus said unto him, If thou wilt be perfect, go *and* sell that thou hast, and give to the poor, and thou shalt have treasure in heaven: and come *and* follow me. 22 But when the young man heard that saying, he went away sorrowful: for he had great possessions.

2 Tim. 4: 10 Demas hath forsaken me, having loved this present world.

625. *Riches and prosperity have a corrupting and dangerous tendency.*

Gen. 13: 10 Lot lifted up his eyes, and beheld all the plain of Jordan, that it *was* well watered every where, before the

LORD destroyed Sodom and Gomorrah, *even* as the garden of the LORD, like the land of Egypt, as thou comest unto Zoar. 11 Then Lot chose him all the plain of Jordan; and Lot journeyed east: and they separated themselves the one from the other. 12 Abram dwelled in the land of Canaan, and Lot dwelled in the cities of the plain, and pitched *his* tent toward Sodom. 13 But the men of Sodom *were* wicked and sinners before the LORD, exceedingly.

Dt. 8: 11 Beware that thou forget not the LORD thy God, in not keeping his commandments, and his judgments, and his statutes, which I command thee this day: 12 Lest *when* thou hast eaten, and art full, and hast built goodly houses, and dwelt *therein;* 13 And *when* thy herds and thy flocks multiply, and thy silver and thy gold is multiplied, and all that thou hast is multiplied; 14 Then thy heart be lifted up, and thou forget the LORD thy God, which brought thee forth out of the land of Egypt, from the house of bondage. — 32: 13 He made him ride on the high places of the earth, that he might eat the increase of the fields; and he made him to suck honey out of the rock, and oil out of the flinty rock; 14 Butter of kine, and milk of sheep, with fat of lambs, and rams of the breed of Bashan, and goats, with the fat of kidneys of wheat; and thou didst drink the pure blood of the grape. 15 But Jeshurun waxed fat, and kicked: thou art waxen fat, thou art grown thick, thou art covered *with fatness;* then he forsook God *which* made him, and lightly esteemed the Rock of his salvation.

2 Ch. 26: 3 Sixteen years old *was* Uzziah when he began to reign, and he reigned fifty and two years in Jerusalem. 5 And he sought God in the days of Zechariah, who had understanding in the visions of God: and, as long as he sought the LORD, God made him to prosper. 15 And his name spread far abroad; for he was marvellously helped, till he was strong. 16 But when he was strong, his heart was lifted up to *his* destruction.

Ps. 30: 6 In my prosperity I said, I shall never be moved. — 55: 19 Because they have no changes, therefore they fear not God. — 92: 7 When the wicked spring as the grass, and when all the workers of iniquity do flourish; *it is* that they shall be destroyed for ever.

Pr. 1: 32 The turning away of the simple shall slay them, and the prosperity of fools shall destroy them. — 30: 8 Remove far from me vanity and lies; give me neither poverty nor riches; feed me with food convenient for me: 9 Lest I be full, and deny *thee,* and say, Who *is* the LORD? or lest I be poor, and steal, and take the name of my God *in vain.*

Ec. 5: 12 The sleep of a laboring man *is* sweet, whether he eat little or much : but the abundance of the rich will not suffer him to sleep.   13 There is a sore evil *which* I have seen under the sun, *namely*, riches kept for the owners thereof to their hurt.

Jer. 22: 21 I spake unto thee in thy prosperity ; *but* thou saidst, I will not hear.

Ezk. 16: 49 Behold, this was the iniquity of thy sister Sodom, pride, fulness of bread, and abundance of idleness was in her and in her daughters; neither did she strengthen the hand of the poor and needy.   50 And they were haughty, and committed abomination before me : therefore I took them away as I saw *good.* — 28: 5 By thy great wisdom *and* by thy traffic, hast thou increased thy riches, and thy heart is lifted up because of thy riches.

Mat. 19: 23 Then said Jesus unto his disciples, Verily, I say unto you, That a rich man shall hardly enter into the kingdom of heaven.   24 And again I say unto you, It is easier for a camel to go through the eye of a needle, than for a rich man to enter into the kingdom of God.

Mk. 4: 19 The cares of this world, and the deceitfulness of riches, and the lusts of other things entering in, choke the word, and it becometh unfruitful.

1 Tim. 6: 8 Having food and raiment, let us be therewith content.   9 But they that will be rich, fall into temptation, and a snare, and *into* many foolish and hurtful lusts, which drown men in destruction and perdition.   10 For the love of money is the root of all evil : which while some coveted after, they have erred from the faith, and pierced themselves through with many sorrows.   11 But thou, O man of God, flee these things ; and follow after righteousness.   [See 741.]

626. *The eager pursuit of riches forbidden and discouraged.*

Pr. 23: 4 Labor not to be rich : cease from thine own wisdom. — 28: 20 A faithful man shall abound with blessings : but he that maketh haste to be rich shall not be innocent.   22 He that hasteth to be rich *hath* an evil eye, and considereth not that poverty shall come upon him.

Is. 5: 8 Wo unto them that join house to house, *that* lay field to field, till *there be* no place, that they may be placed alone in the midst of the earth !

2 Pet. 2: 14 Having eyes full of adultery, and that cannot cease from sin ; beguiling unstable souls : a heart they have exercised with covetous practices ; cursed children : 15 Which have forsaken the right way, and are gone astray, following the

way of Balaam *the son* of Bosor, who loved the wages of unrighteousness; 16 But was rebuked for his iniquity: the dumb
ass, speaking with man's voice, forbade the madness of the
prophet. See [133, 742–3.]

627. *Riches vain and transitory.*

Pr. 23: 5 Wilt thou set thine eyes upon that which is not?
for *riches* certainly make themselves wings; they fly away as
an eagle toward heaven.

Ec. 1: 2 Vanity of vanities, saith the Preacher, vanity of
vanities; all *is* vanity. 14 I have seen all the works that are
done under the sun; and behold, all *is* vanity and vexation of
spirit. — 2: 4 I made me great works; I builded me houses;
I planted me vineyards: 5 I made me gardens and orchards,
and I planted trees in them of all *kind of* fruits: 6 I made
me pools of water, to water therewith the wood that bringeth
forth trees: 7 I got *me* servants and maidens, and had servants born in my house; also I had great possessions of great
and small cattle above all that were in Jerusalem before me;
8 I gathered me also silver and gold, and the peculiar treasure
of kings, and of the provinces: I gat me men-singers and
women-singers, and the delights of the sons of men, *as* musi-
cal instruments, and that of all sorts. 9 So I was great, and
increased more than all that were before me in Jerusalem; also
my wisdom remained with me. 10 And whatsoever mine eyes
desired I kept not from them, I withheld not my heart from
any joy; for my heart rejoiced in all my labor: and this was
my portion of all my labor. 11 Then I looked on all the
works that my hands had wrought, and on the labor that
I had labored to do: and behold, all *was* vanity and vexation of spirit, and *there was* no profit under the sun. 17
Therefore I hated life; because the work that is wrought under
the sun *is* grievous unto me: for all *is* vanity and vexation of
spirit. 18 Yea, I hated all my labor which I had taken under
the sun: because I should leave it unto the man that shall
be after me. 19 And who knoweth whether he shall be a wise
man or a fool? yet shall he have rule over all my labor wherein I have labored, and wherein I have shewed myself wise
under the sun. This *is* also vanity. 10 He that loveth silver
shall not be satisfied with silver; nor he that loveth abundance
with increase: this *is* also vanity. 11 When goods increase, they
are increased that eat them: and what good *is there* to the
owners thereof, saving the beholding *of them* with their eyes.

[See 148.]

628. *Proper use of riches.*

1 Tim. 6: 17 Charge them that are rich in this world that they be not high-minded, nor trust in uncertain riches, but in the living God, who giveth us richly all things to enjoy ; 18 That they do good, that they be rich in good works, ready to distribute, willing to communicate ; 19 Laying up in store for themselves a good foundation against the time to come, that they may lay hold on eternal life. [See 406.]

RIGHTEOUSNESS.

629. *Righteousness, impartiality, truth, and honesty in spiritual and temporal things required and exemplified.*

Lev. 19: 15 Ye shall do no unrighteousness in judgment ; thou shalt not respect the person of the poor, nor honor the person of the mighty : *but* in righteousness shalt thou judge thy neighbor. 36 Just balances, just weights, a just ephah, and a just hin shall ye have : I *am* the LORD your God, which brought you out of the land of Egypt.

Dt. 6: 18 Thou shalt do *that which is* right and good in the sight of the LORD : that it may be well with thee. — 16: 20 That which is altogether just shalt thou follow, that thou mayest live, and inherit the land which the LORD thy God giveth thee.

1 S. 12: 1 Samuel said unto all Israel, Behold, I have hearkened unto your voice in all that ye said unto me, and have made a king over you. 3 Behold, here I *am :* witness against me before the LORD, and before his anointed ; whose ox have I taken ? or whose ass have I taken ? or whom have I defrauded ? whom have I oppressed ? or of whose hand have I received *any* bribe to blind mine eyes therewith ? and I will restore it you. 4 And they said, Thou hast not defrauded us, nor oppressed us, neither hast thou taken aught of any man's hand.

Ps. 51: 6 Behold, thou desirest truth in the inward parts: and in the hidden-*part* thou shalt make me to know wisdom.

Pr. 21: 3 To do justice and judgment is more acceptable to the LORD than sacrifice. — 24: 23 *It is* not good to have respect of persons in judgment.

Is. 56: 1 Thus saith the LORD, Keep ye judgment, and do justice : for my salvation *is* near to come, and my righteousness to be revealed.

Mic. 6: 8 He hath shewed thee, O man, what *is* good ; and what doth the LORD require of thee, but to do justly, and to love mercy, and to walk humbly with thy God ?

Zec. 7: 9 Thus speaketh the LORD of hosts, saying, Execute true judgment, and shew mercy and compassions every man to his brother: 10 And oppress not the widow, nor the fatherless, the stranger, nor the poor; and let none of you imagine evil against his brother in your heart.

Lk. 20: 25 He said unto them, Render therefore unto Cesar the things which be Cesar's, and unto God the things which be God's.

Rom. 13: 7 Render therefore to all their dues: tribute to whom tribute *is due;* custom to whom custom; fear to whom fear; honor to whom honor. 8 Owe no man any thing, but to love one another: for he that loveth another hath fulfilled the law.

Ep. 6: 14 Stand therefore, having your loins girt about with truth, and having on the breast-plate of righteousness.

1 Th. 2: 10 Ye *are* witnesses, and God *also,* how holily, and justly, and unblamably we behaved ourselves among you that believe:

1 Tim. 6: 11 Thou, O man of God, flee these things; and follow after righteousness, godliness, faith, love, patience, meekness.

Tit. 2: 11 The grace of God that bringeth salvation hath appeared to all men, 12 Teaching us, that denying ungodliness, and worldly lusts, we should live soberly, righteously, and godly, in this present world. [See 56, 501, 659, 732.]

630. *Righteousness and honesty rewarded, or the "gain of godliness" and loss by ungodliness.*

Gen. 19: 15 When the morning arose, then the angels hastened Lot, saying, Arise, take thy wife, and thy two daughters which are here, lest thou be consumed in the iniquity of the city. 22 Haste thee, escape thither; for I cannot do any thing till thou be come thither: therefore the name of the city called Zoar.

2 Ch. 16: 9 The eyes of the LORD run to and fro throughout the whole earth, to shew himself strong in the behalf of *them* whose heart *is* perfect toward him.

Ps. 1: 1 Blessed *is* the man that walketh not in the counsel of the ungodly, nor standeth in the way of sinners, nor sitteth in the seat of the scornful. 2 But his delight *is* in the law of the LORD; and in his law doth he meditate day and night. 3 And he shall be like a tree planted by the rivers of water, that bringeth forth his fruit in his season; his leaf also shall not wither; and whatsoever he doeth shall prosper. — 4: 3 Know that the LORD hath set apart him that is godly for himself. — 5: 12 Thou, LORD, wilt bless the righteous; with favor wilt thou compass him as *with* a shield. — 15: 1 LORD, who shall abide in thy tabernacle? who shall dwell in thy holy hill?

Rewarded, or " Gain of Godliness."

2 He that walketh uprightly, and worketh righteousness, and speaketh the truth in his heart. 3 *He that* backbiteth not with his tongue, nor doeth evil to his neighbor, nor taketh up a reproach against his neighbor. 5 *He that* putteth not out his money to usury, nor taketh reward against the innocent. He that doeth these *things* shall never be moved. — 37: 3 Trust in the LORD, and do good ; *so* shalt thou dwell in the land, and verily thou shalt be fed. 9 For evil doers shall be cut off : but those that wait upon the LORD, they shall inherit the earth. 10 For yet a little while, and the wicked *shall* not *be :* yea, thou shalt diligently consider his place, and it *shall* not *be.* 17 For the arms of the wicked shall be broken : but the LORD upholdeth the righteous. 18 The LORD knoweth the days of the upright : and their inheritance shall be forever. 19 They shall not be ashamed in the evil time : and in the days of famine they shall be satisfied. 20 But the wicked shall perish, and the enemies of the LORD *shall be* as the fat of lambs : they shall consume ; into smoke shall they consume away. 25 I have been young, and *now* am old ; yet have I not seen the righteous forsaken, nor his seed begging bread. 26 *He is* ever merciful, and lendeth, and his seed *is* blessed. 27—40.

Ps. 58: 11 Verily *there is* a reward for the righteous : verily he is a God that judgeth in the earth. — 84: 11 The LORD God *is* a sun and shield : the LORD will give grace and glory ; no good *thing* will he withhold from them that walk uprightly. — 92: 12 The righteous shall flourish like the palm-tree : he shall grow like a cedar in Lebanon. 13 Those that he planted in the house of the LORD shall flourish in the courts of our God. 14 They shall still bring forth fruit in old age ; they shall be fat and flourishing. — 112: 1 Blessed *is* the man *that* feareth the LORD, *that* delighteth greatly in his commandments. 2 His seed shall be mighty upon earth : the generation of the upright shall be blessed. 3 Wealth and riches *shall be* in his house : and his righteousness endureth for ever.

Pr. 3: 3 Let not mercy and truth forsake thee : bind them about thy neck ; write them upon the table of thy heart : 4 So shalt thou find favor and good understanding in the sight of God and man. 32 The froward *is* abomination to the LORD : but his secret *is* with the righteous. 33 The curse of the LORD *is* in the house of the wicked : but he blesseth the habitation of the just. — 10: 9 He that walketh uprightly walketh surely : but he that perverteth his ways shall be known. 25 As the whirlwind passeth, so *is* the wicked no *more :* but the righteous *is* an everlasting foundation. 29 The way of the LORD *is* strength to the upright : but destruction *shall be* to

Rewarded, or " Gain of Godliness."

the workers of iniquity. — 11: 17 The merciful man doeth good to his own soul: but *he that is* cruel troubleth his own flesh. 18 The wicked worketh a deceitful work: but to him that soweth righteousness *shall be* a sure reward. 19 As righteousness *tendeth* to life: so he that pursueth evil *pursueth it* to his own death. 20 They that are of a froward heart *are* abomination to the LORD: but *such as are* upright in *their* way *are* his delight. 21 *Though* hand *join* in hand, the wicked shall not be unpunished: but the seed of the righteous shall be delivered. 31 Behold, the righteous shall be recompensed in the earth: much more the wicked and the sinner. — 13: 6 Righteousness keepeth *him that is* upright in the way: but wickedness overthroweth the sinner. 21 Evil pursueth sinners: but to the righteous good shall be repaid. 22 A good *man* leaveth an inheritance to his children's children: and the wealth of the sinner *is* laid up for the just. — 14: 34 Righteousness exalteth a nation: but sin *is* a reproach to any people. — 16: 8 Better *is* a little with righteousness, than great revenues without right. — 20: 7 The just *man* walketh in his integrity: his children *are* blessed after him. — 21: 21 He that followeth after righteousness and mercy, findeth life, righteousness, and honor. — 28: 16 The prince that wanteth understanding *is* also a great oppressor: *but* he that hateth covetousness shall prolong *his* days. 18 Whoso walketh uprightly shall be saved; but *he that is* perverse *in his* ways shall fall at once.

Is. 33: 15 He that walketh righteously, and speaketh uprightly; he that despiseth the gain of oppressions, that shaketh his hands from holding of bribes, that stoppeth his ears from hearing of blood, and shutteth his eyes from seeing evil; 16 He shall dwell on high: his place of defence *shall be* the munitions of rocks; bread shall be given him: his waters *shall be* sure. — 58: 6 *Is* not this the fast that I have chosen? to loose the bands of wickedness, to undo the heavy burdens, and to let the oppressed go free, and that ye break every yoke. 7 *Is it* not to deal thy bread to the hungry, and that thou bring the poor that are cast out to thy house? when thou seest the naked that thou cover him; and that thou hide not thyself from thine own flesh? 8 Then shall thy light break forth as the morning, and thy health shall spring forth speedily; and thy righteousness shall go before thee; the glory of the LORD shall be thy rere-ward.

Dan: 3: 18 But if not, be it known unto thee, O king, that we will not serve thy gods, nor worship the golden image which thou hast set up. 30 Then the king promoted Shadrach, Meshach, and Abed-nego, in the province of Babylon. — 6: 21 Then said Daniel unto the king, O king, live for ever. 22 My God hath sent his angel, and hath shut the lions' mouths, that they have not hurt me: forasmuch as before him innocency was found in me; and also before thee, O king, have I done no hurt. 28 So this Daniel prospered in the reign of Darius, and in the reign of Cyrus the Persian.

Mat. 6: 33 Seek ye first the kingdom of God and his righteousness, and all these things shall be added unto you.

1 Tim. 4: 8 Bodily exercise profiteth little; but godliness is profitable unto all things, having promise of the life that now is, and of that which is to come. 9 This *is* a faithful saying, and worthy of all acceptation. — 6: 6 Godliness with contentment is great gain.

1 Pet. 3: 10 He that will love life, and see good days, let him refrain his tongue from evil, and his lips that they speak no guile: 11 Let him eschew evil, and do good: let him seek peace, and ensue it. 12 For the eyes of the Lord *are* over the righteous, and his ears *are open* unto their prayers: but the face of the Lord *is* against them that do evil. 13 And who *is* he that will harm you, if ye be followers of that which is good?

[See Promises, in the Index, and 87, 286, 344, 362, 470, 550–1, 566, 733.]

RIGHTS OF MAN.

631. *A right to liberty and justice — threats for infringing these rights.*

Job 36: 6 He preserveth not the life of the wicked: but giveth right to the poor.

Is. 10: 1 Wo unto them that decree unrighteous decrees, and that write grievousness *which* they have prescribed; 2 To turn aside the needy from judgment, and to take away the right from the poor of my people.

Lam. 3: 35 To turn aside the right of a man before the face of the Most High, 36 To subvert a man in his cause the LORD approveth not.

Am. 5: 12 I know your manifold transgressions and your mighty sins: they afflict the just, they take a bribe, and they turn aside the poor in the gate *from their right.*

Gal. 5: 13 Brethren, ye have been called unto liberty: only *use* not liberty for an occasion to the flesh, but by love serve one another. [See 682.]

632. *A right to inquire freely, and to express opinions.*

Lk. 12: 57 Why even of yourselves judge ye not what is right?

Jn. 5: 39 Search the scriptures; for in them ye think ye have eternal life : and they are they which testify of me.

1 Cor. 10: 29 Conscience, I say, not thine own, but of the other : for why is my liberty judged of another *man's* conscience ?

1 Th. 5: 21 Prove all things ; hold fast that which is good.

1 Jn. 4: 1 Beloved, believe not every spirit, but try the spirits whether they are of God : because many false prophets are gone out into the world.

633. *A right to pursue mental culture.*

Pr. 4: 13 Take fast hold of instruction ; let *her* not go : keep her ; for she *is* thy life. — 23: 23 Buy the truth, and sell *it* not ; *also* wisdom, and instruction, and understanding.

Lk. 11: 52 Wo unto you, lawyers ! for ye have taken away the key of knowledge: ye entered not in yourselves, and them that were entering in ye hindered. [See 363, 391.]

634. *A right to enjoy the fruits of our own industry.*

Ec. 3: 22 I perceive that *there is* nothing better, than that a man should rejoice in his own works ; for that *is* his portion : for who shall bring him to see what shall be after him ? — 5: 18 Behold *that* which I have seen : *it is* good and comely *for one* to eat and to drink, and to enjoy the good of all his labor that he taketh under the sun all the days of his life, which God giveth him : for it *is* his portion.

635. *A right to our own wives and children.*

Ec. 9: 9 Live joyfully with the wife whom thou lovest all the days of the life of thy vanity, which he hath given thee under the sun, all the days of thy vanity : for that *is* thy portion in *this* life, and in thy labor which thou takest under the sun.

Mat. 19: 6 They are no more twain, but one flesh. What therefore God hath joined together, let not man put asunder.

Ep. 6: 4 Ye fathers, provoke not your children to wrath : but bring them up in the nurture and admonition of the Lord.

ROBBERY.

636. *Robbery forbidden and denounced.*

Lev. 19: 13 Thou shalt not defraud thy neighbor, neither rob *him*: the wages of him that is hired shall not abide with thee all night until the morning.

Pr. 21: 7 The robbery of the wicked shall destroy them; because they refuse to do judgment. — 22: 22 Rob not the poor, because he *is* poor: neither oppress the afflicted in the gate: 23 For the LORD will plead their cause, and spoil the soul of those that spoiled them. — 28: 24 Whoso robbeth his father or his mother, and saith, *It is* no transgression; the same *is* the companion of a destroyer.

Is. 61: 8 I the LORD love judgment, I hate robbery for burnt-offering.

Ezk. 22: 29 The people of the land have used oppression, and exercised robbery, and have vexed the poor and needy: yea, they have oppressed the stranger wrongfully. 30 And I sought for a man among them, that should make up the hedge, and stand in the gap before me for the land, that I should not destroy it: but I found none. 31 Therefore, have I poured out mine indignation upon them; I have consumed them with the fire of my wrath: their own way have I recompensed upon their heads, saith the Lord GOD.

[See 490, 682, 732–3, 736.]

SABBATH.

637. *Instituted in Paradise.*

Gen. 2: 2 On the seventh day God ended his work which he had made; and he rested on the seventh day from all his work which he had made. 3 And God blessed the seventh day, and sanctified it; because that in it he had rested from all his work which God created and made.

Ex. 20: 11 *In* six days the LORD made heaven and earth, the sea, and all that in them *is*, and rested the seventh day: wherefore the LORD blessed the sabbath-day, and hallowed it.

638. *Sabbath enjoined and recognized in the Decalogue, and other parts of the Old Testament.*

Ex. 20: 8 Remember the sabbath-day to keep it holy. 9 Six days shalt thou labor, and do all thy work: 10 But the seventh day *is* the sabbath of the LORD thy God.

Dt. 5: 14 The seventh day *is* the sabbath of the LORD thy God.

Neh. 13: 15 In those days saw I in Judah *some* treading wine presses on the sabbath, and bringing in sheaves, and lading asses; as also wine, grapes, and figs, and all *manner of* burdens which they brought into Jerusalem on the sabbath-day: and I testified *against them* in the day wherein they sold victuals. 16 There dwelt men of Tyre also therein, which brought fish, and all manner of ware, and sold on the sabbath unto the children of Judah, and in Jerusalem. 17 Then I contended with the nobles of Judah, and said unto them, What evil thing *is* this that ye do, and profane the sabbath-day? 18 Did not your fathers thus, and did not our God bring all this evil upon us, and upon this city? yet ye bring more wrath upon Israel by profaning the sabbath.

Ezk. 44: 24 In controversy they shall stand in judgment; *and* they shall judge it according to my judgments: and they shall keep my laws and my statutes in all mine assemblies; and they shall hallow my sabbaths.

639. *Sabbath recognized, and its proper works of mercy asserted by Christ, the " Lord of the Sabbath."*

Mat. 12: 1 At that time Jesus went on the sabbath-day through the corn, and his disciples were an hungered, and began to pluck the ears of corn, and to eat. 2 But when the Pharisees saw *it*, they said unto him, Behold, thy disciples do that which is not lawful to do upon the sabbath-day. 3 But he said unto them, Have ye not read what David did when he was an hungered, and they that were with him; 4 How he entered into the house of God, and did eat the shew-bread, which was not lawful for him to eat, neither for them which were with him, but only for the priests? 5 Or have ye not read in the law how that on the sabbath-days the priests in the temple profane the sabbath, and are blameless? 11 And he said unto them, What man shall there be among you, that shall have one sheep, and if it fall into a pit on the sabbath-day, will he not lay hold on it, and lift *it* out? 12 How much then is a man better than a sheep? Wherefore it is lawful to do well on the sabbath-days. 13 Then saith he to the man, Stretch forth thine hand. And he stretched *it* forth; and *it* was restored whole, like as the other. [Mk. 2: 23—28. Lk. 6: 1—10.] — 24: 20 Pray ye that your flight be not in the winter, neither on the sabbath-day.

Mk. 2: 27 He said unto them, The sabbath was made for man, and not man for the sabbath: 28 Therefore, the Son of man is Lord also of the sabbath. — 3: 4 He saith unto them, Is it lawful to do good on the sabbath-days, or to do evil? to save life, or to kill? but they held their peace.

Lk. 13: 11 Behold there was a woman which had a spirit of infirmity eighteen years, and was bowed together, and could in no wise lift up *herself.* 12 And when Jesus saw her, he called *her to him,* and said unto her, Woman, thou art loosed from thine infirmity. 13 And he laid *his* hands on her; and immediately she was made straight, and glorified God. 14 And the ruler of the synagogue answered with indignation, because that Jesus had healed on the sabbath-day, and said unto the people, There are six days in which men ought to work: in them, therefore, come and be healed, and not on the sabbath-day. 15 The Lord then answered him, and said, *Thou* hypocrite, doth not each one of you on the sabbath loose his ox or *his* ass from the stall, and lead *him* away to watering? 16 And ought not this woman, being a daughter of Abraham, whom Satan hath bound, lo, these eighteen years, be loosed from this bond on the sabbath-day? 17 And when he had said these things, all his adversaries were ashamed.

Jn. 5: 8 Jesus saith unto him, Rise, take up thy bed, and walk. 9 And immediately the man was made whole, and took up his bed, and walked: and on the same day was the sabbath. 10 The Jews therefore said unto him that was cured, It is the sabbath-day; it is not lawful for thee to carry *thy* bed. 16 And therefore did the Jews persecute Jesus, and sought to slay him, because he had done these things on the sabbath-day. 17 But Jesus answered them, My Father worketh hitherto, and I work.

640. *Appropriate Duties of the Sabbath.*

Lev. 19: 30 Ye shall keep my sabbaths, and reverence my sanctuary: I *am* the LORD.

Ezk. 46: 3 The people of the land shall worship at the door of this gate before the LORD in the sabbaths and in the new-moons.

Mk. 6: 2 When the sabbath-day was come, he [Christ] began to teach in the synagogue: and many hearing *him* were astonished, saying, From whence hath this man these things? and what wisdom *is* this which is given unto him, that even such mighty works are wrought by his hands?

Lk. 4: 16 He came to Nazareth, where he had been brought up: and, as his custom was, he went into the synagogue on the sabbath-day, and stood up for to read. 31 And came down to Capernaum, a city of Galilee, and taught them on the sabbath-days.—13: 10 He was teaching in one of the synagogues on the sabbath.

Ac. 13: 14 When they departed from Perga, they came to Antioch in Pisidia, and went into the synagogue on the sabbath-day, and sat down. 15 And after the reading of the law and the prophets, the rulers of the synagogue sent unto them, saying, *Ye* men *and* brethren, if ye have any word of exhortation for the people, say on. 16 Then Paul stood up, and beckoning with *his* hand, said, Men of Israel, and ye that fear God, give audience. 42 And when the Jews were gone out of the synagogue, the Gentiles besought that these words might be preached to them the next sabbath. 44 And the next sabbath-day came almost the whole city together to hear the word of God.—15: 21 Moses of old time hath in every city them that preach him, being read in the synagogues every sabbath-day. —17: 2 Paul, as his manner was, went in unto them, and three sabbath-days reasoned with them out of the scriptures. —18: 4 He [Paul] reasoned in the synagogue every sabbath, and persuaded the Jews and the Greeks.

1 Cor. 16: 2 Upon the first *day* of the week let every one of you lay by him in store, as *God* hath prospered him, that there be no gatherings when I come.

Heb. 10: 25 Not forsaking the assembling of ourselves together, as the manner of some *is ;* but exhorting *one another ;* and so much the more, as ye see the day approaching.

[Is. 66: 23.   Ps. 84: 1—10, and 132: 7.]

641. *Sabbath to be kept holy; secular labor forbidden.*

Ex. 16: 23 He said unto them, This *is that* which the LORD hath said, To-morrow *is* the rest of the holy sabbath unto the LORD : bake *that* which ye will bake *to-day,* and seethe that ye will seethe ; and that which remaineth over, lay up for you to be kept until the morning. 24 And they laid it up till the morning, as Moses bade : and it did not stink, neither was there any worm therein. 25 And Moses said, Eat that to-day ; for to-day *is* a sabbath unto the LORD ; to-day ye shall not find it in the field. 26 Six days ye shall gather it ; but on the seventh day, *which is* the sabbath, in it there shall be none. 27 And it came to pass, *that* there went out *some* of the people on the seventh day for to gather, and they found none. 28 And the LORD said unto Moses, How long refuse ye to keep my commandments and my laws ? 29 See, for that the LORD hath given you the sabbath, therefore he giveth you on the sixth day the bread of two days : abide ye every man in his place, let no man go out of his place on the seventh day. 30

So the people rested on the seventh day.—20: 8 Remember the sabbath-day to keep it holy. 9 Six days shalt thou labor, and do all thy work: 10 But the seventh day *is* the sabbath of the LORD thy God; *in it* thou shalt not do any work, thou, nor thy son, nor thy daughter, thy man-servant, nor thy maid-servant, nor thy cattle, nor thy stranger that *is* within thy gates: 11 For *in* six days the LORD made heaven and earth, the sea and all that in them *is*, and rested the seventh day: wherefore the LORD blessed the sabbath-day, and hallowed it. —23: 12 Six days thou shalt do thy work, and on the seventh day thou shalt rest: that thine ox and thine ass may rest, and the son of thy handmaid, and the stranger, may be refreshed. —31: 13 Speak thou also unto the children of Israel, saying, Verily my sabbaths ye shall keep: for it *is* a sign between me and you throughout your generations; that *ye* may know that I *am* the LORD that doth sanctify you. 14 Ye shall keep the sabbath therefore: for it *is* holy unto you. Every one that defileth it shall surely be put to death: for whosoever doeth *any* work therein, that soul shall be cut off from among his people. 15 Six days may work be done, but in the seventh *is* the sabbath of rest, holy to the LORD: whosoever doeth *any* work in the sabbath-day he shall surely be put to death. 16 Wherefore the children of Israel shall keep the sabbath, to observe the sabbath throughout their generations, *for* a perpetual covenant. 17 It *is* a sign between me and the children of Israel for ever: for *in* six days the LORD made heaven and earth, and on the seventh day he rested and was refreshed.— 34: 21 Six days thou shalt work, but on the seventh day thou shalt rest: in earing-time and in harvest thou shalt rest.— 35: 3 Ye shall kindle no fire throughout your habitations upon the sabbath-day.

Lev. 23: 3 Six days shall work be done; but the seventh day *is* the sabbath of rest, an holy convocation: ye shall do no work *therein:* it *is* the sabbath of the LORD in all your dwellings.—26: 2 Ye shall keep my sabbaths, and reverence my sanctuary: I *am* the LORD.

Dt. 5: 12 Keep the sabbath-day to sanctify it, as the LORD thy God hath commanded thee. 13 Six days shalt thou labor, and do all thy work; 14 But the seventh day *is* the sabbath of the LORD thy God: *in it* thou shalt not do any work, thou, nor thy son, nor thy daughter, nor thy man-servant, nor thy maid-servant, nor thine ox, nor thine ass, nor any of thy cattle, nor thy stranger that *is* within thy gates; that thy man-servant and thy maid-servant may rest as well as thou. 15 And remember that thou wast a servant in the land of Egypt, and *that* the LORD thy God brought thee out thence through a mighty hand and by a stretched-out arm: therefore the LORD thy God commanded thee to keep the sabbath-day.

Jer. 17: 21 Thus saith the LORD; Take heed to yourselves, and bear no burden on the sabbath-day, nor bring *it* in by the gates of Jerusalem: 22 Neither carry forth a burden out of your houses on the sabbath-day, neither do ye any work, but hallow ye the sabbath-day, as I commanded your fathers. [27.]

Mat. 24: 20 But pray ye that your flight be not in the winter, neither on the sabbath-day.

Lk. 23: 56 They returned, and prepared spices and ointments; and rested the sabbath-day, according to the commandment.

642. *Rewards to sabbath-keepers.*

Is. 56: 2 Blessed *is* the man *that* doeth this, and the son of man *that* layeth hold on it ; that keepeth the sabbath from polluting it, and keepeth his hand from doing any evil. 6 Also the sons of the stranger, that join themselves to the LORD, to serve him, and to love the name of the LORD, to be his servants, every one that keepeth the sabbath from polluting it, and taketh hold of my covenant; 7 Even them will I bring to my holy mountain, and make them joyful in my house of prayer: their burnt-offerings and their sacrifices *shall be* accepted upon mine altar; for my house shall be called a house of prayer for all people. — 58: 13 If thou turn away thy foot from the sabbath, *from* doing thy pleasure on my holy day; and call the sabbath a delight, the holy of the LORD, honorable; and shalt honor him, not doing thine own ways, nor finding thine own pleasure, nor speaking *thine own* words: 14 Then shalt thou delight thyself in the LORD; and I will cause thee to ride upon the high places of the earth, and feed thee with the heritage of Jacob thy father: for the mouth of the LORD hath spoken *it*.

Jer. 17: 24 It shall come to pass, if ye diligently hearken unto me, saith the LORD, to bring in no burden through the gates of this city on the sabbath-day, but hallow the sabbath-day, to do no work therein; 25 Then shall there enter into the gates of this city kings and princes sitting upon the throne of David, riding in chariots and on horses, they and their princes, the men of Judah, and the inhabitants of Jerusalem: and this city shall remain for ever.

643. *Punishment of sabbath-breakers.*

Ex. 35: 2 Six days shall work be done, but on the seventh

day there shall be to you a holy day, a sabbath of rest to the LORD: whosoever doeth work therein shall be put to death.

Num. 15: 32 While the children of Israel were in the wilderness, they found a man that gathered sticks upon the sabbath-day. 35 And the LORD said unto Moses, The man shall be surely put to death: all the congregation shall stone him with stones without the camp.

Jer. 17: 27 If ye will not hearken unto me to hallow the sabbath-day, and not to bear a burden, even entering in at the gates of Jerusalem on the sabbath-day; then will I kindle a fire in the gates thereof, and it shall devour the palaces of Jerusalem, and it shall not be quenched.

Ezk. 20: 15 I lifted up my hand unto them in the wilderness, that I would not bring them into the land which I had given *them*, flowing with milk and honey, which *is* the glory of all lands; 16 Because they despised my judgments, and walked not in my statutes, but polluted my sabbaths: for their heart went after their idols. 20 And hallow my sabbaths; and they shall be a sign between me and you, that ye may know that I *am* the LORD your God. 21 Notwithstanding, the children rebelled against me: they walked not in my statutes, neither kept my judgments to do them, which *if* a man do, he shall even live in them: they polluted my sabbaths: then I said, I would pour out my fury upon them, to accomplish my anger against them in the wilderness.

Ezk. 22: 26 Her priests have violated my law, and have profaned mine holy things: they have put no difference between the holy and profane, neither have they shewed *difference* between the unclean and the clean, and have hid their eyes from my sabbaths, and I am profaned among them. 31 Therefore, have I poured out mine indignation upon them.

644. *The first day of the week distinguished and observed after the resurrection of Christ.*

Mk. 16: 9 When *Jesus* was risen early, the first *day* of the week, he appeared first to Mary Magdalene, out of whom he had cast seven devils. [Ps. 118: 24.]

Jn. 20: 19 Then the same day at evening, being the first *day* of the week, when the doors were shut where the disciples were assembled for fear of the Jews, came Jesus and stood in the midst, and saith unto them, Peace *be* unto you. [Mk. 16: 9, Mat. 28: 1, 8, 9.]

Ac. 20: 7 Upon the first *day* of the week, when the disciples came together to break bread, Paul preached unto them, (ready to depart on the morrow) and continued his speech until midnight.

1 Cor. 16: 2 Upon the first *day* of the week let every one of you lay by him in store, as *God* hath prospered him, that there be no gatherings when I come.

Rev. 1: 10 I was in the Spirit on the Lord's day, and heard behind me a great voice, as of a trumpet.

SAINTS.

645. *Saints radically differ from sinners.*

Gen. 7: 1 The LORD said unto Noah, Come thou and all thy house into the ark : for thee have I seen righteous before me in this generation.

Job 2: 3 The LORD said unto Satan, Hast thou considered my servant Job, that *there is* none like him in the earth, a perfeet and an upright man, one that feareth God, and escheweth evil? and still he holdeth fast his integrity, although thou movedst me against him, to destroy him without cause.

Ps. 1: 2 His delight *is* in the law of the LORD ; and in his law doth he meditate day and night. 4 The ungodly *are* not so : but *are* like the chaff which the wind driveth away.

Jer. 15: 19 Thus saith the LORD, If thou return, then will I bring thee again, *and* thou shalt stand before me : and if thou take forth the precious from the vile, thou shalt be as my mouth.

Ezk. 44: 23 They shall teach my people *the difference* between the holy and profane, and cause them to discern between the unclean and the clean.

Jn. 15: 19 If ye were of the world, the world would love his own ; but because ye are not of the world, but I have chosen you out of the world, therefore the world hateth you.

Ac. 8: 21 Thou hast neither part nor lot in this matter : for thy heart is not right in the sight of God.

Tit. 2: 14 Who gave himself for us, that he might redeem us from all iniquity, and purify unto himself a peculiar people, zealous of good works.

1 Pet. 2: 9 Ye *are* a chosen generation, a royal priesthood, an holy nation, a peculiar people ; that ye should shew forth the praises of him who hath called you out of darkness into his marvellous light.

1 Jn. 5: 19 We know that we are of God, and the whole world lieth in wickedness. [See 591.]

SAINTS DISTINGUISHED FROM SINNERS BY OPPOSITE APPELLATIONS.

646. *The godly and ungodly.*

Ps. 1: 1 Blessed *is* the man that walketh not in the counsel of the ungodly, nor standeth in the way of sinners, nor sitteth in the seat of the scornful. 4 The ungodly *are* not so : but *are* like the chaff which the wind driveth away. 5 Therefore the ungodly shall not stand in the judgment, nor sinners in the congregation of the righteous.—4: 3 But know that the LORD hath set apart him that is godly for himself.

647. *The just and the unjust.*

Pr. 29: 27 An unjust man *is* an abomination to the just ; and *he that is* upright in the way *is* abomination to the wicked.

Mat. 5: 45 That ye may be the children of your Father which is in heaven : for he maketh his sun to rise on the evil and on the good, and sendeth rain on the just and on the unjust.

648. *The righteous and wicked.*

Ps. 37: 16 A little that a righteous man hath *is* better than the riches of many wicked. 17 For the arms of the wicked shall be broken : but the LORD upholdeth the righteous.

Mal. 3: 18 Then shall ye return and discern between the righteous and the wicked, between him that serveth God and him that serveth him not.

649. *Friends of God and enemies of God.*

Is. 1: 24 Saith the Lord, the LORD of hosts, the mighty One of Israel, Ah, I will ease me of mine adversaries, and avenge me of mine enemies.

Jam. 2: 23 The scripture was fulfilled, which saith, Abraham believed God, and it was imputed unto him for righteousness : and he was called the Friend of God. [See 690.]

650. *Lovers of God—haters of God.*

Ex. 20: 6 Shewing mercy unto thousands of them that love me, and keep my commandments.

Rom. 1: 30 Backbiters, haters of God.

651. *Believers and unbelievers.*

Ac. 5: 14 Believers were the more added to the Lord, multitudes both of men and women.

2 Cor. 6: 14 Be ye not unequally yoked together with unbe-

Opposite Appellations of Saints and Sinners.

lievers : for what fellowship hath righteousness with unrighteousness ? and what communion hath light with darkness ?

652. *Sheep, and wolves or serpents.*

Mat. 23: 33 *Ye* serpents, *ye* generation of vipers, how can ye escape the damnation of hell ?

Jn. 10: 14 I am the good shepherd, and know my *sheep*, and am known of mine.

Ac. 20: 29 I know this, that after my departing shall grievous wolves enter in among you, not sparing the flock.

653. *Children of God, and children of the devil.*

Mat. 13: 38 The field is the world ; the good seed are the children of the kingdom ; but the tares are the children of the wicked *one.*

1 Jn. 3: 10 In this the children of God are manifest, and the children of the devil : whosoever doeth not righteousness is not of God, neither he that loveth not his brother.

[See 690.]

654. *Children of obedience and children of disobedience.*

Ep. 2: 1 You *hath he quickened,* who were dead in trespasses and sins ; 2 Wherein in time past ye walked according to the course of this world, according to the prince of the power of the air, the spirit that now worketh in the children of disobedience.

1 Pet. 1: 14 As obedient children, not fashioning yourselves according to the former lusts in your ignorance.

655. *Children of light, and children of darkness.*

Is. 42: 18 Hear, ye deaf ; and look, ye blind, that ye may see.

Lk. 16: 8 The lord commended the unjust steward, because he had done wisely : for the children of this world are in their generation wiser than the children of light.

1 Th. 5: 5 Ye are all the children of light, and the children of the day : we are not of the night, nor of darkness.

656. *Children of the kingdom and children of wrath.*

Mat. 13: 38 The field is the world ; the good seed are the children of the kingdom ; but the tares are the children of the wicked *one.*

Ep. 2: 3 Among whom also we all had our conversation in times past in the lusts of our flesh, fulfilling the desires of the flesh and of the mind ; and were by nature the children of wrath, even others.

PECULIAR CHARACTERISTICS OF SAINTS.

657. *Saints hope and delight in God, have fellowship and communion with him, and desire his presence.*

Ex. 15: 2 The LORD *is* my strength and song, and he is become my salvation; he *is* my God, and I will prepare him an habitation; my father's God, and I will exalt him.

1 S. 2: 1 Hannah prayed, and said, My heart rejoiceth in the LORD, mine horn is exalted in the LORD; my mouth is enlarged over mine enemies; because I rejoice in thy salvation.

Ps. 16: 5 The LORD *is* the portion of mine inheritance and of my cup: thou maintainest my lot. 8 I have set the LORD always before me: because *he is* at my right hand, I shall not be moved. — 18: 2 The LORD *is* my rock, and my fortress, and my deliverer; my God, my strength, in whom I will trust; my buckler, and the horn of my salvation, *and* my high tower. — 34: 2 My soul shall make her boast in the LORD: the humble shall hear *thereof*, and be glad. — 38: 15 In thee, O LORD, do I hope: thou wilt hear, O LORD my God. 21 Forsake me not, O LORD: O my God, be not far from me. [32: 22.] — 39: 7 LORD, what wait I for? my hope *is* in thee. — 42: 1 As the hart panteth after the water-brooks, so panteth my soul after thee, O God. 2 My soul thirsteth for God, for the living God: when shall I come and appear before God? — 43: 4 Then will I go unto the altar of God, unto God my exceeding joy: yea, upon the harp will I praise thee, O God my God. — 51: 11 Cast me not away from thy presence; and take not thy Holy Spirit from me. — 63: 1 O God, thou *art* my God; early will I seek thee: my soul thirsteth for thee, my flesh longeth for thee in a dry and thirsty land, where no water is; 2 To see thy power and thy glory, so *as* I have seen thee in the sanctuary. 3 Because thy loving-kindness *is* better than life, my lips shall praise thee. 8 My soul followeth hard after thee: thy right hand upholdeth me. — 73: 25 Whom have I in heaven *but thee?* and *there is* none upon earth *that* I desire besides thee. 26 My flesh and my heart faileth: *but* God *is* the strength of my heart, and my portion for ever. — 119: 57 *Thou art* my portion, O LORD: I have said that I would keep thy words.

Is. 12: 2 Behold, God *is* my salvation; I will trust, and not be afraid; for the LORD JEHOVAH *is* my strength and *my* song; he also is become my salvation. — 26: 8 Yea, in the way of thy judgments, O LORD, have we waited for thee; the desire of our soul *is* to thy name, and to the remembrance of thee. 9 With my soul have I desired thee in the night; yea, with my spirit within me will I seek thee early. — 61: 10 I will greatly rejoice in the LORD, my soul shall be joyful in my God.

Jer. 14: 8 O the hope of Israel, the Saviour thereof in time of trouble, why shouldest thou be as a stranger in the land, and as a wayfaring man *that* turneth aside to tarry for a night? 9 Why shouldest thou be as a man astonished, as a mighty man *that* cannot save? yet thou, O LORD, *art* in the midst of us, and we are called by thy name; leave us not.

Lam. 3: 24 The LORD *is* my portion, saith my soul; therefore will I hope in him.

Hab. 3: 17 Although the fig-tree shall not blossom, neither *shall* fruit *be* in the vines; the labor of the olive shall fail, and the fields shall yield no meat; the flock shall be cut off from the fold, and *there shall be* no herd in the stalls: 18 Yet I will rejoice in the LORD, I will joy in the God of my salvation.

Rom. 5: 2 By whom also we have access by faith into this grace wherein we stand, and rejoice in hope of the glory of God.

1 Cor. 1: 9 God *is* faithful, by whom ye were called unto the fellowship of his Son Jesus Christ our Lord.

1 Jn. 1: 3 That which we have seen and heard declare we unto you, that ye also may have fellowship with us: and truly our fellowship *is* with the Father, and with his Son Jesus Christ. [See 6, 294.]

658. *Saints love and obey God's law, and delight in all his truth and institutions.*

Ps. 1: 2 His delight *is* in the law of the LORD; and in his law doth he meditate day and night. — 119: 20 My soul breaketh for the longing *that it hath* unto thy judgments at all times. 24 Thy testimonies also *are* my delight, *and* my counsellors. 97 O how love I thy law! it *is* my meditation all the day. 103 How sweet are thy words unto my taste! *yea, sweeter* than honey to my mouth. 111 Thy testimonies have I taken as an heritage for ever: for they *are* the rejoicing of my heart. 127 Therefore I love thy commandments above gold; yea, above fine gold. 128 Therefore I esteem all *thy* precepts *concerning* all *things to be* right; *and* I hate every false way. 131 I opened my mouth, and panted: for I longed for thy commandments. 162 I rejoice at thy word, as one that findeth great spoil. 167 My soul hath kept thy testimonies; and I love them exceedingly.

Are honest — Meek and forbearing.

Jer. 15: 16 Thy words were found, and I did eat them; and thy word was unto me the joy and rejoicing of mine heart.

Rom. 7: 22 I delight in the law of God, after the inward man. [See 106.]

659. *Honesty, integrity, and firmness of saints, leaving consequences to God.*

Gen. 22: 10 Abraham stretched forth his hand, and took the knife to slay his son.

Is. 49: 4 Then I said, I have labored in vain, I have spent my strength for nought, and in vain; *yet* surely my judgment *is* with he LORD, and my work with my God. 5 And now, saith the LORD that formed me from the womb *to be* his servant, to bring Jacob again to him, Though Israel be not gathered, yet shall I be glorious in the eyes of the LORD, and my God shall be my strength.

Jn. 1: 47 Jesus saw Nathanael coming to him, and saith of him, Behold an Israelite indeed, in whom is no guile!

2 Cor. 1: 12 Our rejoicing is this, the testimony of our conscience, that in simplicity and godly sincerity, not with fleshly wisdom, but by the grace of God, we have had our conversation in the world, and more abundantly to you-ward. — 4: 1 Seeing we have this ministry, as we have received mercy, we faint not; 2 But have renounced the hidden things of dishonesty; not walking in craftiness, nor handling the word of God deceitfully; but, by manifestation of the truth, commending ourselves to every man's conscience in the sight of God.
[See 56, 294, 460, 504, 629.]

660. *Saints have a meek, gentle, forbearing, and forgiving spirit.*

Mat. 10: 16 Behold, I send you forth as sheep in the midst of wolves: be ye therefore wise as serpents, and harmless as doves.

1 Cor. 4: 12 And labor, working with our own hands. Being reviled, we bless; being persecuted, we suffer it: 13 Being defamed, we entreat. — 13: 4 Charity suffereth long, *and* is kind; charity envieth not; charity vaunteth not itself, is not puffed up, 7 Beareth all things, believeth all things, hopeth all things, endureth all things.

Gal. 5: 22 The fruit of the Spirit is love, joy, peace, long-suffering, gentleness, goodness, faith, 23 Meekness, temperance: against such there is no law.

Heb. 10: 34 Ye had compassion of me in my bonds, and took joyfully the spoiling of your goods, knowing in yourselves that ye have in heaven a better and an enduring substance.

Jam. 5: 6 Ye have condemned *and* killed the just; *and* he doth not resist you. [See 62, 437, 499, 737.]

They are benevolent, and grieve at sin.

661. *Saints are self-denying, disinterested, and devoted to God and his cause.*

Ac. 4: 32 The multitude of them that believed were of one heart, and of one soul: neither said any *of them* that aught of the things which he possessed was his own: but they had all things common.

2 Cor. 12: 14 Behold, the third time I am ready to come to you; and I will not be burdensome to you: for I seek not yours, but you. For the children ought not to lay up for the parents, but the parents for the children. 15 And I will very gladly spend and be spent for you; though the more abundantly I love you, the less I be loved. [See 295, 407, 414, 674.]

662. *Saints grieve when sinners dishonor and offend God.*

Ezra 9: 2 They have taken of their daughters for themselves, and for their sons: so that the holy seed have mingled themselves with the people of *those* lands: yea, the hand of the princes and rulers hath been chief in this trespass. 3 And when I heard this thing, I rent my garment and my mantle, and plucked off the hair of my head and of my beard, and sat down astonished. 4 Then were assembled unto me every one that trembled at the words of the God of Israel, because of the transgression of those that had been carried away; and I sat astonished until the evening sacrifice. 5 And at the evening sacrifice I arose up from my heaviness; and having rent my garment and my mantle, I fell upon my knees, and spread out my hands unto the LORD my God. — 10: 6 Then Ezra rose up from before the house of God, and went into the chamber of Johanan the son of Eliashib: and *when* he came thither, he did eat no bread, nor drink water: for he mourned because of the transgression of them that had been carried away.

Ps. 119: 136 Rivers of waters run down mine eyes, because they keep not thy law. 158 I beheld the transgressors, and was grieved; because they kept not thy word.

Ezk. 9: 4 The LORD said unto him, Go through the midst of the city, through the midst of Jerusalem, and set a mark upon the foreheads of the men that sigh and that cry for all the abominations that be done in the midst thereof.

Ac. 17: 16 While Paul waited for them at Athens, his spirit was stirred in him, when he saw the city wholly given to idolatry.

Rom. 9: 1 I say the truth in Christ, I lie not, my conscience also bearing me witness in the Holy Ghost, 2 That I have great heaviness and continual sorrow in my heart. 3 For I could wish that myself were accursed from Christ, for my brethren, my kinsmen according to the flesh.

2 Pet. 2: 7 And delivered Lot, vexed with the filthy conversation of the wicked: 8 (For that righteous man dwelling among them, in seeing and hearing, vexed *his* righteous soul from day to day with *their* unlawful deeds.) [See 538.]

663. *Saints feel their unworthiness, and desire to learn their guilt.*

Gen. 32: 10 I am not worthy of the least of all the mercies, and of all the truth, which thou hast shewed unto thy servant.

Job 13: 23 How many *are* mine iniquities and sins? make me to know my transgression and my sin.

Ps. 26: 2 Examine me, O LORD, and prove me; try my reins and my heart. — 51: 3 I acknowledge my transgressions: and my sin *is* ever before me. — 115: 1 Not unto us, O LORD, not unto us, but unto thy name give glory, for thy mercy, *and* for thy truth's sake. — 139: 23 Search me, O God, and know my heart: try me, and know my thoughts: 24 And see if *there be any* wicked way in me, and lead me in the way everlasting.

Mat. 8: 8 The centurion answered and said, Lord, I am not worthy that thou shouldest come under my roof: but speak the word only, and my servant shall be healed. — 25: 37 Then shall the righteous answer him, saying, Lord, when saw we thee a hungered, and fed *thee*? or thirsty, and gave *thee* drink? 38 When saw we thee a stranger, and took *thee* in? or naked, and clothed *thee*? 39 Or when saw we thee sick, or in prison, and came unto thee?

Rom. 7: 24 O wretched man that I am! who shall deliver me from the body of this death?

1 Cor. 15: 9 I am the least of the apostles, that am not meet to be called an apostle, because I persecuted the Church of God. 10 But by the grace of God I am what I am.

Ep. 3: 8 Unto me, who am less than the least of all saints, is this grace given, that I should preach among the Gentiles the unsearchable riches of Christ. [See 507, 537.]

664. *Saints believe in Christ, and live by faith in him.*

Gal. 2: 20 I am crucified with Christ: nevertheless, I live; yet not I, but Christ liveth in me: and the life which I now live in the flesh, I live by the faith of the Son of God, who loved me, and gave himself for me.

1 Pet. 1: 8 Whom having not seen, ye love; in whom, though now ye see *him* not, yet believing, ye rejoice with joy unspeakable, and full of glory. [See 184.]

665. *Saints delight in devout meditation and prayer.*

Ps. 1: 2 His delight is in the law of the LORD; and in his law doth he meditate day and night.

Ps. 16: 8 I have set the LORD always before me: because *he is* at my right hand, I shall not be moved. — 63: 5 .My soul shall be satisfied as *with* marrow and fatness; and my mouth shall praise *thee* with joyful lips: When I remember thee upon my bed, *and* meditate on thee in the *night* watches. — 77: 11 I will remember the works of the LORD: surely I will remember thy wonders of old. 12 I will meditate also of all thy work, and talk of thy doings. — 119: 23 Princes also did sit *and* speak against me: *but* thy servant did meditate in thy statutes. 24 Thy testimonies also *are* my delight, *and* my counsellors. 48 My hands also will I lift up unto thy commandments, which I have loved; and I will meditate in thy statutes. 97 O how love I thy law! it *is* my meditation all the day. 99 I have more understanding than all my teachers: for thy testimonies *are* my meditation. 148 Mine eyes prevent the *night*-watches, that I might meditate in thy word. — 143: 5 I remember the days of old, I meditate on all thy works; I muse on the work of thy hands. 6 I stretch forth my hands unto thee: my soul *thirsteth* after thee, as a thirsty land.

Dan. 6: 10 When Daniel knew that the writing was signed, he went into his house; and his windows being open in his chamber toward Jerusalem, he kneeled upon his knees three times a day, and prayed, and gave thanks before his God, as he did aforetime. [See 64, 531.]

666. *Saints have peculiar internal peace.*

Ps. 119: 165 Great peace have they which love thy law: and nothing shall offend them.

Jn. 14: 27 Peace I leave with you, my peace I give unto you: not as the world giveth, give I unto you. Let not your heart be troubled, neither let it be afraid.

Gal. 5: 22 The fruit of the Spirit is love, joy, peace, long-suffering, gentleness, goodness, faith.

Ph. 4: 7 The peace of God, which passeth all understanding, shall keep your hearts and minds through Christ Jesus. [See 582.]

667. *Saints make progress in knowledge and holiness.*

Ps. 92: 12 The righteous shall flourish like the palm-tree: he shall grow like a cedar in Lebanon. 13 Those that be planted in the house of the Lord, shall flourish in the courts of our God.   14 They shall still bring forth fruit in old age; they shall be fat and flourishing.

Mat. 13: 33 Another parable spake he unto them; The kingdom of heaven is like unto leaven, which a woman took, and hid in three measures of meal, till the whole was leavened.

Mk. 4: 26 He said, So is the kingdom of God, as if a man should cast seed into the ground; 27 And should sleep, and rise night and day, and the seed should spring and grow up, he knoweth not how.   28 For the earth bringeth forth fruit of herself; first the blade, then the ear, after that the full corn in the ear.

2 Cor. 4: 16 For which cause we faint not; but though our outward man perish, yet the inward *man* is renewed day by day.

2 Th. 1: 3 We are bound to thank God always for you, brethren, as it is meet, because that your faith groweth exceedingly, and the charity of every one of you all toward each other aboundeth.   [See 515.]

668. *Saints made to differ — boasting excluded.*

Rom. 3: 27 Where *is* boasting then?   It is excluded.   By what law? of works?   Nay; but by the law of faith.

1 Cor. 4: 7 Who maketh thee to differ *from another?* and what hast thou that thou didst not receive? now if thou didst receive *it*, why dost thou glory, as if thou hadst not received *it?*

Ep. 2: 1 You *hath he quickened*, who were dead in trespasses and sins; 2 Wherein in time past ye walked according to the course of this world, according to the prince of the power of the air, the spirit that now worketh in the children of disobedience: 3 Among whom also we all had our conversation in times past in the lusts of our flesh, fulfilling the desires of the flesh and of the mind; and were by nature the children of wrath, even as others.   8 For by grace are ye saved, through faith; and that not of yourselves: *it is* the gift of God.

[See 482.]

669. *Real saints have been comparatively few, but will be very numerous.*

Gen. 7: 1 The LORD said unto Noah, Come thou and all thy house into the ark: for thee have I seen righteous before me in this generation.   [Gen. 6: 11, 12.]

Gen. 18: 32 He said, Oh, let not the Lord be angry and I will speak yet but this once: Peradventure ten shall be found there.   And he said, I will not destroy *it* for ten's sake.

Num. 14: 23 Surely they shall not see the land which I

sware unto their fathers, neither shall any of them that provoked me see it: 24 But my servant Caleb, because he had another spirit with him, and hath followed me fully, him will I bring into the land whereinto he went; and his seed shall possess it.

Mat. 7:14 Strait *is* the gate, and narrow *is* the way, which leadeth unto life, and few there be that find it. — 20: 16 The last shall be first, and the first last: for many be called, but few chosen.

Lk. 12: 32 Fear not, little flock; for it is your Father's good pleasure to give you the kingdom. — 13: 23 Then said one unto him, Lord, are there few that be saved? And he said unto them, 24 Strive to enter in at the strait gate: for many, I say unto you, will seek to enter in, and shall not be able. — 18: 8 I tell you that he will avenge them speedily. Nevertheless, when the Son of man cometh, shall he find faith on the earth?

2 Tim. 1: 15 This thou knowest, that all they which are in Asia be turned away from me; of whom are Phygellus and Hermogenes.

Rev. 7: 9 After this I beheld, and lo, a great multitude which no man could number, of all nations, and kindreds, and people, and tongues, stood before the throne, and before the Lamb, clothed with white robes, and palms in their hands. [See 440.]

670. Saints, the light and salvation of the world.

Jer. 5: 1 Run ye to and fro through the streets of Jerusalem, and see now, and know, and seek in the broad places thereof, if ye can find a man, if there be *any* that executeth judgment, that seeketh the truth; and I will pardon it.

Ezk. 22: 29 The people of the land have used oppression, and exercised robbery, and have vexed the poor and needy: yea, they have oppressed the stranger wrongfully. 30 And I sought for a man among them, that should make up the hedge, and stand in the gap before me for the land, that I should not destroy it; but I found none.

Mat. 5: 13 Ye are the salt of the earth: but if the salt have lost his savour, wherewith shall it be salted? it is thenceforth good for nothing, but to be cast out and to be trodden under foot of men. 14 Ye are the light of the world. A city that is set on a hill cannot be hid. [See 545.]

671. Singularity of Saints

Dt. 14: 2 The LORD hath chosen thee to be a peculiar people unto himself, above all the nations that *are* upon the earth.

Rom. 7: 15 That which I do, I allow not: for what I would, that do I not; but what I hate, that do I. 16 If then I do

that which I would not, I consent unto the law that *it is* good.
17 Now then it is no more I that do it, but sin that dwelleth
in me. 18 For I know that in me (that is, in my flesh,)
dwelleth no good thing: for to will is present with me; but
how to perform that which is good, I find not. 19 For the
good that I would, I do not; but the evil which I would not,
that I do. 20 Now if I do that I would not, it is no more I
that do it, but sin that dwelleth in me. 21 I find then a law,
that when I would do good, evil is present with me. 22 For I
delight in the law of God, after the inward man: 23 But I see
another law in my members warring against the law of my
mind, and bringing me into captivity to the law of sin which is
in my members. 24 O wretched man that I am! who shall
deliver me from the body of this death? 25 I thank God,
through Jesus Christ our Lord. So then, with the mind, I
myself serve the law of God: but with the flesh the law of sin.

2 Cor. 6: 8 As deceivers, and *yet* true; 9 As unknown, and
yet well known; as dying, and behold, we live; as chastened,
and not killed; 10 As sorrowful, yet always rejoicing; as poor,
yet making many rich; as having nothing, and *yet* possessing
all things.

Tit. 2: 14 Who gave himself for us, that he might redeem
us from all iniquity, and purify unto himself a peculiar people,
zealous of good works.

672. *God's delight in saints, and prospective view of their perfection, preëminence and glory.*

Num. 23: 21 He hath not beheld iniquity in Jacob, neither
hath he seen perverseness in Israel.

Dt. 32: 9 The LORD's portion *is* his people; Jacob *is* the lot
of his inheritance.

Job 7: 17 What *is* man, that thou shouldest magnify him?
and that thou shouldest set thine heart upon him? 18 And
that thou shouldest visit him every morning, *and* try him every
moment?

Ps. 50: 2 Out of Zion, the perfection of beauty, God hath
shined.

Song 4: 7 Thou *art* all fair, my love; *there is* no spot in
thee.

Is. 43: 4 Since thou wast precious in my sight, thou hast
been honorable, and I have loved thee: therefore will I give
men for thee, and people for thy life. — 46: 13 I will place
salvation in Zion for Israel my glory. — 62: 3 Thou shalt also
be a crown of glory in the hand of the LORD, and a royal diadem in the hand of thy God. 5 For *as* a young man marrieth

a virgin, *so* shall thy sons marry thee: and *as* the bridegroom rejoiceth over the bride, *so* shall thy God rejoice over thee.

Zep. 3: 17 The LORD thy God in the midst of thee *is* mighty; he will save, he will rejoice over thee with joy; he will rest in his love, he will joy over thee with singing.

Mal. 3: 16 Then they that feared the LORD spake often one to another: and the LORD hearkened, and heard *it:* and a book of remembrance was written before him for them that feared the LORD, and that thought upon his name. 17 And they shall be mine, saith the LORD of hosts, in that day when I make up my jewels; and I will spare them, as a man spareth his own son that serveth him.

Mat. 13: 43 Then shall the righteous shine forth as the sun in the kingdom of their Father.

Lk. 7: 42 When they had nothing to pay, he frankly forgave them both. Tell me therefore, which of them will love him most? 43 Simon answered and said, I suppose that *he,* to whom he forgave most. And he said unto him, Thou hast rightly judged. 47 Wherefore, I say unto thee, Her sins, which are many, are forgiven; for she loved much: but to whom little is forgiven, *the same* loveth little. — 15: 7 I say unto you, that likewise joy shall be in heaven over one sinner that repenteth, more than over ninety and nine just persons which need no repentance. 22 But the father said to his servants, Bring forth the best robe, and put *it* on him; and put a ring on his hand, and shoes on *his* feet.

Jn. 14: 21 He that hath my commandments, and keepeth them, he it is that loveth me: and he that loveth me, shall be loved of my Father, and I will love him, and will manifest myself to him. 22 Judas saith unto him, (not Iscariot) Lord, how is it that thou wilt manifest thyself unto us, and not unto the world? 23 Jesus answered and said unto him, If a man love me, he will keep my words: and my Father will love him, and we will come unto him, and make our abode with him.— 15: 9 As the Father hath loved me, so have I loved you: continue ye in my love. 15 Henceforth I call you not servants; for the servant knoweth not what his lord doeth: but I have called you friends; for all things that I have heard of my Father, I have made known unto you.— 20: 17 Go to my brethren, and say unto them, I ascend unto my Father and your Father, and *to* my God and your God.

Rom. 8: 29 Whom he did foreknow, he also did predestinate *to be* conformed to the image of his Son, that he might be the first-born among many brethren.

1 Cor. 6: 3 Know ye not that we shall judge angels?

2 Cor. 8: 23 Whether *any do inquire* of Titus, *he is* my partner and fellow-helper concerning you: or our brethren *be inquired of, they are* the messengers of the churches, *and* the glory of Christ.

Ep. 5: 25 Husbands, love your wives, even as Christ also loved the church, and gave himself for it; 26 That he might sanctify and cleanse it with the washing of water by the word, 27 That he might present it to himself a glorious church, not having spot or wrinkle, or any such thing; but that it should be holy and without blemish.

Col. 1: 21 You, that were sometime alienated and enemies in *your* mind by wicked works, yet now hath he reconciled, 22 In the body of his flesh through death, to present you holy, and unblamable, and unreprovable, in his sight.

Heb. 12: 23 To the general assembly and church of the first-born, which are written in heaven, and to God the Judge of all, and to the spirits of just men made perfect.

Rev. 1: 6 And hath made us kings and priests unto God and his Father. — 14: 3 They sung as it were a new song before the throne, and before the four beasts, and the elders: and no man could learn that song but the hundred *and* forty *and* four thousand, which were redeemed from the earth. — 21: 9 Come hither, I will shew thee the bride, the Lamb's wife.

[See 94, 340, 504, 584–5.]

SCORN AND CONTEMPT.

673. *Unhallowed scorn and contempt reprobated.*

Pr. 3: 34 Surely he scorneth the scorners: but he giveth grace unto the lowly. — 9: 12 If thou be wise, thou shalt be wise for thyself: but *if* thou scornest, thou alone shalt bear it. — 12: 5 For the oppression of the poor, for the sighing of the needy, now will I arise, saith the LORD; I will set *him* in safety *from him that* puffeth at him. — 14: 21 He that despiseth his neighbor sinneth: but he that hath mercy on the poor, happy *is* he. — 15: 20 A wise son maketh a glad father: but a foolish man despiseth his mother. — 19: 29 Judgments are prepared for scorners. — 22: 10 Cast out the scorner, and contention shall go out; yea, strife and reproach shall cease. — 29: 8 Scornful men bring a city into a snare: but wise *men* turn away wrath.

Mat. 18: 10 Take heed that ye despise not one of these little ones: for I say unto you, That in heaven their angels do always behold the face of my Father which is in heaven.

SELF-DENIAL.

674. *Self-denial required, exemplified and encouraged.*

Gen. 22: 10 Abraham stretched forth his hand, and took the knife to slay his son. 12 Lay not thine hand upon the lad, neither do thou any thing unto him: for now I know that thou fearest God, seeing thou hast not withheld thy son, thine only *son*, from me.

Mat. 10: 37 He that loveth father or mother more than me, is not worthy of me: and he that loveth son or daughter more than me, is not worthy of me. 38 And he that taketh not his cross, and followeth after me, is not worthy of me. 39 He that findeth his life shall lose it: and he that loseth his life for my sake, shall find it. — 16: 24 Then said Jesus unto his disciples, If any *man* will come after me, let him deny himself, and take up his cross, and follow me. 25 For whosoever will save his life, shall lose it: and whosoever will lose his life for my sake, shall find it. 26 For what is a man profited, if he shall gain the whole world, and lose his own soul? or what shall a man give in exchange for his soul? [Mk. 8: 34—37.] — 19: 29 Every one that hath forsaken houses, or brethren, or sisters, or father, or mother, or wife, or children, or lands, for my name's sake, shall receive an hundred-fold, and shall inherit everlasting life.

Mk. 10: 28 Then Peter began to say unto him, Lo, we have left all, and have followed thee. 29 And Jesus answered and said, Verily I say unto you, There is no man that hath left house, or brethren, or sisters, or father, or mother, or wife, or children, or lands, for my sake, and the gospel's, 30 But he shall receive an hundred-fold now in this time, houses, and brethren, and sisters, and mothers, and children, and lands, with persecutions; and in the world to come, eternal life. [Lk. 18: 28—30.]

Lk. 14: 26 If any *man* come to me, and hate not his father, and mother, and wife, and children, and brethren, and sisters, yea, and his own life also, he cannot be my disciple. 27 Whosoever doth not bear his cross, and come after me, cannot be my disciple. 33 Whosoever he be of you that forsaketh not all that he hath, he cannot be my disciple. — 18: 28 Then Peter said, Lo, we have left all, and followed thee. [See 356.]

SENSUALITY.

675. *Improper sensual indulgences forbidden and reproved.*

Am. 6: 3 Ye that put far away the evil day, and cause the seat of violence to come near; 4 That lie upon beds of ivory, and stretch themselves upon their couches, and eat the lambs out of the flock, and the calves out of the midst of the stall; 5 That chant to the sound of the viol, *and* invent to themselves instruments of music, like David; 6 That drink wine in bowls, and anoint themselves with the chief ointments: but they are not grieved for the affliction of Joseph. 7 Therefore, now shall they go captive with the first that go captive, and the banquet of them that stretched themselves shall be removed.

Rom. 6: 12 Let not sin therefore reign in your mortal body, that ye should obey it in the lusts thereof. — 13: 13 Let us walk honestly, as in the day: not in rioting and drunkenness, not in chambering and wantonness, not in strife and envying. 14 But put ye on the Lord Jesus Christ, and make not provision for the flesh, to *fulfil* the lusts *thereof.*

2 Cor. 7: 1 Having therefore these promises, dearly beloved, let us cleanse ourselves from all filthiness of the flesh and spirit, perfecting holiness in the fear of God.

Tit. 2: 11 The grace of God that bringeth salvation hath appeared to all men, 12 Teaching us, that denying ungodliness, and worldly lusts, we should live soberly, righteously, and godly, in this present world.

1 Pet. 2: 11 Dearly beloved, I beseech *you*, as strangers and pilgrims, abstain from fleshly lusts, which war against the soul. [See 366, 698.]

SERVANTS AND SERVITUDE.

676. *Were the civil rights and religious privileges of the patriarchal servants so secured, as to gain their confidence?*

Gen. 14: 14 When Abram heard that his brother was taken captive, he armed his trained *servants*, born in his own house, three hundred and eighteen, and pursued *them* unto Dan. — 17: 12 He that is eight days old shall be circumcised among you, every man-child in your generations, he that is born in the house, or bought with money of any stranger which *is* not of thy seed. — 24: 2 Abraham said unto his eldest servant of his house, that ruled over all that he had, Put, I pray thee, thy hand under my thigh: 3 And I will make thee swear by the

LORD, the God of heaven, and the God of the earth, that thou shalt not take a wife unto my son of the daughters of the Canaanites among whom I dwell: 4 But thou shalt go unto my country, and to my kindred, and take a wife unto my son Isaac. 10 And the servant took ten camels, of the camels of his master, and departed; (for all the goods of his master *were* in his hand,) and he arose, and went to Mesopotamia, unto the city of Nahor.

Job 31: 13 If I did despise the cause of my man-servant or of my maid-servant, when they contended with me; 14 What then shall I do when God riseth up? and when he visiteth, what shall I answer him?

677. *Hebrew laws and usages on procuring, holding, and releasing servants.*

1. *Voluntary servants, and service for life, or for a term, and laws of release.*

Ex. 21: 5 If the servant shall plainly say, I love my master, my wife, and my children; I will not go out free: 6 Then his master shall bring him unto the judges: he shall also bring him to the door, or unto the door-post; and his master shall bore his ear through with an awl; and he shall serve him for ever.

Lev. 25: 47 If a sojourner or a stranger wax rich by thee, and thy brother *that dwelleth* by him wax poor, and sell himself unto the stranger *or* sojourner by thee, or to the stock of the stranger's family: 48 After that he is sold he may be redeemed again: one of his brethren may redeem him: 49 Either his uncle, or his uncle's son may redeem him, or *any* that is nigh of kin unto him of his family may redeem him; or if he be able, he may redeem himself. 50 And he shall reckon with him that bought him, from the year that he was sold to him, unto the year of jubilee: and the price of his sale shall be according unto the number of years, according to the time of an hired servant shall it be with him. 51 If *there be* yet many years *behind,* according unto them he shall give again the price of his redemption out of the money that he was bought for. 52 And if there remain but few years unto the year of jubilee, then he shall count with him, *and* according unto his years shall he give him again the price of his redemption. 53 *And* as a yearly hired servant shall he be with him: *and the other* shall not rule with rigor over him in thy sight. 54 And if he be not redeemed in these *years,* then he shall go out in the year of jubilee, *both* he, and his children with him.

Dt. 15: 16 It shall be, if he say unto thee, I will not go away from thee; because he loveth thee and thine house, because he is well with thee; 17 Then thou shalt take an awl and thrust *it* through his ear unto the door, and he shall be thy servant for ever. And also unto thy maid-servant thou shalt do likewise.

2. Hebrews and their children, sometimes sold for debt — laws of release, of reward, etc.

Ex. 21: 2 If thou buy an Hebrew servant, six years he shall serve: and in the seventh he shall go out free for nothing. 3 If he came in by himself, he shall go out by himself: if he were married, then his wife shall go out with him. 4 If his master have given him a wife, and she have borne him sons or daughters, the wife and her children shall be her master's, and he shall go out by himself.

Lev. 25: 39 If thy brother *that dwelleth* by thee be waxen poor, and be sold unto thee; thou shalt not compel him to serve as a bond-servant: 40 *But* as an hired servant, *and* as a sojourner he shall be with thee, *and* shall serve thee unto the year of jubilee: 41 And *then* shall he depart from thee, *both* he and his children with him, and shall return unto his own family, and unto the possession of his fathers shall he return. 42 For they *are* my servants which I brought forth out of the land of Egypt; they shall not be sold as bond-men. 43 Thou shalt not rule over him with rigor, but shalt fear thy God.

Dt. 15: 12 If thy brother, an Hebrew man, or an Hebrew woman, be sold unto thee, and serve thee six years; then in the seventh year thou shalt let him go free from thee. 13 And when thou sendest him out free from thee, thou shalt not let him go away empty: 14 Thou shalt furnish him liberally out of thy flock, and out of thy floor, and out of thy wine-press: *of that* wherewith the LORD thy God hath blessed thee thou shalt give unto him. 15 And thou shalt remember that thou wast a bond-man in the land of Egypt, and the LORD thy God redeemed thee: therefore I command thee this thing to-day. 18 It shall not seem hard unto thee, when thou sendest him away free from thee: for he hath been worth a double hired servant *to thee*, in serving thee six years: and the LORD thy God shall bless thee in all that thou doest.

2 K. 4: 1 There cried a certain woman of the wives of the sons of the prophets unto Elisha, saying, Thy servant my husband is dead; and thou knowest that thy servant did fear the LORD: and the creditor is come to take unto him my two sons to be bond-men.

Neh. 5: 2 There were that said, We, our sons, and our daughters, *are* many: therefore we take up corn *for them*, that we may eat, and live. 5 Our flesh *is* as the flesh of our brethren, our children as their children: and lo, we bring into bondage our sons and our daughters to be servants, and *some* of our daughters are brought into bondage *already:* neither *is it* in our power *to redeem them ;* for other men have our lands and vineyards.

3. *Permanent servants were of the heathen, or of strangers, and not Hebrews*

Lev. 25: 44 Both thy bond-men, and thy bond-maids, which thou shalt have, *shall be* of the heathen that are round about you; of them shall ye buy bond-men and bond-maids. 45 Moreover, of the children of the strangers that do sojourn among you, of them shall ye buy, and of their families that *are* with you, which they begat in your land: and they shall be your possession. 46 And ye shall take them as an inheritance for your children after you, to inherit *them for* a possession, they shall be your bond-men for ever: but over your brethren the children of Israel, ye shall not rule one over another with rigor.

678. *Mosaic penalty for maiming servants.*

Ex. 21: 20 If a man smite his servant, or his maid, with a rod, and he die under his hand; he shall be surely punished. 21 Notwithstanding, if he continue a day or two, he shall not be punished: for he *is* his money. 26 And, if a man smite the eye of his servant, or the eye of his maid, that it perish; he shall let him go free for his eye's sake. 27 And if he smite .out his man-servant's tooth, or his maid-servant's tooth; he shall let him go free for his tooth's sake.

679. *Justice and kindness to servants enjoined — oppression forbidden.*

Dt. 23: 15 Thou shalt not deliver unto his master the servant which has escaped from his master unto thee : 16 He shall dwell with thee, *even* among you in that place which he shall choose in one of thy gates where it liketh him best : thou shalt not oppress him. — 24: 14 Thou shalt not oppress a hired servant *that is* poor and needy, *whether he be* of thy brethren, or of thy strangers that *are* in thy land within thy gates : 15 At his day thou shalt give *him* his hire, neither shall the sun go down upon it, for he *is* poor, and setteth his heart upon it: lest he cry against thee unto the LORD, and it be sin unto thee.

Jer. 22: 13 Wo unto him that buildeth his house by unrighteousness, and his chambers by wrong; *that* useth his neighbor's service without wages, and giveth him not for his work.

Col. 4: 1 Masters, give unto *your* servants that which is just and equal; knowing that ye also have a Master in heaven.

1 Tim. 5: 18 The scripture saith, Thou shalt not muzzle the ox that treadeth out the corn. And, The laborer *is* worthy of his reward. ̄[Ezk. 16: 49.] [See 490, 636, 687.]

680. *Apostolic precepts respecting the duties of masters and servants.*

Ep. 6: 5 Servants, be obedient to them that are *your* masters ̄according to the flesh, with fear and trembling, in singleness of your heart, as unto Christ; 6 Not with eye-service, as men-pleasers; but as the servants of Christ, doing the will of God from the heart; 7 With good will doing service, as to the Lord, and not to men: 8 Kowing that whatsoever good thing any man doeth, the same shall he receive of the Lord, whether *he be* bond or free. 9 And, ye masters, do the same things unto them, forbearing threatening: knowing that your Master also is in heaven; neither is there respect of persons with him. ̄

Col. 3: 22 Servants, obey in all things *your* masters according to the flesh; not with eye-service, as men-pleasers; but in singleness of heart, fearing God: 23 And whatsoever ye do, do *it* heartily, as to the Lord, and not unto men; 24 Knowing that of the Lord ye shall receive the reward of the inheritance: for ye serve the Lord Christ.

1 Tim. 6: 1 Let as many servants as are under the yoke count their own masters worthy of all honor, that the name of God and *his* doctrine be ̃not blasphemed. 2 And they that have believing masters, let them not despise *them,* because they are brethren; but rather do *them* service, because they are faithful and beloved, partakers of the benefit. These things teach and exhort. 3 If any man teach otherwise, and consent not to wholesome words, *even* the words of our Lord Jesus Christ, and to the doctrine which is according to godliness, 4 He is proud, knowing nothing.

Tit. 2: 9 *Exhort* servants to be obedient unto their own masters, *and* to please *them* well in all *things;* not answering again; 10 Not purloining, but shewing all good fidelity; that they may adorn the doctrine of God our Saviour in all things.

1 Pet. 2: 18 Servants, *be* subject to *your* masters with all fear; not only to the good and gentle, but also to the froward. 19 For this *is* thank-worthy, if a man for conscience toward God endure grief, suffering wrongfully. 20 For what glory *is it,* if, when ye be buffeted for your faults, ye shall take it patiently? but if, when ye do well, and suffer *for it,* ye take it patiently, this *is* acceptable with God.

681. *Ancient merchandise in " slaves and the souls of men."*

Ezk. 27: 13 Javan, Tubal, and Meshech, they *were* thy merchants : they traded the persons of men and vessels of brass in thy market.

Joel 3: 3 They have cast lots for my people ; and have given a boy for an harlot, and sold a girl for wine, that they might drink. ·6 The children also of Judah and the children of Jerusalem have ye sold unto the Grecians, that ye might remove them far from their border.

Rev. 18: 2 Babylon the great is fallen, is fallen, and is become the habitation of devils, and the hold of every foul spirit, and a cage of every unclean and hateful bird. 11 And the merchants of the earth shall weep and mourn over her ; for no man buyeth their merchandise any more : 12 The merchandise of gold, and silver, and precious stones, and of pearls, and fine linen, and purple, and silk, and scarlet, and all thyine wood, and all manner vessels of ivory, and all manner vessels of most precious wood, and of brass, and iron, and marble, 13 And cinnamon, and odors, and ointments, and frankincense, and wine, and oil, and fine flour, and wheat, and beasts, and sheep, and horses, and chariots, and slaves, [Gr. bodies,] and souls of men. [See 488, 636.]

682. *Penalties for man-stealing, and infringing human liberty, in procuring and holding servants.*

Ex. 21: 16 He that stealeth a man, and selleth him, or if he be found in his hand, he shall surely be put to death.

Dt. 24: 7 If a man be found stealing any of his brethren of the children of Israel, and maketh merchandise of him, or selleth him; then that thief shall die ; and thou shalt put evil away from among you.

Jer. 5: 26 Among my people are found wicked *men :* they lay wait, as he that setteth snares ; they set a trap, they catch men. — 34: 17 Thus saith the LORD ; Ye have not hearkened unto me, in proclaiming liberty, every one to his brother, and every man to his neighbor : behold, I proclaim a liberty for you, saith the LORD, to the sword, to the pestilence, and to the famine ; and I will make you to be removed into all the kingdoms of the earth.

1 Tim. 1: 9 Knowing this, that the law is not made for a righteous man, but for the lawless and disobedient, for the ungodly and for sinners, for unholy and profane, for murderers of fathers, and murderers of mothers, for manslayers, 10 For whoremongers, for them that defile themselves with mankind,

for men-stealers, for liars, for perjured persons, and if there be
any other thing that is contrary to sound doctrine.
[See 489—491, 631, 636.]

683. *Freedom at the year of jubilee for servan's.*

Lev. 25: 10 Ye shall hallow the fiftieth year, and proclaim
liberty throughout *all* the land unto all the inhabitants thereof:
it shall be a jubilee unto you ; and ye shall return every man
unto his possession, and ye shall return every man unto his
family.

684. *Freedom recommended as preferable to servitude.*

1 Cor. 7: 21 Art thou called *being* a servant? care not for
it; but if thou mayest be made free, use *it* rather.   22 For he
that is called in the Lord, *being* a servant, is the Lord's free-
man: likewise also he that is called, *being* free, is Christ's
servant.   23 Ye are bought with a price ; be not ye the servants of men.

Philemon 15 Perhaps he therefore departed for a season,
that thou shouldest receive him for ever; 16 Not now as a
servant, but above a servant, a brother beloved, especially to
me, but how much more unto thee, both in the flesh, and in the
Lord?   20 Yea, brother, let me have joy of thee in the Lord:
refresh my bowels in the Lord.   21 Having confidence in thy
obedience I wrote unto thee, knowing that thou wilt also do
more than I say.

685. *General precepts respecting the duty of man to man in all the relations
of life.*

Mal. 2: 10 Have we not all one father? hath not one God
created us? why do we deal treacherously every man against
his brother, by profaning the covenant of our fathers?

Mat. 7: 12 All things whatsoever ye would that men should
do to you, do ye even so to them: for this is the law and the
prophets. — 22: 37 Jesus said unto him, Thou shalt love the
Lord thy God with all thy heart, and with all thy soul, and
with all thy mind.   38 This is the first and great commandment.   39 And the second *is* like unto it, Thou shalt love thy
neighbor as thyself.   40 On these two commandments hang
all the law and the prophets.

Gal. 5: 13 Brethren, ye have been called unto liberty ; only
use not liberty for an occasion to the flesh, but by love serve
one another.   14 For all the law is fulfilled in one word, *even*
in this, Thou shalt love thy neighbor as thyself.   15 But if ye
bite and devour one another, take heed that ye be not consumed
one of another.   [See 412—414, 631-5.]

484

686. *Encouragement to treat those " in bonds," and in poverty and oppression, with sympathy and liberality.*

Is. 58: 6 *Is* not this the fast that I have chosen? to loose the bands of wickedness, to undo the heavy burdens, and to let the oppressed go free, and that ye break every yoke? 7 *Is it* not to deal thy bread to the hungry, and that thou bring the poor that are cast out to thy house? when thou seest the naked, that thou cover him; and that thou hide not thyself from thine own flesh? 8 Then shall thy light break forth as the morning, and thine health shall spring forth speedily: and thy righteousness shall go before thee; the glory of the LORD shall be thy rere-ward. 9 Then shalt thou call, and the LORD shall answer; thou shalt cry, and he shall say, Here I *am*. If thou take away from the midst of thee the yoke, the putting forth of the finger, and speaking vanity; 10 And *if* thou draw out thy soul to the hungry, and satisfy the afflicted soul; then shall thy light rise in obscurity, and thy darkness *be* as the noonday: 11 And the LORD shall guide thee continually, and satisfy thy soul in drought, and make fat thy bones: and thou shalt be like a watered garden, and like a spring of water, whose waters fail not.

Heb. 13: 3 Remember them that are in bonds, as bound with them; *and* them which suffer adversity, as being yourselves also in the body. [See 527.]

687. *Duty to espouse the cause of the injured and oppressed.*

Ps. 82: 3 Defend the poor and fatherless: do justice to the afflicted and needy, 4 Deliver the poor and needy: rid *them* out of the hand of the wicked.

Pr. 21: 13 Whoso stoppeth his ears at the cry of the poor, he also shall cry himself, but shall not be heard. — 24: 11 If thou forbear to deliver *them that are* drawn unto death, and *those that are* ready to be slain; 12 If thou sayest, Behold, we knew it not; doth not he that pondereth the heart consider *it?* and he that keepeth thy soul, doth *not* he know *it?* and shall *not* he render to *every* man according to his works? — 31: 8 Open thy mouth for the dumb in the cause of all such as are appointed to destruction. 9 Open thy mouth, judge righteously, and plead the cause of the poor and needy.

Is. 1: 17 Learn to do well; seek judgment, relieve the oppressed, judge the fatherless, plead for the widow. — 16: 3 Take counsel, execute judgment; make thy shadow as the night in the midst of the noon-day; hide the outcasts; bewray not him that wandereth. 4 Let mine outcasts dwell with thee, Moab: be thou a convert to them from the face of the spoiler:

for the extortioner is at an end, the spoiler ceaseth, the oppressors are consumed out of the land.

Jer. 21: 12 O house of David, thus saith the LORD; Execute judgment in the morning, and deliver *him that is* spoiled out of the hand of the oppresor, lest my fury go out like fire, and burn that none can quench *it*, because of the evil of your doings. [See 490, 526–7.]

SINNERS.

688. *Sinners destitute of holiness.*

Is. 1: 5 Why should ye be stricken any more? ye will revolt more and more : the whole head is sick, and the whole heart faint. 6 From the sole of the foot even unto the head *there is* no soundness in it ; *but* wounds, and bruises, and putrifying sores : they have not been closed, neither bound up, neither mollified with ointment.

Jn. 5: 42 I know you, that ye have not the love of God in you.

Rom. 6: 20 When ye were the servants of sin, ye were free from righteousness. — 7: 18 I know that in me (that is, in my flesh,) dwelleth no good thing. — 8: 8 They that are in the flesh cannot please God.

1 Cor. 2: 14 The natural man receiveth not the things of the Spirit of God : for they are foolishness unto him : neither can he know *them*, because they are spiritually discerned.

Ep. 2: 12 That at that time ye were without Christ, being aliens from the commonwealth of Israel, and strangers from the covenants of promise, having no hope, and without God in the world. [See 165, 589.]

689. *Sinners full of selfishness and unrighteousness.*

*Job 21: 15 What *is* the Almighty, that we should serve him? and what profit should we have, if we pray unto him?

Is. 56: 11 Yea, *they are* greedy dogs *which* can never have enough, and they *are* shepherds *that* cannot understand : they all look to their own way, every one for his gain, from his quarter.

Jer. 6: 13 From the least of them even unto the greatest of them every one *is* given to covetousness; and from the prophet even unto the priest every one dealeth falsely. — 22: 17 Thine eyes and thine heart *are* not but for thy covetousness, and for to shed innocent blood, and for oppression, and for violence to do *it*.

Ezk. 22: 12 In thee have they taken gifts to shed blood; thou hast taken usury and increase, and thou hast greedily gained of thy neighbors by extortion, and hast forgotten me, saith the Lord GOD.—33: 31 Their heart goeth after their covetousness.

Hos. 10: 1 Israel *is* an empty vine, he bringeth forth fruit unto himself.

Mat. 5: 46 If ye love them which love you, what reward have ye? do not even the publicans the same? 47 And if ye salute your brethren only, what do ye more *than others?* do not even the publicans so?

Lk. 6: 32 If ye love them which love you, what thank have ye? for sinners also love those that love them. 33 And if ye do good to them which do good to you, what thank have ye? for sinners also do even the same. 34 And if ye lend *to them* of whom ye hope to receive, what thank have ye? for sinners also lend to sinners, to receive as much again.

Ph. 2: 21 All seek their own, not the things which are Jesus Christ's.

1 Tim. 6: 5 Perverse disputings of men of corrupt minds, and destitute of the truth, supposing that gain is godliness: from such withdraw thyself.

2 Tim. 3: 2 Men shall be lovers of their own selves, covetous, boasters, proud.

[See 137, 191, 194, 411, 609, 623, 728, 732–3.]

690. *Sinners enemies to God, children of the adversary, and prone to wicked works.*

Ps. 36: 1 The transgression of the wicked saith within my heart, *that there is* no fear of God before his eyes.—53: 1 The fool hath said in his heart, *There is* no God. Corrupt are they, and have done abominable iniquity: *there is* none that doeth good. 2 God looked down from heaven upon the children of men, to see if there were *any* that did understand, that did seek God. 3 Every one of them is gone back: they are altogether become filthy; *there is* none that doeth good, no, not one.—55: 9 I have seen violence and strife in the city. 10 Day and night they go about it upon the walls thereof: mischief also and sorrow *are* in the midst of it. 11 Wickedness *is* in the midst thereof: deceit and guile depart not from her streets.—73: 6 Therefore pride compasseth them about as a chain; violence covereth them *as* a garment. 7 Their eyes stand out with fatness: they have more than heart could wish. 8 They are corrupt, and speak wickedly *concerning* oppression:

they speak loftily. 9 They set their mouth against the heavens, and their tongue walketh through the earth.

Hos. 4: 2 By swearing, and lying, and killing, and stealing, and committing adultery, they break out, and blood toucheth blood.

Mat. 13: 38 The tares are the children of the wicked *one*. —23: 33 *Ye* serpents, *ye* generation of vipers, how can ye escape the damnation of hell?

Jn. 7: 7 The world cannot hate you; but me it hateth, because I testify of it, that the works thereof are evil.—8: 44 Ye are of *your* father the devil, and the lusts of your father ye will do: he was a murderer from the beginning, and abode not in the truth; because there is no truth in him. When he speaketh a lie, he speaketh of his own: for he is a liar, and the father of it.—15: 24 If I had not done among them the works which none other man did, they had not had sin: but now have they both seen, and hated both me and my Father. 25 But *this cometh to pass*, that the word might be fulfilled that is written in their law, They hated me without a cause.

Ac. 7: 51 Ye stiff-necked, and uncircumcised in heart and ears, ye do always resist the Holy Ghost: as your fathers *did*, so *do* ye.—13: 10 O full of all subtilty, and all mischief, *thou* child of the devil, *thou* enemy of all righteousness, wilt thou not cease to pervert the right ways of the Lord?

Rom. 1: 30 Haters of God.—3: 13 Their throat *is* an open sepulchre; with their tongues they have used deceit; the poison of asps *is* under their lips: 14 Whose mouth *is* full of cursing and bitterness. 15 Their feet *are* swift to shed blood. 16 Destruction and misery *are* in their ways: 17 And the way of peace have they not known. 18 There is no fear of God before their eyes.—8: 7 Because the carnal mind *is* enmity against God: for it is not subject to the law of God, neither indeed can be. [See 68, 86, 165–6, 511, 702, 740.]

691. *Sinners disobedient to God.*

Ex. 5: 2 Pharaoh said, Who is the Lord, that I should obey his voice to let Israel go? I know not the Lord, neither will I let Israel go.

Dt. 31: 27 I know thy rebellion, and thy stiff neck: behold, while I am yet alive with you this day, ye have been rebellious against the Lord; and how much more after my death.

Neh. 9: 26 They were disobedient, and rebelled against thee, and cast thy law behind their backs, and slew thy prophets which testified against them to turn them to thee, and they wrought great provocations.

Ps. 81: 11 My people would not hearken to my voice; and Israel would none of me.

Pr. 1: 24 Because I have called and ye refused, I have stretched out my hand, and no man regarded; 25 But ye have set at nought all my counsel, and would none of my reproof.

Is. 1: 2 I have nourished and brought up children, and they have rebelled against me.—30: 8 Now go, write it before them in a table, and note it in a book, that it may be for the time to come for ever and ever: 9 That this *is* a rebellious people, lying children, children *that* will not hear the law of the LORD.—65: 2 I have spread out my hands all the day unto a rebellious people, which walketh in a way *that was* not good, after their own thoughts; 3 A people that provoketh me to anger continually to my face.

Jer. 5: 23 This people hath a revolting and a rebellious heart; they are revolted and gone.—25: 4 The LORD hath sent unto you all his servants the prophets, rising early and sending *them;* but ye have not hearkened, nor inclined your ear to hear.

Ezk. 2: 7 Thou shalt speak my words unto them, whether they will hear, or whether they will forbear: for they *are* most rebellious. 8 But thou, son of man, hear what I say unto thee; Be not thou rebellious like that rebellious house.

692. *Sinners prone to forget God.*

Dt. 32: 18 Of the Rock *that* begat thee thou art unmindful, and hast forgotten God that formed thee.

Jud. 3: 7 The children of Israel did evil in the sight of the LORD, and forgat the LORD their God, and served Baalim, and the groves.

1 S. 12: 9 When they forgat the Lord their God, he sold them into the hand of Sisera.

Ps. 9: 17 The wicked shall be turned into hell, *and* all the nations that forget God.—50: 22 Consider this, ye that forget God, lest I tear *you* in pieces, and *there be* none to deliver.—106: 21 They forgat God their saviour, which had done great things in Egypt.

Jer. 2: 32 Can a maid forget her ornaments, *or* a bride her attire? yet my people have forgotten me days without number.—3: 21 A voice was heard upon the high places, weeping *and* supplications of the children of Israel: for they have perverted their way, *and* they have forgotten the LORD their God.

Ezk. 22: 12 Thou hast greedily gained of thy neighbors by extortion, and hast forgotten me, saith the Lord God. [See 22.]

693. *Sinners stupid, and inattentive to God.*

Ps. 10: 4 The wicked, through the pride of his countenance, will not seek *after God:* God *is* not in all his thoughts.— 50: 21 These *things* hast thou done, and I kept silence; thou thoughtest that I was altogether *such an one* as thyself.— 94: 8 Understand, ye brutish among the people: and *ye* fools, when will ye be wise?

Pr. 6: 9 How long wilt thou sleep, O sluggard? when wilt thou arise out of thy sleep?

Is. 5: 12 The harp, and the viol, the tabret, and pipe, and wine are in their feasts: but they re ard not the work of the LORD, neither consider the operation of his hands.

Jer. 4: 22 My people *is* foolish, they have not known me; they *are* sottish children, and they have none understanding: they *are* wise to do evil, but to do good they have no knowledge.— 8: 7 The stork in the heaven knoweth her appointed times; and the turtle, and the crane, and the swallow, observe the time of their coming; but my people know not the judgment of the LORD.

Hos. 7: 11 Ephraim also is like a silly dove without heart. [See 132, 707, 739.]

694. *Sinners depart from God.*

Gen. 3: 8 They heard the voice of the LORD God walking in the garden in the cool of the day: and Adam and his wife hid themselves from the presence of the LORD God amongst the trees of the garden.

Job. 11: 12 Vain man would be wise, though man be born *like* a wild ass's colt.

Jer. 2: 5 Thus saith the LORD, What iniquity have your fathers found in me, that they are gone far from me, and have walked after vanity, and are become vain? 13 My people have committed two evils; they have forsaken me the fountain of living waters, *and* hewed them out cisterns, broken cisterns, that can hold no water.

Hos. 7: 13 Wo unto them! for they have fled from me.

695. *Sinners hate the divine presence, government, and restraints.*

Job. 27: 22 He would fain flee out of his hand.

Is. 30: 11 Cause the Holy One of Israel to cease from before us.

Lk. 19: 14 His citizens hated him, and sent a message after him, saying, We will not have this *man* to reign over us. 27

Those mine enemies, which would not that I should reign over them, bring hither, and slay *them* before me.
[See 22, 23, 272, 705.]

696. *Sinners self-righteous, proud, and opposed to grace.*

Ps. 10: 4 The wicked, through the pride of his countenance, will not seek *after God*.

Mat. 20: 10 When the first came, they supposed that they should have received more; and they likewise received every man a penny. 11 And when they had received *it*, they murmured against the good man of the house, 12 Saying, These last have wrought *but* one hour, and thou hast made them equal unto us, which have borne the burden and heat of the day. 13 But he answered one of them, and said, Friend, I do thee no wrong: didst thou not agree with me for a penny? 14 Take *that* thine *is*, and go thy way: I will give unto this last, even as unto thee. 15 Is it not lawful for me to do what I will with mine own? is thine eye evil because I am good? 16 So the last shall be first, and the first last: for many be called, but few chosen.

Lk. 15: 28 He was angry, and would not go in; therefore came his father out, and entreated him. 29 And he answering, said to *his* father, Lo, these many years do I serve thee, neither transgressed I at any time thy commandment; and yet thou never gavest me a kid, that I might make merry with my friends: 30 But as soon as this thy son was come, which hath devoured thy living with harlots, thou hast killed for him the fatted calf.

Rom. 10: 3 They, being ignorant of God's righteousness, and going about to establish their own righteousness, have not submitted themselves unto the righteousness of God.

1 Cor. 1: 18 The preaching of the cross is to them that perish, foolishness. 23 We preach Christ crucified, unto the Jews a stumbling-block, and unto the Greeks foolishness.
[See 373, 510, 549, 550.]

697. *Sinners rather perish, than come to Christ.*

Pr. 8: 36 He that sinneth against me wrongeth his own soul: all they that hate me love death.

Jn. 5: 40 Ye will not come to me that ye might have life.

Ac. 13: 46 Paul and Barnabas waxed bold, and said, It was necessary that the word of God should first have been spoken to you: but seeing ye put it from you, and judge yourselves unworthy of everlasting life, lo, we turn to the Gentiles.
[See 373.]

698. *Sinners inclined to sensual pleasures and lusts.*

Lev. 18: 24 Defile not ye yourselves in any of these things: for in all these the nations are defiled which I cast out before you: 25 And the land is defiled: therefore I do visit the iniquity thereof upon it, and the land itself vomiteth out her inhabitants.

Gal. 5: 19 The works of the flesh are manifest, which are *these*, Adultery, fornication, uncleanness, lasciviousness, 20 Idolatry, witchcraft, hatred, variance, emulations, wrath, strife, seditions, heresies, 21 Envyings, murders, drunkenness, revellings, and such like: of the which I tell you before, as I have also told *you* in time past, that they which do such things shall not inherit the kingdom of God.

Ep. 2: 3 Among whom also we all had our conversation in times past in the lusts of our flesh, fulfilling the desires of the flesh and of the mind; and were by nature the children of wrath, even as others.

2 Tim. 3: 4 Traitors, heady, high-minded, lovers of pleasures more than lovers of God.

Tit. 3: 3 We ourselves also were sometimes foolish, disobedient, deceived, serving divers lusts and pleasures, living in malice and envy, hateful, *and* hating one another.

Jam. 5: 5 Ye have lived in pleasure on the earth, and been wanton; ye have nourished your hearts, as in a day of slaughter.

1 Pet. 4: 3 The time past of *our* life may suffice us to have wrought the will of the Gentiles, when we walked in lasciviousness, lusts, excess of wine, revellings, banquetings, and abominable idolatries: 4 Wherein they think it strange that ye run not with *them* to the same excess of riot, speaking evil of *you*. [See 675.]

699. *Sinners naturally inclined to idolatry.*

Ex. 32: 1 When the people saw that Moses delayed to come down out of the mount, the people gathered themselves together unto Aaron, and said unto him, Up, make us gods which shall go before us: for *as for* this Moses, the man that brought us up out of the land of Egypt, we wot not what is become of him.

Dt. 31: 16 The LORD said unto Moses, Behold, thou shalt sleep with thy fathers, and this people will rise up, and go a whoring after the gods of the strangers of the land, whither they go *to be* among them, and will forsake me, and break my covenant which I have made with them. 20 When I shall have brought them into the land which I sware unto their fathers, that floweth with milk and honey; and they shall have eaten and filled themselves, and waxen fat; then will they turn unto other gods, and serve them, and provoke me, and break my covenant.

Jer. 44: 17 We will certainly do whatsoever thing goeth forth out of our own mouth, to burn incense unto the queen of heaven, and to pour out drink-offerings unto her, as we have done, we, and our fathers, our kings, and our princes, in the cities of Judah, and in the streets of Jerusalem: for *then* had we plenty of victuals, and were well, and saw no evil.

[See 362.]

700. *Sinners inclined to murmur.*

Ex. 16: 2 The whole congregation of the children of Israel murmured against Moses and Aaron in the wilderness: 3 And the children of Israel said unto them, Would to God we had died by the hand of the LORD in the land of Egypt, when we sat by the flesh-pots, *and* when we did eat bread to the full; for ye have brought us forth into this wilderness, to kill this whole assembly with hunger. 8 Moses said, *This shall be* when the LORD shall give you in the evening flesh to eat, and in the morning bread to the full: for that the LORD heareth your murmurings which ye murmur against him: and what *are* we? your murmurings *are* not against us, but against the LORD.

Num. 17: 10 The LORD said unto Moses, Bring Aaron's rod again before the testimony, to be kept for a token against the rebels; and thou shalt quite take away their murmurings from me, that they die not.

Mat. 20: 11 When they had received *it*, they murmured against the good man of the house, 12 Saying, These last have wrought *but* one hour, and thou hast made them equal unto us, which have borne the burden and heat of the day.

Jude 16 These are murmurers, complainers, walking after their own lusts. [See 9, 171, 272.]

701. *Sinners ungrateful and cruel.*

Gen. 40: 23 Yet did not the chief butler remember Joseph, but forgat him. — 49: 5 Simeon and Levi *are* brethren; instruments of cruelty *are in* their habitations. 6 O my soul, come not thou into their secret: unto their assembly, mine honor, be not thou united! for in their anger they slew a man, and in their self-will they digged down a wall. 7 Cursed *be* their anger, for *it was* fierce : and their wrath, for it was cruel : I will divide them in Jacob, and scatter them in Israel.

Dt. 32: 6 Do ye thus requite the LORD, O foolish people and unwise? *is* not he thy father *that* hath bought thee? hath he not made thee, and established thee? 15 But Jeshurun waxed fat, and kicked : thou art waxen fat, thou art grown thick, thou art covered *with fatness ;* then he forsook God *which* made him, and lightly esteemed the Rock of his salvation.

2 Ch. 24: 22 Thus Joash the king remembered not the kindness which Jehoiada his father had done to him, but slew his son. And when he died, he said, The LORD look upon *it*, and require *it*.

Ps. 35: 11 False witnesses did rise up; they laid to my charge *things* that I knew not. 12 They rewarded me evil for good, *to* the spoiling of my soul. 13 But as for me, when they were sick, my clothing *was* sackcloth : I humbled my soul with fasting; and my prayer returned into mine own bosom. 14 I behaved myself as though *he had been* my friend *or* brother : I bowed down heavily, as one that mourneth *for his* mother. 15 But in mine adversity they rejoiced, and gathered themselves together : *yea*, the abjects gathered themselves together against me, and I knew *it* not; they did tear *me*, and ceased not : 16 With hypocritical mockers in feasts, they gnashed upon me with their teeth.—41: 9 Yea, mine own familiar friend, in whom I trusted, which did eat of my bread, hath lifted up *his* heel against me.—74: 20 Have respect unto the covenant : for the dark places of the earth are full of the habitations of cruelty.

Pr. 1: 11 If they say, Come with us, let us lay wait for blood, let us lurk privily for the innocent without cause : 12 Let us swallow them up alive as the grave ; and whole, as those that go down into the pit : 13 We shall find all precious substance, we shall fill our houses with spoil : 14 Cast in thy lot among us ; let us all have one purse : 15 My son, walk not thou in the way with them ; refrain thy foot from their path : 16 For their feet run to evil, and make haste to shed blood.

Ec. 9: 15 There was found in it a poor wise man, and he by his wisdom delivered the city : yet no man remembered that same poor man.

Is. 1: 2 Hear, O heavens, and give ear, O earth : for the LORD hath spoken, I have nourished and brought up children, and they have rebelled against me.

Deceitful, and fond of Ensnaring.

Rom. 3: 15 Their feet *are* swift to shed blood. 16 Destruction and misery *are* in their ways.

[See 68, 205, 467, 488, 511, 523, 689, 690, 734.]

702. *Sinners deceitful, and inclined to flatter, and lay snares.*

2 S. 15: 5 When any man came nigh *to him*, to do him obeisance, he put forth his hand, and took him, and kissed him. 6 And on this manner did Absalom to all Israel that came to the king for judgment: so Absalom stole the hearts of the men of Israel.

2 Ch. 24: 17 After the death of Jehoiada came the princes of Judah, and made obeisance to the king. Then the king hearkened unto them. 18 And they left the house of the Lord God of their fathers, and served groves and idols.

Ps. 5: 9 *There is* no faithfulness in their mouth; their inward part *is* very wickedness ; their throat *is* an open sepulchre; they flatter with their tongue. — 10: 7 His mouth is full of cursing, and deceit, and fraud. — 12: 2 They speak vanity every one with his neighbor: *with* flattering lips *and* with a double heart do they speak. — 28: 3 Draw me not away with the wicked, and with the workers of iniquity, which speak peace to their neighbors, but mischief *is* in their hearts. — 38: 12 They also that seek after my life lay snares *for me:* and they that seek my hurt speak mischievous things, and imagine deceits all the day long. — 52: 2 Thy tongue deviseth mischiefs; like a sharp razor, working deceitfully. — 64: 5 They encourage themselves *in* an evil matter: they commune of laying snares privily; they say, Who shall see them? 6 They search out iniquities ; they accomplish a diligent search : both the inward *thought* of every one *of them*, and the heart, *is* deep. — 140: 5 The proud have hid a snare for me, and cords; they have spread a net by the way side: they have set gins for me. — 141: 9 Keep me from the snare *which* they have laid for me, and the gins of the workers of iniquity. 10 Let the wicked fall into their own nets, whilst that I withal escape.

Pr. 7: 21 With the flattering of her lips she forced him. — 11: 18 The wicked worketh a deceitful work. — 12: 5 The counsels of the wicked *are* deceit. — 20: 14 *It is* naught, *it is* naught, saith the buyer: but when he is gone his way, then he boasteth.

Is. 29: 20 The scorner is consumed, and all that watch for iniquity are cut off: 21 That make a man an offender for a word, and lay a snare for him that reproveth in the gate, and turn aside the just for a thing of nought. — 66: 5 Hear the

word of the LORD, ye that tremble at his word: Your brethren that hated you, that cast you out for my name's sake, said,
Let the LORD be glorified: but he shall appear to your joy,
and they shall be ashamed.

Jer. 3: 10 Her treacherous sister Judah hath not turned
unto me with her whole heart, but feignedly, saith the Lord.
— 8: 5 They hold fast deceit, they refuse to return. — 9: 2
Oh that I had in the wilderness a lodging-place of way-faring
men; that I might leave my people, and go from them! for
they *be* all adulterers, an assembly of treacherous men. 3
And they bend their tongues, *like* their bow, *for* lies; but they
are not valiant for the truth upon the earth: for they proceed
from evil to evil, and they know not me, saith the LORD. 4
Take ye heed every one of his neighbor, and trust ye not in
any brother: for every brother will utterly supplant, and every
neighbor will walk with slanders. 5 And they will deceive
every one his neighbor, and will not speak the truth: they
have taught their tongue to speak lies, *and* weary themselves
to commit iniquity. 6 Thine habitation *is* in the midst of
deceit: through deceit they refuse to know me, saith the
LORD. 8 Their tongue *is as* an arrow shot out; it speaketh
deceit: *one* speaketh peaceably to his neighbor with his mouth,
but in heart he layeth his wait. — 17: 9 The heart *is* deceitful above all *things*, and desperately wicked: who can
know it?

Ezk. 33: 30 Also, thou son of man, the children of thy people still are talking against thee by the walls and in the doors
of the houses, and speak one to another, every one to his brother,
saying, Come, I pray you, and hear what is the word that cometh forth from the LORD. 31 And they come unto thee as
the people cometh, and they sit before thee as my people, and
they hear thy words, but they will not do them: for with their
mouth they show much love, *but* their heart goeth after their
covetousness.

Dan. 11: 21 In his estate shall stand up a vile person, to
whom they shall not give the honor of the kingdom: but he
shall come in peaceably, and obtain the kingdom by flatteries.
32 And such as do wickedly against the covenant shall he corrupt by flatteries: but the people that do know their God shall
be strong, and do *exploits.*

Hos. 11: 12 Ephraim compasseth me about with lies, and
the house of Israel with deceit.

Mic. 3: 10 They build up Zion with blood, and Jerusalem
with iniquity. 11 The heads thereof judge for reward, and
the priests thereof teach for hire, and the prophets thereof

divine for money: yet will they lean upon the LORD, and say, *Is* not the LORD among us? none evil can come upon us.

Mat. 26: 48 He that betrayed him gave them a sign, saying, Whomsoever I shall kiss, that same is he; hold him fast. 49 And forthwith he came to Jesus, and said, Hail, Master; and kissed him.

Rom'. 1: 29 Being filled with all unrighteousness, fornication, wickedness, covetousness, maliciousness; full of envy, murder, debate, deceit, malignity, whisperers, 30 Backbiters. — 16: 18 By good words and fair speeches, deceive the hearts of the simple.

2 Th. 2: 9 *Even him,* whose coming is after the working of Satan, with all power, and signs, and lying wonders, 10 And with all deceivableness of unrighteousness in them that perish: because they received not the love of the truth, that they might be saved.

Heb. 3: 13 Exhort one another daily, while it is called To-day; lest any of you be hardened through the deceitfulness of sin.

Rev. 18: 23 By thy sorceries were all nations deceived.
[See 191, 194, 198, 411, 416, 474, 728.]

703. *Sinners inclined to ostentation, boasting, and glorying in their shame.*

2 K. 10: 16 Come with me, and see my zeal for the Lord.

Ps. 39: 6 Surely every man walketh in a vain shew: surely they are disquieted in vain.

Pr. 3: 35 Shame shall be the promotion of fools. — 20: 6 Most men will proclaim every one his own goodness: but a faithful man who can find?

Hab. 2: 16 Thou art filled with shame for glory.

Mat. 6: 5 When thou prayest, thou shalt not be as the hypocrites *are:* for they love to pray standing in the synagogues, and in the corners of the streets, that they may be seen of men. 16 When ye fast, be not as the hypocrites, of a sad countenance: for they disfigure their faces, that they may appear unto men to fast. — 23: 5 All their works they do for to be seen of men: they make broad their phylacteries, and enlarge the borders of their garments, 6 And love the uppermost rooms at feasts, and the chief seats in the syna-gogues, 7 And greetings in the markets, and to be called of men, Rabbi, Rabbi.

Lk. 16: 15 He said unto them, Ye are they which justify yourselves before men; but God knoweth your hearts: for that which is highly esteemed among men, is abomination in the sight of God. — 18: 9 He spake this parable unto certain, which trusted in themselves that they were righteous, and despised others: 10 Two men went up into the temple to pray; the one a Pharisee, and the other a publican. 11 The Pharisee stood and prayed thus with himself, God, I thank thee, that I am not as other men *are*, extortioners, unjust, adulterers, or even as this publican. 12 I fast twice in the week, I give tithes of all that I possess.

2 Cor. 10: 12 We dare not make ourselves of the number, or compare ourselves with some that commend themselves.

Ph. 3: 19 Whose end *is* destruction, whose God *is their* belly, and *whose* glory *is* in their shame, who mind earthly things. [See 482, 549, 550.]

704. *Sinners inclined to self-deception — warnings.*

Dt. 11: 16 Take heed to yourselves, that your heart be not deceived, and ye turn aside, and serve other gods, and worship them.

Pr. 16: 25 There is a way that seemeth right unto a man, but the end thereof are the ways of death.

Is. 44: 20 He feedeth on ashes; a deceived heart hath turned him aside, that he cannot deliver his soul, nor say, *Is there* not a lie in my right hand?

Mat. 7: 22 Many will say to me in that day, Lord, Lord, have we not prophesied in thy name? and in thy name have cast out devils? and in thy name done many wonderful works? 23 And then will I profess unto them, I never knew you: depart from me, ye that work iniquity.—24: 4 Jesus answered, and said unto them, Take heed that no man deceive you. 5 For many shall come in my name, saying, I am Christ: and shall deceive many.

Lk. 21: 8 He said, Take heed that ye be not deceived: for many shall come in my name, saying, I am *Christ;* and the time draweth near: go ye not therefore after them.

1 Cor. 3: 18 Let no man deceive himself.

Gal. 6: 3 If a man think himself to be something, when he is nothing, he deceiveth himself. 7 Be not deceived; God is not mocked; for whatsoever a man soweth, that shall he also reap.

Ep. 5: 6 Let no man deceive you with vain words.

2 Th. 2: 3 Let no man deceive you by any means. 11 For this cause God shall send them strong delusion, that they should believe a lie: 12 That they all might be damned who believed not the truth, but had pleasure in unrighteousness.
[See 25, 397, 476, 510.]

705. *Sinners inclined to deny or resist obligation to God.*

Ps. 2: 2 The kings of the earth set themselves, and the rulers take counsel together, against the LORD, and against his Anointed, *saying,* 3 Let us break their bands asunder, and cast away their cords from us. — 12: 4 Who have said, With our tongue will we prevail; our lips *are* our own: who *is* lord over us?

Mat. 25: 24 He which had received the one talent came, and said, Lord, I knew thee that thou art an hard man, reaping where thou hast not sown, and gathering where thou hast not strewed: 25 And I was afraid, and went and hid thy talent in the earth; lo, *there* thou hast *that* is thine. [See 22, 695.]

706. *Sinners prone to deny or palliate their sins.*

Gen. 3: 12 The man said, The woman whom thou gavest *to be* with me, she gave me of the tree, and I did eat. 13 And the LORD God said unto the woman, What *is* this *that* thou hast done? And the woman said, The serpent beguiled me and I did eat.

1 S. 15: 13 Samuel came to Saul: and Saul said unto him, Blessed *be* thou of the LORD: I have performed the commandment of the LORD. 14 And Samuel said, what *meaneth* then this bleating of the sheep in mine ears, and the lowing of the oxen which I hear? 15 And Saul said, They have brought them from the Amalekites: for the people spared the best of the sheep and of the oxen, to sacrifice unto the LORD thy God, and the rest we have utterly destroyed.

Pr. 14: 9 Fools make a mock at sin.

Jer. 7: 9 Will ye steal, murder, and commit adultery, and swear falsely, and burn incense unto Baal, and walk after other gods, whom ye know not: 10 And come and stand before me in this house, which is called by my name, and say, We are delivered to do all these abominations?

. Mat. 25: 44 Then shall they also answer him, saying, Lord, when saw we thee an hungered, or athirst, or a stranger, or naked, or sick, or in prison, and did not minister unto thee? [See 272, 373.]

707. *Voluntary ignorance, blindness, and infatuation of sinners.*

Job 5: 14 They meet with darkness in the day-time, and grope in the noon-day as in the night. — 12: 25 They grope in the dark without light, and he maketh them to stagger like *a* drunken *man.*

Ps. 50: 17 Thou hatest instruction, and castest my words

behind thee. — 21: Thou thoughtest that I was altogether *such an one* as thyself. — 58: 4 *They are* like the deaf adder *that* stoppeth her ear; 5 Which will not hearken to the voice of charmers, charming never so wisely. — 82: 5 They know not, neither will they understand: they walk on in darkness: all the foundations of the earth are out of course.

Pr. 1: 22 How long, ye simple ones, will ye love simplicity? and the scorners delight in their scorning, and fools hate knowledge? 29 For that they hated knowledge, and did not choose the fear of the LORD: 30 They would none of my counsel: they despised all my reproof. — 4: 19 The way of the wicked *is* as darkness: they know not at what they stumble.

Jer. 17: 23 They obeyed not, neither inclined their ear, but made their neck stiff, that they might not hear, nor receive instruction. — 32: 33 They have turned unto me the back, and not the face: though I taught them, rising up early and teaching *them*, yet they have not hearkened to receive instruction.

Dan. 12: 10 Many shall be purified, and made white, and tried; but the wicked shall do wickedly; and none of the wicked shall understand; but the wise shall understand.

Zec. 7: 11 They refused to hearken, and pulled away the shoulder, and stopped their ears, that they should not hear. 12 Yea, they made their hearts as an adamant stone, lest they should hear the law, and the words which the LORD of hosts hath sent in his Spirit by the former prophets: therefore came a great wrath from the LORD of hosts.

Jn. 3: 19 This is the condemnation, that light is come into the world, and men loved darkness rather than light, because their deeds were evil. 20 For every one that doeth evil hateth the light, neither cometh to the light, lest his deeds should be reproved. — 17: 25 O righteous Father, the world hath not known thee.

Ac. 26: 17 Delivering thee from the people, and *from* the Gentiles, unto whom now I send thee, 18 To open their eyes, *and* to turn *them* from darkness to light, and *from* the power of Satan unto God, that they may receive forgiveness of sins, and inheritance among them which are sanctified by faith that is in me.

Rom. 1: 21 When they knew God, they glorified *him* not as God, neither were thankful, but became vain in their imaginations, and their foolish heart was darkened. 28 And even as they did not like to retain God in *their* knowledge, God gave them over to a reprobate mind, to do those things which are not convenient.

1 Cor. 2: 14 The natural man receiveth not the things of the

Spirit of God : for they are foolishness unto him : neither can he know *them*, because they are spiritually discerned.

Ep. 4: 18 Having the understanding darkened, being alienated from the life of God through the ignorance that is in them, because of the blindness of their heart.

1 Jn. 4: 8 He that loveth not, knoweth not God; for God is love. [See 26, 693.]

708. *Sinners inclined to theoretical and practical unbelief — Threat,*

Num. 14: 11 The LORD said unto Moses, How long will this people provoke me? and how long will it be ere they believe me, for all the signs which I have shewed among them?

Ps. 10: 11 He hath said in his heart, God hath forgotten : he hideth his face; he will never see *it.* 13 Wherefore doth the wicked contemn God? he hath said in his heart, thou wilt not require *it.* — 73: 9 They set their mouth against the heavens, and their tongue walketh through the earth. 10 Therefore his people return hither : and waters of a full *cup* are wrung out to them. 11 And they say, How doth God know? and is there knowledge in the Most High? — 94: 5 They break in pieces thy people, O LORD, and afflict thy heritage. 6 They slay the widow and the stranger, and murder the fatherless. 7 Yet they say, The LORD shall not see, neither shall the God of Jacob regard *it.*

Ezk. 8: 12 Then said he unto me, Son of man, hast thou seen what the ancients of the house of Israel do in the dark, every man in the chambers of his imagery? for they say, The LORD seeth us not; the LORD hath forsaken the earth.

Zep. 1: 12 I will search Jerusalem with candles, and punish the men that are settled on their lees : that say in their heart, The Lord will not do good, neither will he do evil.

Mk. 6: 6 He marvelled because of their unbelief. — 16: 16 He that believeth and is baptized, shall be saved ; but he that believeth not, shall be damned.

Jn. 3: 18 He that believeth not, is condemned already. 36 He that believeth not the Son, shall not see life ; but the wrath of God abideth on him. — 5: 44 How can ye believe, which receive honor one of another, and seek not the honor that *cometh* from God only? — 8: 43 Why do ye not understand my speech? *even* because ye cannot hear my word. — 16: 8 When he is come, he will reprove the world of sin, and of righteousness, and of judgment : 9 Of sin, because they believe not on me.

Rom. 11: 20 Because of unbelief they were broken off, and thou standest by faith.

Heb. 3: 12 Take heed, brethren, lest there be in any of you an evil heart of unbelief, in departing from the living God. [See 22, 568.]

709. *Idleness of sinners.*

Ezk. 16: 49 Behold, this was the iniquity of thy sister Sodom, pride, fulness of bread, and abundance of idleness was in her and in her daughters, neither did she strengthen the hand of the poor and needy.

Mat. 20: 6 About the eleventh hour he went out, and found others standing idle, and saith unto them, Why stand ye here all the day idle? 25: 18 He that had received one, went and digged in the earth, and hid his lord's money. 26 His lord answered and said unto him, *Thou* wicked and slothful servant, thou knewest that I reap where I sowed not, and gather where I have not strewed: 27 Thou oughtest therefore to have put my money to the exchangers, and *then* at my coming I should have received mine own with usury. 28 Take therefore the talent from him, and give *it* unto him which hath ten talents. 29 For unto every one that hath shall be given, and he shall have abundance: but from him that hath not, shall be taken away even that which he hath. 30 And cast ye the unprofitable servant into outer darkness: there shall be weeping and gnashing of teeth. -

Lk. 13: 6 He spake also this parable: A certain *man* had a fig-tree planted in his vineyard; and he came and sought fruit thereon, and found none. 7 Then said he unto the dresser of his vineyard, Behold, these three years I come seeking fruit on this fig-tree, and find none: cut it down, why cumbereth it the ground? [See 358.]

710. *Presumption and procrastination of sinners. — death put far away.*

Ps. 49: 11 Their inward thought *is, that* their houses *shall continue* for ever, *and* their dwelling places to all generations; they call *their* lands after their own names.

Pr. 24: 33 *Yet* a little sleep, a little slumber, a little folding of the hands to sleep.

Is. 28: 15 Because ye have said, We have made a covenant with death, and with hell are we at agreement; when the overflowing scourge shall pass through, it shall not come unto us: for we have made lies our refuge, and under falsehood have we hid ourselves. — 56: 12 Come ye, *say they*, I will fetch wine, and we will fill ourselves with strong drink; and to-morrow shall be as this day, and much more abundant.

Am. 6: 3 Ye that ·put far away the evil day, and cause the seat of violence to come near. •

Lk. 12: 19 I will say to my soul, Soul, thou hast much goods laid up for many years; take thine ease, eat, drink, *and* be merry.

Ac. 24: 25 As he reasoned of righteousness, temperance, and judgment to come, Felix trembled, and answered, Go thy way for this time; when I have a convenient season, I will call for thee. [See 22, 479, 726–7.]

N. B.—For other characteristics of sinners, especially for their vices, see " Threats of Evil," in the Index.

SOBRIETY AND GRAVITY.

711. *Sobriety and gravity required.*

Tit. 2: 11 The grace of God that bringeth salvation hath appeared to all men, 12 Teaching us, that denying ungodliness, and worldly lusts, we should live soberly, righteously, and godly, in this present world; 13 Looking for that blessed hope, and the glorious appearing of the great God and our Saviour Jesus Christ.

1 Pet. 1: 13 Gird up the loins of your mind, be sober, and hope to the end for the grace that is to be brought unto you at the revelation of· Jesus Christ: 14 As obedient children, not fashioning yourselves according to the former lusts in your ignorance: 15 But as he which hath called you is holy, so be ye holy in all manner of conversation: — 4: 7 The end of all things is at hand: be ye therefore sober, and watch unto prayer. — 5: 8 Be sober, be vigilant; because your adversary the devil, as·a roaring lion, walketh about, seeking whom he may devour. [See 479.]

STEADFASTNESS.

712. *Steadfastness and firmness required.*

1 Cor. 15: 58 My beloved brethren, be ye steadfast, immovable, always abounding in the work of the Lord, forasmuch as ye know that your labor is not in vain in the Lord. — 16: 13 Watch ye, stand fast in the faith, quit you like men, be strong.

Ph. 1: 27 Only let your conversation be as it becometh the gospel of Christ: that whether I come and see you, or else be absent, I may hear of your affairs, that ye stand fast in one spirit, with one mind striving together for the faith of the gospel: 28 And in nothing terrified by your adversaries. — 4: 1

Therefore, my brethren dearly beloved and ·longed for, my joy and crown, so stand fast in the Lord, *my* dearly beloved.

Col. 1: 23 If ye continue in the faith grounded and settled, and *be* not moved away from the hope of the gospel. — 2: 5 Though I be absent in the flesh, yet am I with you in the spirit, joying and beholding your order, and the steadfastness of your faith in Christ. 6 As ye have therefore received Christ Jesus the Lord, *so* walk ye in him: 7 Rooted and built up in him, and established in the faith, as ye have been taught, abounding therein with thanksgiving.

2 Tim. 1: 13 Hold fast the form of sound words, which thou hast heard of me, in faith and love which is in Christ Jesus.

Heb. 10: 23 Let us hold fast the profession of *our* faith without wavering; for he *is* faithful that promised.

1 Pet. 5: 8 Be sober, be vigilant; because your adversary the devil, as a roaring lion walketh about, seeking whom he may devour: 9 Whom resist steadfast in the faith.

2 Pet. 3: 17 Ye therefore, beloved, seeing ye know *these things* before, beware lest ye also, being led away with the error of the wicked, fall from your own steadfastness.

[See 187, 364.]

STEALING.

713. Stealing forbidden.

Ex. 20: 15 Thou shalt not steal.

Lev. 19: 11 Ye shall not steal, neither deal falsely, neither lie one to another.

Ep. 4: 28 Let him that stole, steal no more: but rather let him labor, working with *his* hands the thing which is good, that he may have to give to him that needeth.

1 Pet. 4: 15 Let none of you suffer as a murderer, or *as* a thief, or *as* an evil-doer, or as a busybody in other men's matters.

714. Punishment of stealing — Threats.

Ex. 21: 16 He that stealeth a man, and selleth him, or if he be found in his hand, he shall surely be put to death.

Jos. 7: 11 Israel hath sinned, and they have also transgressed my covenant which I commanded them: for they have even taken of the accursed thing, and have also stolen, and dissembled also, and they have put *it* even among their own stuff. 12 Therefore the children of Israel could not stand before their enemies, *but* turned *their* backs before their enemies, because they were accursed: neither will I be with you any more, except ye destroy the accursed from among you. 15 It shall be, *that* he that is taken with the accursed thing shall be burnt with fire, he and all that he hath : because he hath transgressed the covenant of the LORD, and because he hath wrought folly in Israel.

Hos. 4: 2 By swearing, and lying, and killing, and stealing, and committing adultery, they break out, and blood toucheth blood. 3 Therefore, shall the land mourn, and every one that dwelleth therein shall languish, with the beasts of the field, and with the fowls of heaven ; yea, the fishes of the sea also shall be taken away.

1 Cor. 6: 10 Nor thieves, nor covetous, nor drunkards, nor revilers, nor extortioners, shall inherit the kingdom of God.

STRANGERS.

715. *Justice, kindness and hospitality to strangers required.*

Ex. 22: 21 Thou shalt neither vex a stranger, nor oppress him : for ye were strangers in the land of Egypt. — 23: 9 Also thou shalt not oppress a stranger : for ye know the heart of a stranger, seeing ye were strangers in the land of Egypt.

Lev. 19: 10 Thou shalt not glean thy vineyard, neither shalt thou gather *every* grape of thy vineyard ; thou shalt leave them for the poor and stranger : I *am* the LORD your God. 33 And if a stranger sojourn with thee in your land, ye shall not vex him. 34 *But* the stranger that dwelleth with you shall be unto you as one born among you, and thou shalt love him as thyself ; for ye were strangers in the land of Egypt : I *am* the LORD your God.

Dt. 1: 16 I charged your judges at that time, saying, Hear *the causes* between your brethren, and judge righteously between *every* man and his brother, and the stranger *that is* with him. — 10: 18 He doth execute the judgment of the fatherless and widow, and loveth the stranger, in giving him food and raiment. 19 Love ye therefore the stranger : for ye were strangers in the land of Egypt.

Job 31: 32 The stranger did not lodge in the street : *but* I opened my doors to the traveller.

Mat. 25: 35 I was an hungered, and ye gave me meat : I was thirsty, and ye gave me drink : I was a stranger, and ye took me in.

Heb. 13: 2 Be not forgetful to entertain strangers : for thereby some have entertained angels unawares. [See 354.]

SUING AT THE LAW.

716. Suing, especially before the unbelieving and unjust, discountenanced.

Mat. 5: 40 If any man will sue thee at the law, and take away thy coat, let him have *thy* cloak also.

1 Cor. 6: 1 Dare any of you, having a matter against another, go to law before the unjust, and not before the saints? 6 But brother goeth to law with brother, and that before the unbelievers. 7 Now therefore there is utterly a fault among you, because ye go to law one with another. Why do ye not rather take wrong? why do ye not rather *suffer yourselves to* be defrauded? [Pr. 19: 11.]

SURETY.

717. Suretyship discountenanced — cautions.

Pr. 6: 1 My son, if thou be surety for thy friend, *if* thou hast stricken thy hand with a stranger, 2 Thou art snared with the words of thy mouth, thou art taken with the words of thy mouth. 3 Do this now, my son, and deliver thyself, when thou art come into the hand of thy friend; go, humble thyself, and make sure thy friend. 4 Give not sleep to thine eyes, nor slumber to thine eyelids. 5 Deliver thyself as a roe from the hand *of the hunter*, and as a bird from the hand of the fowler. — 11: 15 He that is surety for a stranger shall smart *for it*: and he that hateth suretyship is sure. — 22: 26 Be not thou *one* of them that strike hands, *or* of them that are sureties for debts. 27 If thou hast nothing to pay, why should he take away thy bed from under thee? [Pr. 17: 18, and 20: 16.]

SWEARING.

718. Profane swearing forbidden and punished — Threats.

Ex. 20: 7 Thou shalt not take the name of the LORD thy God in vain: for the LORD will not hold him guiltless that taketh his name in vain.

Lev. 19: 12 Ye shall not swear by my name falsely, neither shalt thou profane the name of thy God: I *am* the LORD. — 24: 10 The son of an Israelitish woman, whose father *was* an Egyptian, went out among the children of Israel; and this son of the Israelitish *woman* and a man of Israel strove together in the camp; 11 And the Israelitish woman's son blasphemed the name *of the LORD*, and cursed; and they brought him unto Moses: (and his mother's name *was* Shelomith, the daughter of Dibri, of the tribe of Dan :) 12 And they put him in ward, that the mind of the LORD might be shewed them. 13 And the LORD spake unto Moses, saying, 14 Bring forth him that hath cursed without the camp, and let all that heard *him* lay their hands upon his head, and let all the congregation stone him. 15 And thou shalt speak unto the children of Israel, saying, Whosoever curseth his God shall bear his sin. 16 And he that blasphemeth the name of the LORD, he shall surely be put to death, *and* all the congregation shall certainly stone him : as well the stranger, as he that is born in the land, when he blasphemeth the name *of the LORD*, shall be put to death.

Jer. 23: 10 Because of swearing the land mourneth; the pleasant places of the wilderness are dried up.

Hos. 4: 2 By swearing, and lying and killing, and stealing and committing adultery, they break out, and blood toucheth blood. 3 Therefore, shall the land mourn.

Zec. 5: 3 Then said he unto me, This *is* the curse that goeth forth over the face of the whole earth: for every one that stealeth shall be cut off *as* on this side, according to it ; and every one that sweareth shall be cut off *as* on that side, according to it.

Mat. 5: 34 I say unto you, Swear not at all : neither by heaven; for it is God's throne: 35 Nor by the earth; for it is his footstool : neither by Jerusalem ; for it is the city of the great King: 36 Neither shalt thou swear by thy head, because thou canst not make one hair white or black. 37 But let your communication be, Yea, yea; Nay, nay : for whatsoever *is* more than these cometh of evil.

Jam. 5: 12 Above all things, my brethren, swear not neither by heaven, neither by the earth, neither by any other oath ; but let your yea, be yea; and *your* nay, nay; lest ye fall into condemnation.

719. *Examples of rash swearing.*

Jud. 11: 30 Jephthah vowed a vow unto the LORD, and said, If thou shalt without fail deliver the children of Ammon into mine hands, 31 Then it shall be, that whatsoever cometh forth of the doors of my house to meet me, when I return in peace from the children of Ammon, shalt surely be the LORD's, and I will offer it up for a burnt-offering.

Mat. 14: 6 When Herod's birth-day was kept, the daughter of Herodias danced before them, and pleased Herod. 7

Whereupon he promised with an oath to give her whatsoever she would ask. 8 And she, being before instructed of her mother, said, Give me here John Baptist's head in a charger. 9 And the king was sorry: nevertheless for the oath's sake, and them that sat with him at meat, he commanded it to be given *her*.

Ac. 23: 12 When it was day, certain of the Jews banded together, and bound themselves under a curse, saying that they would neither eat nor drink till they had killed Paul.

720. Oaths of confirmation — examples.

Dt. 10: 20 Thou shalt fear the LORD thy God; him shalt thou serve, and to him shalt thou cleave, and swear by his name.

Neh. 5: 12 Then said they, We will restore *them*, and will require nothing of them; so will we do as thou sayest. Then I called the priests, and took an oath of them, that they should do according to this promise.

Ps. 15: 1 LORD, who shall abide in thy tabernacle? who shall dwell in thy holy hill? 4 *He that* sweareth to *his own* hurt, and changeth not.

Ec. 8: 2 I *counsel thee* to keep the king's commandment, and *that* in regard to the oath of God.

Mat. 26: 63 The high priest answered and said unto him, I adjure thee by the living God, that thou tell us whether thou be the Christ the Son of God. 64 Jesus saith unto him, Thou hast said.

2 Cor. 1: 23 I call God for a record upon my soul, that to spare you I came not as yet unto Corinth.

Heb. 6: 16 Men verily swear by the greater: and an oath for confirmation *is* to them an end of all strife. 17 Wherein God, willing more abundantly to shew unto the heirs of promise the immutability of his counsel, confirmed *it* by an oath.

TEMPERANCE.

721. Temperance required — its importance.

1 Cor. 9: 25 Every man that striveth for the mastery is temperate in all things. Now they *do it* to obtain a corruptible crown; but we an incorruptible.

Gal. 5: 22 The fruit of the Spirit is love, joy, peace, long-suffering, gentleness, goodness, faith, 23 Meekness, temperance: against such there is no law. 24 And they that are Christ's have crucified the flesh, with the affections and lusts.

Tit. 1: 8 A lover of hospitality, a lover of good men, sober, just, holy, temperate.

2 Pet. 1: 5 Giving all diligence, add to your faith, virtue; and to virtue, knowledge; 6 And to knowledge, temperance; and to temperance, patience; and to patience, godliness.

[See 199, 368.]

TEMPTATION.

722. *Temptation, in the sense of trial, common to man.*

Gen. 22: 1 It came to pass after these things, that God did tempt Abraham, and said unto him, Abraham : and he said, Behold, *here I am.* 2 And he said, Take now thy son, thine only *son* Isaac, whom thou lovest, and get thee into the land of Moriah ; and offer him there for a burnt-offering upon one of the mountains which I will tell thee of.

Gal. 4: 14 My temptation which was in my flesh ye despised not, nor rejected ; but received me as an angel of God, *even* as Christ Jesus.

Heb. 4: 15 We have not a high priest which cannot be touched with the feeling of our infirmities : but was in all points tempted like as *we are, yet* without sin.

Jam. 1: 2 My brethren, count it all joy when ye fall into divers temptations; 3 Knowing *this,* that the trying of your faith worketh patience.

723. *Temptation, or solicitation to sin, not of God.*

Jam. 1: 13 Let no man say when he is tempted, I am tempted of God : for God cannot be tempted with evil, neither tempteth he any man : 14 But every man is tempted, when he is drawn away of his own lust, and enticed. [See 269.]

724. *Duty to pray and watch against tempters and temptations.*

Pr. 1: 10 My son, if sinners entice thee, consent thou not. [11—16.]

Mat. 6: 13 Lead us not into temptation, but deliver us from evil. For thine is the kingdom, and the power, and the glory, for ever. — 26: 41 Watch and pray, that ye enter not into temptation : the spirit indeed *is* willing but the flesh *is* weak.

[See 18, 738 .]

725 *Believers shall be helped out of all their temptations — promises.*

Ps. 71: 20 *Thou,* which hast shewed me great and sore troubles, shalt quicken me again, and shalt bring me up again from the depths of the earth. — 138: 7 Though I walk in the midst of trouble, thou wilt revive me : thou shalt stretch forth thine hand against the wrath of mine enemies, and thy right hand shall save me.

1 Cor. 10: 13 There hath no temptation taken you but such as is common to man : But God *is* faithful, who will not suffer you to be tempted above that ye are able; but will with the temptation also make a way to escape, that ye may be able to bear *it.*

Heb. 2: 18 In that he himself hath suffered, being tempted, he is able to succor them that are tempted.

2 Pet. 2: 9 The Lord knoweth how to deliver the godly out of temptations, and to reserve the unjust unto the day of judgment to be punished.

Rev. 3: 10 Because thou hast kept the word of my patience I also will keep thee from the hour of temptation, which shall come upon all the world, to try them that dwell upon the earth.

[See 3—6.]

TIME.

726. *Time short.*

Ps. 89: 47 Remember how short my time is : wherefore hast thou made all men in vain?

1 Cor. 7: 29 This I say, brethren, The time *is* short. It remaineth, that both they that have wives, be as though they had none ; 30 And they that weep, as though they wept not; and they that rejoice, as though they rejoiced not; and they that buy, as though they possessed not ; 31 And they that use this world, as not abusing *it.* For the fashion of this world passeth away. [See 148.]

727. *Time should be improved; or procrastination forbidden.*

Job 22: 21 Acquaint now thyself with him, and be at peace: thereby good shall come unto thee.

Ps. 95: 7 He *is* our God; and we *are* the people of his pasture, and the sheep of his hand. To-day if ye will hear his voice, 8 Harden not your heart, as in the provocation, *and* as *in* the day of temptation in the wilderness: 9 When your fathers tempted me, proved me, and saw my work.

Pr. 27: 1 Boast not thyself of to-morrow: for thou knowest not what a day may bring forth.

Ec. 9: 10 Whatsoever thy hand findeth to do, do *it* with thy might, for *there is* no work, nor device, nor knowledge, nor wisdom, in the grave, whither thou goest.

2 Cor. 6: 2 (For he saith, I have heard thee in a time ac-

cepted, and in the day of salvation have I succored thee: behold, now *is* the accepted time; behold, now *is* .the day of salvation.)

Héb. 2: 1 We ought to give the more earnest heed to the things which we have heard, lest at any time we should let *them* slip. [See 156, 553–6, 710.]

TONGUE.

728. *The tongue often very injurious and mischievous.*

Ps. 52: 2 Thy tongue deviseth mischiefs; like a sharp razor, working deceitfully. 4 Thou lovest all devouring words, O *thou* deceitful tongue.—55: 21 *The words* of his mouth were smoother than butter, but war *was* in his heart: his words were softer than oil, yet *were* they drawn swords.—57: 4 My soul *is* among lions: *and* I lie *even among* them that are set on fire, *even* the sons of men, whose teeth *are* spears and arrows, and their tongue a sharp sword.

Pr. 11: 9 A hypocrite with *his* mouth destroyeth his neighbor: but through knowledge shall the just be delivered.— 12: 18 There is that speaketh like the piercings of a sword: but the tongue of the wise *is* health.—15: 4 A wholesome tongue *is* a tree of life: but perverseness therein *is* a breach in the spirit.—16: 27 An ungodly man diggeth up evil: and in his lips *there is* as a burning fire. 28 A froward man soweth strife; and a whisperer separateth chief friends.—17: 9 He that covereth a transgression seeketh love; but he that repeateth a matter, separateth *very* friends.—18: 7 A fool's mouth *is* his destruction, and his lips *are* the snare of his soul. 8 The words of a tale-bearer *are* as wounds, and they go down into the innermost parts of the belly. 21 Death and life *are* in the power of the tongue: and they that love it shall eat the fruit thereof.—25: 18 A man that beareth false witness against his neighbor *is* a maul, and a sword, and a sharp arrow.—26: 20 Where no wood is, *there* the fire goeth out: so where *there is* no tale-bearer, the strife ceaseth.

Jer. 9: 8 Their tongue *is as* an arrow shot out; it speaketh deceit: *one* speaketh peaceably to his neighbor with his mouth, but in heart he layeth his wait.

Jam. 3: 5 The tongue is a little member, and boasteth great things. Behold, how great a matter a little fire kindleth! 6 And the tongue *is* a fire, a world of iniquity: so is the tongue among our members, that it defileth the whole body, and setteth on fire the course of nature; and it is set on fire of hell. 7

For every kind of beasts, and of birds, and of serpents, and of things in the sea, is tamed, and hath been tamed, of mankind: 8 But the tongue can no man tame; _it is_ an unruly evil, full of deadly poison. [Pr. 11: 11.] [See 198, 416, 702.]

729. *Censoriousness, railing, tale-bearing, whispering, backbiting, slander, and other sins of the tongue forbidden — Threats.*

Lev. 19: 16 Thou shalt not go up and down *as* a tale-bearer among thy people; neither shalt thou stand against the blood of thy neighbor; I *am* the LORD.

Ps. 101: 5 Whoso privily slandereth his neighbor, him will I cut off: him that hath an high look and a proud heart will not I suffer.

Pr. 4: 24 Put away from thee a froward mouth, and perverse lips put far from thee. — 10: 8 The wise in heart will receive commandments: but a prating fool shall fall. — 24: 28 Be not a witness against thy neighbor without cause; and deceive *not* with thy lips.

Rom. 14: 10 Why dost thou judge thy brother? or why dost thou set at nought thy brother? for we shall all stand before the judgment-seat of Christ.

1 Cor. 5: 11 Now I have written unto you not to keep company, if any man that is called a brother be a fornicator, or covetous, or an idolater, or a railer, or a drunkard, or an extortioner: with such a one no not to eat.

Ep. 4: 29 Let no corrupt communication proceed out of your mouth, but that which is good to the use of edifying, that it may minister grace unto the hearers. 31 Let all bitterness, and wrath, and anger, and clamor, and evil-speaking, be put away from you, with all malice. — 5: 3 Fornication, and all uncleanness, or covetousness, let it not be once named among you, as becometh saints; 4 Neither filthiness, nor foolish talking, nor jesting, which are not convenient: but rather giving of thanks.

Col. 3: 8 Now ye also put off all these; anger, wrath, malice, blasphemy, filthy communication out of your mouth.

2 Tim. 2: 16 Shun profane *and* vain babblings: for they will increase unto more ungodliness.

Tit. 3: 1 Put them in mind to be subject to principalities and powers, to obey magistrates, to be ready to every good work, 2 To speak evil of no man, to be no brawlers, *but* gentle, shewing all meekness unto all men.

Jam. 4: 11 Speak not evil one of another, brethren.

1 Pet. 2: 1 Wherefore, laying aside all malice, and all guile, and hypocrisies, and envies, and all evil-speakings, 2 As new-

born babes, desire the sincere milk of the word, that ye may grow thereby. — 3: 9 Not rendering evil for evil, or railing for railing: but contrariwise, blessing; knowing that ye are thereunto called, that ye should inherit a blessing.

Jude 9 Yet Michael the archangel, when contending with the devil, he disputed about the body of Moses, durst not bring against him a railing accusation, but said, The Lord rebuke thee. [See 200, 417.]

730. *Railing at dignities, and reviling superiors forbidden.*

Ex. 22: 28 Thou shalt not revile the gods, nor curse the ruler of thy people.

Ac. 23: 4 They that stood by, said, Revilest thou God's high priest? 5 Then said Paul, I wist not, brethren, that he was the high priest: for it is written, Thou shalt not speak evil of the ruler of thy people.

2 Pet. 2: 9 The Lord knoweth how to deliver the godly out of temptations, and to reserve the unjust unto the day of judgment to be punished: 10 But chiefly them that walk after the flesh in the lust of uncleanness, and despise government. Presumptuous *are they*, self-willed; they are not afraid to speak evil of dignities. 11 Whereas angels, which are greater in power and might, bring not railing accusation against them before the Lord.

Jude 8 Likewise also these *filthy* dreamers defile the flesh, despise dominion, and speak evil of dignities. [See 10.]

731. *Bridling the tongue enjoined and exemplified.*

Ps. 34: 13 Keep thy tongue from evil, and thy lips from speaking guile. — 39: 1 I said, I will take heed to my ways, that I sin not with my tongue: I will keep my mouth with a bridle, while the wicked is before me.

Pr. 10: 19 In the multitude of words there wanteth not sin: but he that refraineth his lips *is* wise. — 13: 3 He that keepeth his mouth keepeth his life: *but* he that openeth wide his lips shall have destruction. — 21: 23 Whoso keepeth his mouth and his tongue, keepeth his soul from troubles.

Ec. 10: 20 Curse not the king, no, not in thy thought; and curse not the rich in thy bed-chamber: for a bird of the air shall carry the voice, and that which hath wings shall tell the matter.

Mic. 7: 5 Trust ye not in a friend, put ye not confidence in a guide: keep the doors of thy mouth from her that lieth in thy bosom.

Jam. 1: 26 If any man among you seem to be religious, and

bridleth not his tongue, but deceiveth his own heart, this man's religion *is* vain.

1 Pet. 3: 10 He that will love life, and see good days, let him refrain his tongue from evil, and his lips that they speak no guile.

UNRIGHTEOUSNESS.

732. *Unrighteousness and dishonesty forbidden.*

Lev. 19: 11 Ye shall not steal, neither deal falsely, neither lie one to another. 13 Thou shalt not defraud thy neighbor, neither rob *him*: the wages of him that is hired shall not abide with thee all night until the morning. 35 Ye shall do no unrighteousness in judgment, in mete-yard, in weight, or in measure.—25: 14 If thou sell aught unto thy neighbor, or buyest *aught* of thy neighbor's hand, ye shall not oppress one another.

Dt. 19: 14 Thou shalt not remove thy neighbor's land-mark, which they of old time have set in thine inheritance, which thou shalt inherit in the land that the LORD thy God giveth thee to possess it.—25: 13 Thou shalt not have in thy bag divers weights, a great and a small. 14 Thou shalt not have in thine house divers measures, a great and a small: 15 *But* thou shalt have a perfect and just weight, a perfect and just measure shalt thou have; that thy days may be lengthened in the land which the LORD thy God giveth thee.—27: 17 Cursed *be* he that removeth his neighbor's landmark: and all the people shall say, Amen.

Ps. 82: 2 How long will ye judge unjustly, and accept the persons of the wicked?

Pr. 11: 1 A false balance *is* abomination to the LORD: but a just weight *is* his delight.

1 Th. 4: 6 That no *man* go beyond and defraud his brother in *any* matter: because that the Lord *is* the avenger of all such, as we also have forewarned you and testified.

[See 629, 636.]

733. *Unrighteousness, extortion, etc., inexpedient, or the tendency of sin to ruin sinners here and hereafter — Threats.*

Num. 32: 23 If ye will not do so, behold, ye have sinned against the LORD: and be sure your sin will find you out.

2 Ch. 28: 19 The LORD brought Judah low because of Ahaz king of Israel: for he made Judah naked, and transgressed sore against the LORD.

Job. 21: 17 How oft is the candle of the wicked put out?

Destructive tendency of.

and *how oft* cometh their destruction upon them? *God* distributeth sorrows in his anger. 18 They are as stubble before the wind, and as chaff that the storm carrieth away. 19 God layeth up his iniquity for his children: he rewardeth him, and he shall know *it*. 20 His eyes shall see his destruction, and he shall drink of the wrath of the Almighty.—27: 13 This *is* the portion of a wicked man with God, and the heritage of oppressors, *which* they shall receive of the Almighty. 14 If his children be multiplied, *it is* for the sword: and his offspring shall not be satisfied with bread. 15 Those that remain of him shall be buried in death: and his widows shall not weep. 16 Though he heap up silver as the dust, and prepare raiment as the clay ; 17 He may prepare *it*, but the just shall put *it* on, and the innocent shall divide the silver.

Ps. 1: 4 The ungodly *are* not so: but *are* like the chaff which the wind driveth away. 5 Therefore the ungodly shall not stand in the judgment, nor sinners in the congregation of the righteous. 6 For the LORD knoweth the way of the righteous : but the way of the ungodly shall perish.—9: 15 The heathen are sunk down in the pit *that* they made: in the net which they hid is their own foot taken. 16 The LORD is known *by* the judgment *which* he executeth: the wicked is snared in the work of his own hands.—34: 16 The face of the LORD *is* against them that do evil, to cut off the remembrance of them from the earth. 21 Evil shall slay the wicked: and they that hate the righteous shall be desolate.—55: 23 But thou, O God, shalt bring them down into the pit of destruction: bloody and deceitful men shall not live out half their days.—58: 11 Verily, *there is* a reward for the righteous: verily he is a God that judgeth in the earth.—73: 12 Behold, these *are* the ungodly, who prosper in the world. 18 Surely thou didst set them in slippery places: thou castedst them down into destruction. 19 How are they *brought* into desolation, as in a moment! they are utterly consumed with terrors.

Pr. 3: 33 The curse of the LORD *is* in the house of the wicked: but he blesseth the habitation of the just.—11: 31 Behold, the righteous shall be recompensed in the earth: much more the wicked and the sinner.—13: 5 A righteous *man* hateth lying: but a wicked *man* is loathsome, and cometh to shame. 15 Good understanding giveth favor: but the way of transgressors *is* hard.—28: 8 He that by usury and unjust gain increaseth his substance, he shall gather it for him that shall pity the poor. 18 Whoso walketh uprightly shall be saved ; but *he that is* perverse *in his* ways shall fall at once.

Jer. 17: 11 *As* the partridge sitteth *on eggs*, and hatcheth

Destructive tendency of.

them not; *so* he that getteth riches, and not by right, shall leave them in the midst of his days, and at his end shall be a fool.—22: 17 Thine eyes and thine heart *are* not but for thy covetousness, and for to shed innocent blood, and for oppression, and for violence, to do *it.* 18 Therefore thus saith the LORD concerning Jehoiakim the son of Josiah king of Judah; They shall not lament for him, *saying,* Ah my brother! or, Ah sister! they shall not lament for him, *saying,* Ah lord! or, Ah his glory! 19 He shall be buried with the burial of an ass, drawn and cast forth beyond the gates of Jerusalem.

Ezk. 22: 12 In thee have they taken gifts to shed blood; thou hast taken usury and increase, and thou hast greedily gained of thy neighbors by extortion, and hast forgotten me, saith the Lord GOD. 13 Behold, therefore I have smitten mine hand at thy dishonest gain which thou hast made, and at thy blood which hath been in the midst of thee. 14 Can thine heart endure, or can thine hands be strong, in the days that I shall deal with thee? I the LORD have spoken *it,* and will do *it.*— 28: 15 Thou *wast* perfect in thy ways from the day that thou wast created, till iniquity was found in thee. 16 By the multitude of thy merchandise they have filled the midst of thee with violence, and thou hast sinned: therefore I will cast thee as profane out of the mountain of God: and I will destroy thee, O covering cherub, from the midst of the stones of fire.

1 Cor. 6: 9 Know ye not that the unrighteous shall not inherit the kingdom of God? Be not deceived; neither fornicators, nor idolaters, nor adulterers, nor effeminate, nor abusers of themselves with mankind, 10 Nor thieves, nor covetous, nor drunkards, nor revilers, nor extortioners, shall inherit the kingdom of God.

Jam. 5: 3 Your gold and silver is cankered; and the rust of them shall be a witness against you, and shall eat your flesh as it were fire. Ye have heaped treasure together for the last days. 4 Behold, the hire of the laborers who have reaped down your fields, which is of you kept back by fraud, crieth; and the cries of them which have reaped are entered into the ears of the Lord of Sabaoth.

2 Pet. 2: 5 And spared not the old world, but saved Noah the eighth *person,* a preacher of righteousness, bringing in the flood upon the world of the ungodly; 6 And turning the cities of Sodom and Gomorrah into ashes, condemned *them* with an overthrow, making *them* an ensample unto those that after should live ungodly. [See 87, 138, 303, 362, 381, 478, 486, 489, 497, 513, 551, 555–6, 630, 735.]

WAR AND FIGHTING.

734. *War and fighting have been prevalent.*

Gen. 6: 11 The earth also was corrupt before God; and the earth was filled with violence.

2 K. 19: 11 Behold, thou hast heard what the kings of Assyria have done to all lands, by destroying them utterly: and shalt thou be delivered?

Is. 1: 15 When ye spread forth your hands, I will hide mine eyes from you; yea, when ye make many prayers, I will not hear: your hands are full of blood. — 10: 13 I have removed the bounds of the people, and have robbed their treasures, and I have put down the inhabitants, like a valiant *man.*

Ezk. 33: 25 Say unto them, Thus saith the Lord GOD; Ye eat with the blood, and lift up your eyes toward your idols, and shed blood: and shall ye possess the land? 26 Ye stand upon your sword, ye work abomination, and ye defile every one his neighbor's wife: and shall ye possess the land?

[See 488, 701.]

735. *Sin and folly of anger, and other warlike passions — wisdom of suppressing them.*

Job 5: 2 Wrath killeth the foolish man, and envy slayeth the silly one.

Ps. 37: 8 Cease from anger, and forsake wrath: fret not thyself in any wise to do evil.

Pr. 11: 17 The merciful man doeth good to his own soul: but *he that is* cruel troubleth his own flesh. — 14: 16 A wise *man* feareth and departeth from evil: but the fool rageth, and is confident. 17 *He that is* soon angry dealeth foolishly: and a man of wicked devices is hated. 29 *He that is* slow to wrath *is* of great understanding: but *he that is* hasty of spirit exalteth folly. — 15: 18 A wrathful man stirreth up strife: but *he that is* slow to anger appeaseth strife. — 16: 32 *He that is* slow to anger *is* better than the mighty; and he that ruleth his spirit, than he that taketh a city. — 19: 19 A man of great wrath shall suffer punishment: for if thou deliver *him,* yet thou must do it again. — 22: 24 Make no friendship with an angry man; and with a furious man thou shalt not go. — 24: 17 Rejoice not when thine enemy falleth, and let not thy heart be glad when he stumbleth: 18 Lest the LORD see *it,* and it displease him, and he turn away his wrath from him. — 25: 28 He that *hath* no rule over his own spirit *is like* a city

44
517

that is broken down, *and* without walls. — 26: 21 *As* coals *are* to burning coals, and wood to fire ; so *is* a contentious man to kindle strife. — 27: 4 Wrath *is* cruel, and anger *is* outrageous; but who *is* able to stand before envy? — 29: 22 An angry man stirreth up strife, and a furious man aboundeth in transgression.

Ec. 7: 9 Be not hasty in thy spirit to be angry : for anger resteth in the bosom of fools.

Ep. 4: 31 Let all bitterness, and wrath, and anger, and clamor, and evil speaking, be put away from you, with all malice. [See 200,(21,) 733.]

736. *Carnal fighting, and returning evil for evil, foolish, and forbidden — Threats.*

Gen. 49: 5 Simeon and Levi *are* brethren; instruments of cruelty *are in* their habitations. 6 O my soul, come not thou into their secret: unto their assembly, mine honor, be not thou united! for in their anger they slew a man, and in their self-will they digged down a wall. 7 Cursed *be* their anger, for *it was* fierce: and their wrath, for it was cruel: I will divide them in Jacob, and scatter them in Israel.

Ex. 20: 13 Thou shalt not kill. [Lk. 18: 20.]

Lev. 19: 18 Thou shalt not avenge, nor bear any grudge against the children of thy people, but thou shalt love thy neighbor as thyself: I *am* the LORD.

Ps. 5: 6 The LORD will abhor the bloody and deceitful man.

Pr. 17: 14 The beginning of strife *is as* when one letteth out water: therefore leave off contention before it be meddled with. — 18: 6 A fool's lips enter into contention, and his mouth calleth for strokes. — 20: 22 Say not thou, I will recompense evil ; *but* wait on the LORD, and he shall save thee. — 24: 29 Say not, I will do so to him as he hath done to me: I will render to the man according to his work. — 26: 17 He that passeth by, *and* meddleth with strife *belonging* not to him, *is like* one that taketh a dog by the ears. — 30: 33 Surely the churning of milk bringeth forth butter, and the wringing of the nose bringeth forth blood: so the forcing of wrath bringeth forth strife.

Ezk. 25: 12 Thus saith the Lord GOD; Because that Edom hath dealt against the house of Judah by taking vengeance, and hath greatly offended, and revenged himself upon them ; 13 Therefore thus saith the Lord GOD ; I will also stretch out my hand upon Edom, and will cut off man and beast from it ; and I will make it desolate from Teman ; and they of Dedan shall fall by the sword. 14 And I will lay my vengeance upon Edom by the hand of my people Israel: and they shall do in Edom according to mine. anger and according to my fury; and they shall know my vengeance, saith the Lord GOD. — 35: 5 Because thou hast had a perpetual hatred, and hast shed *the blood of* the children of Israel by the force of the sword in the time of their calamity, in the time *that their* iniquity *had* an end: 6 Therefore, *as* I live, saith the Lord GOD, I will prepare thee unto blood, and blood shall pursue thee: since thou hast not hated blood, even blood shall pursue thee.

Hos. 4: 2 By swearing, and lying, and killing, and stealing, and committing adultery, they break out, and blood toucheth blood. 3 Therefore shall the land mourn, and every one that dwelleth therein shall languish, with the beasts of the field, and with the fowls of heaven; yea, the fishes of the sea also shall be taken away.

Am. 1: 11 Thus saith the LORD; For three transgressions of Edom, and for four, I will not turn away *the punishment* thereof: because he did pursue his brother with the sword, and did cast off all pity, and his anger did tear perpetually, and he kept his wrath for ever.

Hab. 2: 12 Wo to him that buildeth a town with blood, and establisheth a city by iniquity!

Mat. 26: 52 Then said Jesus unto him, Put up again thy sword into his place: for all they that take the sword, shall perish with the sword.

Lk. 3: 14 The soldiers likewise demanded of him, saying, And what shall we do? And he said unto them, Do violence to no man, neither accuse *any* falsely; and be content with your wages.

Rom. 12: 17 Recompense to no man evil for evil. 19 Dearly beloved, avenge not yourselves, but *rather* give place unto wrath: for it is written, Vengeance *is* mine; I will repay, saith the Lord.

1 Th. 5: 14 Now we exhort you, brethren, warn them that are unruly, comfort the feeble-minded, support the weak, be patient toward all *men.* 15 See that none render evil for evil unto any *man;* but ever follow that which is good, both among yourselves and to all *men.*

Jam. 2: 11 He that said, Do not commit adultery; said also, Do not kill. Now, if thou commit no adultery, yet if thou kill, thou art become a transgressor of the law. — 3: 16 Where envying and strife *is,* there *is* confusion, and every evil work. — 4: 1 Whence *come* wars and fightings among you? *come they*

not hence, *even* of your lusts that war in your members?   12
There is one lawgiver, who is able to save, and to destroy: who
art thou that judgest another?

. Rev. 13: 10 He that leadeth into captivity shall go into captivity : he that killeth with the sword, must be killed with the
sword. [See 488—490, 630, 733.]

737. *How to treat enemies, and to prevent war and fighting.*

Pr. 10: 12 Hatred stirreth up strifes : but love covereth all
sins. — 16: 7 When a man's ways please the LORD, he maketh
even his enemies to be at peace with him. — 18: 24 A man
that hath friends, must show himself friendly. — 25: 15 By
long forbearing is a prince persuaded, and a soft tongue breaketh the bone.   21 If thine enemy be hungry, give him bread
to eat; and if he be thirsty, give him water to drink: 22 For
thou shalt heap coals of fire upon his head, and the LORD shall
reward thee. — 29: 8 Scornful men bring a city into a snare:
but wise *men* turn away wrath.

Mat. 5: 38 Ye have heard that it hath been said, An eye for
an eye, and a tooth for a tooth.   39 But I say unto you, That
ye resist not evil : but whosoever shall smite thee on thy right
cheek, turn to him the other also.   40 And if any man will
sue thee at the law, and take away thy coat, let him have *thy*
cloak also. 43 Ye have heard that it hath been said, Thou shalt
love thy neighbor, and hate thine enemy: 44 But I say unto
you, Love your enemies, bless them that curse you, do good to
them that hate you, and pray for them which despitefully use
you, and persecute you: 45 That ye may be the children of
your Father which is in heaven.

Lk. 6: 30 Give to every man that asketh of thee; and of
him that taketh away thy goods, ask *them* not again.   35 But
love ye your enemies, and do good, and lend, hoping for nothing
again; and your reward shall be great, and ye shall be the
children of the Highest: for he is kind unto the unthankful
and *to* the evil.   36 Be ye therefore merciful, as your Father
also is merciful.   37 Judge not, and ye shall not be judged:
condemn not, and ye shall not be condemned: forgive, and ye
shall be forgiven.

Rom. 12: 14 Bless them which persecute you: bless, and
curse not.   20 Therefore, if thine enemy hunger, feed him; if
he thirst, give him drink: for in so doing thou shalt heap coals
of fire on his head.   21 Be not overcome of evil, but overcome
evil with good.

1 Pet. 3: 8 Finally, *be ye* all of one mind, having compassion
one of another; love as brethren, *be* pitiful, *be* courteous: 9

Not rendering evil for evil, or railing for railing: but contrariwise, blessing; knowing that ye are thereunto called, that ye should inherit a blessing. 13·And who *is* he that will harm you, if ye be followers of that which is good?
[See 62, 201, 203, 204, 437, 498–9, 660.]

WATCHFULNESS .

738. Watchfulness, and fighting the good fight of faith, required, exemplified, and encouraged.

Mat. 26: 41 Watch and pray, that ye enter not into temptation: the spirit indeed *is* willing, but the flesh *is* weak.

Mk. 13: 33 Take ye heed, watch and pray: for ye know not when the time is. 34 *For the Son of man is* as a man taking a far journey, who left his house, and gave authority to his servants, and to every man his work, and commanded the porter to watch. 35 Watch ye, therefore: for ye know not when the master of the house cometh, at even, or at midnight, or at the cock-crowing, or in the morning: 36 Lest coming suddenly, he find you sleeping. 37 And what I say unto you, I say unto all, Watch.

Lk. 12: 37 Blessed *are* those servants, whom the lord when he cometh shall find watching: verily, I say unto you, that he shall gird himself, and make them to sit down to meat, and will come forth and serve them.

1 Cor. 10: 12 Wherefore let him that thinketh he standeth, take heed lest he fall. — 16: 13 Watch ye, stand fast in the faith, quit you like men, be strong.

Ep. 5: 15 See then that ye walk circumspectly, not as fools, but as wise, 16 Redeeming the time, because the days are evil. — 6: 10 Finally, my brethren, be strong in the Lord, and in the power of his might. 11 Put on the whole armor of God, that ye may be able to stand against the wiles of the devil.

1 Th. 5: 6 Let us not sleep, as *do* others: but let us watch and be sober.

1 Tim. 6: 12 Fight the good fight of faith.

2 Tim. 2: 3 Thou therefore endure hardness, as a good soldier of Jesus Christ. — 4: 5 Watch thou in all things, endure afflictions, do the work of an evangelist, make full proof of thy ministry.

1 Peter 4: 7 The end of all things is at hand: be ye therefore sober, and watch unto prayer. [See 18, 477, 724.]

WORLD.

739. *The world, ignorant of God.*

Jn. 17: 25 O righteous Father, the world hath not known thee.

1 Cor. 1: 20 Where *is* the wise? where *is* the scribe? where *is* the disputer of this world? hath not God made foolish the wisdom of this world? 21 For after that in the wisdom of God the world by wisdom knew not God, it pleased God by the foolishness of preaching to save them that believe.

[See 693.]

740. *The world opposed to God and to his people.*

Ps. 82: 2 Lo, thine enemies make a tumult; and they that hate thee have lifted up the head. 3 They have taken crafty counsel against thy people, and consulted against thy hidden ones. 4 They have said, Come, and let us cut them off from *being* a nation; that the name of Israel may be no more in remembrance. 5 For they have consulted together with one consent: they are confederate against thee.

Mat. 10: 22 Ye shall be hated of all *men* for my name's sake: but he that endureth to the end shall be saved.

Jn. 17: 14 I have given them thy word; and the world hath hated them, because they are not of the world, even as I am not of the world. — 18: 36 Jesus answered, My kingdom is not of this world: if my kingdom were of this world, then would my servants fight, that I should not be delivered to the Jews: but now is my kingdom not from hence.

Ep. 2: 1 You *hath he quickened,* who were dead in trespasses and sins; 2 Wherein in time past ye walked according to the course of this world, according to the prince of the power of the air, the spirit that now worketh in the children of disobedience.

Jam. 4: 4 Ye adulterers and adulteresses, know ye not that the friendship of the world is enmity with God? whosoever therefore will be a friend of the world is the enemy of God.

1 Jn. 2: 16 All that *is* in the world, the lust of the flesh, and the lust of the eyes, and the pride of life, is not of the Father, but is of the world.

[See 68, 86, 467, 511, 690.]

741. *The world corrupting and dangerous — cautions.*

Mat. 13: 22 He also that received seed among the thorns

is he that heareth the word; and the care of this world, and the deceitfulness of riches choke the word, and he becometh unfruitful.

Lk. 21: 34 Take heed to yourselves, lest at any time your hearts be overcharged with surfeiting and drunkenness, and cares of this life, and *so* that day come upon you unawares.

Gal. 1: 4 Who gave himself for our sins, that he might deliver us from this present evil world, according to the will of God and our Father.

Ph. 3: 18 (Many walk, of whom I have told you often, and now tell you even weeping, *that they are* the enemies of the cross of Christ: 19 Whose end *is* destruction, whose God *is their* belly, and *whose* glory *is* in their shame, who mind earthly things.)

2 Tim. 4: 10 Demas hath forsaken me, having loved this present world. [See 122, 625.]

742. *Worldly idolatry forbidden — the contrary required.*

Jer. 45: 5 Seekest thou great things for thyself? seek *them* not: for behold, I will bring evil upon all flesh, saith the LORD.

Mat. 6: 19 Lay not up for yourselves treasures upon earth, where moth and rust doth corrupt, and where thieves break through and steal: 20 But lay up for yourselves treasures in heaven, where neither moth nor rust doth corrupt, and where thieves do not break through nor steal. 21 For where your treasure is, there will your heart be also. 24 No man can serve two masters: for either he will hate the one, and love the other; or else he will hold to the one, and despise the other. Ye cannot serve God and mammon. 25 Therefore I say unto you, Take no thought for your life, what ye shall eat or what ye shall drink; nor yet for your body, what ye shall put on. Is not the life more than meat, and the body than raiment? 32 (For after all these things do the Gentiles seek) for your heavenly Father knoweth that ye have need of all these things. 33 But seek ye first the kingdom of God, and his righteousness, and all these things shall be added unto you.

Mk. 8: 36 What shall it profit a man, if he shall gain the whole world, and lose his own soul? 37 Or what shall a man give in exchange for his soul?

Lk. 6: 24 Wo unto you that are rich! for ye have received your consolation. 25 Wo unto you that are full! for ye shall hunger. — 12: 19 I will say to my soul, Soul, thou hast much goods laid up for many years; take thine ease, eat, drink, *and* be merry. 20 But God said unto him, *Thou* fool, this night thy soul shall be required of thee: then whose shall those things be which thou hast provided? 21 So *is* he that layeth up treasure for himself, and is not rich toward God. 33 Sell that ye have, and give alms: provide yourselves bags which wax not old, a treasure in the heavens that faileth not, where no thief approacheth, neither moth corrupteth. 34 For where your treasure is, there will your heart be also.

Jn. 6: 27 Labor not for the meat which perisheth, but for that meat which endureth unto everlasting life, which the Son of man shall give unto you: for him hath God the Father sealed.

Rom. 12: 2 Be not conformed to this world: but be ye transformed by the renewing of your mind, that ye may prove what *is* that good, and acceptable, and perfect will of God.

Col. 3: 2 Set your affection on things above, not on things on the earth.

Jam. 1: 27 Pure religion and undefiled before God and the Father is this, To visit the fatherless and widows in their afflic-tion, *and* to keep himself unspotted from the world.

1 Jn. 2: 15 Love not the world, neither the things *that are* in the world. If any man love the world, the love of the Father is not in him. 16 For all that *is* in the world, the lust of the flesh, and the lust of the eyes, and the pride of life, is not of the Father, but is of the world. [See 626.]

743. *World, overcome by grace.*

Gal. 6: 14 God forbid that I should glory, save in the cross of our Lord Jesus Christ, by whom the world is crucified unto me, and I unto the world.

1 Jn. 5: 4 Whatsoever is born of God, overcometh the world: and this is the victory that overcometh the world, *even* our faith. [See 59.]

WORSHIP OF GOD.

744. *God the only proper object of religious worship.*

Ex. 20: 2 I *am* the LORD thy God, which have brought thee out of the land of Egypt, out of the house of bondage. 3 Thou shalt have no other gods before me.

Ps. 96: 4 For the LORD *is* great, and greatly to be praised: he *is* to be feared above all gods. 5 For all the gods of the nations *are* idols: but the LORD made the heavens. 8 Give unto the LORD the glory *due unto* his name: bring an offering, and come into his courts. 9 O worship the LORD in the beauty of holiness: fear before him, all the earth.

Mat. 4: 10 Thou shalt worship the Lord thy God, and him only shalt thou serve. [See 80, 280, 295.]

745. *Public worship of God required, encouraged, and exemplified.*

Ps. 40: 7 Then said I, Lo, I come: in the volume of the book *it is* written of me, 8 I delight to do thy will, O my God: yea, thy law *is* within my heart. 9 I have preached righteousness in the great congregation: lo, I have not refrained my lips, O LORD, thou knowest. 10 I have not hid thy righteousness within my heart; I have declared thy faithfulness and thy salvation: I have not concealed thy loving-kindness and thy truth from the great congregation.

Mat. 18: 20 Where two or three are gathered together in my name, there am I in the midst of them.

Ac. 11: 25 Then departed Barnabas to Tarsus, for to seek Saul: 26 And when he had found him, he brought him unto Antioch. And it came to pass, that a whole year they assembled themselves with the church, and taught much people. — 13: 14 When they departed from Perga, they came to Antioch in Pisidia, and went into the synagogue on the Sabbath-day, and sat down. 15 And after the reading of the law and the prophets, the rulers of the synagogue sent unto them, saying, *Ye* men *and* brethren, if ye have any word of exhortation for the people, say on. 16 Then Paul stood up, and beckoning with *his* hand, said, Men of Israel, and ye that fear God, give audience.

. Heb. 10: 25 Not forsaking the assembling of ourselves together, as the manner of some *is;* but exhorting *one another;* and so much the more, as ye see the day approaching. [Neh. 8: 1—7, Ac. 13: 42—45.]

746. *Public worship with religious instruction exemplified.*

Neh. 8: 8 They read in the book in the law of God distinctly, and gave the sense, and caused *them* to understand the reading.

Mk. 2: 1 Again he entered into Capernaum, after *some* days; and it was noised that he was in the house. 2 And straightway many were gathered together, insomuch that there was no room to receive *them*, no, not so much as about the door: and he preached the word unto them.

Lk. 4: 43 He said unto them, I must preach the kingdom of God to other cities also, for therefore am I sent. 44 And he preached in the synagogues of Galilee.

Jn. 8: 1 Jesus went unto the mount of Olives: 2 And early in the morning he came again into the temple, and all the people came unto him; and he sat down and taught them. — 18: 20 Jesus answered him, I spake openly to the world; I ever taught in the synagogue, and in the temple, whither the Jews always resort; and in secret have I said nothing.

Ac. 18: 4 He [Paul] reasoned in the synagogue every Sabbath, and persuaded the Jews and the Greeks. 5 And when Silas and Timotheus were come from Macedonia, Paul was pressed in the spirit, and testified to the Jews, *that* Jesus *was* Christ. [See 430.]

747. *Public worship with social prayer, praise and reverence.*

Lev. 18: 30 Ye shall keep my Sabbaths, and reverence my sanctuary: I *am* the LORD.

1 K. 8: 22 Solomon stood before the altar of the LORD in the presence of all the congregation of Israel, and spread forth his hands toward heaven.

Ps. 89: 7 God is greatly to be feared in the assembly of the saints, and to be had in reverence of all *them that are* about him.

Mat. 26: 30 When they had sung an hymn, they went out into the mount of Olives.

Heb. 12: 28 Receiving a kingdom which cannot be moved, let us have grace, whereby we may serve God acceptably, with reverence and godly fear; 29 For our God *is* a consuming fire. [See 528–9.]

ZEAL.

748. *False Zeal exemplified.*

1 K. 18: 28 They cried aloud, and cut themselves after their manner with knives and lancets, till the blood gushed out upon them.

Mat. 23: 15 Wo unto you, scribes and Pharisees, hypocrites! for ye compass sea and land to make one proselyte; and when he is made, ye make him two-fold more the child of hell than yourselves.

Ac. 22: 3 I am verily a man *which am* a Jew, born in Tarsus, *a city* in Cilicia, yet brought up in this city at the feet of Gamaliel, *and* taught according to the perfect manner of the law of the fathers, and was zealous toward God, as ye all are this day.

True Zeal exemplified and required — necessary, to overcome.

Rom. 10: 2 I bear them record that they have a zeal of God, . but not according to knowledge.

Gal. 1: 13 Ye have heard of my conversation in time past in the Jews' religion, how that beyond measure I persecuted the church of God, and wasted it; 14 And profited in the Jews' religion above many my equals in mine own nation, being more exceedingly zealous of the traditions of my fathers. — 4: 17 They zealously affect you, *but* not well; yea, they would exclude you, that ye might affect them.

749. *True Zeal exemplified and required.*

Num. 25: 11 Phinehas, the son of Eleazar, the son of Aaron the priest, hath turned my wrath away from the children of Israel (while he was zealous for my sake among them) that I consumed not the children of Israel in my jealousy. 12 Wherefore say, Behold, I give unto him my covenant of peace: 13 And he shall have it, and his seed after him, *even* the covenant of an everlasting priesthood; because he was zealous for his God, and made an atonement for the children of Israel.

Ps. 119: 139 My zeal hath consumed me; because mine enemies have forgotten thy words.

2 Cor 7: 11 Behold this self-same thing, that ye sorrowed after a godly sort, what carefulness it wrought in you, yea, *what* clearing of ourselves, yea, *what* indignation, yea, *what* fear, yea, *what* vehement desire, yea, *what* zeal, yea, *what* revenge!

Gal. 4: 18 It *is* good to be zealously affected always in *a* good *thing*, and not only when I am present with you.

Col. 4: 12 Epaphras, who is *one* of you, a servant of Christ, saluteth you, always laboring fervently for you in prayers, that ye may stand perfect and complete in all the will of God. 13 For I bear him record, that he hath a great zeal for you, and them *that are* in Laodicea, and them in Hierapolis.

Tit. 2: 14 Who gave himself for us, that he might redeem us from all iniquity, and purify unto himself a peculiar people, zealous of good works. [See 1.]

750. *Zeal necessary, to overcome "the world, the flesh and the devil," and obtain the heavenly inheritance.*

Lk. 13: 24 Strive to enter in at the strait gate: for many, I say unto you, will seek to enter in, and shall not be able.

1 Cor. 9: 26 I therefore so run, not as uncertainly; so fight I, not as one that beateth the air: 27 But I keep under my body, and bring *it* into subjection: lest that by any means

when I have preached to others, I myself should be a cast-away.

Ep. 6: 12 We wrestle not against flesh and blood, but against principalities, against powers, against the rulers of the darkness of this world, against spiritual wickedness in high *places.* 13 Wherefore take unto you the whole armor of God, that ye may be able to withstand in the evil day, and having done all, to stand. 14 Stand therefore, having your loins girt about with truth, and having on the breast-plate of righteousness; 15 And your feet shod with the preparation of the gospel of peace; 16 Above all, taking the shield of faith, wherewith ye shall be able to quench all the fiery darts of the wicked. 17 And take the helmet of salvation, and the sword of the Spirit, which is the word of God: 18 Praying always with all prayer and supplication in the Spirit, and watching thereunto with all perseverance and supplication.

1 Pet. 4: 7 The end of all things is at hand: be ye therefore sober, and watch unto prayer.

528

THE END.

Lightning Source UK Ltd.
Milton Keynes UK
UKHW010604110219
337000UK00006B/372/P